ENTREPRENEURIAL FINANCE

A CASE BOOK

Paul A. Gompers

Harvard Business School

William Sahlman

Harvard Business School

John Wiley & Sons, Inc.

Dedication

To Mary and Stephen (z"l)

To Carol, Stephen, and Charlie

Editor	Leslie Kraham
Associate Editor	Cindy Rhoads
Marketing Manager	Charity Robey
Senior Production Editor	Kelly Tavares
Senior Designer	Kevin Murphy
Cover Photo	AFP/Corbis

This book was set in 10/12 New Caledonia by Matrix Publishing, and printed and bound by Hamilton Printing. The cover was printed by Lehigh Press.

This book is printed on acid-free paper. ∞

ISBN: 0-471-08066-7

Printed in the United States of America

10 9 8 7 6 5 4 3 2

Acknowledgments

This book draws on our research and case writing about entrepreneurial firms that we have undertaken over the past two decades. As such, we are grateful to far too many people to recount (or even remember) all of them. First, without the cooperation and input from the many case protagonists and companies that we have examined, this volume would not have been possible. We owe a great deal to those individuals and firms that were willing and open to this process.

This book follows and builds on the long tradition of the Harvard Business School in exploring issues related to entrepreneurial firms. This history dates back to 1946 when the first entrepreneurship course was taught at the Harvard Business School. Our efforts in putting together this case book stand as a testament to the work done by colleagues here over the past six decades. In particular, John McArthur, our former Dean, made a commitment in the early 1980s to re-invent the Entrepreneurial Management Unit. Kim Clark, our current Dean, has been extremely supportive of building an even stronger, more vibrant Entrepreneurial Management Unit. In addition, Howard Stevenson, who served as Area Chair for many years, rebuilt the Unit here at the Harvard Business School over the past two decades and has served as a teacher and mentor to several generations of entrepreneurship scholars.

More directly, the ideas in this volume were refined in many hours of conversations with academic colleagues and practitioners. Our colleagues in the Entrepreneurial and Service Management Unit at the Harvard Business School have provided encouragement as well as diverse insights into the process of new business formation. In particular, we wish to thank Hank Chesbrough, Felda Hardymon, Myra Hart, Walter Kummerle, Joe Lassiter, Jay Light, and Paul Marshall. We also received valuable comments from instructors who reviewed our text as it was evolving: Frank Demmler (Carnegie Mellon University), Steven Spinelli (Babson College), Wei Guan (Delaware State University), and Leroy Ashorn (Sam Houston State University). We are especially grateful to Josh Lerner and Mike Roberts who allowed us to use some of their course materials in this volume.

The production of this volume was greatly enhanced by research assistance provided by numerous research associates over the past twenty years. In particular, Jeff Anapolsky, Amy Burroughs, Jon Biotti, Catherine Conneely, Jeff Ferrell, Larry Katz, Ben Kaplan, Matt Lieb, Howard Reitz, Nicole Tempest, and Alex Tsai helped in the production of cases or notes for this volume. Chris Allen in Baker Research Services was always particularly helpful in collecting the necessary data to fill out our cases. Chris Darwall and the California Research Center also played a pivotal role in development and writing of several of the cases in this volume. Our assistants, Peggy Moreland and

Wendy Wilson, were of a great deal of assistance in many stages of the process. The Division of Research of Harvard Business School provided us with financial support to make this whole endeavor possible.

The project was shepherded from its earliest stage by our editor, Leslie Kraham, and associate editor, Cindy Rhoads. With a great deal of enthusiasm (but also persistence!), they kept us on track. We owe them a great deal of thanks.

Finally, our families provided a great deal of support while we toiled in writing the cases and notes over the years. We appreciate their understanding and patience through this entire process.

About the Authors

Paul A. Gompers, Professor of Business Administration and Director of Research at the Harvard Business School, specializes in research on financial issues related to venture capital and private equity funds as well as start-up, high growth, and newly public companies. He received his A.B. *summa cum laude* in biology from Harvard College in 1987. After spending a year working as a research biochemist for Bayer Chemical AG, he attended Oxford University on a Marshall Fellowship where he received an M.Sc. in economics. He completed his Ph.D. in Business Economics at Harvard University in 1993. Professor Gompers spent two years as an Assistant Professor of Finance at the Graduate School of Business, the University of Chicago where he created a new course entitled "Entrepreneurial Finance and Management." His course development efforts at the Harvard Business School focuses on issues affecting entrepreneurial firms and their investors, sources of financing for emerging companies, and private equity funds.

His research on private equity funds has examined the relationship between general partners and their portfolio companies. Similarly, he has examined the relationship between institutional investors and private equity fund managers. Gompers has also examined factors affecting the valuation of private equity transactions as well as the risk and return of private equity investments. Other research efforts examine the institutional and market factors that influence the performance of newly public companies. His papers have been published in many academic journals including the *Journal of Finance,* the *Journal of Financial Economics, Brookings Proceedings on Economic Activity, Journal of Private Equity,* the *Quarterly Journal of Economics,* and the *Journal of Law and Economics.* He is also co-author of *The Venture Capital Cycle* published by MIT Press and *The Money of Invention* from Harvard Business School Press.

Professor Gompers is currently on the advisory board of several private companies and has served as a consultant for many large corporations, top private equity funds, and institutional limited partners. He is also a Faculty Research Fellow in the National Bureau of Economic Research's Corporate Finance Program.

William Sahlman is the Dimitri V. d'Arbeloff - Class of 1955 Professor of Business Administration at Harvard Business School. The d'Arbeloff Chair was established in 1986 to support teaching and research on the entrepreneurial process. The Chair honors the late Dimitri d'Arbeloff (HBS '55), whose entrepreneurial skills helped make Millipore Corporation a world leader in its industry.

Professor Sahlman received an A.B. degree in Economics from Princeton University, an M.B.A. from Harvard University, and a Ph.D. in Business Economics, also from Harvard. His research focuses on the investment and financing decisions made in entrepreneurial ventures at all stages in their development. His writings have been widely published in a variety of academic and business journals. Professor Sahlman's most recent article, "The New Economy is Stronger Than You Think" (Harvard Business Review—November/ December 1999), describes the positive role of entrepreneurship in the economy. He emphasizes the impact of enabling technologies like the Internet on critical factors like inflation and productivity. In "How to write a great business plan" (Harvard Business Review—July/August 1997), Professor Sahlman describes the appropriate role of the business plan in new venture formation, whether in a new company or within an existing enterprise. The article emphasizes the role of people in making businesses succeed.

In 1985, Professor Sahlman introduced a new second-year elective course called Entrepreneurial Finance. During the academic 1999-2000 year, over 500 students enrolled in the course. In 2000, he helped introduce and teach a new course in the first year called The Entrepreneurial Manager. Professor Sahlman is currently the co-chair of the Entrepreneurship and Service Management Unit. From 1991 to 1999, he was Senior Associate Dean, Director of Publishing Activities, and chairman of the board for Harvard Business School Publishing Corporation. From 1990 to 1991, he was chairman of the Harvard University Advisory Committee on Shareholder Responsibility. He is a member of the board of directors of several private companies.

Table of Contents

1

Introduction to Entrepreneurial Finance

This chapter presents an overview of the structure and material that will be covered in Entrepreneurial Finance. In addition to presenting the outline and themes of the course, this chapter provides resources from both the popular media and the academic literature to use as reference material. The listing of books, magazines, and articles, while not exhaustive, covers a broad range of topics in entrepreneurial finance at various technical levels.

When looking through the description, many of you may have asked, "What is entrepreneurial finance?" The best way to understand it is to define the individual terms. Finance is the easier of the terms to define. It is the study of value and resource allocation. Cash is central to any working definition of finance. The value of any cash stream is influenced by its magnitude, timing, and riskiness. Finance is also concerned with the cost of capital and determining the least expensive source of funds for an investment project. This issue is especially important for start-up and growing firms that may face internal financial constraints and have different costs of debt and equity capital.

Entrepreneurship has had many definitions over the past two and one half centuries since Richard Cantillon first used the term in the early eighteenth century. Some have focused on the risk-bearing nature of entrepreneurship, while others have focused on the innovations that entrepreneurs create. Both are important elements of what entrepreneurs do, but neither is entrepreneurship. Entrepreneurship focuses on a way of thinking, managing a career, business, or anything else. While most of us associate entrepreneurship with small, start-up companies, large firms can also be "entrepreneurial." The important element of entrepreneurship is the relentless pursuit of opportunity without regard to resources currently controlled.[1]

Professor Paul Gompers prepared this note as the basis for class discussion rather than to illustrate either effective or ineffective handling of an administrative situation.

[1] Howard H. Stevenson and William A. Sahlman, "The Importance of Entrepreneurship," *Entrepreneurship, Intrapreneurship, and Venture Capital*, Robert D. Hisrich, ed. (Lexington, MA: Lexington Books, 1986).

Entrepreneurial Finance will focus on financial management within entrepreneurial firms. Most of these will be young firms, although some are more established. The course will examine these firms at all phases of their life cycle, from the initial idea generation to the ultimate harvesting of the venture. The course will cover firms in a diverse set of industries, including high technology, low technology, and service. A significant proportion of the cases will focus on non-U.S. ventures.

Financial management in entrepreneurial firms entails understanding both sides of the balance sheet. Consequently, we will look at issues related to both sides as well. The first section of the course will explore how to evaluate entrepreneurial business opportunities. The skills necessary to make good investment decisions include developing a framework of analysis for business opportunities. The process also entails reinforcing and enhancing valuation skills. With these tools, you will be able to qualitatively and quantitatively assess markets and opportunities.

The second section of the course examines how entrepreneurial investments are financed. An emphasis will be placed on understanding financial institutions and deal terms. The course then continues with an examination of harvesting. Unless an entrepreneur plans for the future realization on investment, he or she could get left holding the bag with little value having been created. We conclude the course by examining how entrepreneurial firms that have succeeded need to continually reinvent and reinvigorate themselves in order to remain successful. This transition to the second product or opportunity is often the most difficult time for the entrepreneurial enterprise.

Finally, we will make use of notes throughout the course. These notes provide background information about industry facts and figures. They are meant to be references that you can use often, both during the course and as you start your venture.

MODULE 1: INVESTMENT ANALYSIS

Sources of Value

The first module explores the structural model of entrepreneurship. We will use it as a framework for evaluation. The behavioral model defines entrepreneurship as the pursuit of opportunity without regard to resources currently controlled.[2] The four stages of entrepreneurship include: identifying opportunities; acquiring the financial, professional, and productive resources to exploit the opportunity; implementing a plan of action; and harvesting the rewards.[3] Entrepreneurship should not, however, be seen as a linear process. True entrepreneurship involves any or all the elements at any one particular time and should be viewed as a constantly repeating cycle.

William Sahlman developed a framework that identifies four critical success factors for entrepreneurial ventures: people, opportunity, deal, and context.[4] The cases in this course are selected to highlight how these various factors influence success and failure for firms in various industries. Each element is dynamic and can change over time, and the entrepreneur must constantly reevaluate the four factors that are critical to entrepreneurial value creation. Three questions can help center your analysis as you go forward:

What can go right?

What can go wrong?

---

[2] Ibid.

[3] William A. Sahlman, "Entrepreneurial Finance," Harvard Business School Case, 288-004 (1987).

[4] Ibid.

What actions can be taken to increase the probability that things will go right or minimize the chances that things will go wrong?

People

An important task in each case is to identify the key players. What is their experience? How does this experience prepare or not prepare them for the opportunity that exists? What are the strengths and weaknesses of the people involved on all sides of the transaction? Are there key individuals that the company should add or replace?

Opportunity

The opportunity that arises may be a new product or service, a new method of delivery, or a new production technique that provides a cost advantage. The entrepreneur must answer many questions before he or she commits to the venture. What is the nature of the opportunity? Is there a sustainable competitive advantage, or is the idea easily replicated? Must the opportunity be exploited immediately, or is there the possibility of delaying investment until further information is available? Are there intermediate milestones that can be used to assess the success of the project?

Deal

Once the people and opportunity pass a litmus test, a proper deal must be structured. Throwing money at good projects and good people will not guarantee success. Incentives and contingencies are important considerations. The proper deal structure can minimize moral hazard and adverse selection problems. From whom should the firm raise money: wealthy individuals (angels), banks, venture capitalists? What is the proper financing instrument: debt, equity, convertible securities, or a combination? Is a "no-compete" clause important? Can the deal create stakeholders that increase the probability of success? Who bears the downside (upside) risk?

Context

Often the most difficult part of the analysis is identifying contextual issues that are relevant to the success or failure of the project. Potential competitors may not be easily identified but will always be waiting to enter potentially profitable markets. The government is important because regulations and restrictions can aid or harm the firm's profitability. The entrepreneur must attempt to forecast what policies the government might pursue in response to political pressure. The opening of markets and the collapse of foreign regimes may be important in creating a favorable environment for new ideas. Economic conditions and trends will also influence a particular market and should be analyzed and understood.

The Concept of "FIT"

While most of the analysis may be divided into these four areas, it is important to understand the big picture. In other words, how do the four elements relate to each other? Do the people have the requisite skills and experience to exploit the opportunity? Does the deal provide the proper incentive to all players given the necessity of their input and the level of their skills? Will the context change the nature of the opportunity?

VALUATION

The second module of the course will address valuation techniques. Value is one of the fundamental concepts of finance and should be familiar to you from other coursework. To make proper investment decisions, it is always necessary to undertake a valuation. Stating that the uncertainty is too great to "value" a given project or company misses the point. Uncertainty affects the distribution of possible values, not the ability to undertake a valuation. Valuation in finance is a way to ask the right questions and understand what important assumptions determine the ultimate value. In fact, if the range of potential outcomes is quite high, that is, there is high uncertainty, a thorough valuation can give information about when to invest, when to discontinue a project, or when to investigate further. The sole purpose of valuation is not the production of a single number.

The first set of valuation problems are discounted cash flow valuation models. Although we discuss various discounted cash flow models, under the right assumptions, they should all give similar answers. The most important lesson is to fully understand the assumptions made in the process. We analyze discounted cash flow models in the case of both mature leveraged buyout situations and young, start-up ventures. The analysis emphasizes the strengths and weaknesses of such models. In fact, for many young firms, simple discounted cash flow models can give misleading values.

The shortcomings of standard discounted cash flow models often stem from the inability to account for real option value. Many projects have embedded optionality. A project that requires a small investment today to allow for information gathering and a possible future investment is like a financial option. The ability to delay investment until the acquisition of more information is a real option. The ability to halt a project creates an option to abandon. The payoff curve is similar to a call option where the only downside is the price of the option, but the upside is substantial. The entrepreneur who does not understand the value of these options may make improper investment decisions.

Entrepreneurial Finance will also examine real options in entrepreneurial firms. We will discuss their importance in the decisions of young, emerging companies. The course will develop tractable methods to deal with real option value and use it in the planning and structuring of investments.

MODULE 2: FINANCING THE ENTREPRENEURIAL FIRM

Once the entrepreneur identifies an investment opportunity, a financing strategy needs to be outlined. The opportunity may be a new firm, a new project, an expansion of a plant, or even the hiring of new employees. Any of these types of investments presents particular financing problems. An entrepreneur who cannot raise the required resources will not succeed. A firm needs cash to survive.

Discussion will identify financial institutions and players that actively provide resources to entrepreneurial firms. We will also examine the nature of contracting between investors and entrepreneurial firms. Understanding the terms and conditions of financing is important for all entrepreneurs to determine payoffs and incentives. Similarly, terms and conditions determine who controls the firm under various circumstances. Control rights such as board membership, information rights, covenants, and restrictions are often employed in the financing of entrepreneurial firms. Careful crafting of the financing document often increases the likelihood of success. Various factors drive firms to seek capital from a multitude of capital providers. Four primary factors that influence the source of funds can be identified.

The Four Factors

Uncertainty is a measure of the array of potential outcomes for a company or project. The greater the uncertainty, the wider the dispersion of potential outcomes. By their very nature, young companies are associated with significant levels of uncertainty. Uncertainty may exist about whether the research program or new product will succeed. Uncertainty may also exist about the response of rival firms to the introduction of a new product. High uncertainty means that investors and entrepreneurs cannot confidently predict how the firm will perform, what investment opportunities the company will identify, or what resources the firm will require.

Uncertainty affects the willingness of investors to contribute capital, the desire of suppliers to extend credit, and the decisions of a firm's manager. If managers are risk averse, it may be difficult to induce them to make the right decisions. Conversely, if entrepreneurs are overoptimistic, then investors want to curtail various actions. Uncertainty and the revelation of new information also affect the timing of investment. Should an investor contribute all the capital at the beginning, or should he stage the investment through time? Investors need to know how information-gathering activities can address these concerns and when to undertake them.

Asymmetric information is distinct from uncertainty. Because of her day-to-day involvement with the firm, an entrepreneur knows more about her company's prospects than investors, suppliers, or strategic partners. Similarly, investors may know more about their resources or ability to add value than the entrepreneur. Various problems develop in settings where asymmetric information is prevalent. Moral hazard can result when the entrepreneur takes potentially detrimental actions that investors cannot observe. For example, the entrepreneur may undertake a riskier strategy than initially suggested or may not work as hard as the investor expects. The entrepreneur might also invest in projects that build up her reputation at the investors' expense.

Asymmetric information can also lead to adverse selection problems when the entrepreneur knows more about the project or his abilities than investors do. Investors may find it difficult to distinguish between competent entrepreneurs and incompetent ones. Without the ability to screen out unacceptable projects and entrepreneurs, investors are unable to make efficient and appropriate decisions.

The third factor dynamically affecting a firm's corporate and financial strategy is *the nature of its assets*. Firms that have tangible assets—for example, machines, buildings, land, or physical inventory—may find financing easier to obtain or may be able to obtain more favorable terms. The ability to abscond with the firm's source of value is more difficult when it relies on physical assets. When the most important assets are intangible, such as trade secrets, raising outside financing is often more challenging.

Market conditions also play a key role in shaping a firm's evolution. The supply of capital from public and private investors and the price at which this capital is available may vary dramatically. These changes may be a response to regulatory edicts or shifts in investors' perceptions of future profitability. Similarly, the nature of product markets may vary dramatically due to shifts in the intensity of competition or in the nature of the customers.

The ability of young companies to grow rapidly and respond swiftly to the changing competitive environment is a key source of competitive advantage, but also a major problem for those who provide resources to these firms. The key characteristics of the firm—uncertainty, asymmetric information, the nature of its assets, and market conditions—will change dramatically over time. Because the firm may be different in the future, investors and entrepreneurs need to be able to anticipate change.

The combination of case studies and notes in this course develops recommendations for optimal capital raising and ownership structures in entrepreneurial firms. The materials demonstrate that careful crafting of financing strategies and contracts can alleviate many potential roadblocks. For instance, the best source of capital is not always obvious. Each source may be appropriate for a firm at different points in its life. The various factors identified above play a critical role in determining the optimal decision.

In addition, the *form* of financing (e.g., debt, equity, or convertible security) plays a critical role in reducing potential conflicts. Financing can be simple debt or equity, or may involve hybrid securities like convertible preferred equity or convertible debt. These financial structures can potentially screen out overconfident or underqualified entrepreneurs because they have very different payoffs for the entrepreneur in good and bad outcomes. The structure and timing of financing can also reduce the impact of uncertainty on future returns.

Another important element is the *division* of the profits between entrepreneurs and investors. Compensation contracts can be written that align the incentives of managers and investors. Incentive compensation can be in the form of cash, stock, or options. Performance can be tied to several measures and compared to various benchmarks. Carefully designed incentive schemes can avert destructive behavior.

Firms can also alter the nature of their assets and thus obtain greater financial flexibility. Patents, trademarks, and copyrights are all mechanisms to protect firm assets. Understanding the advantages and limitations of various forms of intellectual property protection, and coordinating financial and intellectual property strategies are essential to ensuring a young firm's growth. Firms can also affect the nature of their assets through strategic decisions, such as encouraging the creation of a set of "locked-in" users who rely on its products.

Monitoring and *evaluation* are also critical elements of the relationship between entrepreneurs and investors. Both parties must ensure that proper actions are taken and that appropriate progress is being made. Critical control mechanisms—for example, active and qualified boards of directors, the right to approve important decisions, and the ability to fire and recruit key managers—need to be effectively allocated in any relationship between an entrepreneur and investors. By examining theory and evidence, this course makes both descriptive and prescriptive comments on the effective use of monitoring, evaluation, and control.

MODULE 3: HARVESTING THE ENTREPRENEURIAL VENTURE

Every entrepreneur needs to consider harvesting at some point. Harvesting can take many forms. Successfully planning for harvesting of the entrepreneurial venture is critical to maximizing the value of your input. We will explore various modes of harvesting like initial public offerings (IPOs) and acquisitions. The emphasis is on assessing whether the entrepreneurial firm is "ready" for harvesting. In addition, we will emphasize the structural, legal, and dynamic issues of various modes of harvest.

The public markets are a significant source of capital for emerging companies. For many firms, accessing the public market is just the next phase of their dynamic capital process. For others, it represents the beginning of the ability to receive the fruits of their labors. We explore the various motivations for "going public" and the advantages and disadvantages of being a public company. Structural and legal issues will be discussed. In addition, we explore the impact that the cyclical nature of the initial public offering market has on firms access to capital. The role of various intermediaries will be examined, and the motivations of various parties discussed.

The course then covers acquisitions. Most firms will never be large enough for the public market and will therefore need to find one specific buyer. The ability to find the best buyer and negotiate the best deal terms for the entrepreneur is critical. We emphasize the role of bargaining and auctions in the context of acquisitions. The motivations of buyers and sellers must be understood to ensure the conclusion of a successful deal.

MODULE 4: RENEWAL IN THE ENTREPRENEURIAL ENTERPRISE

In the final module of the course, we discuss the importance of future opportunities in the sustainability of the entrepreneurial firm. If an entrepreneurial firm refuses to innovate and find new opportunities, it will fade away. The true entrepreneur continues to search for new opportunities, strives to find the right investors, implements the next project, and harvests his or her efforts. We examine a firm that has been successful in its initial project and is thinking of pursuing new opportunities. The issues revolve around whether the company should invest in a new project? Will it be a distraction? How should the new program be financed and structured? Does the company have any comparable advantage in this area? The cases will emphasize the difficulties that many young firms face. Being short-run focused yields quick results; being long-run focused may ensure the viability of the company for many years.

CONCLUSION

Entrepreneurial Finance is a course that examines the issues confronting entrepreneurial firms at all stages of their existence. The course presents various frameworks and builds new skills needed to identify important business ideas, raise and structure financing, and ultimately harvest the project. The knowledge and skills learned are invaluable for all students, whether they find a job in an entrepreneurial enterprise, work in a traditional firm, or start a company of their own.

SELECTED BIBLIOGRAPHY

The books and articles listed below are only for reference. They are not required reading and are not in the case packet.

BOOKS ON ENTREPRENEURSHIP, VENTURE CAPITAL, AND SMALL BUSINESS

ACS, ZOLTAN AND DAVID AUDRETSCH, 1991, *Innovation and Small Firms*, MIT Press, Cambridge, MA.

ACS, ZOLTAN AND DAVID AUDRETSCH, 1993, *Small Firms and Entrepreneurship*, Cambridge University Press, New York.

BARTLETT, JOSEPH, 1988, *Venture Capital Law, Business Strategies, and Investment Planning*, John Wiley and Sons, New York.

BIRCH, DAVID, 1987, *Job Creation in America: How Our Smallest Companies Put the Most People to Work*, Free Press, New York.

BORTON, JAMES, 1992, *Venture Japan*, Probus Publishing Co., Chicago.

BRANDT, STEPHEN, 1986, *Entrepreneurship in Established Companies*, Dow Jones-Irwin, Homewood, IL.

BYGRAVE, WILLIAM AND JEFFRY TIMMONS, 1992, *Venture Capital at the Crossroads*, Harvard Business School Press, Boston.

DRUCKER, PETER, 1985, *Innovation and Entrepreneurship*, Harper and Row, New York.

GIOVAGNOLI, MELISSA AND JOAN-MARIE MOSS, 1992, *The Chicago Entrepreneurs Sourcebook*, Enterprise Dearbom, Chicago.

GOMPERS, PAUL AND JOSH LERNER, 1999, *The Venture Capital Cycle*, MIT Press, Boston.

GOMPERS, PAUL AND JOSH LERNER, 2001, *The Money of Invention: How Venture Capital Creates New Wealth*, Harvard Business School Press, Boston.

HISRICH, ROBERT AND MICHAEL PETERS, 1989, *Entrepreneurship: Starting and Managing New Enterprise*, BPI-Irwin, Homewood, IL.

KANTER, ROSABETH, 1983, *The Change Masters: Innovation and Entrepreneurship in the American Corporation*, Simon and Schuster, New York.

KANTER, ROSABETH, 1989, *When Giants Learn to Dance*, Simon and Schuster, New York.

KAO, JOHN, 1989, *Entrepreneurship. Creativity. and Organization*, Prentice Hall, Englewood Cliffs, NJ.

KENT, CALVIN, 1984, *The Environment for Entrepreneurship*, D.C. Heath and Co., Lexington, MA.

KUNZE, ROBERT, 1990, *Nothing Ventured*, HarperCollins, New York.

LIPPERS, ARTHUR AND GEORGE RYAN, 1984, *Venture's Guide to Investing in Private Companies*, Dow Jones-Irwin, Homewood, IL.

PRATT, STANLEY AND JANE MORRIS, annual, *Pratt's Guide to Venture Capital Sources*, Venture Economics, Needham, MA.

RONSTADT, ROBERT, 1988, *Entrepreneurial Finance*, Lord Publishing, Natick, MA.

SEXTON, DONALD AND JOHN KASARDA, 1991, *The State of the Art of Entrepreneurship*, PWS-Kent, Boston.

SHEFSKY, LLOYD, 1995, *Entrepreneurs Are Made, Not Born,*

STEVENSON, HOWARD, MICHAEL ROBERTS, AND IRVING GROUSBECK, 1998, *New Business Ventures and the Entrepreneur*, Richard D. Irwin, Homewood, IL.

Periodicals

Black Enterprise
Buyouts
Entrepreneur
European Venture Capital Journal
Inc.
Journal of Business Venturing
Journal of Small Business Finance
Journal of Private Equity
Latin American Private Equity Analyst
Private Equity Analyst
Red Herring
Success
Venture Capital Journal
Wired

Articles from Academic Journals and Working Papers

AKERLOF, GEORGE, 1970, The market for "lemons": Qualitative uncertainty and the market mechanism, *Quarterly Journal of Economics* 84, 488–500.

BARRY, CHRIS, CHRIS MUSCARELLA, JOHN PEAVY, AND MICHAEL VETSUYPENS, The role of venture capital in the creation of public companies: evidence from the going-going public process, *Journal of Financial Economics* 27, 447–472.

BERGER, ALLEN, ANTHONY SAUNDERS, J. SCALISE, AND GREG UDELL, 1997, The effects of bank mergers and acquisitions on small business lending, New York University working paper.

BERGER, ALLEN AND GREG UDELL, 1995, Relationship lending and lines of credit in small firm finance, *Journal of Business* 65, 351–381.

BERGER, ALLEN AND GREG UDELL, 1996, Universal banking and the future of small business lending, in A. Saunders and I. Walters, eds, *Financial System Design: The Case for Universal Banking*, Irwin Publishing, Homewood, IL.

BRAV, ALON AND PAUL GOMPERS, 1997, Myth or reality? The long-run underperformance of initial public offerings: Evidence from venture and nonventure-backed companies. Forthcoming in *Journal of Finance*.

BYGRAVE, WILLIAM AND M. STEIN, 1989, A time to buy and a time to sell: a study of 77 venture capital investments in companies that went public, *Frontiers of Entrepreneurship Research*, 1989.

CARTER, RICHARD AND STEVEN MANASTER, 1990, Initial public offerings and underwriter reputation, *Journal of Finance* 45, 1045–1067.

DIAMOND, DOUG, 1989, Reputation acquisition in debt markets, *Journal of Political Economy* 97, 828–862.

FAZZARI, STEVE, R. GLEN HUBBARD, AND B. PETERSEN, 1988, Investment and finance reconsidered, *Brookings Papers on Economic Activity*, 141–195.

GOMPERS, PAUL, 1994, The rise of venture capital, *Business and Economic History* 23, 1–24.

GOMPERS, PAUL, 1995, Optimal investment, monitoring, and the staging of venture capital, *Journal of Finance* 50, 1461–1489. December 1995. Reprinted in Michael Wright and Ken Robbie, editors, *Venture Capital* (International Library of Management) (Aldershot: Dartmouth Publishing, 1997).

GOMPERS, PAUL, 1996, Grandstanding in the venture capital industry, *Journal of Financial Economics* 42, 133–156.

GOMPERS, PAUL, 1997, Ownership and control in entrepreneurial firms: An examination of convertible securities in venture capital, Harvard Business School working paper.

GOMPERS, PAUL, 1999, Resource allocation, incentives, and control: The importance of venture capital in financing entrepreneurial firms in *Entrepreneurship, SMEs, and the Macroeconomy*. Cambridge University Press, New York.

GOMPERS, PAUL, 1997, Venture capital growing pains: Should the market diet? *Journal of Banking and Finance* 22, 1089–1104.

GOMPERS, PAUL AND JOSH LERNER, 1996, The use of covenants: An empirical analysis of venture partnership agreements, *Journal of Law and Economics* 39, 463–498.

GOMPERS, PAUL AND JOSH LERNER, 1997, Risk and reward in private equity investments: The challenge of performance assessment, *Journal of Private Equity* 1, 5–2.

GOMPERS, PAUL AND JOSH LERNER, 1997, Venture capitalists and the creation of public companies, *Journal of Private Equity* 1, 15–32.

GOMPERS, PAUL AND JOSH LERNER, 2000, Money chasing deals? The impact of fund inflows on private equity valuations, *Journal of Financial Economics* 55, 281–325.

GOMPERS, PAUL AND JOSH LERNER, 1999, Reputation and conflict of interest in the issuance of public securities: Evidence from venture capital. *Journal of Law and Economics* 52, 1–28.

GOMPERS, PAUL AND JOSH LERNER, 1998, What drives venture capital fundraising? Forthcoming in the *Brookings Proceedings on Microeconomic Activity*.

GORMAN, MICHAEL AND WILLIAM SAHLMAN, 1989, What do venture capitalists do?, *Journal of Business Venturing* 4, 133–147.

GREENWALD, BRUCE, JOSEPH STIGLITZ, AND ANDREW WEISS, 1984, Information imperfections in the capital market and macroeconomic fluctuations, *American Economic Review Papers and Proceedings* 74, 194–199.

HARRIS, MILTON AND ARTUR RAVIV, 1989, The design of securities, *Journal of Financial Economics* 24, 255–287.

HARRIS, MILTON AND ARTUR RAVIV, 1990, Financial contracting theory, University of Chicago working paper.

HART, OLIVER, 1991, Theories of optimal capital structure: a principal-agent perspective, Harvard University working paper.

HART, OLIVER AND BENGT HOLMSTROM, 1987, The theory of contracts, in T. Bewly (ed.), *Advances in Economic Theory*, Fifth World Congress, Cambridge, Cambridge University Press.

HART, OLIVER AND JOHN MOORE, 1990, Property rights and the nature of the firm, *Journal of Political Economy* 98, 1119–1158.

HART, OLIVER AND JOHN MOORE, 1989, Default and renegotiation: a dynamic model of debt, Harvard University working paper.

HART, OLIVER AND JOHN MOORE, 1994, A theory of debt based on the inalienability of human capital, *Quarterly Journal of Economics*, 841–880.

HERMALIN, BENJAMIN AND MICHAEL WEISBACH, 1988, The determinants of board composition, *Rand Journal of Economics* 19, 589–606.

HOLMSTROM, BENGT AND RICARTI-I-COSTA, 1986, Managerial incentives and capital management, *Quarterly Journal of Economics*, 839–860.

HOSHI, T., ANIL KASHYAP, AND DAVID SCHARFSTEIN, 1991, Corporate structure, liquidity, and investment, *Quarterly Journal of Economics* 106, 33–60.

JAMES, CHRISTOPHER, 1987, Some evidence on the uniqueness of bank loans: A comparison of bank borrowing, private placements, and public offerings, *Journal of Financial Economics* 19, 217–235.

JAMES, CHRISTOPHER AND PEGGY WEIR, 1990, Borrowing relationships, intermediation, and the cost of issuing public securities, *Journal of Financial Economics* 28, 149–171.

JENSEN, MICHAEL, 1986, Agency cost of free cash flow, corporate finance and takeovers, *AER Papers and Proceedings* 76, 323–329.

JENSEN, MICHAEL, 1989, Eclipse of the public corporation, *Harvard Business Review* 5, 61–74.

JENSEN, MICHAEL AND WILLIAM MECKLING, 1976, Theory of the firm: managerial behavior, agency costs, and capital structure, *Journal of Financial Economics* 3, 305–360.

LERNER, JOSH, 1994, The syndication of venture capital investments, *Financial Management* 23 (Autumn), 16–27.

LERNER, JOSH, 1995, Venture capital and the oversight of privately-held firms, *Journal of Finance* 50, 301–318.

LERNER, JOSH, 1994, Venture capitalists and the decision to go public, *Journal of Financial Economics* 35, 293–316.

MEGGINSON, WILLIAM AND KATHLEEN WEISS, 1991, Venture capitalist certification in initial public offerings, *Journal of Finance* 46, 879–903.

MODIGLIANI, FRANCO AND MERTON MILLER, 1958, The cost of capital, corporation finance, and the theory of investment, *American Economic Review* 48, 261–297.

MUSCARELLA, CHRIS AND MICHAEL VETSUYPENS, 1989, Initial public offerings and information asymmetry, SMU working paper.

MYERS, STEWART, 1984, The capital structure puzzle, *Journal of Finance* 39, 575–592.

MYERS, STEWART AND N. MAJLUF, 1984, Corporate financing and investment decisions when firms have information that investors do not have, *Journal of Financial Economics* 13, 187–221.

PAGANO, MARCO, F. PANETTA, AND LUIGI. ZINGALES, 1997, Why do firms go public? An empirical analysis, University of Chicago working paper.

PATEL, JAY, RICHARD ZECKHAUSER, AND D. HENDRICKS, 1991, The rationality struggle: Illustrations from financial markets, *American Economic Review* 81, 232–236.

PETERSON, MITCHELL AND RAGHU RAJAN, 1994, The benefits of lending relationships: Evidence from small business data, *Journal of Finance* 99, 3–37.

PETERSON, MITCHELL AND RAGHU RAJAN, 1995, The benefits of firm-creditor relationships: A study of small business financings, *Quarterly Journal of Economics* 110, 407–443.

PLUMMER, J., 1987, QED report on Venture capital analysis, Palo Alto, QED Research.

RAJAN, RAGHU, 1992, A theory of fluctuations in bank credit policy, mimeo.

RITTER, JAY, 1984, The "hot issue" market of 1980, *Journal of Business* 57, 215–241.

RITTER, JAY, 1987, The cost of going public, *Journal of Financial Economics*, 269–281.

RITTER, JAY, 1991, The long run performance of initial public offerings, *Journal of Finance* 46, 328.

SAHLMAN, WILLIAM, 1990, The structure and governance of venture capital organizations, *Journal of Financial Economics* 27, 473–524.

SAPIENZA, HARRY, 1992, When do venture capitalists add value, *Journal of Business Venturing* 7, 9–27.

SCHWARZ, J., 1991, The future of the venture capital industry, *Journal of Business Venturing* 6, 89–92.

STIGLITZ, JOSEPH AND ANDREW WEISS, 1981, Credit rationing in markets with incomplete information, *American Economic Review* 71, 393–409.

STIGLITZ, JOSEPH AND ANDREW WEISS, 1983, Incentive effects of terminations: Applications to the credit and labor markets, *American Economic Review* 73, 919–927.

THACKRAY, JOHN, The institutionalization of venture capital, *Institutional Investor*, August 1983, 73–76.

TITMAN, SHERIDAN AND R. WESSELS, 1988, The determinants of capital structure choice, *Journal of Finance* 43, 1–19.

TOWNSEND, ROBERT, 1979, Optimal contracts and competitive markets with costly state verification, *Journal of Economic Theory* 21, 265–293.

WETZEL, WILLIAM, 1987, The informal venture capital market, *Journal of Business Venturing* 2, 299–314.

WILLIAMSON, OLIVER, 1988, Corporate finance and corporate governance, *Journal of Finance* 43, 567–591.

2

The Knot

David Liu, co-founder and CEO of The Knot, peered out his sixth-floor window at the eclectic streets of the Soho district in New York City. It was November 5, 1997, and Liu had just finished proofreading the final version of The Knot's business plan that had been prepared by Schroder & Co. Inc.'s investment banking arm. Liu's "Silicon Alley" company was at a critical juncture in its two-year history. Despite success as one of the early America Online (AOL) Greenhouse companies, a three-book deal with Bantam Doubleday, strong interest from advertisers, and significant traffic at its World Wide Web site, the future of The Knot was in jeopardy. With a forecasted "fume" date sometime in January of 1998, Liu desperately needed cash. The race for scale economies on the Internet also meant that he needed to capitalize on his company's current momentum by increasing investments in marketing and retail operations. Without some or all of the $10 million sought in the business plan, Liu's dream of building the country's number-one wedding resource would be all for "knot."

BACKGROUND

The Knot's core management team of Liu, Carley Roney, Michael Wolfson, and Rob Fassino (see Exhibit 2-1 for management biographies) first met in the late 1980s as students at New York University's Film School. The year 1993 proved to be a landmark year for Liu and Roney: the longtime couple married in July and co-founded RunTime, Inc., a CD-ROM development company, later the same year. Wolfson and Fassino were reunited with Liu and Roney in 1995 as a result of a RunTime project. Sotheby's, the legendary auction house, was preparing to auction off various pieces of impressionistic art and wanted to develop a CD-ROM as a promotional item. Fassino and Wolfson, founders of the Digital Media Division for Margeotes Fertitta + Partners, were managing the Sotheby's account. Lacking an internal CD-ROM development capability, Fassino and Wolfson turned to RunTime. The Sotheby's project was a resounding

Entrepreneurial Studies Fellow Matthew C. Lieb prepared this case under the supervision of Professor William A. Sahlman and Lecturer Michael J. Roberts as the basis for class discussion rather than to illustrate either effective or ineffective handling of an administrative situation.

EXHIBIT 2-1

THE "KNOT" MANAGEMENT

David Liu, Chief Executive Officer, has over nine years of digital production and management experience. In 1993 he founded RunTime Inc., a CD-ROM development firm producing award-winning titles for clients such as the Smithsonian Institution and Sotheby's. Prior to Run-Time, Liu managed a staff of 40 as Director of Production at VideOvation, a subsidiary of the Reader's Digest, which produced over 300 half-hour video programs annually.

Rob Fassino, VP of Marketing, has eight years of experience in the advertising industry. In 1994, he founded the Digital Media Division of Margeotes Fertitta + Partners advertising, producing award-winning Web sites and CD-ROMs for Stolichnaya Vodka, Sotheby's, and Infoseek. Prior to establishing the division, Fassino produced television commercials for clients such as CBS, General Foods, and New York Newsday.

Carley Roney, VP of Creative Development, was president of RunTime Inc. before founding The Knot. Prior to forming RunTime, she spent six years as creative director and editor for clients including the National Museum of American history, the McGraw-Hill Companies, Simon and Schuster, Prentice Hall, and Worth Publishing. She has an M.A. in Cultural Studies from New York University.

Michael Wolfson, VP of New Business Development, was founder and president of Luna Pictures, Inc., a production company providing creative and post-production services for clients such as MTV Networks, Lifetime Television, and Miramax Films. As a consultant, Wolfson co-founded the Digital Media Division of Margeotes Fertitta + Partners advertising and developed new media brands for clients such as PBS's Trailsides, CyberShop, and America Online.

Russ Casenhiser, Director of Operations, was co-founder and president of Bridal Search, Inc., where he developed the industry's largest, searchable datatbase of bridal gowns. Prior to founding Bridal Search, he co-owned La Galleria, a high-end women's apparel store. Prior to La Galleria, Casenhiser, as president of Contractors Resource, grew the company's annual revenue from $1 million to over $10 million. He has an M.B.A. from Pepperdine University.

Becky Casenhiser, Director of Merchandising, was co-founder and vice president of Bridal Search, Inc., where she procured and maintained relationships with all of the bridal gown manufacturers. Prior to Bridal Search, she co-owned La Galleria, where she managed the buying, sales, and customer service. After significantly increasing La Galleria's sales, she successfully sold the store in 1995. She has an M.B.A. from Pepperdine University.

Erik Herz, Director of Advertising Sales, has over six years of sales experience in the publishing industry. As the National Advertising Manager of <u>M@x</u> racks, he oversaw the restructuring of its advertising department and increased sales by 400%. Prior to <u>M@x</u> racks he was an advertising account manager at The Hearst Corporation, where he helped launch the French magazine *Marie Claire* in the American market.

success and planted the seed for future collaboration among the four entrepreneurs. Liu described the results of the Sotheby's project:

> Working together while producing the Sotheby's CD-ROM really opened our eyes to the potential of our team. We each brought different skills to the table, and the chemistry between us was really powerful. We believed that our collective experience gave us the know-how to build a successful media business if we could find an appropriate consumer market niche on which to focus. We founded Element Studios in 1995 to capitalize on our abilities.

Element's founders wanted the yet-to-be-determined consumer niche to offer high advertising revenue, stable demand, and stagnant competition. They began their research by looking at the magazine business. They felt that magazines offered an excellent proxy for the attractiveness of niche markets because there were magazines for nearly every consumer interest imaginable. The wedding industry immediately caught their attention. The 2.4 million weddings that occur each year generate close to $35 billion in annual sales and services. In studying the dominant wedding magazines (*Bride's*, *Modern Bride*, and *Bridal Guide*), the management team realized that the $170 in advertising revenue per subscriber for these publications far outpaced the ratios seen in other consumer segments. High advertising rates were explained by the attractive demographic and spending patterns of people who were planning a wedding. Nearly 43% of engaged couples had a household income of $50,000 or more and an average age of only 26. More important, engaged couples were on the verge of making significant purchasing decisions regarding everything from furniture to investments.

Further analysis supported the attractiveness of the wedding industry. In 1996 alone, *Modern Bride*, *Bride's*, and *Bridal Guide* garnered a combined $168 million in advertising revenue (see Exhibit 2-2). These three magazines, with an average of 40 years in the bridal business, had developed strong relationships with advertisers and represented the dominant media brands in the wedding segment. Liu described the competitive landscape in 1996:

> The three magazines were deeply entrenched, given their long history in this market. Fortunately, the lack of any new competition in recent years had resulted in a somewhat stale and old feel for each of these magazines. They simply lacked a fresh voice and were too married to their old ways to change. We saw an opportunity to really differentiate ourselves in a segment that had seen a good deal of brand blurring.

The decision to build the business's foundation online was done more out of necessity than anything else. Realizing that infrastructure and development costs for a traditional magazine were prohibitively expensive, the founders decided to develop content for the burgeoning online audience. In Liu's words:

> We are traditional media people; the decision to be an online company was really more of an afterthought. We really liked the lower investment cost associated with an online venture and we felt that the online world offered some competitive advantages vis-à-vis our magazine competition. We strongly believed that the possibility of cannibalization to their existing businesses would deter the three big magazines from moving to the Internet in the short term. With these thoughts in mind, we set out to build a branded media company that would initially be online, but would then grow to encompass more traditional mediums. We chose the name *The Knot* instead of something like *Wedding.com* so we wouldn't pigeonhole ourselves in the online world.

In December 1995, The Knot was formed as the first full-time venture of Element Studios. The team immediately began to solicit an initial investment to get the business

EXHIBIT 2-2

WEDDING MAGAZINE ADVERTISING FIGURES

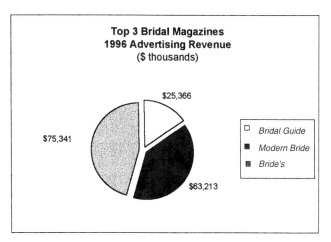

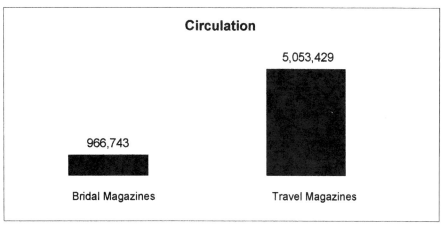

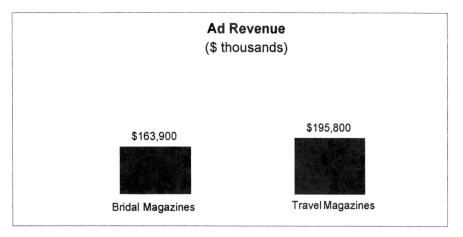

Source: Company Resources.

off the ground. Liu and his management team made a calculated bet on the future of online usage. Despite only one million subscribers at the time, Liu firmly believed that America Online would become the commercial site of choice for the developing online consumer base. In Liu's words:

> Although we needed the money to make things happen, our real goal was to find a strategic partner that brought more than just dollars to the deal. We felt that AOL would eventually dominate the online consumer space, so we saw their new Greenhouse program as an avenue for eventually garnering a substantial proportion of the online wedding consumer market. We used a variety of business contacts to get a foot in the door in hopes of getting money, exposure, and distribution.

It took only three months to convince AOL's Greenhouse Network to sign a letter of intent outlining a substantial investment in The Knot. In February 1996, Greenhouse began making incremental investments in The Knot as the formal financing negotiations between the two sides moved forward. It was not until January 1997 that AOL formally agreed to invest $1.85 million in exchange for warrants for up to 45% of The Knot's equity. In addition to the equity stake, the deal called for AOL to receive 20% of the revenue from advertising inventory sold on The Knot's yet-to-be-developed AOL property as well as a percentage of the revenue from advertising inventory sold on The Knot's own web site (based on the percent of The Knot's web traffic originating from AOL).

Since The Knot's initial incremental funding from AOL, Liu and his team had made significant strides toward achieving their goals of becoming a full-service online wedding resource and a recognizable brand in the industry. In September 1996, the Knot appeared on AOL for the first time, becoming the service's sole wedding property. The response was impressive. User figures quickly rose to a total of over 65,000 unique users per month. The attractiveness of The Knot's audience was not lost on advertisers. In the first two months alone, The Knot generated over $25,000 in advertising revenue from the likes of Nicole Miller and Godiva Chocolates.

The contemporary content of The Knot and the rapid growth of America Online's subscriber base gave the company a great deal of credibility and exposure. The Knot's comprehensive bridal content and services had broad-based appeal. The content attracted couples interested in traditional wedding experiences as well as "to-be-weds" that found themselves in more "nontraditional" marriage situations. The Knot developed content dealing with issues such as second marriages, elopement, same-sex marriages, and premarital pregnancy (see Exhibit 2-3). In addition to its creative content, The Knot made a concerted effort to provide value-added services to users (see Exhibit 2-4). It was not long before The Knot had developed a strong community of users who frequently exchanged information, recommended solutions to other users' problems, and recounted the endless stories surrounding the assorted details leading up to their wedding days.

Building the Brand

Contributing to The Knot's substantial momentum was a creative promotional strategy aimed at increasing brand awareness. Traditional public relations efforts resulted in news coverage from a number of major publications including the *Wall Street Journal*, *Washington Post*, and *USA Today*. Liu also targeted potential partners to promote The Knot brand. Liu's strategy of creating a large inventory of content to be placed within easy reach of potential users began to pay off. Michael Wolfson, The Knot's vice president

EXHIBIT 2-3

SAMPLE CONTENT OF THE KNOT'S ONLINE INFORMATION OFFERINGS

Topic	Title	Description
Wedding Planning	Volumes of Vows	Whether traditional or personal—your vows speak volumes
	Ethnic Customs	Introduce a bit of your background to make your wedding unique
	Eloping 101	Where, why, and how of eloping
	Invitation Issues	Musts to remember for ordering and prepping those invites
Fashion	Dress Talk	Terms you'll need to know to gab intelligently
	Veiled Looks	The latest trends in veils and headpieces
	Same-Sex Wedding	An opportunity for creativity can also mean difficult decisions
Beauty	The 'do for You	Don't let the big day be a bad hair day
	A Tub for Two	A bath is not always a bath . . .
	Many Manicures	Twenty (finger) tips to get a handle on hand care
Advice/Etiquette	Ready or Not	Are you *both* prepared to get engaged?
	Will It Be Different?	What marriage does to your relationship
	Different Strokes	First wedding for one/second for the other
	Fight Right	Correctly confronting confrontations
Grooms/Guys	Sizing Her Up	Tips to sneak her ring size and keep the surprise
	Dance Fever	Don't have a lot of natural rhythm? It's time for some lessons . . .
	Groom's Toasts	Everything you need to know to sound cool when you talk
Attendant/Guest	Fresh Shower Ideas	Themes that'll put a blissed-out smile on any bride's face
	Stifling In-Laws?	When you're getting a bit too much input
	Speak Now	Advice for when you simply *can't* forever hold your peace
Travel	Biking Honeymoons	Roughing it by day, luxuriating by night
	Pack Like a Pro	Tried and true packing tips from a travel-aholic
	The U.S.V.I.	Honeymooning in an American paradise
Gift/Registering	Flatware 101	Making sure your spoons match your forks
	Tooling Around	What a pair of fixer-uppers need in their box
	Want Cash Gifts?	Got enough home stuff? How to roll in the dough
Home/Life	The Electronic Marital Aid	How Sony could save your marriage
	What's Feng Shui?	Use the art of placement for a harmonious home
	Breakfast in Bed	How to pull off this most romantic of capers

of New Business Development, convinced AOL to allow The Knot to create a holiday called "Wedding Day" on June 21, 1996. The results exceeded all expectations. Nearly 1,200 AOL subscribers visited the site, far outpacing sites devoted to more traditional holidays such as Father's Day. The "Wedding Day" chat room was filled with couples exchanging vows before going to their official ceremony in an effort to give guests who were unable to attend the traditional service an opportunity to witness a piece of the wedding.

Liu also looked outside AOL to build strategic partnerships. In December 1996, Rob Fassino, vice president of Marketing launched The Knot's Registry Partner Program with nationwide retailers such as Bloomingdale's. In exchange for The Knot's promotion of registry information kits, the retailers distributed The Knot promotional pieces containing The Knot-branded free-trial AOL disks in their registry kits. Bloomingdale's alone had distributed 10,000 disks since the inception of the Registry Partner Program. Liu signed numerous other partnership deals to continue to build awareness of The Knot brand (see Exhibit 2-5). The significant public relations, advertising, and promo-

EXHIBIT 2-4

SAMPLE COMMUNITY AND INTERACTIVE SERVICES

Service	Description
Chat	24-hour chat room with over 70 hours of scheduled chat sessions every week, moderated by one of The Knot's 35 remote chat hosts.
Message Boards	Discussion boards where The Knot's users ask questions, swap ideas, and share advice.
Membership Benefits	Users who join The Knot (subscribing is free) post their wedding announcements, search for other couples in their region who share common interests, and provide information—such as where they are registered—for their guests.
Daily Interactive	Users participate in surveys, polls, trivia; The Knot's experts offer daily advice on everything from etiquette to travel.
911 Hotline	Users post their latest wedding trauma and find the immediate help they need from both experts and other users.
Bridal Gown Search[a]	The only online bridal gown database allowing brides-to-be the ability to search for and view 6,000 gown images, representing approximately 70% of gowns available from major manufacturers.
Big Day Budgeter[a]	An interactive budgeting program that estimates and tracks wedding budgets throughout the planning process.
Countdown Calendar[a]	An interactive calendar program that creates a timeline of planning tasks leading to the wedding date
Honeymoon Center	Travel reservation service with capability to allow users to bid on unique honeymoon packages in biweekly travel auctions.
Local Listings	A searchable, national database of local wedding vendors sorted by categories such as florists, caterers, and limousines.
Denis Reggie Photographers Network	An interactive national database like Local Listings, dedicated to finding wedding photographers. Denis Reggie is a well-known celebrity-wedding photographer.

[a] The above services are personalized, allowing users to calculate, save, and adjust their personal data throughout their wedding planning period.

tional relationship deals struck by The Knot fueled the growth of the company's user base. The AOL audience alone grew from 65,000 unique users in September 1996 to 260,000 users only seven months later.

The summer of 1997 proved to be the beginning of a series of major achievements for The Knot. In May, The Knot's World Wide Web site was launched (see Exhibit 2-6), garnering over 2.7 million page views per month by July. The Web site encompassed The Knot's first venture into retail sales via The Knot Gift Shop. The Gift Shop began by selling Kodak disposable cameras. Within two months, The Knot had generated $25,000 in disposable camera revenue alone at an average price per order of over $150. Other products that addressed specific needs of to-be-weds were quickly added.

In June, The Knot signed an agreement that would lay the foundation for a future acquisition of Bridal Search, Inc., the only comprehensive online bridal gown database. Under the terms of the agreement, Bridal Search agreed to be acquired in exchange for 10,000 shares of common stock issuable upon completion of The Knot's proposed

EXHIBIT 2-5

SAMPLE OF THE KNOT PARTNERSHIPS

Online Partnerships

Partner	Description	Relationship
Excite	Internet Search Engine	Featured partner, Lifestyle channel
Yahoo!	Internet Search Engine	Developing Yahoo! "I Do" weddings
AOL/Web: Digital Cities	Local listings content	Featured wedding resource
AOL/Web: Preview Travel	AOL's exclusive travel agency	Exclusive honeymoon resource
AOL: Net Noir	Largest Afro-centric community	Featured wedding content partner

Marketing Partnerships

Partner	Description	Relationship
Bloomingdale's	National Retailer	Online and in-store marketing
1-800 Flowers	Largest online floral retailer	Marketing and promotion partner
Atlantic Records	Record Label	Marketing and promotion partner
Great Bridal Expo	National consumer bridal exposition	Featured online wedding resource
Museum of the City of New York	Hosts NY's "Get married" exhibit	"The Future of Weddings"
Harley Davidson Café	National chain of theme restaurants	Special promotions, live events
WEDCON '97	Bridal Industry's online conference	Keynote speaker/online partner

round of financing (see Exhibit 2-10 for ownership information). In addition, Bridal Search had the opportunity to earn up to an additional 32,857 shares of The Knot if certain triggering events occurred. In the meantime, The Knot agreed to cover the operating expenses of Bridal Search in exchange for access to the bridal gown database. Liu commented on the importance of this deal:

> Partnering with Bridal Search was a great move for us. The obvious benefit was that it gave us the only comprehensive online database of wedding dresses. This was a service that our customers really appreciated. Perhaps more importantly, the deal allowed us to improve our management team by adding Russ and Becky Casenhiser. Not only were they successful entrepreneurs in their own right, but their experience in retail would benefit us greatly as we continued to develop our business model.

The unique services of The Knot coupled with relatively high online usage figures and a targeted demographic continued to attract advertisers. The Knot signed one-year deals with Lord West, Riunite Wine, and JLM Couture (the only publicly traded bridal gown manufacturer). These three deals alone represented a combined $750,000 in advertising revenue. The Knot was quickly becoming one of the few success stories among advertising-based online businesses.

Offline Promotional Efforts

Growing brand awareness and successful publicity efforts motivated Liu to implement The Knot's first offline brand building effort. In August of 1997, The Knot signed a

EXHIBIT 2-6

THE KNOT'S WORLD WIDE WEB SITE

TABLE A Sample of The Knot Gift Shop Products

Wedding Accessories	Groomsman Gifts	Bridesmaid Gifts
Kodak cameras	Swiss Army Knife	Swiss Army Knife Key Chain
Bridal Gown Catalogs	Fossil Sport Watch	Handmade Paper Journal/Pen
Ring Bearer Pillows	Cigar Case with Cigar	Glass Perfume Bottle
Toasting Glasses	German Beer Steins	Jewelry Box/Travel Case

three-book deal with Bantam Doubleday. The deal called for The Knot to develop three books over a two-year period, with publishing efforts handled by Broadway Books, a division of Bantam Doubleday Dell. *Just Tie It: The Knot's Real-World Guide to Getting Married*; *Weddings 202: The Knot's Guide to Re-Marrying*; and *The Great Escape: The Knot's Guide to Honeymooning* were to be developed by The Knot's editorial team, utilizing content from the interaction of The Knot users with each other and The Knot experts. The intent was to develop "real-world" publications with unique online tie-ins to encourage readers to participate in The Knot's online properties. In exchange for committing to develop the editorial content of the three books, The Knot received a $350,000 advance and a 7.5% royalty fee.

Liu continued to develop offline promotional deals by signing an agreement in September 1997 with WHYY-TV, Philadelphia's public television station and the second-largest PBS station in the country. The agreement stipulated that The Knot would co-produce a 13-part television program entitled *Weddings for the Real World*. Liu hoped to use the television deal to promote the online service and books. Additional revenue would come from the sale of videos as well as redistribution deals with cable television programmers following the initial three-year programming run on public television.

GIFT REGISTRY

With numerous partnership deals signed, advertising revenue agreements in place, and ancillary products under development, Liu turned his attention to the enormous potential of the bridal registry business:

> There are a lot of things to like about the wedding business. It is recession proof, garners a great deal of advertising revenue, and represents one of the most important times in peoples' lives. We felt that we had developed a model that captured some of the value that existed in the wedding segment, but we knew that if we really wanted our company to prosper we would have to become a player in the registry side of the wedding experience.

Bridal registry alone represented a $17 billion business—nearly half of all wedding-related revenue. Over 90% of all soon-to-be-weds registered, and 79% of these customers registered at two or more stores. Competition for wedding registry was fierce, dominated by well-established department stores such as Macy's and Bloomingdale's. Department stores alone garnered close to 90% of the gift registering business. Bridal registry merchandise tended to be concentrated in a few areas: china and flatware, crystal glassware, cookware, small appliances, and home electronics. Several aspects of the bridal registry business were unique in relation to traditional retail operations. The current bridal registry business model implemented by retailers called for soon-to-be-weds to visit the retail store and develop a comprehensive list of gifts that the couple desired from their wedding guests. Because the items were specified by the engaged couple but purchased by the guests, there was a fair degree of price insensitivity. As a result, wedding registry gifts were almost never discounted. The average price per gift was around $70, and the typical couple received 171 gifts. In addition, because couples registered well in advance of the actual purchase of gifts, and guests tended to follow the protocol of only purchasing gifts from the registry list, sales were extremely predictable once the registration was completed.

Liu saw an enormous opportunity in bridal registry. Not only was the market huge, but the operational and economic aspects of registry boded well for an online solution. Despite well-entrenched competitors, Liu saw a number of competitive advantages for The Knot. Large department stores were burdened by significant investments in "bricks and mortar" as well as legacy computer systems that were not Internet-ready. The fact that gifts were often purchased by out-of-town guests also made the purchasing logistics complicated in the traditional model. Guests would have to find a retail establishment that maintained the engaged couple's registry in order to purchase an appropriate gift. The majority of retail players in this segment used registry as a complementor to their existing businesses. As a result, these competitors were retailers first and registry specialists second. Liu saw an opportunity to build an online registry function that allowed engaged couples to register, and guests to purchase gifts, through The Knot's World Wide Web and AOL sites. Liu believed that leveraging The Knot's existing audience and technological infrastructure would give his company a head start in developing a significantly more efficient and effective method of serving soon-to-be-weds and their guests.

Liu needed to look no further than his existing customers to test the validity of the registry option. User surveys strongly supported his view of the registry potential (see Table B for results of the survey).

Armed with positive consumer feedback, The Knot's management team developed the model further. To address the most important registry issue, offering a wide variety of products, The Knot developed a comprehensive list of items that covered traditional wedding gifts and more contemporary items such as outdoor gear, home mortgage down payments, and mutual funds. Liu commented on the development of gift ideas:

> Most wedding gifts tend to be things that new married couples need. Our goal was to provide gift options that met couples' needs as well as their wants. We simply asked our customers and ourselves what people really wanted and started putting together a list of responses.

To assist couples through the time-consuming gift selection process, Liu decided to organize gifts into distinctive "registry packs." These packs served as custom groupings of products and services designed to match the interests of particular lifestyles arranged under the headings "adventurous," "romantic," "casual," "connoisseur," and "cosmopolitan" (see Exhibit 2-7). In addition to the registry pack option, registrants would be able

TABLE B The Knot Gift Registry Customer Survey Data

Survey Topic	Percentage of Respondents
A wide variety of products is the most important factor in choosing a registry	50%
Convenience is the second-most important factor in choosing a registry	40%
Deciding what gifts to list is the most difficult part of the registering process	40%
We would be likely to use The Knot Online Registry	63%

EXHIBIT 2-7

SAMPLE OF REGISTRY GIFTS

Romantic	Adventurous
His/her terry cloth bathrobes	His/her mountain bikes
Hammock for two	Tent for two
Wine rack	Roof rack
Candlesticks/holders and candles	Coleman lantern
Case of fine wine	Micro-brew-of-the-month club
Dance lessons	Scuba lessons
Champagne glasses & bucket	Margarita glasses & mix
Massage oils	Compass and road atlas
Breakfast-in-bed tray	Camping cook stove
Picnic basket	Cooler
Espresso maker	Barbecue grill
Formal china settings	Casual china settings
Ice cream maker	Wok and utensils
Coffee/tea service	Sport thermos
Classical CD set	Sony Sport portable stereo
Movie rental gift certificates	Lift ticket gift certificates
Luggage set	His/her backpacks
Double shower head	Snorkel gear

to utilize agenting technology to further hone product suggestions. Agenting technology would allow The Knot to essentially match the tastes of new registrants to those of previous registrants who exhibited similar interests. Couples would also have the option of browsing traditional categories like home appliances by criteria such as price.

Convenience was perhaps the most compelling advantage of The Knot's online registry model. Liu developed a strategy to improve the convenience for both the engaged couple and the gift purchasers. To streamline the process for the couple, The Knot would allow them to modify, monitor, and save their registry selections at any time during the engagement via The Knot Web site. In addition, couples would maintain the option of having The Knot send e-mail messages to guests notifying them of the couple's registration. Additional options such as customized delivery dates and preaddressed thank-you notes that accompanied the gifts would add to the convenience of registering with The Knot. Related services would include registry completion programs for couples who did not receive the requested quantity of a specified gift as well as online chats with wedding guests, contests, and sweepstakes.

To enhance the registry process for guests, Liu envisioned a toll-free phone number, fax, and standard mail service that provided the couple's custom list of desired gifts. For purchasers with Internet access, The Knot's online properties would offer a password-protected interface that provided access to an updated registry list complete with a display of gift items that were not yet purchased. The continually updated registry information would give The Knot a significant advantage vis-à-vis traditional retailers. Statistically, 80% of gifts were purchased within three days of the wedding. As a result, retailers who were unable to update registries with real-time data could not help guests avoid duplicate purchases. The end result was a 40% return rate on wedding gifts, which created an inconvenience for both the newlyweds and the retailer.

While The Knot had little online retail experience, the inventory and customer service characteristics of the registry business appeared to further support Liu's vision of an online bridal registry. Because gifts were selected months in advance, Liu saw an opportunity to efficiently organize drop ship and/or just-in-time delivery arrangements with manufacturers. Dealing directly with the manufacturers, as opposed to working with established retailers, would allow The Knot to maintain more control over its brand, pricing, and merchandising. These arrangements in combination with the extensive listing of products and services that did not require inventory to be held (e.g., mutual funds, mortgage down payments, etc.) would allow Liu to manage his balance sheet effectively. Furthermore, because of the nature of registry purchasing, The Knot's customer service effort would be streamlined by dealing almost exclusively with the registered couple (post-purchase) rather than the guests who actually made the purchases.

FINANCING THE KNOT

Liu's decision to seek outside financing was the result of both strategic necessity and financial reality. Liu knew that to capitalize on The Knot's momentum, he needed to increase investment to further develop The Knot brand, build out the technological infrastructure, and develop the gift registry business. On a more practical level, Liu needed capital to fund the payroll and pay for day-to-day operating expenses. As of November 1997, The Knot had only enough money in its coffers to sustain operations for another three months. Despite all of The Knot's achievements to date, the financial pressures were beginning to take their toll. Liu desperately needed cash.

Liu and the management team developed a comprehensive business plan outlining the company's successes to date and the significant opportunities for growth. The early efforts to develop the plan raised many questions. How much money did they really need? Who should they look to for financing? How should they value their enterprise? In attempting to answer these questions, Liu sought the counsel of a New York attorney named Alan Siegel who happened to be the father of a friend of Liu and Roney. Siegel assisted in developing an initial term sheet and a rough valuation of the business. Siegel became intrigued with The Knot's business model and introduced Liu to Ivan Lustig, a managing director in Schroder's U.S. Media & Communications Group. Lustig quickly assembled a team of investment bankers to devise a financing strategy. Scott Blankman, a Schroder's vice president, commented on the arrangement:

> We were really impressed with the business that Liu and his team had built, and our team of bankers agreed that The Knot would be an attractive investment for both venture capitalists and strategic investors. Given the state of the venture capital industry in late 1997 and the buzz surrounding Internet companies (see Exhibits 2-8a and 2-8b), we recommended trying to get as much capital as possible. In this business, you have to strike while the iron is hot.

Ensuing discussions between The Knot's management team and Schroder's investment bankers resulted in a comprehensive Private Placement Prospectus. The management team and its financial advisors agreed that The Knot would seek $10 million in exchange for Series B Convertible Preferred Stock (see Exhibit 2-9). The prospectus also included a solicitation to enter into a formal licensing relationship to develop a magazine utilizing The Knot's content and brand name.

EXHIBIT 2-8A

SELECTED INTERNET FINANCING DEALS

Venture Capital Investments

Company	Business Description	Round of Financing	Amount Raised ($millions)	Post Money Valuation ($millions)	Most Recent Investor	Date
Ticketmaster Online–CitySearch	Provider of Internet content regarding local community activity and businesses	5	40.00	192.00	Washington Post	Nov-97
Value America	Online retailer of branded products	1	0.96	N/A	Individual investors	Nov-97
Salon Internet	Online magazine	2	3.00	N/A	ASCII Ventures	Nov-97
Quote.com	Provider of financial market data over the Internet	3	3.00	53.00	Shawmut Capital Partners	Oct-97
Virtual Vineyards	Provider of gourmet food and wine service over the Internet	3	3.90	N/A	Mitsubishi	Oct-97
Zip2	Provider of Internet directory services	3	25.00	125.00	Hearst New Media and Technology	Oct-97
Internet Gift Registries	Online gift registry services and software for the retail industry	1	0.60	N/A	Individual investors	Oct-97
Total Sports	Online cybercasts for sports events	2	2.50	10.00	Piedmont Venture Partners	Oct-97
GolfWeb	Provider of golf-related information	3	8.20	40.00	Knight Ridder	Oct-97
Baby Center	Online articles and interactive tools focused on pregnancy and infancy issues	1	2.50	N/A	Broderbund Software	Sep-97
Third Age Media	Internet product and service provider for active older adults	2	9.40	22.00	U.S. West Interactive Services	Sep-97
NetBuy	Distributor of standard electronic components over the Internet	1	3.00	8.00	Sprout Group	Aug-97

Initial Public Offerings

Company	Business Description	1996 Revenue ($ millions)	IPO Proceeds ($ millions)	IPO Post Money Valuation ($ millions)	IPO Date	Market Capitalization on 11/05/97 ($ millions)
N2K	Online music retailer	1.66	63.27	310	Oct-97	316
Peapod	Online grocery delivery service	29.17	64.00	337	Jun-97	154
Amazon.com	Online book retailer	15.75	54.00	504	May-97	1,396
OnSale	Online auction house	14.30	15.00	121	Apr-97	523

Sources: VentureSource; Data Stream.

25

EXHIBIT 2-8B

VENTURE CAPITAL-BACKED IPO AND DISBURSEMENT DATA

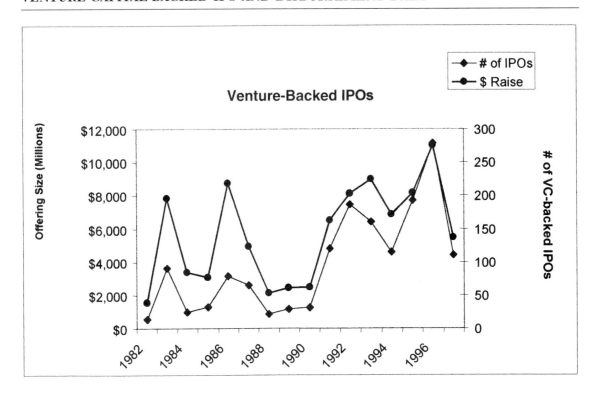

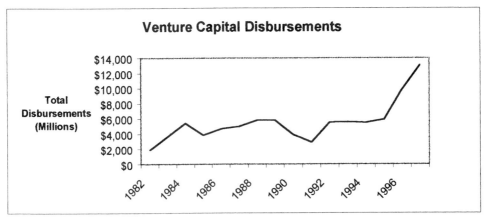

EXHIBIT 2-9

SUMMARY OF OFFERING TERMS

Issuer:	The Knot, Inc.
Type of Security:	Series B Convertible Preferred Stock (the "Preferred Stock")
Par Value:	$.001 per share
Gross Offering Size:	$10,000,000
Dividend:	Dividends on shares of the Preferred Stock shall accrue and accumulate on a semiannual basis at the rate of 5% per annum from the date of issuance to the date on which the Liquidation Value is paid on such shares or the date on which such shares are converted into Common Stock. Accrued dividends will be payable in cash or stock, at the option of the Company.
Use of Proceeds:	The Company expects to use the net proceeds of this Offering to develop its registry service and to accelerate marketing and promotion of its online services and ancillary properties.
Conversion Feature:	The Preferred Stock is convertible into an equal number of the Company's Common Stock.
Redemption Option:	Each holder of Preferred Stock may elect to require the Company to redeem all of the shares of Preferred Stock held by such holder on or after the seventh anniversary of the date of issuance.
Voting Rights:	Prior to the conversion of the Preferred Stock into Common Stock, holders of the Preferred Stock will have voting rights as if converted.
Other Agreements:	Each Purchaser will be required to enter into a Subscription Agreement and the Shareholders Agreement between The Knot and its shareholders. Copies of these documents will be provided to prospective investors on request and in any event prior to acceptance of a subscription.
Licensing Agreement:	The Company seeks to enter into a formal licensing relationship to develop The Knot Magazine.

EXHIBIT 2-10

OWNERSHIP TABLE

Current Equity Ownership

	Shares	Percent
Greenhouse Warrants[a]	100,000	30.4%
Series A Convertible Preferred[a]	0	0.0%
Total Preferred Shares	100,000	30.4%
Element Common Shares[b]	165,714	50.5%
Other Common Shares[c]	62,857	19.1%
Total Shares Outstanding[d]	328,571	100.0%

[a] Greenhouse currently holds Warrants on 100,000 shares of Series A Convertible Preferred Stock. The Warrants will be exercised at funding.

[b] Element is the company formed by Liu, Roney, Fassino and Wolfson (each with 25% ownership) which launched The Knot. This figure includes an Element Reserve of 65,714 shares that Element can earn if certain performance goals are met.

[c] Includes shares for the Employee Reserve and the Bridal Search, Inc., acquisition, including 32,857 shares of Common Stock Bridal Search may earn pursuant to a vesting schedule.

[d] Pro forma based on all employee and management stock options and issuance of shares pursuant to the Bridal Search acquisition.

EXHIBIT 2-11

USE OF PROCEEDS

The Knot expects to use the net proceeds of this offering to develop its registry service and to accelerate marketing and promotion of its online services and ancillary properties. The proceeds from this offering will be used as follows:

Use of Proceeds

Production Expenses	$ 2,911,000
Marketing Expenses	$ 2,670,000
Registry Start-Up Expenses	$ 785,000
Capital Expenditures	$ 1,040,000
Operating Expenses	$ 594,000
Working Capital Purposes	$ 2,000,000
Total	$10,000,000

EXHIBIT 2-12A

CONSOLIDATED HISTORICAL AND FORECASTED INCOME STATEMENT ($000S)

			Year Ending December 31,			
	1996	1997E	1998P	1999P	2000P	2001P
Total Revenue	79	675	2,836	6,638	18,915	49,467
Total Cost of Goods Sold	26	904	2,937	4,613	11,296	29,437
Gross Profit	53	(229)	(101)	2,025	7,619	20,030
SG&A	199	720	4,245	4,565	4,998	5,383
EBITDA	(146)	(949)	(4,346)	(2,540)	2,621	14,647
Dep & Amortization	38	134	291	313	323	305
EBIT	(184)	(1,083)	(4,637)	(2,853)	2,298	14,342
Income Tax	—	—	—	—	580	6,328
Net Income	(184)	(1,083)	(4,637)	(2,853)	1,718	8,014

EXHIBIT 2-12B

DETAILED REVENUE AND COST OF GOODS SOLD FORECAST ($000S)

		Year Ending December 31,			
	1997E	1998P	1999P	2000P	2001P
Revenue					
Advertising	396	1,071	1,738	3,091	4,331
AOL Usage	91	76	76	76	76
Retail Transaction Fees	28	314	800	2,874	6,452
Travel Auction Commissions	18	178	693	2,073	2,371
Registry Revenue	—	840	2,954	10,174	35,034
Book Revenue	137	187	25	—	76
Magazine Revenue	—	—	—	—	—
Mailing List Revenue	5	170	352	627	1,127
Total Revenue	675	2,836	6,638	18,915	49,467
Cost of Goods Sold					
Direct Costs					
Online Advertising	5	271	347	295	377
Retail Transaction	23	251	604	2,025	4,222
Travel Auction	4	45	173	518	593
Registry	—	672	2,225	7,155	22,886
Books	5	60	15	—	—
Magazine	—	—	—	—	—
Indirect Cost					
Production Costs	656	735	180	180	180
Staff Payroll	134	746	883	928	975
Benefits	28	157	186	195	204
Total Cost of Goods Sold	1,055	2,937	4,613	11,296	29,437

EXHIBIT 2-12C

HISTORICAL AND FORECASTED BALANCE SHEET ($000S)

	June 30, 1997	Year Ending December 31,				
		1997E	1998P	1999P	2000P	2001P
Current Assets						
Cash	529	9,973	4,726	1,967	3,855	14,048
Inventory	—	11	99	343	1,067	2,085
Accounts Receivable	93	58	179	314	543	754
Common Stock Subscription	1	1	1	1	1	1
Total Current Assets	623	10,043	5,005	2,625	5,466	16,888
Fixed Assets						
Office Furniture & Equipment	123	168	564	614	664	714
Leasehold Improvements	14	14	414	429	431	434
Less Accum. Dep	(22)	(36)	(221)	(427)	(644)	(871)
Total Fixed Assets	115	146	757	616	451	277
Other Assets						
Deposits	7	7	7	7	7	7
Development/Org. Costs	532	532	532	532	532	532
Accum. Amortization	(82)	(136)	(242)	(348)	(455)	(532)
Total Other Assets	457	403	297	191	84	7
Total Assets	1,195	10,592	6,059	3,432	6,001	17,172
Current Liabilities						
Accounts Payable	87	7	111	338	1,096	3,282
Taxes Payable	—	—	—	—	94	1,065
Total Current Liabilities	87	7	111	338	1,190	4,347
Noncurrent Liabilities						
Notes Payable	1,850	—	—	—	—	—
Total Noncurrent Liabilities	1,850	—	—	—	—	—
Total Liabilities	1,937	7	111	338	1,190	4,347
Stockholder's Equity						
Preferred Stock	—	10,000	10,000	10,000	10,000	10,000
Common Stock	1	1	1	1	1	1
APIC	—	1,850	1,850	1,850	1,850	1,850
Retained Earnings	(743)	(1,266)	(5,904)	(8,757)	(7,039)	974
Total Stockholder's Equity	(742)	10,585	5,947	3,094	4,812	12,825
Total Liabilities & Equity	1,195	10,592	6,058	3,432	6,002	17,172

EXHIBIT 2-12D

FORECASTED STATEMENT OF CASH FLOWS ($000S)

	Year Ending December 31,				
	1997E	1998P	1999P	2000P	2001P
Cash Flow from Operations					
Net Income	(1,083)	(4,637)	(2,853)	1,718	8,014
Dep. & Amortization	134	291	313	323	305
Accounts Payable	(150)	104	227	757	2,186
Taxes Payable	—	—	—	94	971
Deposits	—	—	—	—	—
Inventory	(11)	(87)	(245)	(724)	(1,018)
Accounts Receivable	(9)	(121)	(135)	(230)	(211)
Net Cash from Operations	(1,119)	(4,450)	(2,693)	1,938	10,247
Cash Flow from Investing Activities					
Fixed Assets	(74)	(797)	(65)	(53)	(53)
Development/Organization Costs	—	—	—	—	—
Net Cash from Investing	(74)	(797)	(65)	(53)	(53)
Cash Flow from Financing Activities					
Notes Payable	(700)	—	—	—	—
Equity Contributions	11,850	—	—	—	—
Net Cash from Financing	11,150	—	—	—	—
Change in Cash	9,957	(5,247)	(2,758)	1,885	10,194
Beginning Cash	16	9,973	4,726	1,968	3,853
Ending Cash	9,973	4,726	1,968	3,853	14,047

READY OR "KNOT?"

Liu took little comfort in the fact that the prospectus had finally been completed. The Knot needed capital infusion quickly to build on the momentum of the company and to invest in the future. Complicating matters was the recent news on the competitive front. Internet Gift Registries, an online gift registry and software firm serving retailers, had recently received a venture capital investment (see Exhibit 2-8a) and was turning its attention to enabling traditional retailers to serve newly married couples via the Internet. Further competition came from online businesses that had recently launched Web sites targeting The Knot's current and potential customers. Bride, USA Bride, and the Wedding-Channel had all recently begun operations. The WeddingChannel, in particular, posed a formidable threat. The WeddingChannel was the most recent venture spun out of the California-based Idealab, an incubator for Internet businesses that went on to develop eToys, CitySearch, and eTicket among others. Further enhancing the competitive threat of the WeddingChannel was the company's financial backers. Recently, the Wedding-Channel had begun negotiations with legendary financier Ronald O. Perelman and his business partner Donald Drabkin for a $4 million investment. The stage appeared to be set for a race to dominate the online wedding segment. Liu and his management team's current financing efforts would go a long way toward shaping the future of The Knot.

3

Beta Golf

Bob Zider, founder and managing partner of The Beta Group, placed his handmade golf club prototypes into the back of his Chevrolet Suburban and drove out of the parking lot of San Francisco International Airport. It was June 6, 1997, and he and his partner, John Krumme, had just returned from visiting Callaway Golf in San Diego, where they had introduced executives at the industry's leading golf club maker to their proprietary HXL golf club technology. They were tired—they had arrived at Callaway's test facility at 6 A.M. to witness "Iron Byron," Callaway's mechanical golf swing simulator, test Beta's golf clubs. Later that morning, Zider and Krumme had watched as five of Callaway's in-house professionals tested their prototypes. As they prepared to leave for the airport, Callaway's chief engineer had indicated that the company was not interested in Beta's technology because "it did not offer a significant improvement over their existing technology." The engineer was unwilling to disclose "Iron Byron's" test results, but Zider and Krumme had learned that two of the five in-house professionals had rated Beta's club excellent, two had rated it average, and one had rated it below average. Zider considered the feedback:

> I have often been told that Beta's inventions have been insignificant. I have learned to listen carefully to the naysayers. We went to Callaway because we expected the industry leader to kill the technology through data or engineering logic, but they couldn't. Actually, if all the pros had said it was average or below average, I'd know that we didn't have anything. But two of the them really liked it. I don't consider 1 of 5 "below average" ratings to be a fatal strike. We're not done with HXL until someone presents a logical reason not to pursue it.

In 1983, Zider had founded The Beta Group (Beta) as an "incubator" for technology-based businesses. Over the past 14 years, Beta had successfully built a portfolio of businesses in the medical, consumer products, and industrial technology sectors by systematically matching proprietary technologies to unmet market needs.

Senior Researcher Laurence E. Katz prepared this case at the HBS California Research Center under the supervision of Professor William A. Sahlman and Lecturer Michael J. Roberts as the basis for class discussion rather than to illustrate either effective or ineffective handling of an administrative situation.

In January 1996, Krumme, Beta's chief engineer, had designed a golf club prototype using a new metal "pixel" club face that offered an enlarged "sweet spot." Initial test data sponsored by Beta indicated that the club face reduced shaft vibration and the dispersion of miss-hit balls. At first, Zider had been skeptical about Beta's ability to commercialize this technology. Eight years earlier, Beta had declined an investment in the golf club industry because the market was growing slowly, dominated by entrenched brands, and resistant to technological innovation. Since 1990, however, growth in the golf club market had increased significantly, sparked by enhancements in technology, improved marketing from new club makers such as Callaway, and the emergence of Tiger Woods as a leader on the Men's PGA Tour. Encouraged by the industry trends, Zider and Krumme had focused on refining the technology, developing alternate business models, and addressing key risks. After 18 months, they were confident that the technology was sound and that they could manufacture a quality product within specified tolerances.

However, Zider and Krumme had not resolved one remaining question: how would they commercialize the technology? They had identified five options. First, they could license it to leading club makers, on either an exclusive or nonexclusive basis. This strategy could play off the intense competition in the golf equipment industry for the latest generation of technology. Second, they could manufacture and distribute club inserts that would be inserted into a machined cavity in the club face during assembly. Aldila and True Temper, both club shaft makers, had been successful with this OEM model, supplying shafts to multiple club makers. Several leading club makers recently had adopted inserts because they enabled club makers to market new materials while minimizing design and obsolescence costs. Third, they could buy a former leading club maker that had lost share and revive its brand by promoting HXL. One former industry leader was reportedly for sale, and Beta could leverage its existing brand and distribution infrastructure. Fourth, they could start a new club company from scratch and develop a new line of equipment around Beta's new technology. Cobra, Callaway, and Odyssey each had successfully pursued this strategy and sold for a multiple of three times sales within five years. Finally, Beta could form an exclusive joint venture with a leading club maker to develop a new line of equipment around HXL. Beta had successfully experimented with this model in other businesses but was unaware of a precedent in the golf equipment industry.

As Zider and Krumme reviewed each of these options, they needed to consider the associated capital requirements, risk profiles, and exit options. At the same time, they needed to evaluate which, if any, of these options was feasible, given investor skepticism of the industry and the industry's reluctance to invest in outside technologies.

THE BETA GROUP

The Beta Group[1] was founded by Zider in 1983 to develop and apply a systematic, multidisciplinary approach to innovation. Zider, a 35-year-old partner at the Boston Consulting Group (BCG), had been an engineer at Pratt & Whitney Aircraft prior to attending Harvard Business School. (See Exhibit 3-1 for profiles of Beta's principals.) Through several of his engagements at BCG, Zider had determined that large corporations did not have the internal systems to successfully exploit most innovations from their research departments. He also observed that venture capitalists rarely funded re-

[1] Beta was an acronym for Business Engineering and Technology Applications.

EXHIBIT 3-1

PROFILES OF BETA GROUP PRINCIPALS

John Krumme   John Krumme initially joined The Beta Group in 1986. John served as president and later chairman of *Beta Phase* from 1986 to 1993. In 1993, John formally returned to The Beta Group to participate in the firm's new investment activities. Prior to joining The Beta Group, John was a founding general partner of two start-up companies: Metcal (1981–1986), a self-regulating heating technology company; and Alchemia (1981–1986), a shape memory alloy product development company that became *Beta Phase* in 1986. Prior to his start-up of Metcal and Alchemia, John was a development engineer at Raychem (1973–1979), Hewlett-Packard (1969–1973), and General Electric Medical (1967–1969). John graduated from Stanford in 1967 with a MS/MSE degree in mechanical engineering. John holds more than 20 issued patents.

Bob Newell   Bob Newell joined The Beta Group in 1997. From 1992 to 1997, Bob was CFO of Cardiometrics, a medical device company. In 1985, Bob assisted Bob Zider and John Krumme in the formation of Beta Phase and was CFO of Beta Phase from 1985 to 1992. Bob has held financial management positions with WordStar International Corporation, Donaldson, Lufkin, & Jenrette and Bank of America. He has helped start several medical companies. Bob was also an Air Force pilot. He received a Bachelor of Arts degree in mathematics from the College of William and Mary in 1970 and a Master in Business Administration from Harvard Business School in 1976.

Dave Plough   Dave Plough joined The Beta Group in 1986. Dave has led the firm's investments in *CollOptics* and *Altair Eyewear*. He served as initial president of two portfolio companies, *CollOptics* and *Reflex Sunglasses*, and as general manager of another portfolio company, *FOxS Labs*. From 1982 to 1984, Dave was an associate with The Boston Consulting Group where, among other activities, he had The Beta Group as a client. Dave received a Bachelor of Arts degree in 1981 from Dartmouth College where he graduated cum laude and a Master of Business Administration degree in 1986 from the Stanford Graduate School of Business.

Bob Zider   Bob Zider founded The Beta Group in 1983 with backing from The Boston Consulting Group. Bob initiated and led the firm's investments in *Beta Phase, FOxS Labs, CVI/Beta Ventures, Beta Optical, Marchon, Eschenbach, CVIBeta Japan, Nitinol Devices and Components,* and *Reflex Sunglasses*. Bob served as initial president of *CVI/Beta Ventures* and initial chairman of *Nitinol Development, Reflex Sunglasses,* and the Business Engineering, Inc. consulting firm. Bob spent seven years from 1976 to 1983 at The Boston Consulting Group, where he developed the *Business Engineering* investment approach. Bob began his career from 1969 to 1971 as an analytical engineer with Pratt & Whitney in the Advanced Engines Group. From 1971 to 1973, and on a part-time basis from 1974 to 1976 while attending school, Bob was a lieutenant with the National Oceanic and Atmospheric Administration. Bob received a Bachelor of Science degree in civil engineering in 1969 from the University of Virginia and a Master of Business Administration degree with Distinction in 1976 from the Harvard Business School, where he was class president.

Source: The Beta Group.

---

search and development projects and avoided many industries that required significant investment in R&D. He reflected on what he termed "the innovation gap":

> I believe there are structural reasons that systematic innovation has not fully evolved in corporations or venture capital firms. Most successful corporations focus on managing vast numbers of people and resources efficiently, not innovation. To the extent that an explicit

R&D process exists in these companies, it is often functionally oriented and usually narrowly tied to an existing strategic product area. The typical corporate compensation structure also makes it very difficult to reward innovation, which discourages ground-breaking R&D and drives the best talent out of companies.

VCs do invest capital in others who innovate, but over 90% of their capital goes to fund working capital requirements and operating losses. In the early 1980s, VCs allocated about one-fourth of their investment dollars to seed and start-ups; today it's less than 6%. In fact, many companies themselves invest more in R&D than the entire VC community. Today, VCs focus on investments with low technology risk and high market growth potential. Typically, technology development occurs before the VCs enter the picture.

Zider founded Beta to foster a systematic approach to innovation through a process that he called Business Engineering.[2] Business Engineering referred to the development of a concept and business strategy through rigorous analysis of markets and technologies by a multidisciplinary team. Through Business Engineering, Beta matched an identified market opportunity with a proprietary technology, such as a patented technology or innovative process. Zider compared Business Engineering to the aircraft engine development process he had participated in at Pratt & Whitney Aircraft: "Just as engineers 'flight test' new engine designs on paper before they build them, we want to 'flight test' new businesses through the Business Engineering process before we invest significant capital. Like jet engines which work the first time they fly, we believe our businesses should 'fly' the first time out." Zider believed that Business Engineering would increase the probability of an investment's success while limiting the cost of its failure. (See Exhibit 3-2 for a description of Beta's mission.)

Zider reflected on his vision for Beta's strategy:

> I wanted to create an investment process that could not only develop ideas and concepts but also could test and implement them. My idea was not to start another venture capital fund, but to originate ideas, develop business plans around them, identify key operating officers, assemble financing, and actually bring small companies to the point of operation. To that end, I wanted to pull together the functional expertise of the corporation, the judgment of the venture capitalist, the creativity and fire of the entrepreneur, and the analytic rigor of the strategic consultant.

Zider recruited one of his BCG partners and incorporated the Beta Group, Inc. with a $300,000 investment from BCG and an in-kind donation of $1.5 million of consulting services. In return, BCG received an equity position in Beta's projects. BCG viewed its investment in Beta not only as an opportunity to achieve attractive returns on its partners' capital, but also as an opportunity to attract and retain talented consultants by promoting its affiliation with Beta.

Investment Strategy From the beginning, Beta adopted several operating principles that distinguished its investment strategy. First, Beta funded investments on a deal-by-deal basis with corporate and financial partners:

> We believe that the discipline of having to ask for money lowers our probability of failure. We believe that by forcing ourselves to pass each idea through two external screens—the funding search and the management search—we help to validate the concept. If we fail to complete either, we don't start the business.

[2] Business Engineering is unrelated to Business Re-engineering, which was popularized in the early 1990s.

EXHIBIT 3-2

BETA GROUP MISSION

The Beta Group

The Beta Mission

Exploring for gold was exciting 140 years ago. Upon learning of a random discovery, thousands of men with little or no experience would pick up and "rush" to the gold fields in the hopes of finding gold. A few became fabulously rich. The majority ended up flat broke.

Mineral exploration today is far less exciting. Pattern recognition, pathfinders, air, and satellite reconnaissance have replaced the mule and pick. Information and analysis have replaced random exploration. The simple task of mining has evolved into a systematic, highly engineered process designed to increase the odds of success and reduce the probability of failure.

Business innovation today is exciting. Billions of dollars are standing by to be invested in engineers, scientists, and marketers who have an innovative new idea. Most of these "business explorers" lack a comprehensive knowledge of the market, finances, the competition, and the multitude of other key factors required to build a business and grow it to long-term success. A few will become fabulously rich. The majority will not.

Just like yesterday's gold miners, today's "business explorers" face long odds in the attempt to create wealth as they strive to find a new product, provide a new service, or restructure an obsolete means of doing business. Despite seemingly endless enthusiasm, many fail to achieve their objectives. Successful businesses, like yesterday's gold fields, are not easy to find.

The Beta Mission is to develop and apply a systematic, multidisciplinary approach to innovation that we refer to as Business Engineering. The Business Engineering process utilizes analytic systems to assist business development. It relies less heavily on chance. As in exploration, it relies on the art of pathfinders and pattern recognition to provide clues. As in engineering, it relies on data and analysis of competitors, market, and product characteristics to develop options and simulate their success or failure on paper or in a highly focused test before committing major resources. Business Engineering is the natural extension of disciplined approaches applied elsewhere. Business Engineering coupled with creativity and drive is a powerful approach to innovation.

Robert B. Zider

Business Engineering

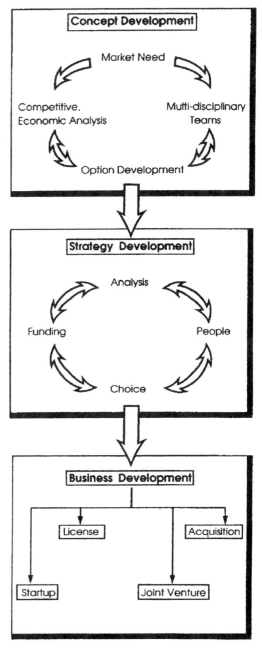

Source: The Beta Group.

Second, Beta created and sponsored its own investment opportunities, usually in sectors such as metallurgy and optometrics in which it had little or no investment competition. (See Exhibit 3-3 for a description of Beta's investments.) Specifically, they targeted opportunities in which a "trailing edge" technology could be applied to a market need. They believed that this strategy allowed them to avoid overpaying for ideas in "hot" sectors, such as multimedia, genetic engineering, or Internet commerce, while also allowing them to maximize control of their investments.

Third, Beta only pursued opportunities for which it had a superior technology, process, or other significant competitive advantage. Zider commented on this strategy:

> Since we fund each deal on its own merits, we have learned that good ideas alone are not fundable. We cannot convince investors that we have a competitive advantage in restaurants, for example. But we have found that if we can patent a technology to insulate ourselves from competition and build a business around that technology, we can fund it and attract a management team.

By 1997, Beta had registered over 40 patents and had successfully defended against patent infringements in the United States and Europe.

Fourth, Beta customized its approach to developing a business to meet the needs of the specific market. Beta was prepared to build a business as a start-up, as a joint venture, under license, or via acquisitions. Zider discussed this approach: "We want to fund a business in a way that will give it the best chance of long-term success. There isn't one cookie cutter way to commercialize a technology." Of Beta's 12 investments since 1983, 30% had been start-ups, 40% joint ventures, 20% licenses, and 10% acquisitions.

Fifth, Beta was rigorous in conducting a feasibility study of the concept and market opportunity prior to investing significant capital. Typically, Beta outlined the steps and timeline that needed to be met for commercial success and then prioritized key risks. Beta preferred situations in which the risks were highly focused, so that they could be analyzed and assessed with limited investment. Zider explained Beta's approach to capital allocation:

> We believe that capital efficiency can be accomplished by staging investments and minimizing investment during high-risk phases. We avoid investing in infrastructure, overhead, and outside management until we feel the primary risks have been adequately addressed. We usually invest less than $250,000 of our own money over a 12–18 month period while we identify and explore key risks.

Finally, Beta adopted a hands-on management relationship with the company throughout its life. Typically, at least one of Beta's partners initially served as a key member of the company's management team. Later in the company's life cycle, Beta would replace themselves with outside managers but would continue to work closely with the company to implement the strategic plan.

Sourcing New Technologies Zider commented on Beta's approach to identifying new technologies:

> Lots of people believe that inventions happen only in a moment of brilliance. We don't believe that innovation is simply a spark of naïve creativity. We believe that idea generation is the convergence of several linked but independent events, which include rigorous analysis of market needs, an open mind, and awareness of technical feasibility. We live by Louis Pasteur's quote, "Chance favors only a prepared mind."[3]

[3] Louis Pasteur, Inaugural Address, University of Lille, December 7, 1854.

EXHIBIT 3-3

DESCRIPTION OF BETA GROUP INVESTMENTS

Medical Sector

The Beta Group believes that the ongoing structural changes that are taking place in the health care industry will create significant investment opportunities. In particular, the historical focus on *quality of care*, irrespective of cost, has been replaced by a focus on the *cost of care*, as long as the care provided is consistent with or superior to the existing quality of care. The Beta Group believes this new *cost of care* focus will be the dominant theme in medical care throughout this decade. The Beta Group believes that technologies, proprietary processes, or other competitive advantages that lower the total cost of care, while maintaining or increasing the quality of care, will create attractive investment opportunities. Examples of medical sector investments that The Beta Group has made include:

Medical Sensors   The Beta Group successfully developed a fiber-optic blood gas sensor technology, achieving a 132% internal rate of return on a staged investment of $3.8 million in a start-up company it founded called *FOxS Labs*. The *FOxS Labs* investment was the result of a methodological exploration of medical sensors opportunities. The Beta Group, working in conjunction with The Boston Consulting Group, conducted an in-depth assessment of the opportunities within blood gas continuous sensing. Interviews and field research were conducted in cardiology, intensive care medicine, surgery, and other specialties. The work team assessed the four most promising technology options and evaluated a fiber-optic technology as the superior option. After an in-depth patent review and a rigorous assessment of the technology by outside technical consultants, The Beta Group acquired a fiber-optic technology patent from Richard G. Buckles. After successful development to the point of human clinical trials, *FOxS Labs* was sold to Puritan-Bennett Corporation, a corporate strategic partner that The Beta Group had brought in to aid in the development and marketing of the Buckles fiber-optic sensor technology.

Medical Devices   The Beta Group has made several investments in shape memory metal alloy applications, including an intravenous flow controller, surgical tools, and incontinence devices.

The Beta Group extended its experience and expertise in shape memory alloys with its 1991 start-up of Nitinol Devices and Components ("NDC"). NDC is a manufacturing company dedicated to the engineering, design, and fabrication of shape memory alloy components. Products include guidewires, catheters, and coronary stents. Beta's $2.0 million investment in NDC achieved a 125% compound annual return with its sale to Johnson and Johnson's Cordis division in 1997.

In January 1992, Beta started up *CollOptics, Inc. CollOptics*, which is jointly owned by The Beta Group, Collagen Corporation, and GE Medical, acquired the GE Medical Systems Laser Adjustable Synthetic Epikeratoplasty (LASE) technology in January 1992. *CollOptics'* mission is to provide a semipermanent contact lens to the consumer on a minimally invasive, reversible, and adjustable basis. The semipermanent contact lens would be placed under the epithelium of the eye in a simple, outpatient procedure. Unlike other refractive surgery approaches, the LASE approach is only minimally invasive and is reversible. It is too early to tell whether The Beta Group's $800,000 investment in the company will prove successful.

(Continued)

At times, Beta identified a market need through analysis and then hunted for a technology to meet that need. For example, Beta uncovered a market need for continuous arterial blood gas monitoring for intensive care patients through a consulting engagement that BCG had completed at a medical device company. At that time, no medical device existed to immediately notify medical professionals when a patient's

EXHIBIT 3-3   (Continued)

Consumer Products Sector

The Beta Group believes the diverse and constantly evolving consumer marketplace offers significant investment opportunities. The principals of The Beta Group believe that the development of new consumer product concepts that address underlying consumer cultural, demographic, and behavioral trends will create attractive investment opportunities. The Beta Group believes this is particularly true where a proprietary technology or process or other competitive advantage is brought to the consumer marketplace. Examples of consumer sector investments that The Beta Group has made follow:

Eyewear   The Beta Group has acquired significant experience and expertise in the development of shape memory alloy applications. Beta applied this expertise to the consumer products arena by developing and commercializing shape memory eyeglass frames in the *CVI/Beta Ventures* start-up company. Beta Group developed and patented the use of nitinol metals in ophthalmic frames. The shape memory properties of nitinol eyeglass frames (primarily known by the "Flexon" trade name) allow the frames to maintain a consistent, comfortable fit despite wear and handling. Beta Group achieved a *134%* compound annual return on a staged investment of $500,000 in *CVI/Beta Ventures*.

Electronic Music Distribution   The Beta Group funded the start-up of *Personics* in 1984. *Personics* permits the music retail consumer to make in-store custom mixes of artists and songs. The consumer samples songs at a listening booth located in the music retail store and has hundreds of songs and artists to choose from. Once the consumer has made selections, he or she submits the choices to a sales clerk. In approximately 10 minutes, the consumer receives an audio cassette tape with the mix of songs he or she selected. The Beta Group achieved a 73% compound annual return on *Personics*, on a staged investment of $3.3 million.

Industrial Technology Sector

The Beta Group believes that the industrial technology sector presents significant investment opportunities, particularly where a new technology, proprietary process, or other competitive advantage is transplanted from an existing application into either a new application or an entirely new market. Examples of industrial technology sector investments that The Beta Group has made follow:

Electronic Connectors   One of Beta's first start-ups, Beta Phase (1984), developed a high-density (up to 500 lines per inch) zero insertion force connector system using a flex print and shape memory actuator combination. Though technically successful (it is still used in Cray's supercomputers), Beta suffered two dilutive financings prior to the sale of the company to Molex.

Other Industrial Products   As part of its continuing development efforts, Beta has obtained rights to FOxS's fiber-optic sensor technology for use in industrial applications such as hazardous waste and hydrocarbon monitoring. Beta also developed under contract a PC-based communications test system for Motorola, launched commercially in 1997. Beta continues development of shape memory applications including pipe couplings, electrical cable connectors, sporting goods, and resettable fuses.

Source: The Beta Group.

blood-oxygen, carbon dioxide, or ph level was dangerously low. Through a concentrated technology search, Beta identified and acquired a fiber-optic sensor technology which it believed could be applied to the blood gas market to provide a procedure that was lower cost and less invasive than other competitive technologies. Beta founded FOxS Labs (Fiber-optic Oxygen Sensors) in 1985 with a $50,000 investment and later found a joint venture partner who invested $2.2 million to test the device in human clinicals. Beta sold its interest to their joint venture partner at a $30 million valuation in 1989.

At other times, Beta identified a technology and then looked for an appropriate market need. For example, Krumme previously had worked with a titanium-based alloy called "nitinol" which could bend but then return to its original shape when heated. As nitinol had been refined, a version had been developed that would "spring" back to its original shape at room temperature. Based on Zider's market analysis of the eyeglass and contact lens businesses while at BCG, Beta identified an opportunity to apply this memory alloy to eyeglass frames. Beta commercialized the technology in the United States through a joint venture with Marchon, a U.S. eyeglass frame distributor, and internationally through license agreements with Japanese and European eyeware manufacturers. When Beta sold its patents to Marchon in 1995, the frames, known domestically by the trade name Flexon, had retail sales worldwide of about $200 million.

Not all of Beta's innovations were ready to be commercialized when developed. At any given time, Beta was actively developing only two to three businesses. Beta kept a file, internally called the "Refrigerator," which contained nearly 50 ideas of lower priority. Each year at its annual retreat, Beta would review its "refrigerator" to identify ideas that might be ready to be commercialized:

> The "refrigerator" is distinct from the "dumpster," where we throw away bad ideas. The "fridge" preserves the ideas that we don't have time for or that don't seem fundable at the time. There are lots of reasons a concept may go into the "fridge"—the market may not be big enough, the technology may not be ready, the industry may not be in favor, or there may not be an identifiable exit strategy. We have never rescued an idea from the dumpster, but several of our successful ideas have come from the refrigerator.

Over the past 13 years, Beta had achieved strong investment returns for its investors. See Exhibit 3-4 for an analysis of investment returns.[4]

BETA'S HXL GOLF TECHNOLOGY

In the late 1980s, Beta identified golf equipment as a potential application of nitinol. The initial idea had been generated by one of Zider's BCG partners who had remarked that golf club shafts would be a good application of this alloy, "It would be great joke if I could bend a club over my knee or wrap it around a tree when I'm frustrated with my game, but then could heat it up at home to return it to its original shape." Zider dismissed this idea as only a gag, but did briefly consider making nitinol inserts that could be placed into a machined cavity in the club face during assembly. After making a prototype in 1989, Zider put the idea in the "refrigerator." Zider commented on the decision, "We couldn't make nitinol work in clubs because the price/value relationship was out of line. At that time, our prototype didn't show any discernible performance differences and a nitinol insert would have cost $100, raising the consumer price way beyond then-current price points."

Beta's technological breakthrough occurred in 1996 when Krumme designed a club face with a thin cross section of a bundle of metal wires. While a traditional club face used a cast or forged slab of monolithic metal, Krumme's design used a series of small

---

[4] In 1989, Beta and BCG agreed to a buyout of BCG's equity position by the Beta principals. Between 1983 and 1989, Beta's realized returns were 55%, while the average venture capital returns of funds raised in 1983 was 11%.

EXHIBIT 3-4

**BETA GROUP FINANCIAL PERFORMANCE SUMMARY
(ONLY INVESTMENTS EXCEEDING $250,000)**

Investment	Description	Investment Date	Internal Rate of Return
Beta Phase	Electronic connectors	1984–1989	Loss
FOxS	Blood gas sensors	1985–1989	132%
Personics	In-store custom music	1984–1989	73%
Beta Optical	U.S. eyeglass frame manufacturing LBO	1986–1988	Loss
Total (1983–1989)			55%
CVI/Beta[8]	Shape memory eyeglass frames	1990–1997	86%
Nitinol Devices and Components	Coronary stents	1992–1997	125%
Reflex Sunglasses	Shape memory sunglasses	1992–1994	Loss
CollOptics	Reversible refractive eye surgery	1992–1997	Loss
Altair Eyewear	Ophthalmic products marketing	1992–1997	34%
Total (1990–1997)			86%

Source: The Beta Group.

metal rods aligned together and attached to the back plate of the club like pixels on a television screen. (See Exhibit 3-5 for a computer diagram of the club face with insert.) Krumme described how his previous inventions had led him to this design: "Several years earlier, I had invented and patented a connector for circuit boards which used a bunch of tiny nitinol threads, each the width of piece of human hair, to connect a microprocessor to a circuit board. While the application and performance needs are very different in circuit boards, this batch of threads provided the seed for the golf idea."

By decoupling the metal "pixels," Krumme's design altered the club's vibration response pattern so that the "sweet spot"—the ideal impact position—was enlarged and vibration feedback was reduced. This resulted in a better feel for the golfer, better ball speed after impact for off-center hits, and reduced dispersion of golf balls.[5] Beta expected that the characteristics would be more apparent to mid- to low-handicap golfers.[6]

Zider described Beta's new technology by analogy:

The club face on a standard club is analogous to a metal trampoline: when the ball impacts the center of the club, energy is transferred from the club to the ball with little feedback. As in a trampoline, however, if the impact is off-center, the ball does not travel the same distance because the energy transfer is imperfect and the response is asymmetrical. Beta's technology makes the club face act more like a mattress, which uses a decoupled support system, so that motion on one part of the mattress is isolated from other parts.

[5] Tests showed that ball speed lost 8% to 10% on miss-hits (i.e., toe or heel hits) with traditional clubs, but only 3% to 5% on similar miss-hits with HXL inserts.

[6] A golfer's handicap referred to the number of strokes above par that the golfer, on average, recorded in a round of 18 holes of golf. Lower handicaps indicated greater proficiency.

EXHIBIT 3-5

COMPUTER DIAGRAM OF HXL CLUB INSERT

Source: The Beta Group.

Zider also compared HXL to recent innovations in tennis equipment:

In the last ten years, golf has moved much the way tennis rackets did earlier: from wood to metal to composites and oversized racquets. But tennis has moved back to newly designed mid-sized rackets which provide bigger sweet spots on a smaller face while improving control and feel. Golf has not yet moved back to the middle. In golf, larger is not necessarily better. The continually increasing size of the club face means that the club will encounter more grass and dirt resistance, often catching the ground before the shot and completely ruining it. Therefore, a mid-sized club, like a mid-sized tennis racket, with the larger sweet spot might be very marketable. Our technology allows that to happen.

Beta commissioned Golf Laboratories, an independent testing center, to evaluate Beta's HXL prototypes. Initial test results showed that HXL designs produced slightly longer shots with less dispersion than the standard club. However, Beta believed that a finished prototype that had been balanced, sanded, and grooved might reduce the flight distance of a well-hit drive 2 to 3 yards. Beta had also conducted a computer simulation of the HXL technology which demonstrated the increased size of the sweet spot of the HXL insert over monolithic club faces. These test results and simulations confirmed Beta's engineering theory.

In addition to improved performance, HXL offered a distinctive new look to the club face. HXL looked like a honeycomb, which reinforced its unique technology and allowed design innovation unavailable with existing mono-faced clubs. Club makers could vary the pixel numbers, size, design, and material, all using their existing molds and designs which could extend product life cycles and reduce tooling, inventory, and obsolescence costs. HXL allowed the face to be dimpled or grooved, like existing club faces, as well as processed for different surface friction characteristics within USGA rules.

THE GOLF INDUSTRY

In 1997, the wholesale golf club industry had $1.5 billion in sales, having grown 15% over the previous 10 years. There were 24.7 million golfers in the United States who spent, on average, $1,000 for a complete new set of clubs (eight iron clubs and three wood clubs). In 1996, nearly 2.0 million sets of woods and 1.3 million sets of irons were sold, an increase of 4% and 7%, respectively, over 1995. Wholesale prices had risen rapidly in recent years, as technological innovation allowed wood and iron prices to rise 16% and 6%, respectively, in 1996. Analysts forecast that the market would grow 12% to 15% over the next five years.

Radical market share changes had accompanied this rapid market growth. Historically, five companies—Wilson, Spalding, Hogan, Dunlop, and MacGregor—had dominated the new golf club market. After decades of little innovation, however, the industry had been shaken by four waves of design and technology improvements. In the early 1970s, Karsten Manufacturing introduced perimeter-weighted Ping irons which allowed more forgiveness for beginner and intermediate players. In the mid-1970s, Aldila, a shaft manufacturer, began marketing a graphite club shaft that had a higher strength to weight ratio, allowing the golfer to increase club speed through a swing without compromising strength. In the 1980s, Taylor Made introduced metal woods, which were 70% stronger than traditional woods. In the 1990s, Callaway Golf introduced the Big Bertha clubs which dramatically increased the size of the club's "sweet spot." As a result of these innovations, Hogan, Dunlop, and MacGregor together captured less than 5% of the market in 1997.

In their place, new brands such as Callaway, Taylor Made, Cobra, and Odyssey emerged. With the introduction of its Big Bertha clubs, Callaway's sales had increased from $55 million in 1991 to $683 mil in 1996, resulting in a market value of over $2 billion. Similarly, Cobra, which had gained the endorsement of Australian-born PGA leader Greg Norman, had achieved great success through the design innovation of its oversized irons. In 1995, Cobra had been acquired by American Brands for $700 million, or four times sales. In 1996, Taylor Made had introduced the Bubble Shaft, a graphite composite design in which the shaft swelled dramatically beneath the grip and tapered to a reinforced lip just above the club head. Lastly, Odyssey Sports had entered the putter business in the late 1980s by offering an unmistakable metal-headed club with a "stronomic" black insert that was marketed to put "more feel into the putt." In 1997, Callaway acquired Odyssey for $130 million, or approximately 3× sales.

In 1996, no one company led all market segments. Callaway, for example, led the woods segment, while it captured virtually no share of specialty clubs (i.e., wedges and putters). Similarly, Ping, Cobra, and Tommy Armour led the irons market, but Ping had almost no share of the woods market, and Cobra and Tommy Armour had only a small share of the putter market. Exhibit 3-6 presents Beta's analysis of leaders by market segment.

Accompanying the rapid innovation, marketing budgets for golf clubs had skyrocketed. While technology appeared critical to success, Callaway, Taylor Made, and Odyssey had proven that adopting a strong consumer marketing focus was necessary as well. Industry analysts estimated that Callaway would spend over $100 million on sales and marketing in 1997.

EXHIBIT 3-6

MARKET SEGMENTATION

	Woods	Irons	Wedges	Putters
Super Premium	>$400	>$1,000	>$120	>$120
	Callaway	Armour Titanium	Armour Titanium	Snake Eyes
	Lynx	Callaway	Callaway	Taylor Made
	Taylor Made	Daiwa	Ping	
		Ping	Taylor Made	
High	$300	$800	$100	$100
	Cleveland	Armour	Cleveland	Callaway
	Cobra	Hogan	Hogan	Cobra
	Nicklaus	Cobra	Cobra	Ping
		Mizuno	Ram	Odyssey
		Nicklaus	Wilson	Alien
		Taylor Made		
Medium	$200	$600	$80	$50
	Golfsmith	MacGregor	Golfsmith	Dunlop
	Ping	Powerbilt	Dunlop	Powerbilt
	Wilson	Ram	Ram	Golfsmith
		Wilson		
Low	$80–$120	<$500	$40	$30
	Dunlop	Dunlop	Golfworks	Golfworks
	Golfsmith	Golfsmith	Magique	Magique
	Mitsushiba	Rawlings		

Source: The Beta Group.

The industry was known for rapid "knock offs" of popular club designs, as most patents in the golf industry were on "design" or "method" which offered very little protection from imitators. Nearly every club sold under a brand name was available through mail order catalogs and at discount retailers under a private label brand at less than half price.

Golf club makers generally performed research and development internally but outsourced production of components to both American and Asian companies. Club makers assembled the three subcomponents—grip, shaft, and club head—and spent heavily to market both to retailers and consumers. Wholesale gross margins for club makers were attractive, approaching 60% for clubs made from standard materials and 50% for more specialized materials, such as titanium.

Since 1894, the United States Golf Association (USGA) had served as the oversight body that had monitored and enforced equipment standards to protect the rules of the game. Rules for equipment, particularly clubs and balls, were strict and specific. The USGA received submissions for approval for nearly 400 club designs per year, about 40% of which were for putters. The USGA approved about half of these submissions each year. Rarely would a manufacturer try to commercially market a club not approved by the USGA. Exhibit 3-7 presents excerpts from the USGA rules book on club faces.

BUSINESS ENGINEERING HXL

In January 1996, Zider turned his attention to address the risks that Beta considered hurdles to HXL's success: USGA approval, patent approval, manufacturing economics, and pricing. While Beta had dedicated only minimal financial resources to explore HXL, Zider began spending nearly half his time evaluating HXL's potential.

Beta initially submitted the pixel design to the USGA for approval. The USGA replied within several weeks that their design, which used round pixels, did not meet specifications because the round pixels and epoxy filler constituted two materials on the impact surface, which was prohibited by their rules. At the same time, they commented that they had never seen a submission analogous to Beta's proposal. Beta resubmitted a revised proposal using hexagonal pixels that fit tightly together. This time, the USGA responded within several weeks that the prototypes "Conformed with USGA Rules." (See Exhibit 3-8.)

After finding no related patents, Beta applied for product patents for HXL covering several materials, including plastics, elastomers, traditional metals and shape memory alloys, and several pixel shapes, including hexagonal, rectangular, and triangular patterns. Product patents provided significantly more protection than the process or design patents typical to club manufacturers. Beta received a notice of allowance by the U.S. Patent and Trademarks Office within six months, which was significantly expedited over the usual 12- to 18-month process. From prior experience, however, Beta was aware that patents were continually subject to review and reversal.

From the beginning, Krumme believed that the manufacturing process would not be a barrier to success but that product costs needed to be determined. The manufacturing process for the pixel technology was different from the traditional monolithic casting or forging process, requiring precision tolerances (plus or minus one-thousandth of an inch) and additional assembly operations. However, it employed standard electronics industry manufacturing techniques that did not pose major technical hurdles and allowed the use of existing club designs. Individual hexagonal wires first would be cut and machined, using standard screw machine technology, to create the pixels. They would then be aligned in a close-packed pattern and inserted into the club head cavity[7] for bonding to the back plate. Finally, they would be machined for grooves as well as surface treatment. Beta estimated that HXL inserts would initially cost $5 to $40, depending on volumes, material selection, and pixel density.

Finally, Zider attacked the pricing model. Initially, he was concerned that there might not be enough room in the industry pricing structure for a technology that was higher cost. Through industry analysis and interviews, Beta pieced together the cost structure of club manufacturers. On average, assemblers spent $20 to make a club that sold at wholesale for $40. The same club would be sold at retail for $60. Based on manufacturing cost analysis, Beta expected that a $10 to $20 price per insert would require a $20 to $40 premium at wholesale and a $30 to $60 premium at retail. Zider's analysis of the retail market indicated that, at the higher end of the market which Beta would target, a $30 to $60 incremental price per club for eight irons was acceptable. Zider

---

[7] Club head makers had routinely made cavities in the club face for other monolithic inserts.

EXHIBIT 3-7

THE RULE OF GOLF 1997–1998

App. II

b) transparent material added for other than decorative or structural purposes,

c) appendages to the main body of the head such as knobs, plates, rods or fins, for the purpose of meeting dimensional specifications, for aiming or for any other purpose. Exceptions may be made for putters.

Any furrows in or runners on the sole shall not extend into the face.

4-1e. Club Face

General

The material and construction of the face shall not have the effect at impact of a spring, or impart significantly more spin to the ball than a standard steel face, or have any other effect which would unduly influence the movement of the ball.

Impact Area Roughness and Material

Except for markings specified in the following paragraphs, the surface roughness within the area where impact is intended (the "impact area") must not exceed that of decorative sandblasting, or of fine milling.

The impact area must be of a single material. Exceptions may be made for wooden clubs (see Fig. VIII, illustrative impact area).

Impact Area Markings

Markings in the impact area must not have sharp edges or raised lips, as determined by a finger test. Grooves or punch marks in the impact area must meet the following specifications:

(i) Grooves. A series of straight grooves with diverging

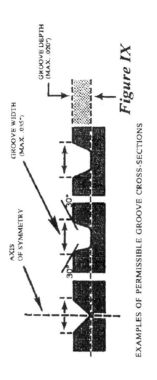

ILLUSTRATIVE IMPACT AREA

Figure VIII

sides and a symmetrical cross-section may be used (see Fig. IX). The width and cross-section must be consistent across the face of the club and along the length of the grooves. Any rounding of groove edges shall be in the form of a radius which does not exceed 0.020 inches (0.5 mm). The width of the grooves shall not exceed 0.035 inches (0.9 mm), using the 30 degree method of measurement on file with the United States Golf Association. The distance between edges of adjacent grooves must not be less than three times the width of a groove, and not less than 0.075 inches (1.9 mm). The depth of a groove must not exceed 0.020 inches (0.5 mm).

AXIS OF SYMMETRY

GROOVE WIDTH (MAX. .035")

30° 30°

GROOVE DEPTH (MAX. .020")

EXAMPLES OF PERMISSIBLE GROOVE CROSS-SECTIONS

Figure IX

Note: Exception—see US Decision 4-1/100.

(ii) Punch Marks. Punch marks may be used. The area of any such mark must not exceed 0.0044 square inches (2.8 sq. mm). A mark must not be closer to an adjacent mark than 0.168 inches (4.3 mm) measured from center to center. The depth of a punch mark must not exceed 0.040 inches (1.0 mm). If punch marks are used in combination with grooves, a punch mark must not be closer to a groove than 0.168 inches (4.3 mm), measured from center to center.

Source: United States Golf Association (USGA).

EXHIBIT 3-8

USGA LETTER TO BETA GROUP

United States Golf Association
Golf House   PO Box 708   Far Hills, NJ 07931-0708
908 234-2300   Fax 908 234-9687
http://www.usga.org
   Technical Department Fax: 908 234-0138

September 25, 1997

Mr. John Krumme
President
Beta Development
2454 Embarcadero Way
Palo Alto, CA 94303

Dear Mr. Krumme: Decision: 97-291 & 97-306

This is in reference to your letter dated July 24, 1997 and the iron (97-291) and putter (97-306) which you submitted for an official ruling. The cavity back iron has an insert in the face made of a copper alloy material, that is formed from hexagonal steel columns which join together creating a smooth surface. The toe-heel weighted putter has a similar face insert made of stainless steel.

I am pleased to advise you that the clubs, as submitted, have been inspected and it has been determined that they conform with the Rules of Golf.

In advertisements of this iron (97-291) and putter (97-306), you are authorized to make the statement: "Conforms with USGA Rules." Use of such statements as "USGA Approved" or "USGA Tested" are prohibited. Use of the USGA seal or logo, without specific permission, is prohibited.

We are retaining the samples as a record of this decision.

The USGA reserves the right to change the Rules and interpretations regulating equipment at any time.

Yours sincerely,

Frank Thomas

Frank W. Thomas
Technical Director

FWT: wp
cc: Reed K. Mackenzie, Chairman, I&B Committee
      O. Gordon Brewer, Jr.
      David B. Fay
      Michael Butz
      John Matheny

concluded, "When golfers spend $100,000 to join a country club, spending an extra $250 to $500 on clubs is not extraordinary, if they think the technology is worthwhile."

THE DECISION

After successfully addressing the key initial risks of patentability, performance, USGA approval, and market potential, Beta turned its attention to evaluate alternative business models for commercializing its HXL technology. Among its options, Beta evaluated licensing its technology to an existing company, supplying a component insert, acquiring an existing company, starting a new equipment company, or entering into a joint venture. Beta had employed each of these strategies in at least one previous investment.

License Beta considered trying to license its patented technology, on either an exclusive or nonexclusive basis, to a leading club maker. An exclusive license might command an 8% to 10% royalty on wholesale sales and a $10 million marketing commitment, while a nonexclusive license might command a 6% to 8% royalty. Licensees would have control over all aspects of production and marketing, including pricing and quality standards. Beta would retain responsibility for research and development and patent defense. In the past, Beta had spent over $3 million defending patents against infringement. Beta expected that any licensee would be able to command a 20% to 50% price premium for the technology.

OEM Supplier Beta also considered manufacturing pixel inserts and selling them to several leading club makers, who would insert them into the club heads during assembly. Club makers were accustomed to purchasing monolithic club inserts, made of different materials, and placing them into a pre-machined cavity in the club head during assembly. Aldila and True Temper, both leading club shaft manufacturers, had been successful with the OEM supplier model, building companies with a market value of approximately one times sales.

Based on detailed costing studies, Beta believed that it would be able to manufacture club inserts for $5 to $40 per insert and sell them at a 30% to 60% gross margin. Beta could acquire machines with 1,200 to 2,000 pixels per hour capacity (depending on materials) for $70,000 each. Beta expected that it would need to charge club makers an 80% to 100% markup on direct cost and a 8% to 10% "technology license" on the wholesale value of the club. But would club makers buy the product?

Beta referred to this strategy as the "Gore-Tex approach." Like Gore-Tex, the waterproof fabric sold to garment makers, Beta would sell branded inserts to several golf club makers who would compete on their own pixel designs and materials as well as on the features of their own clubs.

Acquisition Beta considered bidding for a former leading golf club brand ("Acorn"), which recorded a loss of $2 million in 1996 on sales of $20 million. At its peak in the 1970s and 1980s, Acorn had consistently recorded sales of $90 million and profits of $10 million. Since 1990, the company continually had been losing money on declining sales volumes.

Zider had identified a financial investor, The Parkside Group, which was prepared to join Beta in bidding for Acorn. Together, they would form a newly capitalized company ("Newco"), which would hold the assets of both Acorn and Beta's HXL technology. Terms of the proposed agreement specified that Parkside would acquire Acorn's brand and tangible assets for 50% of 1997 projected sales, or $10 million, and contribute them to Newco along with $15 million to fund working capital requirements. Beta would contribute to Newco its technology, which would be valued at $5 million. The investor would assume operating responsibilities for the merged company, while Beta would continue to manage research and development as well as defend against patent infringement.

Beta was interested in this opportunity because it would provide a "platform" to enter the business with an existing distribution organization and brand franchise. Together, Beta and Parkside planned to try to revitalize the brand by introducing a new product line that incorporated Beta's HXL technology. Re-launching the brand would require $35 million in marketing expenses over the next three years. Exhibits 3-9 and 3-10 present the details of the proposed transaction and associated financial projections. Beta was aware that other strategic buyers also were considering bidding for the company.

Start-up Following the model of Callaway, Cobra, and Odyssey, all of which had introduced new golf brands within the past 10 years, Beta explored starting a new club company. Beta considered Odyssey to be a model of a successful start-up golf equipment business. Odyssey, which had started in 1990 with $5 million of capital from financial partners, had grown to $35 million in sales in 1996 when it was bought by Callaway for $130 million.

To launch a start-up, Beta would need to find a financial partner willing to commit $10 million in start-up capital and would need to recruit a management team with significant experience in the golf industry. The new company would outsource manufacturing but would manage R&D and marketing internally. Beta needed to address several strategic questions that would impact the start-up's economics, including how they would market their brand. Would they try to market clubs through professionals, who had expensive golf contracts, or through infomercials, which cost nearly $1 million each to run? How would they secure distribution through the retail channel? How would they price their clubs?

Joint Venture Beta also considered trying to form an exclusive joint venture with a leading club maker to develop and market Beta's technology. This option would be structured similar to a start-up but would require that Beta partner with a strategic investor, such as a leading club maker, rather than a financial investor. Under this structure, Beta expected to contribute its technology and patents to the joint venture while the partner contributed intangible assets, including its sales and distribution systems, and up to $10 million of capital. Beta expected that the division of the joint venture's equity would be 30% Beta, 50% club maker, and 20% management. If Beta entered a joint venture, it would likely need to accept a buyout clause that could limit its upside in the event of success.

CONCLUSION

As Zider pulled out of San Francisco International Airport's parking lot and headed toward Beta's offices in Menlo Park, he considered which launch strategy he would recommend to his partners:

> We hate businesses like golf. Investing in sporting goods goes against every principle we have at Beta. It's a hobby industry which attracts many people with deep pockets who are in it to stroke their ego—just like boats and wineries. It's a trendy consumer business based on image and perception, and many smart people have lost a lot of money in it. We also are violating the single most basic tenet of business—know something about the industry. We don't know a damn thing about golf.

EXHIBIT 3-9

PROPOSED ACQUISITION STRUCTURE AND FINANCIALS

THE PARKSIDE GROUP
Strategic Equity Investors

September 1, 1997

Barry L. Schneider
Managing Partner

Mr. Bob Zider
Beta Group

Via Fax

Dear Bob:

I was not able to fax you the financials tonight because Cory and I finished them after midnight. The plan is for Cory to get you this letter and our latest pro forma financials so that you and I can talk at some point Monday.

Our understanding has always been that we would create a Newco by merging a newly capitalized "Acorn" with HXL. You can refer to the handwritten schematic that I faxed to you several months ago, indicating such a structure. We specifically asked you the value you placed on HXL, so we would be able to value it as a "contributed asset" in the business combination. Your response was clear; you wanted somewhere near a $5 million valuation.

Attached are our sources and uses, and forecasted financial statements. Please feel free to call Cory to inquire about any part of the financials, and I will try and call you either from the plane or from the hotel Monday night.

The bottom line is that Beta is getting its $5 million valuation, both in terms of a preferred return of $5 million, and in a 16.6% carried ownership interest ($5M/$30M post $). It is likely that the Seller will also want a carried interest, and coincidentally, he will swap $5 million in assets that would otherwise have been purchased for cash. If he does so, we will require $5 million less cash to close, but the seller will maintain a 16.67% carried interest (no dilution; the IRRs would essentially stay the same).

It is contemplated that The Parkside Group (TPG) will be the managing general partner, and in exchange for our work, we will receive a $300,000/year management fee and 20% of the distributions in excess of the preferred distributions (invested capital). Thus, Beta would receive $5 million before the general partner received any of the 20%. Finally, TPG will receive all of the tax loss allocations.

The ironic part of this structure is that we are planning to fund 100% of the LP share as well. However, given the interest in this industry, it would not surprise me if ultimately, there were LPs other than just TPG. Hopefully, after reviewing this financial structuring information, you will agree it is responsive to the issues we have been discussing. Obviously, this information is extremely confidential.

We expect that the operating responsibilities will reside with TPG, and that The Beta Group would continue with research, development and commercialization of the technology, and use their experience to help protect any patent infringements. Certainly, in addition to equity in Newco, we could discuss a technology consulting agreement. I guess it depends a bit on how many generations of technology you have, and ultimately, how well the market accepts HXL.

One point of interest, you will note that we are planning on spending $15 million to support brand in '98 (leading to a pro forma $40 million in sales for the year). In 1996, for the year, Callaway spent $37 million in marketing on its way to $650 million in sales for the year.

Talk to you soon.

Barry Schneider

Barry L. Schneider

EXHIBIT 3-10

PROPOSED ACORN FINANCIAL PROJECTIONS AND ACQUISITION STRUCTURE

Income Statement ($000)

	Post-Closing	1997 (4 mos)	1998	1999	2000
Revenues	—	$4,000	$25,000	$40,000	$60,000
Cost of goods sold	—	2,400	14,000	20,500	30,000
Gross profit	—	$1,600	$11,000	$19,500	$30,000
Gross profit %	—	40.0%	44.0%	48.8%	50.0%
Operating Expenses					
Management fees	—	$ 75	$ 300	$ 300	$ 300
Selling, general and administrative	—	750	5,000	8,500	14,000
Marketing	—	2,200	15,000	10,000	10,000
R&D/innovation	—	150	500	500	500
Depreciation	—	17	21	88	186
Amortization of goodwill	—	—	—	—	—
Total operating expenses	—	$3,192	$20,821	$19,388	$24,986
EBIT	—	$(1,592)	$(9,821)	$113	$5,014
EBIT %	—	(39.8%)	(39.3%)	0.2%	8.4%
Nonrecurring asset liquidation	$2,000	—	—	—	—
Interest income	—	$820	$97	—	—
Interest expense	—	—	—	349	859
Pretax income	$(2,000)	$(772)	$(9,724)	$(237)	$4,155
Income taxes	—	$(772)	—	—	1,620
Net income	$(2,000)	$(772)	$(9,724)	$(237)	$2,534
Net income %	—	(19.3%)	(38.9%)	(4.6%)	4.2%
Preferred dividends	—	—	—	—	—
Convertible preferred dividends	—	—	—	—	—
Net income to common	$(2,000)	$(772)	$(9,724)	$(237)	$2,534

Sources and Uses of Funds

Sources	
Contributed cash	$20,000
Seller contributed assets	5,000
Contributed HXL	5,000
Total Sources	$30,000

Uses	
Cash reserves	$ 2,950
Accounts receivable	6,000
Inventory	10,200
Other assets	5,500
Intangible assets	5,000
Net PP&E	150
Long-term assets	200
Total Uses	$30,000

51

However, we've seen the combination of technology and good marketing lead to significant market share changes very rapidly at the expense of old line brands. Our technology is new. As Callaway and Cobra have proven, there seems to be little loyalty in the retail channel or at the consumer level, and people seem to be willing to pay for the "next thing." The price points and margins are high, and the few companies who have been successful have been extremely well rewarded. To date, we've taken some of the risk out and limited our downside. But we're outsiders to the industry so we're unlikely to find friendly investors. The VCs are into the Internet and medical devices. Even if we do have a preferred model, who can we find to invest?

4

Cachet Technologies

$50K CONTEST: MAY 1998

Danny Lewin, Jonathan Seelig, and Scott Tobin walked down Memorial Drive just outside the MIT campus in Cambridge. The three now were thoroughly dejected and wondered what to do next. Their thoughts turned to the outcome of the 1998 MIT $50K Business Plan Competition that had just finished. Each year, the contest drew the best business plans for new products and services at the university. The audience had been full of venture capitalists, and they knew that a win in the competition would have meant a lot in terms of obtaining financing. Lewin and Seelig thought that they had assembled one of the most compelling new business propositions with their entry, Cachet Technologies. The company proposed to establish a potentially revolutionary way to distribute content over the Internet.

Lewin, an Israeli Ph.D. student who had worked for IBM in Haifa, was studying under Professor Tom Leighton, a world-renowned scientist in the Laboratory of Computer Science (LCS) at MIT. Lewin had seen an advertisement for the business plan contest in the fall and had hopes of being able to pay off some of his mounting debts. Considering his wife, family, and his substantial student loans, the $50,000 prize would have gone a long way to defraying his expenses. Lewin had brought both Seelig, a first-year Sloan MBA student, and Tobin, an associate at Battery Venture Partners and a long-time friend, into the project. A team of computer scientists had made tremendous progress on a prototype, and the team had identified potential partners and customers. Evidently, they were misguided.

First prize in the $50K Competition was shared by two firms: Direct Hit, a company that had been established to develop software that improved the searching capability of Internet search engines, and an Internet nonprofit named Volunteer Commodity Connection. The runner-up was Car Soft, a company that produced software that would enable individuals to run diagnostics on their automobiles by connecting a personal computer to their automobile's computer.

Research Associate Howard Reitz prepared this case under the supervision of Professor Paul Gompers as the basis for class discussion rather than to illustrate either effective or ineffective handling of an administrative situation.

How could a company like Cachet Technologies that had developed a revolution-ary new product to speed content around the Internet have lost to a company that had developed merely an evolutionary new technology to speed up Internet searches such as Direct Hit? Losing to a nonprofit made it even worse. The three friends walked along, recalling their experience and cursing in Hebrew, asking themselves: Why didn't the venture capitalists and entrepreneurs judging the contest understand the potential of Cachet Technologies? What had they not foreseen prior to the competition? Was Ca-chet Technologies' software worthy of being commercialized? Should Lewin and Seelig just call it quits? Perhaps most important, what did they need to do to determine the answer to these questions? Lewin and Seelig had attractive offers to pursue for the sum-mer and Tobin needed to continue screening deals and making investments for Battery Venture Partners. Maybe they would all be better served by pursuing those other opportunities?

WORLD WIDE WEB

The rapid evolution of the World Wide Web (WWW) in less than a decade had been well documented by the late 1990s. The development of the programming language known as hypertext mark-up language (HTML) in 1992 by Tim Berners-Lee enabled content to be displayed easily and accessed universally. Previously, the Internet had been used primarily as a means of transferring files. However, the development of HTML enabled programmers to create individual Web sites featuring the rich content and multimedia applications common in many complex Web sites. The creation of ad-vanced graphical user interfaces and commercial browsers enabled personal computer users for the first time to access a broad range of information from a variety of sources, facilitating the rise of Internet, ushering in the possibility of e-commerce, and chang-ing forever how individuals transacted business.[1]

The promise of the Internet was that it represented a global, interactive, and trans-active new medium. No other distribution channel had those qualities. First-generation Internet sites were often one-dimensional, static, and lacked interactivity. They did not actively engage users, nor did they exploit the information revealed by each user dur-ing every session. Second-generation Web sites promised to be more dynamic and en-abled, leveraging the interactive, and transactive nature of the new medium. This re-quired a substantial investment in Internet infrastructure in order to handle the expansion in bandwidth needed to process this additional information. As recently as 1995, the Internet had only 5 to 10 million pages of content. By the year 2000, how-ever, the Internet was projected to have as many as one billion Web pages.[2]

As users moved to more sophisticated multimedia applications, the existing rout-ing system on the Internet had become overloaded. This created a delay in the system or the feeling of slow Web page access during peak periods, even for individuals with high-speed access lines. Event-driven supersites accessed by broadband placed a sys-temic load on the network that caused a spike in usage, dropping information packets, and sometimes causing outages. Several examples of this phenomenon included the at-tempt to distribute the Starr Report, Victoria's Secret's promotional event during the Super Bowl, and the heavily trafficked Heaven's Gate's Web site after the cult made the headlines. This critical problem, called the "hot spot problem" by Berners-Lee, was

---

[1] Stephen Mahedy, "Talkin' bout a Net-volution," Salomon Smith Barney, December 8, 1999, p. 20.
[2] Ibid., p. 20.

caused when too many users accessed the system during peak periods or during a special event and reduced user access. The costs to companies were even higher with critical applications like online auction, e-commerce, and trading sites. New applications were planned to be introduced into the marketplace that would place even greater loads on the existing network, including advanced streaming media, voice-over-the-Internet, virtual private networks, and Internet roaming services.

CURRENT SOLUTIONS

Internet service providers (ISPs), that is, the companies that actually connected customers to the Internet, and other Internet infrastructure companies, were addressing the problem of net congestion in a number of ways, including building out their system to accommodate larger network loads and creating server farms that enabled them to host content for their customers. These investments in infrastructure were promising and were fueling the dramatic growth in new Internet infrastructure companies. They were, however, very expensive and time consuming to implement. In order to make these investments, Internet infrastructure companies had to make significant capital expenditures. Many of these companies, however, earned relatively low returns. [See Exhibits 4-1 and 4-2 for detailed information on ISPs.] Furthermore, Internet service providers expected substantial competition in the future. Once the large telcos gained entry into the long-distance market, they would be able to offer bundled services of local and long-distance phone service as well as Internet access to their customers. This created a market for a whole new class of Internet service providers. The most rapidly growing segments of the market were companies that provided hosting services to content providers.

One of the most promising solutions to net congestion was mirroring, whereby the entire content of a particular Web site would be replicated on a number of different servers at different locations. Mirroring companies provided their services to bandwidth-intensive, e-commerce companies that were looking to improve both the speed and reliability of their Web sites. Mirroring enabled content providers to spread out their traffic over multiple servers at different locations. It was, however, costly, time consuming, and inefficient. Content providers were required to duplicate the entire site at every server location, regardless of whether all of the information was requested by a user. A mirroring company made its margin by purchasing large volumes of bandwidth, negotiating discounts of as much as 30% to 50% and reselling bandwidth to content providers. Early purchasers of mirroring services were bandwidth-intensive online auction, e-commerce, and trading sites. Investment analysts believed that these companies would continue to outsource their content delivery requirements as their business expanded because no one could do it a cheaper than mirroring companies.[3] Companies such as Alteon, Bright Tiger, F5 Labs, and Resonate were developing software and hardware that would help keep sites synchronized and load balanced. These solutions, however, did not provide large-scale data replication. Although the software solution was helpful to content providers, it did not address the issue of scalability. It still cost more than twice as much to maintain two sites as it did to maintain a single site. [See Exhibit 4-3 for information on the financing of competitor firms.]

Another promising solution to net congestion was caching. Caching involved the temporary data replication and storing of a Web site on servers that were closer to the

[3] Ibid., p. 22.

EXHIBIT 4-1

SUMMARY STATISTICS ON GLOBAL AND NATIONAL ISP NETWORKS

Global and USA National ISPs	Major U.S. Peering Points	U.S. Backbone Cities	International Peering	International Backbone Cities	Revenue ($million 1997)	Business Accounts
AGIS	5	48				300
AT&T	5	11	6	16		
BELL (Canada)	1	12				
CAIS Internet	3	5		2		
Concentric	2	15				
CRL	6	32				5,000
CWIX	4	42	4	56		
DataXchange	5	8	2	2		
Digex	7	63				
Electric Lightwave	4	9				
Epoch Networks	12	9				3,000
Exodus	8	7		3		
Fibre Network Solutions	6					300
GeoNet Communications	4	14			$ 5	
GetNet International	3	5			$ 5	60
Frontier GlobalCenter	4	10				100
GridNet International	4	9		28		250
GTE/BBN	6	28				3,400
GTE/Genuity	10	12	1	1		
GTE/Nap.net	3	6				
IBM Global Network	5	14	10	62		30,000
IDT Corp	4	9				
Icon CMT	6	38			$ 40	800
Inet Solutions	4	51				
MCI Communications	5	19		10		
Netcom	6	11	2	3		
NetRail	2	7				
Priori Networks	4	11				
PSINet	4	37	9	35	$ 500	
PSINet/iSTAR (Canada)	1	19			$ 34	1,300
SAVVIS Communications	8	19				
Sprint IP Services	6	11			$1,000	2,800
TCG CERFnet Services	7	29				
Verio	5	20			$ 85	36,000
VisiNet	8	11			$ 250	
Vnet	3	10				
Worldcom/ANS	5	19		6		
Worldcom/Compuserve	5	11	3	3		
Worldcom/UUNET	5	69	14	14		
WinStar GoodNet	6	25				
ZipLink	3					
TOTAL	204	785	51	241		83,310
AVERAGE	5	20	4	17	0	2,083

Source: Company documents.

EXHIBIT 4-2

ISP FINANCIAL INFORMATION ($ IN THOUSANDS)

Global ISPs

	1996	1997	1998
AT&T CORP			
Market Value	$70,419	$99,584	$132,835
Sales	$52,184	$51,319	$ 53,223
SG&A	$15,589	$14,902	$ 12,695
Capital Expenditures	$ 6,339	$ 7,143	$ 7,817
Operating Income Before Depreciation	NA	$10,798	$ 14,950
Net Income	$ 5,608	$ 4,472	$ 5,235
Total Assets	$55,552	$58,635	$ 59,550
Total Current Assets	$18,310	$16,179	$ 14,118
Total Current Liabilities	$16,318	$16,942	$ 15,442
Total Long-Term Debt	$ 7,883	$ 6,826	$ 5,556
Beta	0.93	0.70	0.86
Price/Earnings	12.50	25.65	25.85
GTE CORP			
Market Value	$43,701	$50,056	$ 62,920
Sales	$21,339	$23,260	$ 25,473
SG&A	$ 4,010	$ 4,560	$ 4,821
Capital Expenditures	$ 4,088	$ 5,128	$ 5,609
Operating Income Before Depreciation	$ 9,258	$ 9,497	$ 9,911
Net Income	$ 2,798	$ 2,794	$ 2,492
Total Assets	$38,422	$42,142	$ 43,615
Total Current Assets	$ 6,033	$ 6,537	$ 6,781
Total Current Liabilities	$ 8,314	$ 9,841	$ 10,355
Total Long-Term Debt	$13,210	$14,494	$ 15,418
Beta	0.84	0.67	0.67
Price/Earnings	15.70	17.89	25.10
MCI WORLDCOM INC			
Market Value	$23,067	$27,503	$131,717
Sales	$ 4,485	$ 7,351	$ 17,678
SG&A	$ 829	$ 1,540	$ 4,312
Capital Expenditures	$ 657	$ 2,645	$ 5,418
Operating Income Before Depreciation	$ 1,199	$ 1,994	$ 4,950
Net Income	−$ 2,189	$ 384	−$ 2,558
Total Assets	$19,862	$22,390	$ 86,401
Total Current Assets	$ 2,296	$ 1,683	$ 10,639
Total Current Liabilities	$ 1,910	$ 2,048	$ 16,029
Total Long-Term Debt	$ 4,804	$ 6,527	$ 16,833
Beta	1.15	1.29	1.51
Price/Earnings	NM	131.52	NM
SPRINT FON GROUP			
Market Value	$17,150	$25,209	$28,981
Sales	$14,045	$14,874	$16,017
SG&A	$ 3,098	$ 3,225	$ 3,741
Capital Expenditures	$ 2,434	$ 2,863	$ 3,159
Operating Income Before Depreciation	$ 3,918	$ 4,198	$ 4,675
Net Income	$ 1,191	$ 953	$ 1,540
Total Assets	$16,953	$18,185	$19,275
Total Current Assets	$ 4,353	$ 3,773	$ 4,042
Total Current Liabilities	$ 3,314	$ 3,077	$ 3,293
Total Long-Term Debt	$ 2,982	$ 3,749	$ 4,683
Beta	1.02	0.78	0.66
Price/Earnings	14.29	26.53	23.37

EXHIBIT 4-2 *(Continued)*

National ISPs

	1996	1997	1998
CRL NETWORK SERVICES			
Market Value	NA	NA	NA
Sales	$6,353	$10,375	$11,692
SG&A	$2,185	$ 3,519	$ 4,495
Capital Expenditures	NA	NA	NA
Operating Income Before Depreciation	$ 822	$ 2,216	$ 1,031
Net Income	$ 161	$ 885	−$ 151
Total Assets	NA	$ 4,455	$ 4,855
Total Current Assets	NA	$ 2,606	$ 2,365
Total Current Liabilities	NA	$ 2,052	$ 1,935
Total Long-Term Debt	NA	$ 402	$ 847
Beta	NA	NA	NA
Price/Earnings	NA	NA	NM
FRONTIER CORP			
Market Value	$3,704	$ 3,938	$ 5,835
Sales	$2,576	$ 2,353	$ 2,594
SG&A	NA	NA	NA
Capital Expenditures	$ 247	$ 277	$ 630
Operating Income Before Depreciation	$ 643	$ 482	$ 550
Net Income	$ 218	$ 55	$ 178
Total Assets	$2,222	$ 2,475	$ 3,059
Total Current Assets	$ 469	$ 484	$ 567
Total Current Liabilities	$ 418	$ 475	$ 568
Total Long-Term Debt	$ 675	$ 930	$ 1,351
Beta	0.83	0.97	0.74
Price/Earnings	17.14	133.33	33.01
GST TELECOMM INC			
Market Value	$ 242	$ 378	$ 238
Sales	$ 41	$ 106	$ 163
SG&A	$ 35	$ 74	$ 97
Capital Expenditures	$ 76	$ 222	$ 219
Operating Income Before Depreciation	−$ 34	−$ 55	−$ 59
Net Income	−$ 60	−$ 113	−$ 155
Total Assets	$ 302	$ 728	$ 1,151
Total Current Assets	$ 101	$ 148	$ 182
Total Current Liabilities	$ 45	$ 75	$ 89
Total Liabilities	$ 280	$ 716	$ 1,223
Total Long-Term Debt	$ 234	$ 628	$ 1,112
Beta	1.43	1.73	1.78
Price/Earnings	NM	NM	NM

(Continued)

user, often co-located in ISP access facilities. In fact, ISPs were most interested in caching because it sped the delivery of content to their customers. In a typical example, a user requested content from a particular site. If the information had already been requested by another user, it would be held in cache (i.e., short-term memory) and could be served to the new user. If the Web page had not been requested recently, then the content would be served from the provider's server. While content providers might

EXHIBIT 4-2 *(Continued)*

	1996	1997	1998
PSINET INC			
Market Value	$436	$207	$1,087
Sales	$ 84	$122	$ 260
SG&A	NA	NA	NA
Capital Expenditures	$ 13	$ 13	$ 118
Operating Income Before Depreciation	−$ 33	−$ 21	NA
Net Income	−$ 55	−$ 46	−$ 262
Total Assets	$177	$186	$1,284
Total Current Assets	$ 82	$ 79	$ 565
Total Current Liabilities	$ 59	$ 78	$ 290
Total Long-Term Debt	$ 27	$ 34	$1,065
Beta	NA	1.45	2.16
Price/Earnings	NM	NM	NM
VERIO INC			
Market Value	NA	NA	$ 742
Sales	$ 2	$ 36	$ 121
SG&A	$ 7	$ 49	$ 111
Capital Expenditures	$ 3	$ 15	$ 23
Operating Income Before Depreciation	NA	−$ 30	−$ 45
Net Income	−$ 5	−$ 46	−$ 112
Total Assets	$ 83	$246	$ 934
Total Current Assets	$ 68	$106	$ 614
Total Current Liabilities	$ 7	$ 31	$ 56
Total Long-Term Debt	$ 0	$142	$ 675
Beta	NA	NA	1.85
Price/Earnings	NA	NA	NM

Source: Compiled from Compustat.

benefit from having their content served more quickly, they sacrificed control over any content that was cached. This was not important for static information, but it could be costly for information that had to be updated regularly. Some content providers had gone so far as to code some of their content as "uncacheable" in order to prevent other sites and ISPs from serving old content. This was particularly important for entertainment, news, and financial services firms.[4] Companies such as CacheFlow, Inktomi, and Netcache were developing software and hardware that would enable large-scale data replication. These solutions did not, however, provide load balancing.

DISCOVERY OF AN ALGORITHM

In 1995, Tim Berners-Lee challenged his colleagues in the Laboratory for Computer Science at MIT to find a more efficient way of managing traffic congestion over the Internet. Professor Tom Leighton, head of the Algorithms Group in MIT's famous Laboratory of Computer Science, took up this challenge. As one of the world's preeminent authorities on mathematical algorithms, Professor Leighton believed that the solution

[4] Ibid., p. 23.

EXHIBIT 4-3

COMPARABLE DEAL STATISTICS FOR CACHET TECHNOLOGIES

CACHEFLOW

Business Brief:	Provider of Internet caching appliances
Founded:	03/96
Employees:	86
Stage:	Shipping Product
Industries:	Connectivity/Communications Tools
Internet Focus:	Infrastructure

INVESTORS:

Investment Firm	Participating Round #(s)
Benchmark Capital	1*, 2, 3
Kelly Hanna Capital	1, 2
Individual Investors	1, 4
U.S. Venture Partners	2*, 3
Technology Crossover Ventures	3*

FINANCINGS TO DATE:

Round #	Round Type	Date	Amount Raised ($MM)	Post $ Valuation ($MM)	Company Stage
1	1st	11/96	5.1	14.0	Product Development
2	2nd	02/98	9.3	54.0	Product in Beta Test

INKTOMI

Business Brief:	Developer of networked information and infrastructure applications
Founded:	02/96
Employees:	89
Stage:	Shipping Product
Industries:	Connectivity/Communications Tools
Internet Focus:	Software/DB

INVESTORS:

Investment Firm	Participating Round #(s)
Oak Investment Partners	2*
Intel Corporation	3*
Individual Investors	1*

FINANCINGS TO DATE:

Round #	Round Type	Date	Amount Raised ($MM)	Post $ Valuation ($MM)	Company Stage
1	Indiv	06/96	4.6	N/A	Product Development
2	1st	04/97	8.0	58.7	Shipping Product
3	Corp	10/97	2.0	58.7	Shipping Product
4	Mezz	03/98	12.0	104.0	Shipping Product

NETWORK APPLIANCE

Business Brief:	Manufacturer of network data storage devices
Founded:	04/92
Employees:	53
Stage:	Shipping Product
Industries:	Data Storage

INVESTORS:

Investment Firm	Participating Round #(s)
Vanguard Venture Partners	1, 2
Sequoia Capital	2, 3
TA Associates	1
Individual Investors	1
Sutter Hill Ventures	2

* = Lead Investor

(Continued)

EXHIBIT 4-3   (Continued)

NETWORK APPLIANCE (*continued*)
FINANCINGS TO DATE:

Round #	Round Type	Date	Amount Raised ($MM)	Post $ Valuation ($MM)	Company Stage
1	1st	09/93	1.5	6.0	Shipping Product
2	2nd	10/94	4.8	11.5	Shipping Product
3	3rd	02/95	6.6	32.1	Shipping Product
4	IPO	11/95	36.45	214.5	Shipping Product

ALTEON WEBSYSTEMS

Business Brief:	Developer of gigabit Ethernet switches
Founded:	03/96
Employees:	58
Stage:	Shipping Product
Industries:	Connectivity Products
Internet Focus:	Infrastructure

INVESTORS:

Investment Firm	Participating Round #(s)
Matrix Partners	1, 2, 3
Sutter Hill Ventures	1, 2, 3
Onset Ventures	2, 3
TOW Partners	2
Mventure	2
GCC Investments, LLC	2
Glynn Ventures	2
New Enterprise Associates	2, 3
GC&H Investments	2
KTB Venture Capital	2
Trailhead Ventures	3
GE Capital	3
Velocity Capital Management	3
W.K. Technology (Taipei)	3
Charter Venture Capital	3

FINANCINGS TO DATE:

Round #	Round Type	Date	Amount Raised ($MM)	Post $ Valuation ($MM)	Company Stage
1	1st	05/96	4.0	10.0	Shipping Product
2	2nd	05/97	18.0	88.5	Shipping Product
3	3rd	05/98	15.0	146.43	Shipping Product

BRIGHT TIGER TECHNOLOGIES

Business Brief:	Developer of software products that provide systems-administration capabilities for intranets
Founded:	06/96
Employees:	39
Stage:	Shipping Product
Industries:	Network/Systems Mgt Tools
Internet Focus:	Software/DB

INVESTORS:

Investment Firm	Participating Round #(s)
North Bridge Venture Partners	1*, 2, 3
Accel Partners	2*, 3
Oak Investment Partners	3*

* = Lead Investor

(*Continued*)

EXHIBIT 4-3 *(Continued)*

BRIGHT TIGER TECHNOLOGIES *(continued)*

FINANCINGS TO DATE:

Round #	Round Type	Date	Amount Raised ($MM)	Post $ Valuation ($MM)	Company Stage
1	Seed	08/96	0.35	1.9	Product Development
2	1st	01/97	4.0	8.6	Product Development
3	2nd	11/97	6.0	30.7	Product Development

CISCO SYSTEMS

Business Brief:	Developer of high performance, multi-protocol internetworking systems that enable users to build large scale integrated networks of computer networks
Founded:	12/84
Employees:	175
Stage:	Profitable
Industries:	Connectivity Products

INVESTORS:

Investment Firm	Participating Round #(s)
Sequoia Capital	1*
Indosuez Ventures	1
VenCap International	1
Stanford University	1

FINANCINGS TO DATE:

Round #	Round Type	Date	Amount Raised ($MM)	Post $ Valuation ($MM)	Company Stage
1	1st	11/87	2.4	4.0	Profitable
2	IPO	02/90	50.4	226.0	Profitable

F5 NETWORKS

Business Brief:	Developer of server array-controller technologies that enable organizations to provide reliable, consistent access to mission-critical Internet, intranet, and extranet applications by enabling the fail-safe use of scalable content servers.
Founded:	02/96
Employees:	44
Stage:	Shipping Product
Industries:	Connectivity/Communications Tools
Internet Focus:	Software/DB

INVESTORS:

Investment Firm	Participating Round #(s)
Encompass Ventures	1*, 2
Britannia Holdings	1, 2*
Individual Investors	
Cypress Partners	3*

FINANCINGS TO DATE:

Round #	Round Type	Date	Amount Raised ($MM)	Post $ Valuation ($MM)	Company Stage
1	PPE	04/96	1.2	12.0	Startup
2	2nd	12/97	2.3	13.0	Shipping Product
3	3rd	04/98	1.5	19.0	Shipping Product

* = Lead Investor

(Continued)

EXHIBIT 4-3   (Continued)

EXODUS COMMUNICATIONS

Business Brief:	Provider of services enabling customers to outsource the management and day-to-day operations of their Internet and intranet servers
Founded:	02/95
Employees:	120
Stage:	Shipping Product
Industries:	Business Services (not Financial)
Internet Focus:	Business Services

INVESTORS:

Investment Firm	Participating Round #(s)
Bay Partners	2, 4
Information Technology Ventures	2, 3, 4
Apex Investment Partners	2, 3, 4
First Analysis Venture Capital	2, 3
J.F. Shea & Co.	1, 2, 3, 4
CE Unterberg Towbin Capital Partners	2, 4
Fleet Equity Partners	3, 4*
Oak Investment Partners	3, 4
Chisholm Private Capital Partners	3, 4
JK&B Capital	3, 4
Draper Richards	4
John R. Dougery	1, 2
Rekhi Family Trust	1, 4

FINANCINGS TO DATE:

Round #	Round Type	Date	Amount Raised ($MM)	Post $ Valuation ($MM)	Company Stage
1	1st	03/96	3.22	5.5	Shipping Product
2	2nd	10/96	6.5	17.64	Shipping Product
3	3rd	06/97	21.5	53.0	Shipping Product
4	Later	12/97	7.5	117.0	Shipping Product

DIGITAL ISLAND

Business Brief:	Provider of a high-performance applications network designed to provide worldwide deployment of Internet applications
Founded:	02/94
Employees:	65
Stage:	Shipping Product
Industries:	Internet Service Providers
Internet Focus:	Business Services

INVESTORS:

Investment Firm	Participating Round #(s)
Vanguard Venture Partners	1*, 2, 3
Crosspoint Venture Partners	1, 2, 3
Bay Partners	1, 2, 3
HMS Investments	1, 2, 3
Crescendo Ventures	2*, 3
Cassin, BJ	2
Stanford University	
Cisco Systems	
National Semiconductor	
JAFCO America Ventures	3
Partech International	3
Japan Associated Finance Company	3
US Information Technologies	3
Nippon Enterprise Development Corp.	3
Tudor Investment Corporation	3*

* = Lead Investor

EXHIBIT 4-3   *(Continued)*

DIGITAL ISLAND *(continued)*

FINANCINGS TO DATE:

Round #	Round Type	Date	Amount Raised ($MM)	Post $ Valuation ($MM)	Company Stage
1	1st	03/97	4.0	8.0	Shipping Product
2	2nd	07/97	7.5	27.5	Shipping Product
3	3rd	02/98	15.0	55.0	Shipping Product

SANDPIPER NETWORKS

Business Brief:	Provider of Internet and system-software architecture, implementation, and maintenance services
Founded:	01/96
Employees:	65
Stage:	Shipping Product
Industries:	Connectivity/Communications Tools
Internet Focus:	Business Services

INVESTORS:

Investment Firm	Participating Round #(s)
Media Technology Ventures	1
Brentwood Venture Capital	1

FINANCINGS TO DATE:

Round #	Round Type	Date	Amount Raised ($MM)	Post $ Valuation ($MM)	Company Stage
1	1st	11/97	6.6	12.6	Shipping Product

INTERNAP NETWORK SERVICES

Business Brief:	Provider of fault-tolerant, Internet network infrastructure, and connectivity services
Founded:	05/96
Employees:	105
Stage:	Shipping Product
Industries:	Internet Service Providers
Internet Focus:	Business Services: Connectivity/Communications Tools

INVESTORS:

Investment Firm	Participating Round #(s)
H&Q Venture Associates, LLC	2
Vulcan Ventures	2*
Kirlan Venture Capital, Inc.	2
Individual Investors	1
TL Ventures	2

FINANCINGS TO DATE:

Round #	Round Type	Date	Amount Raised ($MM)	Post $ Valuation ($MM)	Company Stage
1	Seed	10/96	1.0	8.0	Product Development
2	1st	11/97	7.7	15.0	Shipping Product

* = Lead Investor

Source: Compiled from VentureOne.

to the problem of net congestion lay in an intelligent application of mathematical algorithms to the routing of traffic through the network. He solicited the help of one of his talented graduate students named Danny Lewin. Lewin was a mathematician who had earned degrees from the Israel Institute of Technology (Technion), where he graduated summa cum laude and was named "Outstanding Student in Computer Engineering" while also working as a research fellow for IBM in Haifa.

Lewin was interested in the important theoretical questions that the Internet congestion problems raised and applied himself to developing solutions to the problem. The two scientists developed elaborate white boards with graphs of nodes representing configurations of gateways and individual routers throughout the network. The results of their work produced several early ideas that culminated in Lewin's master's degree thesis. Lewin broke down the overall problem and developed a solution to a subset of the problem posed by Berners-Lee. The problem involved how to evenly distribute traffic among individual routers once it had been distributed through a regional gateway. Lewin's solution was called a "double randomized hashing algorithm," with which he won a coveted award from MIT for the best new master's degree. Simple hashing programs divided traffic evenly but often ran into difficulty when nodes dropped out. Lewin's solution addressed this problem in an elegant way.[5]

After several semesters of work, the computer scientists began to develop additional algorithms to solve other elements of the problem and to outline a solution to the overall problem. Some of their work was published, but some remained proprietary. The solution addressed questions such as how to resolve routing problems by taking advantage of the distributed nature of the Internet. The computer algorithms simultaneously minimized both the download time and packet loss. It could potentially protect a content provider even during a dramatic run on its Web site. The software minimized download time by minimizing the time between locations and by finding the least congested route for the information to travel. It took into consideration a user's location, the location of the content, the status of Internet peering, and backbone congestion conditions. The software minimized packet loss by minimizing the number of router hops (i.e., the number of routers that the information needed to pass through) and the accuracy of individual router links. In its essence, the program was a giant linear program that minimized the most significant problems regarding traffic congestion over the Internet.

THE LEIGHTON-LEWIN SOLUTION

Though none of the computer scientists realized it at the time, the solution to the problem posed by Berners-Lee was a dramatic new way of delivering content over the Internet. As they continued to work on algorithms and software development, they began to realize that they had discovered not only a new way to distribute content over the Internet but a fundamental new way that would forever change the way the Internet worked.[6]

Leighton and Lewin recognized that part of the problem of slow downloading lay in the composition of the web page. Over 70% of the information required to serve a page was from embedded objects rather than text.[7] The first solution enabled portions

[5] Paul Spinrad, "The New Cool," *Wired* Magazine, August 1999.

[6] Mahedy, pp. 42–43.

[7] Ibid., p. 46.

of a Web site to be tagged by software and served throughout a geographically dispersed network of servers. This enabled content providers to decide which elements of their Web pages they wished to serve from their own computers, allowing the remaining elements to be geographically distributed throughout the network developed by Cachet Technologies' customers. This enabled bandwidth-intensive information to be stored and retrieved rapidly without regard to a central server. In addition, it enabled replication of content to be based on the frequency and geographic location of demand. This enabled content producers to scale up to hundreds or perhaps thousands of nodes while maintaining control over relevant data such as number of user hits, user profile, and user location.

A second element of Cachet Technologies' approach called for continuous monitoring of traffic congestion over the Internet. When bottlenecks were discovered, content could be dynamically served from the least congested servers. A third component of Cachet's software dynamically balanced the traffic load, spreading content evenly throughout the network. This was the first software solution that created a truly intelligent network of networks. Individual nodes would communicate with one another to monitor traffic and distribute content in the most efficient way. The benefits of their overall approach—which combined content provider control over their content, ability to scale, and compatibility with all server types—were unique.

TURNING AN IDEA INTO A BUSINESS

Lewin had seen an advertisement for the business plan contest while walking across the MIT campus in the fall of 1997. Earlier in the fall, he had met a bright MIT Sloan student named Preetish Nijhawan who had previously worked as a program manager for a computer-aided design team that produced the Pentium Pro processor. Nijhawan's wife had done some babysitting for Lewin's children, and when Lewin saw the $50K poster, he decided to ask Nijhawan his opinion about his research. Nijhawan believed that there was a market for Lewin's algorithms and was interested in assisting him prepare a business plan for the annual entrepreneurship competition.

While Lewin and Nijhawan began work on the plan, Lewin was introduced to a first-year MIT Sloan student named Jonathan Seelig. Two mutual friends—Marco Greenberg (a public relations expert with Burston-Marsteller in New York) and Roy Navon (an investment banker with Goldman Sachs)—had introduced Lewin and Seelig. Seelig had worked as a product manager for ECI Telecom in Tel Aviv and was interested in becoming involved in a start-up out of the LCS. While at ECI, he led teams that were involved with network design, equipment deployment, and customer training for several major international telecommunications projects. He had also been involved in product marketing of very sophisticated hardware solutions to large telecommunications customers. Seelig became intrigued with the software solution that Leighton and Lewin had devised and agreed to join the team. Seelig brought his business insights to the team, and Cachet Technologies was born.

Leighton, Lewin, and Seelig recognized that they had a good team but not necessarily a complete team. [See Exhibit 4-4 for company bios.] In addition, the team had not yet identified someone who could serve as the company's CEO. Leighton, Lewin, and Seelig knew that the existing group had to be supplemented with additional management. They felt, however, that they had assembled a team that had enough collective technical knowledge to produce an alpha and beta product. The team could draw

EXHIBIT 4-4

CACHET TECHNOLOGIES TEAM

Technology Team

F. Tom Leighton (B.A., Princeton '78, Ph.D. MIT '81) was a professor of Applied Mathematics at MIT and the head of the Algorithms group in MIT's Laboratory for Computer Science. Professor Leighton was one of the world's most eminent authorities on algorithms for network applications. He published more than 100 research papers, and his seminal text on parallel algorithms and architectures were translated into several languages. Dr. Leighton had substantial experience in the development of hi-tech intellectual property. Several of his patents have been licensed or sold to major corporations. He was a former two-term chair of the 2,000-member ACM Special Interest Group on Algorithms and Computation Theory, and former editor-in-chief of the Journal of the ACM—ACM's flagship research publication.

David Karger (B.A. Summa Cum Laude, Harvard '89, Ph.D. Stanford '94) was a professor of Computer Science and member of the Algorithms Group at MIT's Laboratory for Computer Science. Professor Karger was one of the best young researchers in Network Algorithms. His doctoral dissertation won the Association for Computing Machinery's award for best dissertation in 1994. He won several competitive fellowships to support his work, including an NSF career award, an Alfred P. Sloane foundation fellowship, and a David and Lucille Packard foundation fellowship, which was given to only 10 scientists in the country each year. He had published more than 20 research papers in the premier computer science conferences. Previously, David worked in the Text Database Group at the Xerox Palo Alto Research Center. He developed novel interfaces for efficiently browsing massive text collections, helping to spark the current interest in document clustering as a retrieval tool.

Daniel Lewin (B.A., B.Sc. Summa Cum Laude, Israel Institute of Technology—Technion '94, M.Sc. MIT '98) was a Ph.D. student working with Professor Tom Leighton at MIT's Laboratory for Computer Science. He had published several important papers at top computer science conferences. Prior to graduate school, Daniel was a research fellow and project leader at IBM. At IBM, Daniel was responsible for the development and support of the most widely used tool for processor verification within IBM.

Robert Thau (B.A. Magna Cum Laude Harvard '87, Ph.D. MIT '97) was one of the three architects of the Apache Server. This software was used on over 50% of the Internet Web servers online today. He was intimately familiar with the issues involved in creating high performance proxy Web servers. From 1986 to 1993 Robert worked at Thinking Machines Corporation where, among other tasks, he performed performance studies of document retrieval on parallel machines.

Bill Bogstad (Electric Engineering major, Johns Hopkins University '84) had over 12 years of experience in software development and computer systems management. His operating system development experience included networking, file system, and device driver software for various UNIX systems. He had experience in benchmarking and bottleneck analysis of computer and network systems, which was relevant to Global Hosting. He was the lead developer of AT&T Systems Inc.'s XMaster product that allowed benchmarking of multi-user systems via remote workstation emulation of X Window System user machines.

Alex Sherman (undergraduate degree) was an M.Eng. candidate in Computer Science at MIT. His experience included software development at Rational Software Inc., SQA Inc., and Fidelity Investments. Alex was a member of the Tau Beta Pi Engineering Honor Society.

(Continued)

EXHIBIT 4-4 *(Continued)*

Marketing Team

Preetish Nijhawan (B. Eng., Birla Institute of Technology and Science, India, '89 M.Sc. Computer Engineering, University of Southern California, '90) was a second-year student at the MIT Sloan School of Management. Prior to business school, he worked for Intel Corporation as a program manager where he was responsible for the delivery of the CAD suite used to design the Pentium and Pentium Pro processors. This suite had more than 3 million lines of code and was developed by 100 software developers at two sites. Preetish was responsible for gathering customer requirements, planning, schedule and delivery. Before being promoted to program manager, Preetish was a developer on a state-of-the-art interconnect measurement and simulation environment at Intel.

Jonathan Seelig (B.Sc. Physics, with honors, Stanford '94) was a first-year student at the MIT Sloan School of Management. His major was new product and venture development. Prior to attending Sloan, Jonathan worked for ECI Telecom in Tel-Aviv, Israel. Jonathan's work with ECI was primarily in the fields of speech and data compression. He was responsible for the marketing, implementation and design of bandwidth saving equipment in the international telephone networks of over 20 countries.

Marco Greenberg (B.A. History and Political Science, UCLA, M.A. International and Public Affairs, Columbia University) was the founder of NYPR, a high profile New York public relations agency. Until December 1997, Marco served as a manager in the corporate practice at Burson-Marsteller, one of the industry's largest firms.

Board of Advisors

Dr. Michael Dertouzos had been head of MIT's Laboratory for Computer Science since 1974. Under Michael's leadership, the lab had come to be recognized as one of the most important computer science research institutions in the world. With several start-up companies and technology patents to his credit, Dertouzos advised the leaders of Fortune 500 companies and of the U.S. and European governments on the future direction of information technology and its impact.

Dr Albert Vezza (B.Sc., Rochester Institute of Technology, New York, M.Sc. Northeastern University, Boston) is currently head of the Boston office of the Corporation for National Research Initiatives (CNRI). He was previously the Associate Director and Senior Research Scientist at the MIT Laboratory for Computer Science, which in partnership with INRIA, hosted the W3C. He was the chairman of the W3C and was responsible for creating it in 1994. Albert's career at MIT spanned over 32 years. He took a leave of absence from MIT-LCS from 1984 to 1986 to become the chairman and chief executive officer of Infocom, Inc., of Cambridge, Massachusetts.

Randall Kaplan (B.A., highest distinction, Psychology, Michigan, Juris Doctor with honors, Northwestern University School of Law) was managing director of Corporate Development at SunAmerica, a $52 billion financial services company based in Los Angeles. Randall specializes in performing financial analysis, strategic planning, and research functions as part of SunAmerica's mergers and acquisitions and investment efforts. Prior to joining SunAmerica, Randall practiced corporate, securities, and tax law for several years.

Todd A. Dagres, General Partner, Battery Ventures (M.S. Economics, Trinity College, Hartford, CT, MBA, Boston University) focuses on the communications industry where he was involved in all phases of the investment program. He joined Battery in February 1996 from Montgomery Securities where he was a Principal and Senior Technology Analyst focusing on the networking industry.

Scott R. Tobin, Associate, Battery Ventures (B.A. International Relations, Brandeis University) joined Battery Ventures in 1997 and focuses on software investments. Tobin was most recently an Associate in the technology group of First Albany's corporate finance department where he worked on initial public offerings, private placements and merger & acquisition related assignments.

Sean Dalton (BSEE Electrical Engineering, University of Delaware, MSEE University of Pennsylvania) was a second-year student at the Harvard Business School. Prior to business school, Dalton was product manager for Internet services at GTE Telephone World Headquarters. Dalton had served as an advisor to dozens of local high tech companies and joined Highland Venture Partners as an associate upon graduation.

Source: Company documents.

on the expertise of David Karger, a computer science professor at LCS, and Yoav Yerushalmi and Alex Sherman, two graduate students at MIT. In addition, the current Sloan students, Nijhawan and Seelig, had the experience necessary to conduct the initial market research and beta customer recruitment to determine whether the project was feasible to launch. Leighton and Lewin also had to negotiate with MIT's technology licensing office to gain permission to use their work for a business. Even though they had developed the algorithms, MIT owned them. This was a significant issue and neither had any experience with this type of negotiation. In order to help with these and other issues, Lewin believed that Cachet Technologies needed to assemble a credible advisory board. One of Lewin's outside advisers was his close friend, Scott Tobin. Tobin was a young venture capitalist at Battery Ventures in Wellesley. Lewin and Tobin discussed the idea for Cachet Technologies at the Milk Street Café in downtown Boston. Lewin wanted to explore the possibility that Battery would serve as an adviser to their business plan. About a month later, Tobin brought the company to the attention of Todd Dagres, a general partner at Battery. Dagres was a former senior technology analyst with Montgomery Securities in San Francisco and had developed an enviable track record in the venture capital world.

BATTERY VENTURE PARTNERS

Founded in 1983, Battery Ventures was one of the leading venture capital firms in the information technology industry. The Partnership managed six individual funds with more than $800 million of committed capital. Battery was actively investing Battery V, a $400 million investment pool, and the Battery Convergence Fund, a $40 million side fund. Battery Ventures Funds I through IV was fully invested in over 100 companies. Year after year, venture capital industry performance rankings consistently gave Battery Funds among their highest ratings. As lead investor of some of the most successful technology companies, Battery relied on a developed methodology that combined focused industry expertise with an intense commitment to its portfolio companies. This approach allowed it to quickly identify firms with significant potential and to shape strategies for growing them into market leading companies.

Battery Ventures invested worldwide in private companies within the communications, software, and Internet/e-Commerce markets from its offices in Wellesley, Massachusetts, and San Mateo, California. It had a 16-year history of guiding the emergence of many of the world's most successful information technology companies. Battery focused on helping its companies to become category leaders of their particular industry segment. Battery was typically the first institutional investor in a start-up, usually taking a proactive approach to deal generation, utilizing aggressive sourcing and marketing programs, reinforced by focused research into emerging technologies and promising market segments. Employing a team approach, Battery committed several individuals to the pre-investment analysis of target companies. That same team would remain in place post-investment and was at the disposal of the start-up to assist in the building process.

Battery invested at all stages of the growth cycle, from incubations and seed situations to mezzanine and technology buyouts. Their investments typically ranged from $5 million to $25 million per deal. Most important, however, in addition to financial resources, Battery would commit its time, people, and network to a venture's success. Battery tried to leverage the institutional knowledge built through 16 years of technology and industry focus to identify companies with the ingredients for category leadership.

TESTING THE ALPHA PRODUCT

Todd Dagres was intrigued with the technology that Leighton and Lewin had developed. He had enough experience working with engineers and scientists, however, to recognize that the team needed the expertise of an individual who had built a business. Dagres recalled that the first time he really peppered the team with questions, one of the team members broke into a profuse sweat all over his body. Dagres was concerned that this member would not be able to stand up to the competitive pressure of launching a new business. Dagres felt, however, that the idea was good enough to mentor for the time being. After all, if Cachet Technologies turned into something real, Battery Ventures would have an early look at it. Tobin met continuously with Leighton, Lewin, and Seelig until the date of the business plan contest in May 1998. Tobin and Dagres had provided Lewin, Nijhawan, and Seelig with a road map on how they should think about building their business. Lewin was inexperienced but was willing to learn, picking up almost everything published about building a start-up and dealing with venture capitalists.

Leighton and Lewin knew that their first priority was to test the software under real market conditions. The company's innovative mathematical software had been rigorously analyzed, but it had not been put through its paces on a real network. The development of an initial prototype had begun, and the first test was expected to be conducted sometime during the summer. The first trial would be conducted at LCS and then would be expanded to include the entire MIT campus. Professor Leighton was prepared to contribute some of his funding from the Department of Defense's Defense Advanced Research Projects Agency (DARPA) grant to assist in the proof of the concept. In addition, Leighton would be helpful in identifying potential customers for the company's product. Because of his world-renowned reputation, Professor Leighton could get almost any senior scientist at a major communications company to take his call.

As the engineering team progressed, Nijhawan and Seelig began to investigate the market for the company's software product. One of the first tasks for the team was to determine who the customer was. Most current solutions to net congestion problems such as mirroring and caching were sold as a product to Internet service providers (ISP) and other Internet infrastructure companies. ISPs were in the business of connecting users to the Internet. While the team believed that ISPs were a potential paying customer, the team believed that their solution also had to appeal to content providers who would ultimately adopt the technology. The two MIT Sloan students were intrigued because the market was one of the fastest-growing new segments of the Internet market. [See Exhibit 4-5 for Cachet Technologies' business strategy.]

THE GLOBAL HOSTING MARKET

During 1996 and 1997, the number of Internet users had grown rapidly, doubling almost every hundred days. During this period, the Internet had also moved from being a U.S.-based phenomenon to a truly worldwide phenomenon. Though over 70 million users still resided in North America, there were almost 113 million users on a worldwide basis. Typically, consumers chose between a dial-up or dedicated service which connected them to the Internet through a local phone company or competitive local exchange carrier.

Internet service providers were projected to penetrate 30 million of the more than 55 million personal computers in U.S. households by 1999. Dial-up Internet access was estimated to represent a total market value of $6.5 billion by the year 1999 and was in-

EXHIBIT 4-5

CACHET TECHNOLOGIES' BUSINESS MODEL

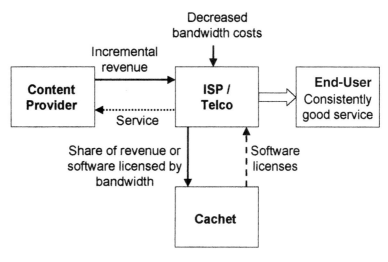

Source: Company documents.

creasing at a rate of 30% per year. The Web hosting market was estimated to be a $1 billion market in 1998 and was growing rapidly. It was projected to grow to $10.5 billion by 2002. Web hosting had two market segments: hosting of simple sites and complex sites. While a simple site was intended to establish an Internet presence with a set of static pages, a complex site was dynamic, interactive, and transactive. The simple site hosting market was estimated to be approximately $300 million in 1998 and was expected to grow to $1 billion by 2002. The complex site hosting market was estimated to be $600 million in 1998 and was expected to grow to $8 billion by 2002. This large and rapidly growing market segment was the one that was targeted by the marketing team.

Nijhawan and Seelig believed that by targeting ISPs, their software would enable the ISPs to speed the delivery of their customers' content while protecting them against spikes in demand. Cachet Technologies targeted 54 of the leading global and national Internet service providers as potential customers for their products. The key driver in this plan was that the key decision makers were few in number and geographically con-

TABLE A Segmentation of the U.S. and Global ISP Market

ISP Market	United States	World Wide
Global ISPs	17	17
Global Regional ISPs	27	25+
U.S. ISPs	500	N/A
U.S. Local ISPs	4000+	2000+

Source: Company documents.

centrated. The leading content and service providers were concentrated in Boston, Washington D.C., San Francisco, and Los Angeles. The team had already identified Bell South, a Californian ISP, and a Florida ISP as potential first clients for their software product.

PRICING THE PRODUCT

One of the first decisions that had to be made was whether the product should be leased or sold. Typically, products of this sort were sold to end-users as a complete solution; some also included product and service solutions. Given the nature of the software, the team believed that it lent itself to being sold as a complete shrink-wrapped solution. Another decision involved how to price the software and whether the software should be sold directly by the company's sales force or through distributors. Nijhawan and Seelig had put together a list of potential competitors. They examined each company to determine how each priced and distributed its company's software product.

Cachet Technologies' software represented a dramatic improvement over alternative software solutions in the marketplace. While Cachet Technologies competed directly with companies in some of the product spaces, it was alone in the range of services that the software provided. Companies that competed in the market for mirroring enabling software included Alteon, Cisco, F5, and Resonate. These companies provided software solutions that assisted their clients in balancing traffic loads on their system but did not provide large-scale data replication for their customers. Companies in the caching market included Cache Flow, Inktomi, and Netcache, which offered software that provided large-scale data replication for their customers but did not provide solutions that load balanced their systems. Only Cachet Technologies provided both.

For this reason, Nijhawan and Seelig suggested that the company's product should be priced at a premium. They looked at comparable companies in the marketplace considering Bright Tiger, CacheFlow, Cisco, F5 Labs, Inktomi, and Resonate. Pricing of their comparable products ranged from $5,000 to $40,000. Inktomi's solution was the most comparable product, according to Seelig. Inktomi, like Cachet, was a software-only solution that required no additional proprietary hardware. Their product was priced at $20,000 but did not include the features of Cachet, that is, its scalability and fault tolerance, nor did it have the capability of load balancing and protecting against peak usage. Nevertheless, as a new entrant, the marketing team decided to price at a discount to Inktomi, or $17,000. [See Exhibit 4-6 for pricing information for competitors' products.]

FINANCIAL PROJECTIONS

Based on a target market of the largest Internet service providers, the team began to build financial projections for the company. Beginning in the second quarter of 1998, the team targeted 14 global and 40 national Internet services providers. Based on a formula for the number of backbone cities served and the number of 45 Mbps hosting servers, Cachet projected a target market of 643 potential global hosting servers that could utilize its products. Cachet projected to scale up rapidly from 1 customer in the fourth quarter of 1998 to 16 by year 2000, adding 3 new customers per quarter, until it had penetrated 16 major accounts, or 28% of its customer base. The marketing team had already identified several beta customers who had expressed an interest in the product, including Bell South, Global One, and @Home.

EXHIBIT 4-6

PRICE COMPARISONS ON SELECTED COMPETITIVE PRODUCTS

Company	Product	Price (US$ 1998)	Comments
F5	Big IP	$40,000 to support two web servers	Dedicated hardware
Bright Tiger	ClusterCATS	$10,000 to support two web servers	Works with Microsoft's IIS web server software only. Software, only available for NT
Resonate	Central Dispatch	$10,000 to support two web servers	
Flying Fox Computer System	Fox Box Network Access Gateway	$5,250 to support two web servers	
Hydraweb Technologies	Hydraweb	$7,900	Hardware solution
IBM	Interactive Network Dispatcher	$1,500 per web server supported	
Cisco	Local Director	$14,000	Hardware
RND	WebServer Director	$14,552	
SGI	WebForce Director	$5,000	Runs on SGI hardware only
BBN	Hopscotch	20% to 30% premium over single site hosting	7 data centers on 3 continents
Cacheflow	Cacheflow 1000	$39,500	Caching software, placed in the network.
Inktomi	Traffic Server	$20,000 per cpu	Caching software, runs on Sun SPARCs
NetWork Appliances	Netcache	Priced per cpu	Caching software, runs on Sun Sparcs, and Microsoft NT.

Source: Company documents.

Based on an initial price of $17,000 per 45 Mbps hosting server plus an average incremental revenue of 10% per server, Cachet projected to scale up rapidly from initial revenues of $200,000 in the fourth quarter of 1998 to approximately $21 million by year 2000. This was based on an average of five global servers per customer. Initially, the company would price at a premium but projected that in a highly competitive market, the projections would build in an average 5% price decline per quarter. [See Exhibits 4-7 and 4-8 for financial details.]

Total costs were scaled off of the projected number of total employees in a given quarter. In the fourth quarter of 1998, Cachet estimated that it would need approximately 26.5 employees (0.5 represented half-time employment) to launch their first product. Based on an average cost per employee per year (including benefits) of $80,000, total personal costs were estimated to be $530,000. All additional costs were estimated to be variable and based on the total number of employees added each quarter. The company hoped to raise approximately $2.5 million in financing, which was expected to provide it with liquidity through the short period until it turned profitable in the second quarter of 1999.

In more ways than one, Inktomi's market penetration and financial success represented a standard that Cachet hoped to achieve. (See Table B.) Inktomi was a devel-

EXHIBIT 4-7

FINANCIAL PROJECTION ASSUMPTIONS FOR CACHET TECHNOLOGIES

Summary Statistics (from Boardwatch Q4 1997)

Number of 45Mbps connections per node	2
Number of 155Mbps connections per node	0.1
Average number of 45Mbps equivalent connections per node (Q4 97)	2.3
Average number of 45Mbps Hosting Servers per node (Assume that 20% of traffic can use Distributed Hosting)	0.5
Growth in average bandwidth per node per quarter	2.5%
Number of Global ISPs (1997)	13
Growth in number of Global ISPs per quarter	2.5%
Growth in average Countries per Global ISP per quarter	10.0%
Average Countries per Global ISP (Q4 1997)	17
Total number of International nodes	221
Total number of 45Mbps connections at International nodes	518
Number of US National ISPs (1997)	40
Growth in number of US National ISPs per year	0%
Growth in average backbone US cities per National ISP per quarter	5%
Average backbone US cities per National ISP	20
Total number of National nodes	800
Total number of 45Mbps connections at National nodes	1876
Countries with Internet Access 1997 (ftp.cs.wisc.edu)	195
Countries without Internet Access 1997 (ftp.cs.wisc.edu)	42
Average initial sale per new customer	5
Average time to complete installation (Quarters)	4
Percentage price decline per quarter	5%

Source: Company documents.

oper of network information and infrastructure. Its solutions utilized parallel processing technology to maximize speed and minimize cost of network information solutions. In particular, Inktomi had developed innovative caching software that enabled content providers to improve the speed and reliability of distributing their content over the Internet. In addition to providing pricing data for product positioning in the market place, Inktomi's financing and valuation achievement provided guideposts for Cachet Technologies. Inktomi had obtained $8.0 million in April 1997 in its first round of venture financing, achieving a post-money valuation of $58.7 million. Inktomi was currently registered to go public in June 1998 with a $400 million valuation. The team felt that their solution was better at solving the content providers' problem than Inktomi's product was.

EXHIBIT 4-8

CACHET TECHNOLOGIES FINANCIAL PROJECTIONS

	1998	1998	1998	1998	1999	1999	1999	1999	2000	2001
	Q1	Q2	Q3	Q4	Q1	Q2	Q3	Q4	Year	Year
Potential Market Size Global Hosting										
Average number of 45Mbps Hosting Servers per node	0.5	0.5	0.5	0.5	0.5	0.5	0.6	0.6	0.6	0.7
Average Countries per Global ISP	17	19	21	23	25	27	30	33	50	75
Number of Global ISPs	13	13	14	14	14	15	15	15	17	19
Total potential market for 45Mbps Global Hosting Servers	106	123	142	164	189	219	253	292	531	963
Potential Market Size National Hosting										
Average number of 45Mbps Hosting Servers per node	0.5	0.5	0.5	0.5	0.5	0.5	0.6	0.6	0.6	0.7
Average backbone US cities per National ISP	20.0	21.0	22.1	23.2	24.3	25.5	26.8	28.1	33.8	40.5
Number of National ISPs	40	40	40	40	40	40	40	40	40	40
Total potential market for 45Mbps National Hosting Servers	384	414	445	479	516	555	598	643	849	1121
Potential Market Size Global and National	**490**	**537**	**587**	**643**	**705**	**774**	**851**	**935**	**1380**	**2084**
Potential Average number of Hosting Servers per ISP	*9*	*10*	*11*	*12*	*13*	*14*	*15*	*17*	*24*	*36*
Sales of T3 Global Hosting Software		Alpha	Beta	FCS						
Number of new customers				1	3	3	3	3	3	3
Total number of customers				1	4	7	10	13	16	19
Penetration of customer base				2%	7%	13%	18%	23%	28%	32%
T3 sales to new customers				2	15	15	15	15	15	15
T3 sales to existing customers				0	8	37	74	123	258	501
Total T3 sales				*2*	*23*	*52*	*89*	*138*	*273*	*516*
Penetration of potential market				0%	3%	7%	10%	15%	20%	25%
Revenues										
Price per T3 software (constant 1998 dollars)				$100,000	$95,000	$90,250	$85,738	$81,451	$77,378	$73,509
Revenue (constant 1998 dollars)				$200,000	$2,208,794	$4,657,226	$7,637,246	$11,238,043	$21,115,791	$37,929,426

(*Continued*)

EXHIBIT 4-8 (*Continued*)

	1998				1999				2000	2001
	Q1	Q2	Q3	Q4	Q1	Q2	Q3	Q4	Year	Year
Staffing										
General										
CEO			1	1	1	1	1	1	1	1
Office Manager			1	1	1	1	1	1	1	1
Recruiter (external, equivalent people)		1	1.5	1.5	0.5	0.5	0.5	0.5	0.5	0.5
Marketing										
VP Marketing			1	1	1	1	1	1	1	1
Director Market Communication			1	1	1	1	1	1	1	1
External PR (external, equivalent people)			1	1.5	1	1	1	1	1	1
Product Manager			1	1	1	1	1	1	1	1
Technical Writer (external, equivalent people)			0.5	0.5	0.25	0.25	0.25	0.25	0.25	0.25
Web Master (initially external)			1	1	1	1	1	1	1	1
Logistics (packaging, licensing etc)			1	1	1	1	1	1	1	1
Sales										
VP Sales				1	1	1	1	1	1	1
Regional Sales					2	3	3	3	3	3
International Sales					1	1	2	2	2	2
Sales Support Engineers					2	3	3	3	4	4
Support										
Director Support			1	1	1	1	1	1	1	1
Support Team			1	1	1	2	2	2	3	3
Finance										
VP Finance		0.5	0.5	1	1	1	1	1	1	1
Engineering										
Chief Technology Officer		1	1	1	1	1	1	1	1	1
VP Engineering		1	1	1	1	1	1	1	1	1
Algorithm Team Leader		1	1	1	1	1	1	1	1	1
Algorithm Team		4	4	4	4	4	4	4	4	4
Remote Management and Billing Team Leader		1	1	1	1	1	1	1	1	1
Remote Management and Billing Team				2	2	2	2	2	2	2
Director QA and System Test				1	1	1	1	1	1	1
QA						1	1	1	1	1
System Test		1	1	1	1	1	1	1	1	1
Computer Support/System Admin			1	1	1	1	1	1	1	1
Total Team Size		10.5	22	27.5	30.75	34.75	35.75	35.75	37.75	37.75
Average cost per employee (including benefits) per year		$80,000	$80,000	$80,000	$80,000	$80,000	$90,000	$90,000	$90,000	$90,000
Total Personnal Cost		$210,000	$440,000	$550,000	$615,000	$695,000	$804,375	$804,375	$3,397,500	$3,397,500

(*Continued*)

EXHIBIT 4-8 (Continued)

	1998 Q1	1998 Q2	1998 Q3	1998 Q4	1999 Q1	1999 Q2	1999 Q3	1999 Q4	2000 Year	2001 Year
Budgets										
Total Personnal Cost		$ 210,000	$ 440,000	$ 550,000	$ 615,000	$ 695,000	$ 804,375	$ 804,375	$ 3,397,500	$ 3,397,500
Computing Infrastructure		$ 85,500	$ 103,500	$ 49,500	$ 29,250	$ 83,500	$ 66,500	$ 27,500	$ 200,000	$ 200,000
Furniture		$ 38,000	$ 46,000	$ 22,000	$ 13,000	$ 16,000	$ 4,000	$ —	$ 8,000	$ —
Rent		$ 36,000	$ 36,000	$ 36,000	$ 36,000	$ 36,000	$ 36,000	$ 36,000	$ 288,000	$ 288,000
Leasing Charges (15%/annum)		$ 4,631	$ 5,606	$ 2,681	$ 1,584	$ 3,731	$ 2,644	$ 1,031	$ 31,200	$ 30,000
Travel and Entertainment		$ 24,000	$ 24,000	$ 36,000	$ 50,000	$ 50,000	$ 50,000	$ 50,000	$ 200,000	$ 200,000
Legal		$ 10,000	$ 10,000	$ 10,000	$ 10,000	$ 10,000	$ 10,000	$ 10,000	$ 50,000	$ 50,000
Marketing (Trade shows, advertising, sponsorship)		$ 10,000	$ 50,000	$ 50,000	$ 50,000	$ 50,000	$ 50,000	$ 50,000	$ 250,000	$ 250,000
Packaging, Printing		$ 5,000	$ 5,000	$ 5,000	$ 5,000	$ 5,000	$ 5,000	$ 5,000	$ 5,000	$ 5,000
Total Budgets		$ 403,131	$ 700,106	$ 741,181	$ 789,834	$ 929,231	$ 1,006,019	$ 3,307,031	$ 4,339,700	$ 4,330,500
Total Financing Required		$ (403,131)	$(1,103,238)	$(1,644,419)	$ (225,459)	$ 3,502,536	$10,133,764	$18,064,775	$34,840,866	$ 68,439,793
Financing										
Capital		$2,500,000	$ 2,500,000	$ 2,500,000	$2,500,000	$ 2,500,000	$ 2,500,000	$ 2,500,000	$ 2,500,000	$ 2,500,000
Leasing		$ 123,500	$ 149,500	$ 71,500	$ 42,250	$ 99,500	$ 70,500	$ 27,500	$ 208,000	$ 200,000
Total Financing Available		$2,623,500	$ 2,649,500	$ 2,571,500	$2,542,250	$ 2,599,500	$ 2,750,500	$ 2,527,500	$ 2,708,000	$ 2,700,000
Liquidity		$2,220,369	$ 1,546,263	$ 1,127,081	$4,525,585	$10,759,262	$20,341,510	$31,830,318	$58,664,658	$109,069,219

TABLE B   Comparison of Cachet Technologies versus Inktomi

Comparison	Inktomi	Cachet
Architecture	Clusters of workstations to provide single-node caching. Nodes work independently of one another.	Distributed network of workstations located at strategic points in ISP network. Nodes work in concert with one another to manage overall load.
Caching control	ISP controls the caching of information. Content provider can mark either an entire Web page cacheable or noncacheable.	Content provider decides which elements of each page must be served from origin server. The ISP does not have control.
Benefits	Content users get faster access to content providers' sites, but content providers lose demographic information.	Content users gain improved access to content providers' sites while capturing online demographic information.

Source: Company documents.

"GO" OR "NO GO"

The final business plan for the company was entered into the MIT $50K Entrepreneurship Competition. This was the ninth annual contest organized by MIT. Each year the contest had grown in size and prestige. In 1998, there were over 84 entrants and 30 semifinalists. Four of the six finalists were Internet-related companies. Lewin, Nijhawan, Seelig, and Tobin were confident that Cachet Technologies stood a great chance to win the contest. The presentation of the plan during the finals did not go well, however, and there was concern about how well their approach had been received.

The results were devastating to the team. First prize in the competition was shared by two companies: Direct Hit, a company that had been established to develop software to improve the searching capability of Internet search engines, and an Internet nonprofit company named Volunteer Commodity Connection. As the three friends, Lewin, Seelig, and Tobin, left the competition, they felt dejected. Again they wondered: How could the company that had developed a revolutionary new product to speed content around the Internet have lost to a company that developed merely an evolutionary new technology to speed up Internet searches? What had they not foreseen prior to the competition? Was Cachet Technologies' software worthy of being commercialized? Or should the three friends just call it quits?

In a very early meeting, Todd Dagres, the general partner at Battery Ventures, had challenged the team to think about delivering a service. Dagres felt that the benefits and potential value creation from offering a service were very large for the team. In addition, he suggested that the primary customer should be the content providers themselves rather than the Internet service providers. The team had considered the idea initially, but the challenge of establishing a service company appeared to be too great, at least relative to the ease of selling a shrink-wrapped software product. Building a service company would be capital intensive and fraught with many dangers. First, they would have to operate 24 hours a day, 7 days a week. No one on the team had experience building or running a service company, and the prospect of doing just that was daunting. Such an offering might also be seen as competing directly with Internet service providers and some of the largest and most successful Internet infrastructure companies.

Now that Cachet Technologies had been relegated to last place in the finals, Lewin, Seelig, and Tobin began to ponder what path they should take. What would it take to reinvent Cachet Technologies as a service company? The three friends each had at-

EXHIBIT 4-9

COMMERCIALIZATION TIME LINE (BEGINNING IN MAY 1998 AND ENDING IN FEBRUARY 1999)

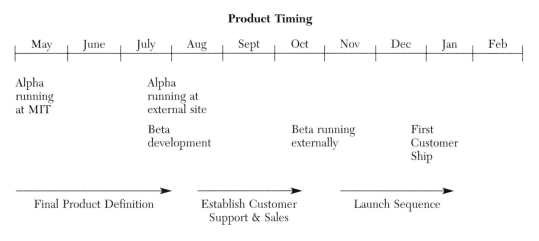

Source: Company documents.

tractive alternative opportunities to pursue. Lewin had an offer from Bell Labs to do research for the summer while Seelig had accepted a summer position from the technology management consulting firm Pittiglio, Rabin, Todd & McGrath on the West Coast. Tobin was looking at several other deals and was feeling the pressure to show that he had the makings of a great venture capitalist. Maybe they could talk to prospective Internet service providers and content providers over the summer to get a better idea about which direction they should take, but how much time should they devote to the project? Maybe they should drop the whole thing now? The sun was beginning to set over the Charles River as the three friends headed for home.

5

Some Thoughts on Business Plans

INTERNET WICKED ALE

Bill Sahlman, Dimitri V. D'Arbeloff Professor of Business Administration, smiled as he was handed the business plan for Internet Wicked Ale, Inc. (IWA), an interactive, on-line marketing company being formed to sell premium beers made by microbreweries over the Internet. According to the president of the company—a soon-to-graduate MBA candidate at a well-known eastern business school—a prototype Web site had already been developed using the now ubiquitous Java programming language. Literally thousands were visiting the site each day: an early review had described the Web site as "way cool." Participating in the meeting were two other MBA candidates. Prior to jointly founding IWA, the three had worked in management consulting and investment banking: each, however, did have substantial experience with beer.

Sahlman glanced over the shoulder of the IWA team and took note of his ever growing stack of Internet-based business plans, each proposing to "revolutionize" an industry, each "conservatively" projecting at least $50 million in revenues within five years based on a modest market share of under 10%, and each containing a projection of likely investor returns of over 100% per annum. He quickly averted his stare from the business plans in the corner of his less than tidy office so as not to offend his eager audience. They looked so young—they were so enthusiastic. Their business plan was so meticulously printed on the new color laser printers in the technology lab. . . . Sahlman wondered what to say next.

INTRODUCTION

This note is about entrepreneurial ventures and the role of business plans. Few areas of new venture creation receive as much attention. There are MBA and undergradu-

Professor William A. Sahlman prepared this note as the basis for class discussion rather than to illustrate either effective or ineffective handling of an administrative situation.

ate courses on business plan writing. There are countless books describing how to write a business plan. There is even software that will help create a business plan, complete with integrated financial projections. All across the United States, and increasingly in other countries, there are contests designed to pick the "best business plan."

Judging by the amount of attention paid to business plans in graduate business schools and the popular press, you would think that the only thing standing between a would-be entrepreneur and spectacular success is a well-crafted and highly regarded business plan. Yet, in my experience, nothing could be further from the truth: on a scale from 1 to 10, business plans rank no higher than 2 as a predictor of likely success. There are many other factors that dominate the business plan per se.

The disparity between my view and that implicit in the business plan feeding frenzy is rooted in over 15 years of field research and personal experience in the world of entrepreneurship. The rest of this note develops a conceptual framework for understanding entrepreneurial venture creation and management, which is based on studying hundreds of successful and unsuccessful companies. The goal is to give the reader insights into sensible entrepreneurial management, and, by implication, into the business plan used to describe a venture.

In my framework, there are four dynamic components of any entrepreneurial process or venture:

- the people
- the opportunity
- the external context
- the deal

By people, I mean those individuals or groups who perform services or provide resources for the venture, whether or not they are directly employed by the venture. This category encompasses managers, employees, lawyers, accountants, capital providers, and parts suppliers, among others. By opportunity, I mean any activity requiring the investment of scarce resources in hopes of future return. By context, I mean all those factors that affect the outcome of the opportunity but that are generally outside the direct control of management. Examples of contextual factors include the level of interest rates, regulations (rules of the game), macroeconomic activity, and some industry variables like threat of substitutes. Finally, by deal, I mean the complete set of implicit and explicit contractual relationships between the entity and all resource providers. Examples of deals range from contracts with capital suppliers to the terms of employment for managers.

The fundamental insight gained from studying hundreds of successful and unsuccessful ventures is the concept of integration, referred to as "fit," which is defined as the degree to which the people, the opportunity, the deal, and the context together influence the potential for success. Phrased differently, the degree of fit is the answer to the following questions:

- To what degree do the people have the right experience, skills and attitudes, given the nature of the opportunity, the context and the deals struck?
- To what degree does the opportunity make sense, given the people involved, the context and the deals struck?
- To what degree is the context favorable for the venture, given the people involved, the nature of the opportunity, and the deals struck?

- To what degree do the deals involved in the venture make sense, given the people involved, the nature of the opportunity, and the context?

These questions focus attention on the fact that excellence in any single dimension is not sufficient: the proper perspective from which to make an evaluation takes into account all of the elements simultaneously. An appropriate analogy might be that of a sports team. It is not sufficient to have the best individual players at each position; rather, success will be a function of how they play together, how the team is managed, what deals have been struck inside and outside the team, and what else goes on in the league. A diagram of the basic framework is provided in Appendix 5-1.

Nor is it sufficient to focus on these elements and their relationship from a static perspective. The people, opportunity, context and deal (and the relationship among them) are all likely to change over time as a company goes from identification of opportunity to harvest. To focus attention on the dynamic aspects of the entrepreneurial process, three related questions can be asked to guide the analysis of any business venture:

- What can go wrong?
- What can go right?
- What decisions can management make today and in the future to ensure that "what can go right" does go right, and "what can go wrong" is avoided, or failing that, is prevented from critically damaging the enterprise? Phrased another way, what decisions can be made to tilt the reward to risk ratio in favor of the venture?

This framework and set of questions are extremely powerful in understanding how ventures evolve over time and how managers can affect outcomes. The balanced emphasis on anticipating (as opposed to predicting) good and bad news is a distinctive feature of the framework. Most students (and practitioners) are adept at identifying risks, far fewer are practiced at foretelling the good news, and even fewer have thought systematically about how they can manage the reward to risk ratio. Yet, there are some recurrent themes in the world of venturing. That projects often take more time and money than originally estimated should not surprise people. Indeed, part of the goal in a course like the one I teach on Entrepreneurial Finance is to provide people with a rich sense of the patterns that underlie real-world entrepreneurship.

The questions described above concerning potential good and bad news also shed light on the fact that current decisions affect future decisions: some decisions open up or preserve options for future action, while others destroy options. Managers must be cognizant of this relationship between current and future decisions.

According to this framework, great businesses have some easily identifiable (but hard to assemble) attributes. They have a world-class managerial team in all dimensions, from the top to the bottom and across all relevant functions. The teams have directly relevant skills and experiences for the opportunity they are pursuing. Ideally, the team has worked successfully together in the past. The opportunity has an attractive, sustainable business model: it is possible to create a competitive edge and to defend it. There are multiple options for expanding the scale and scope of the business, and these options are unique to the enterprise and its team. There are a number of ways to extract value from the business either in a positive harvest event or in a scale down or liquidation mode. The context is favorable both with respect to the regulatory environment and the macroeconomic situation. The deals binding the people to the opportunity are sensible and robust: they provide the right incentives under a wide range of scenarios. The venture is financed by individuals or firms who add value in addition to their capital, thereby increasing the likelihood of success. The financing terms provide the right incentives for the provider and the recipient. There is access to additional capital on an as-warranted basis. In short, the venture is characterized by a high degree of dynamic fit (see Appendix 5-2 for a diagram of the expanded fit management framework).

A great business may or may not have currently, or have ever had for that matter, a great business plan. In the beginning, moreover, a great business may not even have demonstrated a high degree of fit: the important issue is whether the deficiencies are recognized and fixable. Phrased differently, the role of management is to continuously adapt a business to improve the degree of fit: doing so does not guarantee success, but it does increase the odds.

This assessment raises the obvious issue of what role a business plan plays in entrepreneurship. I believe that a useful business plan is one that addresses the elements of the venture—people, opportunity, context, and deal—in the proper dynamic context. In the end, the business plan must provide reasonable answers to the following questions:

- Who are the people involved? What have they done in the past that would lead one to believe that they will be successful in the future? Who is missing from the team and how will they be attracted?

- What is the nature of the opportunity? How will the company make money? How is the opportunity likely to evolve? Can entry barriers be built and maintained?

- What contextual factors will affect the venture? What contextual changes are likely to occur, and how can management respond to those changes?

- What deals have been or are likely to be struck inside and outside the venture? Do the deals struck increase the likelihood of success? How will those deals and the implicit incentives evolve over time?

- What decisions have been made (or can be made) to increase the ratio of reward to risk?

Each of these areas will be addressed in the sections that follow.

PEOPLE

When reading any business plan, or assessing any business, for that matter, I start with the resume section, not with the description of the business. I ask a series of structured questions, some of which include the following:

- Who are the founders?
- What have they accomplished in the past?
- What directly relevant experience do they have for the opportunity they are pursuing?
- What skills do they have?
- Whom do they know and who knows them?
- What is their reputation?
- How realistic are they?

- Can they adapt as circumstances warrant?
- Who else needs to be on the team? Are the founders prepared to recruit high quality people?
- How will the team respond to adversity?
- Can they make the inevitable hard choices that have to be made?
- What are their motivations?
- How committed are they to this venture?
- How can I gain objective information about each member of the team including how they will work together?
- What are the possible consequences if one or more of the team members leaves?

We can now come full circle and begin to evaluate the Internet Wicked Ale (IWA) proposal and the team of MBA founders. Starting first with the people lens, I am not sanguine about IWA's prospects. The founding team has experience drinking, not starting an online business or a beer distribution business. Typically, the business plan for such a team talks about the need to recruit experienced people, but it's rather like trying to draw four cards to complete a five-card straight in poker: a low probability event. Moreover, having a founding team without tremendous experience but large equity ownership often makes it extremely difficult to attract high-quality people on "acceptable" terms.

The framework described above and the pessimistic assessment of the prospects for IWA are not foolproof. Lots of inexperienced teams succeed, occasionally because they are not weighted down by conventional wisdom. This is particularly true in new markets, the Internet representing a very important current illustration. In such markets, commercial innovation is often driven by relatively inexperienced entrants, teams that are repeatedly told they are unlikely to succeed. At the same time, starting a new enterprise with little or no management experience is a little like crossing the Mass Turnpike blindfolded: yes, you can make it to the other side, but having done so, you shouldn't assume the trip was riskless.

Reading a business plan from the resume section first also illustrates a truism of professional venture capital investing. A typical venture capital firm receives approximately 2,000 business plans per year. A nonscientific survey of several prominent firms reveals that they only invest in plans that come in with a specific letter of referral from someone well known by the partners of the firm. That is, they do not invest in, nor do they even investigate fully, plans that are unsolicited.

My colleague Myra Hart has a useful way of describing the process of attracting financial and other resources to a venture. Her research suggests that successful venture founders have two characteristics: they are "known" and they "know." Tackling the latter first, the founders know the industry for which they propose to raise capital and launch a venture—they know the key suppliers, the customers, and the competitors. They also know who the talented individuals are who can contribute to the team. At the same time, they are known in the industry: people can comment on their capabilities and can provide objective referrals to resource suppliers like professional venture capitalists. Suppliers, customers, and employees are willing to work with them in spite of the obvious risks of dealing with a new company.

Thus, the model in venture capital is to back teams with great (directly relevant) track records who are pursuing attractive opportunities. The old adage in venture capital circles is: "I'd rather back an 'A' team with a 'B' idea than a 'B' team with an 'A' idea." Of course, the goal is to only back high-quality teams with high-quality opportunities, but that is not always feasible.

In sum, the IWA business plan doesn't pass the threshold for consideration by professional investors even if the idea is a pretty good one. Again, a truism from the world of venture capital is that ideas are a dime a dozen: only execution skills count. Arthur Rock, a venture capital legend associated with the formation of such companies as Intel, Apple, and Teledyne, stated bluntly, "I invest in people, not ideas."[1]

OPPORTUNITY

Rather than rejecting the IWA plan out of hand, however, let's assume that the team is acceptable or that there are indications that an appropriate team can be built. What is the next step? What other questions do investors or entrepreneurs ask to evaluate prospective ventures?

In my experience, the next major issue is the nature of the opportunity, starting first with an assessment of the overall market potential and its characteristics. Two key initial questions are:

- Is the total market for the venture's product or service large and/or rapidly growing?
- Is the industry one that is now or can become structurally attractive?

Entrepreneurs and investors look for large or rapidly growing markets for a variety of reasons. First, it is often easier to obtain a share of a growing market than to fight with entrenched competitors for a share of a mature or stagnant market. Professional investors like venture capitalists try to identify high-growth potential markets early in their evolution: examples range from integrated circuits to biotechnology. Indeed, they will not invest in a company that cannot reach a significant scale (e.g., $50 million in annual revenues) within five years.

Obviously, all markets are not created equal: some are more attractive than others. Consider, to illustrate, the independent computer disk drive business as it has evolved over the past 20 years. Disk drives were first developed by IBM in the late 1960s and early 1970s. Some of the original engineering team members ultimately left IBM to form independent companies to develop products based on the same technology. Indeed, over the next two decades, scores of new companies were formed to exploit the rapidly growing market for data storage. Examples include Memorex, Seagate, Priam, Quantum, Conner Peripherals, and EMC.

The problem with disk storage, however, is that the industry is not structurally attractive, nor is it ever likely to be. Disk drive manufacturers must design their products to meet the perceived needs of OEMs (original equipment manufacturers) and end-users. Selling a product to OEMs is complicated and often has low margins. The customers are large relative to the supplier. There are lots of competitors, each with high-quality offerings in the same market segment. Because there are so many competitors, product life cycles are short and ongoing technology investments high. The industry is subject to major shifts in technology and customer base (e.g., the shift in form factors or storage medium and the shift from minicomputers to microcomputers). Rivalry also

---

[1] Michael W. Miller, "How One Man Helps High-Tech Prospects Get to the Big Leagues," *Wall Street Journal*, December 31 1985, p. 1.

leads to lower prices and hence, lower margins. In the end, it is extremely difficult to build and sustain a profitable business.

In this regard, the disk drive business looks suspiciously like the tire industry. When the tire industry developed, there were many competitors, each trying to sell their tires to the automobile manufacturers and to end-users. Rivalry was intense. The customers got larger and larger, squeezing the profitability of the tire suppliers. Ultimately, the industry evolved to the point where there were a handful of competitors, each with modest margins and highly cyclical results.

Compare the situation described for disk drives to that confronting biotechnology companies. If a biotech company creates a new product, intellectual property laws grant a certain amount of protection from competitive forces. Competitors must invent new approaches to the same underlying problem, or they must license the product from the inventor. The extended duration of patent protection makes it possible as well to build a brand image that provides a certain amount of economic protection even after patent coverage expires. In the end, a model for a successful biotechnology company is a pharmaceutical company. On average, the latter companies are far more profitable than most precisely because of the structural attractiveness of their industry.

This extended discussion of growth and industry illustrates another important factor in venture formation and investing. What are the appropriate analogies? If a venture is successful, what will it look like? Identifying opportunities is a complex game of pattern recognition which is aided by experience and by honest assessment of business history. Knowing that the disk drive business is like the tire industry and that biotech is like the pharmaceutical industry is helpful in determining where to invest capital or human resources. Tom Stemberg once described what he was trying to accomplish in founding Staples: "I said I wanted to build the Toys R Us of office supplies." He picked a successful model, one that spoke volumes about what he intended to do and the consequences if he were successful.[2]

To reiterate, the goal is to pick industries that have lots of potential to create and protect value. Growth in sales is not equivalent to growth in value. Also, marrying great management to such markets is the primary tool for increasing the likelihood of success. Consider, to illustrate, the story of the formation of Compaq Computer. The founders were senior executives at Texas Instruments. Their original business plan described a plan to enter the disk drive business. They sent the plan to L. J. Sevin and Ben Rosen, venture capitalists with extensive experience in the electronics industry. Sevin and Rosen rejected the plan but liked the team. Ultimately, on a place mat in a local diner in Texas, a plan was sketched out to design, manufacture, and market a portable personal computer. The rest, as they say, is history.[3]

I am also reminded of what the immensely successful venture capitalist, Don Valentine, says about venture investing. Most in the venture industry focus on the three determinants of venture success—people, people, and people. Valentine insists that the real trick is to find markets with explosive potential, to back great technology, and to put management in place as needed. He wants to invest in industries where growth can overcome the shortcomings of management. Valentine cites as Exhibit A his $2.0 million investment in Cisco, a networking company, that seven years later was worth over $6 billion.[4] In like vein, Peter Lynch, the famous manager of Fidelity's Magellan Fund,

---

[2] For information on the launch of Staples, see Thomas G. Stemberg, *Staples for Success* (KEX Press, 1996).

[3] Benjamin Rosen, "Rosen's Ten Rules," in *Raising Money* (Amacom Press, 1990), pp. ix–xxv.

[4] Valentine's perspective is described in "Rise of the Silicon Patriots," *Worth Magazine*, December/January 1996, pp. 86–92, 137–146.

tried to invest in companies whose fundamental industry factors were so favorable that even incompetent management couldn't cause the stock to go down.

What is most important in new venture formation—the market being served, the specific product or service, or the quality of the people involved? I suspect that the correct answer is "yes." In the final analysis, the issues are not unrelated. Great people are those who can identify attractive markets and build compelling strategies. As General Doriot, one of the early pioneers in the venture capital industry once stated, "The problem is to judge ideas and men and the value of the possible combination—a very difficult task."[5]

The next major issue in evaluating a venture is the specific plan for building and launching a product or service. I will not dwell on this topic in spite of its obvious importance but will instead focus on some very simple questions that can help sort out good ideas from potential disasters. I can also quote Arthur Rock to remind the reader of the proper perspective for evaluating business proposals, "If you can find good people, if they're wrong about the product they'll make a switch, so what good is it to understand the product that they're talking about in the first place?"[6] Rock's admonition notwithstanding, a business plan must address a few issues, including the following:

- Who is the customer?
- How does the customer make decisions?
- To what degree is the product or service a compelling purchase for the customer?
- How will the product or service be priced?
- How will the venture reach the identified customer segments?
- How much does it cost (time and resources) to acquire a customer?
- How much does it cost to produce and deliver the product or service?
- How much does it cost to support a customer?
- How easy is it to retain a customer?

Often, asking and answering these kinds of questions will reveal a fatal flaw in a plan. For example, it may be too costly to find the customers and convince them to buy the product. Economically viable access to customers is the key to business, yet many entrepreneurs take the Hollywood approach to this area: "Build it and they will come." That strategy is great in the movies but not very sensible in the real world.

I should note that it is not always easy to answer questions about possible customer response to new products or services. One entrepreneur I know proposed to introduce an electronic news clipping service. He made his pitch to a prospective venture capital investor who rejected the plan, stating, "I just don't think the dogs will eat the dogfood." Later, when the entrepreneur's company went public, he sent the venture capitalist an anonymous package comprised of an empty can of dogfood and a copy of his prospectus. If it were easy, there wouldn't be any opportunities.

The issue of pricing is particularly important in analyzing a business proposal. Sometimes the "dogs will eat the dogfood," but only at a price less than cost. Investors always look for opportunities that entail value pricing in which the price the customer is willing to pay is high. A good example is Sandra Kurtzig's description of how she set prices in the early days of ASK Computer Systems. ASK developed programs to help

---

[5] *Georges F. Doriot: Manufacturing Class Notes, Harvard Business School, 1927–1966* (The French Library, 1993), p. 85.

[6] Ibid., p. 1.

users monitor and evaluate their manufacturing process (scheduling, cost analysis, etc.). The software was extremely valuable to a user, and there were few competitors or alternatives: Kurtzig called her pricing model the "flinch method." When asked how much the software was, she would respond, "$50,000." If the buyer didn't flinch, she would add, "per module." Again, if there were no visible choking, she would add, "per year." And so on, and so on. Kurtzig was ultimately able to build a very profitable multihundred million dollar business using this kind of "street smart" pricing.

The list of questions above focuses on the top and bottom line of a business—the direct revenues and the costs of producing and marketing a product. That's fine, as far as it goes. Sensible analysis of a proposal, however, also involves assessing the business model from a different perspective that takes into account the investment required (i.e., the balance sheet side of the equation). Consider the following questions that I use to assess the cash flow implications of pursuing an opportunity:

- When do you have to buy resources (supplies, people, etc.)?
- When do you have to pay for them?
- How long does it take to acquire a customer?
- How long before the customer sends you a check?
- How much capital equipment is required to support a dollar of sales?

Underlying these questions on the balance sheet is a simple yet powerful maxim in business:

> Buy low, sell high, collect early, and pay late.[7]

The best businesses are those in which you have large profit margins, you get paid by your customers before you have to deliver the product, and the fixed asset requirements are modest. It goes without saying, in addition, that such a business should also be characterized by insuperable entry barriers.

Consider, to illustrate, the magazine publishing business. Once up and running, a successful magazine has remarkably attractive cash flow characteristics. Subscribers pay in advance of receiving the magazine. Often, magazines can even get subscribers to pay for several years in advance. I once discovered that I had nine years worth of service coming on a magazine because I diligently paid the bill each time they sent it to me, taking advantage of multiyear discounts. If the magazine can maintain compelling content, then current subscribers tend to re-subscribe on a regular basis with low incremental marketing cost. It is always easier to retain a customer than to acquire a new one. If the demographic profile of the readers is attractive, then advertisers use the magazine to reach a target audience, a successful example of "if you build it, they will come." It takes very little plant and equipment to run a magazine: printing and fulfillment are often farmed out to vendors who specialize and deliver high-quality service at low cost. The editorial costs of a magazine are typically low. In essence, magazine publishing has all the attractive characteristics listed above.

Of course, the fact that a magazine property is valuable once it is up and running has not escaped people's attention. Each year, hundreds of new magazines are launched:

---

[7] This is the title of a useful book—Richard Levin, *Buy Low, Sell High, Collect Early and Pay Late: The Manager's Guide to Financial Survival*, (Englewood Cliff, NJ: Prentice-Hall, 1983).

most, to quote test pilot Chuck Yeager, "auger in." The Achilles heel in publishing is the cost of acquiring a customer in a world where most niches have already been recognized and served.

Some other attractive business models warrant mention here. When I assess a business, I look for ways in which a company can expand the range of products or services being offered to the same customer base. Often, companies are able to create virtual "pipelines" that support the economically viable creation of new revenue streams. In the magazine business, for example, it is possible to create other lines of products or services that are attractive to subscribers. *Inc.* Magazine, to illustrate, has expanded beyond the basic magazine business to offer seminars, books, and videos for the *Inc.* subscriber (and others). In this example, a virtuous cycle is established in which success in the basic magazine leads to new related business opportunities that might not exist in the absence of the magazine.

A similarly attractive business model is illustrated by Intuit, which is best known for its personal financial program Quicken. The latter program helps users organize their checkbook. After the initial success of Quicken, Intuit was able to offer a wide range of additional services, including electronic banking, personal printing supplies, tax preparation software, and online information services. Because some of these ancillary services are so profitable, Intuit is able to give away the software program in hopes of creating a lifelong customer who buys additional services and products from the company. Intuit also discovered that many users of its personal finance program Quicken were small businesses: they soon introduced a variant of the program, called QuickBooks, which is designed to meet the specific accounting needs of small businesses. The QuickBooks division is now more profitable than the original consumer-focused one, demonstrating how success in one business can lead to success in another that is closely related.[8]

Not all businesses are created equal in terms of the kind of growth opportunities described above. In some businesses, success in one product or service does not necessarily create additional opportunities with the same customer base. Again, the disk drive business is informative because competitors have historically been unable to replicate success in one part of the industry in another. For example, those firms that were successful in producing 5.25″ drives were not, for the most part, successful in producing 3.5″ drives. Catching one technology wave does not always imply an ability to catch the next one. As colleagues Clayton Christensen and Joseph Bower have observed, the old axiom about staying close to the customer works if and only if you choose the right customer.[9]

An obvious extension of the pipeline model relates to geographic expansion possibilities. Some businesses are attractive because a successful model in one region can be rolled out to other regions. Such is the case in the theme restaurant business. If Hard Rock Cafe works in Paris and London, then it will probably work in New York and Chicago. This kind of business is rich in growth options that result from success.

There are many other successful business models that entrepreneurs and investors look for when making resource commitments to opportunities. I try, for example, to

---

[8] Interestingly, the original Intuit business plan was sent to quite a few venture capitalists, including two members of Scott Cook's HBS class. The plan was rejected by one and all. Only later did the two classmates get an opportunity to invest in Intuit while it was still private. The potential small-business accounting opportunity was specifically mentioned in the original Intuit plan.

[9] Clayton Christensen and Joseph Bower, "Disruptive Technologies: Catching the Wave," *Harvard Business Review* (January/February, 1995): pp. 43–53.

find companies that "sell ammunition to all sides of the war without end" rather than engage in direct combat. An illustration is A. C. Nielson, which measures marketing response for companies selling products or services but does not have to try to compete in the actual markets (e.g., Coke versus Pepsi, or ABC versus NBC). A similar company called Internet Profiles exists in the Internet world: it measures activity at Web sites rather than trying to compete with other Web site purveyors.

Another illustration of the "ammunition" strategy is a company called Abacus Direct. This company was founded to help catalog merchants improve the effectiveness of their customer acquisition strategies. Briefly, the co-founders convinced a large number of catalog companies (e.g., Lands' End and Orvis) to give them a data file comprised of the purchasing histories of each catalog's customers. The data on customers of many different catalogs were then pooled and analyzed. Using proprietary software, Abacus Direct was able to help the catalog companies identify high-potential customers to whom new catalogs could be mailed and eliminate low-potential customers from their lists.

Six years after starting, Abacus Direct was able to achieve a 75% share of the domestic catalog business. The company was extremely profitable early in its development, with net margins in the 30% range. Three contextual factors helped Abacus Direct enormously. First, competition among catalog companies was fierce, and Abacus Direct benefited by helping competitors be more effective. Second, postage cost increases changed the business model for catalog merchants, making it imperative that direct mail effectiveness be improved. Finally, the cost of managing and analyzing a massive database, one containing purchase histories on almost 90 million people, fell dramatically. What used to take a mainframe computer many hours to analyze now takes minutes on a powerful workstation. The founders of Abacus Direct had previously founded a company that handled warranty card registrations for major appliance manufacturers. Again, that company had sold mailing lists based on purchase histories: the company was successful and was sold to a larger company some five years after it was founded. To use the terminology introduced in the section on "people," the founders "knew" the industry and they were "known," dramatically increasing the likelihood of their success.

Another simple example of an oft-repeated successful business model involves the old "razors and razor blades" strategy made famous by Gillette. The razors are sold at cost, and all the money is made on the blades. There are many companies pursuing a variation of this strategy, Gillette being the best known. The recently introduced data storage device called the Zip Drive by Iomega illustrates a policy of giving away the device at cost or a small profit and making all of the money on the proprietary disks that go with the drive. Nintendo makes most of its money on software, not on the game players it sells.

There are some opportunity traps that also should be mentioned. Some businesses have distinctly unattractive economic prospects, defined as high capital costs (front-loaded), low margins, and high risk. The disk drive business probably fits this description well. So too does the airline business. In such industries, however, the business plans that are written do not really address the problems. Instead they describe the opportunity in glowing terms. They state that the market is large and growing and that all the new entrant needs to do is to attain a 10% market share to achieve great success. Unfortunately, if hundreds of capable teams all enter a market looking for a 10% share, I don't think the math quite works out. In some industries, even great teams can't overcome poor industry business models, as the great investor Warren Buffett discovered when he bought part of US Air.

I have also come to believe that the world of "invention" is fraught with danger. Over the past 15 years, I have seen scores of individuals who have invented a "better mousetrap." They have developed tools or systems in areas that range from bicycle pumps to inflatable pillows for use on airlines to automated car parking systems. Their technology is patented and seems on the surface to be a "no-brainer" to potential adopters. In spite of the seeming attractiveness of the innovation, however, I have seen very few examples of successful commercialization. It turns out that idea-driven companies typically undervalue commercialization capabilities. The inventor frequently refuses to spend the money required or refuses to share the rewards with the business side of the company, the inevitable consequence of which is that the technology never gets implemented regardless of how compelling it seems to be.

My views of the importance of commercialization skills were influenced by one of the first technology-based companies I ever visited. In the early 1980s, a group of Harvard undergraduates acquired the rights to a technology that would help improve the combustion characteristics of certain grades of fuel oil. Essentially, the process would enable fuel burners to use much cheaper oil to accomplish a given task. I was intrigued by the process and admired the dogged determination of the young entrepreneurs.

Ultimately, this company, Fuel Tech, raised $75 million from private investors around the globe. The technology I described never proved to be commercially viable. The company founders scrambled to find an alternative path to business success for Fuel Tech. To my utter amazement, they were able to acquire some operating companies at attractive prices. The company was eventually sold at a price that netted handsome returns for the investors and the founders. Later, the lead entrepreneur, William Haney, acquired the rights to some environmental technology developed at MIT. He founded, and currently is chairman of, a company called Molten Metals, which has a current market capitalization of almost $500 million. During his Fuel Tech days, he learned how to make money, a far more valuable skill, I submit, than the ability to invent.[10]

One final comment on opportunities involves what I call "arbitrage" businesses. Basically, these businesses exist to take advantage of some pricing disparity in the marketplace. The classic entrepreneurial example was MCI Telecommunications, which was formed to offer long-distance service at a lower price than AT&T. Similar current examples of arbitrage exist in the health-care business in which entrepreneurs are finding ways to offer comparable services to hospitals at much lower costs. Or some of the industry consolidations going on today reflect a different kind of arbitrage—the ability to buy small businesses at a "wholesale" price, roll them up into a larger package, and take them public at a "retail" price, all without necessarily adding true value in the process.

Taking advantage of arbitrage opportunities is a viable and potentially profitable way to enter a business. In the final analysis, however, all arbitrage opportunities go away. It is not a question of whether—only when. The trick in these businesses is to use the arbitrage profits to build a more enduring business model.

COMPETITION

The notion that all arbitrage opportunities go away reflects a more general belief that all opportunities go away. For any given opportunity, there are a myriad of potential competitors. In 1995, to illustrate, almost $30 billion was invested in private equity funds, of which perhaps 20% was in traditional venture capital. In 1995, over 1 million new businesses were incorporated in the United States. The situation outside the United

---

[10] Actually, Molten Metals is not yet profitable, and, given the inevitable difficulties confronting any company scaling up a new technology, success is certainly not guaranteed.

States is similar in the sense that many investors are seeking to back competent entrepreneurial ventures around the world. Moreover, all large companies have become more
attuned to opportunity, suggesting a more rapid and competent attempt to identify and
exploit them.

A business plan must address the current competitors and the potential competitors in a sensible way. Among the specific issues a plan should cover are the following:

- Who are the current competitors?
- What resources do they control? What are their strengths and weaknesses?
- How will they respond to our decision to enter the business?
- How can we respond to their response?
- Who else might be able to observe and exploit the same opportunity?
- Are there ways to co-opt potential or actual competitors by forming alliances?

Business is like chess: to be successful, you must anticipate several moves in advance in order to have any chance. A business plan that describes an insuperable lead
or a proprietary position is by definition written by naive people.

GRAPHICAL ANALYSIS TOOLS FOR ASSESSING OPPORTUNITIES (OR HAROLD AND THE PURPLE CRAYON MEET ENTREPRENEURIAL FINANCE)

I like to think of business opportunities in terms of their risk/reward profiles. I have
two graphical tools that I apply to understand a business model. The first entails drawing a simple cash flow diagram for the business and the second entails assigning probabilities to certain outcomes. Starting first with the cash flow diagram, consider, to illustrate, a proposal to start a new airline. The cash flow pattern depicted in the business
plan looks something like the following:

Cash Flow Diagram for an Airline

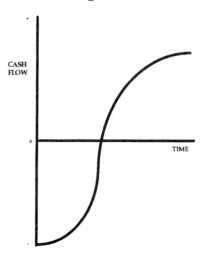

Essentially, starting an airline involves a very large capital commitment up-front followed by some unknown returns in the future. When I look at this pattern, I focus first

and foremost on the likelihood of achieving positive cash flow, when that event might occur, and the potential payoff structure if I am successful. In my view, the airline business is a bad business because the payoffs are too low and risky and too far in the future, given the up-front capital required. The business has high fixed costs of operation, which is often associated with vicious pricing cycles in which prices are driven down to the level of marginal costs. It's rather like what the Harvard freshman football coach said when describing his team, "They're not big, but they're slow." Airlines aren't very profitable, but they require a huge amount of capital.[11]

Compare an airline with an electronically delivered newsletter for which subscribers pay in advance. As noted earlier, the capital requirements in publishing are modest and the potential margins high. If such a plan had a compelling editorial position and could attract subscribers at acceptable costs, then the cash flow pattern might be as depicted below:

Cash Flow Diagram for a Newsletter

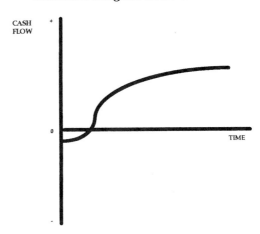

Returning to the earlier discussion of business models, it turns out that successful companies typically have more than one relevant cash flow S-curve. In such companies, there are growth opportunities, defined as opportunities to profitably invest additional funds because of success in the first project. For example, a magazine that is launched and attracts an audience might be able to introduce a related product or service (e.g., seminars or conferences, additional magazines targeted at a segment of the overall readership). Similarly, a single successful restaurant may form the foundation for a chain of restaurants in different areas. Or a successful software company might have international expansion possibilities that are as attractive (or more so) than the domestic one. The goal in investing or in identifying opportunities from the perspective of the entrepreneur is to identify businesses that have many such growth options and to preserve the right to exploit them. The following graph depicts a favorable growth option pattern, one like a magazine or a restaurant.

---

[11] Far better than entering the airline business itself is starting a service for all of the companies in the airline business. Prominent successful examples include Flight Safety, which builds flight simulators, and Sabre Corporation, which was originally started by American Airlines to automate flight scheduling and reservations.

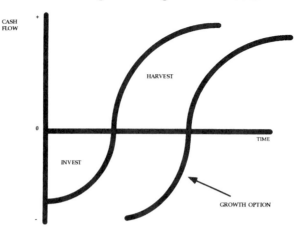

Cash Flow Diagram for a Magazine or a Restaurant

Finding opportunities with ample growth options is a goal: many industries, however, have a pattern that looks attractive but is not. In the disk drive business, for example, success in one investment category does not necessarily lead to success in another: indeed, there is some evidence that success leads to disaster. In such industries, which might be called "wave" industries, it is very hard, if not impossible, to catch successive waves without crashing and burning. The disk drive industry is portrayed as follows:

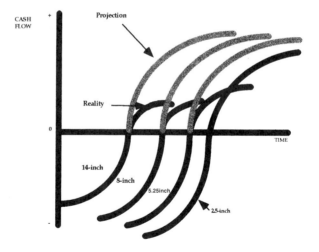

Cash Flow Diagram for the Disk Drive Business

A question that leaps out of the cash flow diagrams depicted above is: how do I make decisions that involve tradeoffs between the present and the future? How do I decide whether the potential future cash is big enough to justify the initial investment? To answer these questions, it is clear that you have to assess the riskiness of the bet you are making.

There are two ways to portray the riskiness of a project such as a new airline or an online publication. One is to draw the same diagrams as above but to depict reasonable scenarios as well as the expected values. The following graph shows three scenarios: the original business plan model, a success scenario in which the company achieved its goals but only after investing more time and money (a frequent event for companies that succeed), and a third scenario in which the company failed after a considerable investment and time period.

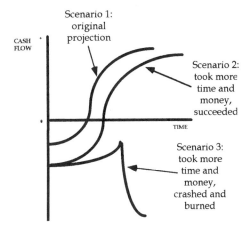

Cash Flow Scenarios

The other way to shed light on the riskiness of a project is to assign probabilities to different outcomes for returns on investment. The following diagram shows the payoff structure for an investment in a new software company:

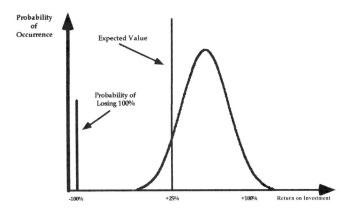

Probability Distribution for a High-Risk/High-Reward Software Company

If I make an investment in a new software company, there is considerable risk that I will lose all of my money. At the same time, I might well invest in the next Microsoft or Netscape, in which case I will have very high returns, perhaps in excess of 100% per year. The picture above suggests that there is a small, perhaps even negligible probability of earning a small rate of return on an investment in a software company. The rationale is that most small software companies are not very profitable and are therefore not worth much very much. Unless the venture reaches escape velocity, it probably won't succeed.

There is a broad class of investments whose payoff structures look like that for the hypothetical software company. There are other investments where the risk/reward pattern looks quite different. Consider an investment in a franchise of a well-established fast food company. In such an investment, there is an extended history of profitable operations. The company has a solid business plan and reasonably predictable results. In this case, the payoff structure might be as depicted as follows:

Payoff Structure for a Mature Company

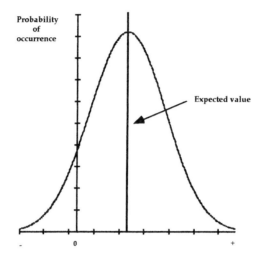

In this example, the likelihood of losing all of your money is modest, but so too is the upside potential. Of course, return on investment depends on who is asking the question and on the price paid to invest. If you have to pay a high franchise fee, then you lower your potential return and increase the likelihood of a loss. Or if you are a venture capital investor who strikes a deal with the entrepreneur that is generous to the entrepreneur (e.g., if you pay a high valuation), then the risk/reward pattern looks different.

In general, these graphical tools can be used to describe investment opportunities. Investments involve different combinations of capital requirements and payoffs. They also involve differing degrees of uncertainty. To reiterate the obvious, you want opportunities that offer the prospect of high, safe returns on modest investment, with lots of attractive and proprietary growth options—a simple rule to describe, but one that is almost impossible to follow in the real world.

CONTEXT

Opportunities exist in a context. At one level, there is the macroeconomic environment, including the level of economic activity, inflation, exchange rates, and interest rates. There are also a wide range of rules and regulations that affect opportunity and how resources are marshaled to exploit it. Examples range from tax policy to the rules concerning raising capital for a private or public company. Then, there are factors like technology, which affect what a business or its competitors can accomplish.

I will not dwell on context here except to remark that context often has a tremendous impact on every aspect of the entrepreneurial process, from identification of opportunity to harvest. In some cases, changes in some contextual factor create opportunity. For example, when the airline industry was deregulated in the late 1970s, over one hundred new airlines were formed. The context for financing was also favorable, enabling new entrants like People Express to go to the public market for capital even before starting operations.

Conversely, there are periods when the context makes it hard to start new enterprises. In the early 1990s, to illustrate, there was a difficult recession, combined with a difficult financing environment for new companies: venture capital disbursements were low as was the amount of capital raised in the public markets. Paradoxically, these relatively tight conditions, which made it harder for new entrants to get going, were associated with very high investment returns later in the 1990s as the capital market environment heated up.

Sometimes, a shift in context turns an unattractive business into an attractive one, and vice versa. A colleague was on the board of a struggling packaging company some years ago. The board had decided to sell the business. Within weeks of that decision, however, there was an incident in which bottles of Tylenol were tampered with, resulting in multiple deaths. The particular company happened to have an efficient mechanism for putting tamper-proof seals on Tylenol bottles. What had been a poorly performing business quickly turned into a spectacular one, all in a matter of weeks. Conversely, for companies in the real estate business, the tax reforms enacted in 1986 in the United States created havoc: almost every positive incentive to invest in real estate was reversed. Many previously successful firms in the real estate industry went out of business soon after the new rules were put in place.

When I read a business plan, I look for two pieces of evidence related to context. First, I want to see that the entrepreneurial team is aware of the context and how it helps or hinders their specific proposal. Second, and more importantly, I look for sensitivity to the fact that the context will inevitably change. If so, how might the changes affect the business? And, what can management do in the event the context worsens? Finally, are there ways in which management can affect context in a positive way? For example, can management have an impact on regulation or on setting industry standards? We will address the issue of dealing with contextual factors in more detail shortly.

DEALS

Most people think of valuation and terms when considering deals. What share of the company will they have to give to the investors to raise capital? What are the terms of the financing? These are the prominent questions. In this section, I will address these issues but only after considering the sources of capital and the amount raised. The rationale for this sequencing will become apparent shortly.

When I talk to young (and old) entrepreneurs looking to finance their ventures, they obsess about valuation. Their explicit goal seems to be to minimize the dilution they will suffer in raising capital. Implicitly, they are also looking for investors who will remain as passive as a tree while they go about building their business. On the food chain of investors, it seems, doctors and dentists are best and venture capitalists worst because of the degree to which the latter group demands a large share of the returns and demands control rights.

I confess to a bias on the subject of financing ventures. My rule is the following:

> From whom you raise capital is often more important than the terms.

Let me explain. Ventures are inherently risky. Murphy often is a member of the management team—what can go wrong will. Most ventures end up taking more time and more money than the entrepreneur ever imagined. The name of the game, then, is not to minimize dilution at each stage of a company's existence but rather to maximize the value of your share at the end of the process.

I have seen quite a few examples of entrepreneurs raising money from unsophisticated investors at high prices. When the inevitable bad news arrives, the investors panic and get angry. They refuse to advance the company more money. They are surprised that results are disappointing. In such situations, it is often difficult to recruit new investors. The new investor has to worry about the old investor group—if they're not putting up more money, what's wrong? The old investors are also reticent to accept the valuation proposed by the new investor.

I view the financing decision as having two fundamental elements: a capital-raising decision and a hiring decision. Consider, to illustrate, raising capital from a professional venture capitalist. The investor typically seeks to earn high returns, perhaps 50% per year or greater. This seems on the surface like very high-cost money, almost loan-shark like. Suppose, however, that the venture capitalist is the leading expert in the world in the business being financed. Suppose as well that the venture capitalist can increase the potential reward and decrease the potential risk by being involved in the business. In this case, the value of the entrepreneur's share of the company assuming the venture capitalist invests may be higher than it would have been if the company had raised money from less competent investors. Phrased differently, the total pie is increased in size so much that the value of the entrepreneur's smaller slice of the pie is larger.

There are many examples of venture capitalists whose presence in a deal helps enormously. John Doerr, for example, is a partner of the highly successful firm Kleiner, Perkins. He was a top-ranked salesman at semiconductor powerhouse Intel in the mid-1970s. Doerr has invested in such companies as Sun Microsystems, Intuit, and Netscape. He knows the process of building large and successful companies. He has a world-class rolodex, which helps his portfolio companies form valuable connections. I would want John Doerr on my team, and I would be prepared to pay a high price to get him. The same is true of other similarly skilled and experienced investors like Arthur Rock or L. J. Sevin. I should also note that if these individuals work with my company, they won't work with my competitor.

I believe that every high potential venture needs an investor who is "process literate." By this, I mean that they have been through the game many times. They are very good at helping companies grow. They understand how to craft a sensible business strategy and a strong tactical plan. They help recruit, compensate, and motivate great team members. They are coaches and cheerleaders, and they understand the distinction between being an investor and being the entrepreneur. I believe as well that good investors do not panic when bad news arrives. They roll up their sleeves and help the company solve its problems.

There are many decisions in a venture that entrepreneurs will have to face only once or twice in their careers. An example is the decision to go public. The entrepreneur is pitted against highly experienced but not necessarily disinterested service providers like investment bankers, lawyers, and accountants. It is extremely useful in such a situation to have advisors who have "been there and done that." The same is true about other process decisions, such as introducing a new product, dealing with a lawsuit, recruiting a VP of Marketing, or selling a business.

There are other areas in which the choice of a financial partner can help a company. For example, sometimes it is advantageous to raise money from customers. Those customers can help sell the product or service. The best form of customer money is a prepaid order, but it might also make sense to have the customer own equity. The same might be true of suppliers. Even potential competitors are on the list of possible investors, if by investing they forgo the option of entering the business directly. Raising money from these nontraditional sources might seem to create conflicts of interest. As Howard Stevenson says, however, "without conflict, there is no interest."

Though I have started this discussion of "deals" by focusing on who invests, an issue of great importance is how much money to raise and in what stages. Most ventures need more money than they are initially able to raise. Investors are loath to hand over large sums of capital up-front to an eager team of business founders. If a company believes it ultimately will need $10 million to develop and introduce a software product, it is likely to find that no investor will invest the full $10 million. Rather, the investor will stage the commitment of capital over time, preserving the right to invest more money and preserving the right to abandon the project in the event the team or the business idea doesn't work out. The investor might offer to invest $1 million, while the software is finished. If the software looks attractive, the investor will put in $4 million for the launch of the product. If the launch is promising, then the investor will put up more money, perhaps the remaining $5 million or more, to support expansion of the company.

The issue of how much money to invest in a company is exceedingly difficult, and the perspective of the players often differs. Entrepreneurs want all the money up-front, while investors want to stage the capital over time in order to "buy" more information. There is no right answer in this ancient debate. There are, however, some useful ways to think about the issues inherent in financing new ventures.

An old saying is "time is money." In entrepreneurial finance, the expression gets turned around: "money is time." By this I mean that money buys time for a venture to find the right combination of people, strategy, and tactics to succeed. Each chunk of money buys an additional chunk of time.

I think of ventures as complicated options such as one finds in financial markets. In this regard, raising money is like extending the expiration date of the option. If the company runs out of money, investors will have to decide whether or not it makes sense to buy more time and, if so, on what terms.

There is also another way in which money is time. Often, a company is pursuing an opportunity for which time to market is critical: the first mover gets the largest share, and the second place finisher is far less attractive. Money can help a company accelerate its entry plan. Some aspects of the business can be done in parallel rather than in sequence. From one perspective, the decision to accelerate spending would seem risky: just the opposite may be true. To go slow is to risk everything. Consider, to illustrate, the famous case on Science Technology used at Harvard Business School. The case mentions that the company invented the oscilloscope after World War II. The case also mentions a sign on the factory floor that stated, "We don't want to grow too large." Unfortunately, they succeeded beyond their wildest dreams: another company pursued the oscilloscope opportunity faster and captured the market leaving Science Technology as small as it apparently aspired to be.

There are other paradoxes in the world of raising money. Sometimes having too much money dooms a company. The founders (and employees) don't view money as a scarce resource: this often occurs in large companies, which have managers who rely on the deep pockets of the parent organization. At other times, a company starves an opportunity.

There are some useful questions that speak to the issue of how time and money should relate to each other in a specific venture, including the following:

- What new information would dramatically change your perception of the likelihood of success for a given venture?
- How much time and money are required to "buy" that information?

- To what degree does the company have control over the rate at which it exploits an opportunity?
- Who else might be pursuing the same opportunity, and what are the consequences of losing the race?

The final issue to be covered in this section on deals relates specifically to their structure. There are two important aspects of deal structure that preoccupy entrepreneurs, judging by the number of phone calls I get asking for advice: valuation and terms (i.e., other aspects of the deal, such as employment contracts, etc.).

Unfortunately, there are very few definitive rules when it comes to structuring deals. On the one hand, I believe in the golden rule: "He who has the gold rules." On the other hand, I believe that deals that are too tough on either side generally don't work.

Over the years, I have developed a set of principles to guide deal making. First, deals fundamentally allocate risk and reward and therefore value. Whenever risk and reward are allocated, the dealmaker has to be concerned with the three issues:

- What are the incentive effects of the allocation?
- Who will be attracted by the terms offered?
- What are the logical implications if the parties to a deal behave in their own perceived best interest?

Consider, for example, a typical deal between a venture capital firm and a venture. During the past 20 years, the structure of such deals has evolved to a recognizable standard. First, venture capitalists invest in stages: they do not give all the money to the entrepreneurial team that will be required to exploit the opportunity. They almost always invest in the form of a convertible preferred. The preferred has liquidation preference: if the company is liquidated, the principal of the preferred must be paid back before the equityholders receive any of the liquidation proceeds. The preferred has a dividend that is payable at the discretion of the board of directors but adds to the liquidation principle, if not paid before liquidation. The preferred is convertible into common stock at some stated price: conversion is typically mandatory if the company goes public. The investors preserve the right to invest additional money by having preemptive rights or rights of first refusal on subsequent financing. The investors have some protection against dilution such as might occur if the company raises additional capital at a lower price. Often, the investors have the right to force the company to repurchase the preferred at some point in the future on some prearranged terms. The investors have certain information rights, enabling them to receive timely (and credible) financial reports and to be notified before major events at the company. The investors also have certain governance rights such as the right to appoint directors or the right to replace the founder or founders. The management team, including the founders, typically receive common stock (or stock options) and are subject to vesting requirements: if they leave the company, they lose the unvested portion of their options or stock.

Implicit in each element of the standard venture capital deal is a notion of how the incentives ought to be set. Any time investors give money to someone else, they have to concern themselves with possible conflicts of interest. The entrepreneur might, for example, pay him/herself a large salary, depleting the funds of the venture. The entrepreneur might decide to keep the company private, never enabling the investor to get a return on investment.

The deal structure described above is designed to protect the investor and provide appropriate incentives to the entrepreneurial venture. Consider, to illustrate, the rationale for staging the commitment of capital—investing less than might ultimately be needed to exploit an opportunity. Suppose a venture needs $20 million to go from concept to commercialization. Why don't investors just give the full $20 million up-front? Well, it's not hard to figure out, when you think about it. I have previously noted that there is often a discrepancy between outcomes and plans. In this hypothetical $20 million venture, it is highly likely that there will be some bad news early in its evolution.

Suppose that six months after the team receives the $20 million, they discover a fatal flaw in their engineering. Will they call the investors, admit to their discovery, and send back the unspent funds? Not on this planet, they won't. Never in the history of entrepreneurship has an entrepreneur announced defeat. The entrepreneur always believes that the problem can be fixed—all that is needed is a little more time and a little more money. By the way, sometimes they are right. Federal Express approached bankruptcy three times before it gained escape velocity.

The point here is that investors need to have the right to decide whether or not to continue to back the team and the project: they should not cede decision rights to the team because the team will almost always make a self-interested choice. Indeed, if the entrepreneurial team were to insist that the entire $20 million be invested up-front, they would likely find no (rational) investors willing to make the bet, regardless of the share of the company they would acquire. Also, because the entrepreneurs are likely to have to agree to a staged infusion of capital—with each additional investment based on new information and a price reflecting that information—the entrepreneurs signal their belief in their ability to bring the project to fruition.

The incentive effects of deal structuring could occupy a book and I will not attempt to describe this topic in detail in this note.[12] Rather, the important lesson for entrepreneurs writing business plans is that they have to structure deals that reflect their incentives and those of investors. There is an implicit balancing act. The specific deal will be tailored to the characteristics of the individuals involved, the nature of the opportunity, and the contextual setting.

One caution is appropriate about deal structuring: there is an old expression—"too clever by half"—which is directly relevant. Often, dealmakers get creative in structuring deals. For example, they design complex valuation schemes that involve conditional pricing of a deal. If the company does as well as management thinks, then management gets some extra options. If the venture only does as well as the venture capitalist thinks, then the terms are more onerously tilted in favor of the investors. Through painful experience, I have come to believe that simple is better than complex. Trying to structure such complex deals often ends up turning partners into adversaries. In the deal described above, perhaps the venture capitalist will be better off if the company does poorly (but not too poorly) for some period and then takes off. Does the venture capitalist really want to be conflicted in this way? I think not.

In my experience, sensible deals have the following characteristics:

- They are simple.
- They are fair.
- They reflect trust rather than legalese.
- They are robust—they do not blow apart if actual differs slightly from plan.

[12] For more information on deals and incentives, see William A. Sahlman, "Note on Financial Contracting: 'Deals,'" Harvard Business School Case # 288-014. See also William A. Sahlman, "The Structure and Governance of Venture Capital Organizations," *Journal of Financial Economics*, October 1990.

- They do not provide perverse incentives that will cause one or both parties to behave in destructive ways.
- They do not foreclose valuable options.
- The papers used to describe the deal are no greater than one-quarter inch.

No discussion of deals would be complete without a section on valuation. How are ventures valued, particularly those for which there is massive uncertainty? The short (and flip) answer is: "aerial extraction." A less curt answer is that venture valuation is an art, not a science. Every entrepreneur I have met says something like the following: "Based on my projections, you (the investor) should be willing to value my company at $10 million. If you do, you will earn a 78% internal rate of return, based on our going public in five years." The response is: "I'll value your company at $3 million—your numbers aren't worth the paper they're written on."

Only if you had omniscience would it be easy to value companies early in their life. The venture investor knows from hard-earned experience that few, if any, ventures come anywhere close to meeting their projections. Only 10% to 20% of the deals in which they invest will do really well. Some 30% will actually result in losses, in some cases complete loss. What seasoned investors do, therefore, is base their valuations on the overall experience they have had. The reasoning goes something like this: "If I value early-stage software companies at $5 million or less, then I will be able—after it is all said and done—to earn a rate of return on my portfolio that is acceptable to me and my limited partners."

My students are always disappointed that there are no formulas for calculating the value of a venture. They do not like the fact that there are a wide range of possible valuations that are okay or "in the ballpark." They do not like the fact that their negotiating skill and assets (i.e., the degree to which the team and the opportunity are outstanding and proprietary) will determine what happens. I too wish it were easier to come up with answers, or at least narrow ranges: it would certainly make my job less stressful![13]

In closing, this section on deals has been implicitly based on a simple set of structured questions, as follows:

- From whom should the money be raised?
- How much money is needed and for what purpose?
- What deal terms are fair and provide the appropriate incentives for each side under a wide range of scenarios?

RISK/REWARD MANAGEMENT

One fascinating aspect of business is the degree to which the future is hard to predict. It is certainly possible to write down a detailed description of a bright future but hard to make it happen. The notion above that there is a known probability distribution for outcomes is useful but slightly misleading. There are no immutable distributions of outcomes. It is ultimately the responsibility of management to change the distribution, to increase the likelihood and consequences of success, and to decrease the likelihood and implications of problems.

---

[13] For more than you ever wanted to know about valuing venture deals, see Daniel R. Scherlis and William A. Sahlman, "A Method for Valuing High-Risk, Long-Term Investments," Harvard Business School Case # 288-006.

One of the great myths about entrepreneurs is that they are risk seekers. My sense is that all sane people want to avoid risk. As colleague Howard Stevenson says, true entrepreneurs want to capture all of the reward and give all of the risk to others. The best business is a post office box to which people send cashiers checks. Yet, risk is unavoidable. So what is a rational person to do?

My answer to this question is that you must assess the risks and find mechanisms to manage them. Consider, to illustrate, a risk inherent in the context, the set of factors outside the control of the entrepreneur. There might be an increase in interest rates: if a venture is highly leveraged, then an increase in interest cost might sink it. To manage this risk, it might make sense to hedge the exposure in the financial futures market so that a contract is purchased that does well when interest rates go up. This is equivalent to buying insurance: you pay a premium to do so, but you can preserve a company's business model by doing so.

In general, a myriad of things can go wrong or right in a venture. Although it is impossible to predict the future, it is possible to change the odds or manage the consequences of adverse events. For example, suppose you write a great novel. You go to an agent. The agent sells the rights to the book to a publisher. What should you worry about?

Clearly, a successful novel has a number of attractive follow-on possibilities/growth options, including a potential movie based on the book. You can insist that the contract you sign enables you—rather than the publisher—to reap the bulk of the rewards from a movie. I promise, however, that the initial contract you receive will grant to the publisher all ancillary rights associated with the book, from software to video. I also promise that the contract will be tilted in favor of the publisher in other ways. To illustrate, the contract will spell out possible royalty rates: you must not become so preoccupied with getting a high royalty rate that you ignore what that rate is applied to. Many naive authors have signed movie deals where they get a share of the net income generated in the movie: lo and behold, the movie grosses $500 million, but the author receives no royalties. She is told the movie was unprofitable. . . .

In this example, you cannot predict the success or failure of the book in the marketplace, but you can preserve the option to benefit if it is a success. You can retain certain rights, and you can pay attention to the nature of those rights, including the incentives of the other party. Or you can cross the Mass Turnpike blindfolded. The basic model of risk/reward management is depicted in the following:

Risk/Reward Management

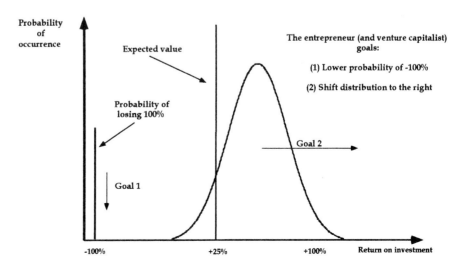

One specific area of importance in the realm of risk/reward management relates to harvesting. Earlier, I suggested that opportunities differed in terms of the implicit growth options defined as opportunities that companies have by dint of their entering a market (e.g., to sell additional products or services to the same customers). Businesses also differ in terms of their harvest potential, by which I mean the ability to reap the rewards of the investment process.

For example, venture capitalists often ask if a company is "IPOable," by which they mean: can the company be taken public at some point in the future? Some businesses are inherently difficult to take public, sometimes because doing so would reveal information that might harm the competitive position of the firm (e.g., reveal profitability, thereby encouraging entry or angering customers or suppliers). Some businesses are not companies, but rather products—they are not sustainable as an independent business.

One important task for entrepreneur and investor alike is to think hard at the beginning about the end of the process. Specifically, how will you get money out of the business, assuming it is successful, or even if it is only marginally successful? Some businesses are rife with harvest potential: they involve products or services that are worth a great deal to many potential buyers. If you are currently in the telecommunications software industry today, for example, you are witnessing one of the great industry consolidations ever. Companies like Cisco, 3Com, and Bay Networks are on acquisition binges. If you have created a successful niche product or service, there is a strong possibility that one of those three companies will try to buy you. Moreover, because each of the three must compete with the other two, the sellers might well get additional (even unwarranted) benefits from playing one firm off against another.

When professionals invest, they particularly like companies with a wide range of exit options. They work hard to preserve and enhance those options along the way. For example, they avoid forming a strategic relationship with a major company early in the process because doing so often forecloses the exit option of having multiple large firms bid against each other for the right to buy the company. There is an old saying: "If you don't know where you are going, any road will get you there." In crafting sensible entrepreneurial strategies, just the opposite is true: you had better know where you might end up and have a plan for getting there.

FINANCIAL PROJECTIONS

No discussion of business plans would be complete without addressing the ubiquitous pro formas that populate them. Most business plan writers spend countless hours on detailed financial projections. They imagine that a potential investor will pore over the numbers, asking a myriad of questions. They also imagine that the investor will propose a deal based on the numbers in the plan.

When I first started to study entrepreneurial ventures, I too turned first to the numbers. Of late, I have gotten to the point where I hardly even look at them. Indeed, if I receive a plan that has five years of monthly projections, I immediately and enthusiastically throw the plan in the circular file next to my desk.

Every business plan contains the following phrase: "we conservatively project." Only about 1 in 20 plans is conservative in the sense that the company comes even close to meeting its plan. If you observe one hundred companies and only five come close to their original projections, then you begin to pick up a pattern.

I have come to believe that spreadsheets have an innate virus that infects the projections made in business plans. The virus turns what might be sensible people into wildly optimistic, nonsensical maniacs.

There are two or three possible explanations for why the virus is so widespread. First, in every business, there is what I call the "horse race between fear and greed." Entrepreneurs want to preserve the largest possible ownership stake when raising capital. At the same time, they are afraid of running out of capital. Very few, if any, entrepreneurs correctly anticipate how much capital and time will be required to accomplish their objectives. Venture capitalists automatically discount what is in a plan to reflect the consistency and predictability of the optimism.

Of course, if the entrepreneurs know that the venture capitalist will discount his or her projections, then they pad the projections to offset the likely haircut to be applied. This sounds to me like a vicious cycle in which reality becomes hard to find.

It's rather like the distinction between "buying pro formas" and "selling pro formas." It all depends on your perspective. Indeed, I always ask a simple question when looking at projections: Who wrote the pro forma and why?

When I read a pro forma projection, I look first and foremost for evidence of a business model that makes sense and an appreciation of the fact that the specific numbers proffered are almost certain to be wrong. I like to see that the entrepreneurial team has thought through the key drivers that will determine success or failure. In a traditional magazine business, to illustrate, among the key business drivers are: total possible subscribers in the target audience; gross response rate (how many respond to a mailing that they are interested in subscribing?); net response (how many who say they will try the magazine actually pay?); and, renewal rate (how many who subscribe actually renew their subscription when it lapses?). These factors help determine the profitability of a magazine because they affect the cost of acquiring and retaining a subscriber. Also important would be the advertising attractiveness of the audience and the costs of creating (editorial), printing, and fulfilling the magazine.

In a software business, the economic drivers differ. Of critical importance are the cost and time schedule for creating the software. Then, the economics of the various distribution channels are at the top of the list. What margins will the retail or OEM channel require? What are the economics of a direct sales force model? How much territory can a salesperson cover? What compensation is required to attract, retain, and motivate a talented sales force and a software development team?

Common to all business models is the issue of breakeven: at what level does the business begin to make a profit? Even more important, at what level does the company turn cash flow positive?

In addition to a clear appreciation of the factors that will affect the economics of the business, I look for sensible sensitivity analysis. What would happen, for example, if net response rates were 20% lower for the magazine? What would happen if the software project took 20% longer than estimated? These are the kinds of questions that I believe the team should address in presenting their model to prospective resource providers.

Many successful companies find that their basic business model is too optimistic. Though ultimately the business model works, more time and capital are required. I was a director of two companies that started out predicting that they would each need less than $2 million to reach escape velocity. One, Avid Technology, went through $25 million before it reached positive cash flow. Avid sells digital video editing software and went from startup in 1988 to over $400 million in 1995. Another company in the information business went through $10 million as compared to its initial guess of $1.5 million. We had a saying at that company when I was a director: "We never wrote a business plan we couldn't miss." This company now does $160 million in revenue, with

$60 million in operating profits. This company also came perilously close to bankruptcy before figuring out its business model.

One final note about pro formas in business plans for high potential ventures—they all look the same. Over the past decade, hundreds of books on entrepreneurship and venture capital have been published. Most of these volumes comment that venture capitalists will not consider making an investment in a company that cannot reasonably project $50 million in annual revenues within five years. It is not surprising that almost every plan I receive shows year five sales of $55 million, representing a 10% cushion over the presumed minimum. They also need only a 10% share, and they all show at least a 10% net margin. And they are all conservative. (See Appendix 5-3 for a glossary of terms found in business plans and an explanation of what they really mean.)

DUE DILIGENCE

A business plan is often used as a blueprint for asking questions. Professional investors conduct due diligence in order to assess the people and the opportunity described in a plan. They will call references, including people not suggested by the entrepreneurs. They will call actual or potential customers, suppliers, and other resource providers. They will talk to competitors, both actual and potential. And, they will grill the team based on the questions they believe must be answered before they will invest.

I recently participated in a meeting at which an entrepreneurial team tried to convince a group of individuals to invest. The team leader had a well-practiced pitch, complete with color slides and attractive props. At several points in the meeting, the presenter noted that "the business model was proved," by which he meant that there was substantial evidence that the company knew how the opportunity would play out. Unfortunately, the individuals to whom the presentation was being made had done some homework. One had called a potential advertiser, and another had called someone in the retail channel. Each gave a sharply divergent story about the company, its business model, and the likely evolution of the relationship with the company. If the presenter had only hedged his bets by describing the process by which he intended to convert promises (or hints) to reality, his pitch would have been successful. It was not.

The process of investigating a potential investment is driven by experience. After investing in a few companies, you begin to build up a sense of what can go right and what can go wrong. You learn to ask questions that you wish you had asked in the last unsuccessful deal you did. You develop a repertoire of tools to ferret out what is really going on in a venture. One friend always asks the same question when he visits a company seeking investment: "Why are sales so bad?" In some cases, the entrepreneur launches into a discussion of the failings of the sales force or the manufacturing problems confronted by the company. In other cases, the entrepreneur takes offense and describes why sales are going great. In either case, my friend has the information he needs to assess the business and its management team.

One final comment about due diligence is appropriate: it is not infallible. Before Bain Capital invested in Staples, it commissioned a survey of small businesses on their use of supplies. The results of the survey were not consonant with the assumptions made in the Staples business plan. The founder, Tom Stemberg, insisted that Bain Capital revisit the issue and check how much small businesses actually spent on supplies as compared with what they thought they spent. As it turned out, Stemberg was right, and Staples is now a multibillion dollar business. Bain Capital did invest, which turned out to be a wise decision.

SUMMARY AND CONCLUSION

In summary, a business plan is neither necessary nor sufficient. Many successful businesses never had a formal plan, and many unsuccessful ventures had a beautifully crafted but irrelevant plan.

A business plan must provide reasonable answers to the following questions:

- Who are the people involved? What have they done in the past that would lead one to believe that they will be successful in the future? Who is missing from the team and how will they be attracted?
- What is the nature of the opportunity? How will the company make money? How is the opportunity likely to evolve? Can entry barriers be built and maintained?
- What contextual factors will affect the venture? What contextual changes are likely to occur, and how can management respond to those changes?
- What deals have been or are likely to be struck inside and outside the venture? Do the deals struck increase the likelihood of success? How will those deals and the implicit incentives evolve over time?
- What decisions have been made (or can be made) to increase the ratio of reward to risk?

Among the many sins committed by business plan writers is arrogance—believing they have a completely proprietary idea or an insuperable lead. In today's economy, few ideas are truly proprietary. Moreover, there has never been a time in recorded history when the supply of capital did not outrace the supply of opportunity. The true half-life of opportunity is decreasing with the passage of time.

A plan must not be an albatross, something that is cast and concrete, hangs around the neck of the entrepreneurial team, and drags them into oblivion. As Steinbeck said, "the best laid plans of mice and men . . . :" the world changes, and the team must change accordingly.

A plan must be a dynamic call for action, one that recognizes that the responsibility of management is to fix what is broken prospectively and in real time. Risk is inevitable, avoiding risk impossible. Risk management is the key, always tilting the venture in favor of reward and away from risk.

A plan must demonstrate mastery of the entire entrepreneurial process, from identification of opportunity to harvest. To paraphrase George Bernard Shaw on the subject of love affairs, "Any fool can start a business—it takes a genius to harvest one."

A plan is not a means for separating unsuspecting investors from their money by hiding the fatal flaw. In the final analysis, the only one being fooled is the entrepreneur.

The ultimate tools in business are people, the leaders of the venture, the people who work at the venture, and all of the suppliers, including the financiers. Picking the A-team is the only way to manage reward and risk in the long term.

PERSONALIZING

Writing a business plan can be a terrific educational experience. It is an integrative exercise, requiring the venture team to bring to bear a wide range of skills and experiences. It is human and it is analytical. Working on a plan can be a useful tool for gaining commitment and consensus among team members, even if the plan turns out to be impractical.

The real purpose of this note is to get MBAs and others to think about their careers using the entrepreneurship lens. To what degree do they know what an opportunity is and how to marshal the required resources? What is missing, and how can the gaps be addressed?

We live in a golden age, one characterized by tremendous opportunity and a myriad of examples of successful entrepreneurship. A young dropout from college, Bill Gates of Microsoft fame, ends up as the wealthiest individual in America. Three young graduates from Harvard Business School, David Thompson, Bruce Ferguson, and Scott Webster, built Orbital Sciences Corporation into a multi-hundred million dollar, publicly traded company whose mission is to commercialize space.

Writing a business plan is useful as part of a lifelong educational experience. If and only if the writer has the skills, experience, contacts, and attitude that are required for the business, then, by all means, the Nike model should be invoked—

Just Do It!
If not,
Just Say No!

THE CONCEPT OF FIT

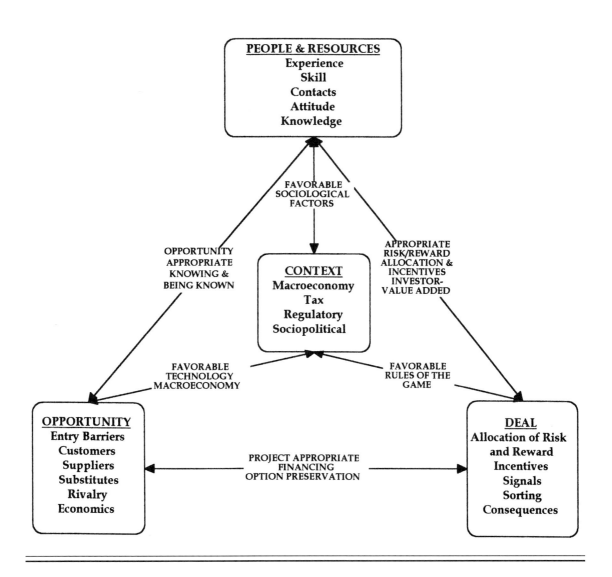

DYNAMIC FIT MANAGEMENT

CHANGE (GOOD AND BAD NEWS)

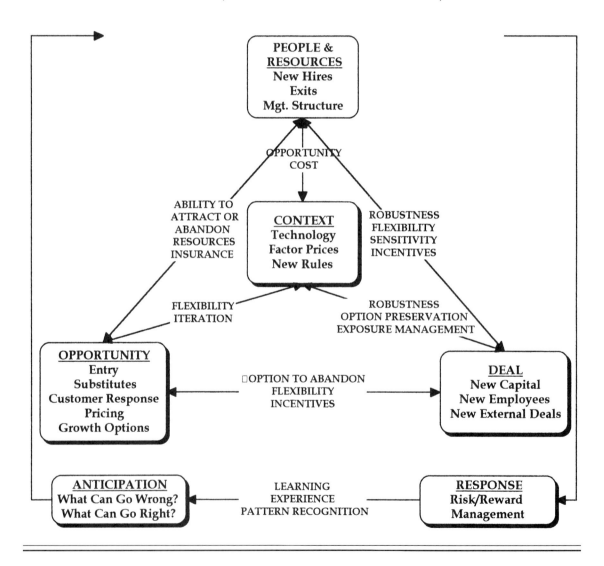

APPENDIX 5-3

TRANSLATION GLOSSARY FOR BUSINESS PLANS

Business Plan Phrase	What It Really Means
We conservatively project . . .	We read a book that said we had to have sales of $50 million in 5 years, and we reverse engineered the numbers . . .
We took our best guess and divided by 2 . . .	We accidentally divided by .5 . . .
We project a 10% margin . . .	We did not modify any of the assumptions in the business plan template we downloaded from the Internet . . .
The project is 98% complete . . .	To complete the remaining 2% will take as long as to create the initial 98%, but will cost twice as much . . .
Our business model is proved . . .	If you take the evidence from the past week for the best of our 50 locations and extrapolate it for all of the others . . .
We have a six-month lead . . .	We have not tried to find out how many other people also have a six-month lead . . .
We only need a 10% market share . . .	So too do all the other 50 entrants getting funded . . .
Customers are clamoring for our product . . .	We have not yet broached the issue of them paying for it. Also, all of our current customers are relatives . . .
We are the low-cost producer . . .	We have not produced anything yet, but we are confident that we will be able to . . .
We have no competition . . .	Only Microsoft, Netscape, IBM, and Sun have announced plans to enter the business . . .
Our management team has a great deal of experience . . .	. . . consuming the product or service . . .
A select group of investors is considering the plan . . .	We mailed a copy of the plan to everyone in Pratt's Guide . . .
We seek a value-added investor . . .	We are looking for a passive, dumb-as-rocks investor . . .
If you invest on our terms, you will earn a 68% IRR . . .	If everything that could conceivably ever go right does go right, you might get your money back . . .

6

NSK Software
Technologies Ltd.

INTRODUCTION

It was July 1993 and "twenty-something"-year-old Gil Shwed was hot. The temperature was over 100 degrees Fahrenheit as Shwed and his two friends, Shlomo Kramer and Marius Nacht, worked in a cramped Tel Aviv apartment without air conditioning which Kramer's family allowed the three to use after the recent death of his grandmother. The partners were working on two borrowed computers to program a new software product that would provide network security for the Internet. A pile of 172 empty Coca-Cola plastic bottles was stacked in the back of the room marking the team's progress as they attempted to quench their thirst and to keep themselves awake. The pile was growing steadily as the entrepreneurs worked feverishly in shifts with four hours sleep per night.

The partners had begun operating under the name NSK Software Technologies Ltd. (NSK) in February, and the three friends worked diligently to finish the business plan (see Exhibit 6-1) for NSK by March. They needed to raise financing quickly in order to take their product to market. They felt timing was critical, and they were working as hard as they could to finish the product by the end of summer. The three partners went to friends and former colleagues for their initial capital, but it was not enough. They realized they needed a financial partner who understood technology but who would not be a potential competitor. Ideally, a partner would have legal, accounting, marketing, and administrative resources to help NSK quickly set up infrastructure for their company.

COMPANY BACKGROUND

Shwed conceived of the concept for NSK in 1990 when he worked on a project during his military service in the Israeli Defense Forces (IDF). His task was to connect two networks, one of which contained classified information that would not be accessible to

JD/MBA student Jeffrey Anapolsky prepared this case under the supervision of Professor Paul Gompers as the basis for class discussion rather than to illustrate either effective or ineffective handling of an administrative situation.

EXHIBIT 6-1

NSK BUSINESS PLAN FROM MARCH 1993

Note: The following Business Plan is presented in its original form without editing.

Guidelines for Investor Agreement

1. Gil Shwed, Marius Nacht and Shlomo Kramer (the founders) will establish a company with the following goals:

   Provide network security solutions to the mass market.

   Security will be simple, transparent, effective and reliable.

2. The founders will be employed full time in the company to achieve the above goals.

3. The first product to be developed by the company is described herein

   Also listed is a budget draft, a development schedule and a sales forecast for the product.

   NSK will develop the product according to the development schedule, and will take all the needed steps to establish the product marketing channels. NSK will support the product and continue its development to ensure its perpetuate success.

4. Subject to the budget enclosed the following finance scheme is suggested:

   The founders will provide 125k$.

   The investor will invest 125k$. In return, the investor will be granted 25% of the company's shares.

FireWall-1

1. The Need

1.1 Introduction

The number of computers and applications is increasing, "right sizing" is gaining momentum, and businesses are going global. This leads to a growing demand for networking computers and network services. Networking is needed in all sizes: Local, Metropolitan and Wide Area Networks, and users want it to be "smooth and transparent". The number of computers connected to networks is growing exponentially and the number of network services is on the rise as well.

1.2 Availability vs. Vulnerability

Connectivity and security are two conflicting musts in the computing solution of any organization. The typical modern computing environment is built around network communication supplying transparent access to a multitude of services. The global availability of these services is perhaps the single most important feature of modern computing solutions.

Protecting network services from unauthorized usage is of paramount importance to any organization. Using current technology, an organization will have to give up much of its availability and connectivity (to a privileged use) in order to prevent vulnerability (availability of services to an unauthorized user).

FireWall-1 enables to enforce, easily and simply, the exact security restrictions needed to prevent vulnerability without having to sacrifice any availability in return.

1.3 Current Status

This implementation of FireWall-1 is focused in the Unix market. Modern Unix system compromise a large part of the world client-server computing environments. Most Unix systems in market are networked in LANs and WANs. Unix systems also compromise the majority of global networks like the Internet.

A Unix based system provides a large set of services in its standard configuration. However, there is no mechanism to control the access to these services from the network. The same holds for other types of systems (e.g. PC, Macintosh).

FireWall-1 is intended to serve as a the doorman to the system. Controlling all network traffic to and from the system.

1.4 An Example

An organization with an R&D department and a Sales & Marketing department will be examined. The computers of each department are clustered in a departmental LAN. The two LANs and maybe those of other departments are, of course, connected to facilitate the joint work of the organization.

The S&M department also works in close collaboration with a growing number of retailers located all over the world. It is only natural that the S&M department will be connected to their retailers (say, using Internet). This connection will provide services such as "E-mail" for orders and other correspondence, "FTP" for file transfers of drawings or bug fixes, "rlogin" for remote login into the organization's computers to demonstrate new features of new releases, etc.

Connection of that sort poses a major problem: By connecting the S&M department to the outside world, all the sensitive information in the R&D department is exposed to intruders from outside the organization. Using current technology, it is difficult, if

(Continued)

EXHIBIT 6-1 *(Continued)*

not impossible, to eliminate that exposure without having to restructure the network or use non-standard communication applications.

The naive solution would be to physically disconnect the S&M network from the R&D network. This is unacceptable, as it makes the communication between the departments cumbersome.

What is really needed here, is a way to discriminate between computers and users by authorizing different services to them according to where they are located: Inside or outside the organization. For example: Restricting inbound connections of "ftp" or "rlogin" that originated from outside the organization only to the S&M department allowing a "rlogin" services from a trusted site to all networks; providing "E-mail" to all in both directions. Connectivity between the departments is not impaired and sensitive R&D data is secured.

FireWall-1 does just that. It enables specifying and enforcing access control rules such as in the example above, in an extremely easy and simple manner, even for the novice network manager. Applications and network setup need not be modified at all.

2. The Product

2.1 Product Highlights

FireWall-1 is a software application for controlling, monitoring and protection computers and computer networks in the context of network access. Six qualities characterize FireWall-1:

1. Prevention of unauthorized communication to or from computers and computer networks.
2. Providing security with minimal restructuring of software and hardware, and negligible performance degradation.
3. Maximization of the usage of information available during access attempts or communication.
4. Facility and simplicity in management and installation.
5. Offering a technique that is invariant to platform and, to large extent, a technology that is invariant to the Operating System.
6. Complementing and co-existing with any other security products available.

2.2 Product Description

FireWall-1 is a software network security package, enabling control of network access to or from the computer system. The application is suitable for utilization on network gateways, servers or end computers. When running on a gateway, communication to and from complete sub-networks can be controlled. On top of controlling network access, FireWall-1 monitors traffic and alert managers of various incidents, such as brake-in attempts.

Once FireWall-1 is activated, it becomes in charge off all communication packets being received, sent and routed by the system.

FireWall-1 inspects any packet, looking for all the information contained in the packet and needed in order to obtain proper security. Security needs are expressed by rules contained in a rule base and by access lists used by the rule base.

FireWall-1 also associates packets to connections. The connection associated with a packet may provide vitally important contextual information unattainable from the packet itself (e.g., authorization data provided in the connection initiation).

The rules applied by inspecting the packets are used to determine the action to be carried for that packets: The most important actions are to route the packet further thus enabling the connection, or to drop it and terminate the connection attempt. Additional actions include logging facilities, warning, and various alert actions.

The system is supplied with a pre-defined set of rule bases. In order to set-up FireWall-1, the network manager should select the appropriate security strategy. Optionally filling forms and providing system specific access lists.

The rule base is specified using high level terms, easy to understand and verify by network managers, e.g., names of hosts, domains, services and protocols are used rather than using address and protocol numbers. System managers do not need to understand nor to deal with the bits and pieces of the various packets and protocols.

Editing rules involves a simple "cut-and-paste" job of selecting conditions and actions, putting them together. However, it is easy and possible for the network manager to modify the rules according to their specific needs or instructions. It is also easy to "teach" the application new protocols (involving different packet's headers and data).

Being able to use all the information carried in the packet, FireWall-1's rule base is extremely comprehensive and flexible. The rules may be based upon any combination of data items such as: The packet's origin, destination, network, user, protocol, service, port, etc. encapsulated in all the communication layers. Additional criteria may include time of day, date, network load and others.

FireWall-1 is an add-on measure to the already existing communication software and hardware installed on the system. Other programs need not be

(Continued)

EXHIBIT 6-1 *(Continued)*

modified, including the networking applications controlled by FireWall-1.

FireWall-1 can co-exist with other security products and serve as a complementary mean for obtaining a better secured network.

On top of controlling network access, FireWall-1 monitors access activity and may be used by the organization to inquire and learn about the current state of network services. Furthermore, the system administrator can use FireWall-1 to get statistics and backlog on network activity.

The main components of FireWall-1 are: The manager's control panel, the rule base builder and the communication control system itself.

FireWall-1 provides additional measures for preventing the system from being tempered, these include: Securing the code itself from being modified, and protecting the various rule bases and access lists.

Current (high) level of performance are not effected by FireWall-1, the system communication throughput and latency are preserved.

Management and installation of FireWall-1 can be done centrally by a single trusted authority (e.g. The network manager trusted workstation). Thus providing a simple and trustable interface.

Since the FireWall-1 technology innovation is generic, independent of the operating environment and communication protocols, it can be a implemented for many system types and multiple application. Providing a complete network security solution.

2.3 Implementation

"Plug 'n Play" software package for Sun Microsystems workstations and servers.

The software protects all IP-based traffic, e.g. TCP, UDP, RPC, NFS, X-Windows, Applications like TELNET, FTP, SMTP, NTP, etc. Any network type can be supported including Ethernet, Point to point interfaces (PPP, SLIP), X25, FDDI, TokenRing, Frame-Relay, etc.

The software can be used and installed by the end user requiring no prior training.

3. Unique Features

1. Transparency
Security is achieved in a transparent manner to applications and users. No changes in application code nor re-compilation is needed to communication program. New commands or operating method need not be learned by end-users.

2. Diversity
FireWall-1 enables to Control access to ALL resources, services and ports that are accessed through the network, without having to modify any of them; unlike other solutions that protect only specific of modified ones.

FireWall-1 is also sensitive to the packet's heading (inbound or outbound with respect to the entity under it's control). It may act differently and intelligently according to the heading. For example: If only one heading is prohibited, it would still allow acknowledge packets of the permitted heading through, even though they travel in the prohibited direction.

3. Generity
Suitable for all packet exchange protocols. The FireWall-1 technology is independent of the communication protocol it is securing, and from the underlying operating environment.

4. Flexibility and Intelligence
Flexible definition of access permissions to various network resources. Allows any combination and definition of access rights according to all layers of data encapsulated in the communication protocol, combined with system information like network interface, direction, time of day etc.

5. Ease of Use
Rules are specified using high level terms, easy to understand and verify by the system users. e.g. names of hosts, domains, services and protocols are used rather than using address and protocol numbers. System managers do not need to understand nor to deal with the bits and pieces of the various packets and protocols.

6. Simple Management
Central control by a network security administrator. Allowing simple and trusted interface for management.

7. Openness
Using FireWall-1 does not force the manager to use new proprietary or special applications. All current setup carries on as before, previous investment is preserved and future investments are not endangered. New network applications need not be aware of FireWall-1 and can be obtained openly, just like before.

8. Lightweight
FireWall-1 provide high level of performance, preserving current communication throughput and latency, for WANs as well as for high-speed LANs.

4. Future Developments
A wide span of products can follow FireWall-1. They are divided into two major categories: Implementations of FireWall-1 technology for other communi-

EXHIBIT 6-1 (Continued)

cation and computer system, and of expanding Fire-Wall-1 innovation to higher levels of security.

Straight forward follow-up implementations could be provided by porting the application to other UNIX platforms: IIP, IBM, etc.

Additional follow ups would be similar products running on Novell servers, PC compatibles and Macintosh computers, each with their own protocols.

Implementation on communication routers and bridges will be examined.

Future products will be directed to the field of trusted computing environments. This includes high level authentication and enhanced privacy. Special purpose hardware may also be part of future products.

5. The Market

5.1 Potential Buyers

Organizations connected to public networks (e.g. The Internet) and wish to secure their internal network from access of the "entire world".

Managers of LANs or MANs that are diverse or segmented and who wish to control the access of various computers or servers according to a more comprehensive set of criteria.

Any network manager, concerned with security but not willing to restructure their network; nor willing to substitute many open server-client applications with proprietary ones.

Public network service providers who wish to protect their customers and provide a better service.

Owners of single workstations who wish to restrict access to their workstation from their organization's network.

Departments within larger organization who wish to control the access to their private network.

End Computer operators/developers or Project Managers who's station provides some services to others and wish to better define and restrict access to their services.

5.2 The Internet

Connecting more than 20 million users, 2 million computers and 10,000 networks worldwide, the Internet is a prime marketing target for FireWall-1. Providing world-wide connectivity, the Internet is plagued with security problems. There is an increasing conciseness to the problem of network security in the internet community.

The Internet is going through a phase of becoming the world's global network, and is growing exponentially. The Internet commercial users now compromise the majority of network sites and traffic, and are the cause to most of the Internet growth.

Any organization connected to the Internet is faced with the problem of exposing its network to the rest of the world. Therefore, security in the Internet is a primary issue for any Internet user.

5.3 The Competition

The following section describes other Internet firewall solutions found in the market.

It describes briefly each product characteristics and features, as well as the major differences between the product and FireWall-1.

5.3.1 Interlock

A product of ANS Co+re sys, A subsidiary of ANS Internet service providers. Controls access to a limited number of network services.

Requires usage and installation on all client computers. Requires user expertise and maintenance. Services not in the package remain unprotected.

Price: 18–29K$/year.

5.3.2 Eagle Network Isolator

A product of Raptor Systems. Isolates private network from public network, controlling traffic. Provides access lists and permissions to network services and workstations. Comprehensive alerts using alarms, tax, telephone etc.

Limited flexibility and performance.

Requires two dedicated high end workstations. Software itself is priced at 60K$.

5.3.3 Gatekeeper

Herve Schauer Consultants, a French consulting firm.

Provide network isolation of private network from the public network. Support special purpose application for authorization. Provide customization and consultancy services together with software.

Requires two dedicated gateway workstations. Price is 1500$/day consulting, 10–20 days are needed. Plus 1500$/Month software usage.

5.3.4 Consult-IGATEWAY

A Product of SunConsult, a Sun Microsystems consulting specialists group.

Provides an Internet gateway that does not pass any traffic between internal and external networks. The gateway provides Telnet and FTP Services to the external network, and from the internal network outside.

Prices at 1800$/gateway.

(Continued)

EXHIBIT 6-1   (Continued)

5.3 Competitive Summary

	NSK FireWall-1	Raptor Network Isolator	ANS CO+RE	HSC Gatekeeper	SunConsult I-Gateway
1. Connectivity					
Traffic routing	YES	YES	LIMITED	YES	NO
Outgoing only mode	YES	LIMITED	NO	NO	NO
Support of communication protocol	YES	NO	NO	NO	NO
2. Security					
Access Lists	YES	YES	YES	YES	NO
Rule Base	YES	LIMITED	LIMITED	NO	NO
Alerts	YES	YES	?	YES	NO
3. Protection					
Entire Network	YES	YES	YES	YES	YES
End User Workstations	YES	LIMITED	LIMITED	NO	NO
4. Transparency					
Preserve current applications	YES	LIMITED	NO	NO	LIMITED
Preserve standard protocol	YES	LIMITED	NO	LIMITED	LIMITED
5. Network Types					
Internet Gateway	YES	YES	YES	YES	YES
LAN Gateway	YES	NO	NO	NO	LIMITED
End-User Workstations	YES	NO	NO	NO	NO
WAN Gateway	YES	LIMITED	NO	LIMITED	YES
6. Functionality					
Applications Supported	ALL	LIMITED	LIMITED	LIMITED	LIMITED
Layers protected	2–7	3 Only	3 Only	3 Only	3 Only
Protocols Supported:					
TCP	YES	YES	LIMITED	YES	NO
UDP	YES	YES	LIMITED	YES	NO
IP	YES	YES	LIMITED	YES	NO
RPC	YES	NO	NO	NO	NO
NFS	YES	NO	NO	NO	NO
Other	YES	NO	NO	NO	NO
Applications Supported:					
TELNET, FTP, SMTP	YES	YES	YES	YES	YES
Other Applications	YES	YES	LIMITED	YES	NO
7. Features					
Packet Mode	YES	YES	NO	YES	NO
Connection Mode	YES	NO	NO	NO	NO
Expansion to new protocols	YES	NO	NO	NO	NO
Programmable Rule Base	YES	NO	NO	NO	NO
Programmable Alert Action	YES	YES	NO	NO	NO
Logging facilities	YES	YES	NO	NO	NO
All Headers Can be Verified	YES	NO	NO	NO	NO
Communication Authentication	NO	NO	NO	NO	NO
Data Encryption	NO	NO	YES	NO	NO
Traffic Control Features	YES	NO	NO	NO	NO
Non-Dedicated Gateway Machine	YES	NO	NO	NO	NO
Installation at defending site only	YES	YES	NO	YES	YES
Product Type	Product	Product	Service	Service	Product
8. Price		60K$	18–29K$/ Year	10–30K$ Setup 1.6K$/Mo	1.8K$

(Continued)

EXHIBIT 6-1 (Continued)

NSK BUDGET DRAFT (in 000s of US$)

	1st Year				Year		
	Q1	Q2	Q3	Q4	1st	2nd	3rd
HR							
Developers	1.5	1.8	2	2	1.825	2	2
Programmers	0	0	0	0	0	1	3
Prod Manager	0.7	0.7	1	1	0.85	1	1
Admin	0.6	0.6	0.6	0.6	0.6	1	1
Salaries							
Developers	12	12	15	15	54	60	65
Programmers						35	40
Prod Manager	12	12	15	15	54	60	65
Admin	4	4	4	4	16	16	16
Cost							
Developers	18	21.6	30	30	98.55	120	130
Programmers	0	0	0	0	0	35	120
Prod Manager	8.4	8.4	15	15	45.9	60	65
Admin	2.4	2.4	2.4	2.4	9.6	16	16
Total Salaries	28.8	32.4	47.4	47.4	154.1	231	331
R&D							
Comm Services	2	1.5	1.5	1.5	6.5	8	8
Documentation		10		5	15	10	20
Travel	5	5	5	5	20	25	25
Capital Expense							
Workstations	22	0	0	0	22	20	20
Comm Equipment	0.5				0.5	1	1
Literature	0.5	0.2	0.2	0.2	1.1	2	2
Data storage	2	2	0	0	4	6	6
Software	0	2	0		2	6	8
Total R&D	32	20.7	6.7	11.7	71.1	78	90
SG&A							
Rent	2.1	2.1	2.1	2.1	8.4	12	12
Comm.	1.5	1.5	1.5	1.5	6	8	8
Accounting & Legal	1.5	1.5	1.5	1.5	6	9	9
Office Supplies	1	1	1	1	4	6	6
Tax & Utilities	1.5	1.5	1.5	1.5	6	8	8
Office Equipment	4	2	0	0	6	4	4
Total SG&A	11.6	9.6	7.6	7.6	36.4	47	47
Summary							
Salaries	28.8	32.4	47.4	47.4	156	231	331
R&D	32	20.7	6.7	11.7	71.1	78	90
SG&A	11.6	9.6	7.6	7.6	36.4	47	47
Total	72.4	62.7	61.7	66.7	263.5	356	468
Accumulated	72.4	135.1	196.8	263.5			

(Continued)

EXHIBIT 6-1 (Continued)

SALES SCENARIOS (in 000s of US$)

Scenario A

	1st	2nd	3rd
		Year	
Unit Price	5	5	5
Units Sold	100	300	600
Total revenues	500	1500	3000

Scenario B

	1st	2nd	3rd
		Year	
Network			
Unit Price	15	12	12
Units Sold	12	60	200
Revenues	180	720	2400
Workstations			
Unit Price	1.5	0.8	0.5
Units Sold	250	1000	6000
Revenues	375	800	3000
Total Revenues	555	1520	5400

(*Continued*)

---

everyone on the other network. He searched for an off-the-shelf software solution, but none was acceptable. Shwed had an idea to use programming methods he knew to create a possible solution. He spent two months working to create and test the new software that included a scripting language that easily expressed the semantics of communication protocols. The system was implemented in C and C++. He then received permission to implement it.

When he left the army in 1991, Shwed considered forming a start-up company based on the software he had created. The initial responses he received indicated that people liked his concept but did not consider the market for his software very exciting or promising. He put the idea on hold and joined Optrotech, an Israeli high-tech company.

In late 1992, Shwed read about many companies moving onto the Internet, and he decided to renew his efforts to start a company. The Internet made network security into a larger issue because companies were exploring Internet connectivity and started discussing the issues of security and firewalls over mailing lists. Shwed approached his friends Nacht, who worked with him at Optrotech, and Kramer, who served with Shwed in the Israeli Defense Forces. Shwed had previously mentioned the network security software idea, and they all agreed that it seemed like the right time to become serious about the business. Nacht and Shwed (see Exhibit 6-2) went to a conference on Internet security in San Diego in February 1993 and discussed firewalls and other network

---

EXHIBIT 6-1 *(Continued)*

SUMMARY (in 000s of US$)

	1st Year				Year		
	Q1	Q2	Q3	Q4	1st	2nd	3rd
Budget							
Salaries	28.8	32.4	47.4	47.4	156	231	331
R&D	32	20.7	6.7	11.7	71.1	78	90
SG&A	11.6	9.6	7.6	7.6	36.4	47	47
Total	72.4	62.7	61.7	66.7	263.5	356	468
Accumulated	72.4	135.1	196.8	263.5			
Sales							
Scenario A		100	150	250	500	1500	3000
Scenario B		111	166.5	277.5	555	1520	5400
Total (R)							
Cash Flow	−72.4	48.3	104.8	210.8	291.5	1164	4932
Accumulated	−72.4	−24.1	80.7	291.5	291.5	1450	6000

MARKETING OPTIONS

	Networks			Workstation			Total	Cash Flow
	Price	Units	Rev	Price	Units	Rev		
WS Units Change	15	12	180	1.5	250	375	555	291.5
B	15	12	180	1.5	100	150	330	66.5
C	15	12	180	1.5	60	90	270	6.5
Network Only	20	15	300				300	36.5
B	20	20	400				400	136.5
C	15	30	450				450	186.5
D	10	40	400				400	136.5
WS Only				1.5	250	375	375	111.5
B				1	350	350	350	86.5
C				0.5	600	300	300	36.5
D				0.25	1500	375	375	111.5
Single Product	5	100	500				500	236.5

(Continued)

---

security concepts with technology insiders. Network security now seemed like an exciting market, but many people told Shwed that NSK should focus on Novell networks as opposed to the Internet. Shwed was convinced, however, that Novell networks did not have the growth potential of the Internet.

The Internet, on the other hand, was hosting increasingly complex applications, and companies were having more and more difficulty keeping criminals and hackers away from confidential information.

EXHIBIT 6-1 (Continued)

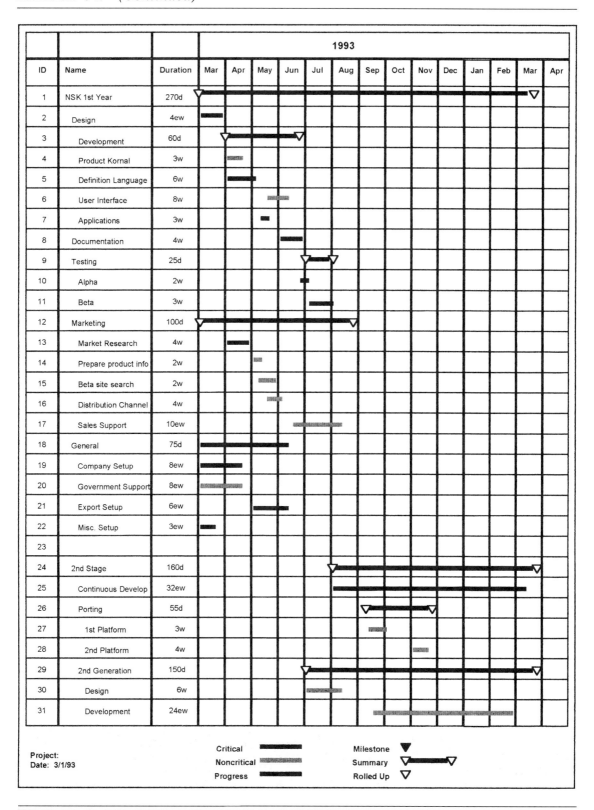

ID	Name	Duration	1993
1	NSK 1st Year	270d	
2	Design	4ew	
3	Development	60d	
4	Product Kornal	3w	
5	Definition Language	6w	
6	User Interface	8w	
7	Applications	3w	
8	Documentation	4w	
9	Testing	25d	
10	Alpha	2w	
11	Beta	3w	
12	Marketing	100d	
13	Market Research	4w	
14	Prepare product info	2w	
15	Beta site search	2w	
16	Distribution Channel	4w	
17	Sales Support	10ew	
18	General	75d	
19	Company Setup	8ew	
20	Government Support	8ew	
21	Export Setup	6ew	
22	Misc. Setup	3ew	
23			
24	2nd Stage	160d	
25	Continuous Develop	32ew	
26	Porting	55d	
27	1st Platform	3w	
28	2nd Platform	4w	
29	2nd Generation	150d	
30	Design	6w	
31	Development	24ew	

Project:
Date: 3/1/93

Critical
Noncritical
Progress

Milestone
Summary
Rolled Up

EXHIBIT 6-2

BIOGRAPHIES OF NSK FOUNDERS

Gil Shwed   Shwed participated in the design and development of operating systems, networking, and network security software for Optrotech, the Israeli Defense Forces, National Semiconductor, and Hebrew University in Jerusalem. He was also a consultant for deploying and developing open systems to corporations in both the United States and Israel.

Shlomo Kramer   Kramer was a cofounder of Algotech, a medical imaging start-up company in Israel, where he directed product analysis, definition, and development. Kramer also managed a large research group in the Israeli Defense Forces, winning the highest Israeli national security award. Kramer earned a B.S. cum laude in Mathematics and Computer Science from Tel Aviv University in 1987 and a M.S. summa cum laude in Computer Science from Hebrew University in Jerusalem. Kramer was 27 in 1993.

Marius Nacht   Nacht was a software development manager at Optrotech, where he co-founded the Graphic Arts Division, developing multidisciplinary software/hardware devices. Previously, he was in charge of the design and development for a large airborne system. Nacht earned a B.S. cum laude in Physics and Mathematics from the Hebrew University in Jerusalem. Nacht was 31 in 1993.

Source: Company documents.

Kramer quit his position at a medical devices company and started working on the software in April 1993. Shwed and Nacht left their jobs in June and joined him.

NETWORK SECURITY

Companies dealt with network security problems by using tools called firewalls. Firewalls were gatekeepers that regulated access to and from private networks while remaining transparent to end-users; at the time, not all application gateway firewalls were transparent. Firewall-1's transparency was a key element of their proposal. Firewalls were usually physically located at the main connection between the private network and an outside network, such as the Internet. Companies could instruct their firewalls to allow access to certain users and generate alarms for unauthorized users. Firewalls needed to be able to relate to many different users, applications, network protocols, operating systems, encryption standards and viruses.

There were two conventional approaches to providing network security with firewalls when Shwed searched for a solution while serving in the Israeli Defense Forces. The fast solution, "packet filtering," filtered packets of data through gateways at routers on the Internet and rejected packets from unauthorized senders. Packet filters could only read the header of packets and could not understand the content of the communication Hackers could circumvent this filter in many ways such as falsifying the return addresses on packets, so this approach could not provide adequate security for corporate networks. The second approach, "proxy server," read every data packet, pieced them together into whole messages, verified the message, broke the message into data packets again, and sent the packets to their final destination. This solution could ensure secure data transmission, but it was unbearably slow, particularly for complicated video and sound data.

NSK's software provided a quick and secure solution by examining each return address like the "packet filter" approach and examining the data like the "proxy server" approach. Instead of reassembling the data packets into whole messages, however, NSK's software analyzed the data packets individually to save significant amounts of time. If a customer desired, NSK could also check for computer viruses or add data encryption at the same time.

INTERNET

In the early 1990s, the Internet experienced explosive growth. Although it was difficult to point to an exact date, sometime in the late spring to early summer of 1992, the Internet entered the general public consciousness in the United States. Companies, universities, students, and individuals began talking about being "on the net." It was estimated that more than 10 million people were connected to the Internet, and the number was doubling every year. It was also estimated that at this rapid rate of growth, everyone would have an e-mail address by the year 2020. The main cause of this growth was the creation of the World Wide Web, which turned the Internet from a black and white text Unix system to a Hyper Text Markup Language (HTML) environment with color, pictures, hyperlinks, sound, music, animations, and video. Still, users found the Web difficult to use because user-friendly browsers were not available.

Uncertainty about intellectual property rights, however, concerned many companies and held back the growth of the Internet. Many commentators questioned how privacy and security should be managed on the Internet. Although commercial use of the Internet was rapidly increasing, many Fortune 500 companies, particularly in the financial services sector, were refraining from using the Internet because of security concerns.

In the January 11, 1993 issue of *Network World*, Paul Saffo, director for the Institute for the Future in Menlo Park, California, said, "You don't have to commission a public opinion poll to know that people are concerned with their privacy and further incursions on it, if you can see how people are reacting publicly to everything from caller ID to credit bureau screwups. The big issue, I think, is to recognize that we need to add some new technology to the mix to help ensure privacy."

ISRAEL

Less than 24 hours after the State of Israel was proclaimed on May 14, 1948, it was invaded by the regular armies of five Arab nations. Israel successfully defended its sovereignty and overcame additional wars with its neighbors in 1956, 1967, and 1974. Given the country's struggle for survival and the urgency of providing for the most basic needs of a population that tripled in its first decade, it was hard to imagine that Israel would make significant progress in economics or technology. By the 1990s, however, Israel had become an economic and technological powerhouse (see Exhibit 6-3). Much of the progress was due to innovative abilities in the applied sciences and technology. As a country almost bereft of natural resources, special emphasis was placed, from the beginning, on the need for advanced education and scientific research. For example, when Israel was faced with well-equipped Arab opponents and Israel had difficulty obtaining weaponry from abroad, the government launched Israel Aircraft Industries and the

---

EXHIBIT 6-3

SELECTED STATISTICS ON ISRAEL

	1965	1975	1985	1992
People				
Population	2,150,000	3,022,000	3,922,000	5,300,000
Number of cities with more than 5,000 residents	53	76	97	120
Pupils in school system	578,000	824,000	1,201,000	1,577,000
Percentage of population with 13 years or more of formal schooling	9%	11.4%	18.7%	27.3%
Economy				
GNP ($ billions)	$2.5	$6.8	$19.1	$64.3
Exports ($ millions)	$749	$4,022	$11,223	$22,863
Imports ($ millions)	$1,269	$8,038	$15,138	$30,583
External debt ($ millions)	$1,540	$8,119	$25,339	$22,516
Inflation	50.0%	28.5%	304.6%	11.9%
T-Bill rate	NA	NA	9.1%	11.0%
Exchange rate per US$1.00	0.0003496	0.0007092	1.4995	2.764

Source: Israel Information Service Gopher.

Technion, the Israel Institute of Technology, opened an aeronautical engineering department in 1951 to provide Israeli-made weapons.

Israel is located on the eastern seaboard of the Mediterranean at the crossroads of Europe, Asia, and Africa. Israel's population was about 5 million in 1991. Created as a homeland for the Jewish people, over 80% of Israel's population are Jews. Israel has experienced more than a fivefold growth in its population since its establishment in 1948. Israel's education system faced the challenge of integrating large numbers of immigrant children from over 70 countries. The mass immigration of the 1950s, mainly Holocaust survivors from postwar Europe and Arab countries, was succeeded in the 1960s by a large influx of Jews from North Africa. In the 1970s the first sizable immigration of Soviet Jews arrived, followed intermittently by smaller groups. In two mass movements, in 1984 and 1991, almost the entire Jewish community from Ethiopia was brought to the country. After the dissolution of the Soviet Union in 1989, over half a million Russian Jews made their way to Israel by 1991 and a steady stream of tens of thousands continued to arrive each year. The government estimated there would be a total of 650,000 Russian immigrants by the end of 1993 and 1 million by 1995. There were approximately 1,500 scientists and researchers per 100,000 Russian Jews which amounted to a massive influx of highly educated, highly motivated intellectuals into Israel.

Education is the second largest functional item in the Israeli national budget after defense. Education is compulsory and tuition-free for ages 5 to 15. The language of instruction is Hebrew in Jewish schools and Arabic in Arab schools. English is the major foreign language taught in Jewish schools and is an optional second language in Arab schools. To address the growing need for technical manpower in industry, Israel's schools have begun implementing computer science courses and bolstering the physical science and mathematics curriculum in the junior high and high schools. A program launched in 1992 called for the installation of a computer in every kindergarten and of one terminal per 10 students in primary and secondary schools.

Although they are autonomous, Israel's universities receive about 60% of their operating budget from the government. Over 240,000 Israelis are university graduates, and they accounted for 15% of the labor force in 1990, up from 7% in 1972. About 20% of these graduates worked in R&D. Israeli universities played an important role in developing and commercializing new technology. For example, the Weitzmann Institute of Science established one of the world's first organizations to commercialize academic research. Such organizations existed in the 1990s on the campuses of all major Israeli universities. Israeli universities also pioneered science-based industrial parks adjacent to their campuses in the 1960s. Many leading Israeli high-tech firms spent their "incubator stage" in these parks.

Israel's government was the primary source of R&D funding. Much of the expenditure was directed toward developing technologies with defense applications. This technology, however, often ended up in the commercial sector as civilian applications were found. In fact, most Israeli high-tech start-ups could trace their technology back to the IDF. Israel was spending more—relative to its size—on R&D than any other developed Western country and invested 3% of the entire GDP on R&D. Over 60% of these funds went to the electronics sector, which was broadly defined to include telecommunications, data communications, medical electronics, defense systems, and software. As a result, Israelis produced over $4 billion of high-technology exports annually. Although they were high quality, Israel's research and development resources were limited because of the small size of the country. The Israeli R&D community, therefore, had to concentrate on selected areas in which it had a competitive advantage. At the same time, it had to maintain some R&D capacity in a broad spectrum of scientific fields to retain an indigenous capacity to absorb new science and technology from other countries. Such diversification had also promoted essential interdisciplinary cross-fertilization. In Israel, there was a growing need to launch more industrially oriented R&D projects to absorb a surplus of new Israeli university graduates as well as highly trained immigrants from the former Soviet Union. According to estimates in 1990, the total number of people engaged in R&D in Israel was expected to reach 76,000 by 1995 and 83,000 by the year 2000. At this rate, Israel would have the world's highest ratio of scientists per capita and an absolute research population equal to that of Switzerland or Sweden by 1995.

Government involvement in the Israeli economy was a hotly debated topic. Many of Israel's early pioneers attempted to mold the state into a government-intensive, socialist-leaning environment. As the economy struggled in the 1970s and 1980s, this socialist legacy came increasingly into question as free market proponents introduced an increasing number of reforms. In 1985, the Israeli government unveiled the Economic Stabilization Plan, which included (1) cutting government subsidies to balance the budget, (2) depreciating the currency, and (3) instituting temporary price controls. This plan successfully reduced inflation from a monthly rate of 20% to 1.5%. At the same time, foreign debt was contained and GDP resumed modest annual growth.

Another government initiative in 1985 was the Law for the Encouragement of Industrial Research and Development. The Law's major objectives included: (1) the development of science-intensive industry while utilizing and expanding the technological and scientific infrastructure and the human resources existing in the state, (2) the improvement of the balance of payments in the state by manufacturing and exporting science intensive products developed herein and reducing the import of such products, and (3) the creation of places of employment in industry and the absorption therein of scientific and technological manpower. The Office of the Chief Scientist was charged with the implementation and administration of this Law. With a 1990 budget of $110 million, the Office of the Chief Scientist received over 1,000 requests annually from about 400 companies of varying sizes.

By 1990, the economy of Israel was approaching the level of development found in Western countries. One-fifth of the civilian labor force was employed in manufacturing, 47% in the services sector, 15% in commerce and finance, and 12% in construction, utilities, transportation and communications. Only about 5% were employed in agriculture. GNP per capita had grown nearly fourfold from 1950 to 1990 at fixed prices. GNP per capita in 1990 was $11,000, which was approximately 75% of Western European countries and about 50% of the $21,000 GNP per capita in the United States. Much of Israel's economic expansion was fueled by exports, which grew as a percentage of net imports from 51% in 1970 to 67% in 1980 and 81% in 1989. Israel expected its economy to grow by 6% annually in the 1990s, compared to 5% in the 1970s and a mere 2% during the 1980s. The Tel Aviv Stock Exchange (TASE) was the best performing exchange in the world in 1992.

Hyperinflation, geopolitical risk, and significant government intervention in the economy deterred much potential foreign investment in Israel before the 1990s. Those investments that had made their way to Israel were in many cases motivated primarily by religious and Zionist sentiment rather than pure economics. The Arab boycott directed at firms doing business with Israel also historically deterred foreign investment. Foreign investors began to reconsider Israel after noticing the government's success in containing prices and reducing foreign debt, the emergence of successful world-class exporters, and the beginnings of improved relations with neighboring nations. Israel established binational industrial R&D agreements with foreign countries including the United States, Canada, France, Holland, and Spain. By 1990, more than 150 foreign companies were involved in R&D investments in Israel. For example, Applied Materials, Digital Equipment Corporation, IBM, Intel, Microsoft, Motorola, Octel Communications, and Sterling Software performed R&D and manufacturing activities through subsidiaries based in Israel. In addition, a growing number of Israeli firms were listed on overseas stock exchanges.

FINANCING OPTIONS

It was against this backdrop that Shwed, Nacht, and Kramer started their company. The first order of business once the software was finished was to find financing. Shwed and his partners considered several financing alternatives.

The Office of the Chief Scientist offered to support 50% of a start-up company's expenses, to $150,000 of annual R&D costs. After the first project (usually at least a year), companies could get 50% of any approved sum in excess of that amount. A start-up company was defined by the Office of the Chief Scientist as any Israeli company that was embarking on its first and only R&D program and whose equity was provided solely by the principal research personnel. In most cases, support recipients were required to repay their grants based on a 2% sales royalty. The Office of the Chief Scientist review of the project requests weighed a number of factors, including innovativeness, export potential, and technological and marketing feasibility before recommending approval to a Research Committee.

Discount Investment Corporation (DIC) of the IDB Holding Group was established in 1961 to participate and invest in the initiation, development, and direction of a diversified portfolio of business enterprises. The criteria for DIC's investment policy included the following: (1) to invest in businesses involved with the Israeli economy with good growth and profit potential in cooperation with overseas and local partners, (2) to place strong emphasis on the industrial and high-technology sectors, particularly in export-oriented companies where the potential exists for long-term growth, (3) to diversify the activities represented in DIC's portfolio in accordance with the changes occurring within the economy, in order to spread the risks involved in long-term operations, and (4) to ensure that the investee companies continually improve the quality of their operations and management while maintaining proper business standards. DIC sought to hold a sufficiently large percentage ownership in investee companies to enable it to influence their direction and management by way of active participation in the activities of their Boards of Directors and their committees. It was DIC's policy to enable additional investors to participate in the development of affiliates by supporting and assisting these companies to issue shares in capital markets in Israel, the United States, and other countries. At the end of 1992, DIC portfolio companies included 23% electronics and communications; 33% energy, shipping, and services; 6% construction and development; 6% investments and finance; and 32% other industry.

DIC's sister company within the IDB Holding Group was PEC Israel Economic Corporation (PEC). PEC organized, acquired interests in, financed, and participated in the management of companies, predominately Israeli or Israel-related companies that had long-term growth potential. PEC was often involved in the early development of a company and participated in the organization, financing, or increase in capital of over 150 Israeli enterprises since its incorporation in 1926. PEC acquired large equity stakes to influence significantly the management and operation of investee companies and to participate actively in management through representation on Boards of Directors. Among other factors, PEC considered quality of management, global or domestic market share, export sales potential, and ability to take advantage of the growth of the domestic Israeli market. PEC emphasized long-term capital appreciation over the ability or intention of an enterprise to provide a cash return in the near future. PEC was involved in a broad cross-section of Israeli companies, including telecommunications and technology, manufacturing, real estate, retailing, shipping, and consumer products. In 1992, PEC went public on the American Stock Exchange. PEC and DIC would often invest in the same companies.

In 1977, Israel and the United States each contributed $30 million to form the Israel-United States Binational Industrial Research and Development Foundation (BIRD). The objective of BIRD was to promote and support joint, nondefense, industrial research and development activities of mutual benefit to the private sectors of the two countries. The endowment was later raised to $110 million. BIRD shared 50% of the cost for each partner in a U.S. company-Israeli company team which convincingly proposed the development and commercialization of any innovative, nondefense high-technology product or process. The investment was a "conditional grant" and could be an off-balance sheet financing. BIRD acquired neither equity nor intellectual property rights. If a project failed, all parties lost their investments. If it succeeded, BIRD received royalties up to a maximum of 150% of the conditional grant. BIRD's royalties could be accounted as a pretax expense. BIRD targeted U.S. companies that (1) were preferably public, (2) developed, manufactured, sold, and supported high-technology products, (3) were perceived to be limited in growth only by their capacity to devise and develop new products, (4) were run by founders or others with a high stake, and

(5) were willing to enter into strategic partnerships with companies having complementary skills and resources. In Israel, BIRD focused on companies that had leading-edge technological capabilities and had the willingness and flexibility to apply their skills to the development of products that fit the business strategy of a proven U.S. company. BIRD was willing to consider any size Israeli company and medium-sized U.S. companies with $10–$500 million in annual sales.

Yozma Venture Capital Ltd. (Yozma means "initiative" in Hebrew) was a $100 million venture capital fund established and wholly owned by the Israeli government in June 1992. Yozma had three goals: (1) to promote the growth of promising high-technology firms in Israel, (2) to encourage the involvement of major international corporations in the Israeli technology sector, and (3) to stimulate the development of a professionally managed, private sector venture capital industry in Israel. Yozma served as a catalyst for international investment in Israel by cooperating with experienced venture firms and major corporations in the establishment of new venture capital funds and also by investing directly up to $2 million per company with one or more partners that could add value to Israeli companies with high-growth potential. Yozma shared the risks associated with its venture investments, but offered its partners an option to increase their upside by buying out Yozma's share of the investment within five years on attractive terms, usually LIBOR plus 1%. Yozma's direct investments could not exceed 49% of the equity in a particular company and needed to carry a proportionate share of voting rights and Board of Directors representation in the company. One of Yozma's first direct investments was AG Associates (Israel) Ltd., a subsidiary of the American firm AG Associates, which was a $30 million company that developed and manufactured chemical vapor deposition equipment and flexible cluster tools for the semiconductor industry. Yozma invested $1 million along with an additional $1 million from the Investment Company of Bank Hapoalim.

Yozma partnered with Advent International Corporation (Advent), which was a Boston-based international investment organization, and DIC in 1992 to create a $30–50 million fund to target small to medium sized Israeli technology companies. Advent managed over $750 million for venture capital investment from both financial institutions and major corporations. Advent and its international affiliates were known as the Advent Network and collectively managed $1.75 billion worldwide. Advent provided access to its international network of investment affiliates to provide management training, assistance in the evaluation of investment opportunities, and support for international development.

Yozma was in the progress of raising funds in 1993 to form another partnership with the Walden Group, an international venture capital firm that had invested extensively in the United States and the Far East, and Oxton International Capital Corporation, a specialist in later-stage investments with strong ties to Taiwan. The fund was expected to raise $30 million to invest in early-stage Israeli companies with a focus on high-growth technology start-ups and offshore companies that had businesses related to Israel. Walden offered potential portfolio companies access to relationships in the United States and the Pacific Rim to help them establish and expand marketing and distribution.

Elron Electronic Industries Ltd. (Elron) was a multinational company formed in 1962 and based in Israel. PEC held a significant interest in the company, which was publicly traded on NASDAQ and TASE. Elron conducted global businesses through a group of subsidiaries and affiliated companies in well-defined market segments that included medical diagnostic imaging, advanced defense electronics, data communications, manufacturing automation, semiconductor products, software products, and sophisti-

EXHIBIT 6-4

COMPARABLE PUBLICLY TRADED COMPANIES (DOLLARS IN MILLIONS)

Borland International, Inc.	1989	1990	1991	1992
Sales	$397.8	$378.6	$457.3	$482.5
SG&A	$187.9	$217.8	$274.2	$306.6
Cap Ex	NA	$25.1	$39.9	$59.7
Op Inc Bef Dep	$61.8	($12.2)	$7.8	$12.6
Net Income	$41.3	($9.3)	$4.8	($14.1)
Total Assets	$355.1	$349.4	$373.5	$364.8
Current Assets	NA	NA	$255.2	$240.4
Current Liab.	NA	NA	$111.3	$106.8
Debt	$20.2	$17.6	$15.8	$29.6
Net Worth	$258.7	$247.5	$246.5	$228.3
Beta	NA	NA	NA	1.86
P/E Ratio		NM		NM

Corel Corporation	1989	1990	1991	1992
Sales	NA	$29.2	$52.2	$90.1
SG&A	NA	$11.1	$19.9	$37.8
Cap Ex	NA	$1.9	$6.5	$15.5
Op Inc Bef Dep	NA	$9.7	$19.0	$22.3
Net Income	NA	$7.1	$12.1	$12.3
Total Assets	NA	$41.9	$59.4	$105.3
Current Assets	NA	NA	$51.6	$86.5
Current Liab.	NA	NA	$9.6	$6.5
Debt	NA	$0.0	$0.0	$0.0
Net Worth	NA	$33.9	$49.8	$98.8
Beta	NA	NA	NA	NA
P/E Ratio	NA			

Microsoft Corporation	1989	1990	1991	1992
Sales	$803.5	$1,183.4	$1,843.4	$2,758.7
SG&A	$246.9	$356.9	$595.6	$944.2
Cap Ex	$89.4	$158.1	$264.4	$316.6
Op Inc Bef Dep	$242.2	$393.2	$649.8	$996.0
Net Income	$170.5	$279.2	$462.7	$708.1
Total Assets	$720.6	$1,105.3	$1,644.2	$2,639.9
Current Assets	$468.9	$719.9	$1,028.5	$1,769.7
Current Liab.	$158.8	$186.8	$293.4	$446.9
Debt	$25.4	$6.5	$19.5	$8.3
Net Worth	$561.8	$918.6	$1,350.8	$2,193.0
Beta	1.36	1.36	1.36	1.23
P/E Ratio	17.49	32.48	27.58	29.05

Sun Microsystems, Inc.	1989	1990	1991	1992
Sales	$1,765.4	$2,466.2	$3,221.3	$3,588.9
SG&A	$432.6	$588.0	$812.2	$983.6
Cap Ex	$204.8	$212.9	$192.3	$185.6
Op Inc Bef Dep	$88.5	$177.3	$294.9	$261.1
Net Income	$60.8	$111.2	$190.3	$173.3
Total Assets	$1,269.1	$1,778.6	$2,326.3	$2,671.6
Current Assets	$879.8	$1,297.4	$1,801.0	$2,148.4
Current Liab.	$462.5	$492.9	$712.6	$838.9
Debt	$144.7	$358.9	$401.2	$347.6
Net Worth	$661.8	$926.8	$1,212.6	$1,485.1
Beta	1.14	1.16	1.21	1.42
P/E Ratio	22.37	28.10	15.07	15.28

Source: Compiled from company financials and the Center for Research on Security Prices.

cated productivity tools. Elron was dedicated to building up electronic industries based primarily on Israeli know-how. By using its expertise in marketing, management, and finance, Elron supported its companies to become successful enterprises. Elron Technologies Inc., a wholly owned subsidiary located in New York, provided marketing support, U.S. investor relations, and other services to Elron's in-house projects. Eltam Technology Incubator Ltd. was formed in 1991 by Elron and Matam, a subsidiary of Haifa Economic Corp., to provide entrepreneurs and scientists, mainly new immigrants, with central services as well as managerial, financial, and technical guidance and to help them develop technological ideas into commercial applications.

Elron invested $2.5 million as a limited partner in Athena Venture Partners L.P., which was formed in 1985 in the United States to invest in high-technology enterprises. The fund raised $29 million and built a portfolio consisting of 18 high-technology companies. Half were based in the United States, and half in Israel.

Finally, there were several investor groups located in Israel and the United States that advertised in Israeli newspapers. Shwed had heard that a software group called BRM was experiencing high growth in their software business and might be interested in investing in additional fields. BRM was started by four young Israeli software engineers in the late 1980s to develop antivirus software. Sales of their product had grown 700% annually through 1993, and the number of employees had grown to 18 software engineers and two administrative support. BRM marketed its products through agents, including PF1 of Tel Aviv, Israel; Infodidact of Paris, France; and Fifth Generation Systems of Baton Rouge, Louisiana. BRM was funded solely by its founders. They avoided government funding sources because of the limitations that accompanied such grants. For example, the Chief Scientist required that the intellectual property from any technology developed with grants from his office remain in Israel.

CONCLUSION

Nacht returned on his motorbike with another box of Coca-Cola bottles. As the three partners opened another bottle of Coke, Shwed wondered how they would be able to access venture capital without any contacts in the venture capital community. Furthermore, Shwed was concerned that the fact that NSK had no track record might scare away potential investors. Shwed also wanted to retain control of NSK. He believed that he, Kramer, and Nacht could run the company.

Even if NSK could attract capital, Shwed realized the company needed help in selling and marketing its product. None of the three partners, however, had any marketing or sales experience, nor had they lived in the United States. Shwed, however, believed NSK must dominate the U.S. market if it was going to become a successful software company.

Shwed understood that the partners would need to hire more people to provide the experience the partners lacked. He did not want to hire any additional employees, however, until NSK had a multimillion dollar contract. The partners prided themselves on being frugal and effective and did not want to spend money unless absolutely necessary. The partners did not plan to create a dedicated sales force and preferred to maintain a low infrastructure by partnering with existing resellers. Shwed wondered if the financial markets would give NSK a valuation like U.S. software companies (see Exhibit 6-4).

7

Tutor Time (A)

John Floegel put down the phone and wondered what to do next. He and a friend, Daniel Hopkins, had offered to partner with Tutor Time Child Care Systems, Inc., an early learning care franchiser, in a complex transaction. Richard Weissman, president of Tutor Time, had just given Floegel his answer. He would not undertake the deal in which Floegel and Hopkins would have ended up with a sizable stake in Tutor Time, but he was so impressed with them that he was making Floegel an offer to join the company as senior vice president of Corporate Development.

This was not the answer Floegel had expected. While he was very excited about Tutor Time's prospects and respected Weissman's business skills, he wondered what the constraints of his new position would be? He had always been an entrepreneur and wanted to participate in running a company. Even though he had taken a somewhat unorthodox route to being an entrepreneur, he was certain he was up to the task.

But now many questions raced through his mind. Was this the right opportunity for him? Did he really bring value to the table? Was Tutor Time the right company to join? If so, what should he demand in the form of ownership and responsibility? These were difficult questions for which he had no answers.

BACKGROUND

John Floegel graduated from Georgetown University and then attended the University of Pennsylvania Law School. After law school, Floegel took a position practicing law at a mergers and acquisitions boutique in Manhattan. Floegel became disenchanted with the practice of law and began looking for a business in which to become involved. He knew that corporate law was not his destiny. He was determined to be an entrepreneur; now he only needed to find the appropriate business.

Floegel had already experienced business success. While still in high school, he had started a landscaping business with a friend in the Long Island Hamptons. After building the company over several summers, Floegel and his partner sold the business for a

Professor Paul A. Gompers prepared this case as the basis for class discussion rather than to illustrate either effective or ineffective handling of an administrative situation. Some information in this case has been disguised.

substantial profit. Rather than starting from scratch again, Floegel intended to purchase into an existing business. During the first several months of his search, Floegel met with business brokers and toured small companies. He let everyone know he was interested in buying or becoming involved with a business and canvassed the opportunities.

He also considered a number of franchise opportunities including child care companies. A chief attraction of starting a child care center was that Floegel knew he could get a quality center director in the person of his wife, Chris, a local school teacher. Chris had a master's degree in primary education and seemed perfect for the job; she truly loved children and she was bright and energetic. Hopkins, who had been unimpressed with the other businesses that Floegel had been considering, liked the child care idea, particularly if Chris agreed to run the center. In addition, Floegel was very familiar with the concept of franchising. His family was a major McDonald's franchisee, at one point owning nine restaurants. With that, the two determined to open the best possible child care center.

THE CHILD CARE INDUSTRY: THE MARKET

In 1994, the for-profit child care was an $8.6 billion industry. U.S. Census data suggested the country's birthrate would remain stable at about 4 million new births per year for the foreseeable future. Other demographic trends, however, indicated a growing market for center-based child care. Women's labor force participation had been growing for decades and was expected to continue (the proportion of mothers of preschool children who worked outside the home grew from 30% in 1970 to 59% in 1990). Likewise, the increasing mobility of the American family and the growing number of single-parent households meant that traditional family-related child care arrangements broke down more frequently. This in turn translated into higher demand for center-based care. Another positive trend was the increasing urbanization of the U.S. population. As the population became increasingly urbanized, the potential for larger, profitable centers increased. (See Exhibit 7-1)

COMPETITION

In early 1995, there were five publicly traded child care companies. The industry was extremely fragmented, however, with the 50 largest providers accounting for just 11% of the market. Providers ranged from large national chains like Kindercare, LaPetite Academy, Inc., and Children's Discovery Learning Centers to single-site mom and pop operations. (See Exhibit 7-2 and Exhibit 7-3)

In general, the national competitors had experienced periods of financial difficulty. Kindercare went through a Chapter 11 bankruptcy reorganization. LaPetite was taken private under distress through a leveraged buyout. Children's Discovery Learning Centers sustained significant losses in the late 1980s when a regulatory shift in Arizona rendered its centers there unprofitable. The sixth largest provider, Nobel Education Dynamics Inc., suffered operating losses in both 1990 and 1991 and was forced to adopt a plan to divest 48 centers after it defaulted on its senior credit facilities. Industry participants tended to dismiss these troubles and suggested they were the result of the unique white collar recession of the early 1990s which hit providers that had become excessively leveraged during the 1980s.

Against this background of financial distress, the terms of competition in the early 1990s got tougher. Larger centers of 10,000 square feet and more were becoming more

EXHIBIT 7-1

PERCENTAGE OF THE U.S. POPULATION LIVING IN URBAN AREAS

% of U.S. Population living in Living in Urban Areas

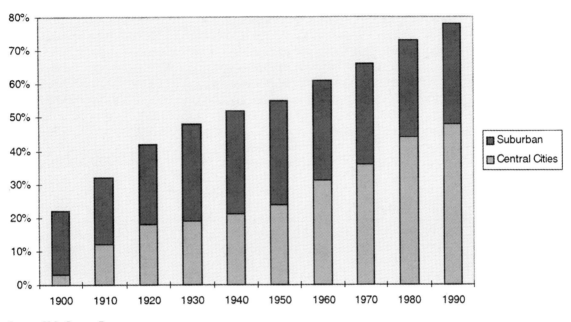

Source: U.S. Census Bureau.

EXHIBIT 7-2

NATIONAL CHILD CARE OPERATORS IN 1995

Rank	Organization	Headquarters	Capacity	Centers
1	KinderCare Learning Centers, Inc.	Montgomery, AL	140,000	1195
2	La Petite Academy, Inc.	Kansas City, MO	94,000	785
3	Children's World Learning Centers	Golden, CO	65,500	525
4	Childtime Childcare, Inc.	Farmington Hills, MI	14,270	127
5	Children's Discovery Centers	San Rafael, CA	11,300	135
6	Nobel Education Dynamics	Cherry Hill NJ	10,200	73
7	Tutor Time Learning Centers	Fort Lauderdale, FL	9,200	46
8	YMCA of Greater Houston	Houston, TX	8,500	219
9	Neighborhood Services Head Start	Detroit, MI	6,192	96
10	Redlands Christian Migrant Association	Immokalee, FL	5,434	67

Source: Child Care Information Exchange, May 1993 [VIA Mabon Securities Analyst Report].

EXHIBIT 7-3

SELECTED FINANCIAL DATA ON NATIONAL CHILDCARE PROVIDERS

Children's Discovery

	1991	1992	1993	1994
Sales	$19.82	$25.66	$38.56	$55.32
SG&A	1.78	2.47	3.51	4.79
Cap Ex	0.60	0.87	1.44	2.37
Op Inc Bef Dep	1.14	1.01	3.65	6.78
Net Inc	−0.30	−0.62	1.11	2.76
Tot Assets	18.84	23.53	36.09	64.69
Current Assets	5.71	3.66	12.62	25.68
Current Liabilities	1.95	2.92	3.79	4.43
Debt	5.14	6.87	8.21	15.43
Net Worth	11.56	13.57	24.42	45.46
Beta	NA	0.66	0.42	0.49
P/E Ratio	−16.96	−14.02	25.71	19.96

Nobel Education Dynamics

	1991	1992	1993	1994
Sales	34.67	33.50	32.59	34.37
SG&A	2.38	2.95	2.56	2.70
Cap Ex	0.57	0.49	0.92	1.37
Op Inc Bef Dep	5.05	4.45	4.45	4.58
Net Inc	−3.82	1.80	1.71	2.34
Tot Assets	27.35	24.23	22.61	23.23
Current Assets	1.39	1.97	2.44	2.32
Current Liabilities	27.10	5.96	5.55	6.52
Debt	25.27	19.81	13.94	10.04
Net Worth	−3.78	−0.28	3.73	8.30
Beta	NA	NA	NA	NA
P/E Ratio	−0.95	NA	8.75	8.65

Childtime Learning Centers

	1994	1995
Sales	$55.34	$65.62
SG&A	6.00	6.18
Cap Ex	1.19	2.21
Op Inc Bef Dep	6.09	7.23
Net Inc	1.85	2.41
Tot Assets	40.97	44.69
Current Assets	3.03	5.84
Current Liabilities	8.23	6.35
Debt	19.42	1.24
Net Worth	11.24	32.95
Beta	NA	NA
P/E Ratio	NA	15.21

Sunrise Preschools

	1991	1992	1993	1994
Sales	$10.42	$10.43	$11.04	$10.63
SG&A	1.42	1.19	1.41	1.40
Cap Ex	0.07	0.10	0.16	0.08
Op Inc Bef Dep	0.18	0.61	0.48	0.77
Net Inc	−0.34	0.15	0.11	0.88
Tot Assets	2.18	1.82	1.85	2.24
Current Assets	0.48	0.39	0.49	0.54
Current Liabilities	1.35	1.13	1.29	1.04
Debt	1.08	0.89	0.73	0.55
Net Worth	−0.83	−0.73	−0.67	0.16
Beta	NA	NA	NA	NA
P/E Ratio	NA	NA	NA	NA

Kinder-Care

	1991	1992	1993	1994
Sales	$411.04	$437.20	$488.73	$506.51
SG&A	NA	NA	NA	NA
Cap Ex	27.49	34.50	35.71	74.38
Op Inc Bef Dep	41.15	59.59	72.31	78.86
Net Inc	−50.71	−10.72	17.43	22.07
Tot Assets	486.94	516.28	456.92	494.26
Current Assets	35.78	65.81	38.31	26.57
Current Liabilities	488.73	84.99	54.22	59.45
Debt	402.15	43.64	178.69	160.39
Net Worth	−34.16	−44.89	206.91	244.24
Beta	NA	0.24	0.60	0.59
P/E Ratio	−0.22	−3.57	12.89	12.38

Source: Compustat.

prevalent due to their superior margins. Expensive investment in the physical appearance of the center was also increasingly important for attracting children and their parents. Furthermore, certain national providers were offering, at least in some centers, creative educational curricula featuring multimedia computers and full age-specific developmental programs for the children. Sophisticated business systems, especially pertaining to labor costs, were increasingly important to center profitability. A small and innovative Florida franchiser, Tutor Time Child Care Systems, Inc., had been the chief initiator of a number of these trends.

To improve profitability, many providers had also begun to experiment with a variety of supplemental programs. These included after-school programs for school-aged children, parent/child gymnastics and other activities, reading programs, summer camps, transportation to and from the child care centers, kindergarten, and schooling for grades one through six. The national providers had also begun to target large corporations in an attempt to jointly provide on-site child care as an employee benefit.

Throughout the early 1990s, it became increasingly apparent that the smaller operators lacked the resources to keep up with the national players' continuous concept innovation. Similarly, long-term leases for smaller centers were becoming a competitive disadvantage. The stiffening terms of competition were beginning to cause a shakeout of the mom and pop operators, with many closing and others selling out to acquisition-hungry Children's Discovery Learning Centers.

CUSTOMERS

The target market for most national providers was middle- to upper-middle-income families with children up to five years old. Anecdotal evidence suggested that in 1995 many areas were still lacking quality, affordable child care. Many centers reported long waiting lists as well as success in pushing through price increases. No meaningful group purchasing had been seen in the industry. Therefore, customers' chief means of resisting the price of child care was to utilize one of many substitutes. The substitutes for for-profit center-based child care included parents, relatives, personal nannies, church organizations, YMCA programs, and government-run programs. These arrangements were only sporadically available and might have been unaffordable. Customer bargaining power was further reduced by the parental tendency to want to provide the best care possible to one's children. Parents had high switching cost because frequent changing of a child's care provider could be mentally and emotionally traumatic for a child.

LABOR

Despite relatively low teacher wages in the industry, the cost of labor was the major expense in running a child care center. On average, labor costs equaled 55% of revenues in the child care industry. Accordingly, management of labor expense was critical to the profitability and viability of a child care business. At the same time, state-mandated teacher/child ratios constrained management of this expense. The uneven flow of students and the large number of part-time students introduced variability into the labor expense ratios as well. Likewise, larger centers tended to decrease the significance of fixed labor such as the administrator and the receptionist. The variability of this expense across providers was demonstrated by the experience of three companies in 1994: Children's Discovery Centers experienced in-center payroll expense equal to 54.6% of revenues; Nobel Education Dynamics reported labor costs of 44.5%; and Tutor Time's labor costs were approximately 38% of revenue.

INVESTMENT DECISION AND STRUCTURE

Trends in the child care industry in late 1992 suggested that although child care was very much a local business, solitary child care providers were unlikely to prosper without the support of a national organization. Floegel and Hopkins felt that if they were to enter the business, it would be best to purchase a franchise from a national franchiser. Because his family had been franchisees for years, Floegel in particular was comfortable with the franchise form of business.

Floegel spearheaded the review of national franchisers. He reviewed their promotional materials, toured their facilities, and interviewed their operators. He also compared the franchisers with the national child care operators to judge the long-term competitive prospects for a franchised center. Floegel's review of industry participants revealed that Tutor Time Child Care Systems, Inc. had the best curriculum and business systems in the industry, franchise, or otherwise. The Tutor Time Centers were far more aesthetically pleasing and ran more smoothly than the competitions' centers. Accordingly, he set up a meeting with Tutor Time's top two executives, Michael Weissman and his son Richard.

Tutor Time's predecessor corporation, led by the Weissmans, opened its first center in 1980 in Boca Raton, Florida. As the business grew to several centers, the company developed and implemented centralized computer systems to track and control the tuitions, financial statements, medical records, labor costs, attendance, payroll budgeting, cash positions and overall profitability of each site. He also developed a strong sense of what demographics were necessary to support a center of a given size. In 1987, the company purchased the exclusive rights to use a preschool education curriculum developed by child development experts at Brigham Young University. The company then combined its business systems with the upgraded curriculum into a franchiseable child care product. Tutor Time was incorporated in 1988 as a vehicle to market and sell Tutor Time's child care franchise system.

Floegel's meeting with the Weissmans went well. He was particularly impressed by the fact that the Weissmans, unlike the heads of their competitors, had personally run child care centers for a decade before setting up their national chain. Floegel also discovered that others believed the Tutor Time operating concept was the best available. NASA's Kennedy Space Center had selected Tutor Time over several national bidders to be the exclusive child care provider for children of Kennedy Space Center scientists, astronauts, and other employees. More critically, Floegel's financial projections indicated that the Tutor Time concept would likely yield an internal rate of return of at least 30% on equity capital.

Floegel and Hopkins determined to pursue the purchase and development of a Tutor Time franchise. Floegel would be the majority owner and capital provider and would be responsible for the bulk of the legwork involved in getting the venture off the ground. Floegel formed a subchapter S corporation named Amerikids Corporation ("Amerikids"), and installed himself, his wife Chris, and Hopkins on the Board of Directors. Tutor Time required a franchise fee of $27,500 and a site development fee of between $80,000 and $100,000. Amerikids would be initially capitalized with $190,000—$120,000 of debt and $70,000 of equity. Floegel strategically invited a few family members and friends to invest in both the debt and the equity in the hope that a syndicate for future deals could be formed. The precise site development fee would be negotiated once the parties had agreed to a site for the Amerikids franchise.

SITE SELECTION

Regardless of the industry, the site selection process for franchisees was uncertain and could be quite protracted. Typically, the franchiser's in-house real estate personnel generated site leads by contacting real estate brokers, landlords, and developers in the franchisee's target area. Franchisees waiting for sites were kept abreast of the search process and could suggest sites that they identified on their own. Although the franchisee might be involved in lease negotiations for a prospective site, more often the franchiser's real estate department simply presented the franchisee with a fully negotiated lease. The franchisee then had the opportunity to accept or reject the lease with minimal additional negotiation.

Tutor Time presented Amerikids with a number of sites. Floegel was also quite active in attempting to locate a site on his own. After months of reviewing demographic information, getting up at 5:00 A.M. to watch traffic flows, and driving through neighborhoods to look for tell-tale swing sets, Floegel decided on a site for their child care center in Succasunna, New Jersey. The site, a stand-alone building in a large shopping center, had an ideal traffic flow. It was directly across the street from a medical office building housing a large number of pediatricians and dentists. The 10,000 square foot site, however, was dilapidated and would require an expensive build-out to convert it into a Tutor Time center.

After extensive negotiations between Amerikids, the building landlord, and Lifecare Acquisitions (Tutor Time's real estate arm), it was agreed that the landlord would finance the build-out at approximately $25.00/square foot and that Lifecare would be responsible for any excess development expense (or would receive any savings). In return for an $80,000 development fee from Amerikids, Tutor Time would be responsible for putting the project out to bid and managing the construction from its offices in Florida. Amerikids had only limited liability for lease payments. Amerikids also obtained a rent and royalty holiday extending four months from the certified opening of the school. These provisions would safeguard Amerikids from both construction delays and the possibility of weak initial market response to its school. Tutor Time's representatives would later remark that they left the Succasunna negotiations with substantial respect for the Amerikids group and, in particular, for Floegel's ability to negotiate a tough, thorough deal in the minimum amount of time.

THE SITE BUILD-OUT

The build-out, which was scheduled to take six months, commenced in January 1993. It was critical to have the school open by midsummer because August and September were by far the largest sign-up months for child care centers. The project was one of Tutor Time's first in the northeastern United States, and it soon became apparent that both Lifecare and its designated general contractor had underestimated the cost of the build-out. Squabbling broke out among Floegel, the landlord, and Tutor Time over responsibility for cost overruns. Both Amerikids and the landlord steadfastly refused to renegotiate the deal or contribute extra cash. Construction on the Succasunna site was delayed off and on for weeks as money for the subcontractors arrived in dribs and drabs. When slow payment by Tutor Time persisted, Floegel began to suspect that the cause of the payment delays might go beyond his site. Calls to other franchisees in the midst of build-outs confirmed that the company was increasingly slow with its construction installment payments. Tutor Time was experiencing cash flow problems. But other than complain, there was little they could do except wait.

In the meantime, Chris had been marketing the center for an early July opening and had received an encouraging response from the community. Based on Floegel's projections (see Exhibit 7-4), the Succasunna center would be very profitable if it met projections. Chris also began to interview prospective teachers. Increasingly, however, she feared that the center would not open on time. Besides the obviously negative effects on the center's first year cash flow, she was concerned about her personal credibility with teachers and parents if the center did not open on time. Her relations with Tutor Time became increasingly strained as construction delays persisted.

The Succasunna center finally opened in late February 1994, seven months late. Final construction overruns totaled more than $130,000. Lifecare incurred liability for seven $15,000 monthly rent payments and was still responsible for four more monthly payments on Amerikids behalf. Worse still, Tutor Time would draw no royalty payments from the Amerikids school for four months. The Succasunna deal put a significant cash strain on the rapidly growing company, but it exposed a number of flaws in the Lifecare lease process. Despite the hit taken by Lifecare and Tutor Time, the principals grudgingly admired the deal that Floegel had managed to cut for Amerikids and the strength with which he clung to it.

From its second month of operation, the Succasunna center was cash flow positive. In the early months, however, the Amerikids operation deviated substantially from Tutor Time operating systems. Communication lines had been strained by the build-out delays, and the relationship between Succasunna's operators and Tutor Time was tense. As the center's enrollment grew, the difficulties of running a child care center became more apparent to Chris. Despite paying wages at the top of the local market, staff turnover was high. Her labor cost ratios were above 50%, more than 10 percentage points above Tutor Time standards. Parents were demanding and, sometimes, unreasonable. Despite working long hours and weekends, Chris felt she was always behind. She was also unhappy with how little time she, as director, got to spend with the children. She was increasingly aware that her experience was not unlike that of many other center directors (see Exhibit 7-5). Ultimately, she decided to hire a new director to return to teaching in the public schools.

Chris's successor, a 20-year child care veteran, also found the director's job to be difficult. She found the center's size to be overwhelming, and she clashed with the staff. Staff dissension became palpable. The new director also did not respond well to the involvement and direction of Tutor Time's field personnel. During a discussion with Floegel regarding possible operational changes, the new director threatened to quit. This uncertainty was intolerable. Floegel and Hopkins determined that another, more dramatic management change was needed. They also knew, however, that there was a limit to how much turnover the parents would tolerate in the director's position. They considered personally managing the center, but neither was available to do so on a full-time basis. Floegel was busy with other business ventures, and Hopkins was halfway through the University of Chicago MBA program.

Instead, they offered to sell the Weissmans the opportunity to buy 51% of Amerikids stock. Tutor Time would also manage the center. The Weissmans and Tutor Time accepted the offer and assumed control of the center in October 1994. The change in control was explained to parents as part of a broader Tutor Time initiative in the Northeast. Succasunna was to become Tutor Time's showcase center in the region. The strategy worked. The center experienced few lost customers, and within months it was running smoothly. The effects of the Tutor Time systems and curriculum on the center were dramatic. Children, parents, and staff were all happier. More tangibly, labor expenses quickly declined to nearly 40% of revenues. Given the widely varying need for teachers, limiting excess personnel was the key to lower labor costs. Tutor Time's systems were able to manage personnel costs much better than Floegel and Hopkins could.

Despite the early difficulties, the Succasunna center had a profitable first year and its future looked bright. In its first year of operation, the center retired $60,000 of its $110,000 in private debt. Monthly revenues in January 1995 had reached nearly $65,000, and the center was expected to net approximately $150,000 on sales of nearly $1 million in 1995.

TUTOR TIME'S RAPID GROWTH

Throughout 1994, Tutor Time seemed to be entering a new league. In January, the company announced to its franchisees that a series of contracts had been signed with a major player in the entertainment industry. Also, Tutor Time was actively exploring the licensing of its Pookie Panda™ and other characters for use in children's video programming, television products, toys, games, and software through a license granted to the entertainment executive. Tutor Time also opened 16 new schools, had 64 schools under construction, and sold nearly 100 franchises in 1994.

Against this backdrop, Hopkins and Floegel decided to explore the possibility of financing more joint-venture schools with Tutor Time. They knew Tutor Time had limited growth capital and that the company had recently enlisted the help of a top-notch regional investment bank to raise money in a stock offering. It appeared that Tutor Time was enamored with the profitability of the northeastern schools and that management was interested in building revenues and profits through the corporate ownership and operation of select schools. In January 1995, Floegel and Hopkins flew to Ft. Lauderdale to gauge the Weissmans' interest in joint-venture schools.

The parties met for a total of eight hours over three days. Floegel and Hopkins obtained a good feel for the Weissmans' expansion plans and financing prospects. The Weissmans' expressed an interest in working with Hopkins and Floegel in the future and made subtle overtures regarding bringing the two in-house. The parties agreed that Floegel and Hopkins should put their ideas in a more concrete form and send it to Tutor Time.

FINANCIAL DIFFICULTIES AT TUTOR TIME

While Floegel and Hopkins were in the process of putting a proposal together, Tutor Time encountered a severe cash flow squeeze. The reasons for the cash flow crisis were many and interrelated. They included: undercapitalization; an ill-advised partnership; construction overruns; and litigation resulting from the first three problems.

UNDERCAPITALIZATION

Tutor Time companies had been built with a minimum of outside capital. The company's 1994 financial statements indicated less than $1 million of contributed equity capital and no debt. Its operations had been sustained and had grown with cash from

EXHIBIT 7-4

PROJECTED PERFORMANCE FOR SUCCASUNNA CENTER

Assumptions

Weeks/month	4.33
Center size	10,000
Student capacity	190
Student days/month capacity	4,117

Month	Mar. 1	Apr. 2	May 3	June 4	July 5	Aug. 6	Sept. 7	Oct. 8	Nov. 9	Dec. 10	Jan. 11	Feb. 12	Year 1 Total
Revenue													
Full-time students	43	52	58	65	71	83	90	92	97	99	103	104	80
Average weekly tuition	125	125	125	125	125	125	125	125	125	125	125	125	125
Full-time tuition	23,292	28,167	31,417	35,208	38,458	44,958	48,750	49,833	52,542	53,625	55,792	56,333	518,375
Part-time students	5	10	15	20	25	25	30	27	33	35	33v	33	291
Average days/month	10	10	10	10	10	10	10	10	10	10	10	10	10
Average tuition/day	27	27	27	27	27	27	27	27	27	27	27	27	324
Part-time tuition	1,350	2,700	4,050	5,400	6,750	6,750	8,100	7,290	8,910	9,450	8,910	8,910	78,570
Total tuition	24,642	30,867	35,467	40,608	45,208	51,708	56,850	57,123	61,452	63,075	64,702	65,243	596,945
Capacity utilization	23.8%	29.8%	34.2%	39.1%	43.4%	49.8%	54.7%	55.0%	59.1%	60.6%	62.2%	62.8%	47.9%
Operating costs (in US $)													
Fixed costs													
Advertising	1,774	309	300	325	500	500	250	457	2,218	—	500	652	7,786
CAMS	650	700	675	650	700	700	750	912	735	900	785	913	9,070
Data fees	250	250	250	250	250	250	250	250	250	250	250	250	3,000
Wages	4,167	4,167	4,167	4,167	6,667	6,667	6,667	6,667	6,667	6,667	6,800	6,800	70,271
Rent	—	—	—	—	12,863	12,863	12,863	12,863	12,863	12,864	12,863	12,863	102,902
General repairs	246	309	355	406	452	517	568	571	615	631	647	652	5,969
Lease guarantee fee	417	417	417	417	417	417	417	417	430	442	442	442	5,089
Insurance	1,240	1,240	1,240	1,240	1,240	1,240	1,240	1,350	1,290	1,325	1,100	1,044	14,789
Janitorial	1,100	1,100	1,100	1,050	1,050	1,050	1,050	1,050	1,050	1,050	1,050	1,174	12,874
P/R prof. fees	271	216	—	—	—	—	—	—	307	500	—	—	1,294
Telephone	1,331	1,111	1,277	1,462	1,627	1,861	2,047	971	1,045	1,236	1,027	457	15,452
Utilities	1,281	1,173	1,383	1,421	1,718	1,836	2,274	1,142	1,966	1,700	2,006	2,135	20,036
Total fixed	12,727	10,991	11,163	11,388	27,484	27,900	28,375	26,651	29,436	27,563	27,470	27,383	268,533

(Continued)

EXHIBIT 7-4 *(Continued)*

Month	Mar. 1	Apr. 2	May 3	June 4	July 5	Aug. 6	Sept. 7	Oct. 8	Nov. 9	Dec. 10	Jan. 11	Feb. 12	Year 1 Total
Variable													
Avg. student/teacher ratio	7	7	7.5	7.5	7.5	7.5	7.5	7.5	7.5	9	10	10	8.0
Avg. teacher wage	6.75	6.75	6.75	6.75	6.75	6.75	6.75	6.75	6.75	6.75	6.75	6.75	6.75
Avg. hrs./day	8	8	8	8	8	8	8	8	8	8	8	8	8
Wages	7,573	9,463	10,128	11,580	12,876	14,748	16,200	16,296	17,508	14,970	13,833	13,950	159,125
Food costs	936	1,173	1,348	1,543	1,718	1,965	2,160	857	922	946	971	1,240	15,778
General supplies	1,109	617	532	711	1,243	1,215	1,137	685	737	1,072	1,488	1,305	11,852
Payroll taxes	1,039	1,206	1,265	1,394	1,730	1,895	2,024	2,032	2,139	1,915	1,826	1,836	20,301
Royalties	—	—	—	—	2,260	2,585	2,842	2,856	3,073	3,154	3,235	3,262	23,268
School & office supplies	1,232	309	532	1,218	904	1,293	995	2,359	1,475	1,514	1,500	1,109	14,440
Miscellaneous	1,109	1,080	1,951	2,640	1,304	2,327	1,876	3,427	2,089	2,523	2,426	2,218	24,971
Total variable costs	12,998	13,848	15,756	19,085	22,036	26,028	27,234	28,513	27,943	26,094	25,279	24,920	269,735
Operating costs	25,725	24,840	26,919	30,473	49,519	53,929	55,610	55,164	57,380	53,657	52,749	52,304	538,269
EBIT	(1,084)	6,027	8,548	10,135	(4,311)	(2,220)	1,240	1,959	4,072	9,418	11,952	12,940	58,676
Operating margin	−4.4%	19.5%	24.1%	25.0%	−9.5%	−4.3%	2.2%	3.4%	6.6%	14.9%	18.5%	19.8%	9.8%

(Continued)

EXHIBIT 7-4 (Continued)

Assumptions

Weeks/month	4.33
Center size	10,000
Student capacity	190
Student days/month capacity	4,117

Month	Mar. 1	Apr. 2	May 3	June 4	July 5	Aug. 6	Sept. 7	Oct. 8	Nov. 9	Dec. 10	Jan. 11	Feb. 12	Year 2 Total
Revenue													
Full-time students	109	113	117	117	117	124	135	136	138	138	140	140	127
Average weekly tuition	130	130	130	130	130	130	130	130	130	130	130	130	130
Full-time tuition	61,403	63,657	65,910	65,910	65,910	69,853	76,050	76,613	77,740	77,740	78,867	78,867	858,520
Part-time students	35	36	36	36	38	39	40	40	40	40	40	40	460
Average days/month	10	10	10	10	10	10	10	10	10	10	10	10	10
Average tuition/day	28	28	28	28	28	28	28	28	28	28	28	28	336
Part-time tuition	9,800	10,080	10,080	10,080	10,640	10,920	11,200	11,200	11,200	11,200	11,200	11,200	128,800
Total tuition	71,203	73,737	75,990	75,990	76,550	80,773	87,250	87,813	88,940	88,940	90,067	90,067	987,320
Capacity utilization	65.9%	68.2%	70.3%	70.3%	70.8%	74.7%	80.8%	81.3%	82.3%	82.3%	83.4%	83.4%	76.2%
Operating costs													
Fixed costs													
Advertising	649	649	649	649	649	649	649	649	649	649	649	649	7,786
CAMS	756	756	756	756	756	756	756	756	756	756	756	756	9,070
Data fees	250	250	250	250	250	250	250	250	250	250	250	250	3,000
Wages	6,800	6,800	6,800	6,800	6,800	6,800	6,800	6,800	6,800	6,800	6,800	6,800	81,604
Rent	12,863	12,863	12,863	12,863	12,863	12,863	12,863	12,863	12,863	12,863	12,863	12,863	154,350
General repairs	—	—	—	—	—	—	—	—	—	—	—	901	901
Lease guarantee fee	442	442	442	442	442	442	442	442	442	442	442	442	5,304
Insurance	1,500	1,500	1,500	1,500	1,500	1,500	1,500	1,500	1,500	1,500	1,500	1,500	18,000
Janitorial	1,100	1,100	1,100	1,100	1,100	1,100	1,100	1,100	1,100	1,100	1,100	1,100	13,200
P/R prof. fees	—	—	—	—	—	—	—	—	—	—	—	—	
Telephone	1,333	1,333	1,333	1,333	1,333	1,333	1,333	1,333	1,333	1,333	1,333	1,333	15,993
Utilities	1,728	1,728	1,728	1,728	1,728	1,728	1,728	1,728	1,728	1,728	1,728	1,728	20,737
Total fixed	27,420	27,420	27,420	27,420	27,420	27,420	27,420	27,420	27,420	27,420	27,420	28,321	329,945

(Continued)

EXHIBIT 7-4 (Continued)

Variable													
Avg. student/teacher ratio	10	10	10	10	10	10	10	10	10	10	10	10	10.0
Avg. teacher wage	6.99	6.99	6.99	6.99	6.99	6.99	6.99	6.99	6.99	6.99	6.99	6.99	6.99
Avg. hrs./day	8	8	8	8	8	8	8	8	8	8	8	8	8
Wages	15,156	15,696	16,180	16,180	16,292	17,195	18,583	18,705	18,947	18,947	19,189	19,189	210,258
Food costs	2,706	2,802	2,888	2,888	2,909	3,069	3,315	1,317	1,334	1,334	1,351	1,711	27,624
General supplies	3,204	1,475	1,140	1,330	2,105	1,898	1,745	1,054	1,067	1,512	2,072	1,801	20,403
Payroll taxes	1,943	1,991	2,034	2,034	2,044	2,124	2,246	2,257	2,279	2,279	2,300	2,300	25,830
Royalties	3,560	3,687	3,799	3,799	3,827	4,039	4,362	4,391	4,447	4,447	4,503	4,503	49,366
School & office supplies	1,709	737	1,140	2,280	1,531	2,019	1,527	2,359	2,135	2,135	1,500	1,531	20,602
Miscellaneous	3,204	2,581	4,179	4,939	2,208	3,635	2,879	5,269	3,024	3,558	3,377	3,062	41,916
Total variable costs	31,482	28,968	31,360	33,450	30,917	33,979	34,659	35,351	33,232	34,211	34,292	34,098	396,000
Operating costs	58,902	56,389	58,781	60,870	58,337	61,400	62,079	62,771	60,653	61,631	61,713	62,419	725,945
EBIT	12,301	17,348	17,209	15,120	18,213	19,374	25,171	25,042	28,287	27,309	28,354	27,647	261,375
Operating margin	17.3%	23.5%	22.6%	19.9%	23.8%	24.0%	28.8%	28.5%	31.8%	30.7%	31.5%	30.7%	26.5%

Source: Company documents.

EXHIBIT 7-5

WALL STREET JOURNAL ARTICLE ON DAYCARE CENTER

A Week in the Life of a Day-Care Center:
Tears, Hugs, Blocks and Bounced Checks
by Clare Ansberry
Staff Reporter of The Wall Street Journal

It's 7 A.M., and 18-month-old Natalie Kusmira is arriving at the Castle Shannon Learning Center clutching her Froot Loops.

The center, in a middle-class suburb outside Pittsburgh, is owned and operated by Joyce Tramonti, a 41-year-old single mother with a two-year degree in human services and more than a dozen years of child care experience. Ms. Tramonti is the center's heart and soul, working from 7 A.M. to 6 P.M. She makes and hangs the ABCs, mops the floor, peels oranges and plays monster.

There are 37 children aged two months to 10 years at the center. A dozen of the older kids come in before and after school and during holidays and vacations. Some younger children come part-time because their parents work irregular hours. The center is homier and more flexible than most. But it's also a business, licensed by the state, with rules and regulations, cinderblock walls, and an alarm that buzzes when the front door opens.

Ms. Tramonti's program has been around for more than a decade, overcoming the long odds that characterize the child care business. A look at the center during a recent week illustrates how millions of the nation's children spend their days—and how the people who look after them struggle to run businesses yet still nurture the children in their care.

Monday

Five-month-old Tommy arrives, pacifier in mouth. He isn't usually here on Mondays so things will be more hectic than usual. But Mondays usually are. Children haven't napped all weekend and don't want to leave their parents. A sobbing four-year-old wraps her arms and legs around her mother. After 10 minutes of gentle pleas, the exasperated mother puts the child back in the car, later calling in sick to her job as a clerical worker.

Tommy is on a rigid feeding schedule; bottle at 8 A.M., two tablespoons of cereal at 10; bottles at noon and 4. He starts to fuss with 19 minutes to go before his first bottle. Maureen Welsh, a mildly retarded, part-time staff member who has worked at the center for 12 years, rocks him, walks with him, and then pushes him in a stroller to distract him.

The center has no infant swings; Ms. Tramonti thinks they make staff members and babies lazy. The center's four babies are held and rocked as often as possible, given the demands on the two full-time and three part-time staff members. "Did you miss me? I missed you," says Jan Eslami, an assistant group supervisor, swinging a baby girl into the air. "This is my rent-a-kid."

The children share two large rooms, rented from the church next door. One doubles as the baby's room and a lunchroom, with a four-foot wall separating sleeping infants from mealtime din. The other functions as a communal playroom, naproom and Ms. Tramonti's office. It is wide open, with no practical place for quiet play or projects. A toddler knocks down seven-year-old Peter Stefano's tower. "I just hate it when the little kids knock my things over," says Peter.

Most child-development experts say babies and toddlers should be separated from bigger children because it's safer, less hectic and helps control illness. You're always watching so the big ones don't knock the little ones down," says Ms. Tramonti. "But you don't separate them at home. Why here?" To control illness, she insists on frequent hand-washing.

After snack, everyone, including infants, goes to a small yard divided in half by a driveway. Little kids play on a plastic slide, seesaw, or toy storefront, which doubles as a boat when tipped over. The big kids and Ms. Tramonti play hide-and-seek in a bigger yard on the other side of the driveway.

The game ends prematurely when a two-month-old newcomer arrives. Ms. Tramonti goes inside, and the big kids glumly walk to the toddler side so that Ms. Welsh and Ms. Eslami can keep watch. When the children go inside, Ms. Tramonti puts on Disney's "The Return of Jafar" video. Ms. Welsh is changing diapers, and Ms. Eslami is picking up school-age kids at the bus stop. "I hate to plug them in but I have to comfort him," says Ms. Tramonti, picking Tommy up to rock him. With an unscheduled baby and a new infant, she adds: "Today, I'm just reacting."

Tuesday

It's noon. Five babies and young toddlers sit strapped in high chairs along the wall. Another 20 kids sit around three tables, waiting for soup to be microwaved and fruit to be cut.

This is the first day for three-year-old Brianna Horan and her baby brother, Kyle. Brianna isn't used to sitting still, and she wanders, cheese slice in hand. "Honey, you have to sit down until everyone is finished," says Ms. Eslami. Brianna does briefly, before popping up.

(Continued)

EXHIBIT 7-5 *(Continued)*

Brandon Slater, his face covered with chocolate pudding, bangs his feet on his high chair to get down. He has another 20 minutes to wait. Ms. Welsh rushes from one child to the next, wiping faces and trays.

At another table, seven-year-old Peter takes a prescription pill. "I get wild," he says. "This calms me down," It will wear off by 4:30. But now he is the perfect gentleman, helping a four-year-old assemble cheese on crackers.

Peter has an attention deficit disorder. He's one of three kids with special needs. Renna Ryce, eight years old, has juvenile diabetes. Every day at 11:30, she pricks her finger and gives herself a blood test. If her sugar level is low, she eats lunch immediately. Last year it was so low, she vomited all over Ms. Tramonti, who called paramedics. The third child, a three-year-old with a speech problem, can barely talk.

These children are one reason why Ms. Tramonti doesn't believe in structured programs. "You can't expect Peter to sit through a half-hour story time when his medication is wearing off," she says.

Wednesday

Ricky spills his juice. Ms. Tramonti mops the floor. She does everything her staff does, and she handles delicate situations. Earlier this week, a child made a racial remark at lunch. Ms. Tramonti privately explained why it was inappropriate and quietly informed his mother.

The center costs $19 a day. Cribs come from a local discount store and toys from clearance sales. Ms. Tramonti's father refurbished a family crib; a sister made curtains. Aides are paid about $5 an hour and assistant group supervisors about $6. "If I paid what I felt they were worth, we'd probably be out of business," Ms. Tramonti says. As it is, she's always struggling. She has received four bad checks, totaling $600 this summer.

Now lunch is over and it's nap time. Everyone has a small blue mat on the floor and a blanket. Some parents complain, saying with naps, their kids won't go to bed at 7:30.

Brianna isn't used to sleeping on the floor and usually naps barefoot, with a bottle of chocolate milk. "Leave them on, honey," Ms. Tramonti tells her, as Brianna starts to remove her shoes. That's one rule. No rubbing backs is another—it would take forever to get everyone asleep—and no toys for little kids. Ms. Tramonti confiscates a ball under Brianna's pillow but then makes an exception, quietly tucking a stuffed rabbit into Brianna's arms.

Once everyone settles down for naps, the staff eats, spreading takeout lunch on the cold linoleum floor in the hallway. It's the only place for privacy and conversation. Ms. Tramonti doesn't think day care has gotten much better or worse over the years. Parents now ask more about staff ratios and qualifications. Ms. Tramonti says that often doesn't matter. "How many parents are qualified to be parents?" she asks.

Nap time is over. A normally cheery two-year-old wakes up crying uncontrollably and has to be cradled. "You never have enough staff," says Ms. Tramonti.

Thursday

It's raining. "If you're done with your snack, find something to do," says Ms. Tramonti. Most of the toys are for toddlers; the bigger kids improvise. One six-year-old tries playing golf, batting a plastic tangerine with a banana.

There are no designated story times or assembly-line art projects. Ms. Tramonti believes children learn through make-believe, dress-up, puzzles, and crafts. Natalie builds block towers. No one taught her; she watched others. Her mother thinks day care has made her more outgoing— and aggressive. Now, Natalie pushes her way onto an already occupied lap, demanding equal attention.

Peter's medication is wearing off. He puts paper under his feet, pretending to skate. Within minutes, seven others join him. Ms. Tramonti stands in the middle, holding an infant and directing skaters. Errant ones go to the "penalty box." Sensing Peter is getting wild, Ms. Tramonti asks him to soothe a fussy baby in the playpen.

As the day comes to an end, time lags. Ms. Tramonti pretends to be a monster sleeping on a table; a half-dozen toddlers sit underneath, waiting for her to wake up and gobble them up. Minutes later, she lines up chairs for "Wheels on the Bus," then proceeds to "Doggie Doggie, Where's Your Bone."

"I go nonstop for 11 hours," says Ms. Tramonti. She has never missed a day's work in 12 years; when she doesn't feel well, she takes aspirin.

Friday

It's a quiet morning. Five kids haven't shown up, and their parents haven't called to say why. But the parents' lives are hectic: Two kids had cookies in the car for breakfast.

At lunchtime, Jayme Jones gets a phone call. Her mom calls every day. "Who was that," asks a five-year-old, when she returns. "My Mom," Jayme answers. The five-year-old's eyes grow large. "My Mom never calls me," she says.

Frank, wearing a Chicago Bulls hat backward, informs Jayme that he just graduated from preschool. "I go to kindergarten," he says. Jayme says she's in the first grade. "My dad died," he tells her. "I have a step dad," she responds, "and one real dad and one real mom and one step mom."

operations, franchise fees, and through its unique lease deals. Through 1994, no Tutor Time centers had failed and the company was building momentum. The concept was sufficiently proven to attract serious capital providers, but Tutor Time was running out of time. The company's reliance on landlord financing meant that the company could not match a prospective franchisee with a site immediately. Although the company's Uniform Offering Circular apprised franchisees of the possibility of delays in getting a site, franchisees became disgruntled as their wait for a site lengthened. The backlog of franchisees without sites grew. Some, in fact, had demanded a return of their franchise fees, and others were threatening to sue. In addition to the increasing risk of litigation, the delay in site sourcing meant that Tutor Time had to wait to collect its $80,000 to $100,000 site development fee. Likewise, the company had to wait for royalties and other fees generated by completed sites. All of this severely strained cash flow. (See Exhibits 7-6–7-7 for Tutor Time financial information.)

AN ILL-ADVISED PARTNERSHIP

Tutor Time was also suffering the effects of a partnership gone bad. In 1992, a Tutor Time representative had been approached by a man named John Martin at a child care trade show. Martin claimed that he was involved in a number of businesses, including child care and real estate development. He showed a balance sheet purporting that his personal net worth was several million dollars. Martin also claimed to have an interest in a real estate development company that was one of the nation's 25 largest. Martin suggested that the two men might be able to help each other. They agreed to meet later. Within weeks the two had formed a joint venture to develop and market Tutor Time child care centers nationally. Tutor Time believed that Martin would give it the capital and real estate expertise it needed to go national quickly.

As it turned out, many of Martin's prior projects were on the brink of insolvency, and his financial statement was a sham. Before Martin's deception was discovered, Martin had managed to saddle Tutor Time with a number of poorly bid lease build-outs. Some of these sites were several hundred thousand dollars over budget in early 1995. The fallout from the Martin partnership included several lawsuits between Tutor Time affiliates and employees and Martin and his associates.

CONSTRUCTION OVERRUNS

The company's third source of cash flow difficulty was its method of school site development which left the company exposed to the vagaries of construction finance. In a typical deal, Tutor Time's real estate affiliate, LifeCare Acquisitions ("LifeCare"), would locate school sites through local real estate brokers. After performing an independent demographic review of the site, Lifecare would approach the landlord and explain the Tutor Time concept. If the landlord was interested, the parties would commence lease negotiations regarding financing the site build-out and other lease terms. Upon agreement, the executed lease would be presented to a franchisee for approval. To get the deal done, Lifecare might have to agree to assume any construction overages and agree to guarantee the lease payments of the franchisee.

The Succasunna lease was a prime example of how a construction build-out could turn against Lifecare. If a build-out financed by the landlord for $25/square foot ended up costing $38/square foot, Lifecare lost $130,000 and the site could not be completed until Lifecare advanced the money to the contractor. Tutor Time bid the project this

EXHIBIT 7-6

TUTOR TIME INCOME STATEMENT ($000S)

	1991	1992	1993	1994
Revenues from Sales				
Franchise fees	$141,250	$ 254,815	$ 305,100	$ 755,405
Royalties	42,990	330,644	434,193	732,327
Site location fees	26,555	120,345	295,009	322,615
Site development fees	0	235,040	759,586	1,414,537
Zone franchise fees	0	818,552	1,085,710	424,697
Insurance	21,733	141,851	121,595	0
Architectural fees	0	0	0	543,732
Commissions	0	0	0	495,204
Operational services	6,752	91,809	197,822	329,068
Total Revenue from Sales	239,280	1,993,056	3,199,015	5,017,586
Costs and Expenses				
Direct cost of sales	0	191,029	431,733	555,111
Licensing fees	0	0	54,240	102,830
Commissions	25,425	107,350	216,480	151,957
Management fee	56,500	406,800	542,400	0
Insurance costs	20,481	0	0	0
Bank charges	125	0	0	0
Amortization expenses	9	0	0	0
General and administrative	0	374,119	1,584,703	3,701,711
Total costs and expenses	102,541	1,079,298	2,829,556	4,511,609
Income from Operations	136,739	913,758	369,459	505,978
Other Income				
Interest	0	33,883	45,495	86,279
Management fees	0	6,780	27,120	9,040
Total Other Income	0	40,663	72,615	95,319
EBT	136,739	954,421	442,074	601,297
Provision for income taxes	51,452	359,128	134,740	222,480
Net Income	$ 85,287	$ 595,293	$ 307,334	$ 378,817

Source: Company documents (data disguised).

way because they had initially made money on this spread. For example, if the bid came in $5 per square foot under what the landlord had agreed to pay, then Tutor Time made $50,000 on a typical 10,000 square foot center. In the spring of 1995, Tutor Time had dozens of sites that they had underbid, and the projected liability was significant.

LITIGATION

Tutor Time's capital raising efforts hit a brick wall in early 1995 when the Federal Trade Commission (FTC) began a confidential investigation of the firm's franchising practices.

EXHIBIT 7-7

TUTOR TIME BALANCE SHEET ($000S)

	1991	1992	1993	1994
Assets				
Current Assets				
Cash	666	0	2,964	5,679
Accounts receivable (Net)	164,415	688,769	1,425,173	4,542,032
Other receivables	0	2,827	795,360	884,156
Due from affiliates (Net)	81,484	1,972,242	651,671	163,597
Notes receivable	14,081	117,641	133,059	699,808
Other current assets	167,445	945,117	620,455	849,642
Total Current Assets	428,090	3,726,596	3,628,681	7,144,914
P, P & E	0	0	24,069	44,214
Other Assets				
Notes receivable*	416,449	435,948	753,092	4,315,428
Due from affiliates*	0	0	2,752,688	0
Investment-unconsolidated subsidiaries	0	0	113	0
Other	189	263	13,718	689,145
Total Other Assets	416,638	436,212	3,519,611	5,004,573
Total Assets	844,728	4,162,808	7,172,361	12,193,701

* Net of current portion

	1991	1992	1993	1994
Liabilities and Shareholder's Equity				
Current Liabilities				
Bounced checks	0	4,156	64,954	0
Accounts payable	0	333,263	1,199,423	2,929,484
Income taxes payable	0	900,735	134,740	357,220
Due to affiliates	0	0	361,486	30,510
Capital lease-current portion	0	0	7,064	1,193
Deferred franchise fees	310,750	1,034,515	875,411	875,411
Deferred coordination fees	0	575,396	0	0
Deferred development fees	0	22,600	704,894	704,894
Deferred marketing fees	0	4,520	0	85,880
Deferred commissions	0	5,650	75,169	110,175
Other deferred liabilities	0	0	170,404	170,404
Total Current Liabilities	310,750	2,880,836	3,593,544	5,265,172
Long-Term Liabilities				
Capital leases	0	0	8,698	0
Deferred fees-net of current portion	0	0	1,726,979	4,293,551
Total long-term liabilities	0	0	1,735,677	4,293,551
Total Liabilities	310,750	2,880,836	5,329,220	9,558,723
Shareholder's Equity				
Common stock	1,130	433,495	1,130	76,224
Paid but not issued shares	0	152,703	0	0
Additional paid in capital	432,365	0	585,068	922,994
Retained earnings	100,483	695,775	1,256,943	1,635,760
Total Stockholder's Equity	533,978	1,281,973	1,843,141	2,634,978
Total Liabilities and Stockholder's Equity	844,728	4,162,808	7,172,361	12,193,701

* Shares Outstanding: 663,200

Source: Company documents (data disguised).

It was believed that the investigation was initiated by a single franchisee disgruntled over the delay in receiving a site. The investigation seemed likely to be limited in scope, but the FTC refused, as a matter of policy, to disclose the nature of an ongoing investigation. If the FTC found Tutor Time to be in violation of federal franchise law, it could prohibit Tutor Time from selling franchises or even shut down the company. On February 6, 1995, the Ft. Lauderdale press broke the story on the FTC litigation. It was also rumored that more litigation was being contemplated by a small band of local plaintiff's attorneys. The uncertainty surrounding these proceedings made an infusion of capital from conventional sources highly unlikely. The confusion surrounding the FTC investigation also made it increasingly difficult for Tutor Time to manage its franchisees waiting for sites. Although the company had no contractual obligation to return franchise fees to franchisees, refusing requests for fee refunds was deemed risky while the FTC investigation was pending.

THE FLOEGEL/HOPKINS PROPOSAL

In February 1995, Floegel and Hopkins discovered most of Tutor Time's problems through other franchisees, acquaintances in Florida, attorney contacts, and from the company itself. They were concerned about what they had heard. They also thought, however, that the company had substantial long-term value if it could survive its present problems. They believed that the situation could not get much worse for the company. If they moved quickly, they might be able to strike a very attractive deal with Tutor Time. Their initial review of the litigation against Tutor Time suggested that the problems were not as bad as they had first appeared. It was, however, quite difficult to get a clear picture of Tutor Time's cash position without returning to Florida for in-depth due diligence.

In late February, Floegel sent a proposal to Richard Weissman. Subject to further due diligence, Floegel and Hopkins offered to create a $1 million line of credit through a new financing entity, a limited liability company, Newco, to fund up to 30 new schools. Newco was to be owned 51% by a Floegel/Hopkins company and 49% by a Tutor Time affiliate. The Weissmans were to contribute a fixed percentage of their Tutor Time stock to the Hopkins/Floegel group for each Newco school that was opened (totaling nearly 40% of the outstanding stock). Furthermore, Tutor Time would issue a note convertible into 15% of the company's stock in return for a $150,000 loan from Floegel and Hopkins. The note would be secured on behalf of Tutor Time by the Weissmans' stock in the Succasunna school. Going forward, Tutor Time would be paid a substantial management fee to run the schools. Newco would have the rights to use all necessary intellectual property to run its schools in select northeastern states. Further, Newco would owe no site development fees or franchise fees.

Floegel and Hopkins conferred extensively with a law school friend to ensure that the deal would survive a bankruptcy court's review. The deal also was structured so that Newco could continue to develop schools regardless of what the FTC did. Tutor Time would get much needed cash immediately. It could also purchase the "corporate" schools from Newco at the time of a future IPO. If current market P/E multiples (around 20) held, the deal could work out fabulously for everyone (see Exhibit 7-8). Floegel and Hopkins worried, however, that their money would be insufficient to get Tutor Time through its difficulties. They also wondered what their deal would be worth if Tutor Time entered bankruptcy.

EXHIBIT 7-8

PROPOSED NEWCO DEAL STRUCTURE

Newco Considerations

Ownership

Floegel/Hopkins	51%
Weissmans	49%

Capitalization

Working Capital	30,000
Number of schools	33
Total Capitalization of Newco Schools	990,000

Newco Revenues

Annual gross revenue per school	800,000
Net Margin	15%
Annual net income per school	120,000
Number of Schools	33
Total Newco Revenues	3,960,002
Less Management Fee (to Tutor Time)	495,000
Net Income (Newco)	3,465,002
Weissmans' Annual Newco Revenues	1,697,851
Floegel/Hopkins Annual Net Income	1,767,151

Private Exit

Private Net Income Multiple	6.5
Total private value of equity (Newco)	22,522,512
IPO Exit	
Public P/E	20
Total public equity value created (Newco)	79,200,041

Tutor Time Considerations

Annual Fees

Tutor Time Franchise Fees	0
Tutor Time revenue royalty	0
Tutor Time management fee	
Monthly fee/school	1,500
Management fee percentage	12.50%
Management Fee	495,000
Tutor Time lease guarantee fee	
Average square footage	10,000
$/Square Foot	0.50
Lease Guarantee Fee	165,000
Tutor Time software licensing fee	
Monthly fee/school	175
Software licensing fee	69,300
Total Annual Tutor Time Fees	729,300
Increase in annual system-wide sales	26,400,014
Public market value of incremental TT fee income	14,586,005

General Assumptions

None of the new schools fail.

There are no major FTC/other regulatory problems, litigation etc., company grows rapidly, drawdown contingencies are met, company is cleaned up and in a position to go public, all else is well, etc. Several substantial operational, legal, competitive and other risks are curtailed and problems overcome. Suitable sites are found promptly and built out quickly without complications.

Revenue Assumptions

Children/school	141
Weekly revenues/child	110
Monthly revenues/child	473
Monthly revenues/school	66,667
Annual revenues/school	800,000

Source: Company documents.

EXHIBIT 7-9

**VOLATILITY OF REPRESENTATIVE DAYCARE/EDUCATIONAL
SERVICE COMPANIES**

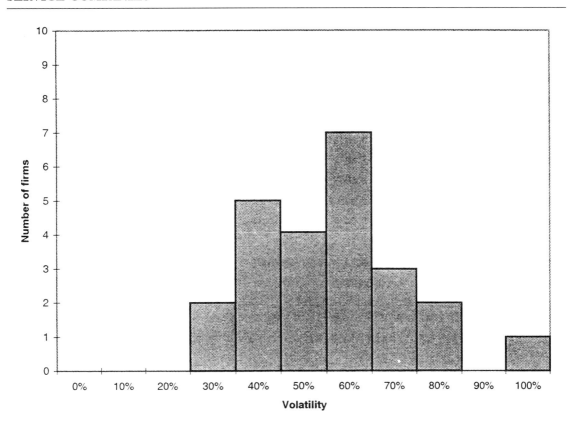

The graph plots the average annualized volatility of 24 daycare and education service firms over the period January 1988 through December 1995. The average annualized volatility was 47%, and the median was 50%.

Source: Casewriter's estimates.

THE COUNTERPROPOSAL

It did not take long for Floegel to get his answer. He received a phone call informing him that the company was not willing to accept his and Hopkins's deal. The Weissmans were so impressed with him, however, that they wanted him to join Tutor Time as senior vice president of Corporate Development. While his responsibilities could be worked out later, Weissman had proposed paying Floegel an initial salary of $70,000 and selling him a substantial percentage of Tutor Time's equity. While the salary was less than he had been making as a lawyer, he realized that Tutor Time could not afford to pay him any more. Anyway, if Tutor Time was half as successful as he thought it could be, then there would be plenty of value in the package. Floegel felt confident in the Weiss-

EXHIBIT 7-10

MACROECONOMIC DATA FOR LAST DAY OF EACH PERIOD

	Dec. 1990	Dec. 1991	Dec. 1992	Dec. 1993	Dec. 1994
A rated bonds	9.63%	8.63%	8.33%	7.39%	8.76%
AA rated bonds	9.40%	8.44%	8.20%	7.21%	8.65%
AAA rated bonds	9.05%	8.16%	7.91%	7.00%	8.49%
Baa rated bonds	10.43%	9.10%	8.76%	7.77%	9.14%
Inflation	5.25%	2.60%	2.89%	2.52%	2.66%
Unemployment rate	6.30%	7.30%	7.40%	6.50%	5.40%
Prime rate	10.00%	7.21%	6.00%	6.00%	8.50%
T-Bill: 1 Mo.	5.35%	3.82%	2.82%	2.80%	3.66%
T-Bill: 1 Year	6.42%	3.91%	3.45%	3.45%	6.75%
Gov't Bond 5 Yr.	7.68%	5.93%	6.04%	5.21%	7.83%
Gov't Bond 10 Yr.	8.08%	6.71%	6.70%	5.83%	7.84%
Gov't Bond 30 Yr.	8.26%	7.41%	7.40%	6.35%	7.89%
Real GDP Growth	−0.24%	0.43%	3.63%	2.37%	3.27%
Wilshire 5000	3101.35	4041.1	4289.74	4657.83	4540.62
S&P 500	330.22	417.09	435.71	466.45	459.27
Hambrecht & Quist Growth Index	633.22	1218.06	1177.79	1285.02	1337.31

Source: Citibase.

mans' management skills and knew that the Tutor Time system was the best in the industry.

The issue was, however, should he take the offer? How much equity should he ask for? How much should he pay for the equity? Would "at-the-money" options be a better choice? Floegel thought that Tutor Time would continue to grow rapidly over the next several years, but what growth rate was reasonable to expect? How did these potential growth rates affect the value of Tutor Time and hence, his stake in it? What were the potential implications for his reputation if Tutor Time went bankrupt? Did he have anything to gain? In addition, what would his responsibilities at Tutor Time be? Up until now, Tutor Time had been run like a family business. How would they respond to some East Coast professional telling them what should be done? In addition, what would Chris say about moving far from her family?

As Floegel pondered his future, he looked out the window of his New Jersey home. A neighborhood child rode her bike down the street, and Floegel's eyes followed the child as he thought about his future. He might soon embark down the road he had always wanted to travel. Too bad it was not the road he had always pictured.

8

Fenchel Lampshade Company

For Steve and Michele Rogers the events of mid-1988 were proceeding at a breakneck pace. They had finally convinced the owners of the Fenchel Lampshade Company to sell their business, a process that had lasted well over a year and that had fallen apart on more than one occasion. Yet, there were many hurdles to be overcome before they could realize their dream of owning their own business: chief among these was raising the capital required to make the deal work.

Although it was exhilarating to think that they would be able to buy Fenchel, Steve and Michele were also painfully aware of the risks. Steve would have to resign from his consulting job at Bain & Company in Boston, and Michele would have to leave her job in the admissions office at Harvard Business School. They and their two small children would have to move from Boston to Chicago, where Michele would find a new full-time job and Steve would take over responsibility for managing Fenchel. They had no illusions about what it would mean to own and run a small company, one that would be highly levered after the deal. On the other hand, that is what they had always wanted to do, and now it seemed it would finally be possible.

BACKGROUND

The search for a business to own had begun for Steve and Michele Rogers while Steve was still in his first year in the MBA Program at Harvard Business School. After careful study, he had decided that he should try to buy a McDonald's franchise. McDonald's was actively seeking black owners for the Boston area, and Steve felt he could find an attractive opportunity with McDonald's help. At the beginning of his second year at HBS, he enrolled in a mandatory McDonald's training program for people interested in owning a franchise. While his classmates ate at the Charles Hotel or flew to New York for meals at Cote Basque, Steve spent 20 hours a week training at a McDonald's store in Lynn, Massachusetts. He did everything from cooking hamburgers to cleaning the lavatories.

This case was prepared by Professor William Sahlaman as the basis for class discussion rather than to illustrate either effective or ineffective handling of an administrative situation. The case facts have been disguised.

After graduating from HBS in June of 1985, Steve took a job as a research associate for the Production and Operations Management course at Harvard Business School: Michele, who was pregnant with their second child, was entering her second year at HBS. Steve continued his duties at the McDonald's restaurant. The work was hard and not very glamorous, but Steve was committed to the program. Owning a McDonald's franchise and ultimately owning a number of stores would be a lucrative and demanding outcome. In the spring of 1986, Steve began serious negotiations with McDonald's about which store he might be able to buy and the terms. Each McDonald's franchise was priced according to its potential sales volume.

McDonald's suggested that Steve buy a franchise in downtown Boston. After considerable investigation, however, Steve became concerned that the opportunity was not very attractive. The price was too high—on the order of $650,000 for a store with sales of approximately $1 million—given what Steve perceived to be the prospects of the location. McDonald's asking price was based on what Steve thought to be unrealistically optimistic assumptions about what the store could do in the future. After exploring several other store possibilities and sometimes heated discussions with McDonald's, Steve finally decided to abandon his two years of training and the related plan to buy a McDonald's franchise.

In the summer of 1986, Steve decided to join Bain & Company, a major international consulting company with headquarters in Boston. After graduation from the MBA Program, Michele stayed on at Harvard Business School in the admissions area. Though both were making a lot of money and enjoyed their work, they still wanted to own their own business.

A number of Steve's consulting assignments with Bain took him to the Midwest where he and Michele had grown up. Steve started the process of trying to find a company to buy in that area. He contacted a number of business brokers, commercial bankers, accountants, and law firms in Chicago, and he also began to subscribe to the Chicago papers. Over time he began to receive proposals from his contacts. On his frequent visits to the area, he would go meet with representatives of the sellers or would go visit the company. In total, he saw some 25 companies between early 1987 and the spring of 1987. Discouragingly, none was particularly attractive.

THE FENCHEL LAMPSHADE COMPANY

Then, in May of 1987, he was contacted by a business broker about the possibility that a lampshade manufacturing company might be for sale. Steve had already seen one lampshade company, which he had rejected because it focused on the highly competitive low end of the market, had terrible management, and was egregiously overpriced. This new company, Fenchel, sounded different. They were a manufacturer of premium price lampshades with total sales volume of about $1 million.

Steve flew to Chicago to meet the broker representing the owners and was favorably impressed by what he heard. The company was managed by 65-year-old Kenneth Fenchel, whose father and uncle had founded the company in 1926. The company was owned by Kenneth and his uncle and aunt, who had assumed control when Kenneth's father passed away. Kenneth's uncle was 88 years old and was effectively retired from the business. The company was profitable and had provided the owners an attractive income stream for many years.

It was also apparent to Steve that the business had not been very aggressively managed. Sales growth had been modest, and Steve was convinced that he could improve the operations of the company.

While Steve's original meeting with the broker representing the Fenchel family was positive, it soon became clear that the Fenchel family was not totally committed to selling the business. Each year they owned Fenchel Lampshades, the income was very high. Aside from a desire to retire and concern about health, there was no real pressure to sell.

Also, the Fenchels had placed a $800,000 total value on the company and had insisted that all of the money be paid up-front. They were unwilling to consider any kind of seller financing. For Steve and Michele Rogers, this was an unacceptable demand, given the inevitable uncertainties associated with taking over any business. Without seller financing, it might also be much more difficult to arrange other elements of the financing plan.

Steve's hope of working out a mutually acceptable deal was dashed on December 7, 1987, when Ken Fenchel called to say that he had decided not to sell and that he intended to take the company off the market. This call came exactly one week after Steve, Ken, and their respective lawyers and accountants had met for over nine hours to finalize the terms of a letter of intent.

While disappointed, Steve and Michele were more committed than ever to buying a company. They also had decided that Fenchel was perfect for their plans. The company was profitable, generated attractive cash flows, and was affordable. Their conversations with the business broker representing the Fenchels had suggested that there might be another opportunity to buy the company if they were patient. As a result, Steve and Michele suspended their active search for another company.

At the same time, they decided to move to Chicago regardless of the outcome at Fenchel. Steve believed that he would be able to continue his work as a consultant for Bain, which was considering opening up a Chicago office. And Michele had arranged to work for James Lowry & Co., a Chicago-based consulting company. They planned to move in midsummer of 1988.

BACK ON TRACK

Then, in April, Steve received a call from the broker representing the Fenchels who said that it made sense to talk again. Ken Fenchel was considering selling the company again. However, a preliminary meeting in May revealed that Ken's uncle was still adamantly opposed to seller financing.

Steve proceeded to line up various potential sources of capital on the assumption that he could work out a reasonable solution to the impasse with the Fenchel family. Steve was convinced that he could get the Fenchel family to take a $75,000 note back for part of the agreed-upon $745,000 purchase price. He and Michele were prepared to invest $50,000 of their own money as a starting point. With respect to the other capital, there were a number of options.

First, Fenchel had certain assets that could be pledged as collateral. Steve intended to apply for a Small Business Administration loan. Under this program, banks agreed to lend money to small businesses, and up to 85% of the principal amount of the loan was guaranteed by the U.S. government. Thus, at least some of the risk was passed off on the government, which resulted in significantly lower interest costs.

Steve hoped to gain access to other debt financing by going to certain state and local programs that had been set up to make investments in local businesses. The City of Chicago had such a program from which Steve hoped to raise $100,000. An additional $50,000 would hopefully come from a State of Illinois loan program.

With respect to the remaining capital required, Steve knew that he would have to gain access to some equity-like financing. There were no other assets to pledge, and every lender would insist on some equity base before lending the money.

One possibility was to go to a MESBIC (Minority Enterprise Small Business Investment Corporation). The MESBIC Program was established by the Small Business Administration in 1969 for the purpose of providing long-term financing and management assistance to new ventures started by minorities. MESBICs were private companies that raised equity from individuals or institutions (often commercial banks) and were able to leverage their equity through government guarantees of loans. Under existing regulations, MESBICs could borrow up to four times their equity capital using government guarantees.

The next step was to turn possibilities into realities. The loan request documentation and related business plan prepared by Steve and Michele Rogers is included as Appendix A.

REMAINING ISSUES

Steve and Michele had debated for hours about how much they should pay for Fenchel, how they should get access to the required capital, and what they should do if they were able to buy the company. Now it seemed that they were finally close. That was very exciting, but it was also slightly frightening. As Steve had discovered more than once during his search for a company to buy, being a Harvard MBA was not an automatic ticket to success. In his more cynical moments, he asked himself what he thought a snot-nosed 31-year-old Harvard MBA knew about running a business. On the other hand, he was ready to find out.

APPENDIX 8-A

FENCHEL LAMPSHADE COMPANY

LOAN REQUEST

Section I
FENCHEL LAMPSHADE COMPANY
Loan Request Summary

Loan Type:	SBA Loan
Amount	$300,000
Borrower	Steven and Michele Rogers
Purpose of Loan:	To purchase Fenchel Lampshade Company
Total Cost of Project:	$745,000—does not include working capital
Other Potential Funding Sources:	• The Chicago Capital Fund
	• The Neighborhood Fund
	• State of Illinois
Collateral:	Assets of Fenchel Lampshade Company and personal guarantees of company's new owners, Steven and Michele Rogers.

(Continued)

Section II
BUSINESS PLAN SUMMARY

Steven and Michele Rogers (both black and from Chicago and Cleveland, respectively) are attempting to buy Fenchel Lampshade Company. Michele will serve as a consultant to the company, while Steve will work as a full-time owner/operator.

Fenchel is recognized as a leading manufacturer of premium quality lampshades in the Midwest. The company has annual sales in excess of $1 million with annual cash flow margins of 15% to 30%. The company is over 61 years old and is owned by Kenneth Fenchel (age 65) and his 88-year-old uncle and 73-year-old aunt. They are selling the business in order to retire.

In 1986, the lampshade industry had total sales of $70 million, a figure that has been growing at a rate of 5% since 1972. There are four identifiable segments in the industry. Fenchel's operates in the premium quality segment (approximately $20 million in 1986 volume) and sells to lamp specialty shops and upscale department stores.

Fenchel sells hard back and fabric lampshades. All of the lampshades are hand made and have wholesale prices of $5 to $35. The company has 65 accounts. Marshall Field's is the company's largest customer accounting for 10% of sales in 1986.

While there are 34 lampshade manufacturers in the country, competition in the industry is generally restricted to geographical regions due to the extremely high cost of transportation. Most manufacturers are in New York or New Jersey.

The acquirers are both graduates of the Harvard Business School. Steven was born and raised on Chicago's South Side where he attended Lewis Champlin grammar school and Englewood High School. He has work experience as a manager, business analyst, and consultant. As supervisor of customer services with Cummins, he managed eight unionized employees. He also has negotiating and financial analysis experience as a result of working as a purchasing agent with Consolidated Diesel Company and as a business analyst with UNC Venture Capital Company. Finally, his work with Bain as a general management consultant has enhanced his ability to solve business problems through the use of analytical tools and has trained him to be an effective task force leader.

Michele has a strong work history in personnel administration. She has worked for Cummins Engine Company in personnel administration and labor relations; Harvard University in development; and Harvard Business School in admissions. Michele will be employed full time with James Lowry and Associates, a Chicago-based consulting firm but will be available for consultation at Fenchel.

John Smith, who has been with Fenchel for 15 years, will continue his position as the supervisor of production. Gerri Wandall, who has been the office manager for the past five years, will also continue in her present position.

The diversified labor force at Fenchel will remain after the acquisition. There are 18 employees of which 15 are female; 13 are black, 2 Hispanic, 2 white, and 1 Asian. Their length of employment with Fenchel ranges from 1 to 21 years.

The combination of all of these characteristics—a loyal and diversified customer base; an experienced and dedicated labor force; and strong cash flow that can meet debt service requirements—makes Fenchel an ideal acquisition candidate.

(Continued)

Section III
BUSINESS PLAN
THE COMPANY

Fenchel Lampshade Company is a manufacturer of premium quality rayon, acetate, and hard back covered lampshades for the replacement market. In addition to diverse materials, Fenchel lampshades vary by style, shape, and color. All of the lampshades are made in response to customer orders, with delivery commitments ranging from 4 to 6 weeks.

Fenchel's customers include department stores, independent lamp and shade retail stores, lighting showrooms, and a few (about 2%) lamp manufacturers. Of the company's sales, 80% are made to customers in the Midwest.

The name "Fenchel" is well regarded in the industry because of the company's strong reputation for high-quality products. To take advantage of Fenchel's strong customer name recognition, customers, such as Gatelys and Marshall Field's, regularly use the name in their advertisements (Exhibit 1).

In 1926 Herbert Fenchel (born in 1900) incorporated the company in Chicago. The corporation became a partnership in 1947 when Herbert's wife Lois Fenchel (born in 1915) joined the company. That same year, Herbert's nephew, I. Kenneth Fenchel (born in 1923), began working for the company as a salesman. In 1957 Kenneth became an equal partner with Herbert and Lois.

For the past five years Kenneth has operated the company alone: Herbert and Lois were silent partners. For health reasons Herbert and Lois live in Florida six months each year.

The Industry

The domestic lampshade industry has total annual volume of approximately $70 million spread over 34 manufacturers. The manufacturers are located in seven states, with over half of them in the New York/New Jersey area. The typical manufacturer is a family-owned business with over 25 years of experience in the industry. Since 1972, the industry's compounded annual growth rate has been 5% (Exhibit 2).

The lampshade industry is seasonal, with the slow season occurring during the summer. During this time, people usually spend most of their time outdoors and are not making internal home improvements. Less than 15% of all sales will be made during the months of June, July, and August. The best sales period occurs through the remaining nine months when people typically spend more

time inside. The strongest months for sales are before holidays such as Thanksgiving, Christmas, and Easter.

There are four categories of lampshade manufacturing; lamp manufacturing companies (e.g., Alsy and Stiffel) with internal lampshade production; independent lampshade manufacturers who sell primarily to lamp manufacturers; low/medium-quality lampshade manufacturers (e.g., Lampshade, Inc.) with discount stores as their primary customer; and premium quality lampshade manufacturers who sell to lamp specialty shops and upscale department stores. The latter category, which includes Fenchel, is a market of approximately $20 million.

Product Description

Fenchel's products serve the premium quality segment of the market. Every lampshade is completely hand made, with all stages of production carefully supervised and inspected. All fabrics are sewn to the frames, not glued. All frames are rust resistant. The trims and folds are bonded to the shade to ensure hand-washability. In addition, the lampshades are wrinkle resistant, glare free, and shadow free. In fact, Fenchel advertises itself as the industry leader of shadow-free lampshades. All of these characteristics in one lampshade are very rare, thereby giving Fenchel a reputation for high quality and workmanship. Only two other lampshade manufacturers, Silko-lite and Diane in the New York/New Jersey area, produce lampshades of similar quality.

Fenchel's lampshades can be divided into two categories; fabric and hard back. Fabric lampshades are manufactured using various fabrics on the exterior with stain internal backings. Fenchel sells fabric lampshades in 6 different styles, 16 shapes, 6 materials, 4 colors, and 7 trims. These lampshades have historically accounted for 63% to 74% of the company's sales and 64% to 76% of the company's profits.

Hard back shades have various fabrics on the exterior and laminated or vinyl internal backings. Fenchel's hard back lampshades are distinctive because, unlike competitive products, they are made with more material, which leads to better defined pleats. In addition, Fenchel's products are made with thicker vinyl or laminated backing and heavier frames than competitive products. The end result is a more durable and beautiful lampshade. The company's hard back lampshades are sold in two different styles and five shapes. These lampshades have his-

(Continued)

torically accounted for 26% to 37% of the company's sales and 24% to 36% of profits.

The wholesale price range of Fenchel lampshades if $5 to $35. The average selling price is $15. These shades will ultimately be sold by a retailer at prices from $20 to $65.

Fenchel's average wholesale price of $15 compares to $6 for a lampshade from a low/medium-quality manufacturer such as Lampshades, Inc., which sells primarily to discount department stores.

In addition to producing a standard line of lampshades highlighted in the Fenchel catalog (Exhibit 3), custom work is accepted. The company will manufacture lampshades to a customer's specifications or even design an exclusive line for a customer such as Marshall Field's.

Customers

As a manufacturer of premium quality lampshades, Fenchel has a stable and loyal customer base. Over 60% of its annual sales are to upscale department stores such as Marshall Field's, headquartered in Chicago; the May Company, headquartered in St. Louis; and Lazarus, headquartered in Indianapolis. The only lampshades sold by these stores are Fenchel's. In fact, the Marshall Field's State Street store in Chicago has an area on the fourth floor (approximately 12 feet by 12 feet) dedicated entirely to Fenchel lampshades.

The balance of sales are to independent retail stores, lighting showrooms, and lamp manufacturers.

Fenchel has 65 customer accounts, of which 50 are located in the Midwest. Some 45 customers account for 80% of total sales. The largest customer is Marshall Field's, which operates 25 stores in metropolitan Chicago, Texas, and Wisconsin: this customer accounts for only 10% of total sales.

Typical orders are $10,000 to $25,000 from department stores and $400 to $2,000 from independent retail stores.

Unlike customers for low/medium-quality lampshades, Fenchel's customers do not base their purchase decisions on price alone. These customers view product quality and delivery to be just as important as price. Thus, Fenchel's reputation for impeccable quality and service for over 50 years has resulted in a very loyal customer base. For example, Marshall Field's has been a Fenchel customer for 20 years.

Competition

Although there are 34 American lampshade manufacturers (Exhibit 4), competition in the industry is regional due to extremely high transportation costs. Lampshades are bulky but light in weight, which creates strong regional barriers to entry. Those premium quality lampshade manufacturers located in the New York/New Jersey area find it cost prohibitive to enter the Midwest region.

The five other lampshade manufacturers in the Midwest are not competitors of Fenchel because their product focus is the low/medium market.

Silk-o-lite, a 60-year-old New Jersey firm with sales in excess of $2 million, is Fenchel's closest competitor.

Fenchel's strong reputation for quality and service, combined with prohibitive shipping costs, make it very difficult for a competitor outside of the Midwest to take away any of Fenchel's market without engaging in predatory pricing.

Marketing and Sales Plan

Fenchel had a 1.3% compound annual growth rate in sales from 1983 to 1986. This minuscule rate of growth reflected Kenneth Fenchel's choice not to aggressively market the company's products. He did not want sales to grow because it would require more of his time, which he did not want to give at this stage of his life. The business cash flow of approximately $140,000 annually was more than enough to satisfy him, his uncle, and aunt.

By taking a more aggressive approach in marketing and sales, the company can grow at $100,000 to $500,000 annually. Steven's strategy for growing the company will include a continuation of Fenchel's present marketing practices such as the co-op advertising program with 20 department stores; the annual product catalog that is mailed to 200 prospective customers; attending the two annual lamp and lampshade trade shows (Kenneth will attend one with Steven); and advertising in lamp and lampshade journals (Exhibit 5). Steven will also continue the practice of employing manufacturing representatives, which is common throughout the industry. Fenchel's representatives account for 33% of sales. Finally, Steven will service the same 20 in-house accounts that are presently being managed by the owner. Kenneth will visit each of the accounts with Steven for introductory purposes and to assure the customers that product quality and service will be maintained.

In addition, Steven will make several changes. First, he will do a thorough analysis of each form of advertising to gauge effectiveness. The data from this analysis will tell him where advertising dollars should be spent in order to achieve a higher return on investment. Next, he will hire and train more manufacturing representatives in an attempt to increase the number of customers in the independent lamp and lampshade retail stores and lighting showrooms. Both of these potential customer groups are ideal for Fenchel lampshades and are experiencing significant growth in affluent suburban areas.

The addition of more manufacturing representatives will be a variable cost since they are entirely compensated via commissions. The present commission system gives a representative 10% of any revenues generated. The commission is paid on the 10th of each month following product delivery. Such a system does not encourage the opening of new accounts since the representative gets the same percentage for a new account order as he does for an order from an existing customer. Therefore, the third change that Steven will make is to give a one-time bonus for new account orders.

Fourth, he will personally market Fenchel's lampshades to the premium quality lamp manufacturers. Opportunities are definitely available in this market based on a statement Peter Gershanov, vice president of Frederick Cooper, made to Steven that only two lamp manufacturers, Frederick Cooper and Stiffel, make their own lampshades, while the others purchase them from an outside manufacturer. This industry, with sales in excess of $2 billion, is too large to continue to ignore.

Steven will also seek to increase sales by pursuing untapped accounts in the Midwest, such as Ehr's Lamp Shade Shoppe in Waukesha, Wisconsin, who carry Silk-o-Lite but not Fenchel lampshades.

Other opportunities will come from new kinds of customers that are not presently served by Fenchel. These potential customers include interior decorating companies, mail order catalogs, upscale hotels, hospitals, colleges, upscale convalescent homes, and the government.

As a minority-owned company, Steven anticipates opportunities to increase revenue by selling to local, state, and federal government agencies through the 8(a) Set Aside Program (Exhibit 6).

As a former purchasing agent, minority supplier coordinator, and member of the National Minority Purchasing Council, Steven is aware that many private corporations have minority supplier programs where buyers actively search to buy from minority-owned businesses. He intends to take advantage of such opportunities.

The opportunity to increase sales in upscale department stores will also present itself because of the presence of minority vendor programs in stores such as Bloomingdale's, I. Magnin, and Lazarus (Exhibit 7). Steven's ability to take advantage of such programs will be enhanced by the efforts of organizations such as the Black Retailers Action Group (BRAG). One of the group's goals, as explained by J. Thomas, president of BRAG and also a vice president of Bloomingdale's, "is to

increase the volume of dollars spent by major retailers with minority-owned manufacturers." Thus, with Fenchel's excellent reputation, it should not be difficult to take advantage of such opportunities.

Another department store opportunity should come from Marshall Field's' expansion. On September 18, 1987 the *Chicago Tribune* newspaper reported that "a new Marshall Field's store will open in Columbus, Ohio next year as the start of an expansion campaign in the midwest." Hopefully, as they expand, their demand for Fenchel lampshades will increase.

The most important thing about Fenchel's future marketing and sales efforts is that an increase in revenues will occur from selling to customers interested in Fenchel's premium quality products. The Fenchel reputation for quality, service, and value will not be compromised or sacrificed to increase short-term sales through price discounting.

Facilities

Fenchel is located at 612 S. Clinton Street in Chicago. The operations are in 17,000 square feet of a beautiful open loft space of an industrial building. Over 16,000 square feet is dedicated to manufacturing and the balance to office space. The rent is $2,841 per month, or $2 per square foot. The lease expires September 31, 1989. The lease is expected to be extended prior to the closing of the business sale.

Operating Plan

The quality control plan will primarily consist of measuring quality throughout each step of the manufacturing process instead of at the end. Each production employee will be held accountable for the quality of his or her added value to the end product. Prior to shipment, each lampshade will have been thoroughly inspected.

The inventory plan will be structured to minimize the amount of inventory-carrying cost without threatening raw material availability.

The production plan will remain as it is today. Fenchel will continue to manufacture lampshades to customer orders. Therefore, there will be virtually no finished goods inventory, which can be extremely expensive and vulnerable to obsolescence. As the volume of orders increases, more production employees will be hired to ensure that product quality and delivery commitments do not suffer.

The purchasing plan will be designed to ensure that the number of suppliers is minimized. This will reduce administrative costs and ensure supplier loyalty and commitment. The plan will also require suppliers to consis-

(Continued)

tently deliver raw materials on time; the quality of their materials must consistently meet expectations without rejects; and their costs must always be competitive. Steven's ability to implement such a plan will be enhanced by his previous work experience as a purchasing agent.

Labor Force

Fenchel's labor force of 16 employees (14 production workers and 2 shipping clerks) has been unionized since 1952. The employees are represented by the Warehouse and Mail Order, Local 743, of the International Brothers of Teamsters. There has never been a strike or any kind of work stoppage. The labor contract, which has usually been for two years, expires in June 1988. Kenneth will work with Steven on the new contract.

The workforce is extremely diverse with respect to ethnicity and experience. The ethnic makeup of the employees is 13 blacks, 2 Hispanics, and 1 Asian. Two of the employees are male. The employees have worked for Fenchel from 1 to 22 years, and their ages range from 20 to 70 (Exhibit 8).

Employees find Fenchel an attractive place to work because they are treated well and have a very good compensation package. The average hourly wage is $5, with $4.30 per hour as the starting wage. The company's noncontributory benefit plan begins 90 days after a new employee's starting date. Fenchel pays $21 per month for each employee to a pension fund. Each employee also receives $10,000 worth of life insurance and $1 million worth of major medical insurance coverage. The employees also have disability and workman's compensation. The total cost of these benefits is approximately $1.50 per hour.

Management Team

The management team will consist of Steven as the owner of Fenchel; Gerri Wandall, the office manager; and John Smith, the production supervisor.

Steven will be intimately involved in the operations of Fenchel. His work experience (Exhibit 9) includes general management duties with Cummins Engine Company, financial analysis with UNC Venture Capital Ltd., and business analysis and problem solving with Bain Consulting, Ltd. Along with this diverse work background, he has an MBA from Harvard Business School.

With the assistance of Kenneth for three months, Steven plans to immerse himself in learning the lampshade business and nurturing relationships with customers and employees. His functional responsibilities will include marketing, sales, and purchasing. Finally, his main objective will be to bring in enough revenue to meet payroll, service debt, and maintain and expand the business.

While Steven will oversee the entire operation, the office manager and production supervisor will continue to manage their respective areas. This strategy will minimize disruptions and make the transfer of ownership as smooth as possible.

Gerri, the office manager for the past 5 years, will continue her present duties of order processing and bookkeeping. Her work in these areas will ultimately be enhanced by the introduction of a personal computer.

John, the 53-year-old production supervisor for the past 15 years, will also continue his present duties of managing production operations.

The skills and personalities of this group will complement each other and continue to result in an effective management team. The goals and objectives of the management team will be consistent on-time product delivery, improved product quality, reduced operating costs, labor productivity gains, increased sales and profits, and a happy labor force.

Potential Risks

While Fenchel has a long history of success in the lampshade business there are several risks, all of which can be managed proactively. The threat of department store consolidation is quite prevalent today. Thus, there is a chance that Fenchel could lose an account such as the May Company if it were purchased by another department store that wanted to stock its stores with lampshades from a company other than Fenchel. To minimize this risk, Steven will continue to keep the customer base diversified and not become too dependent on department stores, in general, or any store, specifically. Steven believes it is safe to have the largest customer account for no more than 15% of total sales.

Another risk is the threat of a competitor locating in Chicago or the Midwest. The Fenchel reputation will be a very difficult obstacle for any new competitor to overcome. But Steven will not rely solely on Fenchel's name. He will maintain close relationships with customers to ensure that Fenchel's lampshades completely meet their quality and delivery expectations. He will also manage costs in order to provide the customer with a product that is competitively priced without discounting. Therefore, Fenchel will be able to maintain and grow market share by emphasizing customer service as it relates to quality, delivery, and costs.

(Continued)

APPENDIX 8-A *(Continued)*

HISTORICAL FINANCIAL STATEMENTS
Fenchel Lampshade Company

Cash Flow

	1987[a]	1986	1985	1984
Owner's salaries	$ 94,000	$ 96,000	$ 94,000	$ 96,000
Owner's automobiles (in Chicago and Florida)	11,976	14,000	12,000	11,500
Life and health insurance	6,000	6,000	4,000	4,000
Owner's personal travel and entertainment	13,000	13,000	11,000	10,000
Herbert and Lois Fenchel's Chicago apartment	9,000	9,000	9,000	8,500
Miscellaneous	2,000	2,000	—	—
Profit	108,386	19,000	(9,291)	(21,000)
Total cash flow	$244,342	$159,000	$120,709	$109,000

Income Statement

	1987	1986	1985	1984
Net sales	$957,558	$805,869	$789,047	$743,166
Cost of sales:				
Materials	330,252	299,361	332,459	271,454
Direct labor	140,486	115,906	106,474	74,269
Other costs	24,929	20,089	28,783	29,391
Total cost of sales	495,667	45,356	467,716	375,114
Gross profit	461,891	360,513	321,331	368,052
Operating expenses:				
Factory	113,842	114,638	109,944	161,119
Selling	103,559	95,385	83,578	80,451
Administrative	42,124	35,111	43,100	51,253
Total operating expenses	259,525	245,134	236,622	292,823
Income before partners' salaries	202,366	115,379	84,709	75,229
Partners' salaries	94,000	96,000	94,000	96,000
Net operating income	108,366	19,379	(9,291)	(20,771)
Interest and other income	14,060	8,626	9,150	12,646
Net income	122,426	28,005	(141)	(8,125)

[a] February–December.

(Continued)

163

HISTORICAL FINANCIAL STATEMENTS
Fenchel Lampshade Company

Balance Sheet

	1987	1986	1985	1984
Assets				
Current assets:				
Cash	63,759	18,360	17,494	37,143
Accounts receivables	121,789	75,263	71,062	45,839
Allowance for uncollectible accounts	0	(8,000)	(8,000)	(8,000)
Inventories	110,835	57,108	51,637	28,195
Prepaid insurance	9,528	2,440	8,150	6,300
Prepaid rent	2,842	2,842	2,842	2,842
Other prepaid expenses	0	0	0	0
Total current assets	308,753	147,013	142,984	117,261
Investments	81,559	90,503	130,607	129,407
Machinery, furniture, and fixtures—at cost	32,132	32,132	32,132	32,132
Accumulated depreciation	(32,132)	(32,132)	(32,132)	(32,132)
Deposits	790	425	425	425
Total assets	391,102	237,941	274,061	247,093
Liabilities and Partners' Equity				
Current liabilities:				
Accounts payable	77,322	63,111	58,412	34,058
Accrued liabilities	29,853	29,932	22,477	21,127
Other expenses	62,220	42,239	48,473	45,113
Total current liabilities	169,395	135,282	129,362	100,298
Partners' equity:				
Balance—beginning of year	102,659	144,654	146,795	168,564
Net income	122,426	28,005	(141)	(8,215)
Withdrawals	(3,378)	(70,000)	(2,000)	(13,644)
Balance—end of year	221,707	102,659	144,654	146,795
Total liabilities and partners' equity	391,102	237,941	274,061	247,093

(Continued)

PROJECTED FINANCIAL STATEMENTS
Fenchel Lampshade Company

Income Statement
(Best case scenario)

	1988	1989	1990
Net sales	$1,500,000	$2,000,000	$2,500,000
Cost of sales:			
Materials	555,000	740,000	925,000
Direct labor	195,000	260,000	325,000
Other costs	60,000	80,000	100,000
Total costs	810,000	1,080,000	1,350,000
Gross profit	690,000	920,000	1,150,000
Operating expenses:			
Factory	210,000	280,000	350,000
Selling	150,000	200,000	250,000
Administrative	50,000	55,000	60,000
Total expenses	410,000	535,000	660,000
Income before owners' salary	280,000	385,000	490,000
Owners' salary	50,000	60,000	70,000
Income before debt payments	230,000	330,000	430,000

Balance Sheet
(Best case scenario)

	1988	1989	1990
Assets			
Current assets:			
Cash	$ 20,000	$ 25,000	$ 30,000
Accounts receivable	135,000	180,000	225,000
Allowance for uncollectibles	(8,000)	(8,000)	(8,000)
Merchandise inventories	105,000	140,000	175,000
Prepaid rent	4,250	4,250	4,250
Total current assets	256,250	341,250	426,250
Machinery, furniture, and fixtures at cost	50,000	50,000	50,000
Total assets	316,250	391,250	476,250
Liabilities and Equity			
Current liabilities:			
Accounts payable	$105,000	$140,000	$175,000
Other expenses	75,000	100,000	125,000
Total current liabilities	180,000	240,000	300,000
Long-term debt	550,000	440,000	330,000
Total liabilities	730,000	680,000	630,000

(Continued)

PROJECTED FINANCIAL STATEMENTS
Fenchel Lampshade Company

Income Statement
(Worst case scenario)

	1988	1989	1990
Net sales	$1,100,000	$1,200,000	$1,300,000
Cost of sales:			
Materials	407,000	444,000	481,000
Direct labor	143,000	156,000	169,000
Other costs	44,000	48,000	52,000
Total costs	594,000	648,000	702,000
Gross profit	506,000	552,000	598,000
Operating expenses:			
Factory	154,000	168,000	182,000
Selling	110,000	120,000	130,000
Administrative	33,000	36,000	39,000
Total expenses	297,000	324,000	351,000
Income before owners' salary	209,000	228,000	247,000
Owners' salary	50,000	60,000	70,000
Income before debt payments	159,000	168,000	177,000

Balance Sheet
(Worst case scenario)

	1988	1989	1990
Assets			
Current assets:			
Cash	$ 11,000	$ 12,000	$ 13,000
Accounts receivable	99,000	108,000	117,000
Allowance for uncollectibles	(8,000)	(8,000)	(8,000)
Merchandise inventories	77,000	84,000	91,000
Prepaid rent	4,250	4,250	4,250
Total current assets	183,250	200,250	217,250
Machinery, furniture, and fixtures at cost	50,000	50,000	50,000
Total assets	233,250	250,250	267,250
Liabilities and Equity			
Current liabilities:			
Accounts payable	$105,000	$110,000	$115,000
Other expenses	55,000	60,000	65,000
Total current liabilities	160,000	170,000	180,000
Long-term debt	550,000	440,000	330,000
Total liabilities	710,000	610,000	510,000

(Continued)

EXHIBIT 8-1   Fenchel Lampshade Company

Fenchel Ad Copy Prepared for Marshall Field's

19.99 TO 44.99 Lampshades by Fenchel. Give your old lamps a whole new look with these deluxe lampshades. Choose scallop, shirred and pleated styles in empire or drum shapes and many textures. Orig. 40.00 to 65.00.

Save through March 18 or while quantities last. Lamps, Eighth Floor, State Street and all stores except Water Tower and Lake Forest.

(Continued)

Exhibit 8-2 Fenchel Lampshade Company

Historical Lampshade Sales

Year	Lampshade Sales[a]	Year	Lampshade Sales[a]
1972	$36,900,000	1979	$58,900,000
1973	42,800,000	1980	53,400,000
1974	43,300,000	1981	59,100,000
1975	41,500,000	1982	41,800,000
1976	37,800,000	1983	45,300,000
1977	51,400,000	1984	65,400,000
1978	55,400,000	1985	70,100,000

Source: Census Bureau Annual Survey of Manufacturing Value of Product Shipments.

[a] Does not include metal, plastic, or glass lampshades.

Exhibit 8-3 Fenchel Lampshade Company

Description of Fenchel Catalog

It is with great pride that we introduce our first catalog. Its purposes are to simplify and facilitate your ordering and to show, in detail, the wide scope of the Fenchel lamp shade line.

For more than 50 years, Fenchel Lamp Shade Company has built a reputation for value and workmanship.

All fabrics are sewn—not glued—to assure beauty and quality. A wide array of materials is available.

All rust-resistant frames are offered in an extensive variety of shapes and sizes.

We lead the industry in shadow-free shades.

Trims and folds are bonded to the shade to insure washability.

All stages of production are carefully supervised and inspected.

We hope you find this catalog convenient, and that you continue to avail yourselves of Fenchel lamp shades, and the high standards of excellence they represent.

Fenchel
Lamp Shades

(Continued)

EXHIBIT 8-4   Fenchel Lampshade Company

American Lampshade Manufacturers

Lampshade Manufacturer	Location
1. ABC Lampshade Company	New York
2. Artemis Studios	New York
3. Diane Studios	New York
4. Edwards Lamp and Shade Company	California
5. Else Lamp and Shade Studio	New York
6. Elite Lamp Shade Manufacturing	California
7. Gold-Ray Shades	New Jersey
8. H. Grabell and Sons	New Jersey
9. Grabell Industries	California
10. Hamilton Corporation	Illinois
11. Hirks Lane Lamp Parts	Pennsylvania
12. Lake Shore Studios	Mississippi
13. Lampshades, Inc.	Illinois
14. Loumel Corporation	New Jersey
15. MSWV, Inc.	Illinois
16. Natalie Lamp and Shade Company	New Jersey
17. Paladin Lampshade	Pennsylvania
18. Penn Shade Crafters	Pennsylvania
19. Queen Anne Lampshades	New Jersey
20. RLR Industries	New York
21. Robinson Lamp Parts	New York
22. Roseart Lampshades	New York
23. Saxe lampshade	Pennsylvania
24. Silk-O-Lite	New Jersey
25. Springel Sales	Pennsylvania
26. Standard Shade	New York
27. Stiffel	New York
28. William B. Venit	Illinois
29. Versaponents	New York
30. Frederick Cooper	Illinois
31. Foss	California
32. Style Craft	New York
33. Rod International	Florida
34. Fenchel	Illinois

Source: Lamp and Shade Institute of America.

(Continued)

EXHIBIT 8-5 Fenchel Lampshade Company

Fenchel Trade Journal Advertising

Fenchel

lamp shade co.

NOT INC

612 SOUTH CLINTON • CHICAGO, ILLINOIS 60607
(312) 922-6454-55-56 • 1-800-345-1456

WE'RE OVER 64 YRS. YOUNG

And We Thank You For Your
Continued Support And Confidence

We know the needs of the consumer and provide you with the quality, fashion, value and service to meet their demands.

Why tie your money up in inventory carrying costs? We have outstanding delivery!

*We welcome your visit in Dallas
World Trade Center – Room 10015
where you'll see many exciting
new additions to our lines*

certain territories available for
experienced reps

(Continued)

Exhibit 8-6   Fenchel Lampshade Company

SBA Program for Minority Businesses

SBA SEEKS BIDS FOR 8(a) FIRMS   January 1987

Pursuant to Section 8(a) of the Small Business Act (PL95-507), SBA is seeking select set-aside requirements and competitive procurement opportunities on behalf of Illinois 8(a) minority small business in the product and service areas listed below.

Should you have specific set-aside or competitive procurement opportunities in any of the areas listed, SBA would like to receive your set-aside offering letter or IFB solicitation request. Your cooperation and reply will help develop another source of qualified minority small business suppliers. Please direct all information and questions to: *Howard Norris, SBA Assistant Director, Minority Small Business and Capital Ownership Development Division, at (312) 353-9098.*

Product and Service areas:

Fabricated Metal Products, Janitorial Services, Computer Programming, Corrugated and Solid Fiber Boxes, Coal, Sand, Gravel-Bulk, Engineering Consulting, Industrial Supplies, Bridge Painting, Pharmaceutical Preparations, Exterminating Service, Mfg. Molding Fabricator Plastic, Computer Related Services, Resilient Floor Laying, Machine Shop Jobbing and Repair, Uniforms, Men's Suit Coats, Mechanical and Piping Construction, Data Entry and Processing, General Construction, Manufacture Light Fixtures, Management and Marketing Consulting, Nonresidential Construction & Excavating, Common Carrier, Heavy Construction, Electrical Construction, Manufacture Railroad Car Equipment, Chemical and Chemical Preparation, Nutritional Consulting, Technical Publications, Asphalt Paving, Reupholstery and Furniture Repair, Lubricant Distribution, Piping, Plumbing and Heating, Manufacture Electronic Components, Special Dies and Tools, HIghway-Street Construction, Industrial Garments, Design Engineering and Architecture, Wholesaler of Medical Supplies, Radio and Television Repair, Detective and Protective Services, Concrete Construction, Certified Public Accountants, Real Estate Agents/Managers, Landscaping, Management Consulting, Sewerage Installation, Wholesaler of Metal Products, Lawn and Garden Services, Medal Fabrication, Cleaning Compounds, Dental Equipment Wholesale, Paint Varnish Manufacturing, Technical Writing Consulting, Service Facilities Management, and Garbage and Refuse Collection.

**Add Us
To Your Bidders List
and Multiply Your Response
Send Bid Request
And
Information to
Minority Entrepreneur
300 North State Street #3425
Chicago, Illinois 60610**

(Continued)

EXHIBIT 8-7   Fenchel Lampshade Company

Corporate Purchasing Programs for Minority Owned Firms

REACHES OUT

AN INVITATION TO YOU . . .

Minority-owned manufacturers of merchandise made for resale to department stores are invited to contact A&S Department Store, Minority Vendor Coordinator, 150 Fulton Avenue, Hempstead, NY 11550, telephone 516-489-7357.

A&S has successful partnerships with minority-owned businesses. In fact, we are winners of the 1986 New York/New Jersey Minority Purchasing Council "Helping Hand" Award.

WE HOPE YOU'LL REACH OUT TO US.

A&S is a division of Federated Department Stores, Inc., which also includes Bloomingdale's, Bullock's/Bullocks Wilshire, Burdines, The Children's Place, Filene's, Filene's Basement, Foley's, Gold Circle/Richway, Goldsmith's, Lazarus, I. Magnin, Main-Street, Ralphs and Rich's.

All Federated divisions have minority vendor programs. Inquiries may be made through Communiplex Services, 35 East Seventh Street, Cincinnati, OH 45202. Call 513-621-2812.

(Continued)

EXHIBIT 8-8   **Fenchel Lampshade Company**

Selected Data on the Fenchel Workforce

Number of Employees	Years with Fenchel
10	1–2
4	4
1	11
2	15
1	22

Number of Employees	Age
3	20–30 years old
3	31–40 years old
2	40–50 years old
10	50–60 years old

(Continued)

EXHIBIT 8-9   **Steven Rogers**

Education

1983–1985   **HARVARD GRADUATE SCHOOL OF BUSINESS ADMINISTRATION BOSTON, MA**

Master in Business Administration General management curriculum. Member of Venture Capital Club and the Afro-American Student Union. COGME Fellow. Resident Director of Wellesley High School "A Better Chance" program.

1975–1979   **WILLIAMS COLLEGE**   **WILLIAMSTOWN, MA**

Bachelor of Arts. Liberal arts program with a major in history. Deans List. Recipient of Lehman Scholarship, Black Student Leadership Award, and Belvedere Brooks Memorial Medal. Varsity Football. Member of E.C.A.C. Division II All-Star Football Team. Treasurer of Black Student Union. Resident Tutor of Mount Greylock High School "A Better Chance" program. Tutor at Monroe State Prison.

Employment Experience

1986–Present   **BAIN AND COMPANY**

Consultant. Case team member on consulting assignments for *Fortune 500* corporations in the health care, glassware, electronics, and manufacturing industries. Researched and analyzed financial, market, and productivity data for use in developing and implementing performance improvement strategies. Managed client task forces and teams.

1985–1986   **HARVARD BUSINESS SCHOOL**

Research Associate. Wrote and published business school case studies concerning various manufacturing businesses. Collected data through statistical analyses, field work, interviews, and library research. Subjects included rubber products, health care, and communications industries.

Summer 1984   **UNC VENTURES, INC.**   **BOSTON, MA**

Summer Associate. Assessed the market and return potential of proposals for venture capital financing. Performed detailed investigation of selected ventures, analyzed proposed strategy, market conditions, management qualifications, valuation, and pricing terms. Completed legal synopses, business overviews, and internal rate of return and investment recovery analyses for portfolio companies. Attended UNC Ventures Board of Directors meeting. Visited portfolio companies. Reported directly to the President.

1981–1983   **CONSOLIDATED DIESEL COMPANY**   **WHITAKERS, NC**

Original member of company's start-up team on $450MM project. Commodity Manager of direct and indirect materials. Responsible for $15MM in purchases annually. Negotiated long-term commodity and service contracts. Initiated source selection and approval. Implemented engineering changes. Controlled price increases. Purchased material from foreign suppliers. Consolidated Minority Supplier Program. Interfaced with manufacturing, accounting, finance, engineering, quality, transportation, and marketing. Completed 75% of examinations for National Certified Purchasing Manager certification.

1979–1981   **CUMMINS ENGINE COMPANY**   **COLUMBUS, IN**

Supervisor of Customer Services Parts Department. Trained and supervised 8 employees responsible for entering, administering, and expediting parts ordered by distributors. Developed an order entry presentation for visitor orientation program. Coordinated distributor ownership transfers. Supported Marketing's $100MM special parts program.

Personal Background

Head coach, P.A.L. Football team, "A Better Chance" student at Radnor High School in Pennsylvania. Raised in Chicago, Illinois. Guardian of 11-year-old sister for 6 years. Married with two daughters. N.A.C.E.L. host family. Interests include traveling, reading, and participating in all sports.

(Continued)

TABLE 8-1   Fenchel Lampshade Company

Proposed Sources and Uses of Funds—1988

SOURCES OF FUNDS:

Bank (SBA loan)	$300,000
Fenchel Trade Debt	105,000
City of Chicago	100,000
MESBIC/SBIC	115,000
Fenchel Family	75,000
State of Illinois	50,000
Steven and Michele Rogers	50,000
TOTAL SOURCES OF FUNDS	**$795,000**

USE OF FUNDS:

Accounts receivables	$120,000
Inventory	125,000
Machinery, equipment, and patterns	100,000
Noncompete clause (5 years)	400,000
Working capital	50,000
TOTAL USES OF FUNDS	**$795,000**

TABLE 8-2   Fenchel Lampshade Company

Terms of Sources of Funds

Source	Amount	Form	Terms
1. Bank Loan	$300,000	Senior debt	• prime plus 2%
2. City of Chicago	$100,000	Subordinated Debt (2nd position)	• 75% of prime • 60 monthly payments
3. State of Illinois	$ 50,000	Subordinated Debt (3rd position)	• 5% • 60 monthly payments
4. Fenchel family	$ 75,000	Subordinated Debt (4th position)	• 10% • 60 monthly payments of $1,592.95
5. Fenchel Trade Debt	$105,000		• Normal terms of invoices
6. MESBIC/SBIC	$115,000	• Equity (15–25%) • Preferred Stock	• 9% cumulative dividend of $2,600 paid quarterly • Redeem preferred stock at beginning of Year 4

APPENDIX 8-1

GENERAL MACROECONOMIC CONDITIONS

	Q1Y86	Q2Y86	Q3Y86	Q4Y86	Q1Y87	Q2Y87	Q3Y87	Q4Y87	Q1Y88	Q2Y88
Moody's Corporate Yields (A rated)	10.06	9.78	9.76	9.39	9.09	9.94	10.85	10.58	10.05	10.38
Moody's Corporate Yields (AA rated)	9.46	9.35	9.40	8.99	8.83	9.59	10.42	10.26	9.77	10.10
Moody's Corporate Yields (AAA rated)	8.94	9.01	8.95	8.47	8.34	9.25	10.24	10.07	9.55	9.83
Inflation	1.96	1.58	1.38	0.82	3.31	3.74	4.17	3.77	3.37	3.69
Consumer Price Index	1.09	1.09	1.10	1.11	1.12	1.14	1.15	1.16	1.17	1.18
Unemployment Rate	7.20	7.20	7.00	6.60	6.60	6.20	5.90	5.70	5.70	5.40
T-Bill 1 Mo.	6.15	5.82	5.00	4.75	5.10	5.33	6.20	3.70	5.50	6.00
T-Bill 2 Mo.	6.35	5.96	5.22	5.35	5.35	5.65	6.40	5.30	5.68	6.28
T-Bill 3 Mo.	6.32	5.95	5.19	5.65	5.60	5.73	6.60	5.69	5.70	6.55
T-Bill 6 Mo.	6.26	5.93	5.38	5.62	5.73	5.91	6.80	6.17	6.04	6.70
T-Bill 12 Mo.	6.29	6.02	5.49	5.60	5.76	6.29	7.25	6.63	6.35	6.98
Prime Rate	9.10	8.50	7.50	7.50	7.50	8.25	8.70	8.75	8.50	9.00
Gov't Bond 5 Yr.	7.19	7.23	6.98	6.81	7.02	8.02	9.21	8.33	8.04	8.41
Gov't Bond 10 Yr.	7.39	7.35	7.45	7.23	7.51	8.38	9.63	8.83	8.57	8.82
Gov't Bond 30 Yr.	7.44	7.24	7.60	7.49	7.81	8.51	9.79	8.95	8.82	8.87
Real GDP $ bil. (1992 $)	5461	5467	5496	5527	5562	5618	5667	5751	5785	5844
Wilshire 5000	2435.43	2577.65	2360.48	2434.95	2928.33	3004.9	3170.98	2417.12	2591.09	2729.65
S&P 500	238.9	250.84	231.32	242.17	291.7	304	321.83	247.08	258.89	273.5

Source: Compiled from Citibase.

COMPARABLE COMPANY FINANCIAL INFORMAITON

Company Name

	1985	1986	1987		1985	1986	1987
BARRY WRIGHT CORP				**KNOLL INTERNATIONAL**			
Sales	$196.87	$195.14	$205.69	Sales	$202.83	$225.59	$282.84
COGS	$103.01	$105.62	$118.08	COGS	$119.57	$155.47	$176.97
SGA	$ 69.26	$ 70.92	$ 69.54	SGA	$ 52.29	$ 69.82	$ 68.11
Net Income	$ 10.52	$ 7.04	$ 8.36	Net Income	$ 13.01	−$6.99	$ 1.86
Total Assets	$149.75	$133.12	$137.90	Total Assets	$179.80	$247.66	$277.20
Total Debt	$ 6.15	$ 5.84	$ 5.16	Total Debt	$ 56.64	$106.15	$ 96.20
Current Assets	$ 90.20	$ 74.22	$ 79.13	Current Assets	$102.87	$155.95	$162.78
Current Liabilities	$ 30.01	$ 30.75	$ 26.85	Current Liabilities	$ 47.18	$ 67.19	$ 84.13
Market Value of Equity	$182.82	$123.45	$ 83.51	Market Value of Equity	$156.19	$122.89	$124.23
Book Value of Equity	$107.91	$ 90.24	$ 97.02	Book Value of Equity	$ 70.35	$ 65.42	$ 90.83
PE Ratio	16.68	18.70	9.94	PE Ratio	12.62	20.95	NA
Beta			1.146	Beta			1.002
BUSH INDUSTRIES				**NEWELL COMPANIES**			
Sales	$41.67	$65.40	$93.48	Sales	$350.05	$401.36	$719.69
COGS	$30.19	$48.87	$67.05	COGS	$228.46	$274.34	$511.24
SGA	$ 6.85	$ 8.61	$13.14	SGA	$ 79.08	$ 71.17	$105.46
Net Income	$ 1.62	$ 2.51	$ 5.55	Net Income	$ 18.85	$ 24.01	$ 37.22
Total Assets	$37.45	$46.92	$53.39	Total Assets	$275.84	$335.28	$842.04
Total Debt	$22.46	$26.09	$23.12	Total Debt	$ 81.79	$ 63.62	$251.72
Current Assets	$18.99	$27.23	$34.34	Current Assets	$158.03	$164.38	$353.39
Current Liabilities	$15.06	$21.38	$23.48	Current Liabilities	$ 75.09	$ 76.14	$167.74
Market Value of Equity	$16.25	$34.15	$53.96	Market Value of Equity	$191.36	$309.29	$325.13
Book Value of Equity	$10.03	$12.69	$18.41	Book Value of Equity	$120.09	$198.01	$354.63
PE Ratio	9.46	13.49	9.73	PE Ratio	10.59	12.44	10.23
Beta			1.290	Beta			0.923
GF CORP				**SHELBY WILLIAMS INDS INC**			
Sales	$134.51	$130.82	$134.97	Sales	$118.03	$130.52	$159.65
COGS	$ 98.91	$ 90.87	$104.93	COGS	$ 84.66	$ 90.85	$114.59
SGA	$ 34.38	$ 34.05	$ 28.42	SGA	$ 17.87	$ 21.17	$ 25.61
Net Income	$ 0.45	$ 0.69	−$3.59	Net Income	$ 8.42	$ 9.30	$ 9.58
Total Assets	$ 89.57	$ 73.73	$7 2.68	Total Assets	$ 64.31	$ 96.41	$102.48
Total Debt	$ 38.17	$ 24.61	$ 22.87	Total Debt	$ 1.26	$ 25.19	$ 22.21
Current Assets	$ 58.71	$ 45.89	$ 47.23	Current Assets	$ 48.28	$ 68.98	$ 66.28
Current Liabilities	$ 28.20	$ 19.39	$ 23.44	Current Liabilities	$ 15.90	$ 20.21	$ 20.38
Market Value of Equity	$ 22.20	$ 20.37	$ 10.21	Market Value of Equity	$178.23	$175.44	$159.46
Book Value of Equity	$ 31.11	$ 31.83	$ 28.23	Book Value of Equity	$ 46.27	$ 52.73	$ 59.08
PE Ratio	NM	58.33	NM	PE Ratio	21.12	18.89	16.67
Beta			1.700	Beta			1.169

(Continued)

APPENDIX 8-2 *(Continued)*

Company Name

	1985	1986	1987		1985	1986	1987
HILLENBRAND INDUSTRIES				**TAB PRODUCTS**			
Sales	$507.61	$641.07	$724.60	Sales	$121.43	$123.68	$131.96
COGS	$274.57	$286.91	$328.49	COGS	$ 60.02	$ 60.15	$ 66.97
SGA	$134.18	$191.26	$215.91	SGA	$ 45.33	$ 46.80	$ 50.81
Net Income	$ 32.83	$ 50.52	$ 57.43	Net Income	$ 5.69	$ 6.79	$ 7.30
Total Assets	$539.27	$587.28	$660.46	Total Assets	$ 62.52	$ 68.04	$ 71.90
Total Debt	$160.61	$141.25	$141.44	Total Debt	$ 1.67	$ 0.93	$ 0.81
Current Assets	$230.37	$255.16	$283.95	Current Assets	$ 44.09	$ 48.99	$ 51.94
Current Liabilities	$126.60	$102.94	$138.74	Current Liabilities	$ 13.74	$ 13.63	$ 14.03
Market Value of Equity	$471.35	$915.56	$863.97	Market Value of Equity	$ 95.44	$116.92	$ 95.21
Book Value of Equity	$257.61	$290.91	$312.43	Book Value of Equity	$ 47.27	$ 53.18	$ 56.75
PE Ratio	14.36	18.27	15.15	PE Ratio	16.93	17.50	13.42
Beta			0.873	Beta			1.056
INTERLAKE CORP				**VIRCO MANUFACTURING**			
	$850.17	$736.01	$823.06		$168.75	$172.34	$183.42
COGS	$655.64	$529.42	$601.15	COGS	$110.31	$113.99	$132.29
SGA	$122.19	$117.23	$135.42	SGA	$ 41.63	$ 42.00	$ 47.28
Net Income	$ 28.18	$ 32.56	$ 54.37	Net Income	$ 3.52	$ 4.00	−$2.97
Total Assets	$729.40	$597.06	$693.80	Total Assets	$ 80.37	$ 90.98	$ 99.10
Total Debt	$125.88	$135.82	$117.32	Total Debt	$ 27.92	$ 36.22	$ 42.98
Current Assets	$371.11	$331.33	$442.27	Current Assets	$ 60.86	$ 69.96	$ 77.97
Current Liabilities	$191.27	$185.35	$250.97	Current Liabilities	$ 24.45	$ 27.18	$ 37.24
Market Value of Equity	$291.10	$444.65	$467.71	Market Value of Equity	$ 42.72	$ 43.26	$ 13.87
Book Value of Equity	$351.75	$250.36	$281.31	Book Value of Equity	$ 30.71	$ 34.61	$ 31.54
PE Ratio	10.04	14.36	9.06	PE Ratio	8.41	10.04	NM
Beta			0.912	Beta			1.070

Source: Compiled from Compustat.

9

A Note on Valuation in Entrepreneurial Ventures

INTRODUCTION

Valuation is the central concept in finance. Although many entrepreneurs believe that the process of valuation is a meaningless exercise, the tools and techniques discussed in this note are arguably far more important to a young, entrepreneurial firm than they are to a large established one. Without methods to assess value, capital budgeting becomes impossible. While elements of valuation remain an "art," finance theory and its implementation through valuation methodologies have important implications for practice. When reasonable assumptions are made, the techniques discussed in this note can lead to better decision making in whatever setting you work. The margin for error in an entrepreneurial firm, however, is much smaller than it is in a large firm with considerable resources. Maximizing the probability that the "right" decision is made is the goal of proper valuation methodologies.

Valuation methodologies can be widely applied to analyze many of the decisions that a firm faces. Anything that might affect the size or timing of a firm's cash flow or changes its riskiness affects the firm's value. Whether it is a new research project, a new production facility, an acquisition target, or a new product launch, value is the fundamental currency that compares all the firm's potential decisions. The ability to make value-increasing decisions is clearly enhanced by a thorough understanding of the material in this note. In addition, a well-thought-out valuation will provide important information that is useful in managing the firm and monitoring its progress.

This note will discuss various valuation techniques and when they are appropriate. The theory behind much of this discussion will be glossed over in order to keep this note to a reasonable length. A detailed analysis and discussion of these issues would occupy a large book. The reference section of this note contains a detailed list of texts and articles that explore these issues in more detail. Many of the references are highly spe-

Professor Paul A. Gompers prepared this case as the basis for class discussion rather than to illustrate either effective or ineffective handling of an administrative situation.

cialized and can provide a deep understanding of the theory behind the methodologies. This note is intended to present the reason for and the mechanics of several approaches to valuation and to give you a sense of when the various techniques are appropriate. The interested student should refer to the appropriate source for further reading.

The rest of this note is divided into five sections. The note starts by discussing two approaches to discounted cash flow analysis: capital cash flows (CCF) and weighted average cost of capital (WACC). These methods form the basis of other techniques that are applied and should be understood fully. The note then proceeds to discuss scenario analysis, which is an attempt to describe the various potential outcomes for a young, start-up firm. We then move to an analysis of valuation in multistage decisions.

There are two related approaches to valuing these types of situations. Decision tree approaches to valuation are the first and most straightforward approach to analyze these types of situations. Real options analysis is a second method and is the subject of related notes. Finally, this note concludes by discussing what is commonly referred to as the "venture capital" valuation method. Many private equity participants utilize this methodology in their due diligence. The note discusses the rules of thumb that are assumed in the method and show how CCF, or WACC can give you more information in the process of valuation.

DISCOUNTED CASH FLOW VALUATION: CASH FLOWS

Both the CCF and WACC methods of valuation start by determining cash flows from operations. These cash flows are pre-financing; that is, they are independent of the capital structure of the firm. One common mistake that students make when calculating cash flows for CCF or WACC is to take out interest payments from the cash flows and call that number cash flow to equityholders. While this approach has merit (it is referred to as equity cash flow valuation), it does not easily allow an individual to calculate the value of the firm independent of financing and under various financing scenarios. Equation (1) gives a quick refresher on how to calculate cash flows. Subscripts denote time periods.

$$CF_t = EBIT_t^\star \, (1 - \tau) + DEPR_t - CAPEX - \Delta \, WK_t + other_t \qquad (1)$$

where

$$CF = \text{Cash Flow}$$
$$EBIT = \text{Earnings Before Interest and Taxes}$$
$$\tau = \text{Corporate Tax Rate}$$
$$DEPR = \text{Depreciation}$$
$$CAPEX = \text{Capital Expenditures}$$
$$\Delta WK = \text{Increases in Working Capital}$$
$$other = \text{Increases in Taxes Payable, Wages Payable, etc.}$$

These cash flows are what are economically significant to the firm and to an investor. As will be discussed below, estimating cash flows is far more important than determining the discount rate. People valuing risky projects tend to increase the discount rate if they feel that the project's returns are uncertain. This "fudge" factor addition to the discount rate should always be avoided. The critical element of CCF and WACC analysis is to have unbiased estimates of free cash flows. One way to approach this estimation is scenario analysis, which will be discussed below.

VALUING CASH FLOWS WITH THE CCF METHOD

The capital cash flows (CCF) method of valuation takes cash flows estimates and calculates the value of an unlevered (all equity) firm. The value of the debt tax shield is added to the present value of future cash flows in an unlevered firm. CCF also adds other elements of value enhancement if they are present (e.g., present value of investment tax credits, etc.). In order to calculate the value of the firm, the first order of business is to forecast cash flows from Equation (1). After cash flows for periods 1 to T are obtained, a terminal value (TV) is calculated. The firm is assumed to grow forever at the rate g, and the appropriate discount rate for the unlevered firm (more below) is determined by the riskiness of the firm's assets, r_a.

$$TV_T = \frac{CF_T^\star(1 + g)}{r_a - g} \tag{2}$$

Other methods of calculating a TV are possible. Most of you should be familiar with salvage value analysis from your introductory finance course. In the salvage value method, the TV is just the sum of recoverable value in the final year, making sure to take tax considerations into account. A brief comment on growth rates is appropriate. First, always check the reality of your growth rate assumption. Remember that if you are using nominal discount rates, your terminal growth rate should reflect your beliefs about inflation. Real growth is the nominal growth rate minus the expected inflation rate. If you get large negative or large positive numbers, what does that imply? Is the business going to shrink in real terms? Is it going to grow in real terms forever? We often assume a growth rate slightly larger than the expected inflation rate to compensate for faster growth now but zero real growth in the future. In the long-run (when the "long run" starts is dependent on industry maturity, firm strategy, etc.), most firms will probably grow at the rate of inflation. Be aware that if your cash flow estimates are over a short period of time (three years or less), then the terminal value will drive your estimates of net present value.

Once the terminal value is calculated, the net present value of future cash flows is given by Equation (3):

$$PV^U = \frac{CF_1}{1 + r_a} + \frac{CF_2}{(1 + r_a)^2} + \cdots + \frac{CF_T + TV_T}{(1 + r_a)^T} \tag{3}$$

The debt taken on by the firm provides tax advantages because the interest payments are tax deductible. The value of the tax shield, TS, in period t from debt level D paying interest at a rate of r_d is given by (4):

$$TS_t = \tau^\star r_d^\star D \tag{4}$$

These tax shields need to be discounted at a rate appropriate to their riskiness. If firms set debt at a level proportional to firm value, then the tax shields are as risky as the firm's assets, so the proper discount rate is r_a. In that case, the present value of the tax shield for the firm, *PVTS*, having debt of D_t and a long-run equilibrium debt level of D_{eq} is given by Equation (5):

$$PVTS = \frac{\tau^{\star} r_d{}^{\star} D_1}{(1 + r_a)} + \frac{\tau^{\star} r_d{}^{\star} D_2}{(1 + r_a)^2} + \frac{\tau^{\star} r_d{}^{\star} D_3}{(1 + r_a)^3} + \cdots + \frac{\dfrac{\tau^{\star} r_d{}^{\star} D_{eq}}{r_a}}{(1 + r_a)^T}$$

$$= \frac{\tau^{\star} r_d{}^{\star} D_1}{(1 + r_a)} + \frac{\tau^{\star} r_d{}^{\star} D_2}{(1 + r_a)^2} + \frac{\tau^{\star} r_d{}^{\star} D_3}{(1 + r_a)^3} + \cdots + \frac{\tau^{\star} r_d{}^{\star} D_{eq}}{r_a{}^{\star}(1 + r_a)^T} \qquad (5)$$

If D is the constant level of debt, then (5) implies that the debt tax shield is just $(\tau^{\star} r_d{}^{\star} D)/r_a$. The capital cash flow value of the project is now given by Equation (6):

$$PV_{CCF} = PV^U + PVTS$$

$$= \frac{CF_1}{(1 + r_a)} + \frac{\tau^{\star} r_d{}^{\star} D_1}{(1 + r_a)} + \frac{CF_2}{(1 + r_a)^2} + \frac{\tau^{\star} r_d{}^{\star} D_2}{(1 + r_a)^2} + \cdots + \frac{\left[\dfrac{(1 + g)CF_T}{r_a - g}\right]}{(1 + r_a)^T} + \frac{\tau^{\star} r_d{}^{\star} D_{eq}}{r_a(1 + r_a)^T} \quad (6)$$

This value is then compared with the investment cost to determine whether or not the firm or individual should undertake the project. CCF minus the cost of the investment, I, yields a much talked about term, net present value (*NPV*).

$$NPV_{CCF} - APV - I \qquad (7)$$

DISCOUNT RATES

Estimation of discount rates should be familiar to most people from earlier course work. Simple formulas provide a guide to appropriate rates.

$$r_a = r_f + \beta^{U\star}(r_m - r_f) \qquad (8)$$

where

r_a = discount rate for the firm's assets, that is, the rate on unlevered equity

r_f = risk free rate

β^U = unlevered beta

r_m = market rate of return on common stocks

$(r_m - r_f)$ = market risk premium

The underlying basis for (8) is the Capital Asset Pricing Model, and its implications have been extensively discussed in the academic and practitioners' literature. I will discuss some of the potential caveats to the use of betas in estimating cost of capital, but given that we have no better alternative, you should use it with caution.

The first question that (8) brings up is, what are the appropriate rates to use? r_f is the risk-free rate. When determining the appropriate risk-free rate, you should attempt to match the maturity of the investment project with that of r_f. For example, if you are valuing a long-term investment project, r_f would be the yield on long-term Treasury bonds minus 1%. For shorter-term investment projects, you should use the short-term

Treasury rate. The 1% reduction in the long-term Treasury rate reflects the historical regularity that long-term rates have exceeded short-term Treasury rates by about 1% on average.

The market risk premium used can vary. Some evidence indicates that the risk premium has decreased over time to around 6% today. From 1926 to 2000, the return on common stocks (1) exceeded the return on Treasury bills by 8.49%; and (2) exceeded the return on Treasury bonds by 7.13%. More recently, the return on common stocks has: (1) exceeded the return on Treasury bills by 6.70%; and (2) exceeded (since 1970) the return on Treasury bonds by 6.99%. A risk premium of between 7 and 8% is probably appropriate. Whatever you choose, you should maintain consistency. Do not estimate the present value of one project using a risk premium of 7% and evaluate another using a risk premium of 8%.

Choosing an estimate of β^U is more difficult than the market risk premium. β^U is the systematic risk of the investment being evaluated assuming that it is 100% equity financed. For public companies, estimates of β^U can be obtained from a regression of stock returns for that company on the market return. The beta estimates obtained from stock returns are, however, equity betas for levered firms, β^L. To go from the equity beta to the unlevered beta, we need to "unlever" the beta.

$$\beta^U = \frac{\beta^L}{[1 + (D^i / E^i)]} \tag{9}$$

where

    D^i = total debt of company i.

    E^i = market value of equity for company i.

    τ = tax rate.

If the project is substantially different from the firm's existing assets or the firm is privately held, then you should search for comparable firms that have assets and activities that are similar to the investment project. As the following discussion will make clear, the more firms you can find that are similar to the project being evaluated, the more confidence you will have in your estimate of beta.

A question often arises when there are no comparable companies. This often occurs in entrepreneurial or venture capital settings. The firm may be doing something new or have a totally new project. In this case you need to use a little common sense to get "ballpark" estimates of the systematic risk of the firm. If you have accounting data on the firm, you can try to use "earnings betas" which have some correlation with equity betas. You should also try to think about how cyclical the firm is. Is the risk systematic, or can it be diversified away? How does the firm fare in booms and busts? These types of questions will get you close to an appropriate discount rate when trying to do valuation. Remember, however, that you should always see how sensitive the value is to various discount rates. It is also important to worry more about cash flow estimation.

SOME THOUGHTS ABOUT DISCOUNT RATES

When you calculate a beta for a firm, you should not regard this as *the* discount rate. Considerable controversy exists about the validity of the Capital Asset Pricing Model that underlies the calculation of costs of capital in this way. Without going into the academic debate, I just warn you that you should not think that betas somehow represent facts that will exactly estimate value.

The first caution is to note that betas are measured with a significant amount of error. The betas of companies that do very similar things often appear to be quite different. If one looks, however, at the standard errors of the estimate (i.e., the potential range of values), the precision of beta estimates for any one company is quite low. For this reason, it is useful to try to use a number of comparable companies in the search for a proper beta. Using a greater number of firms can average out the noise in the estimation of beta. There is usually a trade-off between picking many comparable firms or only a few. The greater the number of comparables, the greater the reduction in estimation error. At the same time, however, you run the risk of including firms that are not truly comparable.

Even trying to find comparables may prove troublesome. One should try to find companies that are as close to the project or acquisition target as possible. This might entail a detailed analysis of what the comparables actually do and the various weights these activities have within the firm.

Finally, the patterns of betas vary over time even for one particular company. If one looks at the beta for an individual company, the beta can change from year to year. The systematic risk of the firm may vary, the capital structure may vary, or both. This fact should provide some caution about using betas estimated over long time periods.

These points are not intended to dissuade you from using discounted cash flow methods for valuing firms and projects. Alternatives have little justification in most cases. You should remember, however, that considerable care needs to be taken when applying the simple formulas. Think about which firms are closest to the firm being valued. Think about the underlying economics of the firm.

WEIGHTED AVERAGE COST OF CAPITAL (WACC)

Estimation using weighted average cost of capital starts with the same cash flows and asset betas with which CCF starts. The difference between the two methods is where the tax advantages of debt comes into the calculation. In CCF the value of the debt tax shield is calculated each year. Therefore, the value of debt and interest payment can be changing over time. With WACC the debt tax advantage affects the discount rate applied to the cash flows. This implies that we either use some long-run debt-to-equity ratio or some average debt-to-equity ratio for the firm. If debt changes a lot over time, then WACC can be somewhat cumbersome.

The first step in WACC is to determine the appropriate discount rate. Using the same inputs as in the CCF method, the discount rate for WACC, r_{WACC} is given by Equation (10):

$$r_{WACC} = \frac{r_e^{L}{}^{*}E + r_d{}^{*}(1 - \tau)^{*}D}{D + E} \tag{10}$$

To estimate the cost of equity, r_e^{L}, you need to relever beta assuming the appropriate debt to equity ratio.

$$\beta^L = \beta^U {}^{*} \left[1 + \frac{D}{E} \right] \tag{11}$$

The levered cost of equity is then given by Equation (12):

$$r_e^L = r_f + \beta^{L\star}(r_m - r_f) \tag{12}$$

The appropriate net present value of the firm is then calculated by discounting the pre-interest payment cash flows by the appropriate weighted average cost of capital. Equation (13) gives that calculation.

$$PV_{WACC} = \frac{CF_1}{(1 + r_{WACC})^1} + \frac{CF_2}{(1 + r_{WACC})^2} + \cdots + \frac{\left[\dfrac{(1 + g)CF_T}{r_{WACC} - g}\right]}{(1 + r_{WACC})^T} \tag{13}$$

The net present value of the project is then given by Equation (14):

$$NPV_{WACC} = PV_{WACC} - I \tag{14}$$

The values you obtain with WACC and CCF should give you very close answers. Appendix 1 gives an example of both CCF and WACC valuations of a certain hypothetical firm. The values obtained in each are very close to the other, which is comforting.

The advice of this section is to employ the method that you feel most comfortable using. The CCF method is perhaps easier to use and allows you to explicitly calculate the net present value of the tax shield effects of debt financing. WACC may be easier to implement if the numbers are presented with an equilibrium debt-to-equity ratio. Remember that whichever method you use, the values you get are only as good as what you put in. Garbage in, garbage out! Make reasonable and justifiable assumptions when you attempt to value firms.

SCENARIO ANALYSIS

Scenario analysis is one attempt to analyze the value of a firm that has considerable uncertainty about cash flows. If we think that the cash flows in the pro formas are an unbiased estimate, then CCF or WACC should be applied to those cash flows. Sometimes, however, you may not believe the cash flows that are presented in a business plan or proposal. In that case, you can try to simulate the distribution of potential outcomes by creating various values for various outcomes.

The number of scenarios should be enough to capture the shape of the distribution without becoming overly complex. Two to five scenarios is probably sufficient. Once an estimate of cash flows is made in each of the scenarios, the net present value of each scenario is calculated using either the CCF or WACC method. Exhibit 9-1 shows a simple example of a scenario analysis in diagrammatic form. The dollar figures at the end of each branch would be the present value of the cash flows under each scenario. The scenarios can be more complex than is shown here.

The next step is to assign various probabilities to the outcomes. Although this is inherently subjective, the market and opportunity analysis that we do in Entrepreneurial Finance should help you estimate what these probabilities might be. While you will never be completely accurate, you can usually justify a distribution that looks reasonable. Always provide supporting explanations for why you chose the relative weights that you did. Common sense pays huge dividends. In Exhibit 9-1, the "best case" scenario is assigned a 25% probability of occurring, the "expected case" has a 50% probability of occurring, and the "worst case" has a 25% probability. When scenario present

---

EXHIBIT 9-1

SCENARIO ANALYSIS

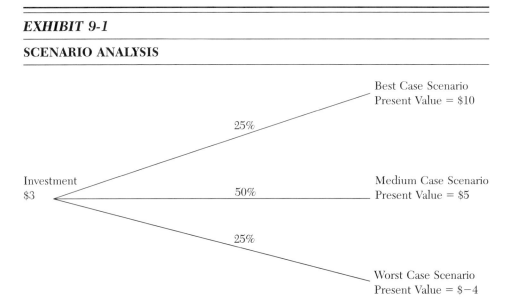

The exhibit displays a hypothetical investment that has three possible scenarios. The present value at the end of each branch is the present value of future cash flows from the project ignoring the initial investment cost. Net present value is just the weighted average of the value of each scenario minus the investment cost, that is, $1.

---

values are weighted by their expected probability of occurring, an expected net present value can be estimated. In the case of Exhibit 9-1, the NPV is $1.

You should not view scenarios as anything mystical or innovative. The use of various scenarios is just a mechanism for you to get an unbiased estimate of cash flows. You can just as easily weight the cash flows from the various scenarios to get your unbiased cash flow estimates. Had I explicitly given you the cash flows of the best, expected, and worst cases, you could have weighted those cash flows by the scenario probabilities. Discounting these cash flows using CCF or WACC will give you the same answer as weighting the value of each scenario.

The use of scenario analysis can be very helpful. Many companies provide a best, expected, and worst case scenario to start the process. Other firms actually use a continuous distribution of outcomes and use computers to estimate the value of these distributions.

Scenario analysis is also useful because it gives you a sense of how well you are doing. Attaining a certain milestone may indicate whether or not you are on a best case track. The forecasts also give you a way to institute monitoring and controls by identifying the value drivers of the business.

MULTISTAGE INVESTMENT PROJECTS UNDER UNCERTAINTY

Many entrepreneurial ventures are staged investments in which the entrepreneur or investors have multiple points to reevaluate the project and choose whether or not to continue the project. These sorts of projects often entail many decision points along the way. An entrepreneur can gather more information and decide what is the best course of action. These types of projects are difficult to value using simple discounted cash flow techniques. We will discuss two approaches to addressing the valuation of these multistage projects. The first is decision tree analysis, which uses discounted cash flow analysis matched with an explicit consideration of various decisions that are made along the way and the various probabilities of certain events occurring along the way. We take up this analysis next. In many cases, a second approach is very useful. Real options are also a way to value these types of projects. While this note discusses the real option approach, the mechanics of the analysis are too complex for this note. Later we will explicitly address the issue of real option valuation techniques.

DECISION TREE ANALYSIS

Multistage investments present problems that are difficult to assess with simple discounted cash flow valuation models. It is often the case that a firm can invest only a fraction of the capital required to complete the project but can gather information after a certain amount of time. This information may be helpful in determining if subsequent investment is profitable. Venture capitalists utilize multistage investments for just that reason. Simple CCF or WACC ignores this multistage decision process and may lead to wrong investment decisions. Projects may have a negative NPV but still be attractive opportunities. One way to assess the value of investment is to use decision trees to estimate the value of the project. As will be discussed below, if the project can be well parameterized, the analysis may be amenable to real options approaches.

Exhibit 9-2 shows a simple decision tree example. The values at the end of the decision tree represent the present value of cash flows under each scenario. At point A a decision about investment in a test plant needs to be taken. The test plant requires an investment of $1 million today. Assume that we choose to invest in a full-scale plant next year, the present value of the cost of the investment is $3 million. With 50% probability, the test plant will be successful. If the test plant fails, the investment returns 0 for sure. If the test plant succeeds (i.e., we reach point B) and a full-scale plant is constructed, then the investment "succeeds" with 50% probability. The investment is worthless in the other 50% of the cases.

The proper strategy to begin valuation is to proceed backwards from the end. At point B, would it be worth investing $3 million in present value terms to have a 50% probability of returning $16 million and 50% probability of returning 0? Clearly, the answer is yes. The net present value of that investment is $5 million, that is, 0.5*16 + 0.5*0 = 5. Now start at point A. Is it worth investing $1 million today to have a 50% probability of a $5 million return and a 50% probability of 0? Again the answer is yes. The net present value of that investment is $1.5 million. Another way to see the same result is to realize that with 25% probability, the net present value of the project will be $12 million. With 25% probability the investment will be worth −$4 million. In 50% of the cases, the project's NPV will be −$1 million. Weighting these outcomes by their respective probabilities yields an expected NPV of $1.5 million.

As in the case of scenario analysis, the decision trees can be as complicated or as simple as you want them to be. The probabilities and explicit branches of the tree may seem like an oversimplification of the real investment opportunity, but standard CCF or WACC do not capture the state contingent nature of investment and lead to inappropriate valuations. Certain firms have adopted complicated decision tree analysis that tries to model cash flow, technological uncertainty, competition, and investment simul-

---

EXHIBIT 9-2

DECISION TREE ANALYSIS

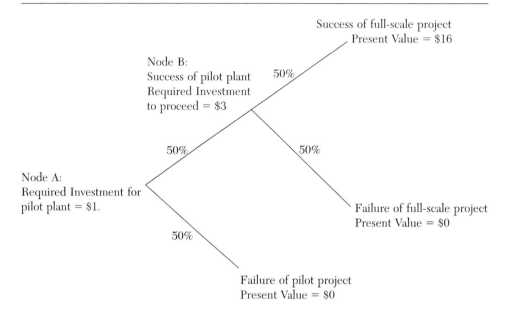

The exhibit displays a hypothetical investment that has two decision points, nodes A and B. The present value at the end of each branch is the present value of future cash flows from the project, ignoring the investment cost at each node.

---

taneously with a continuous distribution of cash flows. Some of the references discuss the actual use of decision tree analysis in high-technology companies. Chapter 10 of Brealy and Myers also has a good discussion of the material.

REAL OPTIONS

While I will not discuss real options extensively in this note, those students who have knowledge of option pricing theory should be able to utilize their knowledge to value investments. A growing academic literature has examined the use of option pricing technology for estimating value. Dixit and Pindyck's (1994) book is an excellent source of information about these techniques. The interested reader should read this book in order to operationalize some of the discussion here. Similarly, there are a number of notes that take up the issue of real options more explicitly.

Option pricing theory and real options are extremely important when determining the value of multistage projects, projects that can be abandoned, or projects that are irreversible. Under various assumptions, you can get more or less projects being funded under option pricing theory than under standard discounted cash flow analysis. Much of the analysis depends on whether the investment can be postponed without affecting the expected value of investment.

Multistage investment is one clear application of real options. For example, if the investment in a firm is to be in two stages and not investing in the second round implies that the project returns 0 for sure, then the first round investment is analogous to a call option on a certain fraction of the firm's equity. If the proportional change in the value of the investment is lognormally distributed, then one can apply the Black-Scholes option pricing formula.

One needs to estimate the current value of the firm assuming that the project is completed. This value may come from using the most recent equity purchase price or using discounted cash flow analysis to estimate value. The volatility of value is estimated from similar public firms. A value of 80–120% is probably not unreasonable. The interest rate is easy enough to obtain. The exercise price of the option is just the estimated amount of the second investment. Once these parameters have been estimated, the Black-Scholes formula will give you a value to compare to the amount of investment that must be made today. If the option value is greater than the amount required to be invested, the project should be undertaken.

It is widely believed that option pricing theory will pervade capital budgeting in the years to come. Many firms are already using these methods in the biotechnology or health care industry. As the theory develops, more uses for option valuation techniques will arise. The application of real options analysis to corporate decision making is clearly in its infancy, but it is gaining momentum. Practitioners who understand its implementation will be at an advantage.

THE "VENTURE CAPITAL" METHOD

Many individuals in practice utilize the "venture capital" method of valuing investments. This method has developed to compensate for various patterns in venture capital-type investments. I will discuss how the venture capital method works and how it is related to the discounted cash flow methodologies that we have discussed earlier. In general, CCF or WACC will be a more consistent and transparent valuation approach.

The method starts by projecting a company's net income in some year of interest (perhaps five years from now). Venture capitalists ignore any scenarios except optimistic ones. This net income is then multiplied by an appropriate price-to-earnings ratio from comparable companies. This projected future value is then discounted back to the present at a discount rate of 50–100% per year. This yields the present value of the firm.

Why do venture capitalists use such high discount rates? They give four reasons. First, the shares purchased are illiquid and therefore need to have a higher discount rate to compensate for the lack of liquidity. Second, the venture capitalist provides services to the firm and therefore this justifies a higher discount rate as compensation. Third, the venture capitalist does not believe the entrepreneur's pro formas; they are considered too optimistic. Finally, the venture capitalist will tell you that it just works.

Each of these reasons may have some merit, but a well-structured CCF or WACC can overcome these obstacles and provide greater intuition and insights. First, the liquidity premium may have some validity, but the estimated premium is much too big. Second, the only time that the venture capitalist makes money on the investment is when the firm goes public, and then the shares will be fully liquid.

Venture capitalists do indeed provide services to the firms that they finance. They provide strategic advice, provide access to industry analysts, consultants, and lawyers, and are very helpful in the going public process. These services do have significant positive value. The venture capitalist should attempt to value these services and estimate how much equity is needed to compensate them for these services. Increasing the discount rate because they provide services implies that the value of the firm is actually smaller with the services provided. The value of the firm, however, is not smaller. Clearly, the higher discount rate is intended to increase the fraction of equity that the venture capitalist receives but that could be accomplished more easily and in a justifiable manner by estimating the true value of services provided.

Most entrepreneurs probably present only the best case estimates to the venture capitalist. Any investor should analyze the pro formas with a large amount of skepticism. This does not mean you should add a fudge factor to the discount rate to compensate for the entrepreneur's optimism. One should do careful analysis and attempt to make reasonable guesses as to the probability of various scenarios. This will give you unbiased estimates of the cash flows of the firms. Remember that cash flow estimation is more important than the estimation of discount rates. Spending time thinking about reasonable estimates of potential outcomes will often help in the due diligence process.

The cogency of the venture capital method can be assessed when one examines the betas and cost of capital of all public companies. Very few companies have betas higher than 3. While the total risk of investing in start-up companies is large, you should only care about the systematic risk of investment. Venture capitalists can diversify away a significant fraction of the idiosyncratic risk associated with start-up companies by investing in multiple projects. Similarly, the ultimate investors in venture capital funds, for example, pension funds and endowments, view these investments as a small part of a larger, diversified portfolio. The cost of capital for the venture capitalist is probably around 15–20%. The median venture capital fund returned less than 20% per year during the period 1975–1996. It would be difficult to justify discount rates much higher than 30–35%.

A better approach to the venture capitalist's problem is to review the comparable companies' experiences. Do reality checks. How much of the market do they need to hit their pro formas? Do they have all they necessary capabilities to implement the plan? How long will it take them? What are the key success factors. The "soft" analysis we do in class is intended to help us estimate the likely effect on the balance sheet and cash flows. Clearly, we can say something about outcomes rather than just taking the entrepreneur's pro formas and discounting at 75%. The information generated in this process will provide milestones to track the progress of the company and allow the investors and entrepreneur to identify the key drivers of value.

RECOMMENDATION

When should you use which method? That depends on the problem. If you are estimating the value of a reasonably stable firm and you are only going to make one investment, then the standard CCF or WACC is appropriate. Each will give you roughly the same answer. If the project has considerable ex ante uncertainty, scenario analysis may help you estimate what the distribution of outcomes may look like and hence better assess the value of the investment. If the project requires multistaged, contingent investment, then decision tree or real option valuation is appropriate. Standard methods of valuation will overlook the value of gathering more information.

This note is meant to provide a review of the valuation material. The references contained at the end of this note are intended to provide an initial source of further data and information. It is important to understand how the methods differ and when to utilize the various methods. The marginal value of this thoughtful analysis is probably substantially higher for private companies than it is for public corporations. One clear lesson from Entrepreneurial Finance should be that analysis pays.

REFERENCES

BALDWIN, C., 1982, Optimal sequential investment when capital is not readily reversible, *Journal of Finance* 37, 763–782.

BREALY, R. AND S. MYERS, 1996, *Principles of Corporate Finance*, 5th edition, McGraw-Hill, New York.

COPELAND, T., T. KOLLER, AND J. MURRIN, 1991, *Valuation: Measuring and Managing the Value of Companies*, John Wiley & Sons, New York.

DIXIT, A., 1992, Investment and hysteresis, *Journal of Economic Perspective*, 107–132.

DIXIT, A. AND R. PINDYCK, 1994, *Investment under Uncertainty*, Princeton University Press, Princeton, NJ.

FAMA, E., 1977, Risk-adjusted discount rates and capital budgeting under uncertainty, *Journal of Financial Economics* 5, 3–24.

GRENADIER, S. AND A. WEISS, 1997, Investment in technological innovations: an option pricing approach," *Journal of Financial Economics* 44, 397–416.

LUEHRMAN, T., 1997, Using APV: a better tool for valuing operations, *Harvard Business Review*, 145–154.

MAJD, S. AND R. PINDYCK, 1987, Time to build, option value, and investment decisions, *Journal of Financial Economics* 18, 7–27.

MODIGLIANI, F. AND M. MILLER, 1958, The cost of capital, corporation finance, and the theory of investment," *American Economic Review* 48, 261–287.

MULLINS, D., 1982, Does the capital asset pricing model work?, *Harvard Business Review*, 105–114.

MYERS, S. AND S. TURNBULL, 1977, Capital budgeting and the capital asset pricing model: good news and bad news, *Journal of Finance* 21, 727–730.

NICHOLS, N. 1994, Scientific management at Merck: an interview with CFO Judy Lewent, *Harvard Business Review*, 88–99.

PINDYCK, R., 1991, Irreversibility, uncertainty, and investment, *Journal of Economic Literature* 29, 1110–1152.

PINDYCK, R., 1993, Investment under uncertain cost, *Journal of Financial Economics* 34, 53–76.

QUIGG, L., 1993, Empirical testing of real option-pricing models, *Journal of Finance* 48, 621–639.

ROBERTS, K. AND M. WEITZMAN, 1981, Funding criteria for research, development, and exploration projects, *Econometrica* 49, 1261–1288.

RUBACK, R., 1986, Calculating the market value of riskless cash flows, *Journal of Financial Economics* 15, 323–339.

SIEGEL, D., J. SMITH, AND J. PADDOCK, 1987, Valuing offshore oil properties with option pricing models, *Midland Corporate Finance Journal* 5, 22–30.

TAGGART, R., 1991, Consistent valuation and cost of capital expressions with corporate and personal taxes, *Financial Management* 20, 8–20.

TRIANTIS, A. AND JAMES HODDER, 1990, Valuing flexibility as a complex option, *Journal of Finance* 45, 549–565.

TRIGEORGIS, L. AND S. MASON, 1987, Valuing managerial flexibility, *Midland Corporate Finance Journal* 5, 14–21.

WEITZMAN, M., W. NEWEY, AND M. RABIN, 1981, Sequential R&D strategy for Synfuels, *Bell Journal of Economics* 12, 574–590.

APPENDIX 9-1

VALUATION EXAMPLE USING CCF AND WACC

Pro Formas

	Year 1	Year 2	Year 3	Year 4
EBIT	5.5	6.2	7.0	7.2
Depreciation	2.5	2.4	2.3	2.2
Capital Expenditure	2.0	3.0	3.0	3.1
Working Capital Investment	1.3	1.9	1.9	1.5
Interest Expense	0.36	0.36	0.36	0.36

Tax Rate	40%
Current Book Value of Debt	3.0
Equity Beta of Comparable Firm	1.90
Debt to Equity Ratio of Comparable Firm	40%
Target Debt to Total Capital Ratio	40%
Long-term T-Bond Rate	10%
Long-term Debt Rate	11%
Long-term Growth Rate	2%

Calculating Free Cash Flows

$FCF = EBIT(1 - \tau) + Depreciation - Capital\ Expenditure - Change\ in\ Working\ Capital$

	Year 1	Year 2	Year 3	Year 4
FCF	2.5	1.22	1.6	1.92

Discount Rate

If we assume an equity risk premium of 8%, we get the following:

$\beta^U = \beta^L/[1 + (D/E)]$

$\beta^U = 1.90/[1 + (0.40/0.60)] = 1.14$

$r_a = r_f + \beta^U * 8$

$r_a = (10.0 - 1.0) + 1.19 * 8 = 18.12\%$

For CCF we will use a discount rate of 18.12%.

In order to calculate the discount rate for WACC, we need to assume some equilibrium debt to equity ratio. I will assume that the firm is financed by 40% debt and 60% equity. If we use our formulas from above, we get:

$\beta^L = \beta^U * [1 + (D/E)]$

$\beta^L = 1.19 * [1 + 0.40/0.60)] = 1.90$

$r_e^L = r_f + \beta^L * 8$

10

Digital Everywhere, Inc.

Jerome Buse stared at the paper in front of him. He had just finished projections for his start-up company, Digital Everywhere, Inc. He intended to use the projections to raise money. He was certain that he would be able to convince others of the potential of his new high-speed digital food technology. He was less certain, however, about what value he should place on the business. He considered the options in front of him.

He considered the projections to be reasonable, although he guessed that he only had a 30% chance of hitting those numbers. He estimated that with 30% probability, the cash flows would be half of those projected in this case. The company would probably be worthless with 40% probability. He wondered how he should take these probabilities into consideration.

In estimating cash flows, Jerome thought that he would only need about $1 million in cash to run the business. Anything above and beyond $1 million would be considered excess cash. Because the company was just getting off the ground, there was no working capital and no property, plant, and equipment at the beginning of 1998. Any working capital and net PPE at the end of the year would be a net investment.

Jerome also thought about the future. He thought that after 2003 he could expect the company to grow at around 5% per year, although he wondered what a somewhat more modest growth rate of 2% would do to the expected value of the firm.

He knew that any venture capitalist would totally ignore a reasonable guess of cash flows, and therefore he decided to show only the best case numbers (see Exhibit 10-1). The venture capitalist from I.M. Greedy Ventures had stated that they would require a 60% rate of return on their investment in Digital Everywhere. Jerome wondered whether he could estimate what the venture capitalist would think his company was worth.

Jerome knew that he would not be taking on any debt for the foreseeable future. His company was just too risky and did not have the history to take on any debt. He wondered how being an all-equity firm would affect his cost of capital. Current 10-year government bonds were yielding 7% on an effective annual rate. A friend, however, had

---

Professor Paul Gompers prepared this case as the basis for class discussion rather than to illustrate either effective or ineffective handling of an administrative situation.

EXHIBIT 10-1

PRO FORMA PROJECTIONS FOR DIGITAL EVERYWHERE, INC.

Digital Everywhere, Inc.   Pro Forma Projections (in $,000s)

INCOME STATEMENT

	1998	1999	2000	2001	2002	2003
Net Sales	$8,500	$15,000	$35,500	$46,000	$52,000	$60,000
COGS	$3,200	$ 5,600	$14,000	$18,100	$20,100	$24,500
Gross Profit	$5,300	$ 9,400	$21,500	$27,900	$31,900	$35,500
SG&A	$3,500	$ 5,410	$ 6,400	$ 5,300	$ 7,200	$ 7,800
R&D	$1,100	$ 2,800	$ 4,100	$ 5,400	$ 6,500	$ 7,000
Earnings before Interest and Tax	$ 700	$ 1,190	$11,000	$17,200	$18,200	$20,700
Income Tax (35%)	$ 245	$ 417	$ 3,850	$ 6,020	$ 6,370	$ 7,245
Net Earnings	$ 455	$ 774	$ 7,150	$11,180	$11,830	$13,455

BALANCE SHEET

	1998	1999	2000	2001	2002	2003
Cash	$1,000	$1,000	$ 4,793	$13,907	$24,699	$37,042
Accounts Receivable	$1,417	$2,500	$ 5,917	$ 7,667	$ 8,667	$10,000
Inventories	$ 400	$ 700	$ 1,750	$ 2,263	$ 2,513	$ 3,063
Other	$ 354	$ 625	$ 1,479	$ 1,917	$ 2,167	$ 2,500
Total Current Assets	$3,171	$4,825	$13,939	$25,753	$38,045	$52,604
Net Fixed Assets	$ 906	$2,300	$ 3,200	$ 4,000	$ 4,300	$ 4,500
Total Assets	$4,077	$7,125	$17,139	$29,753	$42,345	$57,104
Liabilities and Shareholders' Equity						
Accounts Payable	$ 533	$ 933	$ 2,333	$ 3,017	$ 3,350	$ 4,083
Accrued Expenses	$ 607	$1,071	$ 2,536	$ 3,286	$ 3,714	$ 4,286
Current Liabilities	$1,140	$2,005	$ 4,869	$ 6,302	$ 7,064	$ 8,369
Net Worth	$2,936	$5,120	$12,270	$23,450	$35,280	$48,735
Total Liabilities and Net Worth	$4,077	$7,125	$17,139	$29,753	$42,345	$57,104

suggested that Digital Everywhere might be able to take on debt later. Jerome wondered what would happen to the value of the firm if the company were able to take on $2 million in debt in 2001, $5 million in 2002, and $10 million in 2003. He did not feel that Digital Everywhere would want to increase the amount of debt beyond $10 million even after 2003. Jerome thought that any debt would carry an interest rate of 10%.

Jerome knew that he would have to gather information on comparable companies. He found four firms which he thought were directly comparable to the business he was entering (see Exhibit 10-2). He wondered how he should use this information in determining a value for the firm. Did multiples analysis make sense? Digital Everywhere

EXHIBIT 10-2

FINANCIAL DATA ON COMPARABLE DIGITAL FOOD FIRMS

In the Sky, Inc.

	1994	1995	1996	1997
Sales	$79.34	$74.79	$59.39	$54.86
SG&A	$18.58	$17.67	$14.59	$13.97
Cap Ex	$ 1.95	$ 0.37	$ 0.63	$ 0.34
Op Inc Bef Dep	$ 7.30	$ 6.44	$ 2.38	$ 2.76
Net Inc	($ 1.05)	$ 1.54	$ 4.54	$ 5.27
Tot Assets	$77.90	$72.37	$62.99	$54.95
Current Assets	$51.47	$45.86	$38.69	$34.01
Current Liabilities	$15.73	$14.70	$18.76	$42.54
Debt	$ 4.88	$ 5.15	$ 6.28	$ 7.18
Net Worth	$15.73	$13.82	$18.03	$12.10
Beta	NA	NA	NA	1.45
P/E Ratio	NA	21.23	18.63	19.51

We Are Good, Ltd.

	1994	1995	1996	1997
Sales	$154.13	$188.37	$234.68	$312.29
SG&A	$ 19.28	$ 20.92	$ 23.62	$ 33.44
Cap Ex	$176.73	$117.63	$ 76.39	$ 21.81
Op Inc Bef Dep	$ 18.85	$ 26.24	$ 43.22	$ 58.67
Net Inc	($ 13.70)	$ 3.21	$ 16.09	$ 21.75
Tot Assets	$152.21	$149.98	$213.65	$298.32
Current Assets	$ 57.69	$ 70.22	$118.54	$159.93
Current Liabilities	$ 53.58	$ 43.84	$ 59.42	$ 60.56
Debt	$ 2.66	$ 6.01	$ 7.18	$ 6.80
Net Worth	$ 57.32	$ 67.36	$132.20	$211.19
Beta	NA	NA	NA	1.33
P/E Ratio	NA	40	41.05	39.87

Fun in a Can, Co.

	1994	1995	1996	1997
Sales	$17.32	$17.96	$17.10	$18.90
SG&A	$ 2.59	$ 2.72	$ 2.35	$ 2.16
Cap Ex	$ 0.52	$ 0.40	$ 0.28	$ 0.28
Op Inc Bef Dep	$ 0.19	$ 0.18	$ 0.73	$ 1.81
Net Inc	($ 0.38)	($ 0.51)	$ 1.47	$ 3.84
Tot Assets	$ 7.62	$ 7.31	$ 7.11	$ 7.33
Current Assets	$ 3.89	$ 3.98	$ 4.23	$ 4.79
Current Liabilities	$ 1.83	$ 2.23	$ 3.13	$ 2.95
Debt	$ 0.62	$ 0.66	$ 0.67	$ 0.71
Net Worth	$ 2.98	$ 2.34	$ 2.64	$ 3.41
Beta	NA	NA	NA	1.12
P/E Ratio	NA	NA	20.3	18.23

HELP, Inc.

	1994	1995	1996	1997
Sales	$72.39	$82.57	$80.58	$75.35
SG&A	NA	NA	NA	NA
Cap Ex	$ 5.22	$ 3.45	$ 3.05	$ 3.33
Op Inc Bef Dep	$ 6.66	$ 7.65	$ 8.17	$ 4.27
Net Inc	$ 2.96	$ 3.20	$ 3.80	$ 1.50
Tot Assets	$40.66	$45.91	$49.98	$46.85
Current Assets	$22.54	$28.50	$27.59	$22.08
Current Liabilities	$ 5.46	$ 8.92	$10.63	$ 6.41
Debt	$ 0.90	$ 0.71	$ 0.37	$ 0.17
Net Worth	$32.82	$34.53	$36.50	$37.56
Beta	NA	NA	NA	1.23
P/E Ratio	11.81	18.98	23.21	19.38

did not yet have any sales, but he was certain that it would soon. Should he use beta for these publicly traded firms? If so, what about the fact that he was still private and was largely undiversified (i.e., he had invested every penny he had into the company)? As Jerome's list of questions grew, he began to think it would be a very late night. He booted up his laptop and began to stare at the screen.

## 11

The Carlton Polish Company

Charlie Carlton finished looking over his notes. In one week, he would have to decide whether or not to pay $2,500,000 to Jim Miller for Miller's half ownership in the Carlton Polish Company. Each man currently controlled roughly 50% of the shares. If Carlton chose not to buy Miller's shares, then Miller had agreed to buy Carlton's half ownership for the same amount—$2,500,000. Whichever man sold his share would withdraw permanently from the affairs of the company. And they would agree not to compete with Carlton Polish for a period of at least two years.

Charles Carlton was 59 years old. The Carlton Polish Company had been in his family for over 100 years, though for the last five years, he had delegated the responsibility for managing the company to Jim Miller. Buying Mr. Miller's shares would require Mr. Carlton to take active control of the company again.

Carlton and his advisers had spent many hours debating a few key issues. Yet to be resolved were two questions: What was a reasonable value for the Carlton Polish Company? And could the company finance the purchase of Miller's shares?

HISTORY OF THE CARLTON POLISH COMPANY

The Carlton Polish Company was founded in 1883 by Charles Carlton, Sr. The company was the first manufacturer of waxes to be incorporated in the United States. Initially, the company marketed Carlton's Boston Polish, a furniture and hardwood floor paste wax sold to the consumer market. The product was so successful that the name Carlton's wax became a generic name for paste wax.

Charles Carlton II, the founder's grandson, joined the company in 1951 as sales manager. He took over control of the company in 1952, after his father passed away.

On assuming control, Charlie Carlton moved quickly to make the company a more aggressive force in the market. From its founding in 1883 to 1951, sales volume had only grown to $492,000. Carlton's first and boldest move was to redirect the marketing

---

Professor William A. Sahlman prepared this case as the basis for class discussion rather than to illustrate either effective or ineffective handling of an administrative situation. Some of the facts and all of the figures in this case have been disguised.

emphasis of the company from consumer markets to industrial markets. He formed the ICI (Institutional, Commercial, and Industrial) Division.

By 1982, net sales volume at Carlton Polish had increased to $9.3 million. Of this amount, less than 10% represented sales of paste wax to the consumer market.

CARLTON POLISH IN 1982

Carlton Polish sold a complete line of branded floor waxes, finishes, sealers, aerosols, spray buff solutions, disinfectants, detergents, cleaners, deodorizers, carpet care materials, and soaps. A representative list of the company's products is included as Exhibit 11-1.

The company's products were sold by a direct sales force to semi-exclusive sanitary supply distributors throughout the country. These distributors in turn sold their products to end-users such as hospitals, airports, schools, hotels, office building maintenance contractors, and industrial plants. The largest single distributor of Carlton products purchased $350,000 worth of goods in 1982. There were over 300 active accounts at Carlton. Of these, 130 accounts contributed roughly 85% of the company's sales volume.

EXHIBIT 11-1

REPRESENTATIVE LIST OF PRODUCTS

Product Name	Brief Description
Carlton's Floor Care Line:	
Beyond	Co-polymer floor finish
Above	Oligomeric floor finish
Sundance	Nonalkaline floor cleaner
Sgt. Pepper	Neutralizer
Brawny	Floor wax
Hot Springs	Cleaner
Captain Quick	Amine-fortified stripper
Carlton's Disinfectant Cleaners:	
Quantum	Quarternary disinfectant cleaner
Phobe	Phenolic disinfectant detergent
Clockwork	Liquid disinfectant-sanitizer
Bright	Aerosol disinfectant cleaning foam
Charge	Disinfectant bowl cleaner
Clockwork Spray	Aerosol disinfectant/deodorizer
Carlton's Carpet Care Line:	
Royal Plush	Carpet shampoo
Flashback	Carpet prespray, spotter, spin cleaner
Flying Colors	Carpet shampoo
Shot Gun	Power spot and stain remover
Spot Foam	Aerosol spot remover
Deodorant	Liquid concentrate

Carlton also continued to sell the company's original floor and furniture wax product. The consumer product line was distributed to seven manufacturer's representatives, which in turn distributed the product to retail outlets including hardware stores and grocery chains. This sales effort was concentrated in the Northeast and Midwest regions of the country.

The product line was positioned at the high-quality end of the market. Carlton generally charged higher prices for its products than private label or direct marketers and was successful doing so because of its excellent reputation for quality and service to its distribution network.

Charlie Carlton commented about the particular strengths of the Carlton product line:

> If the ultimate user pays $1.00, our distributor pays $0.50, our cost of goods sold is $0.25, and the raw materials cost is $0.15 to $0.20. Some manufacturers sell direct to the ultimate users, in which case their salesmen and warehousing costs are approximately equal to the discount our distributors get. Some manufacturers sell to distributors under the distributor's label (private label). We all compete for the ultimate user. He is a sophisticated buyer and usually can see the advantage of quality over price. Our national name means quality to him because our products are better *and* they cost more. In his view, they save him money because they lower his labor cost. The labor costs of using anyone's product far exceed the cost of the products used. Therefore, if the product is better (i.e., more efficient in cleaning, longer lasting, etc.), his overall costs will be lower.

There were 10 sales managers at Carlton, each with responsibility for a different geographical region around the country. Though Carlton was active in all areas in the country, the bulk of the company's sales were located east of the Rocky Mountains.

A key responsibility of the sales managers was to help train the distributor organizations in selling the Carlton product. Carlton had developed very effective sales training packages, which consisted of videotape films, small product samples in attractive packages, and other related promotional materials.

Most of the distributors to whom Carlton products were sold were relatively small businesses. The company estimated that the distributors employed approximately 600 to 700 salesmen. The Carlton sales force provided very useful services in training the distributor salesmen in how to sell sanitary supplies. Many of the distributors sold private label products that competed directly with the Carlton line; but the companies supplying these goods did not provide the same level of sales support as supplied by the Carlton sales force.

The company's manufacturing facilities were located in Westwood, Massachusetts. The company had a long-term lease on a recently renovated, 75,000-square-foot building on 18 acres. The lease was scheduled to expire in 12 years. The plant area had been effectively doubled in 1981, and the facilities would support growth at levels similar to those realized in the past for at least six years without major additions to capacity.

The manufacturing process at Carlton was quite simple. Raw chemicals were brought into the plant in tank trucks. These materials were then weighed and mixed in various vats and then meted out to the appropriate size containers. The critical task was measuring the proper mixtures of raw materials.

Carlton had an excellent reputation for quality control. The company had a laboratory on the premises, which was responsible for monitoring quality and for doing research on new products or enhancements to existing products.

The company employed approximately 75 people, 5 of whom were executives, 10 were sales managers, and the remaining workers performed sales, clerical, or production-related tasks. Most of the employees belonged to a company union. The average employee had worked at Carlton for over 10 years and received a generous wage and benefits package. The company had not been shut down by strike or walkout in many years. Labor relations were considered excellent.

COMPETITIVE POSITION

The total market for cleaning services and supplies for industrial and institutional facilities in the United States was estimated to exceed $4.5 billion. There were essentially three approximately equal-size segments of the market: independent distributors of cleaning supplies; contract cleaning firms; and manufacturers of cleaning supplies who sold direct to end-users. Of the total $4.5 billion, it was estimated that about 20% represented sales of chemical supplies. The rest was comprised of cleaning equipment (e.g., vacuum cleaners) and labor.

Carlton Polish competed in the first segment described above: they sold chemical supplies to the independent distributor industry. This segment of the industry was highly fragmented. The largest competitor, S.C. Johnson & Sons, had an estimated sales volume of $75 million. The share held by Carlton was under 3%.

Data on four companies involved in the industry are supplied as Exhibit 11-2. No data were available on S.C. Johnson because it was privately owned.

In spite of Carlton's relatively modest market share of the national market, the company occupied a strong competitive position. The Carlton name had an excellent reputation. The company's distributors in each region were perceived as being very strong.

The larger national companies like Johnson and Carlton competed actively for the good distributors in each area. However, once a distributor selected a national brand of products to carry, it was difficult to convince them to change to another company. The same was true of the end-users—satisfied end-users were reluctant to change brands.

The entire market had grown at roughly the same rate as the general economy for many years and was expected to keep pace in the future. Sales of chemical supplies to the industry were relatively immune to economic cycles. People could not postpone cleaning their facilities even when there was a recession. Indeed, just the opposite seemed to be the case. When there was a recession, many firms spent more effort on refurbishing the existing plant than on purchasing a new plant and equipment. And it was often the case that employees who might be laid off from manufacturing positions were assigned to other tasks, including cleaning the plant. In contrast to the chemical supply segment of the industry, sales of cleaning machinery tended to be quite cyclical.

Sales at Carlton had been influenced more by competitive changes than by changes in the overall economy. The company had lost some distributors to the competition but had managed to gain more than it had lost. Carlton had grown at a rate in excess of the industry growth rate for each of the past 10 years. And the company's margins had been extremely stable—much more stable than for most companies in the industry.

Carlton believed this favorable performance could be replicated in the future. The company had a number of avenues to increase market share. First, the company could attempt to enter new geographic areas. For example, the company did not have a strong presence in the West Coast market but could expand its sales efforts in that area at any time. One obstacle to expanding the geographic region served by Carlton was that the company had no manufacturing facility other than the one in Westwood. Freight costs on shipping product to the West Coast might preclude building up sales there unless a new manufacturing plant were added.

EXHIBIT 11-2

SUMMARY INFORMATION ON SELECTED COMPANIES

REV. NOVEMBER 22, 1996

ECONOMICS LABORATORY

Recent price (3/31/1983):	$27.13	Total market value (stock):	$366 MM
Trailing 12-months EPS:	$2.44		
P/E ratio:	11.1×	Estimated beta:	1.10
Dividend yield:	3.8%		

Brief description: Economics Laboratory is a leading manufacturer of cleaning and sanitizing products and related chemical specialties. The company also designs, assembles, and distributes equipment for applying these products. The company has 11 plants in the United States and 15 plants abroad. Approximately 51% of sales and a higher proportion of income are represented by sales of these products to institutions. Economics Laboratory distributes directly to the end-user.

CROMPTON & KNOWLES

Recent price (3/31/1983):	$24.88	Total market value (stock):	$79 MM
Trailing 12-months EPS:	$1.24		
P/E ratio:	20.1×	Estimated beta:	0.85
Dividend yield:	4.2%		

Brief description: Crompton & Knowles is a manufacturer of specialty chemicals, including dyes, cleaning and maintenance chemicals, and pesticides. The company also manufactures plastics and rubber extrusion machinery.

NCH CORPORATION

Recent price (3/31/1983):	$20.00	Total market value (stock):	$218 MM
Trailing 12-months EPS:	$1.26		
P/E ratio:	15.9×	Estimated beta:	0.80
Dividend yield:	3.6%		

Brief description: NCH Corporation is a worldwide distributor of maintenance products, including specialty chemicals, replacement fasteners, welding supplies, and replacement electrical and plumbing parts.

OAKITE PRODUCTS

Recent price (3/31/1983):	$24.00	Total market value (stock):	$42 MM
Trailing 12-months EPS:	$1.81		
P/E ratio:	13.3×	Estimated beta:	0.55
Dividend yield:	6.3%		

Brief description: Oakite produces proprietary chemical products used for cleaning and treating metal and other surfaces as integral phases of the manufacturing process. The company also engages in contract cleaning.

(Continued)

EXHIBIT 11-2   (Continued)

SUMMARY FINANCIAL DATA ON SELECTED COMPANIES
(ALL DATA '000,000, EXCEPT PER-SHARE)

	(Years Ended 6/30)				Compound Growth
	1979	1980	1981	1982	
ECONOMICS LABORATORY					
Sales	464.0	548.0	629.0	670.0	13.0%
Net income	30.0	31.1	29.8	32.9	3.1%
Net interest expense	3.8	9.0	16.9	18.3	68.9%
Earnings per share	2.22	2.31	2.21	2.44	3.2%
Dividends per share	0.89	1.04	1.04	1.04	5.3%
Stock price:					
High	26.00	27.38	23.13	30.35	
Low	20.13	16.13	16.13	15.88	
Average P/E ratio	10	9	9	9	
Cash	68.1	41.0	29.1	37.2	−18.3%
Current assets	211.0	221.0	216.0	211.0	0.0%
Current liabilities	72.5	82.7	81.3	92.6	8.5%
Net working capital	138.5	138.3	134.7	118.4	−5.1%
Total assets	305.0	403.0	424.0	438.0	12.8%
Long-term debt	47.0	116.0	120.0	114.0	34.4%
Shareholders' equity	178.0	195.0	211.0	220.0	7.3%
Year-end shares ('000)				13,504	

	(Years Ended 12/31)				Compound Growth
	1979	1980	1981	1982	
CROMPTON & KNOWLES					
Sales	240.0	242.0	243.0	213.0	−3.9%
Net income	7.1	7.7	8.6	5.2	−9.8%
Net interest expense	4.1	5.2	6.4	4.3	1.2%
Earnings per share	2.03	2.22	2.51	1.44	−10.8%
Dividends per share	0.69	0.80	0.95	1.04	14.4%
Stock price:					
High	12.25	16.50	18.75	19.63	
Low	8.75	10.88	12.88	12.13	
Average P/E ratio	5	6	6	11	
Cash	5.6	3.6	4.9	10.1	21.7%
Current assets	97.8	95.6	94.7	82.3	−5.6%
Current liabilities	42.5	37.2	39.5	31.3	−9.7%
Net working capital	55.3	58.4	55.2	51.0	−2.7%
Total assets	142.0	147.0	143.0	129.0	−3.1%
Long-term debt	33.8	39.2	27.9	25.3	−9.2%
Shareholders' equity	57.3	62.2	66.6	64.1	3.8%
Year-end shares ('000)				3,155	

(Continued)

EXHIBIT 11-2   *(Continued)*

	(Years Ended 4/30)				Compound Growth
	1979	1980	1981	1982	
NCH CORPORATION					
Sales	261.0	322.0	356.0	348.0	10.1%
Net income	22.7	28.0	26.8	15.0	−12.9%
Net interest expense	1.7	2.2	2.1	4.7	40.0%
Earnings per share	2.00	2.60	2.47	1.37	−11.8%
Dividends per share	0.58	0.66	0.72	0.72	7.5%
Stock price:					
High	22.38	23.75	28.75	23.00	
Low	12.75	13.75	17.00	14.50	
Average P/E ratio	9	7	9	14	
Cash	44.6	40.4	36.5	36.7	−6.3%
Current assets	134.0	160.0	164.0	157.0	5.4%
Current liabilities	47.7	63.0	49.8	44.0	−2.7%
Net working capital	86.3	97.0	114.2	113.0	9.4%
Total assets	177.0	216.0	228.0	233.0	9.6%
Long-term debt	2.1	4.3	5.8	5.3	35.6%
Shareholders' equity	120.0	139.0	160.0	167.0	11.6%
Year-end shares ('000)				10,198	

	(Years Ended 12/31)				Compound Growth
	1979	1980	1981	1982	
OAKITE PRODUCTS					
Sales	60.2	67.7	73.6	75.6	7.9%
Net income	4.0	4.4	5.0	3.2	−7.2%
Net interest expense	0.0	0.2	0.1	0.2	NA
Earnings per share	2.21	2.45	2.83	1.81	−6.4%
Dividends per share	1.22	1.31	1.43	1.52	7.6%
Stock price:					
High	20.00	20.00	24.25	25.25	
Low	15.25	15.88	17.13	17.50	
Average P/E ratio	8	7	7	12	
Cash	2.3	4.6	4.2	4.6	26.2%
Current assets	23.5	27.4	27.6	25.4	2.6%
Current liabilities	6.8	10.5	8.1	8.9	9.4%
Net working capital	16.7	16.9	19.5	16.5	−0.4%
Total assets	30.8	36.2	36.3	37.7	7.0%
Long-term debt	0.0	0.0	0.0	1.8	NA
Shareholders' equity	23.0	24.7	27.1	27.0	5.5%
Year-end shares ('000)				1,764	

Second, the company could try to increase the market share held by its distributors. To the extent the distributor increased its own market share, the benefits would accrue to Carlton as well. The important sales tool in this area was enhancing the level of service provided to the distributors.

Third, Carlton could acquire one or several distributors. Many of these companies were family-owned and plagued by problems related to the transition of management and ownership as one generation retired from active participation. The distribution business had very favorable economic characteristics. And Carlton might be able to gather valuable information about its basic business through experimentation with a captive distributor.

Fourth, the company could expand its efforts in selling direct to end-users, including contract cleaners. In certain areas of the country, such an effort would not conflict with the policy of using independent distributors.

Finally, the company could expand and improve its product line through internal means or by acquisition. Carlton and other companies in the industry had successfully launched new products in the past which had had a dramatic impact on sales. A recent example was soft-soap, a product to dispense soap from a container with a small pump. This product had been introduced by another company, but Carlton and its competitors had responded soon thereafter by introducing their own soft-soap products.

FINANCIAL PERFORMANCE

The Carlton Polish Company had been profitable for many years. Indeed, the company had never reported a loss in its 100-plus-year history. Sales and net income had grown at a compound annual rate in excess of 20% for the four years ending on December 31, 1982. Sales in 1982 were $9,302,702, and net income was $276,000. Historical financial statements are provided in Exhibit 11-3.

Several features of the financial statements warrant special comment.

1. *Salary level:*   The company had had a policy of paying relatively large salaries to its top executives. In 1982, for example, the total salaries paid to Jim Miller and Charlie Carlton were almost $800,000. Given the size and profitability of the firm, a more normal level of compensation for the top two officers would be under $300,000 total.

2. *Long-term debt and shareholders' equity:*   The figures shown on the balance sheet for 1982 reflected a major recapitalization of Carlton which took place in 1977. At that time, funds raised from issuing debt securities were used to repurchase some of the shares owned by the Carlton family. The net result was to decrease reported shareholders' equity and to increase long-term debt. Also, interest expense was increased dramatically by this recapitalization. At the end of 1982, the company had total debt (including current maturities) of slightly under $1.3 million. This debt was owed to a trust established by Mr. Carlton's father. The beneficiaries of the trust were Mr. Carlton's mother and Mr. Carlton. The average fixed interest rate on this debt was 13%, and the debt was subordinated. This loan would be unaffected by the proposed buyout.

3. *Lease expense:*   The company leased its principal manufacturing facilities and equipment. The terms of the lease agreement are described in the footnotes to the financial statements. It was estimated that the net present value of the future lease obligations (as of 12/31/82) was $1.6 million. If the company were

THE CARLTON POLISH COMPANY—HISTORICAL FINANCIAL DATA ($000)

	1976	1977	1978	1979	1980	1981	1982	Compound Annual Growth
Income Statement:								
Net sales	$3,368	$3,885	$4,543	$5,259	$6,492	$8,120	$9,303	18.5%
Cost of goods sold	1,886	2,231	2,596	2,964	3,772	4,759	5,445	19.3
Selling, general and administrative	1,227	1,359	1,483	1,814	2,150	2,615	3,055	16.4
Operating profit	255	295	464	481	570	746	803	21.1
Interest income	5	7	5	5	7	12	40	41.4
Interest expense	55	78	187	189	203	192	179	21.7
Other income (expense)	(36)	(19)	(9)	(16)	(7)	(9)	(22)	−7.7
Profit before tax	170	205	273	281	367	557	642	24.9
Taxes	100	118	140	132	212	273	365	24.1
Profit after tax	70	87	133	149	155	284	277	25.9
Dividends	27	23	0	0	0	0	0	−100.0
IRS settlement	0	0	0	0	0	0	115	NA
Note:								
Rental and lease expense (included in cost of goods sold)	149	155	174	157	157	252	343	14.9
Executive salaries (included in SG&A)	336	352	380	406	487	703	795	15.4
Extraordinary legal (included in SG&A)	0	0	0	0	0	0	100	NA
Depreciation and amortization	13	13	13	21	26	38	42	21.6
Balance Sheet:								
Cash	94	140	167	77	121	350	459	30.3
Accounts receivable	613	600	739	975	1,029	1,250	1,480	15.8
Inventory	226	264	242	290	352	394	413	10.6
Other current assets	44	41	44	52	82	71	44	0.0
Total current assets	$ 977	$1,045	$1,192	$1,394	$1,584	$2,065	$2,396	16.1%
Net plant and equipment	114	104	91	129	126	140	100	−2.2
Other fixed assets	97	88	95	98	81	82	62	−7.2
Total assets	$1,188	$1,238	$1,378	$1,621	$1,791	$2,287	$2,558	13.6%
Accounts payable	$ 145	$ 139	$ 168	$ 254	$ 232	$ 342	$ 376	17.2%
Current maturities	58	37	52	50	55	55	60	0.6
Other current liabilities	118	177	190	219	244	443	461	25.5
IRS tax settlement	0	0	0	0	0	0	115	NA
Total current liabilities	$ 321	$ 353	$ 410	$ 523	$ 531	$ 840	$1,012	21.1%
Long-term debt	498	1,450	1,399	1,380	1,387	1,290	1,228	16.3
Shareholders' equity	369	(565)	(432)	(282)	(127)	157	318	−2.5
Total liabilities	$1,188	$1,238	$1,378	$1,621	$1,791	$2,287	$2,558	13.6
Selected Ratios:								
Cost of goods sold/sales	56.0%	57.4%	57.1%	56.4%	58.1%	58.6%	58.5%	
Rental expense/sales	4.4	4.0	3.8	3.0	2.4	3.1	3.7	
Sales, general and administrative/sales	36.4	35.0	32.6	34.5	33.1	32.2	32.8	
Executive salaries/sales	10.0	9.1	8.4	7.7	7.5	8.7	8.5	
Operating profit/sales	7.6	7.6	10.2	9.1	8.8	9.2	8.6	
Profit before tax/sales	5.0	5.3	6.0	5.3	5.7	6.9	6.9	
Tax rate	59.0	57.6	51.3	47.0	57.8	49.0	56.9	
Profit after tax/sales	2.1	2.2	2.9	2.8	2.4	3.5	3.0	
Payout ratio	38.8	26.4	0.0	0.0	0.0	0.0	0.0	
Current assets/sales	29.0	26.9	26.2	26.5	24.4	25.4	25.8	
Current liabilities/sales	9.5	9.1	9.0	9.9	8.2	10.3	10.9	
Total fixed assets/sales	6.3	5.0	4.1	4.3	3.2	2.7	1.7	

See Notes to the Financial Statements.

(*Continued*)

EXHIBIT 11-3   *(Continued)*

NOTES TO THE FINANCIAL STATEMENTS

\#   Summary of Accounting Policies

1. Inventories are stated at the lower of cost or market. Cost is determined on the basis of the first-in, first-out method.

2. Depreciation: Property, plant, and equipment is depreciated over the estimated useful lives of the assets, using the straight-line and sum-of-the-years digits methods.

3. Income Taxes: Investment tax credits are accounted for on the flow-through method, reducing the provisions for income taxes in the year in which the credits offset taxes otherwise payable.

Selected Footnotes

1. Obligations under Operating Leases: The company leases the real estate which it occupies and machinery and equipment. The real estate is owned by a partnership in which Charlie Carlton and Jim Miller have equal shares. The leases are classified as operating leases. The leases expire in 1996. The following table shows the annual lease payments required under the lease agreements:

Year Ending	Amount
1983	$ 287,101
1984	250,318
1985	245,000
1986	245,000
1987	245,000
Later Years	2,082,500

   The present value (as of 12/31/82) of the future lease and rental payments was estimated to be $1.6 million. If the company were required to capitalize these leases, then an asset would be shown on the balance sheet with a value of $1.6 million, and an offsetting liability for the same amount would also appear.

2. Extraordinary Legal Expenses: During 1982, the company incurred extraordinary legal expenses of approximately $100,000.

3. Income Tax Dispute: The Internal Revenue Service has audited the tax returns of the company through 1982. The company and the IRS have agreed that the company will pay $115,000 in taxes and penalties during 1983 to adjust for excess salaries taken in prior years. Shareholders' Equity was reduced by this amount in 1982, and the proposed settlement was included in Current Liabilities.

4. 1977 Recapitalization: In 1977, the company repurchased shares from certain shareholders. The total amount paid was $999,000. This amount was subtracted from shareholders' equity at that time.

required to capitalize these leases, an asset would appear on the balance sheet with a value of $1.6 million, and an offsetting liability for the same amount would also appear.

4. *Legal expenses:* As a result of a protracted legal battle between Jim Miller and Charlie Carlton, the company had extraordinary legal expenses in 1982 of $100,000.

5. *Internal Revenue Service audit:* The company's tax returns had been audited by the IRS several times over the years. One source of disagreement between the company and the IRS was the justifiable level of executive salaries. Essentially, the IRS argued that a part of the salary (the "excess" part) represented a dividend to the owners which would not be tax deductible. In early 1983, the IRS and Carlton Polish reached an agreement calling for the company to make a one-time additional payment of $115,000 in taxes. This payment would occur in 1983. However, the company recorded in 1982 a charge to retained earnings for $115,000. The same amount was also added to Current Liabilities.

6. *Excess cash:* As of December 31, 1982, Carlton Polish had cash and marketable securities in excess of the required transactions balances. At that time, excess cash was estimated at $250,000. Of this amount, $115,000 would be used to pay the IRS as described in item 5. The rest could be used to help finance the buyout of the partner's shares.

The net effect of items 1 to 4 was to lower reported net income and shareholder's equity. Thus, the reported financial statements were not strictly comparable to those for other companies, particularly those publicly traded.

OPERATING PLAN AND FINANCIAL FORECASTS

Charlie Carlton had over the previous year spent a great deal of time reacquainting himself with the situation at Carlton Polish. He felt confident that Jim Miller had done a good job of managing the company and that the future was bright. Carlton and Miller had decided to part company not because of dissatisfaction with the quality of management; rather, their argument was based on economic and personal grounds.

In 1977, Carlton had decided to allow Miller to manage the company while Carlton moved to Boulder, Colorado, to pursue other business (primarily new ventures) and personal interests. The major restructuring of the balance sheet described in item 2 above reflected an agreement between Carlton and Miller to transfer a significant ownership position from Carlton to Miller. At the same time, Miller agreed to retain Carlton as a consultant, paying him an amount based on the profitability of the company. In 1981 and 1982, Miller began to balk at paying Carlton large amounts of money and threatened to stop the payments altogether. This decision reflected economic and other considerations: Miller and Carlton had also argued about Carlton's continued, though indirect, presence in the affairs of the company. Often, employees at Carlton would consult Carlton before making decisions, a situation that Miller felt undermined his authority. The current buyout negotiations were intended to settle the problem once and for all.

If Carlton were to buy Miller's share of the company,[1] he would have to arrange for an orderly transition of management. Carlton had already decided that John Nash,

---

[1] Technically, the shares would be repurchased by the company and then retired.

a long-time friend and employee of the company, would assume day-to-day operating responsibility for the firm. John Nash had held every conceivable job in sales and marketing at Carlton and was fully capable of running the show.

Carlton intended, and John Nash agreed, that Nash would only serve in this new capacity for a limited period of time. He was close to retirement and did not wish to become the permanent replacement for Jim Miller at the company. Charlie Carlton would act as chairman and president. One of Carlton's first duties would be to search for a replacement for Nash. He also had assembled a group of individuals to act as board of directors.

Carlton anticipated that the transition from a Jim Miller-run company to one he headed would go smoothly, both at the plant and with the consumers of Carlton Polish's products. Carlton anticipated no management or personnel changes other than the replacement of Miller.

As part of the process of developing a strategy for determining whether $2,500,000 was a reasonable price to buy out Miller's share of the company, Carlton had developed a set of pro forma financial forecasts. These forecasts and the underlying assumptions are included as Exhibit 11-4.

With regard to financing the acquisition, essentially all of the required funds would come from borrowing. The agreement between Miller and Carlton called for a cash payment of $1,500,000. Charlie Carlton intended to use $135,000 of excess cash on hand (after paying the IRS $115,000) to provide part of the $1,500,000 cash payment.

He had also talked to a local bank about borrowing $1,365,000. Discussions with the banker had led him to believe that he would probably be able to borrow that amount at a rate equal to the prime lending rate plus 2%. The loan would be repaid over a five-year period. The loan would be senior to all existing and future debt at the company. And Charlie Carlton would be required to co-sign the loan. The anticipated loan amortization schedule and a statement of the proposed covenants attached to the loan are included as Exhibit 11-5. Selected economic data, including data on interest rates in the economy, are provided in Exhibit 11-6.

The remainder of the purchase price would be provided by a note issued to the seller. That is, the seller would accept as payment for the difference between the purchase price and $1,500,000 a note issued by the company. Given the $2,500,000 purchase price, the loan provided by the seller would be $1,000,000. The interest rate was set at a fixed 14%. There would be a three-year deferral on principal repayments on the loan. Then, the loan would be repaid in 12 equal annual installments of $83,333. The loan would be subordinated to the proposed bank loan.

Though Carlton intended to use only debt to finance the acquisition, he and his advisers had also addressed the issue of how the company should be financed in the long run. As part of the process of determining a reasonable capital structure, Carlton and his advisers had consulted a table describing the financial characteristics of companies with certain bond ratings. These data are attached as Exhibit 11-7.

LONG-RANGE PLANS

Carlton was enthusiastic about taking control of Carlton Polish. He had a number of ideas about ways to improve the operating performance of the company. And he was confident that the appointment of John Nash would provide stable and strong operating management for the next couple of years.

EXHIBIT 11-4

THE CARLTON POLISH COMPANY—PRO FORMA FINANCIAL DATA[a] ($000)

	Actual 1982	Pro Forma 1983	Pro Forma 1984	Pro Forma 1985	Pro Forma 1986	Pro Forma 1987	Comment
Net sales	$9,303	$10,233	$11,257	$12,382	$13,621	$14,983	Increases 10% per year
Cost of goods sold	5,445	5,612	6,173	6,791	7,470	8,217	
Rental expense	343	287	250	250	250	250	From footnotes, Exhibit 3
Selling, gen. and admin.	3,055	2,486	2,735	3,008	3,309	3,640	
Executive salaries	795	450	495	545	599	659	Raise 10% per year from 450K
Operating profit	803	1,398	1,604	1,789	1,993	2,217	
Interest income	40	0	0	0	0	0	
Interest expense:							
Existing debt	179	156	150	142	133	121	
Seller note	0	140	140	140	140	128	15-year, 14% seller loan
Proposed bank loan	0	184	147	111	74	37	5-year, 13.5% bank loan
Total interest expense	$ 179	$ 480	$ 437	$ 393	$ 347	$ 286	
Other income (expense)	(22)	0	0	0	0	0	
Profit before tax	642	918	1,166	1,396	1,646	1,931	
Taxes	365	477	606	726	856	1,004	
Profit after tax	277	441	560	670	790	927	
Dividends	0	0	0	0	0	0	
IRS settlement	115						
Retained earnings	162	441	560	670	790	927	
Net working capital[b]	1,384	1,440	1,584	1,742	1,917	2,108	
Total net fixed assets	162	178	196	216	237	261	
Debt Amortization:							
Existing debt	60	62	55	62	71	96	
Seller note	0	0	0	0	83	83	See Note a below
Proposed bank loan	0	273	273	273	273	273	5-year bank loan
Total amortization	$ 60	$ 335	$ 328	$ 335	$ 427	$ 452	
Assumptions:							
Inflation rate	3.9%	5.0%	5.0%	5.0%	5.0%	5.0%	
Average interest rate	13.5	13.5	13.5	13.5	13.5	13.5	Avg. rate (above current)
Growth rate	14.6	10.0	10.0	10.0	10.0	10.0	
(COGS-rental)/sales	54.8	54.8	54.8	54.8	54.8	54.8	
Rental expense	343	287	250	250	250	250	
(SG&A-exec. salaries)/sales	24.3	24.3	24.3	24.3	24.3	24.3	
Executive salaries	795	450	495	545	599	659	
Operating profit/sales	8.6	13.7	14.2	14.4	14.6	14.8	
Profit before tax/sales	6.9	9.0	10.4	11.3	12.1	12.9	
Tax rate	56.9	52.0	52.0	52.0	52.0	52.0	
Profit after tax/sales	3.0	4.3	5.0	5.4	5.8	6.2	
Payout ratio	0.0	0.0	0.0	0.0	0.0	0.0	
Current assets/sales[c]	25.8	23.1	23.1	23.1	23.1	23.1	Operating current assets
Current liabilities/sales[c]	10.9	9.0	9.0	9.0	9.0	9.0	Operating current liabilities
Total net fixed assets/sales	1.7	1.7	1.7	1.7	1.7	1.7	

[a] These projections assume that the purchase price for Jim Miller's one-half interest in the company is $2,500,000. Jim Miller agrees to accept a note with a value of $1,000,000. The bank agrees to lend $1,365,000. And excess cash of $135,000 is used to help finance the purchase.

[b] Net working capital is defined above to exclude current maturities of long-term debt or notes payable.

[c] Actual figures for 1982 include some nonoperating current assets and liabilities (e.g., excess cash, short-term debt).

EXHIBIT 11-5

PROBABLE TERMS AND COVENANTS OF THE PROPOSED BANK LOAN

Purchase Price for Miller's Shares: $2,500,000
Loan Amount: $1,365,000
Term: 5 years
        Equal Annual Installments (as per schedule below)
Rate: Prime Interest Rate plus 2%
Compensating Balances: 10% of the Loan Amount

This loan will be senior to all existing debt and to all debt used to finance the purchase of the partner's shares. No additional senior debt can be issued at any time.

Mr. Charles Carlton will be required to co-sign the note. He will be personally responsible for paying the loan and associated interest in the event of a default by Carlton Polish Company.

The probable important covenants of the loan are listed below:

(1) The company will maintain net working capital of at least $750,000.

(2) The company will not make capital expenditures in any one year which exceed $250,000.

(3) The company will not enter into any new operating lease agreement, the present value of which exceeds $250,000.

(4) The company will not pay a dividend until this loan has been completely paid off. Under special circumstances, the bank will consider a request to waive the covenant.

(5) The total compensation paid to the two top officers of the company will not exceed $450,000 in 1983. The allowable level of compensation will increase each year by the same percentage amount as the percentage increase in net sales in the year.

(6) The company will maintain life insurance on the two top officers of the company in an amount at least equal to the remaining principal balance of this loan.

Interest and Amortization Schedule (assuming an interest rate of 13.5%)

	1983	1984	1985	1986	1987
Interest ($000)	$ 184	$147	$111	$ 74	$ 37
Amortization ($000)	273	273	273	273	273
Remaining principal ($000)	1,092	819	546	273	0

EXHIBIT 11-6

THE CARLTON POLISH COMPANY—SELECTED ECONOMIC DATA

Line	Item	1976	1977	1978	1979	1980	1981	1982	March 1983
1	Nominal gross national product (GNP)	1,718	1,918	2,164	2,418	2,633	2,938	3,058	
2	Percent Change—Nominal GNP	10.9	11.6	12.8	11.7	8.9	11.6	4.1	9.6[a]
3	Percent Change—Real (Deflated) GNP	5.4	5.5	5.0	2.8	−0.4	1.9	−1.8	3.5[a]
4	Percent Change—Consumer Price Index	4.8	6.8	9.0	13.3	12.4	8.9	3.9	5.0[a]
5	Price Interest Rate	6.8	6.8	9.1	12.7	15.3	18.9	14.9	10.5
6	Interest Rate—Long-term AAA Corporate Bonds	8.4	8.0	8.7	9.6	11.9	14.2	13.8	11.7
7	Interest Rate—Long-term BBB Corporate Bonds	9.8	9.0	9.5	10.7	13.7	16.0	16.1	12.8
8	Interest Rate—U.S. Treasury Bills (six-month)	5.3	5.5	7.6	10.0	11.4	13.8	11.1	8.7
9	Interest Rate—Long-term Government Bonds	7.6	7.4	8.4	9.4	11.5	13.9	13.0	10.1

[a] These data represent estimates for 1983. All other data represent actuals on March 31, 1983.

Sources: Economic Report of the President (1983).
U.S. Council of Economic Advisors, Economic Indicators.
Casewriter estimates.

EXHIBIT 11-7

STANDARD & POOR'S MEDIAN FINANCIAL RATIOS BY RATING (AVERAGES, 1979 TO 1981)

	AAA	AA	A	BBB	BB	B
Pretax Interest Coverage	18.25×	8.57×	6.56×	3.82×	3.27×	1.76×
Pretax Interest and Full Rental Coverage	8.02	4.95	4.05	2.75	2.41	1.52
Cash Flow/Long-term Debt	231.95%	108.19%	71.75%	43.88%	30.23%	17.89%
Cash Flow/Total Debt	136.23	80.41	57.96	36.58	26.43	13.25
Pretax Return on Average Long-term Capital Employed	31.27	26.29	21.75	18.31	18.44	13.19
Operating Income/Sales	16.15	14.27	12.72	10.90	11.86	9.04
Long-term Debt/Capitalization	11.83	19.02	26.30	34.47	44.09	54.13
Total Debt/Capitalization including Short-term Debt	17.04	23.70	30.41	38.62	48.07	58.77
Total Debt/Capitalization including Short-term Debt (including 8× Rental Expense)	30.93	36.79	41.49	47.93	56.57	64.60
Total Liabilities/Tangible Shareholders' Equity and Minority Interest	70.24	93.16	105.76	131.97	190.37	259.76

Source: Standard & Poor's Credit Overview (Standard & Poor, 1982).

Carlton also knew that, given his age, he would have to arrange for a transfer of ownership in the next few years. Indeed, the banker had indicated that a condition for providing the loan described in Exhibit 5 was that Carlton arrange for more permanent financing within five years.

He had several options. The first was that he could take the company public at some point. Selling shares to public stockholders would create a liquid market for Carlton stock. Of course, for a public stock offering to be feasible and successful, the company's operating performance over the next few years would have to be quite favorable.

Another option was to try to sell Carlton Polish to a larger company. Over the years, a number of companies and business brokers had approached Carlton about selling out. These negotiations had never led to a definitive arrangement, but the option remained open in the future.

Of course, what Charlie Carlton would do if he owned 100% of Carlton Polish would not be a relevant issue unless he succeeded in buying out his partner. Whether he should be willing to pay $2,500,000 for Jim Miller's shares and whether or not the company could raise the funds necessary to finance the purchase were issues yet to be resolved.

12

Record Masters

Kent Dauten returned to his hotel room in August 1994 to find a Federal Express package waiting for him. His associate, Scott Gwilliam, had forwarded to him a Coopers & Lybrand selling memorandum for Record Masters, the leading provider of record and information management services to the health-care industry.

Dauten had been actively looking for a business to buy since March 1994 when he had announced his plans to leave Madison Dearborn Partners, Inc. (MDP), a Chicago-based private equity investment firm. Dauten had been a general partner at MDP and had worked there and at its predecessor, First Chicago Venture Capital, since graduating from Harvard Business School in 1979. While Dauten's investment experience over the previous 15 years had ranged across industries and stages of investment, he had extensive experience leading transactions in the health-care industry. Among other successful investments, Dauten had led a growth equity investment in HMA, a hospital management company that had increased in value by 400×, and Genesis Health Ventures which had become one of the leading publicly traded long-term care management companies. (See Exhibit 12-1 for Dauten's résumé and Exhibit 12-2 for Dauten's professional investment history.) Dauten had decided to leave MDP to sponsor one or more buyouts in which he would provide the majority of equity capital and would play a more active management role than he could at MDP. Based on his experience in private equity, he was targeting investments in which he could earn at least a 35% internal rate of return. He planned to assume the chairman and CEO position of any company he acquired. To guide his search, Dauten had drafted a mission statement with the following objectives: (See Exhibit 12-3 for Dauten's detailed mission statement.)

Mission:	Have fun combining investment and business skills to build a collection of attractive businesses dedicated to the highest standards of excellence, quality, and integrity in working with their customers, suppliers, and employees.
Vision:	Create through acquisitions and internal growth a privately owned holding company with two to three diverse businesses that are leaders in their niche markets.

Senior Researcher Laurence E. Katz prepared this case under the supervision of Professor William A. Sahlman and Lecturer Michael J. Roberts as the basis for class discussion rather than to illustrate either effective or ineffective handling of an administrative situation.

EXHIBIT 12-1

KENT DAUTEN'S RÉSUMÉ

KENT P. DAUTEN

Work Experience

First Chicago Venture Capital/Madison Dearborn Partners, Inc.—*1979 to 1994*
Senior Vice President at FCVC responsible for finding, evaluating, closing and monitoring new management buyout and special equity investments in a variety of industries. Initiated and developed health-care services industry specialization. Overall, completed investments in 28 companies and achieved liquidity through 8 IPOs and 13 sales. Beginning in 1987, assumed managerial and administrative responsibilities supporting FCVC's President in the areas of First Chicago interface, key relationship management, and oversight of junior staff. Board member of First Capital Corporation of Chicago and First Chicago Investment Corporation, the two legal entitles that comprised First Chicago Venture Capital. Past Vice Chairman of the national Association of Small Business Investment Companies Board of Governors, also serving on its Executive, Regulatory and PAC Committees in leading FCVC's battle against proposed SBA regulatory threats during 1991–1992. Also represented FCVC on Merchant Bank Management Committee and assumed responsibility in 1989 for managing and then downsizing mezzanine investment group with a $95 million portfolio in nine companies.

Founding partner in 1992 of Madison Dearborn Partners, Inc., a new private equity investment firm that was the spin-off of First Chicago Venture Capital's entire organization. MDP raised a $550 million pool of capital for new investments and managed an approximately $2 billion portfolio of equity securities for First Chicago Corporation and IFINT Diversified Holdings, Inc.

Booz, Allen & Hamilton—*Summer 1978*
Management consultant for Fortune 50 company business strategy assignment.

Pharmaco, Inc.—*Summers 1976 & 1977*
Assistant to the Chairman/CEO of start-up medical product company.

Education

Harvard Graduate School of Business Administration; M.B.A.—1979
Dartmouth College; B.A. in Economics—1977
  Summa Cum Laude and Phi Beta Kappa
  Two-time President of debate team

Personal

Born 7/9/55
Married with four children.
Interests include real estate, tennis, skiing, soccer coaching, and family.
Guest lecturer at Northwestern, University of Illinois, and NASBIC Institute.
Board Member, Lutheran Social Services of Illinois.
Board Member, Metropolitan Planning Council.

Board of Directors

Health Management Associates, Naples, FL (1980–present)
Southern Foods Group, Dallas, TX (1987–present)
Genesis Health Ventures, Kennett Square, PA (1985–1993)
Surgicare/Medical Care International, Dallas, TX (1982–1985)

EXHIBIT 12-2

KEN DAUTEN'S VENTURE CAPITAL INVESTMENT HISTORY

Date of Investment	Company	Nature of Business	Type of Deal	Internal Rate of Return
05/80	Health Mgmt. Associates I	Hospital Management	Industry Consolidation	45%
03/81	Home Health Care of America	Home Infusion Therapy	Start-up	75%
09/81	American Healthcorp	Hospital Management	Industry Consolidation	27%
09/81	Imperial Clevite	Diversified Industrial	LBO	14%
10/81	PT Components I	Power Transmission	LBO	30%
03/82	Farrells	Restaurants	LBO	(69%)
08/82	Purex	Household Products	LBO	36%
10/82	Surgicare	Outpatient surgery	Start-up	(10%)
04/83	Harris Graphics	Printing Presses	LBO	85%
12/83	Yale	Industrial Hoists	LBO	33%
01/84	Healthcare International	Psychiatric Hospitals	Growth	(37%)
03/84	Hannover Healthcare	Nursing Homes	Industry Consolidation	0%
06/84	J.H. Williams	Hand Tools	Turnaround	(100%)
08/85	Genesis Health Ventures	Nursing Homes	Growth	19%
12/85	Wyndham Foods	Specialty Foods	Industry Consolidation	24%
09/86	PT Components II	Power Transmission	LBO	22%
02/87	Southern Foods Group	Dairy Processing	LBO/Industry Consolidation	64%
09/87	Winkler	Plastic Cutlery	Turnaround	93%
12/87	American Lantern	Residential Lighting	LBO	(96%)
04/88	Tee Jays	Apparel	LBO	46%
09/88	Health Mgmt. Associates II	Hospital Management	LBO	71%
09/88	MC Industries	Fluid Power	Industry Consolidation	(45%)
10/88	Keller	Aluminum Products	Turnaround	(100%)
11/89	Braelan	Textiles	LBO	0%
12/89	EPICOR	Auto Aftermarket Parts	LBO	146%
01/90	Trench	Licensed Apparel	LBO	(100%)
02/90	A–C	Industrial Compressors	LBO	105%
06/91	Titan Tool	Painting Equipment	LBO	63%

EXHIBIT 12-3

KENT DAUTEN'S MISSION STATEMENT

Mission:	Have fun combining investment and business skills to build a collection of attractive businesses dedicated to the highest standards of excellence, quality, and integrity in working with their customers, suppliers, and employees.
Vision:	Create through acquisitions and internal growth a privately owned holding company with two to three diverse businesses that are leaders in their niche markets.

Goals/Strategies:

1) Achieve unique levels of profitability (OI% of 15+%) through high degree of acquisition selectivity, aggressive profit improvement programs, and meaningful management incentives.

2) Achieve $25–$50 million in revenues within five years by closing one core acquisition in the next year.

3) Control own destiny by growing at a deliberate pace, maintaining voting control, employing a conservative financial structure, and having dependable operating management in place.

4) Have fun working with a more concentrated group of referral sources, managers, suppliers, and customers.

5) Build wealth over a long-term time frame through price discipline, reinvestment, growth, debt, paydown, pre-tax compounding of value, and QSBS tax treatment.

Acquisition Criteria:

Purchase price $5–$15 million (low P/E of 3–5×)

Minimum $1 million EBIT (no turnarounds)

Leading and Protected Niche Market Position (under $1–$200 million)

Stable Industry (low cyclicality and diverse customer base) with "Controllable" Revenues/Expenses

Solid and Fun-to-Work-With Management Team

Close Geographical Proximity or Easy Travel Access

Low Tech/Easy to Understand

Quality Reputation and Morally Acceptable Products

"Clean" Business/Minimal Contingent Liabilities

Growth Potential Internally or Add-on Acquisitions

Potential Personal Contribution (prior experience, profit plans, etc.)

Meets "Common Sense" Test

Marketing Gameplan:

1) Focused marketing to high-potential prior relationships.

2) Broader screening of referral sources to cultivate new relationships.

3) High degree of service = personal selling, super responsiveness, periodic communications, unique gifts, and memorable/fun dialogue.

4) Origination efforts through direct company contacts, trade shows, . . .

5) Development of five (5) target industries.

Record Masters Network was an eight-year-old records storage company providing management and retrieval services of active medical records to health-care institutions. Record Masters provided open-shelved storage services, including ancillary services such as copying, purging, and file retrieval. The Record Masters Network had 13 franchisees, each locally operated under the name Record Masters. The Network operated as a co-operative, owned by the shareholders of the franchisees, with equal board representation from each franchisee. The Network provided administrative help to the franchisees but did not control their strategic decisions or day-to-day operations. The Network primarily provided a common name ("Record Masters") and a common file tracking system ("HealthRx") to the franchisees. In 1994, 4 of the 13 Record Masters franchisees, located in Philadelphia, Pittsburgh, New Orleans, and Detroit, decided to sell their businesses collectively. They had hired Coopers & Lybrand to advise them on this process. (See Exhibit 12-4 for excerpts of the selling memorandum.)

Six years earlier, Dauten had considered investing in the records management industry when Bell + Howell had auctioned off its commercial records management division to reduce debt from its own leveraged buyout. Because of this past exposure to the industry, he had accumulated data from other comparable transactions. (See Exhibit 12-5.)

Dauten finished reading the selling memorandum and began considering the investment opportunity. This would probably be the most significant personal investment and employment decision of his life. Was this an attractive opportunity for him to invest both his capital and his time? What were the risks that he needed to consider? What would be a reasonable price to pay, and how would he structure and finance this deal?

EXHIBIT 12-4

EXCERPTS FROM RECORD MASTERS SELLING MEMORANDUM

Record Masters ═══════

July 1994

Coopers	Merger &
& Lybrand	Acquisition
	Services

RECORD MASTERS

SECTION

   I. EXECUTIVE SUMMARY

  II. KEY INVESTMENT CONSIDERATIONS

 III. HISTORY, OWNERSHIP, AND RECENT DEVELOPMENTS

 IV. MARKETS, CLIENTS, AND COMPETITORS

   V. OPERATIONS

 VI. MANAGEMENT, ORGANIZATION, AND PERSONNEL

VII. FACILITIES, EQUIPMENT, AND SYSTEMS

VIII. LEGAL

 IX. HISTORICAL FINANCIAL INFORMATION

  X. EXHIBITS

     A. Corporate Brochure

     B. Organization Charts

     C. Unaudited 1993 Financial Statements

(Continued)

EXHIBIT 12-4 (Continued)

I. EXECUTIVE SUMMARY

- **Introduction**

  Record Masters provides off-site record storage, management and retrieval services to hospitals and medical offices. The proposed transaction presented herein covers the four Record Masters locations (hereafter referred to as the "Business" or "RML") of Detroit, New Orleans, Delaware Valley ("Philadelphia"), and Pittsburgh. The first operation began in October of 1986 in New Orleans, and the most recent began in Detroit in December of 1987.

  Hospitals and clinics generate thousands of linear feet of records each year. The records come from multiple departments within hospitals, the most significant contributors being the Medical Records, Radiology, and Patient Accounting departments. Utilizing, handling, and updating these records, while at the same time locating and providing ready access to them, requires significant human and capital resources, whether within the institution, or as in the case of Record Masters services, via outsourcing to a record management company.

  Hospital space, averaged across the United States is valued at nearly $400/sq. ft. Medical clinic and office space is also purchased or leased at premium rates per square foot. When used for hard-copy record storage this valuable space is nonrevenue producing. The Record Masters' procedures and off-site locations have made it possible for health-care clients to reduce the size of their record rooms and utilize this space for revenue-generating patient care facilities.

  Prior to the advent of the Record Masters proprietary procedures, off-site storage of active hospital records was generally unsatisfactory due to high retrieval charges and the inability of quick turnarounds from requests for records to delivery. The Business utilizes a unique open-shelving procedure for housing records off-site. This procedure for storing records, along with custom-developed record management software, provides faster and more economical recall and refile services than hospitals can achieve themselves. Record Masters provides a level of service sufficient to replace a dedicated hospital record department.

- **Form and Ownership**

  The four locations of the Business are all independently owned corporations and are organized as subchapter S corporations in their respective states. The owners of these independent companies are also the respective CEOs. All locations are franchisees of Record Masters Corporation, of which they in turn are shareholders and Directors. They share a nonbinding relationship with the Network, which is discussed in more detail in Section VIII.

- **Location and Facilities**

  The Business leases facilities that are strategically located within the metropolitan areas served. Location is critical because Record Masters' standard service guarantee promises one-hour "STAT" (emergency requests) record delivery to any client, 7 days per week, 24 hours per day. RML facilities are secure, dry warehouses ranging in size from 36,000 sq. ft. to 76,000 sq. ft. As the buildings approach efficient usage capacity, additional space is leased.

- **Markets, Clients, and Competitors**

  The Business measures market size by the number and size of the hospitals in the metropolitan area. There are 223 hospitals in the four city service area with a total of 57,786 beds. RML currently provides service to 46% of the hospitals, comprising 49% of the beds within their overall service area. The business is the market leader in each of the four cities.

(Continued)

EXHIBIT 12-4 *(Continued)*

- **Financial Summary**

Operating Results

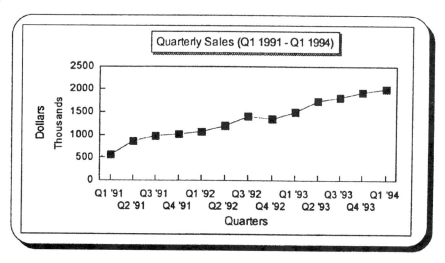

The following table summarizes Record Masters' unaudited operating results for the five-year period 1989–1993 ending December 31 and the unaudited results for the first three months of 1994.

	Fiscal Years Ending December 31 as Indicated ($ Thousands)					3 Months to March 31
	1989	1990	1991	1992	1993	1994
Net sales ($)	$1,420	$2,469	$3,567	$4,971	$6,958	$2,007
Gross profit ($)	$ 407	$ 825	$1,351	$1,863	$2,428	$ 738
Gross margin (%)	28.6%	33.4%	37.9%	37.5%	34.9%	36.8%
(Adjusted) EBIT ($)	$ 118	$ 155	$ 760	$1,180	$1,521	$ 462

Balance Sheet
The pro forma consolidated balance sheet as of December 31, 1993 is summarized below:

ASSETS (000s)		LIABILITIES AND EQUITY (000s)	
Accounts receivable	$1,278	Accounts payable	$ 127
Cash and equivalents	289	Accrued expenses	196
Other (including cash)	75	Current portion of long-term debt	99
Total Current Assets	$1,642	Deferred income	225
		Income taxes payable	30
Fixed assets (gross)	$1,923	Total Current Liabilities	$ 676
Accumulated depreciation	964		
Fixed assets (net of depreciation)	$959	Long-term debt	95
		Deferred rent	41
		Shareholder's Equity	20
		Retained earnings	1,770
Total Assets	$2,602	Total Liabilities and Equity	$2,602

(Continued)

EXHIBIT 12-4 *(Continued)*

- **Reason for Sale**

  The businesses represent a major portion of the net worth of the sellers. The owners have a desire to realize these holdings following a decision by the other nine Record Masters locations not to collectively pursue an aggressive expansion strategy. The owners feel that there is substantial potential for continued growth and that future profitability and growth can best be realized by an organization that is strategically positioned to facilitate growth and invest in new processes, services, and technology to meet the growing needs of their clients. The owners of the four locations have signed a binding agreement to act in concert for the purpose of the proposed transaction.

II. KEY INVESTMENT CONSIDERATIONS

- **INDUSTRY POSITION AND REPUTATION:**   The four locations of Record Masters that comprise the Business enjoy a dominant market position within their respective territories. This position provides a profitable base from which to continue growing an increasingly substantial health-care service and sales organization.

- **PROFITABILITY:**   The Business has generated substantial profit margins and has demonstrated the ability to maintain these margins while building on its history of significant growth. With gross profit of $2.4 million and adjusted EBIT of $1.5 million in 1993, RML anticipates continued substantial progress in 1994.

- **GROWTH PATTERN AND POTENTIAL:**   RML had sales growth of 73%, 44%, 39%, 40% in 1990, 1991, 1992, and 1993, respectively, which equals a 49% compound annual growth rate. The Business anticipates continued sales growth through increased market penetration (current hospital penetration is 47%) and new service initiatives.

- **BARRIERS TO ENTRY:**   Hospital and medical office management have historically shown considerable reluctance to implement changes that necessitate vast movements of valuable and confidential records. While capital requirements for new facilities are not excessive, the proven track record necessary to gain new clients presents a significant barrier to inexperienced market entrants.

- **DISTRIBUTION CHANNELS:**   The Business has developed extensive relationships with major health-care institutions in four of the largest markets in the United States. It is believed that this represents an ideal opportunity to market additional products and services to these institutions.

- **PROPRIETARY SOFTWARE:**   Record Masters has developed proprietary record tracking software known as *HealthRx*. This software integrates bar coding and record indexing to provide access to records on a real-time basis.

- **NEW SERVICES:**   Record Masters has recently developed a capability for providing correspondence copying service, which has been implemented in select locations. This service is in place in Pittsburgh and has recently been launched in Detroit. Although it is relatively new, correspondence copying has generated immediate revenue for these locations and clients have embraced it.

- **INDUSTRY TREND:**   Floor space value and personnel costs are forcing hospitals to pursue outsourcing of their noncore services. RML is ideally positioned to continue to benefit its current clients and expand its client base in the region served.

- **PERFORMANCE:**   The locations are the top four performing locations for Record Masters nationally and represent almost 50% of the Network's total sales and more than 50% of its profits.

- **PERSONNEL:**   The owners of the Business have exhibited the entrepreneurial drive and skills necessary to bring RML to its current level of performance and are poised to continue growing. They are enthusiastic about the prospects of working with a new owner and are seeking to identify parties who share their vision for the future.

(Continued)

EXHIBIT 12-4 *(Continued)*

III. HISTORY, OWNERSHIP, AND RECENT DEVELOPMENTS

* **History**

  The four locations are all independently owned and operated franchisees of Record Masters Network Corporation. The Business, which owns 33% of the outstanding shares of common stock in the franchisor, views the franchise arrangement as more of a cooperative agreement than that of the typical franchise agreement store "chain." The Network provides a dedicated management and administration function, but franchises do not take direction from the Network. The Record Masters Network began franchiser operations on May 1, 1991, and also views itself as a cooperative central administrator rather than a franchising business. The locations that make up the Network began operations as early as 1986.

  The business procedure and methodology that became Record Masters originated in a major hospital in San Jose, California. Aware of problems with retrieving X-ray films in a consistent and timely manner, Dr. Rowen, Radiology Department Chief of Staff, together with his son Steve Rowen, pioneered a solution that provided prompt access to the films and allowed the hospital to free up expensive floor space. The company founded by the Rowens was incorporated under the name Deliverex. Mr. Rowen franchised three West Coast locations in the 1970s before selling a Master Franchise for the entire United States in 1985 to Securex, Inc., also located in San Jose. Between 1985 and 1988, Securex sold 19 franchises which blanketed the major cities throughout the United States. Securex, a start-up company partially financed by venture capital, was poorly managed from the outset. In response to increasing pressure from the franchisees for improved service, decreasing financial resources, and employee problems, the majority owner of Securex sold the company in November of 1989 to Archives Corporation, a box storage vendor in Minneapolis, Minnesota. Archives Corp. was primarily interested in quickly growing the Business through the sale of new franchises rather than devoting resources to providing central leadership to the existing franchisees. In October of 1990, 15 of the 19 franchisees successfully filed for rescission of their franchise agreement with the California Arbitration Association.

  From a legal standpoint, the Network has a Hold Harmless Agreement with Deliverex of San Jose which operates its original location under its own name, and the venture capital organization that financed Securex. Through the purchase of the original venture capital note issued to Securex (which is in default) the Network could, if desired, assume control of the Board of Directors of Securex. Presently, however, there appears to be little incentive to pursue additional legal actions.

* **Ownership**

  Each of the four corporations that make up the Business is organized as a subchapter S corporation under the charter of the state in which it is located. The CEOs of Philadelphia and Pittsburgh each own 100% of their stock. The New Orleans and Detroit locations have multiple shareholders, all but one of whom are involved in business operations. The CEOs are also members of the Board of Directors of the Network. The relationship between franchisee and franchisor is discussed in Section VIII.

* **Recent Developments**

  RML has developed additional products and services for records management departments within hospitals and has realized two recent successes expected to lead a new revenue stream. These services are correspondence copying and file room management, both of which are provided on an outsourced basis. RML believes these services represent significant additional opportunities for future growth.

(Continued)

EXHIBIT 12-4 (Continued)

IV. MARKETS, CLIENTS, AND COMPETITORS

- **Markets**

  RML concentrates its sales efforts on hospitals within one-hour driving time of its warehouse locations. Currently, hospitals comprise 98% of the client base, although medical offices and clinics are also viewed as potential clients. Because of the nature of the services the Business provides, it is in a strong position to protect its client accounts. There exists an inherent resistance to changing record services because the records of the client are in the physical custody of the Business, and there is not only a cost, but also risk involved in moving them (losing or misplacing a patient file). Market share data on the four markets discussed are listed below. Sales ratios are based on data from the first quarter of 1994.

Summary

	Detroit	New Orleans	Philadelphia	Pittsburgh	Total
Total hospitals	41	38	106	38	223
Number of beds	12,584	7,030	27,140	11,032	57,786
Average size in beds	307	185	256	290	260
Hospitals served	26	23	34	21	104
Beds served	8,141	5,551	8,410	7,286	29,388
Penetration: Hospitals	63%	61%	32%	55%	47%
Penetration: Beds	65%	79%	31%	66%	51%

Detroit

	Revenue for First Quarter 1994			
	Record Management Services	New Material Processing	Other	Total
Revenue/hospital	$6,292	$1,634	$1,356	$ 9,282
Revenue/hospital served	$9,921	$2,576	$2,139	$14,636
Revenue/bed	$20.50	$ 5.32	$ 4.42	$ 30.24
Revenue/bed served	$31.69	$ 8.23	$ 6.83	$ 46.75

New Orleans

	Revenue for First Quarter 1994			
	Record Management Services	New Material Processing	Other	Total
Revenue/hospital	$ 8,145	$1,294	$10,117	$19,556
Revenue/hospital served	$13,903	$2,137	$16,715	$32,755
Revenue/bed	$ 25.41	$ 3.91	$ 30.55	$ 59.87
Revenue/bed served	$ 70.26	$10.80	$ 84.47	$165.54

(Continued)

EXHIBIT 12-4 (Continued)

Pittsburgh

	Revenue for First Quarter 1994			
	Record Management Services	New Material Processing	Other	Total
Revenue/hospital	$5,512	$1,918	$ 956	$ 8,386
Revenue/hospital served	$9,974	$3,471	$1,730	$15,175
Revenue/bed	$18.99	$ 6.61	$ 3.29	$ 28.89
Revenue/bed served	$28.75	$10.00	$ 4.99	$ 43.74

Philadelphia

	Revenue for First Quarter 1994			
	Record Management Services	New Material Processing	Other	Total
Revenue/hospital	$ 3,431	$1,113	$0.00	$ 4,545
Revenue/hospital served	$10,698	$3,470	$0.00	$14,168
Revenue/bed	$ 13.40	$ 4.35	$0.00	$ 17.75
Revenue/bed served	$ 43.25	$14.03	$0.00	$ 57.28

- **Clients**

  The percentage of sales to the top 10 clients in each territory is as follows: (Please note that within each hospital there may be from 1 to 12 different departments that are serviced under separate contracts.)

	Percentage of Sales per Client							
	1	2	3	4	5	6–10	Balance	Nonhospital
Detroit	14%	11%	8%	7%	6%	24%	25%	5%
New Orleans	57%	8%	4%	3%	3%	11%	8%	6%
Philadelphia	19%	14%	11%	9%	6%	22%	18%	1%
Pittsburgh	12%	10%	10%	7%	6%	29%	19%	7%

- **Competitors**

  Competition for Record Masters can be divided into four distinct groups: archival vendors who provide box storage or attempt to copy Record Masters service, hospitals, microfilm services, and new technology.

Archival

Prior to Deliverex, which was the pioneer of Record Masters type services, archival vendors served hospitals and professional service firms, such as accountants and attorneys with traditional box storage. Under these systems, the clients are billed for storage space, plus "activity" charges for each retrieval, delivery, return, and refile. Generally speaking, archival competitors are only able to service records that are several years older than those that Record Masters now serves due to the sheer volume of retrieval and refile service activity on newer files. Archival services focus more on attorneys and accountants who customarily request fewer retrievals and who are less sensitive to immediate service. In isolated instances, archival vendors have attempted to alter their method of doing

(Continued)

EXHIBIT 12-4   (Continued)

business by adopting methods similar to Record Masters'. These companies are not viewed as a significant competitive threat.

There are several large chains of archival companies, such as Iron Mountain, Pierce Leahy, and Safesite. There are also local companies, some of which are competent competitors, such as Leonard Archives, and Record Management & Protection ("RMP"). Many archival vendors belong to the Association of Commercial Records Centers ("ACRC") which has about 500 members, 10% of which are international. Record Masters Network is also a member of this organization. A recent survey of Yellow Pages advertisers in the United States under the heading of "record storage" counted almost 2,500 listings, with approximately 1,700 of these clearly identified by name as record storage companies.

Archival vendors that solicit bids in the same market that RML serves are:

Detroit

Name	Approximate Annual Revenue
Leonard Archives	$5,000,000
Safesite	<$1,000,000
Data Retention Center	<$500,000
The Record Center	<$500,000

New Orleans

Name	Approximate Annual Revenue
Record Management & Protection	$1,500,000
CBD Archives	$1,500,000
Record Storage and Storage	$750,000
Gallagher Storage and Service	$750,000

While RMP and CBD Archives are believed to serve a small number of health-care clients, none is of a significant size. The other off-site storage companies in New Orleans serve the oil industry, banking, and legal firms in the area.

Philadelphia

Name	Approximate Annual Revenue
Pierce Leahy Archives	$75,000,000
File Save	<$1,000,000
Security Archives	$500,000–$750,000

Pittsburgh

Name	Approximate Annual Revenue
File Express	$500,000
Business Record Management	>$1,000,000
OPUS	<$500,000

(Continued)

EXHIBIT 12-4 (Continued)

Hospitals

Hospitals maintain extensive file rooms and centers of their own. Usually these are off-site because of the high cost of hospital floor space. The directors are typically mid- or low-level hospital administrators who believe that any move to outsourcing would have clear implications for their own existence. In a number of instances, however, hospital warehouse facilities have been closed because of the cost-effective service that Record Masters has been able to provide. Hospital sites are capable of providing record services for themselves under proper management, but many who service their own records do so as a result of tradition and resistance to change.

Microfilming

Before the advent of Record Masters, many present clients, especially hospital records departments, microfilmed older records. Microfilming cost anywhere from $.025 to $0.65 per page and resulted in a significant expenditure. In a typical 300-bed hospital, microfilming a year's worth of records could cost from $30,000 to $60,000, compared to an annual charge of $5,000 to $7,000 for Record Masters' service. Due to this cost advantage, Record Masters has made significant inroads vis-à-vis microfilm vendors. This cost advantage begins to disappear and becomes a penalty if the hospital requires the records to be stored in hard copy longer than eight to ten years. By this time the linear footage of old records has shrunk significantly as active records are called forward and the recall activity of those remaining records becomes almost negligible. Nevertheless, prices can then be reduced to the point where microfilming still does not make economic sense. In addition to the cost advantage, using microfilm copies takes time, and the copies lose resolution to the point where doctors do not like to use them and greatly prefer the original hard-copy file.

New Technology

At the present time, visionary concepts of computerized patient records and optical disc storage systems are enjoying considerable theoretical debate and attention, but suffer from a lack of hard evidence to support enthusiasm for high-tech systems. Actual use of these systems is very limited, and many institutions that have spent large sums on new and innovative systems have yet to realize a positive payback. Record Masters has extensively investigated the use of optical disc and concluded that the high cost of storage media and transmission of data will make optical disc an ineffective procedure for long-term storage of the entire medical record for some considerable time. Systems and procedures that create the medical record must first change to reduce the number of pages that require scanning onto the disc before this will become an effective solution. Nevertheless, Record Masters' management believes its market position and its capability of serving multiple hospitals with common software and hardware will enable Record Masters to offer this service to hospital clients at some future date. The subject is discussed in greater detail in Section V.

V. OPERATIONS

• **The Business**

Record Masters' approach to off-site storage of hospital and medical records goes beyond a simple warehouse and retrieval service concept. The Detroit, New Orleans, Philadelphia, and Pittsburgh locations have developed their services to the point that they have become an extension of the hospitals' own file rooms.

The service begins with a records system survey performed for the prospective client at no cost or obligation. The survey is performed by Record Masters' personnel and includes exhaustive measurement of the existing filing system, as well as evaluating the effectiveness of the current delivery systems. The results and recommendations are presented to the client in a report that many hospital record managers prize for its thorough and comprehensive information. Included in the report is a proposal to service the needs of the department in a manner unique to their needs for one flat monthly fee. This fee eliminates the need for time-consuming audits by the hospital of monthly invoices and also allows the department to budget this cost with confidence for the coming year. This single cost covers a pre-set delivery schedule and an unlimited amount of retrieval requests as well as refiling of returned records. The service can be quoted in this fashion because of Record Masters' experience in estimating the volume of activity under a wide variety of demand scenarios.

(Continued)

EXHIBIT 12-4 *(Continued)*

If successful in winning the bid (in many cases there are no competing bids that can truly be considered along-side a Record Masters proposal), the first step is to purge records from the client's department. This is usually done by date of its last activity and is performed by a crew of Record Masters personnel after normal working hours who painstakingly go through each record to determine whether it should be purged. Those removed for storage are put in containers and/or carts, transferred by truck to the Record Masters Service Center and then placed in the same order on "open shelving." Record Masters personnel usually complete the purge in a fraction of the time and with greater accuracy than hospital personnel. In fact, because of this efficiency many Record Masters locations often perform contracted in-house purges for hospitals.

The storing of the records on open shelving (individual charts or X-rays are filed side by side on the shelves rather than placed in boxes and then placed on the shelves) is a key element in the success of Record Masters. This allows a fast turnaround time from order to delivery. The retrieval request of records from hospitals is far higher than a general business or law firm, and quick access is essential. Some clients have online order termi-nals, while others fax orders to Record Masters. In two to four hours the records are delivered, depending on the delivery schedule. In many cases this is as fast as a client can retrieve records in their own department. Two daily deliveries are normally provided to each hospital, but certain departments contract for as many as four de-liveries per day. Emergency "STAT" deliveries are guaranteed in one hour to every client. "STAT" services are billed separately from the monthly fee on a per-occurrence basis.

- **Marketing**

The key to Record Masters' success, and the heart of its marketing plan, has been to offer rapid, dependable, and cost-effective record retrieval. From the "guaranteed one-hour 'STAT' delivery" to multiple deliveries per day, Record Masters is organized to support the hospital records department by providing the most accurate, rapid, and reliable retrieval possible.

Several additional factors are at work in creating the market niche for Record Masters. Foremost is the lim-ited filing space and associated high cost in hospital facilities. As noted earlier, estimates of the cost of hospital space average $400 per square foot. Thus, records storage space in hospitals is always expensive, rarely plentiful, and never revenue producing.

As the amount and complexity of filed information grows, the need for more competent and expensive per-sonnel increases dramatically. Qualified personnel must be highly trained to ensure flawless processing. These personnel represent an expensive internal burden which Record Masters alleviates.

Lastly, hospitals require a level of confidentiality that is higher than that normally associated with general busi-ness records. Patient information and treatment are closely guarded matters, and the hospital administration is certain to make confidentiality and security of records a top priority when selecting an off-site facility. The fact that Record Masters concentrates almost exclusively on health-care records is a powerful argument when confi-dentiality issues are being considered.

Thus when space decreases and personnel costs increase, hospital administrators seek other ways to manage their records—ways that are secure, meet the standards of the health-care industry, and are more cost effective than using hospital space and personnel. Record Masters dominates this niche.

- **Computerized Management**

Another key element in the success of Record Masters is the record tracking performed for clients through cus-tomized and proprietary software. The *HealthRx* software program developed by Record Masters provides an in-stant history of all the activity of each record. *HealthRx* gives each Record Masters Service Center the capabil-ity to provide customized record indexing and bar coding services designed for the specific requirements of the healthcare industry.

A unique feature of *HealthRx* is its online ordering capability. This service allows hospital clients to review the history of record deliveries between Record Masters and their department on a real-time basis. Also, online or-dering eliminates duplicate orders for records which can result in lost time at the service center.

Mark Guidry, the CEO of Record Masters of New Orleans, developed *HealthRx* through his knowledge of programming, hardware capabilities of the PC, and his understanding of the operations and requirements of

EXHIBIT 12-4   (Continued)

health-care records management. The concept and initial gap of the capabilities of *HealthRx* allowed the New Orleans center to grow and prosper much faster than any other Record Masters location. The Business's four service centers make full use of this software today, which partially explains why they have outperformed other Record Masters centers.

- **New Services—Correspondence Copying/Release of Information**

  Medical records departments are inundated with requests for copies of patient medical records. These requests come from insurance companies, attorneys, courts, government agencies such as Medicare or Medicaid, and other hospitals or consulting physicians. The determination of proper authorization for release of this confidential information and the work involved in retrieving the record, copying it, mailing it with a cover letter, replacing the original record in its correct place, and billing the recipient if appropriate is a monumental task. The vast majority of hospitals in the United States outsource this task to a company that specializes in this service, called correspondence copying. These services are usually offered with a revenue rebate to a hospital, since the requestor pays the full cost for the service.

  Approximately 25% of the medical records recalled to a hospital client are returned for correspondence purposes. After completion of this process, the record is returned to Record Masters for refiling. Thus, it was somewhat natural for Record Masters to consider offering this service to its clients, for it would further eliminate unnecessary activity within the department.

  Record Masters piloted correspondence copy service in Portland, Oregon, through a subsidiary operation beginning in early 1993. By the end of the third quarter of the same year, this new operation had achieved significant success. Current monthly revenues from seven hospital clients equal approximately two-thirds of the storage and retrieval revenue from 16 hospital clients in that same city. Even more importantly, earnings are running at a rate of 15% before taxes, which exceeded expectations for this start-up operation. As a result of this success, Record Masters Network has written software, integral to the *HealthRx* system, supporting this service. Record Masters is confident that this will reflect state-of-the-art programming and will be a great asset in both management and marketing of this service.

  Two prominent firms offer correspondence copying service nationwide. Industry sources indicate that these firms have revenues in excess of $20 to $30 million and are profitable. There is also a multitude of small local firms providing this service, although correspondence copying is the only service provided by these firms. While Record Masters is new in this field and does not yet have detailed market statistics available, it is apparent that revenues from copy service exceed costs of storage and retrieval by a multiple of two to three. Accordingly, RML feels that this can be a significant and profitable source of new business. The Portland location has already established three hospital contracts from its existing client base. Therefore, the initial focus will be to market this service to current clients.

  The Pittsburgh location was the first to follow Portland in launching correspondence copying and is also experiencing rapid success. Detroit has just recently initiated this new service in its market.

- **Technology and Automation**

  Computerized Records

  One goal of the health-care industry is to computerize the patient record system. Record Masters has determined that this will immediately lead to revisions in existing procedures and also recognizes the challenge and opportunity of providing the next generation of services. Many different kinds of technology and procedures are being proposed and tested in an attempt to reduce or minimize paper usage. Trade journals abound with editorials and advertisements about products claiming to facilitate these goals. Medical Records directors and Management Information Systems managers are deluged with seminars and papers on the subject. There are examples of hospitals from coast to coast that have spent considerable sums on optical disc, bedside terminals, digitized radiology units, and a host of other products. To date, these efforts have not produced a cost-effective solution, and few paper medical records have been eliminated as a result of optical scanning.

(*Continued*)

EXHIBIT 12-4 (Continued)

Record Masters has been advised that the lack of standardization in the computer industry will continue to delay the ultimate solution to this problem, as no technology, company, or product will emerge as the clear leader/winner from this confusion for some time. RML anticipates that in time there will be a significant reduction in the amount of hard-copy file documents, although not a total elimination of them. The Business intends to adapt to its changing marketplace with new services and technological offerings as a viable path to do so becomes clearer.

In the meantime, the Network is closely monitoring this situation and has engaged a leading industry consulting firm to perform a detailed evaluation of the current state of technology and foreseeable innovations and impact. The study reported that from a standing start in 1988 through 1997, approximately 9% of hospitals will have document imaging or other information management systems in place or in the process of being installed. This 9%, however, includes 40% of the hospitals with 400 beds or more. It also concluded that the traditional paper record storage business may never fully disappear, although it will begin to be severely impacted in approximately 10 years' time.

As a result of the study, the Network has been very active in investigating the potential for setting up an imaging center to support the activity of hospital conversion to the electronic hospital record. Institutions such as the University of Cincinnati Medical Center are optically scanning over 90% of a typical medical record into an electronic file. Although this percentage will diminish as the conversion to electronics progresses, it is not expected to fall below 30% of the record. Currently, this hospital had over eight full-time employees engaged in the scanning process, and the cost effectiveness of the process is very much in doubt. Nevertheless, it is perceived as providing improved quality in the health-care delivery systems by permitting multiple users to have simultaneous access to the record, and is vigorously defended by this institution. Record Masters' research has concluded that the imaging process is a function that hospitals will seek to outsource once it becomes more established.

Imaging Centers

Record Masters of New Orleans is currently investigating imaging. If a decision is made to proceed, it will not be with the intent of merely being a low-cost image processing center for the hospital. Consistent with the philosophy in other service lines, Record Masters intends to be a value-added service provider by writing its own software solution for integrating hospital departments' unique needs and/or by attaining a strategic alliance with a firm possessing superior technology. Indexing of material being scanned is a time-consuming and critical characteristic of imaging, and proper forms that facilitate character recognition have yet to be designed. Storage capability, and high-speed data transmission should be provided such that each service center can serve multiple clients, creating an opportunity to expand beyond current geographic limitations.

Record Masters of New Orleans is considering designing a program for imaging Emergency Room ("ER") records. This department has been chosen because it produces a limited number of reports requiring little storage and generates each record within a short period of time while providing a realistic simulation of a hospital-wide system. Multiple users would then be provided access to an electronic file, thereby improving the health-care delivery system downstream of the ER by permitting interfacing with billing and admitting. This information flow will shorten the time between delivery of the service and billing. The resulting service capability will present a competitive advantage in marketing to all hospital clients, regardless of whether they have any immediate plans for instituting an electronic medical record.

Only a handful of hospitals have instituted fully integrated electronic systems, and these hospitals carefully guard the cost of their imaging systems. Record Masters believes that an imaging center suited for its needs would cost approximately $400,000. Payback of this investment is estimated at two years. Record Masters does not intend to invest in such a program until the successful completion of a test site in New Orleans. A search is currently being conducted for an appropriate vendor and potential strategic partner for this program.

(Continued)

EXHIBIT 12-4 *(Continued)*

VI. MANAGEMENT, ORGANIZATION, AND PERSONNEL

- **Management**

Detroit

Barbara A. VanderBrug   President, Founder & CEO—Prior to starting Record Masters of Detroit in December of 1987, Ms. VanderBrug managed a commercial travel agency, held sales positions with several healthcare suppliers, and was also a Registered Nurse in critical care. She is 54 years old, received her RN degree from Blodgett Memorial School of Nursing in 1962, and a BA in accounting from Walsh College of Business in 1982.

Bradley VanderBrug   Vice President—Mr. VanderBrug has been employed by Record Masters since September of 1991. He is in charge of Incoming Material Processing and Facilities Management. Previously, he was employed as Assistant Manager of Deliverex of Chicago. He received his bachelor's degree in Business Management from Calvin College and is attending Wayne State University part-time working on his MBA.

Richard Erwin   Operations Manager—Mr. Erwin has been a Record Masters' employee since April 1991. Mr. Erwin was promoted to Supervisor of File Pullers in 1992 and recently took the position of Operations Manager. He is currently attending Macomb Community College.

Rosemary Konwerski   Medical Records Services Manager—Ms. Konwerski began her employment with Record Masters in July of 1994 and will devote full time to the sales and service of Correspondence Copying. Most recently she was employed as an Account Manager for a large Correspondence Copying firm. Prior to that she was the Medical Records Director of the Lafayette Clinic for 12 years. She has a bachelor's degree in Business Administration and currently is a part-time instructor in Allied Health Sciences at Mercy College.

Cindi Boettcher   Supervisor—Ms. Boettcher began employment with Record Masters in 1992 as a file puller. She was promoted to Supervisor of Order Entry and Refiles in December of 1993.

New Orleans

Mark L. Guidry   President, Founder & CEO—Mr. Guidry founded Record Masters of New Orleans in October of 1986. Prior to this he practiced public accounting for seven years. He is the Network's specialist in computer applications, has been the developer of numerous software packages, and was instrumental in the design and development of Record Masters database applications. Mr. Guidry received a BS and MBA from the University of Southwestern Louisiana, and is a Certified Public Accountant. Mr. Guidry is 38 years old.

Joan P. Guidry   Assistant Director—Ms. Guidry provides support and implementation procedures for existing and new accounts. She also performs personnel functions and monitors quality assurance for all on-site and off-site procedures. She is a former Speech and Language Pathologist and has a Master's degree in Science.

Arnaldo A. Padilla   Supervisor—Mr. Padilla organizes and performs management in various areas, such as client service, deliveries, training, scheduling and general management. He is presently pursuing a degree in Social Science.

Reba G. Verdin   Office Manager—Ms. Verdin performs all accounting and payroll requirements, in addition to facilitating office management and bookkeeping functions.

Philadelphia

Ronald T. Blair   President, Founder, & CEO—Mr. Blair received a BS in Business Administration and attended the MBA Program at Drexel University. Since April 1, 1987 he has been President of Record Masters of Delaware Valley. Prior to this he was Vice President of Prudential Real Estate Affiliates and held other positions in the real estate and home building industries. He is 50 years old.

Nannette Low   Operations Manager—Ms. Low received her Bachelor's degree in Business Administration from Millersville University in 1983, and was employed for eleven years in distribution management prior to joining Record Masters in February of 1989. Her responsibilities include all day-to-day operations, human resources, and overall management and coordination of the Service Center.

(Continued)

EXHIBIT 12-4   *(Continued)*

William J. Walker   Manager—Mr. Walker has more than nine years' experience in the records management field, serving as sales representative and then operations manager for two of the largest micrographics and electronic imaging service bureaus in the Philadelphia area. He is also a graduate of Millersville University and joined Record Masters in November of 1993. He manages the data entry department, acts as co-administrator of the computer network, and is responsible for generating new nonhealth-care business.

Robert F. Keyser   Business Manager—Mr. Keyser is a graduate of Temple University with both a Bachelor's and Master's degree in Accounting. Prior to joining Record Masters, he worked for two years in public accounting, with additional experience in Banking, Import/Export, manufacturing and the wholesale business. He is responsible for all accounting and financial matters, which includes preparation and review of financial statements.

Scott Klemm   Assistant Service Manager—As a college student, Mr. Klemm began working part time at Record Masters as a file puller. He moved through various positions until graduating from college in August of 1993 and began working full time. He is currently responsible for quality assurance of the business process.

Greg Piotti   Accounts Representative, New Jersey—Mr. Piotti worked part time at Record Masters for three years while a student at Rutgers University and began full-time employment upon graduation. As an Account Representative, he brings to this position a solid working knowledge of Record Masters and its commitment to provide quality service to the healthcare field.

Janice Allen   Account Representative, Philadelphia and suburbs and Delaware Counties—Ms. Allen started with Record Masters in January 1994. She has a diversified health-care background, with eight years of experience including marketing of durable medical equipment and nursing services. Ms. Allen has a BA from Allbright College.

Pittsburgh

Dann Scheiferstein   President, Founder, & CEO—Mr. Scheiferstein was a Marketing Program Director for Economics Laboratory for six years prior to opening Record Masters of Pittsburgh in April of 1987. He received his BA from Case Western University and an MBA from Cleveland State University, and is 39 years old.

Don Klein   Operations Manager—Mr. Klein joined Record Masters in 1989 and is responsible for complete day-to-day operations of record service. Prior to coming to Record Masters he was a Manager with Reinhart Amusements. He attended the University of Pittsburgh.

Cathy Aniszewski, RRA, CTR   Medical Records Service Manager—Ms. Aniszewski began working for Record Masters in June of 1993 and is responsible for the development and supervision of medical record services for current clients, which includes correspondence copying. Additional responsibilities include continuous quality improvement for all record services. Prior to coming to Record Masters, she was employed in the Division of registries at Allegheny General Hospital. She has a bachelor degree in Health Information Management from the University of Pittsburgh and is certified as a Registered Records Administrator and a Certified Tumor Registrar.

Geonette Nichol   Day Client Service Supervisor—Ms. Nichol joined Record Masters in February 1993 and coordinates all daily activity with clients and Record Masters' personnel. Ms. Nichol also is responsible for initial orientation of all new clients to Record Masters' service.

Dennis Collage   Evening Client Service Supervisor—Mr. Collage joined Record Masters in June 1993 and coordinates all evening activity with clients and Record Masters' staff.

Carol Yeager   Bookkeeper—Ms. Yeager joined Record Masters in January 1994 and performs daily accounting functions, including the preparation of monthly statements. Prior to coming with Record Masters, she had six years of experience as a bookkeeper at various small businesses.

(Continued)

EXHIBIT 12-4 (Continued)

- **Organization**

  At the present time, each of the four locations operates autonomously and accordingly has its own organization. The President and CEO of each operation is a hands-on owner/operator and is involved in day-to-day operations.

- **Personnel**

  The following table summarizes numbers of employees by function as at March 31, 1994.

Location	Managers	Full Time	Part Time	Off-Site	Total
Detroit	3	18	5	13 part time	39
New Orleans	2	39	0	68	109
Philadelphia	11	26	19	0	56
Pittsburgh	4	22	4	0	30

There is no union representation at any of the four locations of the Business.

VIII. LEGAL

- **Franchisee Relationship**

  All locations of the business are founding franchisees of Record Masters Network Corporation. They are also shareholders, collectively holding 33% of the outstanding stock. As founding franchisees they are accorded certain rights not common in franchise agreements. Key highlights of the franchise agreement are as follows:

  1. A royalty of $750 plus 1% of sales per month, as determined by the Network Board of Directors.
  2. The right to voluntarily terminate the Franchise Agreement with the Network upon 30 days' notice.
  3. Membership on the Network's Board of Directors for each shareholder.
  4. The Network has a 20-day right of first refusal to match any offer for the purchase of any franchisee's business.

  A buyer of the Business thus has the option of remaining in the Network and assuming the obligations accordingly or terminating the Franchise Agreement and "de-imaging" as required under the agreement. Terminating franchisees have the right to the current software (through the clean object code) as of the time of termination.

  Additional Record Masters franchisees have expressed interest in selling their businesses should any prospective purchaser be interested in further expansion, following the acquisition of the four locations described herein. Furthermore, if the buyer wishes to remain part of the Network, the other members of the Network would welcome a buyer that brings technology or marketing capability as a new shareholder of the Network.

  In 1993, the members of the Business spearheaded a proposal to "roll-up" all locations into the Network and pursue aggressive expansion. That effort fell short of achieving a majority vote and led to the decision to seek a buyer for the four locations. The locations have been the top producers in the Network for the past 10 years, and thus there is no expectation that the right of first refusal will be exercised by the Network in their absence.

- **Other**

  The four Record Masters location owners are not aware of any environmental issues or of any material litigation.

(Continued)

EXHIBIT 12-4   (Continued)

IX. HISTORICAL FINANCIAL INFORMATION

- **Financial Commentary**

  Each of the four locations utilizes a local accounting firm to perform a year-end review of their books and records. The financial statements presented below are consolidations of these statements and have not been reviewed or audited.

- **Operating Results**

Summary of Historical Consolidated Unaudited Income Statements for the Years Ended December 31

	1989	1990	1991	1992	1993	1st Qtr. 1994
Revenues	$1,420,405	$2,469,004	$3,567,127	$4,971,171	$6,957,758	$2,007,393
Cost of Goods Sold	1,013,673	1,643,768	2,215,983	3,108,112	4,529,758	1,269,056
Gross margin	406,732	825,236	1,351,144	1,863,059	2,428,000	738,337
G&A expenses	178,556	739,694	709,828	1,118,946	1,261,088	284,953
Operating income	228,176	85,542	641,316	744,113	1,166,912	453,384
Depreciation and amortization	104,544	174,399	247,923	260,441	368,104	92,386
Earnings before interest taxes, depreciation, amortization (EBITDA)	332,720	259,941	889,239	1,004,554	1,535,016	545,770
Adjustment for owners' compensation[a]	(110,300)	69,739	118,555	435,500	354,448	9,000
Adjusted EBITDA	222,420	329,680	1,007,794	1,440,054	1,889,464	554,770
Net interest and local taxes	$ 52,354	$ 53,155	$ 18,617	$ (14,203)	$ (22,091)	$ (5,634)

[a] Actual owner's compensation included in statements	$ 33,700	$261,739	$358,555	$723,500	$690,448	$93,000
Less: Normalized compensation charge	144,000	192,000	240,000	288,000	336,000	84,000
Adjustment	$(110,300)	$ 69,739	$118,555	$435,500	$354,448	$ 9,000

(*Continued*)

EXHIBIT 12-4 (Continued)

EXHIBIT C Unaudited 1993 Financial Statements

Record Masters Profit/Loss Statement Consolidation, Year Ended December 31, 1993

	Detroit	New Orleans	Philadelphia	Pittsburgh	Consolidated
REVENUE					
Record Management Services	$ 960,867	$1,217,485	$1,346,771	$781,249	$4,306,372
Incoming Material processing	265,769	225,798	456,674	203,949	1,152,190
Other	304,548	1,184,269	222	10,157	1,499,196
TOTAL REVENUE	1,531,184	2,627,552	1,803,667	995,355	6,957,758
DIRECT EXPENSES					
Payroll	375,776	1,439,397	547,985	351,854	2,715,012
Payroll tax expense	34,314		61,517		95,831
Vehicle expense	29,466	57,181	49,692	32,987	169,326
Depreciation	30,942	45,808	19,457	50,593	146,800
Royalties	16,090	25,055	17,211	58,356	
Other	4,215	62,854	39,541	3,905	110,515
Total Direct Costs	490,803	1,630,295	735,403	439,339	3,295,840
INDIRECT					
Rent	133,080	107,606	188,270	97,830	526,786
Warehouse repair and maintenance	36,306	8,463	18,431	9,562	72,762
Warehouse supplies	17,497	19,147	11,205	10,813	58,662
Utilities	42,748	24,220	36,274	24,059	127,301
Depreciation	145,428	2,924	70,001	2,951	221,304
Property taxes	14,101		43,211		57,312
Employee benefits	230	27,409			27,639
Insurance—general	40,658	5,073	26,378	7,667	79,776
Equipment rent		2,772	14,853	502	18,127
Box expense	6,016	18,084		4,673	28,773
Other		4,991	8,268	2,217	15,476
TOTAL INDIRECT	436,064	220,689	416,891	160,274	1,233,918
GROSS MARGIN	$ 504,317	$ 776,568	$ 651,373	$395,742	$2,428,000
ADMINISTRATIVE					
Royalties	$ 8,250	$ 9,000	$ 9,000	$ 16,069	$ 42,319
Salary—Administrative	63,811	118,869	259,350	142,278	584,308
Profit sharing-Bonus		280,000		40,125	320,125
Payroll taxes	5,651				5,651
Advertising and marketing	1,953	8,024	6,98	3,284	20,243
Telephone	13,313	17,407	19,541	14,295	64,556
Dues and subscriptions	225	3,761	531	1,248	5,765
Travel and entertainment	920	8,938	5,454	3,924	19,236
Contributions	1,960		510		2,470
Computer and software	14,646		13,296	14,157	42,099
Professional fees	15,932	7,765	12,588	22,843	59,128
Office supplies and expense	7,180	43,931	9,534	13,818	74,463
Taxes—other		2,421		8,902	11,323
Other		523	7,321	1,558	9,402
TOTAL ADMINISTRATIVE	133,841	500,639	344,107	282,501	1,261,088
OPERATING PROFIT	470,476	275,929	307,266	113,241	1,166,912

(*Continued*)

EXHIBIT 12-4   (Continued)

EXHIBIT C   Unaudited 1993 Financial Statements (*continued*)

Record Masters Profit/Loss Statement Consolidation, Year Ended December 31, 1993

	Detroit	New Orleans	Philadelphia	Pittsburgh	Consolidated
OTHER INCOME (expense)					
Interest (net)	3,341	3,691	(7,588)	(7,495)	(8,051)
Miscellaneous income	1,412	(883)	—	—	529
INCOME BEFORE TAXES	475,229	278,737	299,678	105,746	1,159,390
Provision for Local Taxes	18,200		18,974		37,174
NET INCOME	$457,029	$278,737	$280,704	$105,746	$1,122,216
ASSETS					
Cash and equivalents	$160,687	$ 66,259	$ 60,754	$ 904	$ 288,604
Accounts receivable	343,513	322,935	487,803	124,016	1,278,267
Other	10,676	8,835	43,912	11,646	75,069
Total current assets	514,876	398,029	592,469	136,566	1,641,940
Fixed assets	697,076	460,774	441,882	323,633	1,923,365
Accumulated depreciation	409,357	158,645	231,290	164,652	963,944
Net fixed assets	287,719	302,129	210,592	158,981	959,421
Other assets		100	100		200
Total Assets	$802,595	$700,258	$803,161	$295,547	$2,601,561
LIABILITIES AND EQUITY					
Accounts payable	$ 71,107	$ 4,792	$ 27,480	$ 23,123	$ 126,502
Accrued expenses	5,044	86,881	33,680	70,220	195,825
Current portion of long-term debt		650	29,330	69,430	99,410
Deferred income	77,410	97,762		49,544	224,716
Taxes payable	16,135		10,600	2,831	29,566
Total current liabilities	169,696	190,085	101,090	215,148	676,019
Long-term debt	0	0	33,770	61,614	95,384
Deferred rent	0	0	40,840	0	40,840
Total liabilities	169,696	190,085	175,700	276,762	812,243
Shareholders' equity	18,132	100	1,000	300	19,532
Retained earnings	614,767	510,073	626,461	18,485	1,769,786
Total equity	632,899	510,173	627,461	18,785	1,789,318
Total Liabilities and Equity	$802,595	$700,258	$803,161	$295,547	$2,601,561

EXHIBIT 12-4   (*Continued*)

EXHIBIT C   Unaudited 1993 Financial Statements (*continued*)

Record Masters Summary Statement of Consolidated Cash Flows (direct method)
for the Year Ended December 31, 1993

Cash flows from operating activities:	
Cash collections from clients	$6,590,775
Cash paid to suppliers and employees	(5,387,959)
Net interest paid	(15,083)
Net taxes paid	(45,343)
Net cash provided by operating activities	1,142,390
Cash flows from investing activities:	
Net increase in property and equipment	(471,906)
Net repayments of loans from officers	(268,011)
Net cash used by investing activities	(739,917)
Cash flows from financing activities:	
Net borrowings on notes payable	38,759
Distributions to stockholders	(510,410)
Net cash used by financing activities	(471,651)
Net decrease in cash	(69,178)
Cash at beginning of year	357,782
Cash at end of year	$ 288,604

Reconciliation of net income to net cash provided by operating activities:	
Net income for the year	$1,122,216
Adjustments to reconcile net income to net cash provided by operating activities:	
Depreciation and amortization	368,104
Decrease (increase) in:	
Accounts receivable, net	(409,630)
Prepaid expenses	(36,207)
Other assets	(100)
Increase (decrease) in:	
Accounts payable	(18,928)
Accrued expenses	75,898
Deferred income	35,086
Deferred rent	14,120
Taxes payable	(8,169)
Net cash provided by operating activities	$1,142,390

EXHIBIT 12-5

COMPARABLE TRANSACTION STATISTICS

Characteristics	Bekins Records Management	Bell + Howell Records Management
Acquisition date	12/85	12/88
Revenues	$18.3 million	$35.3 million
EBITDA	$4.0 million	$8.1 million
EBITDA %	22%	23%
Revenue growth (last 4 years)	NA	17%/year
Number of centers	NA	37
Revenue/center	NA	$.95 million
% Storage revenues	NA	60%
Revenues/square foot	NA	$23/foot
Number of employees	NA	459
Revenues/employee	NA	$76K/employee
Number of customers	NA	10,000
Customers/center	NA	50–400/center
Accounts receivable/sales	NA	15%–20%
Accounts payable/sales	NA	3%–5%
Purchase price (estimated)	$42.0 million	$60.0 million

## 13

Capital Projects as Real Options: An Introduction

This note introduces an approach to capital budgeting that relies on option pricing theory to analyze and evaluate capital projects. The approach is intended to supplement, not replace, capital budgeting analyses and investment criteria based on standard discounted cash flow (DCF) methodologies. For a wide range of corporate investments, insights from an options-based analysis can improve estimates of project value and, perhaps more important, enhance project management.

MOTIVATION

Why treat a corporate investment proposal as a call option, as suggested here, rather than as a bond or an unlevered equity? The latter are easier to understand and value, and the associated analyses are easier to communicate and defend within a large organization. However, many corporate investment proposals, particularly "strategic" ones, bear a stronger resemblance to a call option than to a stock or a bond. Ignoring the option-like features of such projects can lead to poor decisions. The most likely mistakes are failing to invest in a valuable project because embedded options are overlooked—this will make the corporation appear shortsighted; and not getting the timing right, that is, committing funds earlier or later than would be ideal.

Asset-in-Place vs. Options

Standard DCF valuation methodologies treat projects as follows: managers make a decision to invest (or not) and then wait to see what happens (see Figure 13-1a). For some projects this is an adequate representation of reality, but for others it is backwards. Sometimes managers get to wait and see what happens (at least some uncertainty is resolved) and *then* make a decision to invest or not (see Figure 13-1b). These two are ob-

---

Professor Timothy A. Luehrman prepared this note as the basis for class discussion rather than to illustrate either effective or ineffective handling of an administrative situation.

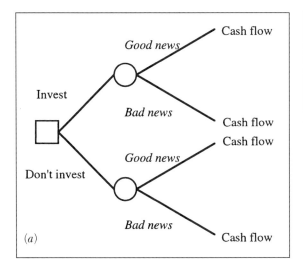 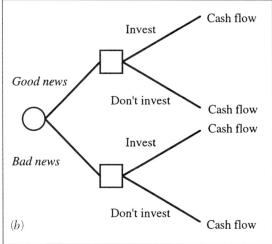

Figure 13-1. (*a*) This is not an option. (*b*) This is an option.

viously quite different. The latter is an option and the former is not. An efficient capital market would not place the same value on both, and neither should a corporation.

A great many corporate investment proposals are complex and fit neither of these pure archetypes exactly. More often they contain elements of both. An R&D program, for example, may create both a cash-producing new product and opportunities for further R&D aimed at yet more new products. Investing in a new market may lead to both immediate cash flow and future expansion opportunities. Creating a brand may simultaneously create future brand-extension possibilities. Replacing a first-generation technology with a second makes it possible to eventually replace the second with a third, and so forth. All of these examples contain both *assets-in-place* (cash-producing assets that can be evaluated with DCF methodologies) and *growth options* (opportunities to make future investments, which require an option-pricing methodology). Growth options and a few other decision opportunities are known, collectively, as "real" options to distinguish them from "financial" options such as exchange-traded puts and calls. Projects with high option content are likely to be misevaluated by DCF techniques: either the options will be ignored (resulting in undervaluation and underinvestment), or they will be poorly approximated (resulting in either under- or overinvestment in addition to poor timing and management).

A sensible solution is to separate a project's assets-in-place from its growth options and to analyze each part accordingly. Unfortunately, this is often difficult, first because a neat separation may not be possible and second because executing the option valuation for a capital project is usually a difficult analytical chore. This note is aimed at the second problem. It explains how to set up a mapping between the simplified project and a call option; how to perform an option valuation and relate it to a DCF valuation; and how to extract some managerial insights from the option-pricing framework.

Preliminaries

As a starting point, this note presumes a working knowledge of basic option pricing and basic capital budgeting. Readers should be acquainted with puts and calls, position diagrams, determinants of call option value, option deltas, and comparative statics. This

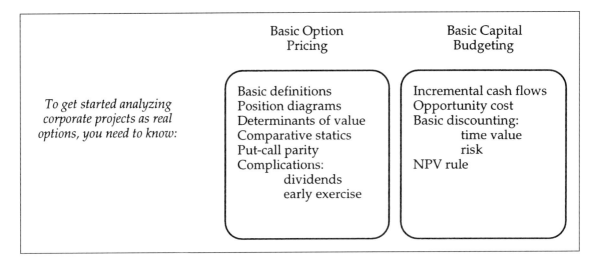

Figure 13-2. Preliminaries.

body of material is covered in most graduate-level corporate finance texts.[1] Readers also need to be familiar with incremental cash flows, time value, opportunity cost, value additivity, net present value, and the NPV rule.[2]

Figure 13-2 shows the topics one needs to have covered in order to use real option methods. From this knowledge base, it is possible to construct a mapping between a corporate investment project and a call option and to see the relationship between a project's NPV and the value of an analogous call option.

PROJECTS AS CALL OPTIONS

An opportunity to invest in a corporate project bears an obvious similarity to an option to invest in a corporation's stock. Both involve the right, but not the obligation, to acquire an asset by paying a certain sum of money on or before a certain time. The right to buy the stock is known as a call option. European calls are exercisable only at expiration, whereas an American call may be exercised at any time prior to expiration. Obviously, an American call must be at least as valuable as an otherwise-identical European call. The Black-Scholes option pricing model gives the value of a European call on a tradable stock that pays no dividends as a function of five variables: the stock price, S; the exercise price, χ; the time to expiration, t; the risk-free rate of return, r; and the standard deviation of returns on the stock, σ.

By establishing a mapping between project characteristics and the determinants of call-option value, a corporate project can be valued in the same way (see Figure 13-3). Most projects involve making an expenditure to buy or build a productive asset. This is analogous to exercising an option: the amount expended is the exercise price (χ) and the value of the asset built or acquired is the stock price (S). The length of time the

---

[1] See, for example, Brealey and Myers, *Principles of Corporate Finance*, 4th ed. (New York: McGraw-Hill, 1991), chapter 20, pp. 483–510.

[2] See ibid., chapters 2–6, pp. 11–128.

Project	*Variable*	*Call Option*
Expenditures required to acquire the assets	**X**	Exercise price
Value of the operating assets to be acquired	**S**	Stock price
Length of time decision may be deferred	**t**	Time to expiration
Riskiness of the underlying operating assets	σ^2	Variance of returns on stock
Time value of money	**r**	Risk-free rate of return

Figure 13-3. Mapping project characteristics onto call option variables.

company can wait without losing the opportunity is the time to expiration (t), and the riskiness of the project is reflected in the standard deviation of returns on the asset (σ). Time value is still given by the risk-free rate (r).

RELATING DCF VALUATION TO OPTION VALUATION

To see how option valuation is related to traditional DCF-based capital budgeting, begin by considering the typical project's NPV. NPV is simply a measure of the difference between how much an asset is worth and what it costs. When it is worth more than it costs, the project has a positive NPV and the corporation goes ahead and invests. Put another way, NPV = PV(expected net cash flows) − PV(capital expenditure), and the decision rule is "invest if NPV > 0."

Notice that NPV can be expressed as a quotient rather than a difference: Define $NPV_q \equiv$ PV(expected net cash flows) ÷ PV(capital expenditure). Similarly, the decision rule can be restated as "invest if $NPV_q > 1$." Figure 13-4 shows a line on which projects can be arrayed according to NPV_q. Those for which $NPV_q > 1$ are accepted; those for which $NPV_q < 1$ are rejected.

Figure 13-4 can be used in the same way to decide whether to exercise a call option *at expiration*. A call option should be exercised if, at expiration, the stock price exceeds the exercise price (the call is "in the money"). Here, the stock price, S, corresponds to PV (expected net cash flows) and the exercise price, χ, corresponds to PV(capital expenditure). Thus, for a call option, $NPV_q = S/PV(\chi)$. If this quotient exceeds 1, the option should be exercised. If $NPV_q < 1$, the option is "out of the money" and should not be exercised. In effect, the traditional approach to deciding whether to invest in a project is identical to deciding whether to exercise a call option at expiration. Notice that NPVq combines four of the five determinants of option value: S; χ; r;

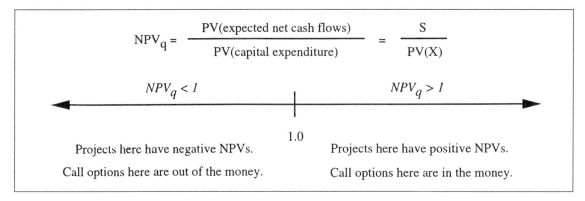

$$NPV_q = \frac{PV(\text{expected net cash flows})}{PV(\text{capital expenditure})} = \frac{S}{PV(X)}$$

NPV$_q$ < 1   *NPV$_q$ > 1*

1.0

Projects here have negative NPVs.   Projects here have positive NPVs.

Call options here are out of the money.   Call options here are in the money.

Figure 13-4. Expressing NPV as a quotient rather than a difference.

and t.[3] Note further that call option value is an increasing function of NPV$_q$: the higher NPV$_q$, the higher the call value.

When a decision cannot be delayed, the call option and the project can *both* be evaluated using simple DCF tools and rules—reality is pretty well represented by Figure 13-1a. But when the decision *can* be delayed, the project is like an option that has not yet expired—reality is better represented by Figure 13-1b. In this case, NPV$_q$ still matters, but so does the riskiness of the project, which is reflected in the remaining option-pricing variable, σ.

The variability, per unit of time, of returns on the project is measured by the variance of returns, σ^2. Multiplying the variance per unit of time by the amount of time remaining gives *cumulative variance*, $\sigma^2 t$. Cumulative variance is a measure of how much things could change before time runs out and a decision must be made. It may be helpful to think of a collection of balls, each with a number on it, that has been placed in an urn. Variance is the amount of variability in the set of numbers written on the balls, and t is the number of draws to be made from the urn. Cumulative variance is simply the variance for each draw times the number of draws. The more cumulative variance, the more valuable the option.

Cumulative variance and NPV$_q$ together are sufficient to value a European call option. Figure 13-5 expands Figure 13-4 to include an extra dimension for $\sigma\sqrt{t}$, which is simply the square root of cumulative variance. Options (or projects) for which either σ or t is zero have no cumulative variance and can be evaluated with standard discounted cash flow techniques, that is, with NPV or NPV$_q$ alone. When both σ and t are nonzero, however, a DCF analysis will certainly give the wrong value and may lead to the wrong exercise decision: in other words, Figure 13-5 should be used rather than Figure 13-4.

The Black-Scholes model, with values for the five variables as inputs, will give a dollar value for a European call option. Some financial calculators and spreadsheet applications come pre-programmed with the Black-Scholes formula. Alternatively, Exhibit 13-1 tabulates European call option value as a percentage of the underlying asset value (S) for combinations of NPV$_q$ and $\sigma\sqrt{t}$. The value of a European call can simply be looked up, without a formula or a computer.

---

[3] The variables r and t come into NPV$_q$ because χ is being discounted to present value. In the Black-Scholes model, discounting is performed on a continuously compounded basis, so the present value of χ is actually given by $\chi(e^{-rt})$. Note, however, that at expiration, $t = 0$; therefore, the present value of χ is simply χ, and NPV$_q$ is simply S/χ as stated in the text. *Prior* to expiration, however, $\chi(e^{-rt}) < \chi$ so, all else equal, NPV$_q$ > S/χ.

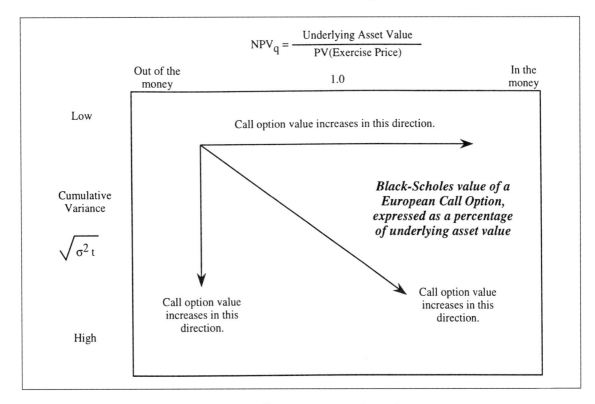

$$NPV_q = \frac{\text{Underlying Asset Value}}{\text{PV(Exercise Price)}}$$

Out of the money   1.0   In the money

Low

Call option value increases in this direction.

Cumulative Variance

$\sqrt{\sigma^2 t}$

Black-Scholes value of a European Call Option, expressed as a percentage of underlying asset value

Call option value increases in this direction.

Call option value increases in this direction.

High

Figure 13-5. Pricing call options: NPV_q and cumulative variance.

To illustrate, consider a simple project that requires an investment of $100, in return for which the company would receive an asset that is currently worth $90. However, the asset is risky, and its value is likely to change: returns on the asset have a standard deviation of about 40% per year. Moreover, the company can wait for up to three years before deciding to invest. Finally, suppose the risk-free rate is 5%. Viewed conventionally, this project's NPV is $90 − $100 = −$10. Clearly, however, having the opportunity to wait three years and see what happens is valuable. In effect, the company owns a three-year European call with an exercise price of $100 on underlying assets worth $90. NPV_q for this option is $90 ÷ [$100/(1.05)^3] = 1.04.[4] Cumulative variance is 0.40 times $\sqrt{3}$, or 0.69. Exhibit 13-1 shows that an option with these characteristics is worth 28.4% of the value of the underlying asset, or .284($90) = $25.56.

MANAGERIAL DECISIONS: OPTIMAL EXERCISE

The simple project just examined had an NPV of −$10 but an option value of more than $25. Are these contradictory? What should the company do? In fact, the NPV and the option value do not contradict one another. The company should not invest in the project now. If it does, it will both forfeit the option and waste $10. But neither should it discard the project. It should wait, watch, and actively cultivate the project over the next three years. Although NPV < 0, the project is very promising because $NPV_q > 1$.

---

[4] The difference between discrete and continuous compounding to compute the present value of χ is negligible in this case.

EXHIBIT 13-1

OPTION-PRICING TABLE

Black-Scholes Value of a European Call Option, Expressed as a Percentage of Underlying Asset Value

NPVq = (Underlying asset value) / PV(Exercise price)

Cumulative Variance: σ[sqrt(t)]	0.30	0.35	0.40	0.45	0.50	0.55	0.60	0.65	0.70	0.75
0.05	0.0	0.0	0.0	0.0	0.0	0.0	0.0	0.0	0.0	0.0
0.10	0.0	0.0	0.0	0.0	0.0	0.0	0.0	0.0	0.0	0.0
0.15	0.0	0.0	0.0	0.0	0.0	0.0	0.0	0.0	0.1	0.2
0.20	0.0	0.0	0.0	0.0	0.0	0.0	0.0	0.1	0.4	0.8
0.25	0.0	0.0	0.0	0.0	0.0	0.1	0.2	0.5	1.0	1.8
0.30	0.0	0.0	0.0	0.1	0.1	0.3	0.7	1.2	2.0	3.1
0.35	0.0	0.0	0.1	0.2	0.4	0.8	1.4	2.3	3.3	4.6
0.40	0.0	0.1	0.2	0.5	0.9	1.6	2.4	3.5	4.8	6.3
0.45	0.1	0.2	0.5	1.0	1.7	2.6	3.7	5.0	6.5	8.1
0.50	0.2	0.5	1.0	1.7	2.6	3.7	5.1	6.6	8.2	10.0
0.55	0.5	1.0	1.7	2.6	3.8	5.1	6.6	8.3	10.0	11.9
0.60	0.9	1.6	2.5	3.7	5.1	6.6	8.3	10.1	11.9	13.8
0.65	1.4	2.4	3.6	4.9	6.5	8.2	10.0	11.9	13.8	15.8
0.70	2.1	3.3	4.7	6.3	8.1	9.9	11.9	13.8	15.8	17.8
0.75	3.0	4.4	6.1	7.9	9.8	11.7	13.7	15.8	17.8	19.8
0.80	4.0	5.7	7.5	9.5	11.5	13.6	15.7	17.7	19.8	21.8
0.85	5.1	7.1	9.1	11.2	13.3	15.5	17.6	19.7	21.8	23.8
0.90	6.4	8.5	10.7	13.0	15.2	17.4	19.6	21.7	23.8	25.8
0.95	7.8	10.1	12.5	14.8	17.1	19.4	21.6	23.7	25.7	27.7
1.00	9.3	11.8	14.3	16.7	19.1	21.4	23.6	25.7	27.7	29.7
1.05	10.9	13.6	16.1	18.6	21.0	23.3	25.6	27.7	29.7	31.6
1.10	12.6	15.4	18.0	20.6	23.0	25.3	27.5	29.6	31.6	33.5
1.15	14.4	17.2	20.0	22.5	25.0	27.3	29.5	31.6	33.6	35.4
1.20	16.2	19.1	21.9	24.5	27.0	29.3	31.5	33.6	35.5	37.3
1.25	18.1	21.1	23.9	26.5	29.0	31.3	33.5	35.5	37.4	39.2
1.30	20.0	23.0	25.9	28.5	31.0	33.3	35.4	37.4	39.3	41.0
1.35	21.9	25.0	27.9	30.5	33.0	35.2	37.3	39.3	41.1	42.8
1.40	23.9	27.0	29.9	32.5	34.9	37.1	39.2	41.1	42.9	44.6
1.45	25.8	29.0	31.9	34.5	36.9	39.1	41.1	43.0	44.7	46.4
1.50	27.8	31.0	33.8	36.4	38.8	40.9	42.9	44.8	46.5	48.1
1.55	29.8	33.0	35.8	38.4	40.7	42.8	44.8	46.6	48.2	49.8
1.60	31.8	35.0	37.8	40.3	42.6	44.6	46.5	48.3	49.9	51.4
1.65	33.8	36.9	39.7	42.2	44.4	46.4	48.3	50.0	51.6	53.1
1.70	35.8	38.9	41.6	44.0	46.2	48.2	50.0	51.7	53.2	54.7
1.75	37.7	40.8	43.5	45.9	48.0	50.0	51.7	53.4	54.8	56.2
2.00	47.3	50.1	52.5	54.6	56.5	58.2	59.7	61.1	62.4	63.6
2.25	56.1	58.6	60.7	62.5	64.1	65.6	66.8	68.0	69.1	70.0
2.50	64.0	66.1	67.9	69.4	70.8	72.0	73.1	74.0	74.9	75.7
2.75	70.9	72.7	74.2	75.4	76.6	77.5	78.4	79.2	79.9	80.5
3.00	76.9	78.3	79.5	80.5	81.4	82.2	82.9	83.5	84.1	84.6
3.50	86.0	86.9	87.6	88.3	88.8	89.3	89.7	90.1	90.5	90.8
4.00	92.0	92.5	92.9	93.3	93.6	93.9	94.2	94.4	94.6	94.8
4.50	95.7	96.0	96.2	96.4	96.6	96.7	96.9	97.0	97.1	97.2
5.00	97.8	97.9	98.1	98.2	98.3	98.3	98.4	98.5	98.5	98.6
6.00	99.5	99.5	99.6	99.6	99.6	99.6	99.7	99.7	99.7	99.7

Cumulative Variance: σ[sqrt(t)]	0.80	0.82	0.84	0.86	0.88	0.90	0.92	0.94	0.96	0.98
0.05	0.0	0.0	0.0	0.0	0.0	0.0	0.1	0.3	0.6	1.2
0.10	0.0	0.1	0.2	0.3	0.5	0.8	1.2	1.7	2.3	3.1
0.15	0.5	0.7	1.0	1.3	1.7	2.2	2.8	3.5	4.2	5.1
0.20	1.5	1.9	2.3	2.8	3.4	4.0	4.7	5.4	6.2	7.1
0.25	2.8	3.3	3.9	4.5	5.2	5.9	6.6	7.4	8.2	9.1
0.30	4.4	5.0	5.7	6.3	7.0	7.8	8.6	9.4	10.2	11.1
0.35	6.2	6.8	7.5	8.2	9.0	9.8	10.6	11.4	12.2	13.0
0.40	8.0	8.7	9.4	10.2	11.0	11.7	12.5	13.4	14.2	15.0
0.45	9.9	10.6	11.4	12.2	12.9	13.7	14.5	15.3	16.2	17.0
0.50	11.8	12.6	13.4	14.2	14.9	15.7	16.5	17.3	18.1	18.9
0.55	13.8	14.6	15.4	16.1	16.9	17.7	18.5	19.3	20.1	20.9
0.60	15.8	16.6	17.4	18.1	18.9	19.7	20.5	21.3	22.0	22.8
0.65	17.8	18.6	19.3	20.1	20.9	21.7	22.5	23.2	24.0	24.7
0.70	19.8	20.6	21.3	22.1	22.9	23.6	24.4	25.2	25.9	26.6
0.75	21.8	22.5	23.3	24.1	24.8	25.6	26.3	27.1	27.8	28.5
0.80	23.7	24.5	25.3	26.0	26.8	27.5	28.3	29.0	29.7	30.4
0.85	25.7	26.5	27.2	28.0	28.7	29.4	30.2	30.9	31.6	32.2
0.90	27.7	28.4	29.2	29.9	30.6	31.3	32.0	32.7	33.4	34.1
0.95	29.6	30.4	31.1	31.8	32.5	33.2	33.9	34.6	35.2	35.9
1.00	31.6	32.3	33.0	33.7	34.4	35.1	35.7	36.4	37.0	37.7
1.05	33.5	34.2	34.9	35.6	36.2	36.9	37.6	38.2	38.8	39.4
1.10	35.4	36.1	36.7	37.4	38.1	38.7	39.3	40.0	40.6	41.2
1.15	37.2	37.9	38.6	39.2	39.9	40.5	41.1	41.7	42.3	42.9
1.20	39.1	39.7	40.4	41.0	41.7	42.3	42.9	43.5	44.0	44.6
1.25	40.9	41.5	42.2	42.8	43.4	44.0	44.6	45.2	45.7	46.3
1.30	42.7	43.3	43.9	44.5	45.1	45.7	46.3	46.8	47.4	47.9
1.35	44.4	45.1	45.7	46.3	46.8	47.4	47.9	48.5	49.0	49.5
1.40	46.2	46.8	47.4	47.9	48.5	49.0	49.6	50.1	50.6	51.1
1.45	47.9	48.5	49.0	49.6	50.1	50.7	51.2	51.7	52.2	52.7
1.50	49.6	50.1	50.7	51.2	51.8	52.3	52.8	53.3	53.7	54.2
1.55	51.2	51.8	52.3	52.8	53.3	53.8	54.3	54.8	55.3	55.7
1.60	52.8	53.4	53.9	54.4	54.9	55.4	55.9	56.3	56.8	57.2
1.65	54.4	54.9	55.4	55.9	56.4	56.9	57.3	57.8	58.2	58.6
1.70	56.0	56.5	57.0	57.5	57.9	58.4	58.8	59.2	59.7	60.1
1.75	57.5	58.0	58.5	58.9	59.4	59.8	60.2	60.7	61.1	61.5
2.00	64.6	65.0	65.4	65.8	66.2	66.6	66.9	67.3	67.6	67.9
2.25	70.9	71.3	71.6	71.9	72.2	72.5	72.8	73.1	73.4	73.7
2.50	76.4	76.7	77.0	77.2	77.5	77.7	78.0	78.2	78.4	78.7
2.75	81.1	81.4	81.6	81.8	82.0	82.2	82.4	82.6	82.7	82.9
3.00	85.1	85.3	85.4	85.6	85.8	85.9	86.1	86.2	86.4	86.5
3.50	91.1	91.2	91.3	91.4	91.5	91.6	91.6	91.7	91.8	91.9
4.00	94.9	95.0	95.0	95.1	95.2	95.2	95.3	95.3	95.4	95.4
4.50	97.3	97.3	97.3	97.4	97.4	97.4	97.5	97.5	97.5	97.5
5.00	98.6	98.6	98.6	98.7	98.7	98.7	98.7	98.7	98.7	98.7
6.00	99.7	99.7	99.7	99.7	99.7	99.7	99.7	99.7	99.7	99.7

Cumulative Variance: σ[sqrt(t)]	1.00	1.02	1.04	1.06	1.08	1.10	1.12	1.14	1.16	1.18
0.05	2.0	3.1	4.5	6.0	7.5	9.1	10.7	12.3	13.8	15.3
0.10	4.0	5.0	6.1	7.3	8.6	10.0	11.3	12.7	14.1	15.4
0.15	6.0	7.0	8.0	9.1	10.2	11.4	12.6	13.8	15.0	16.2
0.20	8.0	8.9	9.9	10.9	11.9	13.0	14.1	15.2	16.3	17.4
0.25	9.9	10.9	11.8	12.8	13.7	14.7	15.7	16.7	17.7	18.7
0.30	11.9	12.8	13.7	14.6	15.6	16.5	17.4	18.4	19.3	20.3
0.35	13.9	14.8	15.6	16.5	17.4	18.3	19.2	20.1	21.0	21.9
0.40	15.9	16.7	17.5	18.4	19.2	20.1	20.9	21.8	22.6	23.5
0.45	17.8	18.6	19.4	20.3	21.1	21.9	22.7	23.5	24.3	25.1
0.50	19.7	20.5	21.3	22.1	22.9	23.7	24.5	25.3	26.1	26.8
0.55	21.7	22.4	23.2	24.0	24.8	25.5	26.3	27.0	27.8	28.5
0.60	23.6	24.3	25.1	25.8	26.6	27.3	28.1	28.8	29.5	30.2
0.65	25.5	26.2	27.0	27.7	28.4	29.1	29.8	30.5	31.2	31.9
0.70	27.4	28.1	28.8	29.5	30.2	30.9	31.6	32.3	32.9	33.6
0.75	29.2	29.9	30.6	31.3	32.0	32.7	33.3	34.0	34.6	35.3
0.80	31.1	31.8	32.4	33.1	33.8	34.4	35.1	35.7	36.3	36.9
0.85	32.9	33.6	34.2	34.9	35.5	36.2	36.8	37.4	38.0	38.6
0.90	34.7	35.4	36.0	36.6	37.3	37.9	38.5	39.1	39.6	40.2
0.95	36.5	37.2	37.8	38.4	39.0	39.6	40.1	40.7	41.3	41.8
1.00	38.3	38.9	39.5	40.1	40.7	41.2	41.8	42.4	42.9	43.4
1.05	40.0	40.6	41.2	41.8	42.4	42.9	43.5	44.0	44.5	45.0
1.10	41.8	42.3	42.9	43.5	44.0	44.5	45.1	45.6	46.1	46.6
1.15	43.5	44.0	44.6	45.1	45.6	46.2	46.7	47.2	47.7	48.2
1.20	45.1	45.7	46.2	46.7	47.3	47.8	48.3	48.7	49.2	49.7
1.25	46.8	47.3	47.8	48.4	48.8	49.3	49.8	50.3	50.7	51.2
1.30	48.4	48.9	49.4	49.9	50.4	50.9	51.3	51.8	52.2	52.7
1.35	50.0	50.5	51.0	51.5	52.0	52.4	52.9	53.3	53.7	54.1
1.40	51.6	52.1	52.6	53.0	53.5	53.9	54.3	54.8	55.2	55.6
1.45	53.2	53.6	54.1	54.5	55.0	55.4	55.8	56.2	56.6	57.0
1.50	54.7	55.1	55.6	56.0	56.4	56.8	57.2	57.6	58.0	58.4
1.55	56.2	56.6	57.0	57.4	57.8	58.2	58.6	59.0	59.4	59.7
1.60	57.6	58.0	58.5	58.9	59.2	59.6	60.0	60.4	60.7	61.1
1.65	59.1	59.5	59.9	60.2	60.6	61.0	61.4	61.7	62.1	62.4
1.70	60.5	60.9	61.2	61.6	62.0	62.3	62.7	63.0	63.4	63.7
1.75	61.8	62.2	62.6	62.9	63.3	63.6	64.0	64.3	64.6	64.9
2.00	68.3	68.6	68.9	69.2	69.5	69.8	70.0	70.3	70.6	70.8
2.25	73.9	74.2	74.4	74.7	74.9	75.2	75.4	75.6	75.8	76.0
2.50	78.9	79.1	79.3	79.5	79.7	79.9	80.0	80.2	80.4	80.6
2.75	83.1	83.3	83.4	83.6	83.7	83.9	84.0	84.2	84.3	84.4
3.00	86.6	86.8	86.9	87.0	87.1	87.3	87.4	87.5	87.6	87.7
3.50	92.0	92.1	92.1	92.2	92.3	92.4	92.4	92.5	92.6	92.6
4.00	95.4	95.5	95.5	95.6	95.6	95.7	95.7	95.7	95.8	95.8
4.50	97.6	97.6	97.6	97.6	97.6	97.7	97.7	97.7	97.7	97.8
5.00	98.8	98.8	98.8	98.8	98.8	98.8	98.8	98.8	98.8	98.9
6.00	99.7	99.7	99.7	99.7	99.7	99.7	99.7	99.7	99.7	99.8

Cumulative Variance: σ[sqrt(t)]	1.20	1.25	1.30	1.35	1.40	1.45	1.50	1.75	2.00	2.50	
0.05	16.7	20.0	23.1	25.9	28.6	31.0	33.3	42.9	50.0	60.0	0.05
0.10	16.8	20.0	23.1	25.9	28.6	31.0	33.3	42.9	50.0	60.0	0.10
0.15	17.4	20.4	23.3	26.0	28.6	31.1	33.3	42.9	50.0	60.0	0.15
0.20	18.5	21.2	23.9	26.4	28.9	31.2	33.5	42.9	50.0	60.0	0.20
0.25	19.8	22.3	24.7	27.1	29.4	31.7	33.8	42.9	50.0	60.0	0.25
0.30	21.2	23.5	25.8	28.1	30.2	32.3	34.3	43.1	50.1	60.0	0.30
0.35	22.7	24.9	27.1	29.2	31.2	33.2	35.1	43.5	50.2	60.0	0.35
0.40	24.3	26.4	28.4	30.4	32.3	34.2	36.0	44.0	50.5	60.1	0.40
0.45	25.9	27.9	29.8	31.7	33.5	35.3	37.0	44.6	50.8	60.2	0.45
0.50	27.6	29.5	31.3	33.1	34.8	36.4	38.1	45.3	51.3	60.4	0.50
0.55	29.2	31.0	32.8	34.5	36.1	37.7	39.2	46.1	51.9	60.7	0.55
0.60	30.9	32.6	34.3	35.9	37.5	39.0	40.4	47.0	52.5	61.0	0.60
0.65	32.6	34.2	35.8	37.4	38.9	40.3	41.7	48.0	53.3	61.4	0.65
0.70	34.2	35.8	37.3	38.8	40.3	41.6	43.0	49.0	54.0	61.9	0.70
0.75	35.9	37.4	38.9	40.3	41.7	43.0	44.3	50.0	54.9	62.4	0.75
0.80	37.5	39.0	40.4	41.8	43.1	44.4	45.6	51.1	55.8	63.0	0.80
0.85	39.2	40.6	41.9	43.3	44.5	45.8	46.9	52.2	56.7	63.6	0.85
0.90	40.8	42.1	43.5	44.7	46.0	47.1	48.3	53.3	57.6	64.3	0.90
0.95	42.4	43.7	45.0	46.2	47.4	48.5	49.6	54.5	58.6	65.0	0.95
1.00	44.0	45.2	46.5	47.6	48.8	49.9	50.9	55.6	59.5	65.7	1.00
1.05	45.5	46.8	48.0	49.1	50.2	51.2	52.2	56.7	60.5	66.5	1.05
1.10	47.1	48.3	49.4	50.5	51.6	52.6	53.5	57.9	61.5	67.2	1.10
1.15	48.6	49.8	50.9	51.9	52.9	53.9	54.9	59.0	62.5	68.0	1.15
1.20	50.1	51.3	52.3	53.3	54.3	55.2	56.1	60.2	63.5	68.8	1.20
1.25	51.6	52.7	53.7	54.7	55.7	56.6	57.4	61.3	64.5	69.6	1.25
1.30	53.1	54.1	55.1	56.1	57.0	57.9	58.7	62.4	65.5	70.4	1.30
1.35	54.6	55.6	56.5	57.4	58.3	59.1	59.9	63.5	66.5	71.1	1.35
1.40	56.0	56.9	57.9	58.7	59.6	60.4	61.2	64.6	67.5	71.9	1.40
1.45	57.4	58.3	59.2	60.0	60.9	61.6	62.4	65.7	68.4	72.7	1.45
1.50	58.8	59.7	60.5	61.3	62.1	62.9	63.6	66.8	69.4	73.5	1.50
1.55	60.1	61.0	61.8	62.6	63.3	64.1	64.7	67.8	70.3	74.3	1.55
1.60	61.4	62.3	63.1	63.8	64.5	65.2	65.9	68.8	71.3	75.1	1.60
1.65	62.7	63.5	64.3	65.0	65.7	66.4	67.0	69.9	72.2	75.9	1.65
1.70	64.0	64.8	65.5	66.2	66.9	67.5	68.2	70.9	73.1	76.6	1.70
1.75	65.3	66.0	66.7	67.4	68.0	68.7	69.2	71.9	74.0	77.4	1.75
2.00	71.1	71.7	72.3	72.9	73.4	73.9	74.4	76.5	78.3	81.0	2.00
2.25	76.3	76.8	77.2	77.7	78.1	78.5	78.9	80.6	82.1	84.3	2.25
2.50	80.7	81.1	81.5	81.9	82.2	82.6	82.9	84.3	85.4	87.2	2.50
2.75	84.6	84.9	85.2	85.5	85.8	86.0	86.3	87.4	88.3	89.7	2.75
3.00	87.8	88.1	88.3	88.5	88.8	89.0	89.2	90.0	90.7	91.8	3.00
3.50	92.7	92.8	93.0	93.1	93.3	93.4	93.5	94.0	94.4	95.1	3.50
4.00	95.8	95.9	96.0	96.1	96.2	96.2	96.3	96.6	96.8	97.2	4.00
4.50	97.8	97.8	97.9	97.9	97.9	98.0	98.0	98.2	98.3	98.5	4.50
5.00	98.9	98.9	98.9	98.9	99.0	99.0	99.0	99.1	99.1	99.2	5.00
6.00	99.8	99.8	99.8	99.8	99.8	99.8	99.8	99.8	99.8	99.8	6.00

Note: Values in the table represent percentages of underlying asset values: e.g., 39.3 denotes a call option worth 39.3% of the underlying asset value.
Values in the table were computed from the Black-Scholes option-pricing model.
The format of the table was adapted from Brealy and Myers, *Principles of Corporate Finance*, 4th edition (New York: McGraw-Hill, 1991), Appendix Table 6, pp. AP12–13.

That is to say, although $\chi > S$, these two variables are relatively close to one another because $S > PV(\chi)$. They are separated only by time value. Over time, we expect the market value of the asset, S, to increase at some rate greater than r. (No one would be willing to hold the asset otherwise.)[5] By the end of three years, there is a good chance that the NPV will exceed zero and the option will be exercised. In any event, at expiration, the option will be worth the greater of zero or $S - \chi$. In the meantime, the option on the project really is worth \$25, not −\$10, provided the company does not (suboptimally) exercise it now.

The difference between NPV and NPV_q contains a useful managerial insight. As time runs out, these two must converge to some agreement: at expiration they will be either greater than 0 and 1, respectively, or less than these values. But prior to expiration, NPV_q may be positive even when NPV is negative (just as in the preceding example). Figure 13-6 shows this diagrammatically. All options that fall in the right half of Figure 13-6 have $NPV_q > 1$. But not all of these are in the money; that is, the NPV of an "exercise-now" strategy is positive for some and negative for others. The locus of points that corresponds to NPV(exercise now) = 0 is a curve that starts at the top, where cumulative variance is zero and $NPV_q = 1$, and runs down and to the right.[6] Options that fall above this curve have both NPV > 0 and $NPV_q > 1$; they are in the money. Those below the curve have $NPV_q > 1$ but NPV < 0; they are out of the money.

[5] This argument assumes that the asset is like a stock that pays no dividends. The exception to this case is quite important and is treated below.

[6] The location of this curve varies with r and σ. The curve is located by holding r and σ constant as t varies and solving for the NPV_q that corresponds to NPV = 0. Note that in the extreme case of r = 0, the curve is a vertical line passing through $NPV_q = 1$. As r increases, the slope of the curve decreases, bending to the right, as shown in Figure 13-6.

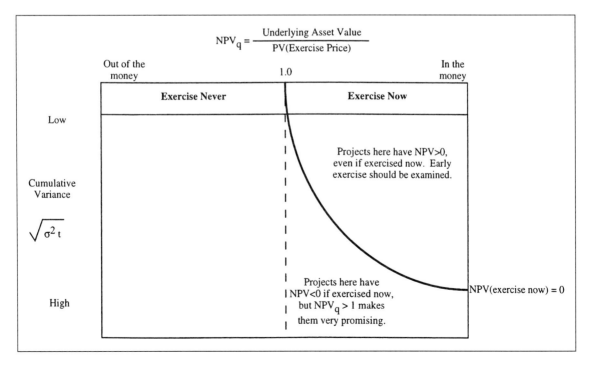

Figure 13-6. Mapping projects into call-option space.

We can now generate three different managerial prescriptions for options with NPVq > 1, each corresponding to a different region in the right half of Figure 13-6. At the very top are options with no cumulative variance—either time has run out or there is no variance. These options are in the money (NPV > 0) and should be exercised immediately—there is no value in waiting.

Just below these are options that are in the money, but for which there is still some cumulative variance. The company should wait, *if possible*, to exercise these options. Early exercise may be desirable when the underlying asset is "wasting." If, for example, its value is subject to erosion due to competitors' actions, or if it is already paying out cash, then it is analogous to a dividend-paying stock. Holders of American call options on a dividend-paying stock sometimes will find it optimal to exercise early, prior to expiration. This is a way to capture the cash being paid out or prevent the value erosion. However, by exercising early, the holder of an American call option foregoes the interest on the exercise price. Hence, a tradeoff must be evaluated in order to determine the better course of action. The distinction between American and European calls is very important for real options. Real options typically *can* be exercised early, and often the value of the underlying asset is subject to erosion by competitors' actions or technical or demographic changes.[7]

Finally, at the bottom of the right half of Figure 13-6 are options like the simple example presented above: they are very promising because $NPV_q > 1$ even though NPV < 0. If, as time runs out, neither S nor χ changes, then NPV_q will fall and these options will expire unexercised. But among a large sample of such projects, we should expect many to end up in the money, especially if they receive active attention and management.

A Stylized Map: The "Tomato Garden"

Pushing the logic of Figure 13-6 a bit further, we can divide the call-option space roughly into six regions, each corresponding to a different managerial prescription as shown in Figure 13-7. The right side of Figure 13-7 is divided into regions I, II, and III, in all of which $NPV_q > 1$. These correspond to the three regions in the right half of Figure 13-6 just described. The left half of Figure 13-7 is divided symmetrically, into regions IV, V, and VI, in all of which $NPV_q < 1$. In region VI at the top, cumulative variance is zero, so these options are never exercised. Region V contains relatively unpromising options. For them, NPV_q and/or $\sigma\sqrt{t}$ is low. Not many of these projects will make it, regardless of the attention they may receive. In region IV are options for which either NPV_q or $\sigma\sqrt{t}$ is reasonably high, but the other is low. These projects require active development to end up in the money. In general, projects will tend to move upward in Figure 13-7 as time passes because time runs out and uncertainty is resolved. Managers have two jobs: to try to move projects to the right before time runs out; and to avoid making mistakes in their exercise decisions in the meantime.

The analogy of a tomato garden located in an unpredictable climate may be a helpful mnemonic device. Managers are the gardeners; they do the cultivating and eventually decide which tomatoes to pick and which not to. At one extreme are perfect, ripe tomatoes (region I of Figure 13-7) which should be picked and eaten immediately. At the other extreme are rotten tomatoes (region VI) which should never be picked. In between are many different tomatoes with varying prospects. Those in region II are ed-

[7] For more on American calls and dividend-paying stocks, see Brealey and Myers, *Principles of Corporate Finance*, chapter 21, pp. 526–529.

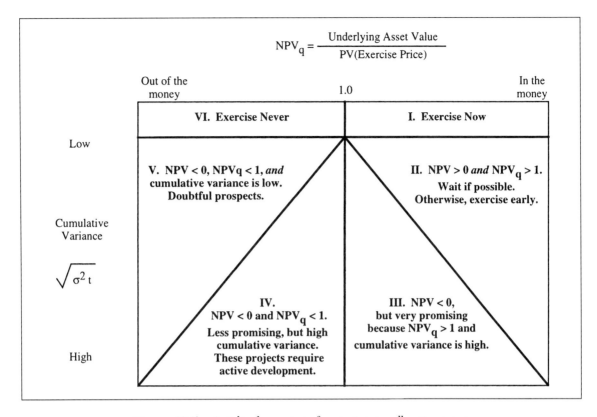

$$NPV_q = \frac{\text{Underlying Asset Value}}{\text{PV(Exercise Price)}}$$

Figure 13-7. A stylized mapping of projects into call-option space.

ible and could be picked, but they would improve with more time on the vine. The gardener will pick them early only if competitors (e.g., squirrels) are likely to get them otherwise. Tomatoes in region III are not edible and should not be picked regardless of competitors. Over time, however, many in region III will ripen and eventually be picked. Region IV contains fruit that is less promising and may not ripen before the season is over. Nevertheless, with more sun or water, fewer weeds, or just good luck, some of these tomatoes may become edible. Finally, region V contains late blossoms and small green tomatoes that have not much chance of growing and ripening before the season ends.

PRACTICAL ISSUES

Using option-pricing models to analyze capital projects presents some practical problems. Comparatively few of these problems have completely satisfactory solutions; on the other hand, some insight is gained just from formulating and articulating the problems. Still more, perhaps, is available from approximations. To interpret an analysis, it helps to remain aware of whether it represents an exact answer to an approximated (simplified) problem, or an approximate answer to an exact problem. Either may be useful.

Simplifying Complex Projects Real corporate projects, especially long-horizon ones, are complex. They are most often combinations of assets-in-place and options. Furthermore, the options are nested; that is, managers face a *sequence* of serially dependent choices. It helps to simplify such problems, not only for formal analytical purposes, but also to make them understandable and discussible within the group of responsible managers. Moreover, an unsimplified problem may be unique (and practically insoluble), whereas a simplified problem may fit in a larger class of problems which will provide hints or boundaries for a solution.

Most real option problems can either be abstracted as fairly simple call options or broken into pieces, each one of which is a fairly simple call option. A useful guide in simplifying is to search for the primary uncertainty against which managers select. That is, by waiting and watching, what is the main thing a manager learns, and how will he or she exploit the learning? Some projects have optionlike characteristics (e.g., the project is risky and managers clearly have a choice about whether to undertake it); yet as long as the company does nothing, it learns nothing. For such projects, a DCF approach may be appropriate; in effect, the company has to make the investment in order to resolve the uncertainty (such projects resemble Figure 13-1a). However, for many other projects, the resolution of a small set of uncertainties determines the outcome, *and* at least some can be resolved without making the entire investment. Such projects resemble Figure 13-1b, and identifying the key uncertainties is the first step toward a useful simplification.

Another useful approach is to construct simplifications such that the simplified project is both priceable and either dominating or dominated, compared to the real project. A dominated project is one that is clearly *less* valuable than the real project. If it also can be priced, then its value provides a lower bound for the project value. For example, a simple European call is clearly dominated by a (more realistic) American call on an asset exposed to erosion by competitors' investments. Dominating simplifications similarly provide an upper bound for project value. Sometimes it is possible to construct and compute both upper and lower bounds.

Estimating Volatility   The option-pricing input managers are least accustomed to estimating its variance, or standard deviation. For a real option, σ cannot be looked up in a table or newspaper, and most people do not have highly developed intuition about, for example, the annual variance of returns on assets associated with entering a new market. Nevertheless, estimating σ is not a completely hopeless task. There are at least three reasonable approaches:

1. *Take a guess.*   Systematic risk (β) and total risk (σ) are positively correlated in large samples of operating assets: those with high asset betas are likelier to have higher standard deviations. What is a high standard deviation? Returns on broad-based U.S. stock market indices had a standard deviation of about 20% per year for much of 1986–1994, with exceptions (upward spikes) associated with events like the 1987 market crash and the 1990–1991 Persian Gulf crisis. Individual projects will have higher volatilities than a diversified portfolio of the same projects. Volatility of 20 to 30% per year is not remarkably high for a single project.

2. *Gather some data.*   Volatility can be estimated for some businesses using historical data on investment returns in certain industries. Alternatively, implied volatilities can be computed from quoted option prices for a very large number of traded equities. The length, breadth, and quality of such data have improved greatly in recent years and should continue to do so. These data do require some adjustment, however. Equity returns are levered and therefore more volatile than underlying asset returns.

3. *Simulate σ.* Spreadsheet-based projections of a project's future cash flows, together with Monte Carlo simulation techniques can be used to synthesize a probability distribution for project returns. Inputs include estimated volatilities for specific items, such as commodity prices or exchange rates. Using these inputs, a computer simulates the project and, in the process, synthesizes a probability distribution for desired output variables, such as project returns. From the synthesized probability distribution, σ can be estimated.[8] Simulation software for desktop computers is commercially available and designed to work as an add-in with popular spreadsheet applications.

Some insight is available from Figure 13-7 even without precise estimates of σ. Simply knowing whether cumulative variance is high or low is enough to locate a project in one part or another of Figure 13-7 and, with some knowledge of NPV_q, to suggest a managerial course of action.

Checking Models and Distributions All formal option-pricing models, including Black-Scholes, assume that the riskiness of an asset can be expressed as a probability distribution for returns (or prices or payouts) for the asset. Some of the assumed distributions are elegantly simple, such as the lognormal distribution assumed by Black-Scholes. But corporate data for some real projects are inelegant and may be inconsistent with, for example, a lognormal distribution. One approach to this problem is to figure out in which direction a simplified distribution biases the analysis and then interpret the output accordingly, as an upper or lower bound for the actual project's value. Another is to choose a model, if one exists, based on a more appropriate distribution. Many models have been constructed and solved, though most are mathematically sophisticated and unwieldy for use with real options.[9]

More fundamental than the particular distribution assumed by a given model is the type of world being modeled. The Black-Scholes world, for example, is one in which underlying assets are securities that are traded continuously. Many real options involve underlying assets that are not traded continuously or, in some cases, not traded at all. For such assets, the five variables (six, if dividends are allowed) of the Black-Scholes model are not sufficient to characterize and price a call option. Whether one model or another remains useful as a way to price a simplified version of the project is a judgment the analyst must make. One alternative to such modeling is brute force, in the form of computing power. High-speed computers and advanced spreadsheet software make it possible to simulate some projects as a complicated decision tree. Decision-tree analysis is not, formally speaking, option pricing, but if well-executed, it provides a better treatment of uncertainty and of managers' scope for decision making than conventional DCF analysis alone.

Interpreting Results To execute a useful analysis, simplification is essential. To interpret the results, some sophistication is equally essential. This typically involves layering complexity back into the problem in the form of sensitivity analyses and the conditioning or qualifying of inferences. To arrive at Figure 13-7 and its useful mapping,

[8] Skillful simulation requires knowledge of probability and statistics, including the forms of distributions, elementary sampling theory, differences between time series and cross-sectional analyses, and so forth. A useful reference is Kelton and Law, *Simulation Modeling and Analysis*, (Cambridge, MA: McGraw-Hill, New York: 1991).

[9] A bibliography of sophisticated models is given in Merton, *Continuous-Time Finance* (Cambridge, MA: Basil Blackwell, 1990). A more narrowly focused reference is Wilmott, Dewynne, and Howison, *Option Pricing: Mathematical Models and Computation* (Oxford: Oxford Financial Press, 1993).

we first took a complicated project and simplified it enough to regard it as a European call option. Then, drawing on an understanding of option pricing and capital budgeting, we further simplified the analysis by combining five variables into two. But now, after valuing a project and locating it in Figure 13-7, we should put some of the complexity back in and begin looking at sensitivity analyses. This will help us understand which of a project's characteristics cause it to fall where it does on the map. For example, in region III, is cumulative variance high primarily because of σ or t? Which of the elements of NPV_q is most readily managed—net cash inflows (S) or capital expenditures (χ)? And so forth. This process is iterative. The results of one analysis suggest a further one until the process converges on an understanding, in both financial and managerial terms, of the project.

## 14

Penelope's Personal Pocket Phones

Penelope Phillips sat in her laboratory at the University of the North and tried to determine whether she should start a company focussed on the next generation of wireless phone technology. Her work in electrical engineering and the 15 patents she held told her that she could enter the market with a new generation of phones. The problem was, however, that the market was quite competitive and she knew that it would therefore be difficult to succeed. Penelope understood that getting into the market today might lead to much bigger opportunities in the future.

Penelope looked at her projections. In order to get the first generation to market, she would have to invest $10 million in the first year. The cash flow forecasts in Exhibit 14-1 show what she expected to earn on this first product. Comparable firms in the industry had unlevered betas of around 1.2 and annual standard deviation of returns of 50%, so she set out to see if the investment was worth the time and energy. The 10-year Treasury bond was yielding 10.0% at the time.

Penelope also knew that by starting the company today, she would have the opportunity to invest in the subsequent generation of phones. Given the expectations about future costs, this opportunity would take $100 million to bring to market. She estimated, however, that she would have to make the investment four years from now when the entire $100 million would have to be invested. She wondered how big the current expected value on the second-generation phone would have to be in order to justify investing in the proposed project. She set about trying to calculate that value.

Thirty minutes into her calculations, Jay Thomas called to tell her that she would be able to start the project using equipment that could easily be sold for $4 million in year two if demand was not high for her phones. By year two, she could be reasonably confident of what the value of her first generation of phones would be; that is, she assumed that the value would be known with certainty at that time. If that were the case, Penelope wondered what the value of the first project would be. She decided to ignore

---

Professor Paul Gompers prepared this case as the basis for class discussion rather than to illustrate either effective or ineffective handling of an administrative situation.

EXHIBIT 14-1

PRO FORMA PROJECTIONS FOR PENELOPE'S PERSONAL POCKET PHONES

	2001	2002	2003	2004	2005	2006
INCOME STATEMENT						
Net Sales	$ 0	$8,600	$14,000	$18,000	$14,500	$8,000
COGS	0	3,500	5,300	7,100	6,500	3,200
Gross Profit	0	5,100	8,700	10,900	8,000	4,800
SG&A	1,900	2,300	3,000	3,700	4,200	4,000
R&D	2,100	2,800	3,000	3,500	3,900	2,000
EBIT	(4,000)	0	2,700	3,700	(100)	(1,200)
Income Tax[a]	0	0	295	1,415	(35)	(300)
Net Earnings	(4,000)	0	2,405	2,285	(65)	(900)
Depreciation	900	900	900	900	900	900
Capital Expenditure	5,400	0	0	0	0	0
Investment in Net Working Capital	1,500	0	0	0	0	(1,500)

[a] If a firm makes a loss but has paid taxes in previous years it receives a refund on previous taxes.

the second-generation phones for a while and focus on this new problem. Did the possibility of selling the equipment at the end of year two make the first project worth it even if there were no follow-on project? If she modeled the annual change in value, Penelope figured that the expected value of cash flows from the first-generation phones would either increase by 64.9% or decrease by 39.3% each year. She wondered how to proceed with her analysis.

## 15

E Ink: Financing Growth

"We signed it!" Russ Wilcox exclaimed to James Iuliano over his cellular phone. Wilcox, E Ink's Vice President of Business Development, was referring to the meeting he had just come out of with executives from JC Penney. It was March 4, 1999, and JC Penney's managers had just agreed to test E Ink's latest prototype large-area display signs in 10 stores located in four different U.S. cities. The JC Penney deal was significant because it gave E Ink its first commercial forum in which to test its revolutionary electronic ink technology.

The timing of Wilcox's call could not have been better. Iuliano, President and CEO of E Ink, was in his Cambridge, Massachusetts, office preparing for his upcoming meeting with Doug Eller, the Chief Financial Officer of Newstime Publishing. The purpose of Iuliano's meeting was to raise a portion of the $20 million needed for E Ink's second round funding. Wilcox's accomplishment with JC Penney represented the company's first commercial deal and could only improve E Ink's attractiveness to Eller. While Iuliano was excited by the leverage Wilcox had just provided, he could not help but wonder if he was making a mistake by bringing this investment opportunity to Newstime Publishing. After all, E Ink still had $9 million in the bank from its $15.8 million first round of financing 10 months earlier. Perhaps more importantly, E Ink had generated an almost unprecedented level of "buzz" regarding its electronic ink technology. Even without a released product, E Ink had already been featured in over 30 publications ranging from *Fortune*'s list of "Cool Companies 1998" to the *L.A. Times* to *Popular Science*, and interest continued to build. The excitement surrounding E Ink had created a unique financing problem for Iuliano—how to politely turn away the numerous venture capitalists, technology companies, and publishers who wanted to participate in the current round of financing.

The interest in E Ink stemmed from the vast potential of the company's electronic ink technology. Iuliano, Wilcox, and the rest of the E Ink team had their sights set on revolutionizing the way people viewed information. The technology would hopefully one day result in an ability to print electronic ink on virtually any surface, enabling peo-

Entrepreneurial Studies Fellow Matthew C. Lieb prepared this case under the supervision of Professor William A. Sahlman as the basis for class discussion rather than to illustrate either effective or ineffective handling of an administrative situation. Some data is disguised.

ple to change displayed information through the use of a paging-type network. If successful, E Ink's technology could be used for a seemingly endless number of applications such as embedding updateable maps on the sleeves of hiking jackets, creating more "readable" displays on cellular phones, and enabling a fleet of billboards to change messages on command. E Ink's technology could alter existing information display mechanisms as well as enable information displays that did not currently exist. Despite the numerous possibilities for the technology, E Ink had fixed its sights on "radio paper," an actual book or newspaper printed with electronic ink and able to receive information wirelessly, as the company's end objective. Iuliano's upcoming meeting with publishing executive Doug Eller highlighted E Ink's commitment to creating a radio paper that would replace the traditional printed newspaper.

BACKGROUND
The Idea

Electronic ink was the brainchild of Joe Jacobson, a professor at the Massachusetts Institute of Technology's (MIT) Media Laboratory. During the summer of 1995, Jacobson was enjoying the California sun at a beach near Palo Alto when he was confronted with a practical problem that formed the genesis of electronic ink. Having just completed the book he was reading, Jacobson had two choices: he could pack up and head home to get another book, or he could bake in the sun with nothing to read. This simple dilemma spurred Jacobson into action. Rather than choosing another book, he began to sketch out possibilities for creating a single book that could morph into other books by changing the ink on the page. Having recently completed his postdoctoral work in quantum mechanics at Stanford University, Jacobson commented on his early vision of electronic ink:

> The idea of an electronic book seemed like an exciting challenge. I knew it had to be done on paper or something pretty similar to paper. People are so used to reading from real paper that the whole notion of using some type of liquid crystal display didn't appeal to me. Second, it needed to use very little power so you could eliminate the need for heavy battery packs or other power sources. Lastly, it needed to be crisp in appearance—just like regular ink on paper. Taking these factors into account, I defined the parameters more narrowly. The electronic book must have 200 or more pages printed on real paper, each capable of displaying information. It must look as good as real ink. The cost per page must be comparable to traditional publishing costs. And the power required to run the book must be sufficiently low that the entire power source could be contained in the spine of the book at almost zero weight.

With rough parameters for electronic ink outlined in his mind, Jacobson turned his attention to various technologies that he could employ to meet his specifications for an electronic book:

> I had experience working with a type of vinyl that could conduct electricity. I figured if you could cover a sheet of paper with millions of two-toned conductive particles you could then create images by carefully applying an electric charge. You could, theoretically, alter the content of each page by simply adjusting the flow of electricity across the page.

The Theory of Electronic Ink

With a vision in mind of what his end product would be, Jacobson came to the MIT Media Lab seeking the best way to develop electronic ink. He formed a team of students that included J.D. Albert and Barrett Comiskey. The two MIT seniors, under the direction of Jacobson, embraced an "Edisonian Approach" in developing the technology. Unlike traditional scientific work where only one variable at a time was modified with results carefully recorded, Albert and Comiskey adopted a more ad hoc approach of changing multiple variables with great frequency in an effort to hone in on a successful combination that would yield the required properties for electronic ink.

Near the end of 1996, after countless hours in the laboratory experimenting across scientific disciplines, Albert and Comiskey produced dramatic, though preliminary, results. Their efforts had yielded a technological foundation for an electronic ink that drew from two typically unrelated fields: electrophoresis and microencapsulation. Electrophoresis is the motion of a charged particle in response to an electric field. It could be used to create an electronic image display by using white particles suspended in a black liquid: when the particles are floating on top the viewer sees white, but when the particles are submerged the viewer sees black. Based on electrophoresis, an array of electrical fields such as a pixel array could move particles up and down to create white and black in a pattern. This formed the basis for making images with true black and white color. The question that remained was how to hold the liquid onto a flexible piece of paper. The answer was microcapsules: hollow shells about the size of a grain of laser toner that could be filled with the electrophoretic liquid and fabricated in bulk. The shells could then be printed onto just about any surface, just like traditional ink. A pattern of pixel electrodes could also be printed using conductive inks, completing the electronic display (see Exhibit 15-1 for a schematic drawing of electronic ink). Thus, the technology allowed for fabricating thin, flexible, low-cost displays with significant economies of scale.

Liquid crystal displays and cathode ray tubes (CRTs), the two most popular forms of electronic displays, suffered from numerous drawbacks that had limited their ability to displace paper for markets such as books and newspapers. The advantages of electronic ink versus traditional display technologies were dramatic. First, electronic ink would be made of the same pigments and dyes as ink on paper. As a result, it would have the superior viewing characteristics of paper such as high contrast, wide viewing angle, and a paper white background. Second, electronic ink could be printed on almost any surface ranging from plastic to metal to paper and could cover large areas inexpensively. Third, the ink was capable of holding its image even after the power was turned off, just like ink on paper, and was legible enough in low light that a backlight would rarely be needed. The team felt this would significantly extend the battery life for portable devices. Lastly, the process was highly scaleable, suggesting that electronic ink could catch up on a cost basis with more mature technologies.

Jacobson and his team dreamed of the day when they could beam digital information from a wireless transmitter directly to a sheet of electronic ink that incorporated a printed antenna and processor. This would allow people to read whatever they wanted, whenever they wanted, wherever they were. Achieving this ambitious goal would require another three to five years of well-funded R&D in both ink technology and pixel circuitry.

The Company

By early 1997, it was clear that electronic ink held strong commercial potential if sufficient resources and passion were committed. At this stage, Jerry Rubin, chairman of the "News in the Future" forum at the MIT Media Lab and a veteran of the publishing and information management industries, offered to help the team incorporate a company to pursue electronic ink and achieve the ultimate vision of radio paper. To-

---

EXHIBIT 15-1

SCHEMATIC DRAWING OF ELECTRONIC INK

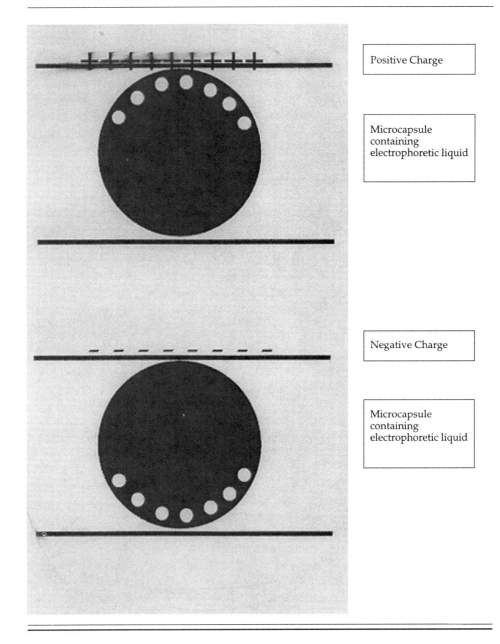

Positive Charge

Microcapsule
containing
electrophoretic liquid

Negative Charge

Microcapsule
containing
electrophoretic liquid

---

gether, Jacobson and Rubin brought Russ Wilcox, a 1995 graduate of Harvard Business School, on board to lead the effort to raise capital. By April 2, 1997, E Ink was incorporated and Wilcox was hard at work on a business plan.

Armed with a potentially revolutionary technology, Wilcox was able to quickly raise a seed round of $1.7 million in convertible debt from three local venture capitalists. In addition to the venture money, Wilcox arranged for a $2 million capital equipment credit facility with Imperial Bank. Wilcox then devoted his time to recruiting both scientists and managers, while Comiskey and Albert built an R&D lab and began to move the technology forward. Wilcox also negotiated term sheets for a first equity round that would convert the $1.7 million in debt and add $14.1 million in new capital from the venture capitalists as well four major corporations (see Exhibit 15-2 for a list of equity investors). By May of 1998, the equity round was closed, and by October 1998, E Ink had a team of 22 people in place focused on advancing the technology.

The surge in employees was highlighted by the arrival of Iuliano and an array of high-profile scientists (see Exhibit 15-3 for the management team and board of directors' biographies). With the nucleus of a team together, Wilcox assumed the role of Vice President for Business Development, and Jacobson refocused on his teaching efforts at MIT while continuing to serve as a consultant to E Ink.

The technical efforts quickly produced results. By March of 1999, the scientists at the company's laboratory had increased the brightness and contrast of the display by a factor of five. In addition, reflectivity increased from 15% to 35% while switching voltage dropped from 300 volts to 90 volts. Prototypes increased in size from 3 square inches to 25 square inches. The progress of the technology was highlighted by E Ink's production of the world's first all-printed flexible reflective display. While the technology was evolving, Iuliano moved aggressively to protect E Ink's technological progress via a series of patents. By the time of Eller's visit, Iuliano and his team had succeeded in acquiring, filing, or licensing a large number of patents, including a license from MIT that gave the university a small ownership stake in E Ink in exchange for rights to the patents filed by Jacobson, Albert, and Comiskey.

The technological improvements had made the company's prototypes sufficiently attractive that E Ink began to receive requests for shipment from potential customers. Strong customer interest and the advancement of the technology led Iuliano to aim for commercial readiness of the technology in the form of large-area retail displays in some form by the end of 1999. The deal with JC Penney represented a significant step forward in achieving Iuliano's goal for retail displays.

THE CRITICAL PATH

E Ink's founders were driven by a desire to answer a single question: How could E Ink provide all of the benefits of digital content, yet retain the pleasures of reading in bed, browsing a newspaper on the subway, or thumbing through a magazine on the beach? Attempting to answer this question had set the company on a course to transform one of the world's largest industries: publishing.

While radio paper was the pot of gold at the end of E Ink's rainbow, there were many other potentially distracting and/or profitable applications along the way. E Ink's technology could one day be used to replace almost any display currently in use or to create displays that had never before been possible. In fact, E Ink's original business plan mentioned applications for electronic ink ranging from sneakers that track the number of steps taken to drug dispensers that indicate remaining doses to cereal boxes that scroll during breakfast reading. The media coverage of E Ink's progress regarding the technology had already led to a flood of interest from potential partners such as JC Penney and other large corporations.

The challenge for Iuliano and his team was in pursuing only the opportunities that could generate short-term profitability while also serving to develop the technology along the path of radio paper. Iuliano explained the company's predicament:

EXHIBIT 15-2

E INK'S FIRST ROUND FINANCING AS OF MARCH 1999[1]

E Ink was funded by a $15.8 million first round of equity that included the following investors:

Applied Technologye*: Appled Technology, a venture capital firm founded in 1983 with more than $80 million in capital under management, maintains offices in Lexington, Massachusetts; Austin, Texas; and Menlo Park, California. Focused on early-stage high-tech companies, it offers a unique framework for maximizing investment returns by coupling an experienced management team with both corporate partners and academic experts. The Partnership is actively investing from its third fund with investments in 32 companies to date.

Atlas Venture*: Venture capital firm focusing on information technology and life sciences with offices in Boston, Menlo Park, Amsterdam, London, and Munich. The firm manages over $850 million, with over $400 million committed from the most recent fund formed in 1999. Since its inception in 1980, Atlas Venture has funded more than 200 companies. Of these companies, 39 have successfully completed initial public offerings, 76 have been acquired, and 81 are still developing.

Creavis GmbH: Headquartered in Marl, Germany, Creavis is a wholly owned subsidiary of Degussa-Huels. Degussa Huels is one of the world's largest specialty chemical companies. Creavis specializes in investing in and developing innovative products with a heavy reliance on chemistry.

The Hearst Corporation: The Hearst Corporation is one of the nation's largest diversified communications companies. Its major interests include magazine, newspaper and business publishing, cable networks, television and radio broadcasting, Internet businesses, television production and distribution, newspaper features distribution, and real estate.

Interpublic Group of Companies, Inc.: Interpublic Group specializes in advertising and communication services. IPG operating companies include McCann-Erickson WorldGroup, Ammirati Puris Lintas, The Lowe Group, and Western International Media.

Motorola, Inc.*: Motorola is a global company specializing in providing integrated communications and embedded electronic solutions. Motorola is a leader in software-enhanced wireless telephone, two-way radio, messaging, and satellite communications products and systems. Motorola also offers networking and Internet access products.

Solstice Capital**: Solstice Capital is a private venture capital partnership formed in 1995 to invest in seed and early-stage private companies. The partnership oversees the investment of $22.75 million of committed capital and has invested in 20 portfolio companies. The basic strategy of the Fund is to identify companies that are positioned to capitalize on major change factors. Solstice believes that a number of long-term trends such as concern for the environment, clean water, whole foods, and quality of life create opportunities for new companies. The primary factors which are determinants of success for investment are quality of management, technology advantage, and market positioning.

[1] Information on investors was taken from the Web sites of the respective companies or was supplied by E Ink management.

* Received a position on the E Ink Board of Directors.

** Received observer rights on the E Ink Board of Directors.

EXHIBIT 15-3

E INK MANAGEMENT TEAM AS OF MARCH 1999

James P. Iuliano, President and CEO. James Iuliano is also a member of the board of directors. Iuliano was recruited to develop and implement the strategy for commercializing electronic ink. Prior to joining E Ink, Iuliano was president, director, and CEO of Molecular Devices Corporation of Sunnyvale, California (NASDAQ: MDCC), an analytical instrumentation company in the life sciences market. At Molecular Devices, Iuliano completed a successful turnaround, generating 20 consecutive quarters of record profits and growing revenues 300% in five years. Iuliano led Molecular Devices through a highly successful initial public offering and grew its market capitalization to nearly $250 million. In his career, Iuliano has raised over $100 million in public and private financing, negotiated several acquisitions and technology licensing deals, and built worldwide market leadership positions in emerging technologies. He earned an M.B.A. from Harvard Business School and a B.S. from Boston College.

F. Javed Chaudhary, Vice President Operations. F. Javed Chaudhary is responsible for all operational and manufacturing activities at E Ink. Most recently as Vice President and General Manager of Seagate Technology (Thailand), Chaudhary was responsible for building over 20 million assemblies annually with a P&L budget exceeding $280 million. He holds an M.S. in Engineering Management from Northeastern University and a B.S. in Mechanical Engineering from the Engineering University Lahore, Pakistan.

Russell J. Wilcox, Vice President and General Manager (co-founder). Russell J. Wilcox holds P&L responsibility for launching the large-area display business, encompassing wireless networks of billboards, signs, and displays. One of the founders of E Ink, Wilcox led the company during its first 10 months of operations as Vice President of Business Development. He was instrumental in recruiting the initial team, securing $18 million in debt and equity financing, licensing intellectual property, and developing corporate relationships. Wilcox was previously Director of PC Products for venture-backed PureSpeech, Inc. Wilcox earned honors degrees from Harvard College in Applied Mathematics and the Harvard Business School MBA Program where he was named a Baker Scholar.

J.D. Albert, Principal Engineer (co-founder). J.D. Albert is the lead design engineer behind the company's large-area display product line. At the MIT Media Lab, he developed novel methods of making electronic ink and flexible displays. He is an MIT graduate, with a B.S. in Mechanical Engineering.

Barrett Comiskey, Principal Scientist (co-founder). Barrett Comiskey works on intellectual property, quality testing, and future technologies. Comiskey pioneered the original research at the MIT Media Lab. He graduated from MIT, earning a B.S. in Mathematics. Comiskey has published several papers and holds patents on technologies related to electronic ink, digital and analog steganography and cryptography.

Dr. Paul Drzaic, Director of Display Technology. Paul Drzaic has extensive experience in both display systems and materials science. Prior to joining E Ink, Drzaic was the principal scientist leading the polymer-dispersed liquid crystal (PDLC) effort for Raychem Corporation, where he developed new materials for use in flat-panel displays. Drzaic is the author of *Liquid Crystal Dispersions* (1995).

Dr. Ian Morrison, Director of Ink Technology. Ian Morrison leads E Ink's ongoing development of enhanced versions of electronic ink. Prior to joining E Ink, Morrison had a distinguished career at Xerox Corporation where he held a variety of high-level research and development positions. Most recently, Morrison researched electrical, rheological and optical properties of nonaqueous dispersions. Morrison holds 19 patents and has written numerous technical articles published in scientific journals.

(Continued)

EXHIBIT 15-3   (Continued)

Tom Grant, Managing Director, Applied Technology   Tom Grant selects and manages investments for Applied Technology and serves actively on the boards of several portfolio companies. Applied Technology focuses on early-stage companies developing enabling information technologies and content.

James P. Iuliano, President and CEO of E Ink Corporation   Mr. Iuliano also serves as the company's chief executive officer.

Dr. Joseph Jacobson, Assistant Professor, MIT Media Lab   Joseph Jacobson is an Assistant Professor at the Massachusetts Institute of Technology (MIT) Media Laboratory, where he initiated a program to develop electronic paperbooks with pages consisting of electronically addressable, rewritable displays formed on real paper. He holds several patents and patents pending in electronic display technology. Dr. Jacobson received his Ph.D. in Physics at MIT in 1992 in femtosecond laser engineering. He created the world's shortest pulse laser (in optical cycles) in 1991. He was a postdoctoral fellow at Stanford from 1992 to 1995, working on experimental and theoretical nonlinear nonlocal quantum systems. His theoretical work, published in the *Physical Review*, has been written up in the *New York Times* and *Physics Today*.

Jerome S. Rubin, Founder Lexis/Nexis, and Managing Director Veronis, Suhler & Associates (Chairman)   Jerry Rubin was first exposed to electronic ink while serving as Chairman of the MIT Media Lab's research initiative, News in the Future. He joined MIT in December 1992 after retiring from the Times Mirror Company, where he was Chairman of the Professional Information and Book Publishing Group. Before joining Times Mirror in 1983, Mr. Rubin developed and brought to commercial success LEXIS, the computer-assisted legal research service (launched in 1973), and NEXIS, the online news research service (launched in 1978). Combined, these constitute the world's largest online textual information service. In 1985 the Information Industry Association inducted Mr. Rubin into its Hall of Fame for his pioneering achievements in electronic publishing. Since September 1995, Mr. Rubin has been a Managing Director of Veronis, Suhler & Associates, the foremost investment banking firm specializing in communications & media (newspaper, magazine & book publishing, radio, TV & cable, and online information systems). Mr. Rubin is a Director of several corporations besides E Ink and also of some not-for-profit organizations. Mr. Rubin holds two Harvard degrees—a bachelor's degree in Physics (1944) and a law degree (1949). He was a co-author of *Toward the Year 2000: New Forces in Publishing* (Bertelsmann, 1989) and of *Mastering the Changing Information World* (Ablex, 1992).

Larry Silverstein, Esq., Partner, Bingham Dana (general counsel)   Larry Silverstein practices as a member of the Entrepreneurial Services Group at Bingham Dana. Mr. Silverstein acts as counsel to many emerging growth, middle-market, and established companies, both public and private.

Christopher Spray, General Partner, Atlas Venture Capital   Christopher Spray founded Atlas Venture's US partnership in 1986. He began his international venture capital career in 1983, when he joined CINVen, a leading European venture fund based in the UK. Atlas Venture is a partnership of international venture capitalists formed to finance high-technology businesses seeking success in the global economy. Investments are concentrated in two sectors—life sciences and information technology.

John Steadman, Vice President, Motorola Messaging Systems Products Group   Mr. Steadman is currently Vice President of Motorola's Messaging Systems Products Group (MSPG). MSPG is responsible for all aspects of Motorola's paging business worldwide. Motorola's 1997 sales were $29.8 billion.

Our stated goal has always been to create radio paper. Having said that, we know that we have a long way to go technologically to make radio paper a reality. In the meantime, we have a consortium of investors and a continual influx of potential customers and partners who all have different views on the best use for electronic ink. In fact, over the past 45 weeks, we have had 40 well-known companies visit our offices hoping to use electronic ink in some way to improve their business. The challenge for us as an organization is to very carefully select only the applications that can advance the technology along the critical path towards radio paper. We can't afford to veer off track by pursuing seductive applications that have no relevance to our end goal. We really need to be creative in developing the technology and disciplined in applying it.

After much analysis and debate, Iuliano had chosen to set E Ink along a well-defined "critical path" toward the ultimate goal of radio paper. The path envisioned by Iuliano would begin with (1) large-area displays, followed by (2) battery-powered flat panel displays, ending with (3) radio paper. All of these steps represented entry to successively larger markets. The relevant portion of the large-area display market exceeded $600 million. The flat-panel display industry was expected to exceed $25 billion by 2004. The U.S. publishing industry alone exceeded $135 billion in annual revenue. With this critical path in mind, Iuliano attempted to profitably steer the company through a series of obstacles en route to radio paper.

Phase I: Large-Area Displays

E Ink's first commercial venture would be in the large-area display market. Convinced that E Ink needed to produce a "single product for a single market and a single market niche," E Ink's focus would be large-area displays for retail signs, such as the prototypes developed for JC Penney. Large-area displays represented an attractive market for E Ink because the opportunity was "big but with no entrenched gorilla," and a commercially viable product could be launched quickly based on the existing state of the technology.

Technically, electronic ink offered dramatic improvements over other large-area display technologies. While other display technologies were glass-based and did not scale readily to large areas, electronic ink could be economically printed over large areas. The lightweight and visual appearance of electronic ink were key advantages over existing technologies.

The market for in-store displays was both large and ripe for improvement (see Exhibit 15-4 for market data on large-area displays). LEK Consulting reported that the presence of machine-printed signs could raise unit sales by an average of 200% based on a study of 143 different items. Despite the impact of signs, field compliance with prescribed messages for signs was remarkably low. In fact, only 33% of in-store displays conformed to specified requirements and the average lead-time to create a point-of-purchase program and deploy it to the field was nearly 90 days.

E Ink's ability to incorporate a wireless communications interface such as an embedded pager offered another dramatic improvement versus existing in-store display options. Electronic ink-enabled signs could be changed instantly from a central location, thus ensuring field compliance and quick response times. E Ink's technology might also allow retailers and manufacturers to display more intelligent information based on factors such as time of day, demographics, and sales trends. In addition to potentially delivering a higher quality product, E Ink also offered a cost advantage. A large two-line LED sign would cost a retailer over $2,000 to install. The higher performing E Ink sign of similar dimensions was expected to sell for less than half the price of existing signs once production was ramped up to manufacture signs at a significant scale.

EXHIBIT 15-4

SEGMENTS OF THE LARGE-AREA DISPLAY MARKET RELEVANT TO E INK ($ MILLIONS)

	LED Matrix Over 2′ Wide	Incandescent Bulbs	Electro-mechanical	Total	%
General purpose	$ 80	$ 50	$15	$145	24%
Casino & bar	20	125	—	145	24
Government	75	35	25	135	22
Retail & food	70	—	—	70	11
Sports	—	35	10	45	7
Transport	10	—	30	50	7
All Other	15	15	—	30	5
TOTAL	$270	$260	$80	$610	100%

Wilcox, who headed up the Phase I effort for E Ink, estimated that the company could exceed a $20 million revenue run rate within three years. Wilcox also believed that the in-store display business could exceed $100 million in revenue by 2004 if the technology advanced to the point of offering higher resolution and color. To fully take advantage of this opportunity, Wilcox estimated that E Ink would need to invest $10 to $20 million.

Despite the economic opportunity available in the in-store display market, it was the advancement of E Ink's technology that interested Iuliano the most. Iuliano saw large-area displays as a building-block opportunity. He described the in-store display opportunity from a technology development perspective:

> The product requirements are right in line with our path to create electronic paper. By subjecting ourselves to marketplace demands early in our lifecycle, we can begin to build a customer and market-driven mentality that will serve us well going forward. As we enter the next phases along our critical path, the large-area display product line should be able to make use of all of the progress being made in our core technology.

Phase II: Flat-Panel Displays

Iuliano intended to make flat-panel displays the second step on E Ink's critical path to radio paper. Flat-panel displays had received pervasive acceptance in the marketplace in a variety of forms for a number of uses. Most consumer electronics, computers, personal digital assistants, and cellular phones utilized flat-panel displays. In 1998, total flat-panel display sales were nearly $14 billion and were expected to grow rapidly to over $25.9 billion by 2004.[1]

E Ink's strategy in the flat-panel display market was to identify specific niches of the market where the attributes of electronic ink created substantial value, permitting the company to price at a premium. Within this market, Iuliano sought applications re-

---

[1] All market-size data in this section are from "Flat Information Displays Market & Technology Trends (1998)" by Stanford Resources, Inc.

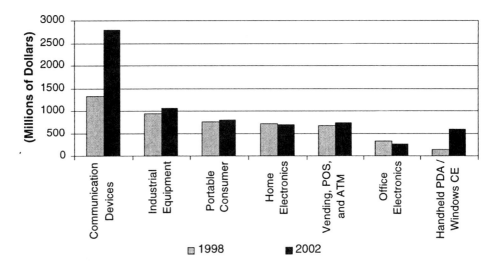

Figure A. Global flat-panel display market of relevance to E Ink ($4.9 billion–$6.9 billion).

quiring a high-contrast, low-power, thin and ultra-lightweight display. Such applications covered a wide array of products, including communications, portable consumer, and handheld devices. The market relevant to E Ink totaled almost $5 billion in 1998 and was expected to grow to almost $7 billion by 2002 (see Figure A for the flat-panel display market relevant to E Ink).

In researching the flat-panel display market, Iuliano and others had engaged in conversations with managers at two major handheld device companies. These managers indicated a willingness to pay a substantial price premium for electronic ink versions of the typical handheld display, which typically cost $30 for volumes over one million. The premium was due to electronic ink's greater visual appeal and lower power consumption.

Liquid Crystal Displays The flat-panel display market was currently dominated by several large manufacturers of liquid crystal displays (LCDs). Despite the fact that Sharp, Toshiba, and other makers of LCDs had significantly improved the technology over time (see Exhibit 15-5 for LCD technology progress), LCDs had many inherent shortcomings. Active-matrix LCD displays were costly because of the need for an ultra high-precision glass-based thin-film transistor (TFT) backplane for switching. The backlight in many LCD displays consumed significant amounts of power, while reflective LCDs tended to be dim under many viewing conditions. Also, LCDs were produced on rigid substrates.

E Ink's Flat-Panel Display Advantages Iuliano believed that E Ink's technology offered the best combination of price and performance for flat-panel displays. When comparing the promise of electronic ink versus traditional LCDs, Iuliano pointed out a number of benefits highlighted in Table A.

Given the current limitations of LCDs and the large and growing market for flat-panel displays, a number of other display technologies were under development. Microdisplays, organic light emitting diodes (OLEDs), field emission displays, plasma displays, microsphere approaches, and further improvements to existing LCDs were all in the works. (See Exhibit 15-6 for information on competing flat-panel display technologies.)

EXHIBIT 15-5

TECHNOLOGICAL PROGRESS OF LIQUID CRYSTAL DISPLAYS

Thickness Trend (10-Inch Class TFT-LCD)

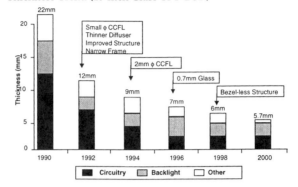

Weight Trend (10-Inch Class TFT-LCD)

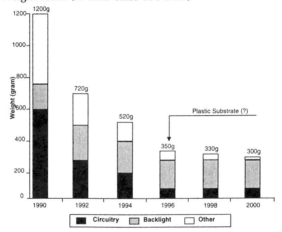

Power Trend (10-Inch Class TFT-LCD)

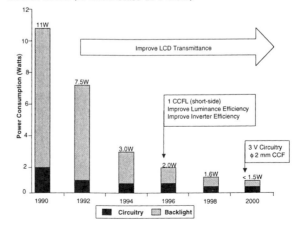

Adapted from: *Flat Panel Displays*; Toshiba America Electronic Components, Inc.

TABLE A Electronic Ink versus LCDs

Electronic Ink	Liquid Crystal Displays
Direct color change	Requires a change in light transmission
Looks like real ink on paper	Lacks the appeal of ink on paper
Less than 1 mm thick	Significantly thicker than 1 mm
Flexible	Rigid
Easily scaled to large sizes	Significant price increase when scaled up
Holds image without power drain (bistability)	Requires significant power to hold images
Lightweight	Power supply and glass makes LCDs relatively heavy
Broad temperature range	Does not perform well in low temperatures
Readable in sunlight	Difficult to see in bright light situations
Wide viewing angle	Limited viewing angle
Does not distort under finger pressure	Distorts when pressure is applied

Technological Hurdles   While E Ink had already made tremendous progress in developing its technology for use in large-area displays, the leap to flat-panel displays was still challenging. Specifically, E Ink's scientists needed to combine their electronic ink with a transistor backplane. The backplane would serve as the "circuitry" by which high-resolution images could be changed through the application of a charge to the ink. E Ink was aggressively pursuing several backplane technologies in parallel. E Ink's team had identified both cooperative and proprietary approaches to solving this problem and expected to demonstrate a crude working device sometime in 2000, with product shipping roughly 18 months later. To successfully launch into the flat-panel display market, Iuliano estimated that E Ink would need an additional $30 to 50 million in financing.

Phase III: Publishing

Radio paper had been the ultimate goal at E Ink since Jacobson's reading dilemma at the California beach. The notion of radio paper captivated the minds of employees, investors, and the press. If Iuliano and the rest of the team could deliver what they were aiming for, E Ink might revolutionize one of America's largest industries.

The U.S. publishing industry generated over $135 billion in revenue in 1998 (see Table B for detailed breakdown) from a variety of sources, including purchases, subscriptions, and advertising. Publishing revenues were surprisingly robust, despite the growth of the Internet and the digital economy. For example, even though overall newspaper circulation had been on the decline since 1987, advertising sales were growing at a rate of nearly 8% per year. The growth in advertising rates yielded a forecasted industry revenue figure of over $160 billion by 2001.

Iuliano intended to leverage technological advancements achieved during the development of large-area displays and flat-panel displays to make radio paper a reality. The possible economic rewards associated with replacing much of traditional publishing with electronic ink technology were astronomical. All sectors of publishing could benefit economically from a paper-free distribution model that required $0 for manufacturing, no inventory, and $0 for distribution. Such expenses typically accounted for 20 to 40% of publishers' costs, suggesting a multibillion problem that was E Ink's opportunity.

EXHIBIT 15-6

COMPETING FLAT-PANEL DISPLAY TECHNOLOGIES

Enhancement of LCDs—The LCD is not a fixed technology. With hundreds of millions of dollars being spent annually on incremental improvements, the LCD is getting cheaper and better with each passing year. Enhancements include new ways of addressing passive displays, filters to improve light transmission, the development of plastic-substrate LCDs, wider viewing angles, and a sustained and massive effort by Asian display companies to drive down costs.

Microdisplays—These are being commercialized by Kopin, DisplayTech, Colorado Microdisplay, Siliscape, and others. These devices consist of a 1-inch or smaller display, which must be magnified for the viewer to discern an image. Microdisplays are suited for virtual reality headgear, camcorders, PDA with lens attachment, and projection TVs where the image can be expanded onto a distant surface.

Organic LEDs (OLEDs)—OLEDs are under study by over 60 companies worldwide, including most major display companies. OLEDs offer full-color capability in a flexible light emitting display (i.e., visible in the dark). This is described as a "high-potential new display technology" but is still in the development stage. OLEDs are likely to achieve commercial status in the next few years.

Field Emission Displays (FEDs)—FEDs are being commercialized by Candescent, Motorola, and PixTech. This technology is based on the same principle as television, but is replicated on a tiny scale with one emitter per pixel. While original prospects were strong for this technology to replace laptop screens, several years of delay have allowed LCDs to narrow the gap in price/performance.

Plasma (PDPs)—PDPs are being commercialized by several Japanese companies, especially Fujitsu. Plasma displays offer a better alternative to the LCD for large displays from 40 to 80 inches. While starting factory prices were at $15,000 for a 42-inch display in 1996, prices reached $7,000 in 1998 projected at $2,600 by 2002, according to Fujitsu. The emphasis in PDP technology has been on large-area displays, competing primarily against projection display systems.

Gyricon—Xerox, as long ago as 1977, began research of the Gyricon in which half black/half white microspheres are encapsulated in a rubber sheet. This is considered a rival technology to E Ink's for creating an electronic paper. No product plans have been announced.

Newspapers   The newspaper industry was particularly ripe for an electronic ink enabled change. Nearly 65% of Americans read a daily newspaper, with 60 million daily newspapers sold on average each day and an average per-copy readership of 2.3. Thus, 138 million people were reached on a daily basis. There were nearly 1,500 daily newspapers in the United States, with the top 10 newspaper companies owning 325 newspapers that accounted for 43% of the total daily circulation.

The average circulation revenue per year per subscriber was $175, with an additional $600 per year in per subscriber advertising revenue. Newsprint was the single largest expense for newspapers besides labor. Newsprint prices were volatile, ranging 40% from peak to trough in the space of a single year. This instability added risk to the newspaper business and made profits hard to predict. In 1996, 11.1 million tons of

Table B   U.S. Publishing Market Revenues in 1998

Market	1998 U.S. Revenues ($ billions)
Newspapers	$ 60
Professional/educational books	30
Consumer magazines	18
Consumer books	18
Business magazines	9
Total	$135

newsprint was purchased by the U.S. newspaper industry at a cost totaling $7 billion. Newsprint alone represented a cost of roughly $115 per subscriber every year. Adding other variable manufacturing and distribution costs, newspapers spent roughly $350 per customer each year.

While Iuliano was unclear as to the specific business model he would employ to exploit the newspaper opportunity, it was clear that the impact of electronic ink could be dramatic (see Exhibit 15-7 for the economics of the newspaper industry). E Ink might one day offer consumers the ability to have one newspaper where content could be updated and customized instantaneously at the push of a button.

EXHIBIT 15-7

POTENTIAL RADIO PAPER ECONOMICS VERSUS TRADITIONAL NEWSPAPERS

Line Item	Traditional Newspapers (billion)	Radio Paper (billion)
Newspapers per year	22.50	22.50
Sales per paper	$2.18	$2.18
Operating costs	$1.75	$1.40
Operating margin	$0.44	$0.78
Net income	$0.18	$0.40

Source: E Ink estimates.

Additional benefits of radio paper versus physical newspapers:

- Faster turnaround eliminates 11:30 P.M. deadlines to deliver by 5:30 A.M.
- Elimination of vulnerability to hypercyclical input cost of newsprint.
- No space constraints (can expand size of paper and therefore advertising space as desired).
- Ability to microsegment delivery zones.

EXHIBIT 15-8

COMPETING ELECTRONIC BOOK PRODUCTS

RocketBook—a small, lightweight device with medium memory but long battery life. Partnered with Sharp to help design and manufacture the device, with Levenger and Franklin Electronics to sell it by mail order and retail outlets, with many publishers to provide content, and with Barnes & Noble to sell electronic versions. Consumer focus, especially popular business books for traveling executives. Users are demanding ability to store user files and HTML on device. Sells for $499. Must buy books from barnesandnoble.com.

SoftBook—a large, heavy device with much memory and short battery life. Fewer partners. Some consumer sales but oriented to fleet sales to corporate customers who must publish many pages of documents to mobile workers. Sells for $599 or $299 with 24 months subscription at $19.95/month. Must buy books from proprietary store.

Everybook—a large, heavy device with much memory and short battery life. Focused on selling to the professional/educational market as a replacement for heavy textbooks. Full-color screens with high resolution for precise book reproduction. Sells for $1,000 to $1,500 with two full side-by-side screens. Must use proprietary store.

Librius—a small, lightweight device with limited memory and long battery life. Focused on selling romance novels to consumers. Sells for $199. Must buy novels in proprietary store; priced at 20 to 25% less than paper.

Books   Books represented another large segment of the publishing industry where E Ink's technology might one day become applicable. Jacobson's initial vision was centered on the ability to provide consumers with a single-paper-based book that could be updated with customized content through a wireless network. While newspapers had not received much attention from other display technology companies, electronic books were not a new phenomenon. In fact, in 1999 several electronic book products were scheduled to be available to consumers (see Exhibit 15-8 for a description of competing electronic book products). In addition, Microsoft was already in the process of devising an industry standard for the operating system that would enable electronic books.

E Ink hoped to differentiate, and eventually dominate, the electronic book industry by utilizing the inherently superior display technology of electronic ink. Iuliano and his team intended to comply with whatever standards were developed and believed that an early electronic ink-based book could be ready in two to three years, with the ultimate radio paper version arriving in four or five years.

Although the rewards associated with transforming the publishing industry were great, the investment required for success was not inconsequential. Depending on the business model, Iuliano could envision needing an additional $50 million to $100 million in capital to fully exploit the publishing opportunity.

FINANCING

Despite still having $9 million on hand from E Ink's first round of financing, Iuliano was now in the process of raising still more capital. His upcoming meeting with Eller would hopefully yield a portion of the $20 million in funds he hoped to raise during the second full round of financing. The company was consuming nearly $500,000 in cash each month, and the burn rate was forecasted to increase to nearly $1 million per month as Iuliano ramped up personnel and development efforts. Iuliano estimated that E Ink would need over $16 million to sustain progress over the next five fiscal quarters. He described his motives and strategy for the company's second round financing:

> We are trying to revolutionize an entire industry within five years, so going slow is not an option. We have quite a bit of momentum right now in terms of the attention we are receiving and the progress we are making. This is critical and a second round of financing, despite our cash position, is integral to keeping that momentum.
>
> This round of funding will be used primarily to fund the large-area display business and second-generation technology development. But I can see additional fund-raising over the next few years. It will not be long before we need another $30 to $50 million to launch the flat-panel display business. Shortly thereafter, we will require another infusion to grow our radio paper business. So I intend for this current round of financing to be a mezzanine round that will allow us to prove some things and give us the ability to go public if we so choose.
>
> Sizing a round is about more than money. I am convinced that raising capital more frequently in smaller rounds as the technology is demonstrated will minimize dilution. On the other hand, raising bigger amounts of capital may block out competitors and improve our flexibility. We need to strike the right balance.

CONCLUSION

Everyone involved with E Ink believed in the company's ability to achieve its end goal of radio paper. To attain this goal, Iuliano knew that he and his team of managers and scientists would need to aggressively maneuver past a series of technological, financial, marketing, manufacturing and human resource obstacles (see Exhibit 15-9 for the goals and responsibilities of E Ink functional areas). The pace of business for E Ink was extremely aggressive, with a 1999 schedule including a move into a new facility, ramping up production of large-area displays, more than doubling the number of in-house scientists, achieving demonstrable progress in the area of transistor backplanes, and raising a second round of funding.

While the critical path to success was both disciplined and well thought out, Iuliano knew there were hundreds of things that could go wrong. In particular, Iuliano was focused on choosing the right partners for both financing and technology development. As he prepared for Eller's arrival, he contemplated the journey ahead:

> While we have a lot of people interested in partnering with us, we must be very careful in choosing the right partners. Financing in particular is going to be very important as we will need a lot of capital in a relatively short period of time to achieve our goals. Our current investors are very valuable, but their resources are limited and we can't count on them to finance all of our efforts.
>
> I spend a lot of time thinking about who the right investors are for this opportunity. Venture capitalists are capable of moving very quickly, which is a positive, but it is not clear to me what new VC's will add above and beyond what our current venture capital investors provide. Corporate investors might also be attractive, but they also have drawbacks. Chemistry companies might give us valuable assistance in our R&D efforts, while sign companies could speed up the development and implementation of our large-area display business. Down the road, handheld device manufacturers and publishers could prove to be invaluable in achieving our Phase II and Phase III objectives. The problem with corporate

---

EXHIBIT 15-9

E INK FUNCTIONAL AREA OBJECTIVES

Marketing

E Ink's goal is to distinguish the company as more than a component supplier. Efforts will involve both consumer marketing and industrial marketing campaigns. The company intends to develop a two-tiered strategy with a flagship E Ink brand and product line names for each major product category (large-area, flat-panel, publishing).

Near-term marketing responsibilities include corporate identity and branding, creation of sales demo kits and printed collateral, public relations, and evaluating customer feedback to display designs.

Research & Development

Near-term R&D objectives include optimizing first-generation ink that can be sold, developing enhanced second-generation ink, and adding more layers of patent protection. Following the achievement of near-term objectives, R&D efforts will focus on minimizing the cost to manufacture the ink, optimizing the visual appeal of the displays, further reducing power and voltage requirements, and exploring third-generation ink possibilities.

Engineering

The engineering department is primarily responsible for applying R&D technologies to products. Near-term priorities for the engineering team include designing large-area text displays, developing volume production processes, engineering custom designs for major corporate partners, and building prototypes to support sales activities.

Manufacturing

E Ink's manufacturing employees will develop and control all critical manufacturing processes to commercialize electronic ink in large-area displays, portable flat-panel displays, and publishing applications. The manufacturing strategy consists of demonstration of process capability ready for scale up by E Ink followed by in-house pilot production of selected key process steps. Volume production of most process steps will be maintained at subcontract supply partners and controlled by E Ink technical support staff for conformance to E Ink specifications.

Near-term manufacturing objectives include start-up of new E Ink consolidated facility and scale production of large-area displays.

---

investors is that they tend to move cautiously, and they may want to tie their investments to specific rights and restrictions that would limit our flexibility.

Getting to radio paper is not going to be easy, and there is not much room for error. We need to make the right decisions in so many areas. Who do we partner with for financing and technology development? Can we beat competing technologies to market? How will the company's culture evolve as we grow so quickly? What will our business model look like as we move along the "critical path"? All of these questions represent inflection points in the growth of this business, and the repercussions of making the wrong decisions could be disastrous.

16

Genset: 1989

Pascal Brandys and Marc Vasseur stared at the many napkins spread out on the conference table. Since first meeting six months ago in October 1988 and exchanging ideas, they had held numerous brainstorming sessions in Paris restaurants. They used the napkins to take notes about their strategy for building a biotechnology company. There were many service and product development options to pursue; now they only needed to choose the right ones. Their choices would determine the success or failure of the firm. Had they developed the right strategy to gain a competitive advantage in this growing industry? Was this the opportunity to start the company they had each been waiting for?

Brandys, a 30-year-old international venture capitalist with experience investing in biotech, had always dreamed of starting his own technology company. Brandys knew that because Genset was not sufficiently developed to present to U.S. venture capital firms, he would have to raise all of his money in Europe, with the majority coming from French venture capital. In addition, U.S. venture firms were more accustomed to regional investing. His experience, however, told him that raising money for a biotech company in France would be difficult. How much money could he expect to raise? His business plan outlined a need for 10 million French Francs ($1.7 million), significantly less than he would realistically need to build a global firm with cutting-edge research. In the United States most biotechnology firms raised between $5 and $20 million in their development stage. Was access to top French scientists worth all the disadvantages of starting the company in France? They were preparing their presentation for Sofinnova, the premier French venture capital firm and one of the only ones that could be their lead investor. Brandys was determined to convince the partners that with his management capabilities and Vasseur's scientific expertise, the risks were low and the opportunities were limitless.

CONDITIONS IN FRANCE

Throughout the mid-1980s, the French economy had been characterized by slow growth, low industrial investment, and high unemployment rates (see Exhibit 16-1). The

Research Associate Amy Burroughs prepared this case under the supervision of Professor Paul Gompers as the basis for class discussion rather than to illustrate either effective or ineffective handling of an administrative situation.

EXHIBIT 16-1

FRENCH ECONOMIC INDICATORS

	1982	1983	1984	1985	1986	1987	1988
GDP (1980 FF)[a] (Billions)	2,913	2,934	2,973	3,028	3,098	3,158	3,270
Real increase[a]	2.5%	0.7%	1.3%	1.9%	1.3%	1.9%	3.5%
GDP/capita (1980 FF)[a]	53,482	53,608	54,097	54,891	55,928	56,772	58,518
Real increase[a]	2.0%	0.2%	0.9%	1.5%	1.9%	1.5%	3.1%
Unemployment[a]	8.1%	8.3%	9.7%	10.2%	10.4%	10.5%	10.1%
% change in consumer prices[a]	11.8%	9.6%	7.4%	5.8%	2.5%	3.3%	2.7%
Stock market index	125	210	252	347	516	371	569
Number of French Initial public offerings					2	6	5
Value of French Initial public offerings (millions of U.S. $)					319.3	1,459.9	1,165.2
7-year Interest rate[a]	16.6%	14.6%	13.3%	11.7%	8.7%	9.6%	9.1%
Exchange rate (FF per U.S. $)	6.7	8.3	9.6	7.5	6.5	5.4	6.1

[a] *Source:* EIU Country Profile—France. The Economist Intelligence Unit.

French government had taken a proactive role in stimulating the economy. Among the initiatives to reverse the economic downturn was a 1981 government program to make France a leader in biotechnology by the end of the century. Like many countries around the world, France was responding to the growth of biotech in the United States and the belief that biotech was an important new industry.[1] In 1982, the Ministry of Research and Technology published a plan to carry France's share of world trade in biology-based products from 7 to 10% by the end of the decade. This included a significant investment of government money, an increased focus on research for the country, and a focus on stronger relationships between academic institutions and industry. Estimates, however, showed that the government spent only $10.6 million of the $122.4 million that it had committed to biotechnology R&D from 1983 to 1985.[2]

The government took a multipronged approach to biotechnology development. It funded basic research, owned stock in all major users of the new technology, controlled key banking and financial institutions, and influenced consumption of new products through socialized medicine (see Exhibit 16-2). The French pharmaceutical industry, however, had always been small relative to that in the United States, Germany, and Japan.

One of France's biggest competitive advantages in the biotechnology area was the availability of world-class research and scientists. France had always had a strong base of academic research in microbiology and genetics, including world-famous centers like the Institut Pasteur, INSERM, and INRA[3] (see Exhibit 16-3). The government also en-

---

[1] Margaret Sharpe, "National Policies Towards Biotechnology," *Technovation*, 5 (1987): 283.

[2] Robert T. Yuan, *Biotechnology in Western Europe* (Washington, DC: U.S. Department of Commerce, 1987), p. A-3.

[3] Sharpe, pp. 291–293.

EXHIBIT 16-2

GOVERNMENT INVOLVEMENT IN BIOTECH IN 1987

	Research Funding	Research Institutes	Technology Transfer Institutes	University/ Institute Funding	Industry Funding	Tax Credits	Loans/Grants	Risk Capital
Finland	X		X					
Norway	X	X						
Italy	X			X	X			
Spain	X	X	planned	X	X		X	X
Switzerland	X		limited	limited				
Denmark	X		X	X	X		X	
Sweden	X	X	X	X	X		X	X
Netherlands	X		X	X	X	X	X	X
France	X	X	X	X	X	X	X	X
U.K.	X	X	X	X	X	X	X	X
Germany	X	X	X	X	X	X	X	X
Japan	X	X	X	X	X	X	X	X
United States	X	NIH			X	X		

Source: Robert T. Yuan, *Biotechnology in Western Europe* (Washington, DC: U.S. Department of Commerce, 1987).

couraged private funding of research-focused companies by granting tax credits to individuals who invested in them.

France had never been considered a world center for biotech development. There were a few French biotech firms developing therapeutics, but none had a major presence in the market. Many French scientists considered it a sin to think about commercial applications of their technology. Most of the biotechnology companies were started by scientists who were more interested in a Nobel Prize than in creating products and profits.

In addition to the academic orientation of its scientists, one of the biggest hurdles facing a biotechnology company in France was the availability of experienced management. It was difficult to find French nationals who knew the intricacies of patents, licensing, and business development. Many believed that French biotech suffered from a state of self-imposed isolation. French scientists did not spend extensive time abroad, few technical managers had international experience, and significant numbers of senior government officials and corporate managers were fluent only in French. French companies had been slow to develop foreign markets in the pharmaceutical industry, particularly in North America and Japan.

ENTREPRENEURSHIP AND VENTURE CAPITAL

Certain structural and psychological barriers prevented the growth of a large venture capital and entrepreneurial base in the 1980s. One of the biggest reasons was the aversion of the French toward risk. The words in French for venture capital, "risk capital,"

EXHIBIT 16-3

FRENCH GOVERNMENT RESEARCH AGENCIES INVOLVED IN BIOTECH

	CNRS[a]	INSERM[b]	INRA[c]	Pasteur Institute
# Staff	600 scientists 700 associate scientists 700 technicians	220 scientists 170 associate scientists 500 technicians	8,000 total (1,400 scientists)	400 scientists 200 associate scientists 1000 technicians
Research priorities	Gene expression Molecular genetics and nervous system Molecular genetics and endocrinology Genetic probes and human disease Applications of biotechnology	Molecular biology with emphasis on eukaryotes Cell biology Immunology Biochemical signals & receptors Medical Applications	Soil microbiology Animal health care Plant molecular biology, physiology & biochemistry Enzymes and fermentation technology	Molecular biology of bacteria and their viruses Eukaryotic molecular biology Immunology; vaccines Virology Applications of genetic engineering

[a] Centre National de la Recherche Scientifique (National Center of Scientific Research).

[b] Institut National de la Sante et de la Recherche Medicale (National Institute of Health and Medical Research).

[c] Institut National de la Recherche Agronomique (National Institute of Agronomic Research).

Source: Robert T. Yuan, *Biotechnolgoy in Western Europe* (Washington, DC: U.S. Department of Commerce, 1987).

EXHIBIT 16-4

**GROWTH IN VENTURE CAPITAL
INVESTED IN FRANCE**

Year	Estimated Amount Invested (millions FF)
1980	100–250
1983	700–900
1984	1,100–1,300
1985	1,300–1,500
1986	1,500–1,800
1987	2,000

Source: European Venture Capital Association.

has a negative connotation whereas there are positive feelings toward the words "venture capital" in the United States.

The French people as a whole did not have a strong entrepreneurial spirit. Unlike the United States, most of the engineers and scientists had little or no management experience. It was uncommon for an employee to leave a stable job at a large corporation to start an independent business. One reason for this was a law, originally passed in 1967 and modified in 1985, that held managers and board members personally responsible for the debts of a firm in bankruptcy if the management was found negligible. This meant that venture capitalists often did not get involved in firm management because they might also be held responsible. In addition, French management was often uncomfortable with the idea of giving up independence to investors in the running of their firm.[4] They liked to maintain their authority and did not want to answer to investors and go back to them for additional equity infusions. The exit possibilities for entrepreneurs and investors were also less promising given an underdeveloped public market and the lack of a NASDAQ-type of stock exchange for smaller market capitalization stocks.

Despite these factors, the venture capital industry grew quickly in the late 1980s. The year 1989 was looking like a particularly promising year for entrepreneurs to attract venture funds. The economy was improving and the fiscal environment was favorable for venture capital. Capital gains taxes stood at 15 to 16%.[5] The amount of venture funds invested rose from 100 million to 250 million FF ($17–$40 million) in 1980 to 2,000 million FF ($330 million) in 1987 (see Exhibit 16-4). In 1988, France was second in Europe to the United Kingdom in total venture capital funds available. An estimated 1,297 new investments were made (see Exhibit 16-5). Most French venture firms invested domestically, and the leading industries were consumer and computer-related goods. In France, 5.4% of total investments were made in biotech versus 2% for all of Europe (see Exhibit 16-6).

Large French banks were the source for more than a third of the capital for venture capital funds. The banks either set up dedicated subsidiaries or sponsored exter-

[4] Pierre-Yves Touati, *Le Capital-Risque Regional et Local en France*, (1989), pp. 28–30.

[5] *European Venture Capital Association Journal*, 1989, p. 72.

EXHIBIT 16-5

VENTURE CAPITAL POSITION OF FRANCE VS. OTHER EUROPEAN COUNTRIES IN 1988

Country	Total Funds Available (millions of ECU)	New Funds Raised (millions of ECU)
Total Europe	17,117	3,484
United Kingdom	9,609	1,895
France	2,705	644
Netherlands	1,227	243
Italy	861	238
West Germany	636	144
Belgium	544	62
Spain	430	94
Other	1,105	164

Country	Amount New Investment (millions of ECU)	Number of Investments
Total Europe	3,451	5,078
United Kingdom	2,003	2,104
France	667	1,297
Netherlands	159	684
Italy	169	130
West Germany	105	224
Belgium	75	124
Spain	91	112
Other	182	403

Note: Exchange rate is 7FF per ECU.

Source: European Venture Capital Association.

nally raised funds.[6] Other important venture capital contributors were corporations and insurance companies. Private individuals only contributed 4.6% of the total funds (see Exhibit 16-7). Venture firms were more focused on the expansion of existing firms than funding start-ups (see Exhibit 16-8).

Sofinnova was one of the oldest and most established venture capital firms in France. In 1989, it had $90 million of venture funds invested domestically. It was a pioneer in learning from the experiences of Silicon Valley and seeing the value of funding high-technology startups. Unlike most other French venture capital firms, it was seeking to fund early-stage companies and to become actively involved in their management.

[6] Ibid., p. 71.

EXHIBIT 16-6

PERCENT OF VENTURE CAPITAL INVESTED BY SECTOR IN EUROPE AND FRANCE

	Europe 1988[a]	France 1988[a]	U.S. 1988[b]
Consumer related	24.8%	18.3%	12%
Manufacturing	18.6	5.5	—
Computer related	9.0	13.6	21
Other services	6.9	5.5	—
Industrial products and services	6.3	7.4	6
Financial services	5.1	3.0	—
Other electronics	4.7	9.5	9
Construction	4.2	5.1	—
Chemicals and materials	3.5	4.3	—
Medical/health related	3.0	6.8	12
Transportation	2.3	1.9	—
Biotechnology	2.0	5.4	7
Industrial automation	2.0	1.2	1
Communications	1.8	2.8	12
Agriculture	1.0	1.6	—
Energy	0.5	0.0	1
Other	4.3	8.1	22

[a] *Source:* European Venture Capital Association.

[b] National Venture Capital Association Annual Report. U.S. data for all areas not available and accounted for in "other."

EXHIBIT 16-7

SOURCES OF VENTURE CAPITAL IN 1988

	France[a]		United States[b]	
	Amount ($millions)	% of total	Amount ($millions)	% of total
Banks	270	36%	—	—
Corporate investors	95	13%	324	11%
Insurance companies	82	11%	271	9%
Private individuals	34	5%	249	8%
Pension funds	14	2%	1,355	46%
Endowments/foundations	—	—	341	12%
Foreign investors	—	—	401	14%
Others	176	24%	—	—
Realized capital gains	71	10%	—	—
Total	739		2,947	

[a] *Source:* European Venture Capital Association.

[b] National Venture Capital Association Annual Report. Includes only money directed to private venture capital funds.

EXHIBIT 16-8

**VENTURE CAPITAL INVESTMENT IN FRANCE AND
THE UNITED STATES, BY STAGE, 1988**

FRANCE	Amount of Investment ($ millions)	%	Number of Investments	%
Seed	1.8	0.2%	9	0.7%
Start-up	12.4	16.2	359	27.7
Expansion	46.5	60.9	669	51.6
Replacement capital	10.2	13.3	116	8.9
Buyout	7.2	9.4	144	11.1

Source: European Venture Capital Association.

UNITED STATES	Amount of Investment ($ millions)	%	Number of Investments	%
Seed	88	3%	126	7%
Start-up	265	9	220	12
Other early stages	442	15	328	18
Expansion	1,179	40	902	50
Buyout	855	29	173	10
Other	118	4	68	4

Source: National Venture Capital Association Annual Report.

BIOTECHNOLOGY WORLDWIDE

Biotechnology was seen as a revolutionary change in the development process for pharmaceuticals. For years, drug company scientists had worked on new products by randomly testing different compounds. They would explore exotic lands and return with bags of dirt, plants, or mold that they could test against a variety of microbes and viruses to see if it could be the next penicillin. The success of this approach, however, was fading as the wars against old diseases, microbial infections like tuberculosis or pneumonia, were won and new challenges arose in areas like heart disease, arthritis, and Alzheimer's disease.[7]

From a scientific perspective, two breakthroughs in the mid-1970s were pivotal. The first was recombinant DNA: the ability to alter genes with the objective of altering the production of proteins. DNA is the code that carries the blueprints for all living cells. A sequence of DNA makes up a gene that directs the cells' "machinery" to manufacture a specific protein. Scientists were able to insert a piece of foreign DNA into a cell that could reproduce and spread the desired genetic change. The second breakthrough was the development of monoclonal antibodies. Antibodies are critical to the immune system's response to foreign threats such as viruses or bacteria. Antibod-

---

[7] Robert Teitelman, *Gene Dreams. Wall Street, Academia and the Rise of Biotechnology* (1989), pp. 15–16.

ies are responsible for identifying foreign intruders into the body. In the past, it had been impossible to generate pure antibodies. This was because, to get an antibody against a flu virus, a researcher would inject the virus into a sheep and collect the resulting antibodies. However, the sheep would produce many different types of antibodies that together would help the sheep's body fight off the flu. The ability to generate monoclonal antibodies was critical to disease research. These discoveries led to an explosion of biotechnology companies and a totally different approach to drug development.

Biotechnology was not only about innovative science. Financing this new technology was prohibitively expensive. In the late 1970s, the interest of investors in biotechnology changed the path of biomedical research and offered scientists a way of getting around the established peer review system and the dominance of institutions like the National Institutes of Health.[8] One of the biggest catalysts for this change occurred in October 1980 when Genentech, the first large biotechnology company in the world, launched its IPO. A venture capitalist and inventor of recombinant DNA technology joined forces to create the firm and took it public before it had a single product on the market. Its human insulin product would not be approved until 1984, and another drug, interferon, was not approved until several years after that. The company's IPO set a record for the largest price increase on the first day of trading. Its shares jumped from the offering price of $35 per share to $89 per share in the first 20 minutes. This offering sent a shock wave through the industry and caused dozens of similar companies to offer their stock to the public. By 1987, over 100 public biotechnology companies had raised about $500 million in new capital from the public markets. This did not include the millions of dollars raised from large pharmaceutical companies and VC firms over the same period. Many people called it biomania.[9]

THE GENSET BUSINESS OPPORTUNITY

Vasseur was one of the top French scientists in the area of molecular biology and had the distinction of earning his academic tenure at an unusually young age. He had held numerous positions at some of the most prestigious research institutions in France. Vasseur, however, had a passion beyond scientific research. He found that much of his scientific work in the laboratories became tedious over time, and he did not want to rely solely on the government for funding. He lamented over the many commercial opportunities that he dreamt about but did not have the management ability or capital to pursue. He spoke with many people about potential applications of his technical expertise in an attempt to find a business partner. A partner with the management vision and talents could not be found until a friend introduced him to Brandys.

Brandys had weaved his way through several jobs, all with the intention of starting his own technology firm. It had been a dream for him since he received his Master's in Economic Systems in 1983 from Stanford where he had his first exposure to technology start-ups in Silicon Valley. Over the next six years, he became a successful venture capitalist with extensive contacts in France, Japan, Britain, and the United States. Much of his work focused on relationship building among pharmaceutical, biotechnology, and venture capital firms. He was a partner in a Pan-European venture capital fund based in London where he had made investments in well-known biotech companies and served

---

[8] Ibid., pp. 4, 8.
[9] Ibid., pp. 11–14.

on several boards. During this time, he had considered several entrepreneurial opportunities. None of them, however, excited him enough to write a business plan and seek funding until he met Vasseur. (See Exhibit 16-9 for a full description of the founders' backgrounds.)

At the urging of a mutual friend, Vasseur and Brandys met over dinner to discuss their entrepreneurial vision. Vasseur told Brandys about an exciting new technology called PCR that would allow scientists to amplify DNA, that is, to create millions of copies of a single DNA fragment. Prior to the discovery, scientists had only one copy of each piece of DNA that they studied. Both Vasseur and Brandys recognized that this would substantially increase the study of DNA and the market for services to support this research. One area that interested them in particular was the use of antisense technology for new drug development. Rather than inserting new DNA into cells like recombinant DNA technology, antisense involved using DNA fragments to block the production of diseased proteins. They felt that scientists in France were well positioned to advance antisense and develop innovative and proprietary pharmaceuticals.

Brandys and Vasseur met over the course of several months to discuss various strategies for their business plan. Their personalities were a good fit from the start, and each recognized the complementary talents of the other. There were many meetings where Vasseur would explain the technological developments as simply as possible to Brandys and others where Brandys explained to Vasseur details about the venture capital market, IPOs, accounting, and other management expertise.

French investors told Brandys from the beginning that they would not have the understanding or patience for a long-term investment in a biotechnology company focused solely on research and one that would incur significant losses in the initial years. To address this concern, Brandys and Vasseur needed to develop some immediate revenue and position the business as a low-risk opportunity to make it attractive to investors.

This led to a three-phase business strategy. In the short term, Brandys planned to generate revenues by selling short strands of DNA called oligonucleotides. The demand for these strands was increasing because they were becoming a basic building block for genetic research with the widespread use of DNA amplification. In the medium term, the company would develop both diagnostic services and diagnostic kits to detect major diseases. This was becoming a well-developed area worldwide and would represent a majority of the company's business in three to four years. They felt that the company's scientists were well positioned to make advances in diagnostics. In the long term, the company hoped to develop drugs based on antisense technology. This research was preliminary and was not incorporated into the financial projections of the business plan. Brandys, however, had high hopes for the future of antisense or some other future technology based on PCR and its ability to contribute to the company's long-term value.

OLIGONUCLEOTIDES

An oligonucleotide is a short fragment of synthetic DNA. Vasseur knew that as amplification technology became more widespread, oligonucleotides would become routine tools in the molecular biology lab. Large molecular biology labs were not able to produce their own oligonucleotides because it was a complex process. The majority of researchers had been getting their supply from scientists who made custom orders. As the demand increased, the problem was that no one had yet figured out how to automate the process. This made production both expensive and slow.

To address this need, Vasseur approached his friend and colleague, Dr. Luc d'Auriol, and asked him to join Genset as a founder and head of oligonucleotide

EXHIBIT 16-9

BACKGROUNDS OF COMPANY FOUNDERS

Mr. Pascal Brandys, Chief Executive Officer and Director—age 30 Mr. Brandys was a partner of Eurocontinental Ventures, a pan-European ECU 27 million venture capital fund operating in London. He has structured and monitored investments in several European biotechnology firms, including Plant Genetic Systems and Innogenetics. In 1986, he founded Unihon Services Limited in Japan and acted as CEO until 1988. During this period, he was involved in the management of a ¥2 billion Japanese venture capital fund, Unihon Partners, and initiated equity participation in BioEurope and Immunotech Partners from Japanese investors. He also negotiated agreements with Orsan and Clause, two major French biotechnology companies, regarding corporate finance activities in the Japanese market. Mr. Brandys joined the Ministry for Industry in Paris in 1983 after his graduate studies and was in charge for one year of the development of projects involving technology in France. He subsequently joined the French Industrial Development Agency as deputy director of the Tokyo office until 1986, and he had extensive experience with international corporate venturing. His university education included both a major in economics from Ecole Polytechnique in Paris and a major in civil engineering from Ecole Nationale des Ponts et Chausees. He also received a Master of Science in Economic Systems at Stanford in 1983.

Luc d'Auriol, PhD, Chief Operating Officer and Director—age 39 Mr. d'Auriol was in charge of research at CNRS and was Staff Scientist at the Institute for the Study of Blood Diseases at Saint-Louis Hospital in Paris. In 1989, he was in charge of the PCR program for monitoring cancer cells in leukemia patients, HLA markers, and for the epidemiology survey of HIV and HTLV infections. From 1983 to 1986, he was in charge of the improvement of oligonucleotide synthesis technologies and use in molecular biology. During this period, he was involved in numerous collaborations, both in academic institutions and hospitals. As a graduate student, he worked in the Laboratory of Retroviruses on the interactions between cell differentiation and retrovirus expression. Dr. d'Auriol was one of the first French molecular biologist to enter the field of oligonucleotide synthesis and applications including PCR. He had 30 publications, and was invited to give seminars and conferences to numerous groups and prestigious academic institutions.

Marc Vasseur, PhD, Chief Scientific Officer—age 39 Mr. Vasseur was Professor of Virology at the University of Paris and Head of the Virology Department. He was a molecular biologist, specializing in genetic engineering applied to the analysis of genetic structure and regulation. From 1980 to 1987, prior to joining the University, he was a scientist at the Pasteur Institute in the laboratory of Cell Genetic directed by Professor Francois Jacob. During this period, he was responsible for the analysis of molecular mechanisms involved in the regulation of gene expression during the early steps of embryonic differentiation. From 1975 to 1980, he worked at the Institute for Cancer Research on DNA tumor viruses expression. He received his Ph.D. in Biochemistry in 1980. As a graduate student, he worked from 1971 to 1974 in the laboratory of nucleic acid chemistry in the Institute of Biological Chemistry on post-transcriptionnal modifications of RNA. From 1985 to date, he had also been a consultant to the International Center for Dermatological Research where he was advisor for the molecular biology aspects of the antiviral drug development program. Professor Vasseur had 16 years of experience in the field of molecular biology and nucleic acid analysis and over 35 publications. He was also author of a book devoted to Tumor Virology and Cancer.

production. In France, d'Auriol was the main supplier of custom synthesized oligonucleotides for other French labs. He filled all of the orders from his university lab. He did not, however, have the resources to expand and develop a system to automate the service. Vasseur knew that d'Auriol had more expertise in oligonucleotide production than any other French scientist and possibly any scientist in the world. Vasseur had confidence that d'Auriol could develop a proprietary process for Genset to automate production and become the leading supplier of oligonucleotides in France. d'Auriol also gave Genset more credibility in both the academic and investment community.

Genset planned to develop a large catalog of standard oligonucleotides for viruses, bacteria, parasites, and genetic disorders. The company would have an advantage through its early entry into the market and a business based on rapid delivery (within 48 hours) and high quality. Researchers and technicians in large public and private R&D or clinical laboratories would be the firm's primary customers. The oligonucleotides would be sold exclusively through a catalog and would require no direct sales support.

Prior to the founding of Genset, d'Auriol sold over 400 customized oligonucleotides at over 2,000 FF per unit without any marketing or sales effort. Brandys believed that this market would grow by more than 50% per year in the near future and that the company could contribute to this demand by aiding the diffusion of DNA amplification techniques. In 1990, the company expected to be the sole producer in France, but it would encounter competition over time as the market grew. In 1990, Genset would sell only in France and expected to expand over the next three years to other EEC countries. By 1993, Brandys projected that Genset would garner 19% of the French market and 6% of other EEC markets, with total revenue from oligonucleotide sales of $6.4 million francs (about U.S. $1 million).

DIAGNOSTICS

Diagnostics would use strands of synthetic DNA to analyze genes and profoundly facilitate diagnostic medicine, including such things as pre- and postnatal analysis of genetic diseases, analysis of a wide range of infectious diseases, and basically anything hard-wired within the genetic code. Genset would first develop a diagnostic services lab in 1990 and then move into selling diagnostic kits by 1991.

The company would offer diagnostic services primarily through its lab in Paris. The company would charge a fixed fee to the lab for each major diagnostic test offered. The company planned to launch diagnostic services for the following areas:

1. *HPV.* Three percent of the population carried this virus that was acknowledged as a primary risk factor for cervical cancer development in women. Since the sexually active population at risk in the Paris area alone exceeded 100,000 women, the company believed the lab could easily market over 1,000 tests per year.

2. *Chlamydia.* Five percent to 20% of the population carried this virus that was responsible for disease and infertility in women. Diagnostic routines were expensive and required several days for cell culture. The lab could market its fast, accurate, and noninvasive test to a population of at least 100,000 women in Paris.

3. *Hepatitis B/Herpes.* All Paris hospitals were considering this type of test for all pregnant women because 1% of pregnant women carried this virus that

caused grave consequences for children. However, there was no fast or reliable service offered. Brandys believed that the lab could command a sizable share of the 300,000 test market.

4. *Prenatal testing* for genetic disorders was an emerging business in France and received support from the government. In 1987, there were 14,000 genetic tests, and the market was growing at 50% per year. Genset's technology was competitive and would focus on chromosomal anomalies, particularly for disorders in the X chromosome that cause serious diseases like muscular dystrophy and hemophilia. Brandys expected the lab to sell at least 500 tests per year at a price of 2,000 FF each (U.S. $333)

5. *Periodontal disease* was the leading cause of teeth loss among adults. Treatment of this disease was significantly improved by early diagnosis. Research showed that there were over 200 dentists in Paris concerned enough about this disease to order 20 tests per week at a cost of 200 FF (U.S. $33) per test. The lab expected to capture at least 5% of this market after four years with a fast and reliable service.

There were other areas that Brandys and Vasseur decided not to pursue. For example, the market for HIV testing was growing at a rapid rate. Although it was impossible to know, they thought that less expensive tests for HIV could be developed and a need for a genetic test would be low. There were also opportunities to develop forensic testing capabilities, but this raised some legal and competitive issues.

Genset's initial customer for diagnostic services would be the reference laboratory. The lab would provide diagnostic services to MDs working in comprehensive health-care centers and hospitals or to other clinical laboratories. The head of the laboratory would work directly with MDs and clinicians as well as major health-care centers to sell the diagnostic services.

Given sales in the five targeted areas, Brandys predicted that the lab would generate revenues of 1.25 million FF in 1990 and grow to 4 million FF in 1993. Genset would charge the lab a fixed fee per type of test and collect the fee over four equal yearly installments from 1990 to 1993. These fees would bring between 700,000 FF and 900,000 FF of Genset revenue per year.

By 1991, Brandys hoped to develop a second generation of products—a proprietary line of DNA diagnostic kits called DNAgnostic®. In 1989, there were fewer than 20 diagnostic kits approved and marketed in the world. The market for these tests was growing quickly, however, particularly in the United States. The company would focus on two large and growing markets in the viral disease areas of HPV and Herpes CMV. There were no suitable diagnostic kits for these two infectious diseases. The company's kits would have a competitive advantage in the areas of sample size, preparation, accuracy and automation. The founders expected to command a large share of the French market and a smaller share of the European market, which would generate revenues of 2 million FF in 1991 and grow quickly to 20 million FF by 1993. The company would market its test to large clinical laboratories and hospitals. The founders did not believe that there was a big opportunity for taking these tests into individual physician offices.

Since the technology was not fully developed, there was a possibility that the company would adjust its product development plan and focus on other disease diagnostics as the market and technical capabilities evolved. The customer would be the MDs, pharmacists, and technicians in labs. The company would use its own small, highly trained sales force to sell to large health-care centers. There were also possibilities for negotiating licensing or distribution agreements with producers outside of France, particularly in the United States, who had complementary products for the French market and would like to use Genset's marketing and sales capabilities in France.

THERAPEUTICS

Although not included in the business plan for fear of scaring investors, the founders' long-term agenda was to use the company's developing expertise in DNA to move into the development of therapeutics. The third-phase product would be the "blockbuster" that would generate substantial value.

One potential area of exploration was the use of antisense technology to treat genetic diseases. Antisense was discovered in 1985, but no one really knew how to apply it. Vasseur felt that the advent of the amplification technology would make antisense development significantly easier. Vasseur had recently opened a molecular virology laboratory with top scientists devoted to looking more closely at antisense technology.

Brandys, however, wanted to keep Genset's options open. The knowledge they would gain by being in the oligonucleotide and diagnostic markets would help them assess potential blockbuster markets. He felt that Genset would have to invest $20 to $30 million in three to four years once they decided to target a specific technology. Brandys was certain, however, that any revenues from therapeutics would be at least 8 to 10 years away.

THE GENSET PLAN

Competition

Genset competition in both France and Europe was limited; Brandys had explicitly designed the strategy to avoid any direct competition.

In France, there were a few small biotech companies, but none had the same focus or management talent to compete with Genset. Appligene, a small four-year-old company, had limited capital to market general products for molecular biology but did not offer DNA probe services. Bioprobe had recently been launched to exploit a technology for labeling DNA probes, but the Genset founders did not view this technology as essential to diagnostic services or products. Neither company had the capability for oligonucleotide synthesis. The competitor with the most potential—Codgene—was a company that offered DNA fingerprinting for legal and forensic applications and had the support of well-regarded scientists and institutions. It could have been a competitor for some segments of diagnostic kits, but it was not expected to compete in the DNA probe market or the diagnostic services market.

In Europe, its primary competitors were two British companies, Cellmark Diagnostics and British Biotechnology Ltd. Both had the resources, scientific expertise, and management talent to become serious competitors in the medium term for oligonucleotide distribution and some diagnostic services. Brandys had access to their current business plans and knew that they did not plan to move into the segments selected by Genset. If they changed their plans, Genset would have at least a two-year head start in these areas. None of these competitors currently planned to move into the therapeutic areas that Genset would target.

Several U.S. companies were pursuing areas related to Genset's core business. None of them could compete in the area of oligonucleotide synthesis or diagnostic services because customer proximity was critical. For diagnostic kits, companies like Enzo Biochem, Gen-Probe, Gene-Trak Systems, Molecular Biosystems, Oncogene Sciences, and Oncor had the resources to compete but were not targeting the same market segments. For therapeutic applications using antisense technology, Gilead Sciences had been recently launched in California with the support of Menlo Ventures.

Financing

Brandys knew that he had to minimize the company's need for money from investors. Most biotechnology companies in the United States could raise between $5 and $10 million in their initial financing round, but Brandys's experience told him that his goal to raise 10 million FF ($1.7 million) was more reasonable given the state of the French capital markets and biotech industry. Without any other successful French biotech company to model itself after, it was more difficult to sell to investors. Brandys wrote a business plan showing that the company would turn a profit in only two years and would then sustain itself for at least another three years without another equity infusion (see Exhibits 16-10 through 16-12). On paper, he projected the majority of his business in France and no business outside of Europe because investors would feel insecure about relying on foreign markets to earn their needed return. Brandys felt it was a conservative plan. In reality, he knew that he would want to raise at least $20 to $30 million in the future to realize his aspiration of turning Genset into a leading international biotech firm with cutting-edge research and alliances with foreign pharmaceutical companies.

The company would keep investment in facilities low by leasing space in the Hall des Biotechnolgies at the University of Paris. This group of labs was specifically devoted to biotech R&D. Vasseur had already secured a two-year lease with a possibility of extending it to four. He thought this location at a prestigious academic institution in the center of Paris would be helpful for developing relationships with research laboratories and giving a positive image to potential customers. Brandys knew that as soon as the company grew large enough to merit its own facilities, he would have to raise more money.

Most of the expenses for initial R&D would be covered through outside revenues like oligonucleotide sales, research grants, contract revenues with public institutions and collaborative research with private corporations. The company would also generate research through the funding of university scientists in exchange for rights associated with the results.

Grants offered by the French Ministry for Research, ANVAR (Aid to Innovation Program) and the EEC covered 50% of the R&D expenses incurred by a private group on specific projects. So far, all reasonable biotech projects submitted to the French Ministry had received funding. Genset Founders were sure that they would be able to cover 50% of all expenses related to the DNAgnostic development and a sizable share of other R&D expenses through such grants. The 1 million FF for research grants shown in the financial statements for 1990 and 1991 were viewed as highly conservative.

Brandys was committed to making sure the contract research would be limited to projects that were in line with the company's research objectives and only involved a small amount of incremental work. The company would retain production and marketing rights on any researched oligonucleotide.

EXHIBIT 16-10

GENSET PROJECTED INCOME STATEMENT (,000S OF FF)

	1989	1990	1991	1992	1993
Revenues					
Oligonucleotide sales	0	1,600	3,200	4,800	6,400
DNAgnostic sales	0	0	2,000	10,000	20,000
Contract revenues	0	2,000	3,000	3,000	3,000
Laboratory revenues	250	950	950	900	900
Gross revenues	250	4,550	9,150	18,700	30,300
Capitalized research[a]	698	2,267	2,889	3,571	4,193
Sales commissions	0	160	520	1,480	2,640
Net Revenues	948	6,657	11,519	20,791	31,853
Cost of Sales:					
R&D personnel	450	1,140	1,380	1,820	2,060
Subcontracted R&D expenses	0	500	750	750	100
Other personnel	100	200	420	820	1,020
Chemicals for oligos	800	1,600	200	300	400
Supplies for kits	0	0	125	500	1,000
Rent	0	100	200	300	400
Services	50	100	200	300	400
Laboratory supplies	150	400	500	700	800
Depreciation	650	800	1040	1190	1210
R&D amortization[b]	140	593	1171	1885	2724
Total Cost of Sales	2,340	5,433	5,986	8,565	10,114
Gross Margin	−1,392	1,224	5,533	12,226	21,739
Sales, General, and Administrative Expenses:					
Personnel	1175	2350	2500	3000	3450
Travel	500	500	500	600	700
Advertising	500	500	700	900	1,000
Other	500	600	700	850	1,000
Total	2,675	3,950	4,400	5,350	6,150
Operating Margin	−4,067	−2,726	1,133	6,876	15,589
Interest income	672	183	30	211	1,005
Net Income[c]	−3,395	−2,543	1,163	7,087	16,594

[a] French accounting standards allowed capitalization of all R&D personnel expenses, and other capitalized R&D expenses were set to 55% of R&D personnel expenses. In the case of Genset, they could also capitalize the subcontracted R&D expense.

[b] French accounting rules allow R&D to be amortized linearly over five years.

[c] No tax is paid until after 1993 due to tax exemptions and carried deficits.

Source: Company documents.

EXHIBIT 16-11

GENSET STATEMENT OF CASH FLOW (,000S OF FF)

	1989	1990	1991	1992	1993
Sources:					
Cash flow	−2,606	−1,150	3,374	10,162	19,628
Paid-in capital	10,000				
Research grants	—	1,000	1,000	—	—
Tax credit-research	—	329	800	—	—
Total	7,395	179	5,174	10,162	19,628
Uses:					
Investments	3,250	750	1,200	750	100
Research	698	2,267	2,889	3,571	4,193
Operating capital		400	900	2,400	2,900
Total	3,948	3,417	4,989	6,721	7,193
Net cash	3,447	209	394	3,835	16,270

Source: Company documents.

EXHIBIT 16-12

GENSET PROJECTED BALANCE SHEET (,000S OF FF)

	1989	1990	1991	1992	1993
Assets:					
Cash	3,447	209	394	3,835	16,270
Accounts receivable	—	400	1,300	3,700	6,600
PPE	2,600	2,550	2,710	2,270	1,160
Research	558	2,232	3,950	5,637	7,106
Total Assets	6,605	5,391	8,355	15,442	31,136
Liabilities and Equity:					
Research grants	—	1,000	2,000	2,000	2,000
Accumulated earnings	−3,395	−5,938	−4,775	2,313	18,007
Tax credit-research		329	1,129	1,129	1,129
Paid-in capital	10,000	10,000	10,000	10,000	10,000
Total Liabilities and Equity	6,605	5,391	8,355	15,442	31,136

Source: Company documents.

EXHIBIT 16-13

FINANCIALS FOR SELECTED GENETICS-FOCUSED BIOTECHNOLOGY COMPANIES (MILLIONS OF DOLLARS)

	1986	1987	1988	1989
CISTRON BIOTECHNOLOGY				
Sales	$0.91	$0.60	$0.75	$1.26
SG&A	NA	NA	NA	NA
Cap Ex	$0.08	$0.17	NA	$0.00
Op Inc Bef Dep	−$1.72	−$2.58	−$1.55	$0.40
Net Inc	−$1.96	−$2.58	−$2.07	$0.30
Tot Assets	$0.84	$1.99	$0.63	$0.82
Current Assets	$0.07	$1.37	$0.20	$0.49
Current Liabilities	$1.68	$0.50	$1.19	$1.38
Debt	$0.76	$0.00	$0.00	$0.00
Net Worth	−$1.25	$1.17	−$0.92	−$0.62
Beta	NA	NA	NA	NA
P/E Ratio	NM	NM	NM	NM
GENOME THERAPEUTICS				
Sales	$10.43	$11.12	$14.91	$11.51
SG&A	$7.24	$6.00	$6.86	$7.79
Cap Ex	$2.83	$2.15	$1.12	$1.11
Op Inc Bef Dep	−$2.34	−$1.22	$0.09	−$2.98
Net Inc	−$2.35	−$1.59	−$0.86	−$4.11
Tot Assets	$21.54	$19.52	$19.50	$15.18
Current Assets	$15.88	$12.76	$13.10	$9.28
Current Liabilities	$2.18	$1.52	$2.10	$1.80
Debt	$0.00	$0.00	$0.58	$0.23
Net Worth	$19.23	$17.82	$17.11	$13.10
Beta	NA	NA	NA	1.65
P/E Ratio	NM	NM	NM	NM

Source: Compustat.

EXHIBIT 16-14

INVESTMENT HISTORY OF BIOTECHNOLOGY FIRMS

Round Number	Number of Companies	Amount Invested ($ millions)	Pre-money Valuation ($ millions)
1	352	$3.39	$7.05
		[$1.78]	[$2.05]
2	261	$5.31	$13.56
		[$3.75]	[$7.0]
3	180	$7.25	$24.63
		[$5.20]	[$15.5]
4	136	$10.30	$45.52
		[$7.0]	[$35.24]
5	85	$16.44	$67.4
		[$10.8]	[$47.8]
6	40	$19.94	$98.05
		[$16.05]	[$67.6]

The table tabulates the investment history of 352 biotechnology companies. The number of companies receiving financing at each round is indicated along with the average [medians are in brackets] amount invested in the round in millions of dollars and the average [medians are in brackets] pre-money valuation in millions of dollars. The declining number of firms in later rounds is caused by some firms not receiving additional follow-on venture financing.

Source: VentureOne.

Brandys planned to actively pursue collaborative research with large private pharmaceutical and health-care companies. These agreements would help cover the expenses for the long-term therapeutic projects. The partner would help fund the research and would receive exclusive production and distribution rights in a specific geographic zone. Brandys had experience with these types of partnerships and felt that he could negotiate these deals with companies, particularly in Japan. Conservative estimates were that these collaborative research partnerships would bring in $1 million FF in 1990 and 1991, and $2 million in 1992 and 1993.

Conclusion

Brandys and Vasseur had one more week to put the finishing touches on his business plan before meeting with Sofinnova. He sometimes wondered if he was doing the right thing by leaving his position as a partner at Eurocontinental Ventures. Although he knew that he wanted to start a company someday, maybe he should wait until he was older and had more experience. Given his position as a venture capitalist, it was possible that he would find something better than the Genset opportunity.

He also wondered what investors would think about his plan. Was it possible that he was being too conservative? Ten million FF was a meager amount of money to start a biotech company. In the ideal case, he would like to raise 50 million FF to give him-

EXHIBIT 16-15

ANNUALIZED VOLATILITY OF THE RETURNS OF 75 BIOTECHNOLOGY FIRMS

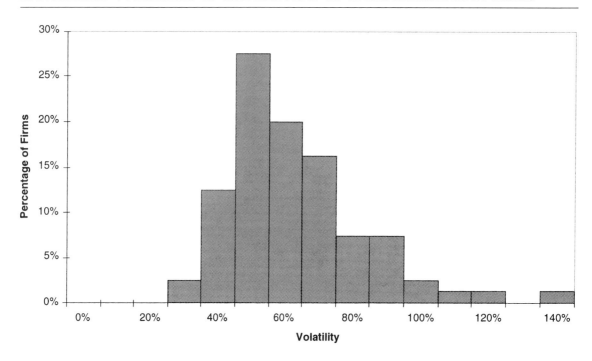

This chart plots the annualized volatility of 75 biotechnology firms' common stocks. Daily volatility was calculated for each stock from the 15th trading day subsequent to the stocks' initial public offering until the end of the third year of trading, with returns observable for approximately 745 trading days. The mean annualized volatility for this sample is 68%, and the median volatility is 67%. In 37% of the 51,771 trading days, these stocks experienced a zero return. The stocks experienced single-day returns exceeding 3%, 5%, and 10% on 31%, 16%, and 4% of all trading days, respectively.

Source: Aberlyn Capital Management: July 1993. Harvard Case No. 294–083.

self more flexibility and the ability to grow faster. The downside of asking for more was that he might scare away his investors and might never get the chance to go back. Maybe he should try to raise money outside of France where investors had more tolerance for risk. Maybe he was crazy for even trying to start a biotechnology company in France.

Brandys and Vasseur looked down at the napkins once again. It would be another late night. They ordered two more cappuccinos and sat down to revise their plan.

17

A Note on Private Equity Securities

IN THE BEGINNING, THERE WAS COMMON STOCK . . .

Common stock is the basic unit of ownership. It does not carry any special rights outside of those described in the company charter and bylaws. It gives the holder ownership, but that ownership is subordinated to (i) all government claims (read "taxes"), (ii) all regulated employee claims (e.g., pension obligations), (iii) all trade debt (accounts receivable), (iv) all bank debt, and (v) all forms of preferred stock. Specifically, were the company liquidated—or sold in an asset sale—the common shareholder stands behind all of those other stakeholders before getting the residual value, that is, what's left after all other obligations are satisfied.

Typically, venture capitalists do not buy common stock. The fundamental reason is illustrated by the following example:

Joe Flash has a great idea for a new Internet company and goes to his local venture capitalist, Rex Finance. Joe and Rex agree that $1.5 million will fund the project to the next big value accretion point, and they further agree to a 50.05/49.95 split, with Joe holding the majority stake. But contrary to standard venture practice, perhaps because the competition to finance Joe's deal is so great, Rex agrees to an all common stock structure. Therefore, immediately after the closing, the company has an implied enterprise value of $3 million (since the market price that Rex paid was $1.5 million for 49.95%), one employee (Joe), one class of tangible assets (cash) and some intangible assets (Joe's Power Point slides and a business plan).

On the day of the closing as they walk out of the lawyers' office, Joe bumps into his old friend, John Terrific, who is Vice President for Business Development of WooWee!, a public Internet company valued in the market at just over $12 billion. WooWee! needs ideas and talent to maintain the promise of their "full" market valuation, so John pulls Joe aside and offers him $2 million for Joe's new company. Seeing a

Senior Lecturer Felda Hardymon and Professor Josh Lerner prepared this note as the basis for class discussion.

quick return on the hours he put in writing his business plan, and realizing WooWee! will use their considerable resources and market clout to enter the market ahead of him should he decline their offer, Joe accepts the offer.

How is the pie divided? Joe and Rex each get $1 million from WooWee! So in a matter of minutes, Joe's investment goes from $0 (sweat equity) to $1 million, while Rex's investment goes from $1.5 million (cash) to $1 million. Rex was powerless through the whole process; and WooWee! was able to recruit Joe and own his idea for a mere $500,000 since they end up with the $1.5 million (less the legal fees) that was in Joe's company. How could Rex have avoided this disaster?

Most venture securities have three features, any one of which would have saved Rex from having to explain to his partners how he lost $500,000 in an afternoon:

1. Preferred stock.
2. Vesting of founder, management, and key employee shares.
3. Covenants and supermajority provisions.

This note will briefly discuss each with the major variations commonly used in practice.

Key to all of these structural features is the concept of the entrepreneur earning his equity through value creation. In the preceding example, Rex was valuing Joe's company based on its potential value, not on its current tangible value. In a perfect, frictionless world, Rex's money might be metered into Joe's company precisely in proportion to value being created and to the expenses incurred. But in the real world entrepreneurs need to finance ahead of their expenses. Moreover, value is created in lumps coincident with important events like first proof of product feasibility, first customer shipment, and major successes in the marketplace, and so on. Venture capital exists to bridge between such value accretion events; at the same time, the entrepreneur's stake should not be perfected until he or she has delivered on the promised value. This is the basis of most deviations of typically used venture securities from common stock. In the above example, Joe had not *earned* his equity interest at the time of the WooWee! buyout, and that violated the principle of reward for performance.

PREFERRED STOCK

Preferred stock has a *liquidation preference* over common stock: that is, in the event of sale or liquidation of the company, the preferred stock gets paid ahead of the common stock. There must be a face value to preferred stock, which is the amount that gets paid to the preferred stock before moving on to paying the common stock. Generally, the face value of a preferred stock in a private equity transaction is the cost basis the venture capitalist pays for the stock. If in the original example Rex had invested his money in Joe's company in the form of preferred stock, then when WooWee! purchased Joe's company, Rex's $1.5 million would have been returned to him through a redemption of the preferred stock. But how would the remainder $500,000 been divided? That leads to the variations of preferred stock used in private equity transactions.

Redeemable Preferred Redeemable preferred, sometimes called "straight preferred," is preferred stock that has no convertibility into equity. Its intrinsic value is therefore its face value plus any dividend rights it carries.[1] In most ways it behaves in a capital structure like deeply subordinated debt. Redeemable preferred stock always carries a negotiated term specifying when it *must* be redeemed by the company—typically, the sooner of a public offering or five to eight years. It is used in private equity transactions in combination with common stock or warrants. For example, had Rex agreed with Joe to the same 50.05/49.95 split, but had specified that his investment would be in the form of a redeemable preferred stock with $1.5 million face value plus 49.95% of the common stock, then the WooWee! transaction would have first redeemed out the straight preferred stock ($1.5 million to Rex) and the remaining $500,000 would have been split proportionally to the ownership of common stock ($250,000 each to Rex and to Joe).

Had the company gone on to a successful public offering, Rex could have expected his initial $1.5 million investment to be returned through a redemption of the redeemable preferred without affecting his basic ownership position held in common stock. He would, in effect, be getting his money back *and* keeping his investment. This aspect of "double-dipping" is sometimes troubling to entrepreneurs. Moreover, when a material portion of the proceeds of a public offering is used to redeem out a venture capitalist's preferred stock, the public market value of the company can be adversely affected. These negatives of the redeemable preferred[2] led to the use of convertible preferred stock in private equity transactions.

Convertible Preferred Stock Convertible preferred stock is preferred stock that can be converted *at the shareholder's option* into common stock. This forces the shareholder to choose whether he will take his returns through the liquidation feature or through the underlying common equity position. Clearly, if the value being offered for the company exceeds the implied total enterprise value at the time of the investment, then the shareholder will convert the preferred stock to common stock in order to realize his portion of the gain in value.

---

[1] Generally, venture securities carry no dividends, or defer dividends considerably out into the future, because venture capitalists are capital gains oriented. In fact, many venture partnerships do not grant a carried interest to the general partners on dividends received. Moreover, dividends can limit the ability of a growth company to raise capital since it raises the question: "Why are you returning cash to your shareholders when you need it to grow?" Finally, dividends create an asymmetry of rewards between the preferred shareholders (typically the investors) and the common shareholders (typically the founders, management, and key employees), which in turn leads to a misalignment of incentives between investor and company. Large public companies often issue preferred stock with high dividends, which are themselves preferential to common stock dividends, in order to attract certain classes of investors who desire high-income streams. The use of preferred stock in venture securities is based on the preference value and the "earn out" principle and should not be confused with this common use of preferred stock in large public companies. We will not discuss dividends in this note since they generally do not play a large role in venture securities.

[2] One might suggest a solution to this problem of assigning more of the value of the unit to the common stock. However, it is accepted practice to assign as much value as possible to the preferred. There are three reasons for this practice: 1. Tax deferral—Since redemption of preferred stock is simply a return of capital with no associated gain, there is no tax on redemption. Moreover, since the preferred is much more likely to be redeemed before the common is sold, then putting more value in the preferred portion of the unit defers tax. 2. Security—The preference is protection from the common receiving value before it is earned and so it makes since to put as much in that instrument as possible. 3. Pricing employee incentive shares—In declaring a fair market value for incentive stock option exercise prices or for employee purchase plans, a board of directors wants as low a share price as possible in order to embed as much value as possible in the incentive shares. Since these incentive plans use common stock as their underlying equity, the board can use the "cheap common" part of the transaction as the basis of a low share price.

In our example, if Rex had proposed a convertible preferred stock, then he would have received his original $1.5 million investment back from the redemption of the unconverted preferred and Joe would have gotten the residual $500,000. Rex would have left his preferred stock unconverted since converting the preferred to common would have left him with 49.95% of the proceeds ($1 million) and in a loss position. Clearly, if WooWee! had chosen to pay more than $3 million for Joe's company, Rex would have had an incentive to convert to common stock in order to enjoy his portion (49.95%) of whatever premium over the $3 million implied enterprise value that WooWee! was offering.

Conceptually, convertible preferred allows the entrepreneur to "catch up" to the investor after the investor's initial investment is secured. Therefore, convertible preferred stock differs from the redeemable preferred plus cheap common as follows:

Portion of Proceeds Received by Investor

Amount of Proceeds	Redeemable Preferred	Convertible Preferred
Up to face value of preferred (FV)	All to Investor	All to Investor
From FV to implied enterprise value at time of investment (IEV)	FV plus common equity proportion of increment over FV to Investor	FV only to Investor
Above IEV	FV plus common equity proportion of increment over FV to Investor	Common equity proportion to Investor

In general, the public markets expect companies to have simple capital structure using only common stock and debt. Therefore, underwriters nearly always insist that all preferred stock be converted coincident with an initial public offering. To avoid a round of negotiations wherein investors demand to be compensated for their conversion to common, convertible preferred stock routinely contains a *mandatory conversion term* which specifies that the company can force conversion as part of an underwritten IPO of a certain (negotiated) size and price. The size is usually large enough to insure a liquid market (recently, these terms tend to specify a $30 million or larger offering) and the price is negotiated to be high enough to insure that it is in the venture capitalist's clear interest to convert (recently, these terms have tended to specify at least a factor of three increase in share price from that at the time the investment).

Convertible preferred stock naturally led to the idea that the conversion ratio need not be fixed. Many convertible preferred stocks contain *antidilution provisions* that automatically adjust the conversion price down[3] if the company sells stock below the share price that the investor has paid. The rationale for these provisions is that the company is presumably selling at a lower price (a "down round") because of underperformance. By having an automatic adjustment, the investor is less likely to oppose or forestall a

---

[3] The adjustment mechanism is a negotiated term and can range from complete adjustment ("full ratchet") to one based on the size of the round and the size of the price decrease ("weighted average formula"). Some antidilution provisions only apply below a certain negotiated price level, and some except smaller financings.

dilutive financing to take on much needed capital when the company needs it most or when the private equity markets are difficult.[4]

Anecdotally, private equity deals in the 1970s tended to be of redeemable preferred structure, reflecting the paucity of capital available and the need to get it back as soon as possible to do more deals. As venture capital became more institutionalized during the 1980s, the market became more competitive and convertible preferred became the standard security. As the pattern of multiple private venture capital rounds became prevalent, later round players who were paying significantly higher prices than early round players insisted on having preferred stock with liquidation preferences over *both* common stock and lower-priced preferred stock.[5] This trend accelerated in the 1990s as later round investors paid higher and higher prices. These investors insisted on structures that gave them more participation in the returns reaped from the early sale of private companies at prices that gave astonishing returns to the early stage investor, but gave considerably less returns to the later stage investor who had paid a high price expecting an exit in the hot public markets. The structure that satisfies this need is participating convertible preferred stock.

Participating Convertible Preferred Stock Participating convertible preferred stock is convertible preferred stock, with the additional feature that in the event of a sale or liquidation of the company the holder has a right to receive the face value *and* the equity participation as if the stock were converted. Like a convertible preferred, these instruments carry a mandatory conversion term triggered on a public offering. The net result is an instrument that acts like the redeemable preferred structure while the company is private and converts to common on a public offering.

A key companion term to a participating convertible preferred is the specification of when the participation term is in effect. Usually, the term reads, "in the event of sale or liquidation," and often goes on to define liquidation as being any merger or transaction that constitutes a change of control. As a result, in a merger transaction between two private firms where the private surviving merged company issues new preferred stock in exchange for the preexisting preferred stock, these clauses may be triggered. This may set off a demand from the holders of the participating convertible preferred for both new preferred stock equal in face value to the old preferred stock plus a participation in the common equity of the new company. All of this can occur without any true liquidity event.

The driver behind the recent acceptance of participating convertible preferred is the willingness of later stage investors to pay very high prices if the terms include a participation feature. If the company goes public, the highly dilutive participating feature goes away.[6] Therefore, companies and their current shareholders feel confident issuing

---

[4] While antidilution provisions became prevalent based on adjusting the conversion ratio of convertible preferred stock, venture capitalists have applied the concept to the redeemable preferred structure by having the company issue free common shares in a down round according to similar formulas. Other antidilution structures include the use of payable-in-kind dividends should the company miss its targets.

[5] In the case of sharply increasing share prices in multiple private rounds, the later round players hold the same relationship to early round players that early round players hold to the founders in the initial financing. If the first financing is at $1/share (that is $1 per *common equivalent share*—the price of the convertible preferred divided by the number of share into which it converts), and the later financing is at $5/share, than the early round investors as well as management would be delighted with an offer to purchase the company for $4/share. Unless the later round investor had a liquidation preference, he would lose money in such a transaction just as Rex lost money in our starting example.

[6] Later stage, high-priced financings are almost always large, so the participating feature can be quite dilutive to management and existing shareholders.

such instruments when the public market is "hot," and a public offering appears feasible if the company has any business success at all.

To summarize the various preferred structures:

Portion of Proceeds Received by Investor

Amount of Proceeds	Redeemable Preferred	Convertible Preferred	Participating Convertible Preferred
Up to face value of preferred (FV)	All to Investor	All to Investor	All to Investor
From FV to implied enterprise value at time of investment (IEV)	FV plus common equity proportion of increment over FV to Investor	FV only to Investor	FV plus common equity proportion of increment over FV to Investor
From IEV to public offering	FV plus common equity proportion of increment over FV to Investor	Common equity proportion to Investor	FV plus common equity proportion of increment over FV to Investor
Above public offering	FV plus common equity proportion of increment over FV to Investor	Common equity proportion to Investor	Common equity proportion to Investor

VESTING

The concept of vesting is simple. It holds that an entrepreneur's stock does not become his or her own until he or she has been with the company for a period of time, or until some value accretion event occurs (e.g., the sale of the company). Typically, vesting is implemented over a time period (currently, four years on the East Coast, three years on the West Coast), and the stock "vests" (i.e., the entrepreneur obtains unqualified ownership of the shares) proportionately over that time period. For administrative purposes, stock vesting usually occurs quarterly, occasionally annually, and maybe even monthly.

In our example, suppose Rex had eschewed preferred stock entirely but had insisted that Joe's shares vest proportionately over four years (1/16th per quarter). Then when the WooWee! transaction occurred, Rex could have insisted the company buy back Joe's stock at cost (probably a nominal 1¢ per share) and theoretically received the entire $2 million of proceeds. Of course, since Joe likely would have objected to receiving no proceeds from the sale to WooWee! and since WooWee! wanted to acquire Joe's talents and wished to see that Joe was a happy WooWee! employee, the transaction may have been called off under those conditions. Having foreseen this situation, Rex may have agreed to a partial acceleration of Joe's vesting in the event of acquisition.[7] If that agreement called for 25% acceleration, then the proceeds would be split 12.5% to Joe (25% of 50.05%) and the remainder to Rex.

---

[7] Often venture terms allow for a 25% to 50% acceleration of vesting for certain managers on acquisition based on the theory that (1) many managers lose their job in an acquisition and it is not fair for those who have created the value to lose a big portion of it by the very act of perfecting that value for the shareholders, and (2) it is better to have the cooperation of management and key employees in the event of a potential acquisition, and acceleration acts as an incentive to get the deal done. Of course, acceleration acts *against* the interest of the acquiring company who may have to spend stock option shares to re-motivate the acquired employees who have had the benefits of acceleration. It also acts against the interest of the nonmanagement shareholders by effectively adding shares to the pool of shares to be bought. The fixed negotiated share price is therefore divided among more shares. For these reasons, acceleration usually is restricted to a few employees and often is only partial.

In general, preferred stock structures do a better job of implementing the "reward for performance" principle since they rely on the investment's terminal value. Furthermore, vesting is contractual: potential events and situations must be anticipated and written down if vesting is to do the same job as preferred stock. However, vesting does perform the very important function of preventing an employee from leaving and taking with him value disproportionate to the time he was employed at the company. Vesting creates the "golden handcuffs" that motivates an employee to stay when other opportunities call. If a company is doing well, and a key employee holds valuable options or stock that would be lost if the employee left before a certain date or event, then the possibility of an early departure is greatly diminished.

Vesting also performs the function of returning shares to the incentive stock pool from employees who in some sense "haven't finished the job," thereby providing incentive stock for their replacements. This allows companies to budget their incentive stock by position or task with some assurance that they are somewhat protected from turnover. Similarly, vesting protects morale by assuring employees that those who leave will not benefit as much as those who stay behind and create value.

COVENANTS

Maybe the most basic way venture capitalists protect their investments is through covenant provisions. Covenants are contractual agreements between the investor and the company and fall into two broad categories: positive covenants and negative covenants. Positive covenants are the list of things the company agrees to do. They include such things as producing audited reports, holding regular board meetings, and paying taxes on time.

In addition to the positive commitments, the preferred equity agreements also contain numerous covenants and restrictions that serve to limit detrimental behavior by the entrepreneur. Certain actions are expressly forbidden or require the approval of a supermajority of investors. For instance, sales of assets are often restricted. Any disposal of assets above a certain dollar value or above a certain percentage of the firm's book value may be limited without the approval of private equity investors. This prevents the entrepreneur from increasing the risk profile of the company and changing the firm's activities from its intended focus. It also prevents the entrepreneur from making "sweetheart" deals with friends.

The private equity investors are also often concerned about changes in control. The contracts may state that the founders cannot sell any of their common stock without approval of the private equity investors or offering the securities to the private equity investors. Similarly, restrictions may prevent a merger or sale of the company without approval of the investors. Transfer-of-control restrictions are important because venture capitalists invest in people. If the management team decides to remove its human capital from the deal, venture capitalists would want to approve the terms of the transfer. Control transfers may hurt the position of the private equity investor if they are done on terms that are unfavorable to earlier investors.

The purchase of major assets above a certain size threshold may also be forbidden without approval of private equity investors. This restriction may be written in absolute dollar terms or may be written as a percentage of book value. The wording is usually broad enough to cover purchases of assets or merger of the firm. Restrictions on purchases may help prevent radical changes in strategy or wasteful expenditure by the entrepreneur. Many such strategy changes could have detrimental effects on the value of the private equity investors' stake.

Finally, the contracts usually contain some provision for restricting the issuance of new securities. Almost all documents contain a provision that restricts the issuance of senior securities without the approval of previous investors. Many documents alter the restriction to include securities on the preferred equity level or any security issuance. Usually, a majority of preferred shares must vote in favor of such an issue. Restricting security issuance prevents the transfer of value from current shareholders to new security holders.

Often negative covenants are coupled with supermajority voting provisions wherein the company agrees not to do certain things unless a greater than 50% majority of shareholders (or in some cases, the board) agrees. So, for example, if Rex had insisted in the original deal that the company could only be sold if two-thirds of common shares agreed in a shareholder vote, then he would have had a veto over the WooWee! transaction, and presumably would have had the negotiating leverage to insist on an acceptable deal.

A few frequently encountered covenants are somewhat different from the positive and negative ones considered above. Many contracts also contain mandatory redemption rights. These are rights of the private equity investors that allow them to "put," or sell at a predetermined price, the preferred stock back to the company. Essentially, the venture capitalists can force the firm to repay the face value of the investment at any time. This mechanism can often be used to force liquidation or merger of the firm. The mandatory redemption provisions are often included for two reasons: (1) most venture partnerships have a limited life so they must have some mechanism to force a liquidity event before the partnership expires, and (2) mandatory redemption clauses help prevent "lifestyle companies," that is, companies that exist only to provide a good living to the management but do not accrete value to the investors. By demanding redemption, the investors can get their money back, or in the event there isn't enough money available in the company, force a negotiation to create a liquidity event.

A contract usually explicitly states the number of board seats that venture capital investors can elect. Typically, in companies that are venture backed from the beginning, private equity investors control the board, or at least the board has a majority of outside (i.e., nonmanagement) directors where the investors at least have approval rights over those seats not held by them or the management. Even if the private equity investors do not own greater than 50% of the equity, the contracts may allocate control of the board to venture capitalists. The board control serves as an important check on management that may try to exploit minority shareholders. Similarly, in any future initial public offering, an outsider-dominated board lends credibility to the firm.

All in all, the most frequent use of covenants is to effectively disconnect control on important issues from owning a majority of the equity. Price and control then become separate items for negotiation. Control issues implemented through covenants and supermajority voting provisions can be settled quite specifically and therefore appropriately to each side's concerns. For example, management often has stronger concerns about operational matters than financing ones, while investors' concerns are typically the reverse. A negotiated set of covenants can leave investors minimally involved in determining operating policy but heavily consulted and involved in financial strategy.

18

edocs, Inc. (A)

Kevin Laracey, Kris Canekeratne, and Jim Moran walked out of the Waltham office of Charles River Ventures (CRV) and were both elated and terrified. It was the spring of 1998 and they had finally found receptive ears for their business proposition to revolutionize online billing via the Internet. Their morning meeting with CRV had gone so well that Jonathan Guerster, the CRV associate responsible for contacting edocs, had asked Laracey, Canekeratne, and Moran to come back after lunch for more discussion. What greeted them upon their return, however, was a term sheet for a $4 million investment in their fledgling company. CRV had committed to financing at least $2 million of the $4 million investment and had promised to bring in a co-investor for the remaining $2 million. While the term sheet appeared to be written in an arcane language that Laracey, Moran, and Canekeratne could not decipher, they knew that this meant instant certification. Their months of searching for a venture capital investor were now over.

Now, however, the tough part began. Guerster had asked that edocs not shop the deal around to other venture capital firms. But was that the right response? Laracey was certain that he could fax this term sheet to five other venture firms and have a "better" deal on the table in a matter of days, if not hours. Should he do that? Laracey wondered what all these terms and conditions meant. Even though he had an MBA from UCLA, he felt ill prepared to negotiate with CRV. How could he find a way to make the deal more to his liking? What could and should CRV change, and which terms were necessary? As Laracey, Moran, and Canekeratne got in their rental car and headed toward Route 128 on their way back to Logan Airport, they began to discuss their strategy.

THE BILL PRESENTMENT MARKET

In 1998, most personalized transactional documents such as bills and statements were printed, stuffed into envelopes, metered for postage, and then delivered by the postal service. If the document was a bill, payment was usually made by paper check. Although

---

Professor Paul A. Gompers prepared this case as the basis for class discussion rather than to illustrate either effective or ineffective handling of an administrative situation.

reliable, this approach to bill presentment and remittance processing had become quite costly. Each year, Americans paid 18 billion bills and many billions were spent each year on the postage and processing of these bills. The U.S. postal service estimated that in 1997 alone, $2.4 billion was spent on postage for bank statements and bills. Of the remittance processing operations that process more than 100,000 transactions monthly, 94% of the transactions were paper-based, while only 6% were electronic. The average cost for processing a paper check payment was $1, while the production and postage costs for the typical bill were 30 to 40 cents.

As the costs of paper bill presentation and remittance processing increased, the costs of connectivity and computing power—two key enabling technologies for *electronic* document delivery, presentation, and remittance processing—had dropped dramatically. In 1998 more than 37% of U.S. households had personal computers, with approximately 22 million households connecting to online services and the Internet. This number was expected to grow to 40 million households by 2000. It was estimated that 55 million people lived in households with e-mail access. The Web browsers and e-mail packages used by consumers and business were capable of displaying multimedia "electronic" documents, including typographic fonts, full-color graphics, and active content, including hypertext links, sound, and video. The security issues associated with transmitting sensitive information over the Internet had been largely resolved, with numerous vendors offering secure payment and information encryption technologies.

The penetration of low-cost computing power and connectivity into homes and businesses had significant implications for producers of personalized documents and vendors of personalized document technologies and services. The U.S. Postal Service estimated that within 10 years, $900 million of the $2.4 billion in annual postage charges for bills and bank statements would be lost due to the rise of electronic presentation and delivery solutions. CyberCash, a vendor of electronic payment technologies and services, estimated that its electronic check payment could reduce check-processing costs by 50%. Similarly, a recent industry trade study suggested that 69% of all large-volume billers (more than 5 million bills/statements per month) were planning to implement or pilot electronic bill presentment in 1998.

Laracey, Moran, and Canekeratne felt that the market was on the edge of a fundamental shift in the way that personalized documents were produced, distributed, and processed. A similar shift had occurred in the 1970s, as all points addressable production laser printing technology began to displace line printers, which were less cost effective and produced less visually rich documents than the new all points addressable technology. The transition from paper to electronic documents would not only affect how documents were produced but would also change the content of the document, the medium through which they were delivered, and the infrastructure required to process return documents and payments. The edocs' founders felt that this trend represented a significant opportunity—and a tremendous risk—for companies whose core business was based on the paper-centric approach to document processing.

THE edocs OPPORTUNITY

Laracey, Moran, and Canekeratne hoped to revolutionize traditional bill and statement production, delivery, and payment process by enabling consumers and businesses to receive personalized documents via e-mail or through their Web browser. edocs would leverage the Internet to dramatically reduce the costs associated with producing, delivering, and paying bills and statements, while simultaneously transforming these documents into dynamic, interactive marketing tools. Rather than simply presenting customers with a facsimile of the document as it was designed for print, edocs would transform documents from their traditional layout into HTML format documents that incorporated hypertext links, animated image files, and "clickable" image maps (see Exhibit 18-1). Such a product would allow edocs to generate documents that could fully utilize the interactive power of the Web. This ability to "re-compose" the document for presentation on-screen—rather than on paper—would make edocs generated documents more inviting, more personalized, and therefore, more effective.

edocs generated messages could also come with content enhancements, or "attachments," that would be used to perform time-saving tasks such as automatically updating a Quicken personal finance register. Through a technology partnership with CyberCash, messages generated by the edocs system would also incorporate a "PAY" button, which could be used to pay the bill by securely debiting the recipient's checking account or credit card via the Internet.

EXHIBIT 18-1

EDOCS INTERFACE

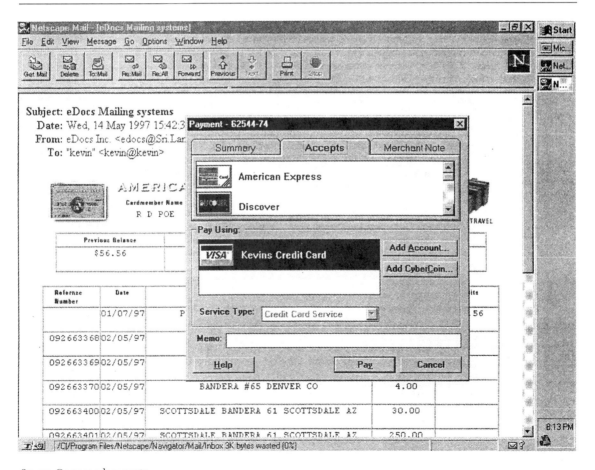

Source: Company documents.

Laracey, Canekeratne, and Moran felt that the edocs system would have tremendous benefits for both the billing entity and the customer. For companies that used the edocs system, the electronic nature of billing would allow them to use bills and statements to facilitate cross-selling on the Web. Similarly, these companies could differentiate themselves from their competitors' "print only" offerings. Because the edocs system interfaced seamlessly with their existing billing infrastructure, it would preserve the investment made in legacy systems. On the cost side, the savings were even more impressive. Document delivery (postage) costs, remittance processing costs (electronic payment vs. paper check processing), as well as printing and finishing cost reductions would all be substantially lower for those firms that adopted the edocs' system.

Equally important, however, the edocs product would provide many benefits to customers who received the bills. First, documents could be "pushed" to the recipient's favorite e-mail package, or retrieved from a central server through any browser allowing ease of use. Similarly, bill payment/reconciliation would be easier and less time consuming. edocs would enable "one-click" bill payment, saving even more time. Because edocs would interface with programs like Quicken, it would automatically update personal finance software files. Over time, as the number of paper bills declined, edocs would be perceived as being environmental friendly. Finally, the electronic format allowed the customer to use the data in spreadsheets or other programs to analyze patterns in usage or expenses.

DEVELOPMENT STRATEGY

Prior to forming edocs, Laracey worked for Elixir Technologies, a company focused on developing graphical software tools that simplified the process of producing personalized bills and statements on high-speed laser printers. (See Exhibit 18-2 for biographies of edocs' management.) Canekeratne met Laracey when his firm, INSCI Corporation, a leading vendor of high-volume customer care solutions for companies that produced bills and statements, licensed document-viewing technology from Elixir. While collaborating on the integration effort, they learned that each shared a strong desire to start a new venture that would leverage the Internet and their experience developing software for high-volume producers of bills and statements.

Laracey and Canekeratne knew that in order to get the best possible deal for their company, they should not approach venture capitalists without having made significant progress on the product. Early investments came from Laracey and Canekeratne's private savings. Canekeratne's family was also very important in making progress quickly and inexpensively. Not only did they invest, but his family owned a software development company in Sri Lanka. edocs utilized his family's company by hiring software development personnel in Sri Lanka. By the time Laracey and Canekeratne began approaching venture capitalists, product development for the first release of the edocs software had been completed. The edocs software was developed both more quickly and less expensively than it would have been had it been developed in the United States. Laracey and Canekeratne believed that these development resources represented a significant competitive advantage because of their unique expertise and the low cost of maintaining resources offshore.

BUILDING VALUE THROUGH ALLIANCES

Laracey knew that edocs would need the services provided by other companies in order to successfully implement all of the elements that their customers would require.

EXHIBIT 18-2

MANAGEMENT BIOGRAPHIES

J.J. Keil, Chairman   Mr. Keil, founder of Keil & Keil, a Washington DC-based consulting firm specializing in sales and marketing consulting to the Fortune 500, was formerly a Vice President in the Xerox Printing Systems Division, where he played a key role in growing this business from $100 million to more than $1 billion in revenue when he left in 1990. Before joining Xerox, Mr. Keil spent 20 years at IBM in various management positions. He has also been involved in a number of technology startups. He served on the board of Document Sciences, a major provider of database publishing solutions that completed a successful IPO in 1996. He also served on the board of NeoMedia Technologies, a provider of digital document solutions that also completed an IPO in 1996. In addition, he served on the board and was chairman of Elixir Technologies Corporation, a leading provider of graphical software tools that simplified the production of printed bills, statements, and other personalized documents on high-speed laser printers. Mr. Keil had a working relationship with Mr. Laracey since 1988. In addition to providing overall guidance to the company, Mr. Keil would play a key role in securing sales and marketing relationships with key technology and services vendors in the print and mail industry.

Kevin E. Laracey, President   Before founding edocs, Mr. Laracey was Vice President of Marketing at Elixir Technologies Corporation. While at Elixir, Mr. Laracey played a key role in setting product strategy and in establishing a leveraged sales model that allowed Elixir to sell its products through the IBM and Xerox printing systems sales forces, and to become the dominant supplier in its market. He also designed Elixir's products that facilitated the conversion of documents in production print file formats to Adobe's Portable Document Format, making it possible to view these documents on the Internet using any browser. Mr. Laracey was a prominent figure in the database publishing/print and mail industry, and had served on the vendor advisory council for the industry's user group, XPLOR. Before joining Elixir, Mr. Laracey worked as an analyst in the Travelers Companies computer science department, where he played a key role in developing the company's corporate electronic publishing strategy, and designed and implemented the first electronic publishing solution that linked desktop publishing software to production speed laser printers. Mr. Laracey received an MBA in Marketing and Finance from the UCLA Anderson School of Business and a B.A. from the University of Notre Dame.

Kris Canekeratne, Director   Mr. Canekeratne was Senior Vice President and Chief Technology Officer at INSCI Corporation (NASDAQ: INSI), the leading provider of high-volume document archiving technology in the document management market. Mr. Canekeratne was the chief architect of the INSCI CoinServ and CoinCD systems, which made it possible to distribute documents in image and print file formats throughout the enterprise. Mr. Canekeratne served as a key technical advisor to the edocs team and was instrumental in helping edocs establish its offshore development capability. While Mr. Laracey was at Elixir Technologies, Mr. Canekeratne and Mr. Laracey worked closely to merge Elixir's document viewing technology with the INSCI CoinServ document archiving system. Mr. Canekeratne received a Bachelor of Science degree in Computer Science from the University of Syracuse and frequently represented INSCI at industry conferences and analyst briefings.

(Continued)

He had identified CyberCash as a prime strategic partner. CyberCash was the leading provider of technology that enabled secure payments to be made over the Internet by debiting a credit card or checking account. James "J.J." Keil, a former Xerox executive from the company's printing systems division and a board member on a number of early-stage technology companies was a member of Elixir's board and had been an early edocs supporter. At Laracey's request, he approached Bill Melton, then CEO of CyberCash

---

EXHIBIT 18-2   (Continued)

Jim Moran, Executive Vice President   As a Founder and Executive Vice President, Mr. Moran was responsible for sales, marketing, and business development. Formerly SVP of Sales in Check-Free's (NASDAQ: CKFR) Electronic Commerce Division, Mr. Moran developed a successful sales strategy and field organization that linked the suite of CheckFree payment solutions with the highly leveraged distribution channels of Banks, Brokerages and Diversified Financial Institutions. This resulted in positioning CheckFree for a successful IPO, four acquisitions, and revenue growth from $25M to $250M in just four years. In addition, Mr. Moran had been an industry spokesperson and featured speaker at events such as Internet World, Financial Forum, Harvard Business School, TeleStrategies, BAI, TMA, and H&Q's Planet Wall Street. Prior to CheckFree, Mr. Moran held senior sales positions with the high-tech organizations Infinium Software (NASDAQ:INFM), Storage Technology (NYSE:STK), and EMC Corporation (NYSE:EMC). Moran served on the Board of Directors at BancFirst Ohio Corporation (NASDAQ:BFOH). He was a graduate of Northeastern University.

Richard K. Crone, Director   Richard K. Crone was Vice President and General Manager at CyberCash, Inc. (NASDAQ:CYCH). He was responsible for the development and release of the PayNow™ Secure Electronic Check Service. He was responsible for leading a team that developed the PayNow service. He also secured several major strategic alliances with other technology and financial service providers, giving CyberCash access to a sales force with relationships in nearly 100% of the accounts targeted for the new PayNow service. The business plan for his service had been used on several occasions to secure both private and public sources of funding and joint development agreements with alliance partners. Prior to joining CyberCash, Mr. Crone led the nation's largest savings bank, Home Savings of America, as Senior Vice President and Co-Director of Electronic Banking, in their successful launch of online banking with Microsoft Money and Intuit's Quicken. Prior to joining Home Savings of America, Mr. Crone spent eight years with KPMG Peat Marwick's Financial Services Consulting Practice, leaving as a Senior Manager and director of the Firm's Center for Electronic Banking. Mr. Crone began working with edocs early in 1997, when edocs and CyberCash consummated a technology partnership agreement, which was expanded to enable CyberCash's sales force to sell the edocs product line along with Cyber-Cash's PayNow service. He received a Bachelor of Science degree and a Master's of Business Administration degree with honors from the University of Southern California.

Source: Company documents.

---

and an AOL board member while Keil was attending an AOL shareholder's meeting. This led to a meeting with Richard Crone, CyberCash's VP and General Manager of the PayNow electronic check division at the April 1997 Internet World conference. At the conference, Laracey demonstrated the edocs product to Crone, who immediately recognized the product's potential, saying, "You've invented a new category of software. . . . Internet bill presentment and payment software."

In December of 1997, Laracey signed an agreement with CheckFree, a leading provider of electronic payment and bill presentment services. Laracey was also able to sign a Technology Partnership agreement with CyberCash and ultimately expanded the relationship to enable the CyberCash sales force to sell the edocs product line. This relationship had provided edocs with the right to integrate CyberCash's Wallet product into its software. The CyberCash Wallet would allow recipients of edocs generated messages to pay bills with the click of a mouse. CyberCash would also present edocs as a key provider of bill presentment technology to its prospective customers. Laracey believed that the CyberCash relationship represented a major competitive advantage and that it would expedite the company's ability to achieve its development and marketing objectives.

THE COMPETITION

Laracey, Moran, and Canekeratne had done an extensive survey of the competitive landscape. Competitors and potential competitors included MSFDC, CheckFree, and document services providers such as International Billing Services. Other potential competitors included vendors in the document archiving market such as IBM with its OnDemand product, FileNet, and start-up firms such as Cephas Multimedia and BlueGill Technologies, which were focusing on enabling document presentment on the Web by providing consulting services.

MSFDC (now known as Transpoint) was a company formed by Microsoft and First Data Corporation to pursue the Internet bill presentment and payment market. FDC was known to have a large group of personnel working on bill presentment and remittance processing solutions. As a multibillion dollar (revenues) processor of credit card transactions in the US, First Data had made significant inroads into the population of bill and statement originators and had access to large amounts of raw statement data. MSFDC intended to use its technology as part of a service offering and would not offer it as a software solution that could be purchased. Instead, the company was employing a "consolidator" service model, in which MSFDC concentrated bills from multiple billers at a single site and charged billers "something less than the cost of a postage stamp" for placing the bill on the MSFDC site.

CheckFree had an electronic bill presentment and remittance processing solution and was also firmly in the consolidator camp. CheckFree planned to use its technology to facilitate a service offering and had no immediate plans to license its software to billers. Industry analysts noted that it would be "difficult" for the company to pursue a biller direct model in which CheckFree would sell its bill presentment capabilities to empower billers to present bills on their own Web site. Laracey, Moran, and Canekeratne felt that because CheckFree was focused on its service center business model, it was unlikely that CheckFree would extensively tailor its presentment solution to meet the needs of each individual biller. Moran's experience as SVP of Sales in CheckFree's Electronic Commerce division helped them reach these conclusions.

IBM was also known to view the Internet as being key to the strategy of its Printing Systems Division. IBM's major investment in the On Demand product, which facilitated presentment of AFP (Advanced Function Presentation) and Adobe PDF format documents over corporate Intranets, had shown their interest in online bill presentment. IBM had developed a Web browser plug-in to facilitate display of AFP data over the Internet. Laracey and Canekeratne expected that IBM would try to extend the AFP architecture to incorporate presentment capabilities like those found in edocs, and so they were considered a potential competitor.

International Billing Services produced 1.5% of all U.S. first class mail and was one of the largest providers of billing services for cable television systems in the United States. The company announced a pilot project in 1997 in which it would convert legacy print files to document formats that could be retrieved from a Web site.

Another group of potential competitors were service firms which provided custom solutions for various billers. Cephas Multimedia was a provider of custom Web site development services and was the systems integrator that created one of the first interactive bill presentment and payment systems available on the Web for Kansas City Power and Light. Laracey and Canekeratne believed that Cephas Multimedia was trying to replicate their experience at KCP&L by selling integration services, but they were not developing a software suite that would enable Internet bill presentment and payment. BlueGill was a start-up firm selling information technology consulting services to convert AFP format print documents to Adobe's Portable Document Format (PDF) to enable the presentation of bills and statements via a browser. They had received initial seed money from five to ten private investors and were believed to have two installations of their product. BlueGill had also approached Laracey and Canekeratne about the possibility of re-selling the edocs product line.

MARKETING STRATEGY

Laracey, Moran, and Canekeratne had developed a two-part marketing approach. The edocs software suite would be marketed to high-volume producers of transactional documents—such as bills and statements—who viewed bill presentment as a strategic asset, who saw innovative bill presentment technologies as a means of achieving competitive advantage, and who were ready to pilot or implement an electronic document presentment system. The cost savings associated with electronic presentation, delivery, and remittance processing were, however, a secondary but important consideration for these early adopters.

Initial sales would likely be to billers or billing services providers looking to offer the edocs service to their more affluent customers who had PCs and Internet connectivity. It was also likely that many initial applications would be business-to-business applications. It was probable that for the first several years after its launch, the edocs system would not reduce the number of paper bills and statements produced. At the start, edocs generated messages would be sent in addition to the paper version of the bill or statement, suggesting that electronic presentment would represent a net new revenue opportunity for vendors of paper-based document production technologies. Over time, billers would offer financial incentives to bill and statement recipients to encourage them to forego the receipt of printed documents.

Prospective edocs customers were likely to be users of specialized database publishing products. Use of these products indicated that the potential customers viewed bill and statement presentment as a valuable marketing opportunity that could yield competitive advantage.

In addition to end-user customers, Laracey, Canekeratne, and Moran felt that a significant opportunity existed to license its technology to vendors of document management and database publishing products. Laracey, Canekeratne, and Moran had already received two inquiries from well-known vendors of these types of products about the possibility of incorporating edocs technology into existing offerings.

BUSINESS MODEL—edocs ADVANTAGES

The decision to offer edocs as a software product—not as a service—provided edocs with a significant competitive advantage over firms such as MSFDC, who only offered Internet document production and delivery as a service. Laracey, Canekeratne, and Moran had learned that these firms experienced problems gaining acceptance for their service-only offerings in the marketplace because of customer concerns about "intermediation"—the introduction of a third party that stood between the biller and its customers to facilitate bill presentment. Among the concerns was the fear that a single service provider could aggregate and "mine" the data provided by several billers. Purchasing a software solution like edocs would give billers and billing services providers complete control of their data, with none of the issues associated with intermediation.

PRICING

Workstation versions of database publishing systems typically ran under a variant of the Unix or Windows NT operating systems and were available from a variety of vendors at prices that ranged from $70,000 to $150,000. This price typically included a server component that converted input data into a composed document, and a designer component that allowed users to define the rules that governed how a document should be composed. Laracey, Canekeratne, and Moran estimated that the average edocs software system would sell for $120,000, since the product's Internet presentment capabilities would allow it to demand a premium over the average price of a database publishing system.

As was customary with complex software solutions, Laracey, Canekeratne, and Moran expected that edocs annual license fees would be 18% of the initial license fee, resulting in a recurring revenue stream of $21,600 for each system sold.

CHARLES RIVER VENTURES

Charles River Ventures (CRV) was one of the nation's leading early-stage venture capital firms. Founded in 1970 and based in Boston, its mission was to contribute to the creation of significant new enterprises by working in constructive partnership with driven, talented entrepreneurs. Through 1998, Charles River had organized nine funds totaling $565 million, providing capital and guidance to more than 235 companies. In 1998 CRV's most recent two venture funds were both returning more than 100% per annum to their investors. Charles River Partnership IX was organized in 1998 with a total capitalization of $175 million. CRV focused on high-potential start-ups in the communications, software, and information services industries. Each principal specialized in a particular subset of these sectors. The firm played an active role in their investments, usually through board representation.

CRV's initial commitment to a company was typically $1 to 5 million; over the course of the company's evolution, they expected to invest roughly $3 to 10 million in the project. Their equity ownership of portfolio companies was generally 10 to 20% prior to an initial public offering. More than 50 of their past investments had gone public, with many going on to become industry leaders (e.g., Cascade Communications, Chipcom, CIENA, Parametric Technology, Sybase, and Vignette). Many others were successfully merged into preexisting public companies.

CRV's investment focus identified opportunities that met several yardsticks. The firm specialized in early-stage projects in communications, software, and e-commerce services—industries where it had an extensive network of contacts and where each general partner had gained operating experience. CRV hoped that companies addressed markets of $250 million per year or more and companies that could reach the $50 million or higher revenue threshold within five to seven years. CRV generally preferred to act as the "lead" investor, and consequently directed most of its attention to companies in the Northeast corridor (Washington, DC to Boston).

At times, CRV would provide seed financing to an outstanding entrepreneur to fund the development of a business concept. In financing a company, CRV typically worked initially with one other top-tier venture firm, bringing the portfolio company a more diverse network and providing a stronger financial syndicate.

CRV'S FOCUS ON BILL PRESENTMENT

Jonathan Guerster had joined Charles River as an associate in late 1997 with an explicit mandate to invest in e-commerce-related businesses. (See Exhibit 18-3 for CRV biographies.) Even though he had only been at Charles River for several months, he knew that Internet bill presentment was a tremendous market opportunity. Prior to joining Charles River, Guerster had worked at OpenMarket on Internet bill presentment and understood the market opportunity that it represented. Guerster had spent several months surveying the landscape and identified three potential investment targets for CRV. Just-in-Time Solutions (JITS), Bluegill, and edocs were all focusing on Internet bill presentment and were all looking for first round venture financing in early 1998.

To try and help with the due diligence process, Guerster contacted Jim Moran, Senior Vice President of Sales for CheckFree, a company that processed electronic payments via the Internet. Moran was interested in the Internet bill presentment space and was actively looking for an opportunity to join in the effort. Guerster and Moran thought that Just-in-Time had the edge and was aggressively trying to finance the firm, even though Norwest, another venture capital firm, seemed to have the inside track.

As it happened, Moran and Laracey had been collaborating prior to Guerster's call to Moran. Laracey and Moran had spent a fair amount of time talking on the phone about the marketplace in great detail. As it happened, Moran and Laracey actually met face-to-face for the first time in JITS offices. Laracey was at Just-in-Time to discuss a potential joint venture whereby Just-in-Time would utilize edocs' software solution, while Moran was there evaluating the possibility of joining Just-in-Time. Moran was waiting in a glass conference room adjoining the glass room in which Laracey was waiting. Becoming bored with the wait, Moran proceeded to walk over to Laracey and introduce himself. When Laracey replied, the pair laughed at the circumstances. Upon concluding their respective meetings, Moran and Laracey shared a cab to the hotel and continued their discussions about Moran potentially joining edocs. Moran had been an executive at CheckFree, where he had been General Manager of the Corporate Commerce Services Division and SVP of Sales for the Electronic Commerce Division. While at CheckFree the company had grown its revenues from $20 million per annum to more than $250 million. Moran played a key role in positioning CheckFree for a successful IPO in 1995. Moran had decided that he wanted to join a start-up and was evaluating firms in the Internet billing space.

The day after the meeting at Just-in-Time, an Electronic Banking Conference was held in San Francisco. Moran and Laracey ended up staying together for a couple of days after the meeting at JITS. In discussions, Laracey told Moran that edocs had been searching for venture financing for six months and had had little success. While he had been able to set up initial meetings with several Silicon Valley venture funds, none of them seemed overly eager to commit. Many of them told Laracey that they would call back. His phone had not been ringing yet. Moran saw that Laracey's software-based strategy gave edocs a potential advantage relative to both Just-in-Time and Bluegill. During the conference, Moran arranged a meeting with Jonathon Guerster to discuss opportunities. Moran indicated that he was 99% certain that he would partner with

EXHIBIT 18-3

CHARLES RIVER VENTURES GENERAL PARTNERS' BIOGRAPHIES

Rick Burnes: Burnes had been a venture capitalist since 1965, nearly his entire professional life. He was a co-founder of Charles River Ventures in 1970 and had played a major role in the firm's development into one of the nation's most successful venture funds. He focused on investments in the fields of communications and information services. Cascade Communications (NASDAQ: CSCC), Chipcom Corporation (acquired by 3COM), Epoch Systems (acquired by EMC), Abacus Direct (NASDAQ: ABDR), Summa Four (NASDAQ: SUMA), Concord Communications (NASDAQ: CCRD), Prominet (acquired by Lucent), and Aptis (acquired by Nortel) were among the successful investments he led on behalf of Charles River. Burnes was also responsible for investments in AirSpan and Sonus, and held Board seats at Concord Communications, OMNIA, and SpeechWorks.

Jonathan Guerster: Guerster joined Charles River in 1997 focusing on e-commerce related software and services. Prior to Charles River, Guerster served as Director of Corporate Development at Open Market (NASDAQ: OMKT), an Internet commerce software company in Burlington, Massachusetts. As Director of Financial Services, Guerster was responsible for building Open Market's overall business in the financial services industry. Prior to Open Market, Guerster worked in marketing and sales management roles with Hewlett-Packard's Apollo Workstation Division and with J.P. Morgan. Guerster was a graduate of Northwestern's Kellogg Graduate School of Management and of Duke University, where he graduated with Distinction, earning a Bachelor of Science in Electrical Engineering and Computer Science.

Ted Dintersmith: Dintersmith had over a decade of experience in early-stage venture investing, focusing on software and information services companies. He had been an early and active investor in several successful start-ups including Flycast Communications (NASDAQ: FCST), Ibis Technology (NASDAQ: IBIS), Individual (NASDAQ: NEWZ), PCs Compleat (acquired by CompUSA), SQA (NASDAQ: SQAX, acquired by Rational), and Vignette (NASDAQ: VIGN). He served on the Boards of Bow Street Software, Be Free, Entelos, Flycast, net.Genesis, Novera, Trellix, and WebSpective Software. Prior to his career in venture, Dintersmith was General Manager of the Digital Signal Processing Division of Analog Devices, which he directed from start-up phase to a leading position in a rapidly growing sector of the semiconductor industry. His work experience also includes two years as a congressional staff assistant, where he contributed to science and technology policy. Dintersmith earned a Ph.D. in Engineering from Stanford University, concentrating on mathematical modeling and optimization theory. His undergraduate degree was from the College of William and Mary, where he graduated Phi Beta Kappa with High Honors in Physics and English.

Mike Zak: Zak joined Charles River in 1991, where he became known for his focus on data communications, telecommunications, and networking software. He led the firm's investments in projects such as Agile Networks (now part of Lucent Technologies), American Internet (now part of Cisco Systems), CIENA (NASDAQ: CIEN), RAScom (acquired by Excel Switching), and ON Technology (NASDAQ: ONTC). Zak organized the seed financing for OMNIA (acquired by Ciena) and Charles River's initial investments in C-Port and Sitara. Prior to joining Charles River, Zak spent 14 years in various sectors of the communications industry and held positions as various as network systems engineer, network operations manager, director of marketing for Motorola, Inc., and co-founder and V.P. of engineering for Concord Communications, Inc., a data communications start-up company. Earlier in his career, he was a management consultant with McKinsey & Company, where his clients included companies in PC software, value-added networking, telecommunications, and semiconductors. Zak was a 1975 graduate of the College of Engineering at Cornell University, and in 1981 he earned an MBA degree from the Harvard Business School. Prior to business school, he served as an officer in the U.S. Marine Corps in both the United States and overseas.

Izhar Armony: Armony joined Charles River in 1997 focusing on enterprise software and services. Previously, in the summer of 1996, he worked with General Atlantic Partners focusing on enterprise software and from 1988 to 1995 with Onyx Interactive, an interactive training software company. At Onyx, Armony held various positions from software designer to director of business development. Prior to Onyx, he spent four years as an officer in the Israeli Army. Armony's investing focus was on the areas of enterprise software and e-commerce. He was responsible for Charles River's investments in Celarix, Oberon, VIP Calling, and Yantra. Armony held an M.A. in Cognitive Psychology from the University of Tel Aviv, an M.A. in International Studies from the University of Pennsylvania, and an MBA from Wharton.

Source: Company documents.

Laracey and Canekeratne to help launch edocs. Guerster viewed this as a material event for edocs and was willing to "fast track" the due diligence process. Guerster knew that he had a "short wick" relative to the timing associated with making a potential investment in Bluegill or JITS. (See Exhibit 18-4 for financial projections for edocs. Exhibits 18-5 & 18-6 contain information on comparable companies.)

MARCH 23, 1998 MEETING

Guerster indicated to Moran that he was very impressed with Laracey and suggested that Laracey fly from Los Angeles, where he was based, to Boston to meet with the Charles River's general partners. Laracey, Canekeratne, and Moran scheduled a meeting for the next week at CRV's Waltham offices.

During the three-hour-long meeting between edocs and CRV, Laracey, Canekeratne, and Moran were very impressed with the knowledge of the market that Guerster and CRV brought to the table. Questions were insightful and challenging. As the presentation concluded, Laracey, Moran, and Canekeratne had a good feeling about the meeting. Most of the general partners at CRV were nodding in agreement during the discussion. The meeting concluded at noon. As Laracey, Moran, and Canekeratne packed up to head back to the airport for their flights, Guerster asked the edocs team to have a quick lunch and return in one hour for further discussions.

EXHIBIT 18-4

EDOCS REVENUE SCENARIOS—FISCAL 1998 THROUGH 2002 ($ MILLIONS)

Target Performance:

Year	1998	1999	2000	2001	2002
Revenue	$3.0	$11.7	$32.1	$56.3	$98.5

Threshold Performance (−35% of Target):

Year	1998	1999	2000	2001	2002
Revenue	$1.9	$7.6	$20.8	$36.6	$64.0

Stretch Performance (+35% of Target):

Year	1998	1999	2000	2001	2002
Revenue	$4.0	$15.7	$43.3	$76.1	$132.9

Target Performance Income Summary:

	1998	1999	2000	2001	2002
Revenue	$2,966,396	$11,671,709	$32,055,412	$56,344,305	$98,504,098
Cost of Revenues	$ 561,496	$ 2,140,705	$ 5,860,619	$ 8,647,045	$15,749,974
Operating Expenses	$4,316,173	$ 8,713,549	$17,266,953	$33,624,550	$57,838,269
Net Income	($1,911,273)	$ 817,455	$ 8,927,842	$14,072,710	$24,844,454
Net Income %	−64%	7%	28%	25%	25%

Source: Company documents. (Data disguised.)

EXHIBIT 18-5

COMPARABLE FIRM VENTURE FINANCING DATA

Netdox
http://www.netdox.com

COMPANY OVERVIEW:

Business Brief:	Provider of secure, electronic message delivery over the Internet
Founded:	01/96
Status:	Private & Independent
Employees:	36
Stage:	Product Development
Spinout of:	Deloitte & Touche
Industries:	Other Online Services
Internet Focus:	Business Services

INVESTORS:

Investment Firm	Participating Round #(s)
Apex Investment Partners	1, 2, 3
Thurston Group	3

FINANCINGS TO DATE:

Round # Type	Round	Date	Amount Raised ($MM)	Post $ Valuation ($MM)	Company Stage
1	1st	08/97	0.8	20.0	Startup
2	2nd	11/97	2.87	N/A	Product Development
3	Bridge	02/98	N/A	N/A	Product Development

Documentum
http://www.documentum.com

COMPANY OVERVIEW:

Business Brief:	Developer of object-oriented document management systems
Financing Status:	As of 02/96 The company completed a $43.2M IPO on 2/5/96 priced at $24/share.
Founded:	01/90
Status:	Publicly-held
Employees:	174
Stage:	Profitable
Spinout of:	Xerox
Industries:	Workflow Software

INVESTORS:

Investment Firm	Participating Round #(s)
Brentwood Venture Capital	2, 3
Norwest Venture Partners	2, 3
Merrill, Pickard, Anderson & Eyre	2, 3
Sequoia Capital	2, 3
Xerox Venture Capital	1*, 2*, 3
Integral Capital Partners	3

* = Lead Investor

(Continued)

EXHIBIT 18-5 *(Continued)*

FINANCINGS TO DATE:

Round # Type	Round	Date	Amount Raised ($MM)	Post $ Valuation ($MM)	Company Stage
1	1st	03/93	2.0	2.7	Product Development
2	2nd	10/93	7.0	13.7	Shipping Product
3	3rd	09/94	4.5	49.7	Shipping Product
4	IPO	02/96	43.2	323.3	Profitable

Dazel
http://www.dazel.com

COMPANY OVERVIEW:

Business Brief: Developer of distributed client/server software which automates the process of sending documents, spreadsheets, reports, orders, and presentations to other parties
Founded: 08/91
Employees: 70
Stage: Shipping Product
Spinout of: Tivoli Systems
Previous Name: Atrium Technologies
Industries: Workflow Software

INVESTORS:

Investment Firm	Participating Round #(s)
Individual Investors	1*, 2, 3, 4
Sevin Rosen Funds	2*, 3, 4, 5
Austin Ventures	2, 3, 4, 5
SSM Ventures	2, 3, 4, 5
Sigma Partners	3*, 4, 5
Integral Capital Partners	4*, 5
Goldman Sachs Group	5*

* = Lead Investor

FINANCINGS TO DATE:

Round # Type	Round	Date	Amount Raised ($MM)	Post $ Valuation ($MM)	Company Stage
1	Seed	08/91	0.13	N/A	Startup
2	1st	05/94	3.5	7.5	Shipping Product
3	2nd	02/95	3.2	14.4	Shipping Product
4	3rd	06/96	9.5	45.0	Shipping Product
5	Later	12/97	7.0	100.0	Shipping Product

Source: Compiled from VentureOne

EXHIBIT 18-6

COMPARABLE FIRM FINANCIAL DATA ($ IN MILLIONS)

IBM

	1994	1995	1996	1997
Sales	$64,052	$71,940	$75,947	$78,508
SG&A	$20,279	$20,448	$21,508	$21,511
Cap Ex	$ 3,078	$ 4,744	$ 5,883	$ 6,793
Op Inc before Dep	$ 9,202	$13,874	$12,707	$13,116
Net Income	$ 3,021	$ 4,178	$ 5,429	$ 6,093
Total Assets	$81,091	$80,292	$81,132	$81,499
Current Assets	$41,338	$40,691	$40,695	$40,418
Current Liabilities	$29,226	$31,648	$34,000	$33,507
Total Debt	$22,118	$21,629	$22,829	$26,926
Market Value	$43,197	$50,053	$76,959	$100,240
Beta	0.87	1.00	1.18	1.33
P/E Ratio	14.30	11.98	14.18	16.45

DOCUMENTUM

	1994	1995	1996	1997
Sales		$25.46	$ 45.30	$ 75.64
SG&A		$19.45	$ 31.90	$ 52.05
Cap Ex		$ 2.75	$ 5.20	$ 6.92
Op Inc before Dep		$ 2.41	$ 6.70	$ 12.23
Net Income		$ 1.26	$ 4.48	$ 7.35
Total Assets		$16.50	$ 74.94	$127.20
Current Assets		$12.79	$ 67.22	$116.87
Current Liabilities		$ 8.16	$ 15.40	$ 25.17
Total Debt		$ 1.44	$ 1.04	$ 0.02
Mkt. Value		NA	$478.81	$657.28
Beta		NA	1.79	1.70
P/E		NA	106.78	89.38

XEROX

	1994	1995	1996	1997
Sales	$17,837	$16,611	$17,378	$18,166
SG&A	NA	$ 5,721	$ 6,118	$ 6,304
Cap Ex	$ 389	$ 438	$ 510	$ 520
Op Inc before Dep	$ 2,967	$ 3,151	$12,707	$ 3,499
Net Income	$ 794	-$ 472	$ 1,206	$ 1,452
Total Assets	$38,585	$25,969	$26,818	$27,732
Current Assets	NA	$ 9,833	$10,152	$10,766
Current Liabilities	NA	$ 6,999	$ 7,204	$ 7,692
Total Debt	$10,939	$11,132	$11,960	$13,123
Mkt. Value	$10,493	$14,843	$17,034	$24,101
Beta	1.27	1.26	0.71	1.00
P/E Ratio	13.22	-31.45	14.12	16.60

DOCUMENT SCIENCES

	1994	1995	1996	1997
Sales		$10.51	$ 15.32	$19.74
SG&A		$ 7.68	$ 11.37	$15.27
Cap Ex		$ 0.30	$ 0.53	$ 1.59
Op Inc before Dep		$ 1.83	$ 1.92	$ 0.44
Net Income		$ 1.05	$ 1.36	$ 0.84
Total Assets		$ 6.29	$ 32.02	$34.23
Current Assets		$ 5.28	$ 30.65	$29.97
Current Liabilities		$ 3.93	$ 4.84	$ 6.07
Total Debt		$ 0.14	$ 0.18	$ 0.12
Mkt. Value		NA	$105.88	$32.23
Beta		NA	1.44	1.60
P/E		NA	77.80	38.46

(Continued)

313

EXHIBIT 18-6 (*Continued*)

	1994	1995	1996	1997
CHECKFREE				
Sales	$39.27	$ 49.33	$ 76.79	$176.45
SG&A	$11.75	$ 18.25	$ 46.99	$ 84.25
Cap Ex	$ 1.04	$ 3.43	NA	$ 9.76
Op Inc before Dep	$ 3.04	$ 0.61	NA	–$ 24.17
Net Income	$ 0.49	–$ 0.22	–$138.86	–$161.81
Total Assets	$30.51	$115.64	$196.23	$223.84
Current Assets	$17.61	$ 90.47	$ 90.80	$ 86.22
Current Liabilities	$ 5.68	$ 8.68	$ 45.30	$ 66.22
Total Debt	$ 9.30	$ 8.44	$ 9.44	$ 9.35
Mkt. Value	NA	$690.30	$825.15	$960.65
Beta	NA	1.24	1.39	1.22
P/E	NA	NM	NM	NM

Source: Compiled from Compustat.

What greeted Laracey, Canekeratne, and Moran upon their return to CRV's office, however, was not more discussions but a term sheet that outlined general terms for an investment. (See Exhibit 18-7 for the preliminary investment term sheet.) Laracey was stunned. He had been hopeful that CRV might invest, but he did not believe that a decision would be made so quickly.

The terms of the deal called for CRV to invest $2 million and for CRV to find a second venture capital firm to invest another $2 million investment with a $10.5 million post-money valuation. The founders would receive 5 million shares, 1.5 million shares would be set aside for employee stock options, and CRV and its syndicate partner would get 4 million shares of convertible preferred equity for their $4 million. The convertible preferred would convert one-for-one into common stock. If no other venture firm was willing to coinvest, CRV would invest the additional $2 million, but would get additional warrants for investing the entire amount. That much, Laracey, Canekeratne, and Moran

---

EXHIBIT 18-7

MEMORANDUM OF TERMS

SUMMARY DRAFT MEMORANDUM OF TERMS
For a Proposed Financing
Series A Preferred Stock of edocs, Inc.
March 23, 1998
Version 1.2

Amount & Securities:	$4,000,000 of Series A Convertible Preferred Stock.
Share Price:	$1.00/share
Dividend:	Annually accruing $0.08 per share, to be paid in case of redemption.
Closing Date:	April 28th, 1998.
Founders:	Kevin Laracey, Kris Canekeratne, Jim Moran
Investors:	Name Amount Charles River Ventures $2,000,000 Additional mutually agreeable venture capital firm $2,000,000
Liquidation:	In case of merger, reorganization or transfer of control of edocs, first pay cost of Preferred Stock. Participating goes away on valuation that corresponds to $50 million. Thereafter Preferred and Common share on as-converted basis.
Redemption:	Redemption at mutual agreement of both Series A Preferred Stock holders, equal annual installments years 5 through 7. Pay back cost plus accrued dividend.
Conversion:	Convertible into one share of Common Stock at the option of the holder, or automatically upon a qualified IPO (at least $5.00 per share and aggregate proceeds of $15 million).
Antidilution:	Conversion ratio adjusted on a Weighted Average basis in the event of an issuance at less than $1.00, with the exception of stock issued to employees, consultants, directors or other individual contributors. Antidilution subject to "pay to play" limitations. Pro rata adjustments for stock splits, combinations, and dividends.
Voting Rights:	Votes on an as-converted basis, but also has class vote.
Representations & Warranties:	Standard.

(Continued)

EXHIBIT 18-7 (Continued)

Proposed Terms
EDocs, Inc.

Non Competition & Nondisclosure: Founders and key employees to execute noncompetition, nondisclosure and invention assignment agreements with edocs.

Negative Covenants: Consent of at least 60% of the outstanding Preferred Stock for: dividends on Common; Preferred or Common repurchase; loans to employees; guarantees; Merger consolidation, sell, or disposal of substantially all of the properties or assets; Mortgage, pledge, or creation of a security interest; Ownership of any security by the edocs; incurring debt senior to the Series A Preferred Stock; Change in the principal business of edocs; investments in third parties; capital expenditures of $250,000 in a single expenditure or in aggregate of $500,000 in a twelve month period.

Right of First Refusal: The Investors shall have a pro rata right, based on their percentage equity ownership of Preferred Stock, to participate in subsequent equity financing of the edocs. If any shareholder of the Common equivalent wants to sell shares, he must offer them first to the holders of Series A Preferred.

Take-Me-Along: If a shareholder of Common or equivalent wants to sell shares, holders of Series A Preferred have a right to participate on a *pro rata* basis in the sale. This does not apply to sales in an IPO or afterward.

Access & Reporting: Standard. Annual business plan and budgets by the fourth quarter. Monthly, quarterly, and annual audited financial statements.

Board of Directors: Five total, until new CEO is hired: two representatives of the Series A Preferred; Kevin Laracey (Founders' representative and CEO), one outsider recommended by the Founders and acceptable to Investors, and one additional outside director (possibly Chairman) acceptable to the board. Upon hiring of new CEO, board total increases to six with new CEO taking additional board seat. Board meetings to take place every four weeks.

Indemnification: Directors and officers will be entitled to indemnification to the fullest extent permitted by applicable law.

Counsel & Expenses: Investor counsel to draft closing documents. edocs to pay all legal and administrative costs of the financing, not to exceed $20,000 plus disbursements.

Registration Rights: On demand registration starting four years from closing or three months after initial registration with aggregate proceeds in excess of $10 million; unlimited piggybacks; limited S-3 registrations of at least $500,000 each. All at eDoc's expense.

Founders' Stock, Options & Vesting: Option pool of 1,500,000 to have 48 months vesting with 12-month cliff and linear vesting thereafter. Founder's shares vest 25% on closing, with the remainder vesting linearly over a 36-month period, and the unvested portion subject to buyback provisions. edocs has right to repurchase unvested shares in the event of employment termination. All vesting will accelerate by 12 months on an acquisition resulting in a change of control.

Founders' Termination: In the event that a Founder is terminated by the incoming CEO, a committee consisting of the remaining Founders and one representative from Charles River Ventures will determine whether some portion of that Founder's unvested equity should be accelerated.

Subject to: —Legal and accounting due diligence
—No significant business or organizational changes prior to closing

Signed: March 23, 1998

(Continued)

EXHIBIT 18-7   (Continued)

March 23, 1998

Kevin Laracey
Chief Executive Officer
edocs, Inc.

Dear Kevin,

This letter confirms that Charles River Ventures is committing $2 million in financing to edocs, Inc. with an expected closing date of April 28, 1998. Our plan is to secure a commitment of $2 million from another top-tier venture fund by that date, for a total financing of $4 million. If no such commitment has been obtained by the target closing date, CRV will close on the $2 million financing.

At the discretion of the Founders and Charles River Ventures, the financing may be held open for an additional time period (no longer than 45 days) as the process for obtaining an additional investor is resolved. If, at the end of that period, no such additional investor has committed to this financing, we will receive a grant of 500,000 warrants (exercisable at $.10 per share, duration of three years) for common shares, and close on a $2 million round.

We are looking forward to working together.

Sincerely,

Jonathan M. Guerster
Associate
Charles River Ventures

Source: Company documents.

---

understood. The three pages of additional terms and conditions, however, were very confusing. Neither Laracey nor Canekeratne had ever seen a venture capital term sheet. Many of the terms looked onerous, but how could they decide? In the meantime, Guerster asked Laracey, Canekeratne, and Moran not to "shop the deal around." CRV was making a commitment to finance the company and wanted to be perceived as a partner, not an adversary.

WHAT TO DO?

As Laracey, Canekeratne, and Moran left CRV's office, all their hard work and sacrifice seemed to be paying off. edocs had suddenly cleared a major hurdle. Charles River was certainly a top-tier venture firm and would bring much needed capital and credibility

---

EXHIBIT 18-8

VENTURE CAPITAL COMMITMENTS ($ IN MILLIONS)

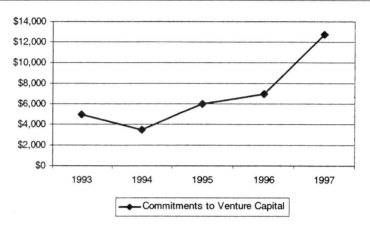

Source: Compiled from Asset Alternatives.

EXHIBIT 18-9

VENTURE CAPITAL-BACKED IPOS ($ IN MILLIONS)

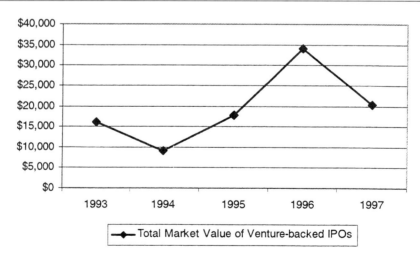

Source: Compiled from VentureOne.

to edocs. They were uncertain, however, what the best course of action was. They knew that they would now have immediate access to other top venture funds and might be able to negotiate better terms if they had competing offers. (See Exhibits 18-8 and 18-9 for information on the state of the venture capital market.) How hard should they negotiate, and which terms were most important to alter? Should they ask for more money? a higher valuation? What about the potential co-investor? Laracey, Canekerantne, and Moran began to discuss how they might make the deal work. First, however, they needed to understand the terms of the proposed financing. Laracey threw 50 cents into the tollbooth bucket and headed down Interstate 90 toward the airport.

edocs, Inc. (B-1): Kevin Laracey

Kevin Laracey knew that he and his partners, Jim Moran and Kris Canekeratne, had had a successful meeting. Charles River Ventures (CRV), one of the premier venture capital firms in the United States, wanted to finance their company. Their enthusiasm was so high that they had given the edocs team a term sheet on the spot. Laracey knew that the venture capital industry was moving quickly, but this seemed to exceed his wildest expectations.

On the flight back to California, he decided to make a list of issues that needed to be hammered out. He had spent most of the flight just trying to decipher the terms of the agreement. Laracey, Moran, and Canekeratne still felt that they needed to understand those terms better in order to negotiate from a position of understanding and strength. They tried to think of who might be able to provide a quick tutorial on venture capital terms and conditions.

The first question that Laracey pondered was whether CRV was offering a fair valuation of edocs. Laracey knew that prices were heating up in the venture capital industry as record amounts of capital began to flow into the sector. Many of his friends had been able to increase the valuation of their venture investments by creating a deal auction. Laracey wondered how he might capitalize on the increased competition for deals to extract concessions. This had to be balanced with the fact that other competitors were waiting in line to take money from CRV and others. First mover advantage was a key factor.

Management issues were also circling around in Laracey's mind. From the financing documents, it appeared that CRV wanted to bring in a new CEO. While he was amenable to that possibility, Laracey thought that he should be given the opportunity to run edocs until it outgrew his capabilities. Yes, he was young, but he had prepared himself to run his own company and felt that he should be given that opportunity. Similarly, he felt that his partner, Canekeratne, should have a place on the board of directors. Canekeratne and his family had been instrumental in the formative stages of the

Professor Paul A. Gompers prepared this case as the basis for class discussion rather than to illustrate either effective or ineffective handling of an administrative situation.

firm's development, and Laracey thought that it was only fair that they have a say in the direction of the company. In addition, Moran brought a considerable amount of operating experience as a former SVP and GM at CheckFree Corporation and lent credibility to the team.

The vesting schedule also appeared onerous. Laracey had built the company and developed the software before any venture money had come into the deal. Why should he suddenly accept vesting of his shares over the next several years? Laracey and his partners were not going anywhere, so why should the venture capitalists try to tie their hands? Was this any way for a partnership to begin?

Other issues were a bit fuzzier to understand. What were the antidilution provision and right of first refusal doing in the agreement? It appeared that CRV was trying to maintain leverage over future financing rounds. Laracey felt that he wanted to maintain maximum flexibility as it related to future investors. The current term sheet seemed to lock edocs into CRV. Was that such a good idea?

Finally, Guerster's letter stating that CRV intended to bring in a co-investor for the additional $2 million seemed problematic. If CRV failed to find a syndicate partner, CRV would not only get the additional 2 million shares of convertible preferred, but they would get cheap warrants. That too seemed to be one-sided. Why should Laracey, Moran, and Canekeratne bear the cost of CRV's inability to find a syndicate partner? That was their job anyway. Laracey felt that CRV should guarantee the entire $4 million of financing without any additional warrants or equity being handed out.

All of this was set in the backdrop of an attractive alternative. Sitting back in California was an offer to purchase edocs for $15 million, Laracey and Canekeratne could make a quick flip and have a nice payday without any of the hassles of negotiating with CRV or their counterparts at other venture firms. This seemed attractive, but Laracey was not certain it was the right path to follow. How could he decide which direction to go? Suddenly, the pilot announced that their plane would be diverted because of bad weather in the Los Angeles area. Laracey had promised to be home in time to take his wife out to dinner, and now it seemed like he would miss that opportunity. Laracey quickly picked up the phone from his seat and dialed his wife's office number, hoping to reach her before she left for the restaurant. He certainly hoped that this was not an omen about what lay down the road that he was about to travel with CRV.

edocs, Inc. (B-2): Jonathon Guerster

Jonathon Guerster sat in his office and looked over the term sheet that he had just handed to Kevin Laracey, founder of edocs. The term sheet looked very reasonable, even though it had been hastily drafted. For Guerster, edocs represented a huge opportunity, but perhaps an even larger risk. He had been working with Charles River Ventures (CRV) for little more than three months and had yet to "do a deal." He had been brought on board to provide expertise in e-commerce and the Internet. Now he had his chance. He appreciated the opportunity in online bill presentment and felt that the market would be very profitable. Guerster was, however, staking his future as a venture capitalist on the line. If edocs ultimately turned out to be a poor investment, he would find it tough going in the future. On the other hand, if the deal turned out well, he would establish his reputation inside and outside of the firm.

Although Guerster had several years of high-technology experience at an Internet start-up, he was still a venture capital novice. He was relying on the partners of CRV to help negotiate the terms. Guerster was trying to determine how hard he should bargain with Laracey. While Laracey had spent some time trying to acquire venture financing, Guerster knew that this term sheet would be like bait for other venture capitalists. One smell, and edocs would have five other offers to finance them. He wondered how he could avoid such an auction like atmosphere? How could he make Laracey, Moran, and Canekeratnee know that he wanted this to be an amicable partnership?

On the terms side, Guerster had little knowledge of what typical venture capital agreements looked like and how many terms were negotiable. Guerster was concerned about keeping Laracey as CEO in the long run. He was in his very early thirties and had relatively little senior management experience. While he had shown his tenacity and insight during the entire edocs idea generation process, Guerster wanted to ensure that CRV had the opportunity to bring in a new CEO at some point in the future. How could he convince Laracey that this was in his own best interests? Moran's addition to

---

Professor Paul A. Gompers prepared this case as the basis for class discussion rather than to illustrate either effective or ineffective handling of an administrative situation.

the founding team helped to reduce some of this risk, but this founding team had never worked together before and significant risks remained.

A related issue was Canekeratne's role in the firm. His family currently owned a significant fraction of the company, providing both financing and software development resources. As such, he was currently a member of the board of directors. Guerster did not know whether Canekeratne's background would make him the best board member. CRV had a method for crafting boards of directors. The board was meant to add credibility and contacts for the firm. If Canekeratne were on the board, it might mean one fewer member that could add value. Guerster was averse to creating a large, unwieldy board of directors. He felt that they just did not work well.

Guerster also knew that Laracey would push on the valuation. He thought, however, that the $10.5 million post-money valuation was extremely generous and fair. There was significant upside for all parties involved if things worked out well. It was very likely that, given the tremendous amount of venture capital that was being raised, edocs could easily raise money at a much higher valuation. Already reports were surfacing of deal price inflation as money began to chase deals, driving up valuations in the interim. Guerster knew that he would need to show some restraint if CRV got into a bidding war.

Finally, Guerster worried that while bringing in another venture firm would not be difficult, if he could not find an investor to co-invest, then the terms he had negotiated might be poor or the edocs might not actually be a great idea. He hoped to give CRV some wiggle room by imposing a penalty on edocs if no one would co-invest. The additional warrants that would be handed out (500,000) in the event of no co-investor showing an interest, would compensate for some of the negative news associated with just such an event. He hoped that Laracey, Moran, and Canekeratne would not view the condition as too onerous.

As he pondered what to do, Guerster opened a stack of mail on his desk. The collection of junk mail and bills seemed to grow every day and demanded ever increasing amounts of time to wade through. The phone on his desk suddenly rang. It was Rick Burns and Ted Dintersmith calling to get an update on the edocs negotiations. They wanted to see him in the conference room in five minutes. Guerster grabbed his cup of coffee and a notepad as he walked down the hall. His heart began to speed up as he thought about what he was going to say. After all, this was going to be the biggest check he had written in his life.

19

A Note on Angel Financing

INTRODUCTION

The role of venture capitalists and banks in financing young, start-up companies has become increasingly documented and studied. A large body of research has examined the types of firms that receive each form of financing and what factors influence the monitoring and control they institute. Little systematic work, however, has been done on the informal risk capital market, or the "angel" market. Angels, in the business sense, are often wealthy businesspeople, doctors, lawyers, and the like, who invest in young companies. While various surveys have tried to address the issue of how much angel financing is invested each year and what form that investment takes, very little has come out of those efforts.

Recent efforts across the country, however, have indicated the belief that too little angel capital is invested. Many of these efforts have been local in scope; that is, they have tried to bring various angels and entrepreneurs together through conferences, workshops, or informal meetings. The efforts are often seen as a way to promote more capital for entrepreneurial firms in areas that are underserved by organized venture capital. The largest and most far-reaching effort to date has been introduced by the U.S. Small Business Administration's (SBA) Office of Advocacy. In order to increase the availability of angel money, the SBA launched a new Internet-based market for angel financing known as the Angel Capital Electronic Network, or ACE-Net. This Internet forum allows small businesses to post business plans and communicate with accredited investors. (For an overview, see U.S. Small Business Administration, Office of Advocacy [1996].) The goal of ACE-Net is to bring angel investors together with worthy entrepreneurs by making information quickly and efficiently available and by enhancing the matchmaking process between entrepreneurs and angels.

The motivation for these programs rests on the belief that young firms face large capital constraints in the market for growth capital. In order to evaluate these programs, we need to examine the financing and strategic needs of young, entrepreneurial firms and ask what potential conflicts can arise in these relationships. Similarly, we will find

---

Professor Paul A. Gompers prepared this note as the basis for class discussion rather than to illustrate either effective or ineffective handling of an administrative situation.

that all angels are not created equally. A carefully chosen angel investor can increase the value fo the firm and the likelihood of success. A poorly chosen angel investor will mire the company in perpetual conflict.

This note provides an overview of the motivations for efforts to encourage individual investors as well as a detailed description of the implementation of ACE-Net. The note explores the underlying challenges that the financing of young growth firms pose, as well as the ways that specialized financial intermediaries address them.

CHARACTERISTICS OF THE ANGEL MARKET

It is difficult to get accurate data on the angel market in the United States because it is so fragmented and informal. Much of the research that has been done has been survey-oriented research, which can be notoriously troublesome. Freear, Sohl, and Wetzel (1996) estimate that between 5 and 10% of start-ups (around 50,000 firms) and 300,000 growing small firms require equity capital each year. If the average required investment was $250,000, the required amount of equity capital would be $87 billion, far more than the venture capital industry currently invests. Estimates by these researchers have placed the annual amount invested by angel investors at between $20 and $30 billion, although these numbers should be regarded with a great deal of suspicion. Other, potentially more reasonable estimates, place the amount of angel capital at around $3 billion per year (1993 National Survey of Small Business Finance).

In addition, Freear, Sohl, and Wetzel (1996) also utilize surveys to draw inferences about the characteristics of angel investors.

- Angels typically invest in technologies that they understand.
- They tend to invest close to where they live.
- They tend to invest in very early-stage companies.
- Typical angel financing rounds are less than $1 million.
- Angels tend to use investment terms and conditions that are briefer and more informal than venture capitalists.
- Angels tend to take bigger risks and accept lower returns if they feel that the entrepreneur's idea is attractive for "nonfinancial" reasons; that is, the idea has the right "bells and whistles."

What is clear from anecdotal evidence, however, is that angels are also a diverse group. Many angel investors may be nothing more than wealthy local doctors, dentists, or businesspeople who have strong desires to "make a fortune." Many are also naïve about the potential conflicts that can arise and are easy prey for unscrupulous entrepreneurs. On the other hand, some angel investors can provide value to the firm and are critical to its success.

Recent work by Fenn, Liang, and Prowse (1997) examines the characteristics of successful high-technology start-ups that had been financed by angels and similar firms that had been financed by professional venture capital firms. Although both angel investors and venture capitalists had invested in a large proportion of successful firms, venture capitalists tended to invest more money, the venture-backed firms had significantly higher sales and significantly more assets, and the venture-backed companies had more patents. It appears that the venture-backed companies are more developed and more productive than similar angel-financed firms. Brav and Gompers (1997) find that venture-backed firms perform significantly better than similar nonventure capital-backed companies after they go public. Venture capitalists potentially add greater value to their companies, or they select better companies at the beginning.

ACE-NET

In late 1996, the Office of the Advocacy of the U.S. Small Business Administration (SBA) unveiled an Internet-based market for the financing of young, entrepreneurial firms. The system, known as the Angel Capital Electronic Network (ACE-Net), was intended to be a national market that would match wealthy individuals with companies that met their investment interest. The targeted size of investments ranged from $250,000 to $2 million. ACE-Net was conceived during the 1995 White House Conference on Small Business.

Entrepreneurs who wish to have their companies listed on ACE-Net fill out an application, file financial statements with ACE-Net, and pay a $450 fee to appear on the network for six months. The company must also have a registered or qualified offering with the SEC and state security agencies. These include Regulation A, Regulation D, Rule 504, or "test the water documents" that comply with state and federal requirements. The companies are listed on a database that is accessible through the Internet by individuals who have a password. Companies are organized by region, industry, and size of investment sought. This allows investors to target the types of investment that they want to make.

ACE-Net got a jump-start when the Department of Defense (DOD) prepaid the listing fees for 200 firms that had won Small Business Innovation Research (SBIR) awards through the DOD. The SBA also had plans to use the ACE-Net search engine to allow investors to search through the more than 35,000 SBIR companies from all government agencies.

Investors receive passwords by registering with a regional ACE-Net office. An individual must verify that he or she meets the SEC's definition of an "accredited" investor (SEC Rule 501). To qualify, an individual must have net worth of at least $1 million or earn more than $200,000 per year.

The stated goal of ACE-Net is to improve the access of young, entrepreneurial firms to equity capital. The belief was that small investments, that is, those less than $250,000 or so, could be financed by the entrepreneur or family and friends. Venture capitalists typically like to make investments of at least $2 million per round. The SBA believed that between those two amounts, no organized financial intermediaries existed.

The SBA also argued that venture capital investments are highly concentrated by region and industry. Almost 50% of venture capital investments are made in California and Massachusetts. Much of the rest of the country is devoid of venture capital. ACE-Net might be a method to utilize information technology to overcome many of these geographic constraints.

ARE ENTREPRENEURIAL FIRMS REALLY THAT DIFFICULT TO FINANCE?

Is the foundation for ACE-Net well placed? A lengthy literature has highlighted the role of financial intermediaries in alleviating moral hazard and information asymmetries. Young firms, particularly those in high-technology industries that are the focus of many of today's policy initiative towards angel capital, are often characterized by considerable uncertainty and informational asymmetries that permit opportunistic behavior by entrepreneurs. Careful screening of potential investors seems critical to improving outcomes.

A large body of economic research has explored the conflicts between managers and outside managers.[1] Jensen and Meckling (1976), in one of the first articles on the subject, demonstrate that agency conflicts between managers and investors can affect the willingness of both debt and equity holders to provide capital. If a firm is financed by outside equity, the manager has an incentive to either spend the money on perquisites that only he or she can enjoy or can decide to not exert as much effort as investors would like. The reason for these inefficiencies is that the manager receives the full benefit from building a big office or relaxing on the golf course, but bears only a small fraction of the monetary cost because he or she only owns a small fraction of the firm's equity. Similarly, if the firm is financed by outside debt, the manager may have an incentive to take excessive risk. If outside investors rationally anticipate these problems, they may not wish to finance the firm.

Even if the manager is motivated to maximize shareholder value, informational asymmetries may make raising external capital more expensive or even preclude it entirely. Myers and Majluf (1984) and Greenwald, Stiglitz, and Weiss (1984) demonstrate that the equity offerings of firms may be associated with a "lemons" problem (first identified by Akerlof [1970]). If the manager is better informed about the investment opportunities of the firm and acts in the interest of current shareholders, then managers only issue new shares when the company's stock is overvalued. Indeed, numerous studies have documented that stock prices decline upon the announcement of equity issues, largely because of the negative signal that it sends to the market.

These information problems have also been shown to exist in debt markets. Stiglitz and Weiss (1981) show that if banks find it difficult to discriminate among companies, raising interest rates can have perverse selection effects. In particular, the high interest rates discourage all but the highest-risk borrowers, so the quality of the loan pool declines markedly. To address this problem, banks may restrict the amount of lending rather than increasing interest rates.

These problems in the debt and equity markets are a consequence of the information gaps between the entrepreneurs and investors. If the information asymmetries could be eliminated, financing constraints would disappear. Financial economists argue that specialized financial intermediaries, such as venture capital organizations, can address these problems. By intensively scrutinizing firms before providing capital and then monitoring them afterward, they can alleviate some of the information gaps and reduce capital constraints.

To address these information problems, the partners at venture capital organizations (venture capitalists) employ a variety of mechanisms. First, business plans are intensively scrutinized: of those firms that submit business plans to venture capital organizations, historically only 1% have been funded (Fenn, Liang, and Prowse[1995]). The decision to invest is frequently made conditional on the identification of a syndication partner who agrees that this is an attractive investment (Lerner [1994]). Once the decision to invest is made, the venture capitalists frequently disburse funds in stages. The entrepreneur must periodically prove that the company is making progress and not squandering money in order to receive additional capital. In addition, venture capitalists intensively monitor managers. These investors demand preferred stock with nu-

[1] This and the following two paragraphs are based on Gompers and Lerner (1997b).

merous restrictive covenants and representation on the board of directors. (Various aspects of the oversight role played by venture capitalists are documented in Gompers [1995, 1997], Lerner [1995], and Sahlman [1990]; the theoretical literature is reviewed in Barry [1994]). Thus, it is not surprising that the capital provided by venture capital firms is the dominant form of equity financing for privately held technology-based businesses.

RATIONALES FOR ENCOURAGING ANGEL INVESTORS

In recent years, the amount of venture capital raised has increased dramatically. The increase in venture capital, however, does not necessarily imply that there is no funding shortfall for young, entrepreneurial firms. A large finance literature has examined the conditions under which firms will be "capital rationed," that is, be subject to significantly higher external financing costs. These papers (Hoshi, Kayshap, and Scharfstein [1991]; Fazzari, Hubbard, and Petersen [1988]; Hubbard [1997]) look at firm characteristics that would be associated with severe informational asymmetries. They find that firms that suffer from large information gaps tend to have more difficulty raising necessary funds. Hall (1992), Hao and Jaffe (1993), and Himmelberg and Petersen (1994) show that small, R&D intensive firms are severely restricted in the capital market.

The argument is often made that very small firms are the most likely to suffer from capital constraints. While venture capitalists, as was argued above, try to overcome these information asymmetries, in order to recoup their monitoring and information-gathering costs, they need to focus on investments that are at least $2 million (Gompers [1995]). The reason for concentrating on larger investments is often that due diligence and monitoring are largely fixed costs, independent of the size of investment. If venture capitalists had to spend their time making very small investments (i.e., $500,000), then they would be unable to make substantial returns for investors.

Even given the desire to make large investments, in recent years there has been increasing pressure to make even larger investments. Several factors have increased that minimum venture investment threshold over the past several years. The increase in fund size, driven by the rapid growth in commitments to the venture capital industry, has meant that each partner at a venture capital firm is managing more money. In order to put that money to use, bigger checks need to be written. Venture capitalists try to write bigger checks by financing later stage companies or reducing syndicate sizes. As the number of dollars per venture fund and dollars per venture partner has grown, so too has the size of venture investments: for instance, the mean financing round for a start-up firm climbed (in 1996 dollars) from $1.6 million in 1991 to $3.2 million in 1996 (VentureOne [1997]).

The SBA and advocates of ACE-Net also argue that venture capital is both geographically concentrated and highly focused on a few industries. First, very few companies actually receive venture capital financing. In recent years, the Department of Commerce has estimated that nearly one million new businesses are begun annually. In 1996, a year of record venture capital investment activity, only 658 firms received a first-time venture capital investment (VentureOne [1997]). In addition, the money that is investment is highly concentrated on certain regions. Companies in California and Massachusetts accounted for 49% of venture capital investments in 1996. Eighty-two percent of the venture capital investments went into information technology and the life science companies (VentureOne [1997]). Companies in regions that have few venture capital firms or companies in industries that are out of favor are unlikely to attract venture investors.

WILL MORE ANGEL FINANCING HELP OR HURT?

Clearly, many firms do not receive venture capital. The issue, however, is how can a program like ACE-Net attract the right type of angel without allowing more fools to rush in as well? There may be a reason why venture capitalists do no invest in these micro-companies; it may be impossible to earn enough money to justify the due diligence and monitoring expenses. Active investors will spend a substantial amount of time advising the company and trying to increase value. If the absolute dollar stake in the company is small, then the potential dollar return might not justify the time.

If the investor does not take the time to monitor the company, however, there exists the possibility that the entrepreneur will take advantage of the angel. In this case, the investor can lose all or most of his investment. The entrepreneur-investor relationship is the quintessential principal-agent relationship with all types of conflicts just waiting to happen. Venture capitalists utilize many different control mechanisms (as was discussed above) for precisely that reason. Good angels will be active investors, providing advice, contacts, and credibility.

In addition, during the last several years, leading venture capital firms have attempted to adopt programs to foster younger, early-stage entrepreneurs through "entrepreneur-in-residence" programs. Similarly, innovative young venture firms like Draper, Fischer Partners increasingly target very small, seed-stage investments. Many of these firms are targeting the smaller investments to avoid competition that is present for the larger, later stage investments. To put it another way, if there is profit to be made, professional investors will attempt to capitalize on it.

ARE ALL ANGELS CREATED EQUAL?

One issue that is critical to the success of angel investing is the potential synergies that are present between an investor and the entrepreneur. Many recent angel investors have considerable experience in a particular industry. Some are highly successful entrepreneurs in their own right. Steve Jobs, Mitch Kapor, Paul Allen, and Jim Clark are just a few examples of entrepreneurs who utilize their wealth and experience to help young entrepreneurial firms. In many ways, these investors harken back to the early entrepreneurial activity in the United States when successful families like the Whitneys and the Rockefellers financed many entrepreneurs. The network of contacts that these families provided often added considerable value to the companies.

Entrepreneurs considering angel financing versus other sources of financing need to think about what each group of investors brings to the table. Often entrepreneurs worry about how much of the firm they own in percentage terms without focusing on the real issue, which is, how valuable is their slice of the equity? Many investors can increase the size of the pie, and this increase in value may justify giving them a greater percentage of the firm. Entrepreneurs need to think about the skills, contacts, and other resources that investors bring. "Dumb money" may not be the best money.

Similarly, entrepreneurs need to think carefully about the terms of the financing. Many terms may look attractive on the surface but may hinder raising additional capital in the future. Some angels lack the sophistication to understand terms and conditions or how they might hinder the firm in the future. Professional investors, both venture capitalists and experienced angels, understand that crafting the proper deal terms can often mean the difference between success and failure.

CONCLUSION

Although many entrepreneurial firms lack outside capital, government policy promoting more angel financing may not necessarily be a solution. First, the entrepreneurial sector has been growing rapidly despite the lack of any centralized policy to foster an angel network. There are several reasons why this might be the case. First, alternatives to angel financing are often available to young entrepreneurs. Bank financing is often available for businesses with assets or cash flow. Trade credit is often a major source of credit for young firms. Similarly, a supplier or customer is often a source of equity capital through a strategic alliance.

How does any policy ensure that the investors who participate are those who can add value to the firm? Surveys (Wetzel and Seymour [1981] and Freear, Sohl, and Wetzel [1994]) have highlighted the differences among angel investors. Many angels are former entrepreneurs who have substantial financial capital and skills to bring to the entrepreneurial company. Jim Clark, seed backer of Netscape and former founder of Silicon Graphics, is just such an angel. Many other private investors, however, are clearly unsophisticated and lack the ability to add value or understand the ramifications of investment. Any policy that seeks to increase the availability of angel capital needs to address the issue of which type of angel is attracted to the market.

Many economists would argue that there is no need for government intervention. If there are good investments to be made, then the free market will see that they are made. In the past several years, many angel networks have been organized by the private sector. Many of these are even Internet-based (e.g., American Venture Capital Exchange, Capital Matchmaker, FinanceHub, MoneyHunter, and Venture Capital Report). Many of these appear to have more sophisticated matching mechanisms that screen angels more carefully than does ACE-Net. It may be debatable whether a government-sponsored scheme like ACE-Net is required to meet the need. What is certain, however, is that the debate about the need for and the value of angel investing will not die out any time soon.

APPENDIX: UNREGISTERED SECURITY OFFERINGS[2]

A Regulation D, Rule 504 offering allows a small company to raise up to $1 million in an offering that does not have to be registered with the U.S. Securities and Exchange Commission (SEC). An offering of securities in a Reg D, Rule 504 offering must meet the following requirements.

- The firm may not have sales that exceed $1 million.
- There are no limitations on the number of investors or no restriction that they be sophisticated.
- The company cannot be an investment company that needs to register under the Investment Company Act of 1940, nor may it be a "blank-check" company. A blank-

---

[2] For a more complete description of unregistered security offerings, see Levin (1994).

check company is a start-up with no specific business plan other than to purchase unidentified acquisition targets.

A regulation A offering is one that permits a small company to raise up to $5 million through a streamlined registration process if it does not meet the criteria for a Reg D offering. Regulation A offerings are a federal small corporation registration exemption, but also require state registration where the offering is intended to be offered and sold. The requirements for a Reg A filing include the following:

- The firm cannot have sales over $5 million.
- The offering may have as much as $1.5 million in secondary shares.
- The firm must file a Reg A offering form with the SEC, but the turnaround time is substantially shorter and the form is less complex than the registration requirements under a full-blown registration.
- There are no limits on the number of investors or no requirement that they be sophisticated.

REFERENCES

AKERLOF, G.A., 1970, The market for "lemons": Qualitative uncertainty and the market mechanism, *Quarterly Journal of Economics* 84, 488–500.

BARRY, C.B., 1994, New directions in research on venture capital finance, *Financial Management* 23 (Autumn), 3–15.

BOLTON, P., AND D. SCHARFSTEIN, 1990, A theory of predation based on agency problems in financial contracting, *American Economic Review* 80, 93–106.

BRAV, A., AND P.A. GOMPERS, 1997, Myth or reality?: Long-run underperformance of initial public offerings; Evidence from venture capital and nonventure capital-backed IPOs, *Journal of Finance*, Forthcoming.

DAS, S.R., AND J. LERNER, 1995, Apex Investment Partners (A) and (B) (Cases No. 9-296-028 and 296-029, Harvard Business School).

FENN, G.W., N. LIANG, AND S. PROWSE, 1995, The economics of the private equity market (Washington, DC: Board of Governors of the Federal Reserve System).

FENN, G.W., N. LIANG, AND S. PROWSE, 1997, The Role of Angel Investors and Venture Capitalists in Financing High-Tech Start-ups (Washington, DC: Board of Governors of the Federal Reserve System).

FIELD, L.C., 1996, Is the institutional ownership of initial public offerings related to the long-run performance of these firms?, Unpublished working paper, Pennsylvania State University.

FREEAR, J., AND W.E. WETZEL, JR., 1990, Who bankrolls high-tech entrepreneurs?, *Journal of Business Venturing* 5, 77–89.

FREEAR, J., J.E. SOHL, AND W.E. WETZEL, JR., 1994, Angels and non-angels: Are there differences?, *Journal of Business Venturing* 9, 109–123.

FREEAR, J., J.E. SOHL, AND W.E. WETZEL, JR., 1996, Creating new capital markets for emerging ventures, A Report for the U.S. Small Business Administration's Office of Advocacy.

GOMPERS, P.A., 1995, Optimal investment, monitoring, and the staging of venture capital, *Journal of Finance* 50, 1461–1489.

GOMPERS, P.A., 1997, Ownership and control in entrepreneurial firms: An analysis of convertible securities in venture capital investments, Harvard Business School working paper.

GOMPERS, P.A., 1998, Venture capital growing pains: Should the market diet?, *Journal of Banking and Finance* 22, 1089–1104.

GOMPERS, P.A., AND J. LERNER, 1996, The use of covenants: An empirical analysis of venture partnership agreements, *Journal of Law and Economics* 39, 463–498.

GOMPERS, P.A., AND J. LERNER, 1997a, Venture capital fundraising, firm performance, and the capital gains tax, Unpublished working paper, Harvard University.

GOMPERS, P.A., AND J. LERNER, 1997b, Venture capitalists and the creation of public companies, *Journal of Private Equity* 1, 15–32.

GOOD, M.L., 1995, Prepared testimony before the Senate Commerce, Science and Transportation Committee, Subcommittee on Science, Technology and Space (Mimeo, U.S. Department of Commerce).

GREENWALD, B.C., J.E. STIGLITZ, AND A. WEISS, 1984, Information imperfections in the capital market and macroeconomic fluctuations, *American Economic Review Papers and Proceedings* 74, 194–199.

GRILICHES, Z., 1986, Productivity, R&D, and basic research at the firm level in the 1970's, *American Economic Review* 76, 141–154.

HALL, B.H., 1992, Investment and research and development: Does the source of financing matter? (Working Paper No. 92-194, Department of Economics, University of California at Berkeley).

HAO, K.Y., AND A.B. JAFFE, 1993, Effect of liquidity on firms' R&D spending, *Economics of Innovation and New Technology* 2, 275–282.

HIMMELBERG, C.P., AND B.C. PETERSEN, 1994, R&D and internal finance: A panel study of small firms in high-tech industries, *Review of Economics and Statistics* 76, 38–51.

HUBBARD, R.G., 1997, Capital-market imperfections and investment, *Journal of Economic Literature* forthcoming.

IRWIN, D.A., AND P.J. KLENOW, 1996, High tech R&D subsidies: Estimating the effects of Sematech, *Journal of International Economics* 40, 323–344.

JENSEN, M.C., AND W.H. MECKLING, 1976, Theory of the firm: Managerial behavior, agency costs and ownership structure, *Journal of Financial Economics* 3, 305–360.

KRUGMAN, P.R., 1991, Geography and trade (MIT Press, Cambridge).

LERNER, J., 1994, The syndication of venture capital investments, *Financial Management* 23 (Autumn) 16–27.

LERNER, J., 1995, Venture capital and the oversight of privately-held firms, *Journal of Finance* 50, 301–318.

LERNER, J., 1997, "Angel" Financing and Public Policy: An Overview, *Journal of Banking and Finance*, Forthcoming.

LEVIN, JACK, 1994, Structuring venture capital, private equity, and entrepreneurial transactions, (CCH, Inc., Chicago.)

MANSFIELD, E., J. RAPOPORT, A. ROMEO, S. WAGNER, AND G. BEARDSLEY, 1977, Social and private rates of return from industrial innovations, *Quarterly Journal of Economics* 91, 221–240.

MYERS, S.C., AND N. MAJLUF, 1984, Corporate financing and investment decisions when firms have information that investors do not have, *Journal of Financial Economics* 13, 187–221.

NOONE, C.M., AND S.M. RUBEL, 1970, SBICs" Pioneers in organized venture capital (Capital Publishing Company, Chicago).

Organization for Economic Co-operation and Development, 1995, Venture capital in OECD countries, (Organization for Economic Co-operation and Development, Paris).

SAHLMAN, W.A., 1990, The structure and governance of venture capital organizations, *Journal of Financial Economics* 27, 473–521.

SAXENIAN, A., 1994, Regional advantage: Culture and competition in Silicon Valley and Route 128 (Harvard University Press, Cambridge).

SPARKMAN, J., 1958, Introduction, in: U.S. Congress, Senate, Small Business Committee, Small Business Investment Act of 1958 (U.S. Government Printing Office, Washington, DC).

STIGLITZ, J.E., AND A. WEISS, 1981, Credit rationing in markets with incomplete information, *American Economic Review* 71, 393–409.

U.S. Congressional Budget Office, 1985, Federal financial support for high-technology industries (U.S. Congressional Budget Office, Washington, DC).

U.S. Small Business Administration, Office of Advocacy, 1996 The process and analysis behind ACE-Net (U.S. Small Business Administration, Washington, DC).

Venture Economics, 1996, Special report: Rose-colored asset class, *Venture Capital Journal* 36 (July) 32–34 (and earlier years).

VentureOne, 1997, National Venture Capital Association 1996 annual report (VentureOne, San Francisco).

WALLSTEN, S.J., 1996, The Small Business Innovation Research program: Encouraging technological innovation and commercialization in small firms?, Unpublished working paper, Stanford University.

WETZEL, W.E., AND C.R. SEYMOUR, 1981, Informal risk capital in New England (Center for Industrial and Institutional Development, University of New Hampshire, Durham, NH).

## 20

Honest Tea

Seth Goldman, President and TeaEO of Honest Tea, looked out the window of his office in Bethesda, Maryland. Honest Tea was a three-year-old start-up in the fast growing ready-to-drink tea market with its sights set on increasing brand awareness and distribution. Goldman had been answering e-mails from customers for the past 30 minutes as he waited to call his co-founder and Yale School of Management professor, Barry Nalebuff, so they could discuss their financing strategy. Many of these e-mails stood as testimonials to the vision he had set out to create in his company. Several drinkers even offered to invest in the company if Goldman was seeking to raise new capital.

The December 2000 cold spell had put a chill on the sales of his company's bottled tea product and he now had a bit of time to reflect on his successes of the past three years and what the future might hold for his company, Honest Tea. Honest Tea had received tremendous media attention in the last several months. Goldman, Nalebuff, and the company had been featured in magazines like *Fortune*, *Entrepreneur*, and *Beverage World* and in papers like the *Washington Post*, the *Washington Business Journal*, and the *New York Times*. The media coverage had been critical in raising public awareness of the company.

Looking forward, however, Goldman and Nalebuff knew that 2001 would be an important year for the company. In order to expand distribution, he figured that Honest Tea would have to raise financing. Goldman had recently received an offer from a prominent West Coast venture capital firm to invest $5 million in the company. Goldman was concerned, however, about what the implications of taking that much money from a professional venture capital group would do to the culture and mission of the company. He was particularly concerned that the valuation and control issues that the venture capital group demanded would be difficult for him or his employees to swallow. On the other hand, he could try to raise money from angel investors who shared a common vision for the company and who could add value at the same time. Goldman and Nalebuff had begun to sketch out their plans for raising that money. They had several op-

---

Professor Paul A. Gompers prepared this case as the basis for class discussion rather than to illustrate either effective or ineffective handling of an administrative situation.

tions and needed to decide soon which one they were going to follow. Goldman reached for the tea kettle to boil some water for a cup of tea and began to work.

THE FOUNDING

In the summer of 1997, Seth Goldman was running in Central Park. The temperature reached the mid-90s and Goldman was parched. On the way back to his friend's apartment, he stopped in a local convenience market to find something to drink. After trying several bottles of iced tea and sports drinks, Goldman found that none of them actually quenched his thirst. This experience led him to call Barry Nalebuff, his Yale School of Management professor. While at Yale, Goldman was intrigued about the beverage industry after reading a case on the cola wars between Coke and Pepsi in Nalebuff's class on competitive strategy. Goldman contacted his former professor, and they soon converged on an untapped opportunity in the beverage market, the space between super-sweet drinks and flavorless waters.

Goldman and Nalebuff both felt that the market for these types of beverages would be quite large. (See Exhibit 20-1 for statistics on the ready-to-drink tea market and the bottled water market.) They convened for several marathon tea-brewing sessions in which pots of water were boiled and various teas were mixed and matched. They were certain that others shared their same tastes and that the right beverage would catch on quickly. Several focus groups confirmed their idea. As ideas and investors for the company gathered critical mass, Seth left his marketing and sales post at Calvert Group, the nation's largest family of socially responsible mutual funds, and launched Honest Tea out of the guest room in his house. Using five large thermoses and label mock-ups, he sold the product to the 18 Fresh Fields stores of the Whole Foods Market chain. Four months later, the recipes were set, the teas were sourced, the labels were designed, and the teas were brewed and bottled. (See Exhibit 20-2 for management bios and Exhibit 20-3 for Honest Tea's mission statement.)

In order to get the tea on the shelves, Goldman actually rented a U-Haul and delivered the tea himself, 50 cases at a time. By the end of the summer of 1998, Honest Tea had become the best-selling tea throughout the Fresh Fields chain and was accepted by several national supermarket chains and distributors.

EXHIBIT 20-1

TEA CONSUMPTION VS. BOTTLED WATER CONSUMPTION

	Tea Consumption		Bottled Water Consumption	
	Gallons	Per capita	Gallons	Per capita
1994	2,682,200	10.4	2,901,900	11.3
1995	2,630,600	10	3,167,500	12
1996	2,590,200	9.7	3,449,300	13
1997	2,528,500	9.4	3,775,800	14
1998	2,548,200	9.4	4,146,000	15.3
1999	2,595,500	9.5	4,646,100	17

Source: Compiled from *Beverage Marketing Directory 2001.*

EXHIBIT 20-2

MANAGEMENT BIOGRAPHIES

President & TeaEO Seth Goldman launched Honest Tea after leaving the Calvert Group where he was Vice President of Calvert Social Investment Fund, the nation's largest family of mutual funds that invest in socially and environmentally responsible companies. In this role, Seth managed the marketing and sales efforts, including a groundbreaking public awareness campaign that increased Web site traffic eightfold and doubled sales in the company's flagship equity fund. His other work at Calvert Group included active involvement in the company's private equity portfolio and a corporate child labor initiative for the Calvert Foundation. As Calvert's most visible presence within the community of socially responsible businesses, Seth's contacts and connections helped give Honest Tea a mark of credibility. In addition, the target customer for Calvert's equity funds was very much in line with the Cultural Creative profile discussed earlier.

His previous work included directing a nationally recognized demonstration project for Americorps, which gave him experience managing a staff of more than 50 employees, and serving as Senator Lloyd Bentsen's Deputy Press Secretary for two and a half years, which helped him develop strong public relations skills as well as contacts. He had also worked for a year in China (1987–1988) and a year and a half in the former Soviet Union (1989–1990), where he developed, among other things, an appreciation for the role tea plays in many cultures.

Goldman graduated from the Yale School of Management in 1995. While at Yale, he and a classmate were winners of the inaugural Connecticut Future Fund New Enterprise Competition for a business plan they developed based on a diagnostic invented at the Yale School of Medicine. Seth is a graduate of Harvard College, where he was a Class Marshal and a member of the Varsity Track team. He served as Chair of the Yale School of Management Annual Fund and was on the board of the Montgomery Public Schools Educational Foundation. He was a former board member of Students for Responsible Business.

Chairman of the Board Barry Nalebuff was the Milton Steinbach Professor at Yale School of Management. He taught at Harvard and Princeton before coming to Yale where he taught competitive strategy, mergers and acquisition, strategic marketing, and decision making and game theory. An expert on Game Theory, he was co-author of *Thinking Strategically and Coopetition*, which was a *Business Week* bestseller. He applied the use of game theory in consulting to companies in banking, consumer products, health care, high-tech manufacturing, insurance, oil, pharmaceuticals software, and telecommunications. He was on the board of Trader.com, Bear Stearns Financial Products, and the Connecticut Citizenship Fund. A graduate of MIT and a Rhodes Scholar, he earned his doctorate in economics at Oxford University.

Chief Financial Officer Christel Bivens, CPA, joined Honest Tea in April of 1999, bringing a wide array of accounting experience, having been involved in all aspects of financial management—from budgeting to collections to cash management and financial analysis. She had worked with Telecorp, a $300 million telecommunications company, managed the IPO of Digene, and oversaw manufacturing plants for Greenstone, a $20 million manufacturing company.

Division Manager (Northeast) Dan Cavanaugh had the beverage business in his blood, having worked as a truck loader as early as the age of 13. He rose from being a route driver to managing Arizona's presence in New Jersey and then Nantucket Nectar's presence in the New York/New Jersey markets. He loved pioneering brands, knows all the players in the Northeast market and has demonstrated tremendous success in DSD and food service channels.

(Continued)

EXHIBIT 20-2   (Continued)

National Sales Manager (Natural/Specialty)   Melanie Knitzer came to Honest Tea in October 1998 from her post as Director of Corporate Sales with Gourm-E-Co Imports, a mid-Atlantic specialty food distributor. Melanie also brought 15 years of experience selling artisan products and coordinating promotions with major chains. She was responsible for managing all natural foods and gourmet foods retail accounts.

Brewmaster   George Scalf joined Honest Tea in March of 1998 to manage the production of the tea. As the founder of numerous natural beverage enterprises including, Blue Range Natural Foods and New Dawn Natural Foods, George brought more than 20 years of expertise and contacts in beverage manufacturing.

Director of Distribution (East)   Larry Vinson joined Honest Tea in March of 2000 from Sobe, where he managed the company's rapid expansion in the Southeast. He had more than 25 years of experience pioneering brands and developing DSD distribution networks from scratch, having also worked with Mistic and Snapple.

National Sales Manager (Food service)   Charlie Woodruff came to Honest Tea from Oregon Chai where he led that fast-growing brand's food service presence on the East Coast. He had pioneered a gourmet beverage into multiple food service channels.

Division Manager (Mountain States)   Larry Ziegler joined Honest Tea in April of 2000 after working with Gatorade/Quaker Oats, where he had managed that brand's presence from Idaho through Arizona. He also has worked with Snapple and Sysco, the nation's largest food service distributor. Based in Denver, Larry understands how to manage and develop beverage distribution networks.

Central-South Regional Manager   Danny Sky-Eagle. Danny joined the team in early 2001, bringing with him a strong network of distributor relationships he had developed during his tenure as a manager for Sobe in Oklahoma, Arkansas, Louisiana, and Missouri. In two years Danny built Sobe's business in that region from 9,000 cases per year to 200,000 cases per year.

Source: Company documents.

THE "READY-TO-DRINK" TEA MARKET

The myth of the origins of tea can be trace to 3000 BCE in China where the emperor Shen Nong is said to have ordered that all drinking water should be boiled to avoid disease transmitted by tainted water. According to the myth, one day when the emperor's servants were boiling water for him to drink, leaves from a nearby tree blew into the pot. The boiling water turned brown. Shen Nong is said to have tasted the liquid and was impressed by the drink. The consumption of tea soon spread throughout China.

In 2000, however, tea had become an international drink and was second in overall consumption only to water. The U.S. tea market, however, was considered quite different from the international market. First, overall tea consumption per capita was far lower in the United States than in most other countries. While the ready-to-drink tea market had experienced steady growth prior to 1990s, through most of the decade total tea consumption and per capita tea consumption declined quite dramatically. From 1998 to 1999, however, tea consumption was once again on the rise. Second, 80% of

---

EXHIBIT 20-3

STATEMENT AND ASPIRATIONS FOR SOCIAL RESPONSIBILITY

Although a statement of social and environmental responsibility is not usually found in most business plans, these issues are central to Honest Tea's identity and purpose. Not only is the value of our brand based on authenticity, integrity, and purity, but our management team is committed to these values as well. We will never claim to be a perfect company, but we will address difficult issues and strive to be honest about our ability or inability to resolve them. For example, we recognize that the labor and environmental conditions on many tea estates are below internationally accepted standards. We will strive to work with our suppliers to promote higher standards while recognizing the limited influence we have as a small company. We value diversity in the workplace and we intend to become a visible presence in the communities where our products are sold. When presented with a purchasing decision between two financially comparable alternatives, we will attempt to choose the option which better addresses the needs of economically disadvantaged communities.

We have taken our first substantive step in that direction with the development of our First Nation Peppermint. After much negotiation with I'tchik, a woman-owned company based on the Crow reservation, we have created a partnership that allows the Crow community to be economically involved in the production and sale of the tea. I'tchik is serving as Honest Tea's buyer for the ingredients, charging a modest administrative fee per kilo of tea with the understanding that over time I'tchik will develop the capacity to harvest the tea on the reservation. In addition I'tchik is licensing the recipe and artwork to Honest Tea in a royalty arrangement. A portion of the royalties are directed to the Pretty Shield Foundation, a nonprofit created to address the needs of at-risk Native American youth.

We are in the process of developing partnerships associated with new tea varieties, including City Year, the national urban peace corps program, and tea estates owned by black South Africans.

Source: Company documents.

---

tea consumed in the United States was consumed iced. No where else in the world was such a high fraction of tea drunk cold. (See Exhibit 20-4 for statistics on U.S. beverage consumption.)

Goldman and Nalebuff were targeting the "ready-to-drink" tea segment of the U.S. market. In 1999, the ready-to-drink tea market totaled $2.67 billion, up 9% from 1998. The average American consumed nearly two gallons of ready-to-drink tea each year. Many experts predicted that the ready-to-drink tea market would more than double in size over the next decade. Data on tea sales showed that while the majority of the ready-to-drink tea was purchased in supermarkets, other distribution channels were growing more rapidly. (See Exhibit 20-5 for a breakdown of beverage sales by channel.)

Several trends were driving the increased interest in tea consumption. First, there was increasing awareness of tea's health benefits versus carbonated soft drinks and alcohol. The growing presence of tea bars around the country was a testament to this trend. As competitors like Arizona Iced Tea and Sobe entered the market and dramatically sought to expand into new markets, ready-to-drink tea moved outside of the exclusive domain of supermarket distribution. By 2000, ready-to-drink teas were available in most warehouse clubs, convenience stores, gas stations, and dining establishments. In 2000 alone, more than $100 million was spent promoting ready-to-drink tea consumption.

EXHIBIT 20-4

DRINK CONSUMPTION IN THE UNITED STATES

	Wholesale Sales		
Drink	1998	1999	Growth
Beer	$ 28.49	$ 28.92	1.5%
Bottled water	$ 4.33	$ 4.94	14.1%
Fruit beverages	$ 12.77	$ 13.41	5.0%
Ready-to-drink teas	$ 1.34	$ 1.46	9.0%
Soft drinks	$ 41.79	$ 42.20	1.0%
Spirits	$ 15.55	$ 15.86	2.0%
Sport drinks	$ 1.59	$ 1.75	10.1%
Wine	$ 10.32	$ 10.63	3.0%
Total beverages	$116.18	$119.17	

	Retail Sales		
Drink	1998	1999	Growth
Beer	$ 54.20	$ 55.05	1.6%
Bottled water	$ 5.20	$ 5.92	13.8%
Fruit beverages	$ 17.50	$ 18.57	6.1%
Ready-to-drink teas	$ 2.45	$ 2.67	9.0%
Soft drinks	$ 54.30	$ 54.84	1.0%
Spirits	$ 34.05	$ 34.80	2.2%
Sport drinks	$ 2.65	$ 2.91	9.8%
Wine	$ 17.38	$ 17.91	3.0%
Total beverages	$187.73	$192.67	

Source: Compiled from *Beverage World's State of the Industry Report,* 2000.

The major competitors in the ready-to-drink tea market were all national brands. Snapple was the top brand with 14.6% of the market. Arizona Iced Tea held 10.6% of the market, while Lipton represented 9.5% of the market.

THE PRODUCT AND TARGET AUDIENCE

Somewhere between the pumped-up, sugar-saturated drinks and the tasteless waters, Goldman and Nalebuff saw a need for a healthier beverage, one that provided genuine natural taste without the artificially concocted sweeteners and preservatives designed to compensate for lack of taste. The concept of Honest Tea was to brew pure tea leaves from around the world in spring water and to add just a hint of honey or pure cane sugar.

Unlike most of the bottled teas in the marketplace, Honest Tea was not made with bricks of tea dust, tea concentrate, or artificial sweeteners. The tea had no bitter after-taste or sugar kick, and did not leave a syrupy film on the tongue. Although taste was

EXHIBIT 20-5

SALES OF BEVERAGE WITHIN VARIOUS CHANNELS

DOLLAR SALES

	Supermarkets		Drug Stores		Mass Merchandise		Total FDM	
	Dollar Sales (in Millions)	% Growth	Dollar Sales (in Millions)	% Growth	Dollar Sales (in Millions)	% Growth	Dollar Sales (in Millions)	% Growth
Carbonated soft drinks	$12,525.2	4.0%	$622.7	8.8%	$2,079.2	26.3%	$15,227.1	6.8%
Bottled water	1,432.0	20.9	120.0	20.2	244.0	55.0	1,796.0	24.6
Coffee	2,868.0	−8.2	47.9	−1.5	547.7	5.8	3,463.6	−6.2
Drink mixes	629.6	1.5	5.2	30.2	103.0	37.7	737.8	5.5
Aseptic juice	645.9	8.4	5.5	−4.3	127.1	36.1	778.5	12.0
Bottled juice (shelf-stable)	3,241.8	8.9	142.0	12.2	449.5	18.0	3,833.3	10.0
Canned juice (shelf-stable)	714.2	−0.6	5.2	−14.3	53.1	35.2	772.5	1.2
Instant tea	263.0	−4.6	1.6	−1.6	20.3	32.0	284.9	−2.7
Loose tea & tea bags	638.9	5.7	14.8	13.9	77.0	6.9	730.8	6.0
RTD tea	450.9	7.5	36.5	8.6	42.2	14.6	529.7	8.1
Isotonics	700.6	7.5	49.2	17.0	121.9	29.4	871.7	12.5
Milk	10,179.7	5.5	N/A	N/A	N/A	N/A	N/A	N/A

(Continued)

EXHIBIT 20-5 *(Continued)*

VOLUME SALES

	Supermarkets		Drug Stores		Mass Merchandise		Total FDM	
	Dollar Sales (in Millions)	% Growth	Dollar Sales (in Millions)	% Growth	Dollar Sales (in Millions)	% Growth	Dollar Sales (in Millions)	% Growth
Carbonated soft drinks	$ 3,341.1	−0.2%	$160.1	10.7%	$626.8	26.5%	$4,128.0	3.5%
Bottled water	1,155.6	14.4	51.7	14.0	205.1	43.6	1,412.4	17.8
Coffee	648.1	−2.2	14.1	17.0	168.0	17.5	830.2	1.6
Drink mixes	6,117.1	−1.2	46.2	19.0	969.6	25.3	7,133.0	1.8
Aseptic juice	1,017.1	5.8	8.6	−5.8	280.0	41.3	1,305.8	11.7
Bottled juice (shelf-stable)	5,615.5	7.4	200.1	9.2	931.3	17.3	6,746.8	8.7
Canned juice (shelf-stable)	1,186.5	−3.2	10.1	−9.3	112.8	33.8	1,309.3	−0.9
Instant tea	2,499.0	−4.8	13.1	−1.2	268.5	34.0	2,780.6	−2.0
Loose tea & tea bags	1,062.4	−0.6	24.4	27.4	171.2	32.5	1,258.0	3.3
RTD tea	952.3	5.6	57.8	7.8	106.9	21.2	1,117.0	7.0
Isotonics	1,141.8	6.6	68.0	13.1	224.6	28.2	1,434.4	9.8
Milk	27,296.2	−1.0	N/A	N/A	N/A	N/A	N/A	N/A

Source: Compiled from *Beverage Industry*, September 2000.

the primary benefit of drinking Honest Tea, the product had several attributes that enhanced its acceptance and marketability to four key audiences:

1. Disenchanted bottled tea drinkers who thought existing drinks were too sweet.
2. Bottled water drinkers who longed for taste and variety.
3. Diet soda drinkers who were interested in a low-calorie beverage that did not contain artificial sweeteners such as Nutrasweet.
4. Tea purists who were resigned to brewing tea at home because they had not been able to find "real tea" in a bottle.

The four attributes that made Honest Tea attractive to these consumers were:

1. *Low in calories:* A 12-ounce serving of Honest Tea had 9 to 17 calories, dramatically less than other bottled teas or comparable beverages.
2. *Health benefits of brewed tea:* The curative properties of tea had been known for thousands of years. Tea was the richest natural source of antioxidants. (Antioxidants impair the development of free radicals which contribute to cancer and heart disease.) The antioxidants in green tea were believed to be at least 100 times more effective than Vitamin C and 25 times better than Vitamin E at protecting cells and DNA from damage believed to be linked to cancer, heart disease, and other potentially life-threatening illnesses. In September 2000 Honest Tea released a comparative study on the antioxidant levels in bottled green teas performed by Analytical Chemical Services of Columbia. (For results of the study, see Exhibit 20-6.) Honest Tea significantly outperformed other bottled green teas. For example, Honest Tea's Moroccan Mint had six times the amount of EGCG, a key antioxidant, found in Arizona's Green Tea.
3. *Organic and all-natural ingredients:* With three bottled varieties that were fully organic and organic ingredients included in almost every variety, Honest Tea held a strong position in one of the fastest growing segments of the food industry. As consumers increasingly looked for products produced without chemical pesticides and fertilizers, Honest Tea represented a very approachable way for people to enjoy organic foods.
4. *Cultural experience of tea:* Each Honest Tea flavor was brewed based on a recipe perfected over generations in a specific region of the world. As a result, drinking Honest Tea became a cultural experience, from the genuine tastes to the distinctive international art and information on the label. While some bottled teas sought to cloak themselves in a cosmopolitan mantle by including exotic-looking drawings on the label, the front of each Honest Tea label featured authentic art from the culture of origin.

WHOLE LEAF TEA BAGS

As their bottled tea gained acceptance, Goldman and Nalebuff began thinking of ways to leverage the brand equity they had established. Ready-to-drink tea sales were highly seasonal, and they hoped introducing new products might dampen the seasonal effects. In March of 2000 the company introduced whole leaf tea bags that were the first fully biodegradable tag-and-bag tea bags. The bags contained whole leaves instead of tea dust, yielding a fuller, fresher taste—the richness of loose tea without the mess and accessories. After some adjustments to the packaging (plastic to paper overwraps), the

EXHIBIT 20-6

HONEST TEA CHARACTERISTICS

Calories per 8-ounce serving

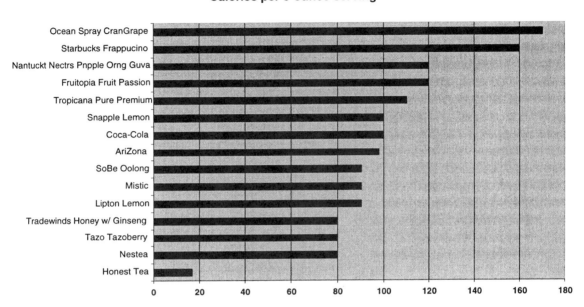

Range of EGCG in bottled green tea samples

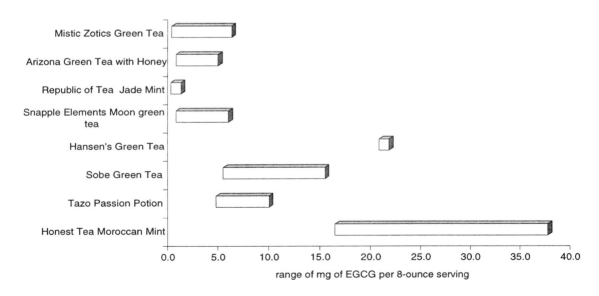

Source: Company documents.

EXHIBIT 20-7

TEA AND COFFEE CONSUMPTION (IN MILLIONS)

	1995	2000
Coffee	$4,023.80	$3,488.80
Ground coffee	$2,447.70	$2,089.20
Instant coffee	$ 720.00	$ 596.20
Whole bean coffee	$ 231.90	$ 283.80
Cocoa mixes	$ 347.80	$ 347.40
Tea bags/loose tea	$ 636.80	$ 751.10

Source: Compiled from *Beverage Industry*, September 2000.

---

bags entered natural foods distribution in the fall of 2000, and by December sales were picking up. The bags had been approved for Fresh Fields, Ukrop's, and Giant Eagle. They were made with unbleached paper and came in eight different varieties, five of which were organic. The first shippers, which merchandise the bags in a supermarket setting, were scheduled to enter distribution in December 2000. Food service merchandisers were scheduled to be completed in March of 2001. (See Exhibit 20-7 for data on tea bags and loose leaf tea sales.)

PRODUCTION AND MANUFACTURING

Initially, Goldman rented time in a bottling plant to brew his tea. During this period of time, Honest Tea developed several proprietary brewing tools and techniques that enabled it to manufacture several thousand cases of tea a day on both coasts with the desired consistency. In March 2000, the company consolidated its bottled tea production at Three Rivers Bottling, LLC, a plant Honest Tea had jointly purchased with Vancol Industries, a beverage company based in Denver, and Devine Foods, a food research and development company based in Philadelphia. While Honest Tea received a very attractive deal on its share of the plant, the operations of the plant had put some financial strain on the company, but Goldman felt that it was important to have the ability to control production. Since Honest Tea owned a third of a bottling plant and had a full-time brewmaster on staff, the company retained the knowledge of manufacturing the product, instead of relying on a co-packer for that information. All of the company's bottled tea was produced in the Three Rivers plant and shipped around the country.

The company had invested $300,000 in acquiring the plant and investing in the working capital to get production up and running. Goldman estimated that the plant had capacity to support approximately $30 million in sales. Because the current revenue run rate was far below this level, Honest Tea rented out production time to Arizona Iced Tea and other brands. The agreement with Arizona Iced Tea, however, was structured as a short-term rental and Honest Tea could increase production in short order if necessary.

The company's whole leaf tea bag line was developed through a strong strategic partnership with a tea bag co-packer on the East Coast. The unique bag-and-tag was patented by the co-packer. Honest Tea had manufactured proprietary equipment for the bags and had exclusive rights to those parts and designs.

PACKAGING AND PRICING

Honest Tea's bottled tea line was sold in 16-ounce glass bottles. All of the company's labels featured culturally authentic artwork. (See Exhibit 20-8 for sample bottle labels.) All caps had a "pop-button safety seal" and a distinctive black matte finish that complemented the black border on the front of the label. In 2001, Goldman had committed the company to use caps that would have fun and philosophical messages underneath, which would help reinforce Honest Tea's spirited, authentic image. The company's packaging was designed to communicate the attributes of the tea inside in four ways:

- *High quality*—By using colorful and artistically sophisticated artwork presented with spot labels, (i.e., front and back instead of wraparound), the bottles evoked comparisons with a bottle of fine wine and other gourmet food.

EXHIBIT 20-8

HONEST TEA BOTTLES

Source: Company documents.

- *Culturally authentic*—By using artwork directly from the culture where the tea came from, Honest Tea presented the tea as it was meant to be, without any "spin" or Westernized interpretation of what an Indian painting might look like.

- *Honest*—By using the spot labels, there was more space for the consumer to see the tea. Since the company used real tea leaves, it had nothing to hide inside.

- *Simplicity*—The essence of this millennia-old drink of water and leaves was its simplicity. Honest Tea's packaging had no flashy slogans, advertising callouts, or marketing hype. The package helped condition the consumer for what they were about to experience, an honest taste of tea.

In 2000 the company introduced a variety pack that contained a selection of flavors. This pack, which was first sold to natural food stores, had been approved by Costco for a test in the Southeast and Mid-Atlantic in 2001.

The retail price for a 16-ounce Honest Tea varied between $1.19 and $2.00. In food service accounts, the price range was from $1.29 to $2.50.

COMPETITIVE ADVANTAGE

The results of 2000 clearly indicated that Honest Tea had tapped into a market opportunity. In 1999, Goldman had planned to spend several years building up a strong presence in a local market before expanding nationally. The rapid growth during 2000, however, had changed his mind. (See Exhibits 20-9 and 20-10 for the historical financial performance of Honest Tea and Exhibit 20-11 for pro forma projections.) He now saw an opportunity to aggressively expand into new markets.

Market opportunity—Goldman and Nalebuff had created a new beverage category and were currently the only company filling that category. If Honest Tea were to hesitate, other companies would eventually move in.

Compelling brand image and story—The packaging, presentation, and profile of the Honest Tea brand fit together extremely well with the product. Although the company might be able to improve on the bottle design in the future, this was a package that came close to selling itself. It was also a brand and a story, which had successfully gained free media coverage.

Management team—Honest Tea had developed a team with the right combination of sales experience and market creativity that was capable of growing the company on a national, and even an international, scale.

Production capability—Even though it was not traditional for a beverage company Honest Tea's size to own a bottling plant, Goldman and Nalebuff made the strategic decision that it was essential to have control over their destiny. In the summer of 1999, several major brands ran into trouble with product shortages. If Honest Tea decided to focus all production at Three Rivers on Honest Tea, it could grow to $30 million in sales before they would need to develop additional production sites.

The excitement that Honest Tea had generated was palpable. In addition to the positive media coverage, the company had received a large number of recognitions in 2000, including:

- Named one of the "100 Most Notable Brands of the Century" by Beverage World
- First prize, National Nutritional Foods Association, best tea
- Socially Responsible Business Award at the Natural Product Expo

EXHIBIT 20-9

HISTORICAL FINANCIAL PERFORMANCE OF HONEST TEA

HONEST TEA, INC.
Income Statements, 1998–2000

	Year Ended Dec. 31		Qtr Ended June 30, 2000
	1998	1999	
REVENUES			
Sales	$273,913	$1,229,882	$630,022
Sales discounts	−$ 7,807	−$ 149,027	−$ 51,756
Other income	$ 5,862	$ 15,167	$ 14,254
Total revenues	$271,968	$1,096,022	$592,520
Cost of goods sold	$222,414	$ 745,321	$360,459
Gross profit, %	$ 49,555	$ 350,702	$232,060
EXPENSES			
Broker commissions	$ 0	$ 38,787	$ 20,649
Consultants	$ 81,464	$ 43,659	$ 27,344
General & administrative	$ 29,970	$ 103,242	$ 56,174
Payroll taxes & benefits	$ 13,191	$ 41,559	$ 17,847
Professional fees	$ 35,467	$ 24,307	$ 675
Research & development	$ 22,254	$ 80,957	$ 8,055
Salaries	$125,976	$ 390,876	$140,175
Sales & marketing	$ 87,016	$ 399,649	$131,278
Travel & entertainment	$ 15,647	$ 65,865	$ 42,519
Total operating expenses	$410,983	$1,188,901	$444,715
Bad debt expense	$ 0	$ 31,136	$ 2,384
Depreciation & amortization	$ 4,090	$ 11,916	$ 13,288
Interest expense	$ 0	$ 1,107	$ 551
Total expenses	$415,073	$1,233,062	$460,939
NET INCOME (LOSS)	−$365,519	−$ 882,359	−$228,879

(Continued)

- First Recipient of the Specialty Coffee Association of America's Award for Best Sustainable Practices/Product
- Gold Medal for its Web site from Art Directors Club of Metropolitan Washington
- Bronze Medal, Beverage Packaging Awards for First Nation bottled tea
- Seth Goldman selected as one of "20 Rising Stars Under 40" by *Gourmet News*

EXHIBIT 20-9 *(Continued)*

HONEST TEA, INC.
Balance Sheets, 1998–2000

	Year Ended Dec. 31		Qtr Ended June 30, 2000
	1998	1999	
ASSETS			
Current assets			
Cash	$ 33,578	$ 450,173	$ 220,982
Accounts receivable	$ 61,066	$ 176,039	$ 272,028
Inventory	$ 98,477	$ 297,571	$ 433,979
Prepaid expenses & other current assets	$ 0	$ 36,131	$ 49,284
Total current assets	$193,121	$ 959,915	$ 976,272
Investment—Three Rivers Bottling	$ 0	−$ 38,207	−$ 38,207
Secured notes receivable— Three Rivers Bottling	$ 0	$ 57,742	$ 82,538
depreciation	$ 22,644	$ 69,022	$ 182,335
of amortization	$ 1,389	$ 25,033	$ 24,737
Deposits	$ 0	$ 58,095	$ 114,336
Total assets	$217,153	$1,131,601	$1,342,011
LIABILITIES			
Current liabilities			
Accts pay & credit card	$ 1,518	$ 217,630	$ 164,945
Total current liabilities	$ 0	$ 217,630	$ 164,945
Long term lease obligation	$ 0	$ 1,843	$ 1,833
Total liabilities	$ 1,518	$ 219,472	$ 166,778
SHAREHOLDER'S EQUITY			
(value $.01/share); issued: 125 shares	$ 1	$ 0	$ 0
(value $.01/share); issued: 174 shares	$ 0	$ 2	$ 2
Additional paid in capital	$581,153	$2,366,662	$3,161,309
Loss from Investment in Three Rivers Bottling	$ 0	−$ 206,657	−$ 206,657
Retained earnings	−$365,519	−$1,247,879	−$1,779,422
Total shareholder's equity	$215,635	$ 912,129	$1,175,233
Total liabilities & shareholder's equity	$217,153	$1,131,601	$1,342,011

Source: Company documents. (Data disguised.)

EXHIBIT 20-10

QUARTERLY REVENUES FOR HONEST TEA

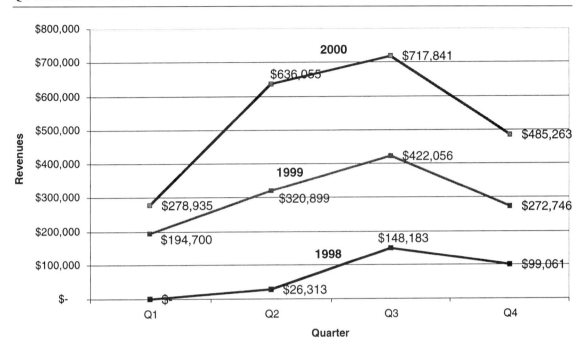

Source: Company documents. (Data disguised.)

EXIT STRATEGIES

Goldman believed that Honest Tea would be capable of financing its own growth through profits within the next 12 to 24 months. Even so, it was likely that the company's success would lead to invitations from strategic partners. Goldman felt that the most likely exit strategy would be either an investment or acquisition by a strategic partner. Sobe, Snapple, and Nantucket Nectars all were either acquired entirely or in part by large, strategic investors at between two and three times sales. In recent years, Coke, Pepsi and Cadbury-Schweppes seemed to be making less effort to build brands internally and more effort to acquire other brands. In addition, other large companies had been interested in the bottled beverage business, including Hain-Celestial, Danone, Unilever (Lipton's parent company), Crystal Geyser, and Suntory.

Although going public was a less traditional form of financing in the beverage industry, if Honest Tea could meet its expectations for growth, the company would consider a public offering to provide liquidity to investors and to raise capital for expansion in the future. Such an exit might eventually provide an opportunity to merge or acquire other beverage brands.

EXHIBIT 20-11

PRO FORMA PROJECTIONS FOR HONEST TEA

2001 Aggressive Growth ($ in thousands)	January	February	March	April	May	June	July	August	September	October	November	December	TOTAL
REVENUE													
Cases sold	38.18	67.38	78.61	87.59	95.46	106.69	101.07	112.30	106.69	89.84	85.35	75.24	1,044.39
RTD sales	$295.9	$522.2	$609.2	$678.9	$739.7	$826.8	$783.3	$870.3	$826.8	$696.3	$661.4	$583.1	$8,094.0
Tea bag/non-RTD sales	$67.4	$61.8	$61.8	$56.2	$56.2	$50.5	$50.5	$89.8	$101.1	$95.5	$106.7	$101.1	$898.4
Gross sales	$261.1	$584.0	$671.0	$735.0	$795.9	$877.3	$833.8	$960.2	$927.8	$791.7	$768.1	$684.1	$8,992.4
Discount/promotion/ allowance	5.00%	4.00%	10.00%	4.00%	4.00%	15.00%	5.00%	7.50%	7.50%	4.00%	4.00%	4.00%	
Discount on sales	($18.2)	($23.4)	($67.0)	($29.4)	($31.8)	($131.6)	($41.7)	($72.0)	($69.6)	($31.7)	($30.8)	($27.4)	($574.5)
Damages %	0.5%	0.5%	0.5%	0.5%	0.5%	0.5%	0.5%	0.5%	0.5%	0.5%	0.5%	0.5%	0.5%
Damages on sales	($1.8)	($2.9)	($3.4)	($3.7)	($3.9)	($4.4)	($4.2)	($4.8)	($4.6)	($3.9)	($3.8)	($3.4)	($44.9)
Net sales	$343.3	$557.7	$600.6	$701.9	$760.2	$741.4	$788.0	$883.4	$853.6	$756.1	$733.5	$653.4	$8,373.0
TOTAL COGS	$196.9	$307.4	$351.4	$382.7	$413.5	$453.6	$431.6	$503.1	$489.0	$419.0	$409.2	$365.6	$4,722.9
Gross Profit	$146.4	$250.3	$249.2	$319.3	$346.7	$287.8	$356.4	$380.2	$364.6	$337.1	$324.3	$287.7	$3,650.1
Three Rivers dividend	$0.0	$0.0	$0.0	$0.0	$4.5	$4.5	$4.5	$4.5	$4.5	$0.0	$0.0	$0.0	$22.5
Net revenue	$343.3	$557.7	$600.6	$701.9	$764.7	$745.9	$792.5	$887.8	$891.8	$756.1	$733.5	$653.4	$8,395.4
EXPENSES													
Slotting fees	$89.8	$89.8	$89.8	$89.8	$89.8	$0.0	$0.0	$0.0	$0.0	$0.0	$0.0	$0.0	$449.2
Coolers	$112.3	$112.3	$112.3	$0.0	$0.0	$0.0	$0.0	$0.0	$0.0	$0.0	$0.0	$0.0	$336.9
Marketing & Promotion	$134.8	$134.8	$134.8	$123.5	$112.3	$112.3	$112.3	$112.3	$101.1	$95.5	$95.5	$89.8	$1,358.8
Brokerage/commissions	$5.2	$8.4	$9.0	$10.6	$11.5	$11.1	$11.8	$13.3	$12.8	$11.3	$11.0	$9.8	$125.6
Consultants/Summer interns	$2.8	$2.8	$2.8	$2.8	$16.8	$16.8	$16.8	$20.2	$2.8	$2.8	$2.8	$2.8	$93.2
Legal & Acctg Fees	$2.2	$2.2	$2.2	$2.2	$2.2	$2.2	$2.2	$2.2	$2.2	$2.2	$2.2	$2.2	$27.0
General & Administrative	$6.7	$6.7	$9.0	$9.0	$11.2	$11.2	$11.2	$11.2	$9.0	$9.0	$9.0	$9.0	$112.3
Rent	$3.9	$3.9	$3.9	$6.2	$6.2	$6.2	$6.2	$6.2	$6.2	$6.2	$6.2	$6.2	$67.4
Research & Development	$11.2	$11.2	$11.2	$3.4	$0.0	$0.0	$0.0	$0.0	$0.0	$0.0	$0.0	$0.0	$37.1
Travel/entertainment	$39.3	$39.3	$39.3	$39.3	$50.5	$50.5	$50.5	$50.5	$39.3	$33.7	$33.7	$33.7	$499.7
Bonus & Prof. Development	$7.9	$9.5	$11.2	$11.2	$11.2	$11.2	$11.2	$11.2	$11.2	$11.2	$11.2	$11.2	$129.7
Salaries/wages/benefits	$78.6	$95.5	$112.3	$112.3	$112.3	$112.3	$112.3	$112.3	$112.3	$112.3	$112.3	$112.3	$1,297.1
EXPENSES	$494.8	$516.6	$537.9	$410.3	$424.2	$334.0	$334.7	$339.5	$296.9	$284.2	$283.9	$277.0	$4,533.9
Net income	($348.4)	($266.2)	($288.8)	($91.1)	($73.0)	($41.7)	$26.2	$45.3	$72.2	$52.9	$40.4	$10.7	($861.5)

(*Continued*)

EXHIBIT 20-11 (*Continued*)

2002 ($ in thousands)	January	February	March	April	May	June	July	August	September	October	November	December	TOTAL
REVENUE													
Cases sold	89.84	101.07	145.99	157.22	168.45	196.53	179.68	224.60	213.37	179.68	168.45	157.22	1,982.10
RTD sales	$696.3	$783.3	$1,131.4	$1,218.5	$1,305.5	$1,523.0	$1,392.5	$1,740.7	$1,653.6	$1,392.5	$1,305.5	$1,218.5	$15,361.2
Tea bag/non RTD sales	$112.3	$101.1	$101.1	$ 95.5	$ 95.5	$ 89.8	$ 89.8	$ 112.3	$ 168.5	$ 157.2	$ 224.6	$ 179.7	$ 1,527.3
Gross sales	$808.6	$884.4	$1,232.5	$1,313.9	$1,400.9	$1,612.9	$1,482.4	$1,853.0	$1,822.1	$1,549.7	$1,530.1	$1,398.1	$16,888.5
Disc/promo/allow	5.00%	4.00%	10.00%	4.00%	4.00%	15.00%	5.00%	7.50%	7.50%	4.00%	4.00%	4.00%	
Discount on sales	($40.4)	($35.4)	($123.2)	($52.6)	($56.2)	($241.9)	($74.1)	($138.9)	($136.7)	($62.0)	($61.2)	($55.9)	($1,078.4)
Damages %	0.5%	0.5%	0.5%	0.5%	0.5%	0.5%	0.5%	0.5%	0.5%	0.5%	0.5%	0.5%	0.5%
Damages on sales	($ 4.0)	($ 4.4)	($ 6.2)	($ 6.5)	($ 7.0)	($ 8.1)	($ 7.4)	($ 9.2)	($ 9.1)	($ 7.7)	($ 7.6)	($ 7.0)	($ 84.4)
Net sales	$764.1	$844.5	$1,103.1	$1,254.7	$1,337.8	$1,362.9	$1,400.8	$1,704.7	$1,676.3	$1,480.0	$1,461.2	$1,335.2	$15,725.6
Cost of Goods Sold													
TOTAL COGS	$423.6	$458.9	$631.4	$670.5	$713.7	$817.5	$752.9	$941.1	$937.3	$800.0	$804.1	$729.5	$8,680.3
Gross Profit	$340.5	$385.8	$471.9	$584.2	$624.3	$545.3	$648.0	$763.6	$739.0	$680.0	$657.2	$605.7	$7,045.3
Three Rivers dividend	$ 0.0	$ 0.0	$ 0.0	$ 0.0	$ 9.0	$ 9.0	$ 9.0	$ 9.0	$ 9.0	$ 0.0	$ 0.0	$ 0.0	$ 44.9
Net revenue	$764.1	$844.6	$1,103.1	$1,254.7	$1,346.9	$1,371.9	$1,409.8	$1,713.7	$1,685.3	$1,480.0	$1,461.2	$1,335.2	$15,770.5
EXPENSES													
Slotting	$ 89.8	$ 89.8	$ 89.8	$ 89.8	$ 89.8	$ 0.0	$ 0.0	$ 0.0	$ 0.0	$ 0.0	$ 0.0	$ 0.0	$ 449.2
Coolers	$112.3	$112.3	$112.3	$112.3	$ 0.0	$ 0.0	$ 0.0	$ 0.0	$ 0.0	$ 0.0	$ 0.0	$ 0.0	$ 449.2
Mktg & Promo	$179.7	$157.2	$157.2	$157.2	$157.2	$157.2	$157.2	$157.2	$157.2	$157.2	$157.2	$157.2	$1,909.1
Brokerage Comm	$ 9.5	$ 10.6	$ 13.8	$ 15.7	$ 16.7	$ 17.1	$ 17.5	$ 21.3	$ 21.0	$ 18.5	$ 18.3	$ 16.7	$ 196.5
Consult/SumIntern	$ 5.6	$ 5.6	$ 5.6	$ 5.6	$ 22.5	$ 22.5	$ 22.5	$ 24.7	$ 5.6	$ 5.6	$ 5.6	$ 5.6	$ 137.0
Legal & Acctg Fees	$ 2.8	$ 2.8	$ 2.8	$ 2.8	$ 2.8	$ 2.8	$ 2.8	$ 2.8	$ 2.8	$ 2.8	$ 2.8	$ 2.8	$ 33.7
Gen'l & Admin	$ 10.1	$ 10.1	$ 10.1	$ 10.1	$ 10.1	$ 10.1	$ 10.1	$ 10.1	$ 10.1	$ 10.1	$ 10.1	$ 10.1	$ 121.3
Rent	$ 6.7	$ 6.7	$ 6.7	$ 6.7	$ 6.7	$ 6.7	$ 6.7	$ 6.7	$ 6.7	$ 6.7	$ 6.7	$ 6.7	$ 80.9
Res & Devel	$ 11.2	$ 11.2	$ 11.2	$ 3.4	$ 0.0	$ 0.0	$ 0.0	$ 0.0	$ 0.0	$ 0.0	$ 0.0	$ 0.0	$ 37.1
Travel/entertainment	$ 50.5	$ 50.5	$ 50.5	$ 50.5	$ 61.8	$ 61.8	$ 61.8	$ 61.8	$ 61.8	$ 50.5	$ 50.5	$ 50.5	$ 662.6
Ben/bonus & prof dev	$ 13.5	$ 14.0	$ 14.6	$ 14.6	$ 14.6	$ 14.6	$ 14.6	$ 14.6	$ 14.6	$ 14.6	$ 14.6	$ 14.6	$ 173.5
Salaries & wages	$134.8	$140.4	$146.0	$146.0	$146.0	$146.0	$146.0	$146.0	$146.0	$146.0	$146.0	$146.0	$1,735.0
EXPENSES	$626.6	$611.4	$620.8	$614.8	$528.3	$438.8	$439.2	$445.3	$425.8	$412.1	$411.9	$410.3	$5,985.0
Net income	($286.1)	($225.6)	($149.0)	($ 30.5)	$105.0	$115.7	$217.7	$327.4	$322.2	$267.8	$245.3	$195.4	$1,105.1

Source: Company documents. (Data disguised.)

351

FINANCING OF HONEST TEA

Honest Tea was formally launched in February 1998 with a $300,000 start-up investment by Goldman and Nalebuff. (See Exhibit 20-12 for proposed financing structure.) The founders felt that going to a large outside investor at this stage would have been a distraction. The money was used to prove the concept, refine the product, and land distribution agreements. In addition to the common stock that they purchased, the founders were given warrants for creating the company.

Nalebuff came up with the novel financing structure to avoid contentious discussions about what the value of the company should be in the first round. While he and Goldman had put together the projections for Honest Tea right from the start, they were entering uncharted waters. The category of beverage they were targeting did not exist and investors could not be certain that the company would take off. Therefore, Nalebuff thought that by including warrants for the founders with exercise prices staged at multiples of the initial price at which family and friends brought in would avoid such disagreements. If the company did very well, as Goldman and Nalebuff believed, then they would be able to exercise their warrants and they would own a greater fraction of the company. If they did not do as well, then the original investors would own a larger piece of the firm.

Shortly after launching the company, Goldman and Nalebuff approached family and friends to gauge their interest in making rather modest investments in the firm. An additional $217,500 was raised in a relatively short time. The pre-money valuation was assumed to be zero for all of the initial financing.

In late 1998, Goldman realized that the company would need additional capital to continue operations. The goal was to raise a significantly more substantial round to provide the money for expanding the production and distribution. While he felt that family and friends could be counted on for some of the round, Goldman hoped to raise enough money to push distribution into several new channels.

In the process of searching for potential angels, Goldman returned to the pile of e-mails he had received from loyal customers. While the company did not solicit funds over the Internet, Honest Tea, like most start-ups, had a Web page devoted to telling the company's story. Many people who tried the tea loved the product so much that they responded by sending e-mails to Goldman praising the clean and refreshing taste of Honest Tea. Several satisfied consumers even wrote that they would consider investing in the company should Honest Tea need financing in the future. Goldman decided to send anyone who had expressed an interest in providing capital the investment letter for the company's second round of financing. Goldman was pleasantly surprised and received commitments for $1.2 million. The round placed a pre-money valuation of $4 million on the company. Despite the success in fundraising, however, Nalebuff and Goldman had spent a significant amount of time over the past eight months fundraising during this round. Even when they were not physically raising money, it was always on their mind.

In early 2000, Honest Tea once again needed to raise financing. Nalebuff and Goldman had discussions with a venture group about coming into the round. Before investing, the group wanted to see what commitment would be found from existing investors. Goldman and Nalebuff went to their existing investors and quickly gained a commitment for all the capital they needed. The financing raised a total of $1 million at a $8.5 million pre-money valuation.

EXHIBIT 20-12

PROPOSED FINANCING STRUCTURE

December 15, 2000

Offering of Honest Tea Shares

Honest Tea is offering a total of 54 share-and-warrants packages, valued at $37,000 each, at a pre-money valuation of $13,113,000, and a $15,111,000 post-money valuation. The offering therefore represents 2/15, or 13.3% of the company. The shares will be issued on a first-come-first-served basis. In the event the offering is oversubscribed, Honest Tea reserves the right to expand the offering by 10%, or five additional shares.

We have designed a share-plus-warrant package that seeks to protect shareholders against future dilution by offering two half warrants with the shares being offered

Each share-and-warrant package being offered consists of the following:

1.00 share

0.50 warrants at 50k exercise

0.50 warrants at 75k exercise

In any liquidity event, all in-the-money warrants can be called and converted into stock and all out-of-the-money warrants expire worthless. This holds true for all warrants in the company.

PRE-FUNDRAISING	Shares	Warrants $5,000	Warrants $10,000	Warrants $15,000	Warrants $25,000	Warrants $50,000	Warrants $75,000
Founders	80		80	80	80	56	63
Employees/consultants	4	4	3	1	7	1	1
Seed investors	45					22	
First Round investors	48					24	
Second Round investors	38					18.5	18.5
TOTAL	215	4	83	81	87	121.5	82.5

POST-FUNDRAISING	Shares	Warrants $5,000	Warrants $10,000	Warrants $15,000	Warrants $25,000	Warrants $50,000	Warrants $75,000
Founders	80		80	80	80	56	63
Employees/consultants	4	4	3	1	7	1	1
Seed investors	45					22	
First Round investors	48					24	
Second Round investors	38					18.5	18.5
Third Round investors	**54**					**27**	**27**
TOTAL	**269**	4	83	81	87	**148.5**	**109.5**

The numbers in bold indicate changes to the equity structure

(*Continued*)

EXHIBIT 20-12   (Continued)

December 15, 2000

Performance Guarantee for offering of shares

We have set aggressive sales targets for 2001 and beyond. We are confident we can meet these sales goals; if not, we are prepared to stand by these targets and a post-money valuation of $15,111,000 with a performance guarantee based on 2001 calendar-year sales. The valuation to the investors participating in this round is based on the following formula:

$$2\times \text{tea bottle sales}$$

$$7\times \text{bag sales}$$

$$\$750,000 \text{ value of the bottling plant}$$

Two Scenarios:

To see how this works, we provide two scenarios:

1. If bottled sales are $8 million and tea bag sales are $400,000, the company would have the following valuation:

$$(2*\$8,000,000) + (7*\$400,000) + \$750,000 = \$19,550,000$$

   Since the resulting valuation exceeds $15.1 million, no adjustment to valuation would be made.

2. If bottled sales are $4 million and tea bag sales are $200,000, the company would have the following valuation:

$$(2*\$400,000) + (7*\$200,000) + \$750,000 = \$10,150,000$$

   Since the resulting valuation is less than $15.1 million, investors would be issued additional shares. Investors in this round would see their share of the company shift from 13.3% to 19.7% (which is $2 million/$10.15 million).

Source: Company documents.

WHERE TO GO FOR FINANCING?

Despite all the company's success over the past year, it still needed financing to bring it to breakeven. Goldman had initially estimated that a $2 million round of financing would carry Honest Tea to profitability. The cash was needed to finance operating losses for the next several quarters as well as to invest in new distribution channels. Capital needs included the hiring of a national sales force. With the acquisition of Sobe by Pepsi, Honest Tea had the opportunity to hire several, well-connected sales managers who had helped make Sobe the fastest growing brand in the country. Funds were also needed to purchase marketing and merchandising materials such as coolers and other sales incentives. The company also required capital to support the launch of Honest Tea in several new supermarket chains including Safeway. The launch of Honest Tea in 500 Safeway's required an introductory allowance of one case per SKU per store. Finally, the company needed capital to help get the Three Rivers Bottling plant to profitability.

Goldman and Nalebuff had had several meetings and conversations trying to hammer out details of the financing strategy. Both wanted to diversify the investor base and potentially bring on an investor that could help with the operational aspects of running a startup. On an early trip to the West Coast, Goldman met with several venture capital groups. One prominent firm had offered to invest $5 million in Honest Tea. While Goldman was excited, he was also concerned. The venture group had proposed a pre-money valuation in the $5 to $7 million range and significant control over the board of directors and future strategic decisions. While the money would help the company grow aggressively and would provide a reputational benefit for the young company, Goldman and Nalebuff were uncertain about whether such a deal made sense at this time. The venture capital firm wanted to push Honest Tea to expand very rapidly and might push Goldman to compromise some of his convictions.

On the same trip, Goldman met with several angel investor groups, including the Investors' Circle (IC), a nonprofit national network of investors. IC was founded in 1992 and had invested more than $70 million in 120 companies. The median investment amount was $225,000, but the group's investments ranged from $10,000 all the way to $6.5 million depending on the company's needs and members' interests. What was unusual about IC was its investment goals. The group invested in socially responsible start-ups. (See Exhibit 20-13 for IC's statement of responsibility and Exhibit 20-14 for a description of previous investments by IC.) Because Goldman had worked with the IC when he worked at the Calvert Group, he believed that IC's investment philosophy coincided with the mission of Honest Tea. He felt that members of IC might be able to provide as much as $500,000 in the next round of financing.

Even if he could count on the Investors' Circle, however, Goldman had considerably more legwork ahead of him. He had to identify other individuals who would be willing to invest and be able to help Honest Tea. In fact, Goldman was convinced that this round of investment must bring in a new, more value-added set of investors. Gold-

---

EXHIBIT 20-13

INVESTORS' CIRCLE STATEMENT OF RESPONSIBILITY

The Board of Investors' Circle has endorsed the following Statement of Responsibility:

We begin the investment management process recognizing that our responsibility as investors does not end with maximizing return and minimizing risk.

We recognize that economic growth can come at considerable cost to community and environment.

We believe that efforts to mitigate environmental degradation and promote social well-being will be successful to the extent that these concerns are brought from the margins to the center of business and investment decision making.

We recognize that addressing such concerns while pursuing financial objectives is an imperfect process. However, we believe that the development of healthier corporate cultures, and through them a healthier, more sustainable economy, depends on the recognition of these concerns by management, directors, employees, and investors.

Investors' Circle encourages companies to articulate their own statement of principles relating to corporate responsibility and sustainability.

Source: Company documents.

EXHIBIT 20-14

INVESTORS' CIRCLE INVESTMENTS

Earth's Best: Organic baby food.

University Access: Internet-based content in broadband content for higher education.

Mosaic Technologies: Minority-owned biotechnology company.

Energia Global: Renewable power and cogeneration, and energy-efficient products and services in Latin America.

Wild Planet Toys: Maker of nonviolent toys.

Sonic Innovations: Developer of hearing instruments.

Biocorp: Manufacturer of fully biodegradable garbage, grocery, and trash bags.

Brush Dance: Distributor of products that inspire and enlighten, featuring the words and images of leading authors, philosophers, and spiritual teachers.

Latina Magazine: Bilingual magazine by and about Hispanic women.

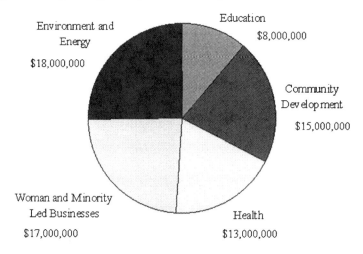

Source: Company documents.

man hoped to identify a lead investor who would agree to valuation and terms. Then other, smaller investors would fall in line. Negotiating terms with multiple parties was a very real challenge. Each angel investor came to the table with his or her own set of issues.

At the same time, Goldman hoped to establish a real board of directors. If he could attract the right angels, putting them on the board could provide value-added advice and direction. Goldman wondered whether he could find the right investors quickly. While sales were currently at a relatively low point in the year, he didn't feel that he could take a lot of time away from the business. Fundraising was meant to allow the business to operate effectively. It was not supposed to be the business.

EXHIBIT 20-15

COMPARABLE FINANCIAL INFORMATION

	1995	1996	1997	1998	1999
TRIARC COS INC					
Sales	1184.22	989.25	861.32	815.04	853.97
Net Inc	−36.99	−13.90	−3.62	14.64	10.12
EBITDA	95.19	113.12	105.17	121.35	123.03
Total Assets	1085.97	854.40	1004.87	1019.89	1123.73
Current Assets	412.83	445.66	355.76	409.50	477.64
Current Liabilities	254.56	250.49	225.67	201.14	239.65
Market Value of Equity	329.05	343.67	861.02	465.09	436.88
Total Debt	846.88	594.10	619.01	708.96	893.05
Net Worth	20.65	6.76	43.99	10.91	−166.73
Beta	NA	0.958	0.975	1.138	0.905
SARATOGA BEVERAGE					
Sales	3.27	4.38	6.27	8.88	50.74
Net Inc	−0.92	−0.15	0.81	0.87	1.76
EBITDA	−0.72	0.23	1.08	1.53	4.87
Total Assets	2.99	2.63	5.70	7.50	41.35
Current Assets	1.07	1.00	3.80	3.96	13.89
Current Liabilities	0.81	0.61	1.29	1.55	5.40
Market Value of Equity	5.45	2.55	6.31	7.00	26.60
Total Debt	0.15	0.31	1.51	1.57	23.61
Net Worth	2.18	2.01	2.91	4.39	11.99
Beta	NA	NA	0.756	0.886	0.632
NATIONAL BEVERAGE CORP					
Sales	350.43	385.43	400.75	402.11	426.27
Net Inc	9.00	10.69	13.10	13.17	13.58
EBITDA	25.50	27.82	30.52	29.52	26.89
Total Assets	177.56	170.90	182.33	180.40	197.75
Current Assets	101.62	96.16	107.34	104.14	113.67
Current Liabilities	58.04	48.54	56.94	46.64	58.77
Market Value of Equity	87.29	184.60	189.56	164.36	151.10
Total Debt	63.50	55.75	41.99	40.27	33.93
Net Worth	47.05	56.70	69.98	82.00	93.69
Beta	0.856	0.831	0.753	1.035	0.887
CLEARLY CANADIAN BEVERAGE, INC.					
Sales	48.20	50.08	47.27	39.93	36.60
Net Inc	−3.97	0.45	−12.27	0.31	−9.94
EBITDA	−2.00	1.00	−0.88	2.46	−2.99
Total Assets	36.50	52.10	46.66	42.83	33.85
Current Assets	22.71	27.50	18.81	15.73	10.10
Current Liabilities	5.89	7.44	7.05	5.59	5.57
Market Value of Equity	15.11	41.69	31.09	13.64	6.17
Total Debt	2.46	4.10	7.08	6.03	5.69
Net Worth	28.46	43.37	34.68	32.89	23.68
Beta	NA	0.660	0.804	1.076	1.051

Source: Compiled from Compustat.

DECISION

Now that the kettle was bubbling away, Goldman opened up a pack of Kashmiri Chai tea and began to let it steep. He knew that the market potential for his company was very large. The real questions, however, was what type of investor made sense. On the one hand, taking venture capital funding would save him time and energy and would provide capital to grow Honest Tea quickly. He wondered, however, whether the strings attached to the funding were worth it. On the other hand, Goldman knew that angels could be incredibly high maintenance, needing significant amounts of handholding and information. Most of Honest Tea's investors were relatively unsophisticated, and on more than one occasion, Goldman had had to spend hours just explaining how to interpret an income statement and balance sheet. Communicating information to more than 50 individual investors often demanded a great deal of Goldman's time.

Until now the choices of financing had been driven out of necessity and ease of access. Now, however, Goldman felt that he and Nalebuff needed to craft a plan to bring Honest Tea to the next level. They had proven that a market for their product existed and had begun to craft a strategy to establish it as the market leader in this segment. With money, advice, and a little luck, they just might become the next "must have" brand.

## 21

A Note on the Venture Leasing Industry

INTRODUCTION TO LEASING[1]

Equipment leasing is among the most ancient of financing mechanisms, dating back to the Phoenician shipping industry of 3,000 years ago. In the U.S. economy, however, rapid growth in equipment leasing did not occur until the boom of the early 1950s. Fast-growing firms then began leasing a wide variety of capital equipment from construction machinery to aircraft to computers.

The essential characteristic of a lease is that the user of the equipment (the lessee) does not own the equipment. Rather, the title rests with the lessor, who receives periodic payments from the lessee. While long-term leasing is similar to purchasing equipment with a secured loan (that is, debt that is guaranteed by a pledge of the firm's assets), leasing has several advantages that can make it an attractive financing option for firms.

The first consideration is taxes. If the firm is in a low-tax bracket, it cannot take full advantage of the tax deduction for the depreciation of its capital equipment. In fact, if the firm is losing money, it will have to defer using the deductions for depreciation until it reaches profitability. Leasing can address this problem. Since the title to the equipment remains with the lessor, he can deduct the depreciation for income taxes as long as certain tests specified by the U.S. Internal Revenue Service are met. But taxes have a limited ability to explain which firms employ leasing and how much equipment they lease.[2]

Professor Joshua Lerner prepared this case as the basis for class discussion rather than to illustrate either effective or ineffective handling of an administrative situation. I thank Paul Gompers for his assistance in preparing the tables, and Jonathan Axelrad of Wilson, Sonsini, Goodrich & Rosanti for helpful comments.

[1] This background section is based primarily on Stephen A. Ross, Randolph W. Westerfield, and Jeffrey F. Jaffe, "Leasing," *Corporate Finance* (Homewood, IL: Irwin, 1993), pp. 673–702, and U.S. Department of Commerce, International Trade Administration, *A Competitive Assessment of the U.S. Equipment Leasing Industry* (Washington, DC: ITC, 1985).

[2] See, for instance, Clifford E. Smith and L. MacDonald Wakefield, "Determinants of Corporate Leasing Policy," *Journal of Finance* 40 (1985): 895–908; and James Ang and Pamela P. Peterson, "The Leasing Puzzle," *Journal of Finance* 39 (1984): 1055–1065.

One of the most important nontax motivations for leasing is the possibility of bankruptcy. In these cases, holders of secured debt often find it hard to obtain the property pledged to them, even if their legal rights to the property are well established. Because the lessor retains title to the asset, and the lessee uses the asset only as long as there are no defaults on lease payments, it is often easier for the lessor to recover his equipment.[3] A consequence of this improved security is that lessors typically provide 100% financing for equipment purchases. Banks will often require that the firm pay up front in cash 10% or more of the purchase price.

Several other explanations for choosing leasing over secured debt are frequently offered. First, many management compensation schemes are based on return on invested capital. Leasing may lead to a lower computed level of invested capital, and consequentially to higher bonuses. Second, lessors may become specialists in assessing the quality of maintenance and the resale value of equipment. Leasing organizations may thus be better at avoiding costly defaults than bankers, who make loans secured by many classes of assets. Finally, managers of risky enterprises often prefer leases to bank loans because of the limited collateral. While bank loans are often secured by all the firm's assets, leases are secured only by the equipment being leased. A default on a lease thus may not entail the same level of disruption to the firm as the failure to meet a bank payment.

THE ORIGIN OF VENTURE LEASING[4]

Venture leasing had its origins in the late 1960s, as the boom in venture capital financing in that decade slowed. Several West Coast venture capital organizations sensed the opportunity to lease equipment to start up firms as well as provide equity financing. As the new firms found it more difficult to obtain equity financing, they had sought to finance major equipment purchases with debt. Bank loan officers, however, had little interest in firms without operating revenues, much less profits. Even when they were willing to extend loans, they typically demanded that the firms purchase the equipment with between 30% and 70% cash up-front. This was usually impossible to manage. Similarly, the start-ups encountered difficulties structuring arrangements with traditional leasing agencies, which often used criteria similar to those employed by commercial banks.

The early venture leasing deals typically involved three parties. Not only was the lessee and the venture capitalist-lessor involved, but frequently another venture fund was as well: the lead venture capitalist investing in the firm. This was because a relatively small number of venture funds undertook venture leasing. Consequently, venture lessors were reliant on the referrals of other venture financiers for deals. As in a traditional lease, the lessor maintained title to the equipment over the life of the lease. Unlike traditional leasing, both the lessor and the lead venture capitalist who had provided the referral received warrants in the firm.

These early leases were usually structured as triple-net full-payout leases. This meant the lessee would make payments that covered the entire cost of the leased equip-

[3] For a detailed description, see Linda L. Boss, "Uniform Commercial Code Article 2A—Leases: Structuring Priorities of Competing Claimants to Leased Property," *Minnesota Law Review* 73 (October 1988): 208–245.

[4] The most comprehensive history of venture leasing—on which this section is largely based—is Venture Economics, *Venture Leasing* (Needham, MA: Venture Economics, 1989).

ment over the course of the lease. In addition, the lessee would assume responsibility for costs such as maintenance, taxes, and insurance.

Although several successful transactions were completed in the early 1970s, the boom was short-lived. This new financial product faced several difficulties. First, the venture capitalists promoting this product encountered considerable resistance from the start-up firms. The new firms were concerned that the leases would add to an already substantial arsenal of mechanisms through which venture capitalists could exercise control over their firms.

Second, the management of these arrangements proved daunting to the venture capital organizations. The administration of the leases called for considerable paperwork on a monthly basis. Many venture capital firms were run as very "lean" organizations, with little capability to handle routine administrative tasks.

Finally, the reduced capital commitments to the venture capital industry during the 1970s led to a retrenchment. Venture capitalists focused primarily on raising funds to support their core business of investing in new firms, rather than on expanding their product offerings.

The rebirth of venture leasing was fueled by the growth of investments in the semiconductor industry in the early 1980s. The chip fabrication equipment that semiconductor manufacturers needed was enormously expensive. In late 1982, a West Coast venture capital fund encouraged Equitec Financial Group, a major real estate syndicator, to extend leases for the purchase of semiconductor manufacturing equipment. Out of these discussions, a new Equitec subsidiary, Equitec Leasing Company, was born. Between 1984 and 1987, Equitec raised 11 limited partnerships of approximately $30 million each, to undertake equipment leases to high-risk firms.

Between the first venture leases and these funds, the treatment of leases had been codified by the Financial Accounting Standards Board (FASB). The new venture leases were structured as capital leases. This was required if at least one of several tests, as stated in FASB's Statement 13, were met. These sought to ascertain if the economic ownership in the leased equipment had been transferred to the lessee.[5] In these cases, the firm was required to include the leased asset as an additional asset, and the lease obligation as a liability. (In other cases, the lease would just be noted in a footnote to the financial statements.)

This success of the early Equitec funds led to entry by a number of other firms. These included other real estate syndicators, investment banks, equipment leasing firms, and several organizations dedicated to venture leasing. These firms active in venture leasing since 1982 are summarized in Exhibit 21-1. The volume of venture leasing in several years, as well as that of traditional venture investments, is reported in Exhibit 21-2.

THE VENTURE LEASING PROCESS

The first step in the venture leasing process, it could be argued, is fundraising. A few of these organizations have employed their internal capital, but it has been far more common for venture lessors to access capital through limited partnerships. These specialized pools of money have been raised through private placements with solo investors and syndicated partnerships with a number of limited partners.

---

[5] These tests included if (1) the present value of the lease payments was at least 90% of the asset value, (2) the lease life was at least 75% of the economic life of the asset, and (3) the lessee was able to purchase the asset at a below-market value price at the end of the period.

EXHIBIT 21-1

MAJOR ACTORS IN VENTURE LEASING BUSINESS, 1982–1998

Aberlyn Capital Management
Waltham, Massachusetts
An investment banking that entered venture leasing in 1992.

Comdisco Ventures (about $500 million in assets under management in the beginning of 1998)
Rosemont, Illinois
Primary line of business: equipment leasing
Entered venture leasing in 1987.

Costella Kirsch
Mountain View, California
Solely devoted to venture leasing.
Established in 1986; apparently exited in the late 1980s.

Dominion Ventures (about $250 million in assets under management in the beginning of 1998)
San Francisco, California
A subsidiary of two venture capital firms and the leasing holding company PLM Co.
Established in 1985 solely to do venture leasing; emphasis on early-stage deals.

Eden Hannon and Co.
Menlo Park, California
Primary line of business: government asset and energy financing.
Entered venture leasing in the mid-1980s, but exited soon thereafter.

Equitec Leasing Company
Oakland, California
A subsidiary of a real-estate syndicator.
Established in 1982 as the first venture leasing organization; acquired by Pacificorp Financial Services (a utility's financial subsidiary in 1990); declared bankruptcy in 1991.

Fairfax Financial Group
Fairfax, Virginia
Primary line of business is tax-exempt leasing.
Entered venture leasing in the mid-1980s; apparently exited in the late 1980s.

Lease Management Services
Menlo Park, California
One of earliest venture leasing organizations.

Lighthouse Capital Partners (about $120 million in assets under management in the beginning of 1998)
Greenbrae, California
Emphasis on early-stage transactions.
Founded in 1994.

Linc Capital Partners (about $125 million in assets under management in the beginning of 1998)
Chicago, Illinois
A subsidiary of a specialist in health-care equipment lease financing for hospitals.

Phoenix Growth, Inc. (about $250 million in assets under management in the beginning of 1998)
San Rafael, California
A subsidiary of Phoenix America, a leasing firm and limited partnership broker, with a strong leasing emphasis.

R&D Funding Corporation
New York, New York
A subsidiary of Prudential Securities. Served as a general partner, beginning in 1984, in two limited partnerships that provided venture leasing: PruTech I and II. Currently inactive and subject to litigation.

Technology Funding Securities
San Mateo, California
Subsidiary of a venture capital organization, Technology Funding, which had marketed R&D limited partnerships in the early 1980s.

Third Coast Capital (about $66 million in assets under management in the beginning of 1998)
Chicago, Illinois
Founded in 1996; acquired by DVI, Inc. in 1998.

Western Technology Investment
San Jose, California

Source: Compiled from numerous media accounts, Web pages, and corporate filings with the Securities and Exchange Commission.

EXHIBIT 21-2

VENTURE LEASING AND TRADITIONAL VENTURE CAPITAL INVESTMENTS BY YEAR

	Venture Leasing				Traditional Venture Capital		
Year	Total Firms Funded[a]	Total Amount Invested ($000)	Average Amount Invested ($000)	Range ($000)	Median Investment ($000)	Total Firms Funded[a]	Total Amount Invested ($Billion)
1986	55	$ 54,511	$991	$57–$4,500	$750	1,504	$3.23
1987	97	92,672	945	150–5,000	750	1,729	3.94
1988	177	154,939	875	50–3,000	500	1,472	3.65
1989	—	200,000[b]	—	—	—	1,355	3.26

[a] Some firms may have received several traditional venture rounds in a single year.

[b] Estimate.

Source: Compiled from Venture Economics, *Venture Leasing* (Needham, MA: Venture Economics, 1989); and Venture Economics, "Special Report: Disbursements Fall for Second Year," *Venture Capital Journal* 30 (July 1990): 14–22.

The venture leasing partnerships are in many respects structured like venture capital partnerships. The foremost of these similarities is in the compensation of the general partners (the venture lessors). Venture lessors will charge the fund a management fee and receive a percentage of profits. The annual management fees are often 2% to 3% of the capital committed to the fund or the assets under management. Other funds structure fees as up to 5% of the partnership's gross revenues from rental fees and equipment sales. Additional charges may be made per each lease signed.

In addition, the general partners will receive between 15% and 30% of the profits from the fund, but most usually 20%. These funds are usually only received after the limited partners receive their initial investment back. In recent years, it has become more common to also provide for a minimum annual rate of return to the limited partners before the general partners begin receiving distributions.

Venture leasing partnerships differ from venture capital organizations, however, in two respects. First, the timing of the cash flows out of the fund is quite different. Venture capital funds typically must wait years until the first investments are "harvested" through an acquisition or an initial public offering. Venture leasing funds, however, generate funds from lease payments almost immediately. Consequently, the funds will typically pay out distributions quarterly, beginning in the first year of operations.

The second difference is the nature of the investors. Venture lessors have found the primary contemporary sources of venture capital, pension funds, and endowments, to be reluctant to invest in their partnerships. The reluctance of the institutions to invest stems from three factors. The first is the information costs associated with educating pension fund managers about venture leasing. Venture investments make up only a small percentage of most pension portfolios. Pension managers are unlikely to spend much time learning about the opportunities inherent in venture leasing, a small subfield of this area. Second, many pension managers are reluctant to invest funds for which they bear a fiduciary responsibility in a relatively unproven asset class.

A final concern is the tax treatment of nonprofit institutional investors' investments in venture leasing funds. In particular, the Internal Revenue Service regards the interest payments from the lessee to the fund as unrelated business income. Many nonprofit institutions are required to pay taxes on such income, even if the lease payments are retained by the partnership and not distributed to the limited partners. Since the vast majority of endowment earnings are not taxable (e.g., traditional dividends), the tax status of leasing funds imposes a substantial administrative burden and may lead to a less attractive financial return.

Thus, the primary limited partners in leasing partnerships funds have been individuals—just as they were in the early days of the venture capital. Increasingly important sources of funds are insurance companies and foreign individuals and institutions. These investors have been attracted to the high returns promised by venture leasing funds, particularly in light of the relatively low yields of Treasury bonds and bills.

Consistent with the origins of the venture leasing industry, these firms have cultivated the venture capital industry. Most firms have close ties with two or three venture capital organizations, who will steer portfolio companies to them. The primary incentive for the venture capitalist is that this provides a chance for their firms to receive additional financing while reducing their stake in the firm by only a small percentage.

In many respects, the venture lessors play a role for the venture capitalists that is akin to that of marginal or fringe venture partnerships. The venture lessors provide financing after the lead venture capitalist makes the bulk of his investment, in exchange for a much smaller share of the firm's equity. The venture lessors will similarly rely on the lead venture capitalist to monitor management through his role on the board and to provide them with accurate information about the firm's prospects. But because the same venture capitalists and venture lessors frequently interact on deals, their relationships avoid the exploitative behavior that has sometimes characterized established the venture capitalists' relationships with less experienced venture funds.

Many of the remaining deals come from the same network of service providers to high-technology firms—law firms, auditors, academic consultants—that venture capitalists employ to generate prospective investments. A small number of firms—most notably, Meier Mitchell and Co. and Venlease Associates—have established themselves as brokers of venture leases. These firms locate prospective lessors and perform preliminary background research on the firms. The one-time fee for the broker's services is usually paid by the venture lessor.

Having identified a prospective deal, venture leasing organizations differ considerably in the ways in which the potential transactions are evaluated. These differences reflect whether the lessor is a specialist in low-risk, late-stage investments or higher-risk, early-stage ones. All venture leasing organizations examine the extent to which the equipment can be resold if the lessee defaults and affects the ability of the firm to meet its lease payments. The ability to resell the equipment is largely a function of the extent to which a liquid secondary market exists and the equipment is standard (i.e., it did not require physical retrofitting or application-specific software).

Venture leasing organizations undertaking deals with higher-risk firms (particularly cases where the equipment is specialized) evaluate the firms like a venture capitalist, considering issues such as the strength of the management team and the competitive dynamics of the market. More traditional lessors, however, stress analyses employed by bank lending officers, such as historical and pro forma ratio analysis.

Four key issues frequently emerge in lease negotiations. The first of these is the size and timing of the equipment purchase. Most venture leases will allow the firm to

EXHIBIT 21-3

AVERAGE SIZE OF VENTURE LEASING AND TRADITIONAL VENTURE CAPITAL INVESTMENTS, BY STAGE

| Stage | Venture Leasing | | | | |
	Amount Invested ($000)	% of Total Invested	Number of Companies	Average Amount Invested ($000)	Average Venture Round[a] ($000)
Seed	4,620	1.5%	11	$ 420	$ 712
Start-up	39,102	13.0	44	889	2,387
Other early stage	51,946	17.3	59	880	1,651
Second stage	102,988	34.2	113	911	2,501
Later stage	102,466	34.0	102	1,005	2,459
Total[a]	$301,122	100.0%	329	$ 915	$1,939

[a] Based on a random sample of 2,138 traditional venture capital rounds at 795 venture-backed firms between 1969 and 1992.

Source: Compiled from Venture Economics, *Venture Leasing* (Needham, MA: Venture Economics, 1989); and Paul A. Gompers, "Optimal Investment, Monitoring, and the Staging of Venture Capital," *Journal of Finance* 50 (December 1995): 1461–1489.

lease a set dollar amount of equipment, which will often be described down to the manufacturer's product number. The average lease has historically been for about $1 million, although this has varied by stage of firm and industry. If the firm does not use all of its lease financing, its interest and principal payments will be reduced, but no adjustment is made to the number of warrants that are provided to the lessor. Exhibits 21-3 and 21-4 summarize the average size of lease by the stage of the lessee and its industry. The exhibits also provide comparative information on the size of traditional venture capital investments.[6]

Second, the timing of the lease payments presents several issues. First, the lessee will frequently have a set period of time after the lease begins in which it can request that the equipment purchase be made. This "takedown" period is often 6 to 12 months. Once the request is made, the lessor purchases the equipment and the lease payments begin. In many cases, not all the principal is repaid over the life of the lease. Thus, the final payment is a "balloon" payment containing the unpaid principal. At the opposite extreme, in some cases lessors demand that the firm make a security deposit of up to 20%. In these cases, a percentage of the loan is withheld. This is somewhat similar to a commercial bank's demand that a lending firm retain a minimum level of deposits (a "compensating balance") in their bank account at all times.

A third issue is the length of the lease. Most venture leases are between three and four years in length. But considerable diversity exists across industries. The longer development times of certain industries—such as medical and biotechnology firms—lead them to opt for longer-term leases. Since the return of principal is delayed longer, lessors

---

[6] Rather than providing funds in one large sum, U.S. venture capital organizations typically provide financings in several stages (rounds). This allows them to terminate funding if the firm does not live up to its initial promise.

EXHIBIT 21-4

AVERAGE SIZE OF VENTURE LEASING AND TRADITIONAL VENTURE CAPITAL INVESTMENTS, BY INDUSTRY

| Industry | Venture Leasing | | | | Average Venture Round[a] ($000) |
	Amount Invested ($000)	% of Total Invested	Number of Companies	Average Amount Invested ($000)	
Biotechnology	$ 13,391	4.4%	21	$ 638	$2,412
Commercial communcations	1,600	0.5	2	800	[b]
Computer hardware and systems	61,751	20.5	65	950	4,197
Computer software and services	24,125	8.0	31	778	1,916
Consumer related	48,450	16.1	38	1,275	3,120
Other electronics	67,834	22.5	71	955	1,649
Industrial automation	4,700	1.5	9	522	[c]
Industrial products and machinery	13,100	4.4	20	655	1,406
Medical/health	40,838	13.6	42	972	1,900
Telephone and data communications	21,833	7.3	27	809	2,644
Other	3,500	1.2	3	1,167	2,829
Total	$301,122	100.0%	329	$ 915	$1,939

[a] Based on a random sample of 2,138 traditional venture capital rounds at 795 venture-backed firms between 1969 and 1992.

[b] Included with "Telephone and data communications."

[c] Included with "Industrial products and machinery."

Source: Compiled from Venture Economics, *Venture Leasing* (Needham, MA: Venture Economics, 1989); and Paul A. Gompers, "Optimal Investment, Monitoring, and the Staging of Venture Capital," *Journal of Finance* 50 (December 1995): 1461–1489.

EXHIBIT 21-5

AVERAGE LENGTH OF VENTURE LEASING AND TRADITIONAL VENTURE CAPITAL INVESTMENTS, BY STAGE

Stage	Venture Leasing							Average Length of Venture Round[a]
	Length of Lease (Months)						Average	
	1–12	13–24	25–36	37–48	49–60	60+		
			(number of companies)					
Seed	—	—	6	3	—	—	39	25
Start-up	—	—	9	22	2	1	44	15
Other early stage	1	—	22	29	2	1	41	13
Second stage	2	4	30	65	6	1	42	12
Later stage	6	—	28	56	7	2	41	13
Total	9	4	95	175	17	5	42	16

[a] Based on a random sample of 2,138 traditional venture capital rounds at 795 venture-backed firms between 1969 and 1992.

Source: Compiled from Venture Economics, *Venture Leasing* (Needham, MA: Venture Economics, 1989); and Paul A. Gompers, "Optimal Investment, Monitoring, and the Staging of Venture Capital," *Journal of Finance* 50 (December 1995): 1461–1489.

EXHIBIT 21-6

AVERAGE LENGTH OF VENTURE LEASING AND TRADITIONAL VENTURE CAPITAL INVESTMENTS, BY INDUSTRY

Stage	Venture Leasing							Average Length of Venture Round[a]
	1–12	13–24	25–36	37–48	49–60	60+	Average	
				Months				
Biotechnology	—	—	1	15	1	1	47	15
Commercial communications	—	—	2	—	—	—	36	[b]
Computer hardware and systems	2	—	21	36	5	—	41	15
Computer software and services	1	—	9	16	1	—	40	13
Consumer related	1	1	9	21	—	2	42	17
Other electronics	1	—	24	39	1	—	41	15
Industrial automation	1	2	3	3	—	—	32	[c]
Industrial products and machinery	1	1	8	9	—	—	38	12
Medical/health	—	—	9	18	8	2	47	17
Telephone and data communications	2	—		15	1	—	40	19
Other	—	—	—	3	—	—	45	13
Total	9	4	95	175	17	5	42	16

[a] Based on a random sample of 2,138 traditional venture capital rounds at 795 venture-backed firms between 1969 and 1992.

[b] Included with "Telephone and data communications."

[c] Included with "Industrial products and machinery."

Source: Compiled from Venture Economics, *Venture Leasing* (Needham, MA: Venture Economics, 1989); and Paul A. Gompers, "Optimal Investment, Monitoring, and the Staging of Venture Capital," *Journal of Finance*, 50 (December 1995) 1461–1489.

regard longer-term leases as riskier. Exhibits 21-5 and 21-6 summarize the average length of leases by the stage of the lessee's development and its industry. It also provides comparative information on the time between rounds of traditional venture capital investments for each stage and industry.

The final area of discussion is the pricing of these transactions. Lessors typically view the pricing of the lease as having two aspects. The first of these, the implicit rate, is the internal rate of return of the promised principal and interest payments associated with the lease, as well as the anticipated cash flows from the final disposition of the property. (The impact of the warrants is not considered.) These rates often range across deals, from just one or two percentage points above the prime interest rate to 10% or more above this rate. Typically, lessors will provide lessees an option to purchase the equipment at the end of the lease. If the equipment is quite firm-specific, the purchase price is likely to be nominal. If the equipment is more generally marketable, the option price may be as high as 25% of the original purchase price. By specifying the price in the transaction, the parties avoid conflicts at the end of the transaction. In the early days of U.S. leasing, the failure to specify the purchase option price led to cases where the lessors would sell equipment—for instance, a telephone system—back to the lessee at *above* the market price, because the disruption entailed by its replacement would be incredibly costly!

The second component of pricing is termed *warrant coverage*. Venture lessors are typically granted warrants that are exercisable at the price paid per share of the last venture round. Venture lessors calculate the amount of warrants that they should receive using a unique method. They compute the ratio of the amount that they would pay to exercise the warrant to the funds advanced in the lease.

Consider, for instance, a firm that undertakes a $1 million venture lease, whose last venture round was priced at $5/share. If the venture lessor desired 10% "warrant coverage," he would seek to have warrants that could be exercised for a total of $100,000. The exercise price of $5/share (the price of the previous venture round) would imply that he would receive 20,000 warrants.

The unique system of compensation must be understood in the context of the venture financing process. Venture capitalists will typically make several rounds of investment in a firm, at progressively higher valuations. First-round investments are often valued at $1/share, subsequent rounds at a few dollars per share, and initial public offerings at $10/share or higher. Thus, a lessor can be confident that the venture firm will—if it is not terminated—appreciate sharply in value.

The extent of "warrant coverage" that venture lessors will obtain ranges from 5% to 40% of the lease amount, with most lessors receiving between 10% and 15%. In many cases, however, the underwriter of a firm going public will purchase the warrants from the venture lessor at the time of the firm's initial public offering (IPO). This may be because the warrants represent a small and potentially confusing complication of the firm's capital structure.

efficient market services: August 1993 (A)

Around the somewhat cluttered table, the senior management of efficient market services (ems) met to discuss the recent conclusion of the company's second full fiscal year. After a long day of discussion, the conversation had turned to the topic of American Stores Company, the second largest chain of supermarkets in the United States. It was August 2, 1993. Just yesterday, ems had received a letter of intent from the Vice President of Marketing from American Stores indicating the supermarket's interest in rolling out ems's information infrastructure in the chain over a two-year period. Kroger, the largest supermarket chain in the United States, had already deployed ems's information service in approximately one-third of their stores. Together, Kroger and American Stores had more than $40 billion in annual sales. No one in the room could deny the strategic importance of servicing both chains.

Even with this apparent triumph, the senior management team were aware of the obstacles that would stand in the way of a smooth deployment. ems was still operating at a net loss and probably would be for at least another year. In order to make American Stores part of the ems wide area network, the company would need to finance the deployment (and maintenance) of its proprietary information infrastructure into the 1,000 stores that American Stores operated.

efficient market services

efficient market services, Inc. (ems), headquartered in Deerfield, Illinois, a suburb of Chicago, was founded on April 2, 1991, by a group of senior executives and entrepreneurs in the packaged goods information services business (see Exhibit 22-1). ems provided information management services in the form of daily, store-specific POS (point-of-sale) data and applications; it provided data within 12 hours of the close of business

Jeffrey A. Ferrell (Harvard College '97) prepared this case under the supervision of Professor Paul Gompers as the basis for class discussion rather than to illustrate either effective or ineffective handling of an administrative situation.

EXHIBIT 22-1

EMS MANAGEMENT TEAM

Dr. Penny Baron,   Vice President of Business Development and Director, has been in general management for over 15 years with experience in the starting and growth of businesses in the information industry. Dr. Baron was President of Baron Consulting Company where she developed business forecasting systems for large packaged goods companies. Prior to that, she was a co-founding Director of Information Resources, Inc. (IRI), currently a $200 million market research company where she developed and patented many aspects of their core service. Dr. Baron co-developed and patented IRI's BehaviorScan testing system. Dr. Baron received her B.A. with distinction from Pennsylvania State University in 1964. She received her M.A. and Ph.D. from the University of Minnesota in 1971 and was a tenured faculty member at the University of Iowa, College of Business Administration until 1981. Dr. Barron plays an important role in strategic planning and partnering and as an advisor for product development.

Wayne Levy,   Vice President of Operations and Development, has had over 15 years of technical and managerial experience in computer technology. His skills provided a broad range of capabilities, including system specification, design, implementation, project management, vendor evaluation, and product acquisition. Mr. Levy was formerly Vice President and Director of Product Development for the A.C. Nielsen Company where he developed its first decision support database service. Prior to this, Wayne was Director of Sales and Decision Support Services at H.J. Heinz USA. He began his career at Needham, Harper and Steers Advertising as Associate Director of Marketing Decision Systems. Wayne received his B.A. from California State University in 1976. He received his M.A. from the University of Chicago in 1978 and was an instructor in the University of Chicago's Department of Statistics in 1979. Levy has specific experience in the application of technology to low-cost, rapid development of information services.

Dr. Danny Moore,   Vice President of Manufacturer Sales and Client Service, was Vice President, Product Development for the A.C. Nielsen Company and SAMI. Prior to this, Dr. Moor was Assistant Professor of Marketing at the University of Florida. Dr. Moore has extensive experience working on both corporate and business unit strategy and new product development. He has consulted for a variety of packaged goods companies and has developed expertise in the impact of marketplace information on product development and corporate strategy. He is co-founder of the current targeted micro-marketing strategy used to efficiently exploit marketing database information. Dr. Moore has an in-depth understanding of all functional areas of business, with particular strengths in sales, marketing, and customer applications development. Dr. Moore received his B.A. with honors and distinction from Indiana University in 1973. He earned his M.A. in 1978 and his Ph.D. in 1980 at the University of Iowa, Department of Psychology. He is widely published in both the consumer packaged goods industry and academic journals.

Bill Purcell,   Vice President of Retail Services and Marketing, began his career working for the nation's largest supermarket retailer, American Stores, Co. He left as Director of Marketing to co-found ABA Groups, Inc., a company that developed the Apollo Space Management System. Mr. Purcell moved to Information Resources, Inc. as Senior Vice President of Sales and Marketing when IRI acquired ABA. He subsequently founded Bill Purcell Marketing, Inc. which offered comprehensive retail consulting and training services for sales merchandising and store technology management and market development. Purcell received his B.A. in Business in 1981 from the Food Industry Management Program, which was part of the Graduate School of Business at the University of Southern California. He also attended the University of California at Berkeley from 1974 to 1977, while beginning his career at American Stores' divisional buying office. Purcell's experience during the past 15 years has given him comprehensive skills in the delivery of data technologies to retailers and in the development of industrywide information strategies for implementing just-in-time distribution systems.

(Continued)

EXHIBIT 22-1   (Continued)

Michael Spindler,   President and Director, had 17 years of experience at the A.C. Nielsen Company. As Vice President, Director of National Sales and Client Service, he was responsible for $300 million of revenues in information products and services covering all segments of the consumer packaged goods industry. Besides broad general management experience and skills needed to sell and support large-scale information database services, Mr. Spindler's significant capabilities were in the areas of prototyping new information services to facilitate rapid development and designing supporting sales and marketing strategies. Spindler earned his B.S. degree in Business Administration and Economics at St. Joseph's College in Collegeville, Indiana, in 1973. He also attended graduate school in Indiana at the University of Evansville from 1975 to 1977 where he majored in Business Economics. During his career, Spindler has managed all functions required to produce the largest retail information service for the consumer packaged goods industry, including data acquisition, processing and distribution.

Bill Feid,   Vice President of Finance and Chief Financial Officer, was formerly with Arthur Andersen & Co. for 11 years. Mr. Feid was a member of Arthur Andersen's Technology Practice team and serves as a board member of the Chicago High Tech Association. He has had extensive experience working with information services companies, providing a broad base of financial consulting services. His specialty was to assist companies through the IPO process. Feid received his B.S. in Accountancy and a B.S. in Industrial Technology in 1982 from Illinois State University. He also received his CPA the same year. Bill's special area of expertise is the financial management of companies prior to going public, including due diligence, deal feasibility assessment, capitalization transactions, and valuation methodologies.

Source: Company documents.

on every item in every store. This service contrasted sharply with currently available information which was reported three weeks after the close of business on an aggregate of sample stores. The company processed the data using data cleaning and enhancement software. The information was then made available to manufacturers, grocery store personnel and retail management through applications designed by ems. Major grocery chains as of August 1993 participating with ems in the data collection process included Kroger, Stop & Shop (Boston), H.E.B. (Southwest Texas), Dominick's (Chicago), Save-Mart (North Carolina), and ABCo (Phoenix). Major customers on the manufacturer side included Heinz Petfoods, Nabisco, Sara Lee, Scott Paper, Anheuser Busch, Miller, RJ Reynolds, Continental Bacon, and several divisions of Kraft General Foods. ems hoped to be able to use the information it collected and processed to reduce inefficiencies within the consumer packaged goods industry—inefficiencies that had been estimated at between $10 billion and $30 billion annually.[1]

INDUSTRY BACKGROUND

The consumer packaged goods industry consisted of manufacturers of consumer goods, distributors of grocery and perishable products, food brokers, warehouses, and

---

[1] Kurt Salmon Associates, *Efficient Consumer Response: Enhancing Consumer Value in the Grocery Industry* (Washington, DC: Research Department of the Foot Marketing Institute, January 1993).

retailers. ems's business was focused on companies that sold products through the largest chain grocery stores in the United States. Distributing and marketing through these stores had become more difficult for manufacturers over the last 10 years because of numerous changes in market conditions. Specifically, the number of items offered in each store had doubled, while the amount of shelf space available to these items had increased by only 20%. This proliferation of products had led consumers to expect variety, limiting the ability of retailers and manufacturers to substitute. At the same time, alternative methods of advertising and promotion had increased, leaving manufacturers and retailers with more complex options and fragmented consumer franchises. Finally, the emergence of new retail discount formats with selected offerings had impacted the profitability of the traditional retail formats.

Manufacturers developed some tools to cope with these changes. What did not change, however, was the nature, accuracy, specificity and timeliness of the data required for these new systems to support the complex market conditions. The net result had been that manufacturers and retailers were unable to efficiently execute their current selling strategies, which resulted in costly stockouts, overstocks, and the inability to monitor and assess advertising and promotional programs. Broad-based, multiproduct manufacturers like Nestles, Procter & Gamble, Kraft General Foods, and ConAgra were continually out of stock on approximately 8% of their product lines in every store, resulting in reduced sales for both manufacturers and retailers. Key selling snack items were out-of-stock 30% of the time on weekends despite huge expenditures by manufacturers on their own distribution network. Baked good manufacturers suffered out-of-stocks, missing sales opportunities on some products, while 12 to 20% of what they baked was wasted due to spoilage.

Traditional syndicated data suppliers (such as IRI and A.C. Nielsen) projected what manufacturers and their competitors sold at the national and local level based on a sample of stores (see Exhibit 22-2). This type of information was adequate for broad strategic uses such as allocating advertising dollars to marketing areas, but it did not support precise store-specific tactics. In 1993, replenishment orders were based on visual inspection of the shelf by a grocery clerk. Even if the clerk had a handheld computer, inefficiency persisted because an accurate timely link to sales data was not available. Promotions were sold into a chain's warehouse based on chain-wide performance averages without regard to significant variances of success in the chain's individual stores. Shelving patterns and prices were also set without the benefit of information on store-by-store variances.

ECR

Concerned that the grocery industry was losing its competitive edge, packaged goods manufacturers, grocery retailers, distributors, suppliers, and brokers cooperated in an attempt to eliminate the inherent inefficiencies of the current system. This cooperation within the grocery industry was characterized as Efficient Consumer Response (ECR). ECR was a grocery industry strategy in which distributors and suppliers worked closely together to bring better value to the grocery consumer. By jointly focusing on the efficiency of the total grocery supply system rather than the efficiency of individual components, they hoped to reduce total system costs, inventories, and physical assets while improving the consumer's choice of high quality fresh grocery products. The ultimate goal of ECR was a responsive, consumer-driven system in which distributors and suppliers worked together as business allies to maximize consumer satisfaction while

EXHIBIT 22-2

ems COMPETITION

Information Resources Inc. (IRI Infoscan) and Nielsen ScanTrack

Both of these services provide POS-based grocery store information to manufacturers. The nature of this data was completely different from the store-specific management tools provided by ems. Both of these companies used an 8 to 10% sample of stores from chains and independents to project the results of the unsampled stores in order to represent that chain's business as part of an overall market. These services retrieved data from the computers of a chain's headquarters' because 65% of scanner data problems occurred when data was removed from the store. Fifteen percent of the numbers brought back to the chain headquarters are bad. These suppliers combined this data with casual promotion data from a sample of stores and then projected it to cover retail sales at the national market and sometimes total chain level. A report could finally be delivered to the manufacturer three to ten weeks after the retail sales actually occurred.

The data supplied by these services was clean enough and timely enough for some purposes. It was an adequate tool for strategic tracking of sales progress and programs at the national and market level. It was a tool for planning and evaluating those programs and for allocating strategic resources between regions, markets, or accounts. It was not, however, a tool for store-specific management, nor did it provide the benefits of the ems information. In order for Nielsen or IRI to enter the store-specific management business, they would have had to start from scratch and build a new database system parallel to their current syndicated data system.

Catalina Information Resources

The formation of this joint venture company was announced in September of 1992 by Catalina Marketing and IRI. It planned to exploit the excess capabilities of the Catalina in-store coupon system to supply daily sales information about particular predefined UPC. The service did not include an in-store database or revenue sharing with the retailer, nor did it provide the manufacturer with comprehensive reporting for an entire category. In addition, the system did not generate baseline sales data or record casual data. The system was currently in tests with three or four chains.

The Logic Connection

This test program run by IRI would be used in conjunction with an updated version of SAMI Warehouse withdrawal service. IRI planned to connect the manufacturer's distribution center with the retailer's warehouse. In addition, it would generate store-specific POS data from the chain headquarters' computer to help manufacturers calibrate the effect of their supply on retail sales. This approach offered some of the benefits that ems provided but was limited to three areas. First, the system only addressed products moving through the retailer's warehouse, which accounted for 40 to 60% of the volume through the store. This area was expected to shrink as manufacturers experimented with direct store delivery and supplemental distribution brokers for seasonal products. Second, the weekly report could not provide quick response benefits to retail stores that wanted to manage product inventories for marketing and sales action. Stockouts were generally a two- or three-day problem and were often undetectable using a weekly report. Third, even if a product was out-of-stock all week and detectable on a weekly report, it would not be reported until well into the next week. At that point the damage was done.

Others

Other potential competitors included technology companies such as IBM or AT&T, other in-store service providers such as Videocard, information companies such as IRI or Nielsen, or networked industries such as banking.

Source: Company documents.

minimizing cost. Accurate information and high-quality products flowed through a paperless system between the manufacturing line and the check out counter with minimum degradation and interruption both within and between trading partners.

The anticipated economic savings of such a System were immense. A report prepared for the Grocery Manufacturers of America claimed that one half of the $100 billion pipeline of inventory was wasted. Between $10 billion and $30 billion of that inventory could be taken out of the pipeline annually and dropped to the bottom line of manufacturers and retailers.

An example of ECR on a micro basis was the highly talked about and progressive partnership between Wal-Mart and Procter & Gamble. In this case P&G used daily, clean-scanned data from each Wal-Mart store to restock shelves, determine minimum made-to-order production ship runs, and schedule cross dock exchanges so that inventory never sat anywhere but on a Wal-Mart shelf. This partnership virtually eliminated paperwork for the supported items. Wal-Mart followed up the success of this program with the announcement of a massive program to align 200 of its largest vendors as partners in a merchandise flow program. Therefore, on a generic basis, ECR meant higher inventory turns and fresher product for the consumer through fast recycle times, lower product carrying costs, and simplified warehouse and handling requirements.

ems POSITIONING

ems sought to leverage off of the ECR revolution by being the sole supplier of timely, accurate, and store-specific management and pricing information on products sold through individual supermarkets. This type of information was not currently available from any other source, and ems maintained that such information was required to optimize inventory levels, reduce out-of-stock conditions, optimize pricing, and more efficiently align promotional efforts with sales response opportunities. Unlike the precedent-setting Wal-Mart and P&G alliance, ems provided a single infrastructure to deliver consumer POS information to retailers, manufacturers, and distributors. This meant capital investment could be leveraged across all participants in the ems service as there was no redundancy in the acquisition, processing, storage, or delivery of information. Manufacturers and retailers did not all need to make large investments in POS information systems.

Store-specific management information would allow manufacturers and retailers to improve control over product assortment, shelving, pricing, promotion, inventory levels, replenishment, and production. ems estimated the systemwide cost savings and increased sales at $30 billion to $50 billion in an industry where total sales were nearly $300 billion. Over half of these savings would directly benefit the manufacturers, the paying customers of ems.

MANUFACTURER SERVICES

Manufacturers received store-specific clean POS scanner information from ems updated daily. This information covered all category-specific products (including competitors) that were selling and their associated selling conditions, including price, feature, advertisement, and in-store display presence. Manufacturers were able to classify stores according to their importance based on sales volume, volume potential, profitability, and efficiency. With this information, manufacturers were able to plan product assortment, shelving, merchandising, pricing, and product promotion across their product portfolio based on each store's potential and past performance rather than on the performance of the chain as a whole. ems believed that the importance of this information could not be overestimated. Manufacturers in 1993 spent nearly $50 billion annually on local store promotions, with no effective method to monitor results. Sixty-five percent of all product sales to retailers were sold on some sort of promotional discount. Less than 15% of these promotional sales incrementally benefited the manufacturer. This was due primarily to the manufacturer's inability to match the performance of a particular promotion with an individual store.

In addition, ems's manufacturers service system included so-called quick response management tools that notified manufacturers through alerts when prices changed, manufacturer's products were out-of-stock, new products had been introduced, promotions had been introduced by competitors, manufacturer's promotions had been improperly executed, and sales were unusually strong leading to out-of-stock situations. A second group of quick response tools effected the supply chain. Shipments to a store from the warehouse or through direct distribution could be modified by up-to-the-minute news about consumer demand and competitive activities that could affect shipments to the warehouse, distribution center inventories, truck packing practices, finished inventory processing, production runs, and scheduling and procurement practices.

Manufacturers who participated in the ems system signed a one-year contract that automatically renewed unless a 120-day cancellation option was exercised. As of July of 1993, ems had signed over 50 manufacturers representing approximately 100 categories. No manufacturer had left the program.

RETAILER SERVICES

ems generated its data through exclusive, three- to five-year contracts with retail grocery store chains. In exchange for this data, ems provided the retail grocery store chain with a standard 3% of profits generated from the chain's particular data. The chain and its particular stores also benefited from store-specific information supplied through the ems in-store platform. ems had designed a number of key applications specifically targeted at a store manager designed to aid in tactical management of the store. These applications included out-of-stock alerts, fast-moving items and display sell-downs, forecasts for bakery and dairy replenishments, price verification, in-store sign printing, store coupon redemptions, standing order adjustments, and consignment sales and scan promotions. Through its in-store platform, ems also supported other retail applications such as shelf space management, back door delivery, and labor scheduling software packages. ems provided clean POS data to chain headquarters as well as allowing a chain headquarters computer to poll each store and receive clean and accurate POS data. Therefore, all subsequent applications could be run with more reliable data by merchandisers and buyers at the regional or national headquarters with ems data.

As of August 1993, ems had signed three- to five-year contracts with five major retail chains, rolling out in six regional markets and approximately 1,700 stores. ems had also signed Kroger, the number one grocery store retailer with revenues of $21.9 billion (see Exhibit 22-3).

BUSINESS ECONOMICS

Revenues and prices were based on the value that ems provided a manufacturer for its brands. The benefits to manufacturers as a result of this information from one store

EXHIBIT 22-3

SUPERMARKET CHAINS .

Rank	Company	Sales ($ billions)
1	Kroger Co.	21.9
2	American Stores Co.	19.0
3	Safeway	16.3
4	SuperValu	15.1
5	Fleming Cos.	12.9
6	A&P	10.7
7	Winn-Dixie Stores	10.3
8	Albertson's	10.2
9	Loblaw Cos.	7.2
10	Food Lion	7.1
11	Ahold USA	6.3
12	Publix Super Markets	6.1
13	Scrivner	5.9
14	Univa	5.8
15	Vons Cos.	5.6
16	Supermarkets General	4.7
17	Oshawa Group	4.0
18	H.E.B. Grocery Co.	3.8
19	Wakefern Food Corp.	3.5
20	Giant Food	3.5
21	Stop & Shop Cos.	3.2
22	Food 4 Less	3.0
23	Grand Union	2.9
24	Ralph's Grocery Co.	2.9
25	Penn Traffic Co.	2.7
26	Fred Meyer Inc.	2.7
27	Bruno's	2.7
28	Smith's Food & Drug	2.6
29	Roundy's	2.5
30	Spartan Stores	2.4
31	Nash Finch Co.	2.3
32	Associated Wholesale Grocers	2.3
33	Certified Grocers of CA	2.3
34	Hy-Vee Food Stores	2.2
35	Randall's Food Market	2.1
36	Dominick's Finer Foods	2.0
37	Hannaford Bros.	2.0
38	Metro-Richelieu	2.0

Source: "Supermarket News," *The Top Seventy-Five*, January 18, 1993, pp. 14–16.

were replicated with each additional store. Consequently, ems charged on both a per store and per category basis. Given the dynamic daily nature of the supermarket business, actions taken in response to specific opportunities in each store required constant adjustment over time, necessitating a constant feed of ems information.

ems priced large or fast-moving categories at higher per store rates than small or slow-moving categories. Furthermore, ems priced bigger brands higher than smaller brands. Each ems client paid a sign on fee for each store and category, ranging from between 35 and 70% of the per year/store/category fee ($50 to $900). Clients were required to give a four-month notice if they desired to drop a store or a group of stores. If the client wished to reinstate the dropped stores at a later date, he or she would be charged another sign on fee. Clients began paying ongoing transaction fees for a store when ems provided them information from it. For example, manufacturer one, category A, purchased ems data from 600 stores in the beginning of the year, adding 120 stores every other month, and had a brand that required a $150 annual per store charge. The original sign on was therefore $63,000 ($150 × 70% × 600 stores). The ongoing cost would be $132,000 in the initial year with the month twelve revenues of $15,000 (1,200 stores × $12.50 per month) (see Exhibit 22-4 and Exhibit 22-5).

EXHIBIT 22-4

BALANCE SHEET FOR ems FOR YEARS ENDING JULY 31

	1992 (Audited)	1993 (Unaudited)	1994 (Projection)	1995 (Projection)	1996 (Projection)
Assets					
Cash and cash equivalents	$2,742,588	$ 8,003,663	($1,758,084)	$13,157,467	$ 43,914,423
Accounts receivable	289,290	307,157	4,315,668	12,627,053	37,787,084
Prepaid expenses and deposits	36,863	79,586	0	0	0
Net property, plant, & equipment	1,449,512	6,652,206	16,145,309	21,522,295	24,594,412
Total Assets	4,518,252	15,042,612	18,702,892	47,306,815	106,295,919
Liabilities & Shareholder's Equity					
Accounts payable & accrued expenses	792,536	994,398	2,157,712	3,045,137	13,745,039
Deferred revenue	29,294	58,456	2,780,370	7,865,448	21,879,000
Current portion of capital lease obligation	247,684	1,299,396	4,289,060	6,384,340	7,155,175
Total Current Liabilities	1,069,515	2,352,250	9,227,142	17,294,925	42,779,214
Notes payable to shareholders	942,773	982,772	1,022,940	0	0
Capital lease obligations net of current portion	921,799	4,984,342	11,710,330	15,397,607	18,033,184
Shareholder's equity	1,584,166	6,723,248	(3,257,520)	14,614,283	45,483,521
Total liabilities & shareholder's equity	4,518,252	15,042,612	18,702,892	47,306,815	106,295,919

Source: Company documents. (Data disguised.)

EXHIBIT 22-5

INCOME STATEMENT FOR ems FOR YEARS ENDING JULY 31

	1992 (Audited)	1993 (Audited)	1994 (Projection)	1995 (Projection)	1996 (Projection)
Number of billable stores	256	1,733	3,528	6,616	9,705
Number of equivalent customer contracts	10	41	121	212	238
Revenues	$ 787,752	$ 1,411,430	$11,069,156	$49,225,994	$152,148,821
Costs					
Operations	$ 563,772	$ 3,185,422	$ 9,724,022	$16,508,067	$ 24,244,132
Sales and service	$1,109,913	$ 2,834,697	$ 3,971,614	$ 6,033,364	$ 9,390,856
Marketing and administration	$ 690,667	$ 1,355,157	$ 2,276,251	$ 2,931,861	$ 2,903,582
Development	$ 781,167	$ 3,015,489	$ 3,915,132	$ 4,188,357	$ 3,446,518
Retailer fees	$ 0	$ 0	$ 40,753	$ 363,349	$ 67,774,627
	$3,145,519	$10,390,765	$19,927,773	$30,024,997	$107,759,716
Income (Loss) before interest and taxes	($2,357,768)	($ 8,979,336)	($ 8,858,618)	$19,200,996	$ 44,389,105
Net interest expense	$ 60,966	$ 319,396	$ 1,129,269	$ 1,843,996	$ 2,180,798
Income taxes	$ 0	$ 0	$ 0	$ 0	$ 11,339,069
Income (Loss)	($2,418,734)	($ 9,298,732)	($ 9,987,886)	$17,357,000	$ 30,869,238

Source: Company documents. (Data disguised.)

INFRASTRUCTURE

ems In-Store Platform ems's in-store computer was connected to that store's POS computer system. The ems computer ran software that extracted item sales and price data from the store's POS system once a day and converted the information into an ems database. The in-store computer could also retrieve retail store applications which used the ems information to help a store manager verify prices, replenish stock, and manage items on promotion.

ems polled the in-store platform to determine item movement data and all active files (e.g., price files, exception files, supplementary item files) on a daily basis. The in-store processor then checked its own files for changes of in-store conditions such as items on promotion and store operating hours. With this information plus sales history and information about an item's past responses to promotion events, the store's sales data were edited and sales projections for the next days were generated. The ems system also evaluated itself by comparing yesterday's expectation for today's sales with today's actual sales and then adjusted its forecast parameters.

ems gathered data regarding the promotional environment through a third-party organization that was contracted to visit stores regularly to gather so-called casual data. This data was inputted into the ems databases to match promotions against sales on a store-by-store basis. This service had cost ems $232 per store per month. Subsequently, ems entered into an alliance with ActMedia whereby sales representatives assumed this function in the usual course of business. This had reduced the per store cost to $70 per month.

ems Information Center The information was moved from the in-store platform over the ems wide area network (WAN) to the ems information center's local area network (LAN) in Chicago. The information center was a LAN connecting various types of processors that received, processed, and delivered information to many classes of users, including ems sales, client service and application developers, manufacturers' headquarters and remote sales sites, retail headquarters, and corporate divisions. All store databases were housed in the ems information center. These databases were updated daily and made accessible to each manufacturer through its ems quick mailbox application.

Technology ems's computer network was built in a modular structure. Costs were, therefore, controlled incrementally as new markets were established. In addition, the in-store computer platform could be upgraded if necessary. Software was platform-independent, meaning that ems's clients did not need to use a particular type of computer system. Information center expansion occurred in relatively small continuous increments, adding about one workstation for each incremental market of about 100 stores. There were no large incremental step functions in hardware requirements as were typically associated with large mainframe implementations.

ems believed the risk of changing technology was minimized by several factors. First, the current technology was upgradable equipment that would be compatible with future generations of similar systems. Second, if technology were to change in a dramatic fashion, ems had built its infrastructure using a modular market methodology. Replacement of current technology could therefore occur over a controlled period of time. Lower technology prices only enhanced ems's profitability and were not considered to be a risk. Third, the ems technology strategy was reactive, utilizing whatever technology strategy each retailer required. ems software was designed to function in various environments. ems systems operated in dozens of different POS environments and under various operating systems, including DOS, AIX, and Unix. ems could export its information to virtually any database a retailer chose.

ems's strategy was to deliver data to the consumer using tools that created no technological hurdles for any user. The ems information center supported remote access by any computer that had a standard modem connection. ems's internal strategy was to develop database structures based on customer application requirements that minimized the cost of data retrieval while keeping processing requirements in the range of the newer downsized processors. ems had several database alternatives, all of which provided a general database structure compatible with SQL (a standardized database protocol) and its major extensions. Current databases were in Paradox and Informix. The in-store databases included daily item trend detail and associated selling conditions. The information center mirrored these databases and sorted the data into customer categories. ems evaluated database alternatives by determining the retrieval requirements of customer applications and measuring the performance of alternative database designs. In addition, ems had developed a sophisticated report writing system to support both applications and customer reports.

All ems databases were on the in-store platform and at the information center. Data and source code were routinely archived and stored off site. Data lost due to store POS failure tended to be for short periods of time, usually less than one day and for only one store. Baseline sales and the store's sale history were used to estimate sales data lost due to a POS or communication failure.

ems had the support of several large hardware, software, and technical support organizations to help develop its products, services, and technologies. The company had contracted with a larger, national organization to handle system installation and service.

BUSINESS STRATEGY

ems's business strategy was predicated on a first-to-market strategy. This strategy was supported by the company's unique ability to provide store-specific data to both manufacturers and retailers within a 12-hour turnaround. ems sought to enhance the value of this data over potential competitors through assuring clean data, providing baseline or normal sales by category, and custom applications where appropriate, and establishing an infrastructure that would guarantee ems as the lowest cost provider. Key to ems's ongoing success was the decision to provide information within a specific category to whoever signed up for that category. Competitors were then compelled to sign up with ems to level the playing field, allowing ems to leverage its cost base.

ems had targeted the largest supermarket chain within the country in an attempt to gain the greatest possible market share through the smallest number of retail locations. The company sought to expand by market and then by category, thereby leveraging the infrastructure required for a new market over a number of different clients. More importantly, this created a multiplier effect against revenues as one category led to multiple customers, which in turn led to participation in other existing categories as well as entirely new categories.

MARKETS

In 1992, the consumer packaged goods industry spent approximately $600 million in syndicated, strategic data services and market research. While ems was not a research tool, some of its revenues initially came from research budgets. As the value of ems's information penetrated the sales and distribution functions, ongoing revenue would come primarily from manufacturer sales, promotion, and distribution budgets, which totaled over $100 billion annually.

Success would be determined by how quickly and thoroughly ems could penetrate the domestic supermarket chains. There were 31,000 supermarkets which made up about 80% of the total dollars flowing through the grocery trade, which was the second largest retail business following the auto industry. There were 20,150 chain supermarkets, which accounted for approximately 70% of $300 billion in industry revenues. ems's revenues were driven by the number of stores providing data to ems and the amount of customer interest in each store. Likewise, the most effective barrier to competition from other information companies was significant prior penetrations of this retail chain universe by ems.

Within the manufacturing community, ems concentrated on selling participation either to companies that sold in large fast-moving categories or to companies that sold in many categories of various sizes. After a category was sold once, ems could gain further penetration into the category across other manufacturers. Using these general strategies, the company had been successful with initial penetration into a number of multiple category companies including Kraft General Foods, Heinz, Nabisco, Scott Paper, Continental Baking, Clairol, Sara Lee Meats, and Church & Dwight. ems had also been successful in penetrating fast-moving category groups including Breyers (ice cream), Anheuser Busch, Miller Brewer Company, and Coors (beer), RJR (cigarettes) and the national carbonated beverage manufacturers. No paying subscribers to ems's services had been lost to date.

Within the retailer segment, ems was currently working with Kroger, the top national supermarket chain. ems was continuing its discussions with the third-ranked player in the supermarket category, Safeway, and eventually hoped to sign the chain. Together Kroger, American Stores, and Safeway operated about 4,500 stores and generated about 12% of total grocery store sales. In addition, ems had participation among key regional chains including Stop & Shop (Boston), Dominick's (Chicago), SaveMart (Northern California), ABCo (Phoenix) and H.E.B. (Southwest Texas). To date, the company had established infrastructure in six regional marketplaces encompassing in excess of 1,200 retail grocery stores.

MARKETING AND SALES

The consumer packaged goods manufacturing community had consolidated over the past 20 years. As a result, personal selling had proven to be quite effective. Each member of the ems senior management team was well known in the industry and was directly involved with selling. The most effective efforts to date had been made with high-level client personnel, usually at the VP of Sales or VP of Marketing level. ems used proprietary evidence of inefficiencies gathered through interviews with company managers to illustrate the problems and uses of the ems quick response mailboxes to solve these problems.

ems supported its selling efforts through a newsletter called *Just in Times*—sent to top executives in the retail, in-store service, and manufacturing communities. Speaking engagements at industry conferences and conventions and retailer co-marketing programs were also critical to the marketing effort.

CAPITALIZATION

To date, ems had raised $14.6 million in four rounds of financing. Although not a venture capital round, ems raised its first founder's round in November 1991 through a group of wealthy individuals located in Chicago. The initial dollar amount raised was $800,000 of convertible debt, which was subsequently converted into a combination of common stock and warrants. The exercise price of the warrants was $2.50.

In April 1992, the Plymouth Fund, Tenor Ventures, and Capital Ventures collectively invested $3 million ($1 million each) at a price of $3.075 per share, resulting in a post-money valuation of $8.07 million. The Plymouth Fund, Tenor Ventures, and Capital Ventures were all private, West Coast venture capital partnerships with decades of experience and substantial amounts of capital under management: since its founding in 1969, Plymouth had over $370 million of capital under management; since its founding in 1976, Tenor had managed five funds with combined capital of $285 million; since its founding in 1965, Capital Ventures had over $180 million of capital under management.

In November 1992, the Plymouth Fund, Tenor Ventures, and Capital Ventures collectively invested $2 million ($666,667 each) at a price of $4.125 per share, resulting in a post-money valuation of $13.3 million. In April 1993, an additional $8.8 million was invested at a per share price of $11.00. Plymouth and Tenor Ventures invested $1 million each; Capital Ventures invested $500,000; Palo Alto Partners came in for $6 million. The remaining $300,000 came from employees of ems. Post-money valuation was $46.9 million (see Exhibit 22-6).

EXHIBIT 22-6

ems CAPITALIZATION

	Common	Stock Rights	Employee Options	Warrants	Series A	Series B	Fully Diluted Capitalization	Percent	Employee Options	Series C	Fully Diluted Capitalization	Percent
Management	975,900	15,620	116,916				1,109,236	34.3%	16,500	19,509	1,145,245	26.8%
Others Issued			55,400				55,400	1.7%			55,400	1.3%
Reserved			5,684				5,684	0.2%	223,500		229,184	5.4%
Total Management and Employees	976,700	15,620	178,000				1,170,320	36.2%	240,000	19,509	1,429,829	33.5%
Total 1991 Investors (12 Families)	320,000			160,000			480,000	14.9%		0	480,000	11.3%
Tenor Ventures					325,220	202,027	527,247	16.3%		90,909	618,156	14.5%
Capital Ventures					325,220	202,027	527,247	16.3%		45,455	572,702	13.4%
Plymouth IV					312,220	193,952	506,172	15.7%		87,273	593,445	13.9%
Plymouth Associates					13,000	8,075	21,075	0.7%		3,636	24,711	0.6%
Palo Alto Partners—Strategic Ptr							0	0.0%		181,818	181,818	4.3%
Palo Alto Partners—High Yield							0	0.0%	363,637	363,637	8.5%	
Palo Alto Partners—Reserve for Board							0	0.0%	3,308	3,308	0.1%	
Total 1992 and 1993 Investors	0	0	0	0	975,660	606,081	1,581,741	48.9%	0	776,036	2,357,777	55.2%
TOTAL	1,296,700	15,620	178,000	160,000	975,660	606,081	3,232,061	100.0%	606,945	795,545	4,267,606	100.0%

Source: Company documents. (Data disguised.)

FUTURE FINANCING

Venture Capital The last round of efficient market services' venture financing closed in April 1993. Following the round, the 1992 and 1993 venture capital investors owned 55.2 percent of ems. The previous round of financing lasted approximately five months. The most recent round, however, raised more than four times the money of the previous round. The management of ems considered it unlikely that another venture round could be raised in 1993. The possibility of another round prior to an IPO, however, had been mentioned at the time of the April financing.

Venture Leasing Since ems was backed by prominent venture capital firms, the management team was aware that a venture lease might also be a financing option. Venture leasing was in many ways similar to venture capital. Venture lease partnerships extended leasing agreements to venture-backed, start-up firms with high-growth prospects who were generally unable to obtain bank loans or standard leasing agreements due to limited or negative cash flow. The venture lessor typically extended a lease to such a firm and took an equity stake in the firm, usually in the form of warrants. The venture leasing industry was a niche market that invested somewhere between $200 and $300 million annually. Because of the specialized nature of the transaction, venture leasing firms were usually referred to a company through the lead venture capital investor, resulting in the close association of venture leasing funds with a handful of venture capital partnerships. The relatively high rates of return characteristic of the venture leasing industry were attributable to the lower default risk as a result of venture financing and the warrants. Typically, the venture lessor retained ownership of the leased equipment for tax purposes: the start-up was unlikely to be able to make use of the depreciation tax shield. Comdisco Ventures was introduced to the management of ems through the venture capital firms that had taken a stake in ems in 1992 and 1993.

The Comdisco Ventures was founded in 1987 and had over $250 million under management. Fully funded by Comdisco, Inc., a New York Stock Exchange-listed leasing company, Comdisco Ventures was an independently managed venture fund that focused on developing a diversified and broad-based portfolio of investments in a variety of industries. The fund had a nationwide presence because of its association with Comdisco, Inc. Since its inception, the Comdisco Ventures had provided venture lease financing to more than 200 venture capital-backed firms. Eighty percent of the fund's transactions were venture lease financings, while the remaining 20% were pure equity investments or various forms of debt financing. Typical venture lease investments, ranging from $300,000 to more than $2 million, were placed in seed-stage, later round, and public companies. In 1992, over $41 million of lease-based capital was provided to 29 new portfolio companies and 28 existing portfolio companies. Jim Labe, Comdisco Venture Group's president, worked out of the company's Rosemont, Illinois, headquarters. Jeff Brody and Rick Stubblefield, senior vice presidents, directed investment activities and managed portfolio companies at the firm's Menlo Park, California and Corte Madera, California offices, respectively. Gwill York, senior vice president, managed activities from the Boston office. The group had worked together as a team for over six years. Don Notman, vice president, joined the Boston office in December 1992. Comdisco Ventures began making direct equity investments in April 1993. Equity investments, which ranged from $250,000 to $500,000, often coincided with an initial venture lease (see Exhibit 22-7).

Comdisco had engaged in a venture lease agreement with the following Plymouth Fund portfolio companies: Nchip, S3, Inc., Tulark, Inc., and Focal, Inc. Comdisco had engaged in a venture lease agreement with the following Tenor Ventures portfolio

---

EXHIBIT 22-7

OTHER COMDISCO VENTURE FINANCINGS

Agile Networks, Inc.
Concord, MA

Provides high-performance Internet-working products based on asynchronous transfer mode (ATM) switching technology. Venture capital investors include Oak Investment Partners, Accel Partners, Charles River Ventures, and ABS Ventures.

Books That Work
Palo Alto, CA

Focused on home-oriented personal productivity software products targeting dual market and demographic trends—the market for home computers and the do-it-yourself home hobby market. Venture capital investors include Hummer Winblad, Mohr, Davidov Ventures, and Accel Partners.

Edify Corp.
Santa Clara, CA

Provides software solutions to automate the process of information access and delivery. Venture capital investors include Sutter Hill Ventures, Technology Venture Investors, Greylock Management, Highland Capital Partners, Sigma Partners, InterWest Partners, and Glynn Ventures.

Human Genome Sciences, Inc.
Rockville, MD

Pharmaceutical company established to develop and market novel and proprietary products derived from genomic (gene typing) research by exploiting a method for rapidly identifying genes. Venture capital investors include HealthCare Investment Corp., Everest Trust, and Oxford BioSciences.

Montage Software, Inc.
Emeryville, CA

Supplier of next-generation database management technology and application development tools for organizations building applications that incorporate multimedia, scientific, and other nontraditional data. Venture capital investors include: Morgenthaler Ventures, Accel Partners, Sequoia Capital, and Oak Investment Partners.

Mitotix, Inc.
Cambridge, MA

Biopharmaceutical company developing unique pharmaceuticals that will inhibit and regulate the cell cycle through control of key regulatory checkpoints in cell growth. Venture capital investors include Greylock Management, Venrock Associates, Plymouth Fund, J.H. Whitney, Weiss, Peck & Greer, and Robertson, Stepehens & Co.

Nvidia Corp.
Sunnyvale, CA

Provides graphics accelerator products for high-volume applications. Venture capital investors include Sequoia Capital and Sutter Hill Ventures.

Pharmacyclics, Inc.
Mountain View, CA

Developer of biomedical products incorporating macrocyclic chemistry. This format has the potential for creating molecules with predetermined properties useful in diagnostic and therapeutic applications. Venture capital investors include Kleiner Perking Caulfield & Byers, Venrock Associates, Plymouth Fund, and Capital Ventures.

Spectrum HoloByte, Inc.
Alameda, CA

Develops and publishes entertainment software for computers and video game machines. Venture capital investors include Kleiner Perkins Caulfield & Byers, Accel Partners, Paramount Chancellor Capital Management, Vertex, Integral Partners, AT&T, and Stanford University are the venture investors.

Tularik, Inc.
South San Francisco, CA

Biopharmaceutical company developing transcription factors (proteins that regulate gene expression) aimed at treating a variety of human diseases. Venture capital investors include Plymouth Fund, Institutional Venture Partners, Medicus Ventures, Frazier & Co., and Delphi Bioventures.

Virus Research Institute, Inc.
Cambridge, MA

Biotechnology company developing and manufacturing the next generation of vaccines and therapeutics designed to prevent and treat infectious and microbial diseases. Venture capital investors include: HealthCare Investment Corp.

Source: "Comdisco Venture Group," *Venture Capital Journal*, November 1993.

companies: Gupta Technologies and Connect, Inc. Comdisco had engaged in a venture lease agreement with the following Capital Ventures portfolio companies: Conductus, Inc. and Pharmacyclics.[2]

ems was currently seeking financing larger than the average venture lease of the Comdisco portfolio. The management of ems, however, was confident that the prominent nature of its venture capital backers, in addition to other factors, would allow the firm to obtain consideration for a larger lease.

Structure of a Venture Lease   A venture lease had a number of contractual components, most of which were typical of a normal leasing agreement; others were features peculiar to venture leasing transactions. There were a number of issues surrounding the possible negotiation of a venture lease agreement between the Comdisco Venture Group and efficient market services, Inc.: What was the optimal lease size? What was an appropriate draw-down period? What type of equipment should ems be able to purchase and at what interest rate? Should there be multiple classifications of equipment? How long should the lease be?

One of the trickiest issues in negotiating the lease revolved around the double pricing issue. First, what was an appropriate implicit rate (the IRR of the promised principal and interest payments associated with the lease, as well as the anticipated cash flows from the final disposition of the property—the impact of warrants is typically not considered)? Second, what was the appropriate "warrant coverage"? Venture lessors computed the ratio of the amount that they would pay to exercise the warrant to the funds advanced in the lease. For example, if a $1 million lease were offered, 10% warrant coverage would mean that the lessor owned warrants that could be exercised for 10% of the total lease or $100,000 in warrants.

There were other issues of significance that should be considered. For example: Which party was responsible for maintenance? What were the rights of the lessor and lessee at the expiration of the lease?

Following the negotiation of the terms of a venture lease, the venture lessor usually engaged in a due diligence process similar to a venture capital due diligence process. In addition, the venture capital investors were consulted. The venture lessor was also interested in the likelihood and timing of a public offering since high returns were directly tied to the ability to exercise the warrants. Typically, the warrants were repurchased by the firm at the time of the IPO to avoid confusion surrounding the capital structure of the firm.

DECISION

ems senior managers thought about the possible venture lease. Initial discussions had produced terms (see Exhibit 22-8). The talk around the table became even more serious as the terms were discussed. How much money did ems need to complete the American Stores project successfully? Clearly, the money had to come from somewhere because ems was not going to turn away one of its potentially most profitable accounts. ems no longer regarded itself as an unproven venture. After all, it had attracted the top two supermarket chains in the United States as clients. Were the terms of the lease too onerous? Someone suggested ordering Chinese. Clearly, this was going to be another long night. The management team began to go over the proposed agreement term by term. The decision would not be easy.

---

[2] "Comdisco Venture Group," *Venture Capital Journal*, November 1993.

EXHIBIT 22-8

PROPOSED VENTURE LEASE AGREEMENT

Lessor	Comdisco, Inc.
Lessee	efficient market services, Inc.
Maximum Cost of Equipment	$3,000,000–$8,000,000
Lease Rate	8% to 12%
Lease Term	Category IA, II, III, IV—48 months
	Category IB—54 months
Draw-down Period	Twelve (12) months beginning 6 weeks after approval
Expiration	At expiration, lessee has the option to (1) purchase the Equipment for a mutually agreed upon value, (2) release the Equipment upon mutually agreeable terms, or (3) return the equipment to the lessor
Net Lease	Yes
Tax Assumptions	Lessor is the owner of the equipment for tax purposes
Equipment Description	IA—computer equipment furnished from Comdisco inventory for in-store use
	IB—computer equipment not furnished from Comdisco inventory for in-store use
	II—computer and peripheral equipment for use in ems headquarters
	III—any other inventory equipment for in-store or headquarters use
	IV—specialized equipment
Advance Rental	One month's lease payment
Warrants	10 to 15% of the maximum equipment value
Approval Process	Approval by Comdisco Investment Committee
Commitment Fee	Commitment fee of $25,000
Information	Lessee agrees to all relevant disclosure

Source: Company documents.

EXHIBIT 22-9

MACROECONOMIC DATA FOR LAST DAY OF EACH PERIOD

Date	1 Month US T-Bills	3 Month US T-Bills	30 Year US T-Bond	US Prime Rate	S&P BBB	Moody's Aaa	Moody's Aa	Moody's A
Dec 1990	7.3	6.6	8.2	9.7	10.	9.0	9.3	9.6
Mar 1991	5.8	5.9	8.2	8.8	10.	8.9	9.2	9.5
Jun 1991	5.4	5.6	8.4	8.5	10.	9.0	9.2	9.5
Sep 1991	5.0	5.2	7.8	8.0	9.4	8.6	8.8	9.1
Dec 1991	3.7	3.9	7.4	6.5	9.2	8.3	8.6	8.8
Mar 1992	3.8	4.1	7.9	6.5	9.3	8.3	8.7	8.8
Jun 1992	3.6	3.6	7.7	6.5	9.1	8.2	8.5	8.7
Sep 1992	2.7	2.7	7.3	6.0	8.9	7.9	8.1	8.3
Dec 1992	2.8	3.1	7.4	6.0	8.8	7.9	8.2	8.3
Mar 1993	2.7	2.8	6.9	6.0	8.3	7.5	7.5	7.8
Jun 1993	2.8	3.0	6.6	6.0	8.5	7.3	7.5	7.7

Source: Moody's Industrial Manual.

EXHIBIT 22-10

SELECTED FINANCIAL DATA ON MARKET RESEARCH COMPANIES ($ MILLIONS)

Audits and Surveys Worldwide

	1989	1990	1991	1992
Sales	$70.21	$66.19	$52.56	$48.55
SG&A	16.44	15.64	12.91	12.36
Cap Ex	1.73	0.33	0.56	0.30
Op Inc Bef Dep	6.46	5.70	2.11	2.44
Net Inc	−0.93	−1.61	4.02	−4.66
Tot Assets	68.94	64.04	55.74	48.63
Current Assets	45.55	40.58	34.24	30.10
Current Liabilities	13.92	13.01	16.60	37.65
Debt	43.34	42.49	30.35	29.43
Net Worth	13.92	12.23	15.96	10.71
Beta	NA	NA	NA	0.42
P/E Ratio	NA	NA	2.75	NA

Information Resources, Inc.

	1989	1990	1991	1992
Sales	$136.40	$166.70	$207.68	$276.36
SG&A	17.06	18.51	20.90	29.59
Cap Ex	156.4	104.1	67.6	19.3
Op Inc Bef Dep	16.68	23.22	38.25	51.92
Net Inc	−12.12	2.84	14.24	19.25
Tot Assets	134.70	132.73	189.07	264.00
Current Assets	51.05	62.14	104.90	141.53
Current Liabilities	47.42	38.80	52.58	53.59
Debt	39.84	25.07	22.21	6.39
Net Worth	50.73	59.61	116.99	186.89
Beta	NA	NA	NA	1.49
P/E Ratio	NA	40.00	41.05	39.87

Biospherics

	1989	1990	1991	1992
Sales	$15.33	$15.89	$15.13	
SG&A	2.29	2.41	2.08	1.91
Cap Ex	0.46	0.35	0.25	0.25
Op Inc Bef Dep	0.17	0.16	0.65	1.6
Net Inc	−0.34	−0.45	0.13	0.68
Tot Assets	6.74	6.47	6.29	6.49
Current Assets	3.44	3.52	3.74	4.24
Current Liabilities	1.62	1.97	2.77	2.61
Debt	1.90	1.93	1.64	0.71
Net Worth	2.64	2.07	2.34	3.02
Beta	NA	NA	NA	0.73
P/E Ratio	NA	NA	206	39.71

M/A/R/C Inc.

	1989	1990	1991	1992
Sales	$64.06	$73.07	$71.31	$66.68
SG&A	NA	NA	NA	NA
Cap Ex	4.62	3.05	2.70	2.95
Op Inc Bef Dep	5.89	6.77	7.23	3.78
Net Inc	2.62	2.83	3.36	1.33
Tot Assets	35.98	40.63	44.23	41.46
Current Assets	19.95	25.22	24.42	19.54
Current Liabilities	4.83	7.89	9.41	5.67
Debt	0.80	0.63	0.33	0.15
Net Worth	29.04	30.56	32.30	33.24
Beta	NA	NA	NA	0.94
P/E Ratio	11.81	8.98	10.28	19.38

(Continued)

EXHIBIT 22-10 *(Continued)*

Ceridan Corp.	1989	1990	1991	1992	**Paychex, Inc.**	1989	1990	1991	1992
Sales	$2,934	$1,691	$1,525	$830	Sales	$120.2	$137.08	$161.27	$190.03
SG&A	830	563	500	211	SG&A	63.04	73.82	89.21	102.66
Cap Ex	156	104	67.6	19.3	Cap Ex	15.36	17.37	13.41	8.67
Op Inc Bef Dep	209.4	130.7	93.3	66.7	Op Inc Bef Dep	19.45	21.57	28.39	37.09
Net Inc	−680.4	2.7	−9.8	−392.5	Net Inc	8.57	9.62	13.70	19.96
Tot Assets	1,861	1,424	1,214	530	Tot Assets	62.11	70.41	86.24	106.92
Current Assets	1,274	951	792	356	Current Assets	31.42	29.70	41.62	64.23
Current Liabilities	843	624	467	298	Current Liabilities	10.17	10.48	13.74	17.84
Debt	379	359	201	188	Debt	2.14	2.41	2.02	1.63
Net Worth	412	457	446	−101	Net Worth	47.16	54.49	67.41	85.19
Beta	NA	NA	NA	1.21	Beta	NA	NA	NA	1.05
P/E Ratio	NA	177.5	7.20	NA	P/E Ratio	23.86	31.25	36.07	39.85

Market Facts, Inc.					**Sandy Corp.**				
Sales	$39.00	$40.17	$40.75	$40.42	Sales	$32.48	$33.47	$34.87	$37.77
SG&A	17.40	17.18	16.62	17.74	SG&A	8.84	8.90	6.64	6.67
Cap Ex	1.28	13.04	1.55	3.74	Cap Ex	0.22	0	0.01	0.21
Op Inc Bef Dep	2.27	2.33	3.14	2.15	Op Inc Bef Dep	−0.08	−0.80	2.11	3.15
Net Inc	1.07	0.91	0.82	−0.44	Net Inc	−2.39	−1.88	0.79	1.97
Tot Assets	22.60	32.83	32.05	27.77	Tot Assets	20.55	15.44	12.75	15.55
Current Assets	17.53	16.71	15.73	10.13	Current Assets	17.17	12.81	10.98	14.14
Current Liabilities	14.55	13.70	13.34	8.68	Current Liabilities	11.94	9.12	5.85	6.40
Debt	0.65	11.54	11.28	12.86	Debt	6.09	4.54	1.18	0.02
Net Worth	7.25	7.47	7.33	8.15	Net Worth	7.28	5.63	6.42	8.50
Beta	NA	NA	NA	0.84	Beta	NA	NA	NA	1.08
P/E Ratio	12.29	11.06	8.51	NA	P/E Ratio	NA	NA	11.43	10.90

Source: Compustat.

EXHIBIT 22-11

ANNUALIZED VOLATILITY FOR 40 MARKET RESEARCH/INFORMATION SERVICE FIRMS

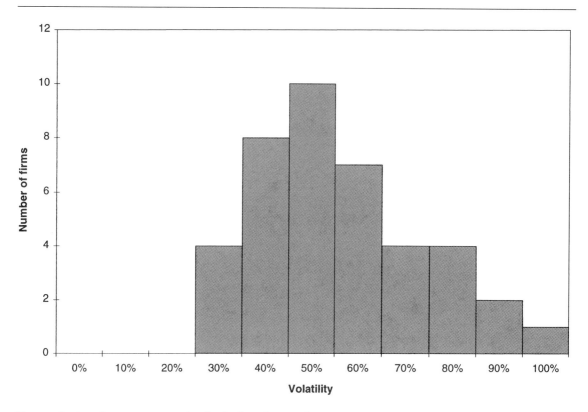

The graph plots the average annualized volatility of 40 market research/information service firms over the period January 1988 through December 1992. The average annualized volatility was 61%, and the median was 57%.

Source: Casewriters' estimates.

efficient market services: August 1993 (B-1) ems Management

Dr. Penny Baron understood the importance of the American Stores contract: While Kroger was certainly an important client, American Stores represented an opportunity to leverage ems's cost base and to prove that ems could successfully deploy in multiple environments. She felt the two successes could trigger a domino-like effect that would put other chains in the position of having to adopt ems's system to remain competitive.

Baron also knew that ems would not be able to finance the deployment without tapping an outside source of capital. Based on her experience with ems's venture capital investors, she understood the value of financing alternatives. At the suggestion of the venture capital firms, the Comdisco Ventures had taken a strong interest in ems. A venture lease seemed like a workable solution; it was a source of money because ems was going to have to purchase computer equipment that Comdisco could supply. In addition, there was the issue of flexibility: while the lease money only applied to equipment, would it free up other funds? Baron felt comfortable that ems would have no problem making lease payments.

She knew the whole negotiation was simple in a sense. ems needed funds, as much as possible because the lease was a relatively inexpensive source of capital. ems needed to successfully deploy into the American Stores chain within two years; otherwise a fantastic opportunity could be lost. For the most part, ems needed computer equipment, which Comdisco already owned. One issue that had to be resolved was the status of the equipment at lease expiration. The majority of the equipment was likely to be installed in stores across the country and could not be removed or replaced without interrupting service. The issue had to be resolved when the lease was signed; otherwise the Comdisco Ventures could exploit the situation when the lease expired.

Research Associate Jeffrey A. Ferrell (Harvard College '97) prepared this case under the supervision of Professor Paul Gompers as the basis for class discussion rather than to illustrate either effective or ineffective handling of an administrative situation.

Baron knew that warrant coverage could become an issue. She felt the trick would be to receive a fair valuation of ems and high price-earnings multiple, which would greatly increase the valuation at the time of the projected IPO and reduce the number of warrants that they would need to give Comdisco.

She knew she had some more work to do before presenting her recommendations to the rest of the ems management team. She would have to determine the amount that ems would need to sustain expanded operations until the next financing. Everything else would fall in place, she told herself. She had gotten along well with Jim Labe during their initial conversations. Surely, the Comdisco Ventures would realize that ems was a great investment; after all, the last venture capital round was four times oversubscribed. Picking up her coat, she headed toward Mike Spindler's office. She would be sure to share some of her thoughts over lunch.

efficient market services: August 1993 (B-2) Comdisco Ventures

Jim Labe sat comfortably in the leather chair of his office at the Comdisco Ventures. The initial negotiation between Comdisco Ventures and ems had produced the framework of a venture lease, but he knew that there were still a number of issues to be resolved.

Labe was somewhat uncomfortable with the industry that ems serviced: he was aware of the paper-thin profit margins, low technology, rapid turnover, and low barrier to entry in the packaged goods industry. Furthermore, he was weary of firms purporting to be in the consulting or market research business. However, he could not deny the fact that ems was the only deal in the Midwest to ever have attracted three major West Coast venture capital firms that were very enthusiastic about their investment: the most recent venture round was oversubscribed and had closed at almost a 3× uptick in less than a year's time. Over the past several years, Comdisco Ventures had invested in a number of portfolio companies of each of the venture capital firms, and the results had been more than satisfactory.

There was no denying that the management team of ems was strong; senior management was known in the industry and had recognized expertise in POS data creation, collection, processing, reporting, and application. Indeed, the management team had substantial experience at a number of ems's most likely competitors, including IRI and Nielsen.

There were a couple of obvious weaknesses in ems's strategy. First, although ems's systems and process were unique, they could and would be replicated over time. ems admitted that its success was predicated on a first to market strategy; it surely was ahead of its competitors, but ems was operating in a market populated by large, experienced,

Jeffrey A. Ferrell (Harvard College '97) prepared this case under the supervision of Professor Paul Gompers as the basis for class discussion rather than to illustrate either effective or ineffective handling of an administrative situation.

and well-funded competitors. Would its lead prove sufficient? Second, Labe knew that Manufacturers' promotion, research, and information budgets had come under increasing pressure as consumers continued to exhibit decreasing brand loyalty, resulting in reduced overall profit margins. Third, Labe was concerned about the speed with which ems could achieve market penetration. Projected revenues and profits were clearly based on ems's ability to move aggressively. Chains could be slower to sign contracts and roll out ems projects than anyone anticipated. Furthermore, each store had a unique information system that could result in implementation problems, thereby slowing deployment. Fourth, the enthusiasm for ECR could wane. ems depended on the cooperation of retail stores and brand owners to be profitable.

Despite these factors, Labe was confident that the inefficiencies in the packaged goods industry could be reduced through better information management. It seemed that ems's customers shared this belief. After all, ems had not lost a paying customer during its first two years of operation. Labe had a positive impression of ems for another reason: unlike so many other companies his fund had invested in, ems had a product that had been deployed and was in use by a large number of paying customers. At the right price, there was clearly an investment opportunity here.

Labe's thoughts turned to the terms of the lease. ems was a computer-intensive company—Comdisco would probably be able to supply refurbished equipment from its inventory to ems. This, coupled with the fact that ems had strong venture capital backing, assured him that it made sense to make a larger than average investment in ems. Also, if things went well for ems, there would be other leasing opportunities that would emerge. While most of the equipment would be of general utility, Labe knew that ems would also need specialty equipment that would be difficult to rent to someone else.

Labe knew that ems needed to finance the deployment of its information service in American Stores' one thousand supermarkets over the next two years; the major deployment costs would be computer hardware upgrades at the company's headquarters and the in-store platform. It seemed reasonable that Comdisco would provide the large majority of this equipment.

Labe leaned back in his chair and started to calculate what an appropriate rate of warrant coverage would be. Much of it depended on when ems would be able to go public and when Comdisco Ventures would be able to cash out. If everything went well, Labe thought ems should be able to generate a 20 to 30% annual return over the lifetime of the investment. Of course, things rarely went completely as planned. Labe considered ways of structuring the lease to leave Comdisco Ventures as protected as possible. He pondered the takedown period; if ems was on track with American Stores, a year seemed reasonable. How long should the lease be? What would happen to the equipment at expiration? Were there any competitors bidding for the business? If there were a problem, how would you dispose of the specialty equipment in the stores? What should the mix be between specialty and regular computer equipment, and should they be priced differently? He continued to scribble down lease terms. He would be meeting with the senior management team of ems next week to work out a final venture lease proposal.

He got up, walked to the office kitchen, hoping to find a bag of potato chips. He now remembered his secretary saying something about the store not having any. Suddenly, ems was looking like an excellent investment opportunity.

23

A Note on Franchising

Franchising, according to the U.S. Department of Commerce,[1] is a form of licensing by which the owner (the franchisor) of a product, service, or business method obtains distribution through affiliated dealers (the franchisees). In return for the franchisor's support in starting the business, the franchisee pays the franchisor an initial fee, which may range from $1,000 to $150,000.[2] In addition the franchisee usually pays a certain percentage from his or her gross revenues annually for the continued support of the franchisor and use of brands, trademarks, or business formats. The annual royalty payment can range between 0 and 50%, and the average royalty rate is 7%.[3] Franchising accounts for approximately one-third of total retail sales in North America. Exhibit 23-1 shows the total number of franchises in the economy broken down into company- or franchisor-owned and number of outlets held by franchisees for 1969–1991.

HISTORY OF FRANCHISING

Franchising, a term that comes from the French language and means to be free from servitude, developed as a business method in the 1850s in the United States. Some business historians argue that as a method of licensing, franchising developed much earlier in feudal times when the head of the Roman Catholic Church gave his clergy the right to collect tithes or church taxes locally. For this right, the clergy sent a portion of the tithes to Rome.[4] English beer brewers in the eighteenth century also engaged in a form

Research Associate Catherine Conneely prepared this note as the basis for class discussion under the supervision of Professor Paul Gompers.

[1] U.S. Department of Commerce—Minority Business Development Agency, *Franchise Opportunities Handbook* (Washington DC: U.S. Government Printing Office, October 1994).

[2] L.W. Stern and A. I. El-Ansary, *Marketing Channels* (Englewood Cliffs, NJ: Prentice-Hall, 1988).

[3] "Data collected for the paper show royalty rates range from 0 to 50%, with 7% as the mean and 4.83% the standard deviation." (Kabir C. Sen, "The Use of Initial Fees and Royalties in Business-format Franchising," *Managerial and Decision Economics* [1993]: 190).

[4] See Chapter 3 of *The Franchise Fraud* for a discussion of the history of franchising (Robert L. Purvin, *The Franchise Fraud: How to Protect Yourself Before and After You Invest* (New York: John Wiley, 1994).

EXHIBIT 23-1

FRANCHISED OUTLETS IN THE UNITED STATES, 1969–1991

Year	Number of Establishments			Sales (millions of dollars)		
	Total	Company-owned	Franchisee-owned	Total	Company-owned	Franchisee-owned
1969	383,908	68,863	315,045	119.53	24.82	94.70
1970	396,314	71,934	324,380	111.24	24.83	86.41
1971	431,169	74,721	356,448	128.88	18.65	110.23
1972	445,281	77,539	367,742	143.68	21.00	122.69
1973	453,632	78,850	374,782	161.90	24.35	137.55
1974	440,701	78,680	362,021	165.62	26.16	139.46
1975	434,538	80,561	353,977	182.31	28.72	153.59
1976	443,263	83,229	360,034	217.38	32.80	184.58
1977	450,800	85,941	364,859	253.37	38.14	215.24
1978	451,790	84,867	366,923	287.31	44.18	243.13
1979	452,487	85,280	367,207	312.19	39.55	272.64
1980	442,371	85,475	356,896	336.22	47.16	289.06
1981	442,418	85,905	356,513	364.72	50.60	314.12
1982	439,384	86,827	352,557	376.43	55.08	321.35
1983	441,181	85,789	355,392	422.83	59.16	363.67
1984	444,299	86,964	357,335	492.09	63.64	428.45
1985	455,220	86,443	368,777	542.97	68.30	474.67
1986	462,123	88,500	373,623	569.08	85.37	483.71
1987	479,087	89,483	389,604	599.43	90.61	508.82
1988	480,789	93,945	386,844	648.11	98.28	549.83
1989	492,498	94,574	397,924	677.91	107.45	570.45
1990	521,215	97,008	424,207	713.86	117.07	596.80
1991	542,496	100,496	442,000	757.83	127.21	630.62

Note: Numbers are estimated by U.S. DoC for 1987.

Source: Years 1969–1987 are from U.S. Department of Commerce, *Franchising in the Economy, 1986–1988,* February 1988; 1988 is from IFA, *Franchising in the Economy, 1988–1990;* years 1989–1991 are from IFA, *Franchising in the Economy, 1991.*

of franchising. Some brewers entered into licensing and financing arrangements with tavern owners for exclusive sale of beer and ale brands.

In the United States, in 1850 Isaac Singer sold licenses to individuals for up to $5,000. These first franchisees established retail outlets for Singer's new invention, the sewing machine, and spread the word of the Singer product line far more quickly than Singer would have been able to if he had sold the machines independently. In 1898, GM established its first independent dealer to sell and service automobiles. In 1899, Coca-Cola sold its first bottling franchise in Chattanooga. Along with the automotive and soft drink industries, the oil industry quickly established itself among the first modern franchisors. Franchising developed in the United States at this time for a variety of reasons; the size of the country meant that there were many logistical problems for producers and manufacturers in distributing goods and establishing national networks. It was also difficult to raise capital for new or expanding businesses. The fees from franchisees helped finance growth.

Two distinct types of franchise systems developed in the United States between the 1850s and 1950s. The first, product franchising, developed in the 1840s when the makers and inventors of new and complex machines used a modification of the agent/licensee system to spread knowledge of their products. The second, business format franchising, first appeared in the 1920s with Howard Johnson's innovation in standardized food preparation techniques. Business format franchising took off in the 1950s as an industry in its own right as fast food chains such as McDonald's and Kentucky Fried Chicken expanded rapidly throughout the country during the decade. The growth of franchising during the 1950s is attributable to another set of reasons. In the postwar United States the population was growing, and increasing mobility meant that it was spreading throughout the country. The country was prosperous, leading to rising disposable incomes and to greater demands for consumer goods and services. The population became familiar with brand names for products and services as technological advances led to television and nationwide advertising and brand recognition.

A recent development in franchise formats is conversion franchising, whereby an independent business converts its name and trade style to that of a large marketing network. An example is the Century 21 Real Estate Corporation franchise system which has allowed independent real estate agencies to be part of a nationwide realty network.

FRANCHISING FORMATS

Product franchising started in the United States as an independent sales relationship between supplier and dealer. The dealer acquired some of the identity of the supplier as a franchisee concentrating on one company's product line and identifying their business with that company. Examples of product franchises are bottling companies, beer distributorships, petroleum and automotive dealerships, or any single line or primary line brand-name retail outlet. Exhibit 23-2 shows the extent of product/trade mark franchising in the economy for 1969–1991.

Business format franchising is the right to license a business or trade style as opposed to selling a particular product. Not only does the franchisee have access to the franchisor's product, but it is also able to utilize the franchisor's business concept, which can include a marketing strategy and plan, operating manuals and standards, quality control, and a continuing process of support and guidance. It has become more difficult to distinguish between product franchising and business format franchising according to Purvin.[5] Most franchisees or dealers of an individual brand look and feel as if they are committed to a common business format. Exhibit 23-3 shows the numbers of business format franchise establishments in the economy for 1969–1991.

Although business format franchises account for approximately 80% of all franchised business in the United States, they only have 31% of the total retail sales from franchising. Product franchisors, on the other hand, represent only 20% of franchising

[5] Purvin, p. 39.

EXHIBIT 23-2

PRODUCT/TRADE NAME FRANCHISE OUTLETS IN THE UNITED STATES, 1969–1991

	Number of Establishments			Sales (millions of dollars)		
Year	Total	Company-owned	Franchisee-owned	Total	Company-owned	Franchisee-owned
1969	N/A	N/A	217,822	N/A	N/A	82.10
1970	N/A	N/A	217,028	N/A	N/A	82.49
1971	255,620	44,401	211,219	104.17	5.91	98.25
1972	262,100	45,693	216,407	115.20	7.55	107.65
1973	251,395	43,557	207,838	131.00	8.62	122.39
1974	230,974	39,611	191,363	131.30	9.77	121.53
1975	223,724	38,281	185,443	144.90	10.70	134.20
1976	220,946	37,744	183,202	171.30	11.74	159.56
1977	211,984	35,675	176,309	195.90	5.51	190.39
1978	207,896	33,057	174,839	217.90	13.81	204.09
1979	199,785	31,585	168,200	241.00	15.71	225.29
1980	189,823	28,762	161,061	250.80	19.44	231.36
1981	181,863	27,350	154,513	275.70	19.59	256.11
1982	174,107	26,119	147,988	277.00	19.92	257.08
1983	164,986	24,668	140,318	312.30	19.85	292.46
1984	160,723	23,869	136,854	369.80	19.56	350.25
1985	153,531	22,533	130,998	401.60	19.56	382.04
1986	149,313	22,354	126,959	413.50	32.07	381.43
1987	144,751	N/A	N/A	429.80	N/A	N/A
1988	141,810	20,843	120,967	469.80	373.37	432.46
1989	139,245	20,536	118,709	484.95	402.24	444.73
1990	135,097	19,791	115,306	500.71	450.08	455.70
1991	134,279	19,691	114,588	525.59	491.11	476.48

Note: Numbers are estimated by U.S. DoC for 1987. N/A: Data not available.

Source: Years 1969–1987 are from U.S. Department of Commerce, *Franchising in the Economy, 1986–1988*, February 1988; 1988 is from IFA, *Franchising in the Economy, 1988–1990*; years 1989–1991 are from IFA, *Franchising in the Economy*, 1991.

companies in the United States but account for 69% of retail sales.[6] Exhibit 23-4 shows the industry breakdown in business format franchising for 1989–1991.

In recent years, the concept of multilevel franchising has modified the classical business format model. Multilevel franchising provides the franchisor with more op-

[6] In 1992 there were an estimated 540,000 franchised businesses in the United States which made $757.8 billion in retail sales (see ibid., 64–65).

EXHIBIT 23-3

BUSINESS FORMAT FRANCHISING IN THE UNITED STATES, 1969–1991

Year	Number of Establishments			Sales (millions of dollars)		
	Total	Company-owned	Franchisee-owned	Total	Company-owned	Franchisee-owned
1969	N/A	N/A	97,223	N/A	N/A	11.63
1970	N/A	N/A	107,352	N/A	N/A	13.44
1971	175,549	30,320	145,229	24.05	12.74	15.97
1972	189,640	33,138	156,502	28.70	13.27	19.43
1973	202,237	35,293	166,944	32.70	15.67	21.63
1974	209,727	39,069	170,658	37.30	16.36	24.54
1975	210,814	42,280	168,534	40.90	19.72	26.88
1976	222,317	45,485	176,832	46.60	34.96	30.84
1977	240,524	50,281	190,243	65.80	24.62	39.68
1978	245,694	51,760	193,934	64.30	29.65	42.75
1979	252,702	53,695	199,007	72.40	35.23	48.27
1980	252,548	56,713	195,835	83.50	34.56	54.55
1981	260,555	58,555	202,000	89.10	40.94	58.06
1982	268,306	60,708	207,598	99.00	46.46	64.04
1983	276,195	61,121	215,074	110.50	51.09	71.21
1984	283,576	63,095	220,481	122.30	63.10	78.21
1985	301,689	63,910	237,779	141.30	62.87	92.63
1986	312,810	66,146	246,664	155.50	67.32	102.28
1987	324,516	N/A	N/A	169.60	N/A	N/A
1988	338,979	73,102	265,877	178.32	60.44	117.37
1989	353,253	74,038	279,215	192.95	67.23	125.73
1990	386,118	77,217	308,901	213.16	72.06	141.10
1991	408,217	80,805	327,412	232.24	78.10	154.14

Note: Numbers are estimated by U.S. DoC for 1987. N/A: Data not available.

Source: Years 1969–1987 are from U.S. Department of Commerce, *Franchising in the Economy, 1986–1988,* February 1988; 1988 is from IFA, *Franchising in the Economy, 1988–1990;* years 1989–1991 are from IFA, *Franchising in the Economy,* 1991.

tions to grow more quickly and at less cost. The three primary methods employed in multilevel franchising are master (or regional) franchising; subfranchising; and area development franchising. A common thread for all three methods is that the franchisor sells development rights in a particular market to one or more franchisees. The differences between the methods involve the depth of the relationship between franchisor, franchisee, and subfranchisees.[7]

---

[7] *Bond's Franchise Guide* (1996 ed.; Oakland, CA: Source Book Publications), p. 15.

EXHIBIT 23-4

INDUSTRY BREAKDOWN OF BUSINESS FORMAT FRANCHISING, 1989–1991

Owned by:	Company			Franchisee			Total		
	1989	1990	1991	1989	1990	1991	1989	1990	1991
Number of Establishments									
Restaurants—All Types	27,596	29,152	30,533	64,359	70,188	72,780	91,955	99,340	103,313
Hotels, Motels, & Campgrounds	1,232	1,261	1,307	8,880	9,785	10,091	10,112	11,046	11,398
Recreation, Entertainment, & Travel	480	587	705	9,322	10,300	10,849	9,802	10,887	11,554
Automotive Products & Services	4,741	5,128	5,618	31,483	34,121	36,604	36,224	39,249	42,222
Business Aids & Services	7,075	7,541	8,205	51,115	56,866	61,330	58,190	64,407	69,535
Accting, Credit, Collection Agencies, & Gen. Bus. Sys.	27	28	31	1,706	1,730	1,904	1,733	1,758	1,935
Employment Services	2,654	2,939	3,227	3,969	4,569	5,038	6,623	7,508	8,265
Printing & Copying Services	195	204	231	6,133	6,641	7,191	6,328	6,845	7,422
Tax Preparation	3,359	3,425	3,456	4,850	4,870	5,000	8,209	8,295	8,456
Real Estate	118	118	130	15,688	16,322	18,039	15,806	16,440	18,169
Miscellaneous Business Systems	722	827	1,130	18,805	22,734	24,158	19,527	23,561	25,288
Const., Home Impro., Maintenance, & Cleaning Svces.	620	615	680	23,468	26,800	29,899	24,088	27,415	30,579
Educational Products & Services	841	1,081	1,106	10,236	11,458	12,744	11,077	12,539	13,850
Laundry & Dry Cleaning Services	131	142	154	2,862	3,054	3,338	2,993	3,196	3,492
Rental Services (Auto-Truck)	731	784	804	1,885	1,962	2,094	2,616	2,746	2,898
Rental Services (Equipment)	2,451	2,485	2,570	7,432	8,255	8,543	9,883	10,740	11,113
Retail (Nonfood)	13,497	14,151	14,621	36,582	40,277	42,414	50,079	54,428	57,035
Retail Food (Nonconvenience)	3,210	3,389	3,546	17,854	21,122	21,832	21,064	24,511	25,378
Convenience Stores	10,864	10,295	10,325	6,703	6,913	6,940	17,567	17,208	17,265
Miscellaneous Business Systems	569	606	631	6,998	7,800	7,954	7,567	8,406	8,585
TOTAL ESTABLISHMENTS	81,113	84,758	89,010	330,330	365,767	388,742	411,443	450,525	477,752

(Continued)

The developers in all three models pay an up-front fee to the franchisor who gives them sole responsibility in developing an area.

- The master franchisee must bear the burden of finding individual franchisees for the area. Once the process is complete, the individual franchisees receive ongoing support from the parent franchisor. The master franchisee shares in the fees and royalties of the individual franchisees in that territory.

- The subfranchisor model is similar to the master franchisee; however, the parent franchisor has no involvement with the individual franchisees in the area once the

EXHIBIT 23-4 *(Continued)*

Owned by:	Company			Franchisee			Total		
	1989	1990	1991	1989	1990	1991	1989	1990	1991
Sales ($ million)									
Restaurants—All Types	25,490	27,901	30,498	44,622	49,954	54,998	70,113	77,855	85,497
Hotels, Motels, & Campgrounds	6,233	6,459	7,073	15,337	18,356	18,912	21,571	24,815	25,986
Recreation, Entertainment, & Travel	818	978	1,105	2,708	3,253	3,704	3,527	4,231	4,809
Automotive Products & Services	4,285	4,685	5,145	8,225	9,181	10,315	12,511	13,866	15,460
Business Aids & Services	4,007	4,408	4,913	12,936	14,231	15,862	16,943	18,640	20,776
Accting, Credit, Collection Agencies, & Gen. Bus. Sys.	8	8	9	178	187	211	186	195	221
Employment Services	2,515	2,825	3,166	2,465	2,906	3,240	4,981	5,731	6,406
Printing & Copying Services	47	50	59	1,544	1,708	1,910	1,592	1,758	1,969
Tax Preparation	349	368	386	294	304	325	643	673	711
Real Estate	680	726	820	5,504	6,060	6,859	6,184	6,786	7,680
Miscellaneous Business Systems	405	428	471	2,948	3,064	3,315	3,354	3,493	3,787
Const., Home Impro., Maintenance, & Cleaning Svces.	1,487	1,609	1,742	4,272	4,844	5,349	5,759	6,454	7,092
Educational Products & Services	540	620	677	1,113	1,411	1,577	1,654	2,031	2,255
Laundry & Dry Cleaning Services	36	41	45	323	360	406	359	401	452
Rental Services (Auto-Truck)	229	243	257	457	488	514	687	731	771
Rental Services (Equipment)	3,860	4,115	4,354	3,042	3,422	3,683	6,902	7,537	8,037
Retail (Nonfood)	9,061	9,831	10,505	17,608	19,433	20,879	26,669	29,264	31,384
Retail Food (Nonconvenience)	1,389	1,504	1,646	8,611	10,201	10,529	10,001	11,705	12,175
Convenience Stores	9,363	9,179	9,607	4,932	5,142	5,385	14,295	14,321	14,992
Miscellaneous Business Systems	424	484	528	1,532	1,815	2,023	1,957	2,300	2,551
TOTAL SALES	71,235	76,470	83,014	138,661	156,329	170,005	209,897	232,799	253,019

Source: Franchising in the Economy 1991, IFA Educational Foundation & Howarth International.

subfranchisor has paid the fee for exclusive development of the area. The individual franchisees are wholly dependent on the subfranchisor for initial training and setup and for ongoing support.

- The area development agreement allows the area developers to either seek independent franchisees or set up individual franchise units of their own. The agreement specifies that a certain number of units must be developed within a given time period. The area developers do not share in the franchise fees or royalties paid by the individual franchisees not owned by them. The area developers gain only from self-owned franchise units in the area. They profit over time because the upfront fee for the area is usually at a discount to the amount they would have had to pay to develop the self-owned franchise units individually.

FRANCHISING IN THE ECONOMY

It is difficult to gather data on the level of franchising in the economy. The U.S. Department of Commerce did not survey the franchise sector until 1988. The International Franchise Association (IFA), which represents the franchising industry, has collaborated with several organizations since then in an effort to produce statistics on the level of franchising in the United States. Unfortunately, data collection by the IFA included only its members, which total approximately 630 out of a possible 2,500 North American franchisors.[8] Only about 22% of relevant participants were contacted.

Another difficulty is finding accurate failure rates in franchise systems. A study by FranData, a Washington, DC-based company specializing in franchise research, analysis, and document retrieval, suggests that 4.4% of franchises leave their franchise systems annually.[9] This rate has been confirmed by Bates in his 1992 study.[10] Exhibit 23-5 shows data from the U.S. Department of Commerce on the number of franchise failures and departures. The definition of franchise failure is quite loose, and it is not certain that franchise units returned to company ownership or franchised by other individuals are included in the numbers of failed franchises. Exhibit 23-6 shows the changes in franchise ownership to company-owned outlets or franchisee-owned units. Among the reasons for a change in ownership of a franchise unit are the ending of the franchise agreement, death of the franchisee, or termination of the franchisee for breach of the franchise contract. Franchisee-owned units that are in danger of failing are sometimes taken over by other franchisees or by the franchisor. It is difficult to ascertain, however, if the changes in franchise ownership are due to failure on the part of the franchisee.

As can be seen from Exhibit 23-7 of franchisor distribution in the United States, franchisors tend to develop in the larger states and the more heavily populated areas of the country.

REASONS COMPANIES FRANCHISE

The advantages of franchising as opposed to expanding with company-owned outlets are many. The franchisor can establish a presence in the market rapidly and quickly lock in a market position for products or services. Another bonus for the franchisor is the initial fees paid by franchisees to become part of the business. The ongoing royalty payments paid in return for continuous support from the franchisor are also revenue for the franchisor. Franchisees typically need less management and capital than company-owned outlets. Franchisees are working for themselves and are therefore more motivated. They generally set up locally and have knowledge of the area.

The drawbacks of franchising for the franchisor include dealing with complaints from franchisees, failure of the interests of franchisees and the franchisor to coincide

---

[8] Ibid., p. 16.

[9] Franchise departures, which cover only terminations and nonrenewals, were categorized as follows: 1.2% of franchise contracts were canceled, terminated, or not renewed for unspecified reasons; 1.0% left for specified reasons (e.g., abandonment, bankruptcy, health reasons, etc.); 0.8% were terminated by mutual agreement between franchisee and franchisor or voluntarily by the franchisee; 0.7% were terminated for failure to pay royalties, for quality control reasons, or for failure to meet other contractual obligations; 0.7% were reacquired by purchase or by other means. (See Robert E. Bond, *The Source Book of Franchise Opportunities*, 1993 ed., Homewood, IL: Dow Jones-Irwin, 1993, p. 11).

[10] Timothy Bates, "A Comparison of Franchise and Independent Small Business Survival Rates," *Small Business Economics* (October 1995): 377–388.

EXHIBIT 23-5

NUMBER OF FRANCHISE FAILURES AND DEPARTURES, 1973–1989

Year	Failures	Departures	Total
1973	33	25	58
1974	49	40	89
1975	55	48	103
1976	39	47	86
1977	24	47	71
1978	30	44	74
1979	55	64	119
1980	42	74	116
1981	50	75	125
1982	59	61	120
1983	57	84	141
1984	56	63	119
1985	46	79	125
1986	78	105	183
1987	104	80	184
1988	105	82	187
1989	107	83	190

Source: Handbook of Successful Franchising, U.S. Department of Commerce survey.

(for example, on issues of quality), and a restrictive legal environment. Franchisees need control and monitoring, which is an additional expense for the franchisor. There may be a lack of trust in the relationship between the franchisor and franchisee, particularly if there are communication problems. Given the popularity of franchising, franchisors in some industries might find it difficult to choose a good franchisee from among the many hundreds of applicants.

Those interested in owning a business choose between the alternatives of franchising, in what is generally a proven business system, or setting up an independent business. If the prospective franchisee lacks knowledge or business expertise, then the training provided by the franchisor will help overcome this disadvantage. Franchisees are eager to become business owners, but with the support and assistance from the franchisor. The franchisee also benefits from the brand name, reputation, and image of an experienced franchisor who generally has built up public goodwill. Not only is the capital commitment usually smaller than that needed in setting up independent business, but the franchisor's know-how makes franchising a more efficient use of capital by the franchisee. The franchisee also benefits from the national scale of franchisor's advertising and promotional activities if a larger franchisor is chosen. The franchisee can also avail of the bulk purchasing and negotiating capacity of the franchisor with suppliers. In addition, the franchisee does not have to independently develop new products; any new products, services, or production techniques are usually available to the

EXHIBIT 23-6

CHANGES IN FRANCHISE OWNERSHIP, 1971–1989

Year	Repurchase for Company Ownership	Converted to Franchisee Ownership
1971	1755	602
1972	1187	601
1973	992	659
1974	878	668
1975	716	725
1976	546	956
1977	619	839
1978	612	718
1979	710	1052
1980	808	1012
1981	760	1068
1982	707	1057
1983	549	1069
1984	577	953
1985	640	1407
1986	827	1726
1987	831	1791
1988	834	1848
1989	832	1839

Note: Changes in ownership include establishments that were repurchased for company ownership, those converted to franchisee ownership, and establishments discontinued that were either company-owned or franchisee-owned units. Those that were discontinued did so for a multitude of reasons. Failure of business is one of the reasons, although the number of failures is unknown.

Source: Handbook of Successful Franchising.

franchisee from the franchisor's R&D process. As part of a franchising system, the franchisee might have access to information not otherwise available to independent business owners.

The disadvantages of franchising for the franchisee include the imposition of controls on the methods of doing business by the franchisor. Franchise contracts are generally restrictive and might be biased toward the franchisor. The initial fee is usually the first cash outflow for the franchisee and one he or she will not recoup unless the business is successful. In addition, royalty payments must be paid out of gross revenues whether or not the franchisee is breaking even. Sometimes it is difficult for the franchisee to assess a franchisor's quality. The Federal Trade Commission's (FTC) disclosure rule states that the prospective franchisees must be told certain things by the franchisor. However, it is still possible for franchisors to omit material facts that are not covered by the FTC rule.

EXHIBIT 23-7

FRANCHISING IN THE UNITED STATES—
ACTIVE FRANCHISORS BY STATE

State	Units	%	State	Units	%
Alabama	14	0.6	Montana	5	0.2
Alaska	1	0.0	North Carolina	46	1.9
Arkansas	13	0.5	North Dakota	7	0.3
Arizona	58	2.3	Nebraska	24	1.0
California	331	13.4	Nevada	12	0.5
Colorado	60	2.4	New Hampshire	7	0.3
Connecticut	54	2.2	New Jersey	105	4.2
Delaware	9	0.4	New Mexico	3	0.1
District of Columbia	6	0.2	New York	150	6.1
Florida	189	7.6	Ohio	123	5.0
Georgia	85	3.4	Oklahoma	19	0.8
Hawaii	8	0.3	Oregon	23	0.9
Idaho	7	0.3	Pennsylvania	101	4.1
Illinois	121	4.9	Rhode Island	19	0.8
Indiana	30	1.2	South Carolina	15	0.6
Iowa	22	0.9	South Dakota	6	0.2
Kansas	21	0.8	Tennessee	64	2.6
Kentucky	29	1.2	Texas	164	6.6
Louisiana	29	1.2	Utah	17	0.7
Maine	10	0.4	Vermont	3	0.1
Maryland	50	2.0	Virginia	36	1.5
Massachusetts	86	3.5	Washington	31	1.3
Michigan	88	3.6	West Virginia	8	0.3
Minnesota	78	3.2	Wisconsin	32	1.3
Mississippi	10	0.4	Wyoming	4	0.2
Missouri	40	1.6	Total	2,473	100

Note: Composition of franchisors listed in *The 1993 Source Book of Franchise Opportunities.*

Source: The 1993 Source Book of Franchise Opportunities.

There is also the possibility that the franchisee might become too dependent on the franchisor through no fault of his or her own. The franchisor can restrict the franchisee from setting up a similar business once the franchise agreement has been terminated. On the other hand, the franchisor might issue policies that affect a franchisee's profitability and the franchisee has no control over the franchisor in this regard. Neither does the franchisee have control over other franchisees who may damage the brand image to his/her detriment.

The most often cited reason for a business organization to embark on licensing its products, services, or business methods to independent operators is availability of capital. However, Rubin[11] in a text on the subject found that lack of capital was not the most important factor in a company's decision to franchise. He maintains that selling shares in the franchise to franchisees would be less costly. Hence, raising capital by selling franchises would seem to be inefficient. The inefficiency of the capital market is not the main impetus for franchising. Rubin argues that franchising is a response to agency problems.

Factors motivating franchising were found to be monitoring and control within the business organization, risk sharing, and ability of franchisors to exploit economies of scale. Business format franchising is on the rise because of the sharing of financial and managerial risks involved.[12] Lafontaine[13] states that the agency-theoretic explanations for franchising include risk sharing, one-sided moral hazard, and two-sided moral hazard. If the parties to a franchise contract are risk averse, then they both benefit from the "insurance" that arises in the mutually binding agreement.

Moral hazard occurs when one party to a contract tends to alter his or her behavior in such a way that costs to the other party are increased. Moral hazard is one-sided when the franchisor is unable to adequately observe the franchisee's behavior. In this case the contract is a compromise between the need to give the franchisee incentives and the need to provide the franchisee with support. Making the franchisee the residual claimant on the firm's profit provides an incentive to maximize profits. Two-sided moral hazard arises when both parties to the contract need incentives. The franchisee is highly motivated to succeed in the franchisor's system and the franchisor reaps the benefit of franchising the outlet through ongoing royalty payments. The efforts of both the franchisee and franchisor are important to the ultimate success of the business. Franchisees must work hard to maintain quality and service. The franchisor must invest in brand name.

These factors and the franchisor's need for capital explain decisions about the terms of franchise contracts and the setting of royalty rates and up-front franchise fees. These factors may also explain the extent to which companies use franchising. Lafontaine finds that the two-sided moral hazard explanation of franchising is most consistent. This suggests that there are incentive issues on both sides. She also finds that firms use franchising more when they want to grow faster.

Brickley and Dark[14] consider franchising to be a "hybrid" between two methods of controlling agency problems, control devices, such as monitoring, and ownership of residual claims restricted to agents bearing the effects of their actions. They find that opening franchisee-owned outlets instead of company-owned outlets reflects a tradeoff among agency problems. Whereas the agency problem associated with "shirking and perquisite taking by unit managers" is low for franchised outlets and high for company-owned outlets, "inefficient risk-bearing," "free-rider problems," and "quasi-rent appropriation" are considered high-risk agency problems with franchisee-owned outlets and low for company-owned outlets. It is obvious that managers in company-owned outlets would have less incentive to work hard and to ensure that inefficiencies are minimized

[11] P.H. Rubin, "The Theory of the Firm and the Structure of the Franchise Contact," *Journal of Law and Economics* 21 (1978): 223–233.

[12] Frank Cavaliere and Marleen Swerdlow, "The Pros and Cons of Franchising: Two Views—Why Franchise?" *Business Forum* (Summer 1988): 11–13.

[13] Francine Lafontaine, "Agency Theory and Franchising: Some Empirical Results," *Rand Journal of Economics* (Summer 1992): 263–283.

[14] J. A. Brickley and F. Dark, "The Choice of Organization Form: The Case of Franchising," *Journal of Financial Economics* (June 1987): 401–420.

than the individual owner of a franchised outlet who would bear most, if not all, of the consequences of his or her actions. However, the franchisee incurs inefficient risk-bearing by having a substantial proportion of his or her wealth and income tied up in one outlet. The franchisee may be more reluctant to take risks, such as investing in new equipment, and may also expect a higher return from the investment. Both the franchisor and franchisee can be free-riders. The franchisee has the incentive to use low-quality goods when the reputation of the chain is shared with fellow franchisees. The franchisor may also free-ride on the backs of the franchisees by not living up to the franchise agreement by, for example, not protecting the chain's trademark or quality. Quasi-rent is the value of an asset above its salvage value. The franchisee or franchisor may be able to appropriate this value when firm-specific assets exist. An example would be a building specially constructed as part of the franchise agreement. Owned by the franchisee, if the franchise contract ended and was not renewed or the franchisor demanded higher royalty payments, the building would be worth less to the franchisee in an alternative use.

The differences in costs of monitoring store managers and franchisees, as well as the geographic location of the outlet, appear to be important factors in a company's decision to franchise a unit. Outlets close to the franchisor's headquarters are more likely to be company-owned because the costs of monitoring these outlets are less. Brickley and Dark also found that locations where there was a higher frequency of repeat customers were more likely to be franchised than company-owned. For example, a fast food outlet located at a highway rest stop or in a busy area of a city is less likely to have repeat customers. The owner/manager of this unit would have little incentive to keep up the quality of the product or brand name when he or she knew that few customers would come back to the outlet. In this case the company would need to monitor the unit more frequently to ensure that standards were being maintained. Therefore, it is more effective for the company to retain ownership of such a unit. According to Brickley and Dark, factors favoring franchising over owning, when all other factors are held constant, include low investment risk on the part of the franchisee, low incentives for free-riding by both the franchisor and franchisee, and low investment in firm-specific assets.

A reason for the success of franchises is the low variance in output quality between franchise outlets. Consumers expect that wherever they are the quality of the product or service they order at a particular outlet is standard across the franchise system. The returns for franchisors rest heavily on strategies that make it difficult, if not impossible, for a franchisee to operate without their assistance, which can be accomplished through restrictions in the franchise contract or agreement.

TYPICAL FRANCHISING ARRANGEMENTS

A franchise agreement is a contract between two firms, the franchisor and the franchisee (see Exhibit 23-8 for a sample franchising contract). Mathewson and Winter[15] state that the principal ingredient in most franchise contracts is the franchisee's right to use a national brand name in exchange for a share of profits to the franchisor. However, the use of national brand names by local retailers involves a number of potential agency problems discussed in this note.

---

[15] G. F. Mathewson and R.A. Winter, "The Economics of Franchise Contracts," *Journal of Law and Economics* 28 (1985): 503–526.

EXHIBIT 23-8

A SAMPLE FRANCHISE AGREEMENT

THIS AGREEMENT made this _____ day of 19___, by and between FRANCHISOR COR-PORATION, a _____ Corporation having its principal office located at _____, here-inafter referred to as FRANCHISOR, and I.M. FRANCHISEE, individual as sole proprietor, trading as _____, located at _____, hereinafter referred to as FRANCHISEE,

   WITNESSETH:

WHEREAS, FRANCHISOR is the owner of the trademark and logo, "FRANCHISOR" (the "Mark"), and other trademarks and trade names, trade secrets and know-how for use in connec-tion with the unique system for performing the special functions of this business, and is the owner of the entire right, title and interest in and to U.S. Trademark Application, Serial No. _____, together with all of the good will connected therewith, which Mark is used in identifying, ad-vertising, promoting and marketing the FRANCHISOR System; and

WHEREAS, FRANCHISEE hereby acknowledges that by reason of FRANCHISOR's high stan-dards of quality and service in connection with the development of the unique System, and that the FRANCHISOR has created over a period of time a clear identification and consumer de-mand thereof, which requires appropriate and adequate safeguards for the maintenance and fu-ture promotion of the FRANCHISOR's System; and

WHEREAS, FRANCHISEE hereby acknowledges the exclusive right of FRANCHISOR in and to the FRANCHISOR System, as presently developed, or as same may be improved and ex-panded during the term of this Agreement, including practices, know-how, trade secrets, designs, trademarks, trade names, logos, signs and slogans, presently in use and to be hereafter devel-oped, all of which may be used thereunder; and

WHEREAS, FRANCHISEE desires, upon the terms and conditions herein set forth, to obtain and enter into the business of owning and operating FRANCHISOR System at and from the lo-cation agreed upon, under the Mark, subject to the supervision of FRANCHISOR and in ac-cordance with the standards of FRANCHISOR.

NOW, THEREFORE, in consideration of the mutual agreements herein contained and for other valuable consideration acknowledged by each of the parties to be adequate and sufficient, the parties hereby agree as follows;

1. *Franchise.* Franchisor hereby grants Franchisee during the life of this Agreement a non-assignable license to use the trademarks, service marks and trade name owned and as designated by Franchisor including "Franchisor System: in the operation of a _____ business (hereinafter referred to as the "franchise business"), which shall be limited to one unit located at _____ (hereinafter referred to as the "Premises"), together with the right to use a system of operation and method of doing business conceived and designed by Franchisor, and to sell the products specified by Franchisor, and to sell the products specified by Franchisor ac-cording to the procedure, system and method defined herein.

2. *Term and Renewal.* This Agreement and the franchise hereby granted shall continue for a period of twenty (20) years subsequent to its effective date, subject to prior revocation or termi-nation in accordance with the provision of Sections A and B. If, upon the expiration of the 20-year period Franchisee is in full compliance with his obligations hereunder, he shall have the op-tion to renew his franchise by executing Franchisor's then current Franchise Agreement; provided, that as a condition to renewal Franchisee must modernize his building and equipment to con-form to Franchisor's standards at the time in effect. No additional franchise fee will be payable upon renewal, but the relationship between the Franchisor and Franchisee during the renewal period will otherwise be governed by the provisions of Franchisor's then current Franchise Agree-ment, including those pertaining to royalties, advertising and duration of franchise.

(Continued)

EXHIBIT 23-8 *(Continued)*

3. *Location and Territory*

A. This Agreement shall be performed by the Franchisee at a location known as _____ _____.

B. The foregoing location is situated in a territory described (1) on the map attached hereto and incorporated herein/ (2) as follows: _____

C. Without the prior written consent of the Franchisee first had and obtained, the Franchisor shall neither itself use, nor shall it license its trademarks, service marks and trade name to any other person, partnership, corporation or other entity for use in the territory described in paragraph (B) of this Section while this agreement remains in force.

4. *Payments by Franchisee.* In consideration of the grant of the franchise contained herein, Franchisee shall pay to Franchisor the following:

(a) Upon the execution hereof, a franchise establishment fee of Fifteen Thousand Dollars ($15,000.00), receipt of which Franchisor hereby acknowledges.

(b) A sum equal to six (6%) percent of Franchisee's total monthly gross billings as hereinafter defined. "Gross Billing" shall mean the total of all sales and/or fees charged for products and/or services furnished in, or upon orders placed at, or completed by delivery in, through or from the Franchisee's Premises whether or not collected by Franchisee, less state and local sales taxes, if any. Within ten (10) days after the end of each month, Franchisee shall send to Franchisor, in a form approved by Franchisor, a statement signed by Franchisee showing all merchandise sold, and all billings therefor during the month, accompanied by a royalty check in the appropriate amount. Royalty fees shall be waived for the first sixty (60) days after opening of the Franchisee's business.

5. *Use of Marks, Trade Secrets and Operations Manual.*

A. *Marks.* Franchisee acknowledges that Franchisee is required by federal law to prevent the unauthorized use of its Marks and to control the quality of goods and services offered through use of its Marks. To assist Franchisors in its compliance with those requirements, Franchisee covenants and agrees to perform and abide by the following provisions.

1. Franchisee shall not use the words FRANCHISOR SYSTEMS or any stylistic or colorable variation thereof as part of the name of any corporation, partnership, proprietorship or other business entity in which Franchisee owns or holds an interest or as the trade name or assumed name of any such business entity except in connection with the subject business and premises.

2. Franchisee shall not use any of the Marks in connection with the advertising, promotion, sale or distribution of any item or other product not listed in FRANCHISOR's approved list or of any service not customarily offered by FRANCHISOR without FRANCHISOR's prior written consent.

3. Franchisee shall not use or allow the use of FRANCHISOR's registered logograph or the words FRANCHISOR SYSTEMS in or any promotional material, advertisement, display, business forms or other printed or graphic material without affixing the symbol thereto in the manner required by law.

4. Franchisee shall use the Marks in the precise form prescribed by the FRANCHISOR and shall observe reasonable directions regarding representations of the Marks and the manner of their display and use. Franchisee shall submit all paper goods, advertising and promotional material not furnished by FRANCHISOR to FRANCHISOR for approval prior to use.

5. Franchisee shall not use the Marks on any goods and/or for any services otherwise than in compliance with specifications issued from time to time by FRANCHISOR and with such other quality control measures which FRANCHISOR may adopt to promote and defend the goodwill associated with the Marks.

6. Upon the expiration, termination or revocation of the franchise hereby granted, Franchisee shall promptly discontinue use of the Marks and shall take appropriate action to remove the Marks from the premises upon which his business is located.

(Continued)

EXHIBIT 23-8   (Continued)

B. *Trade Secrets and Operations.* (Similar limitations and restrictions, as above in A, are set forth in detail in most agreements.)

OBLIGATIONS OF FRANCHISOR AND FRANCHISEE

1. Assistance: Initial training; Follow-up aid; On-going aid; Comprehensive operations manual.
2. Quality and Performance Control: Uniformity; Products and purchases; Right to modify system; Hours of operation; Inspections; Maintenance and repairs.
3. Recordkeeping: Accounting system; Business reports; Inspection of records.
4. Insurance Protection: Allocation of risks not insurable.
5. Taxes, Permits, and Business Certificates

Franchisor Agrees:

a. To make available to Franchisee the benefit of its knowledge and experience in the installation and commencement of FRANCHISOR's SYSTEMS for the business and service establishment.
b. To make available to Franchisee initial required plans and specifications for the building, equipment, furnishing, decor, layout and signs identified with FRANCHISOR's SYSTEM, together with advice and consultation concerning them. Franchisee shall bear the cost of duplicating such plans and specifications and the cost of adapting the same to the Franchisee's Premises. Franchisee shall also return all copies of said plans and specifications to the Franchisor upon the completion of construction.
c. To render advisory service regarding the operation of the franchised business, such as, but not limited to, handling products and services in accordance with the Specification, and the development of personnel policy together with training of Franchisee and Franchisee's employees in the operation of the franchised business.
d. To assist Franchisee in promoting the franchise business through advertising and public relations campaigns coordinated with the respective Franchisee Advertising Councils and national Advertising Council described herein.
e. To protect Franchisee's investment by not granting another franchise or operating a FRANCHISOR'S SYSTEM at any location within the geographic area contained within the granted boundaries.
f. To provide consultation and advice by Franchisor's filed representatives, either by personal visit, telephone, mail or otherwise, as may from time to time be reasonably required.

Franchisee Agrees:

a. To commence to operate the franchised business using the licensed name, marks and style immediately after the premises, in which the franchised business is located, is ready for occupancy. To continue to operate the same, diligently, on the days and during the business hours set forth below, except when it may be impossible because of acts of God or similar circumstances beyond Franchisee's control.
b. To conduct the franchise business in accordance with the standards, procedures and methods established and prescribed by Franchisor from time to time and to comply with all laws, ordinances and regulations relating to the operation of the franchise business.
c. To permit Franchisor to inspect Franchisee's entire Premises at any time during regular business hours, without notice, and observe all aspects of the conduct of the business by the Franchisee. Franchisee will take immediate remedial action to correct any deficiencies and to maintain the standards of quality referred to herein and in the Specifications.
d. That it understands and hereby acknowledges that uniform and high standards of quality and service among all FRANCHISOR'S SYSTEMS are necessary in order to create and maintain good will and widespread consumer acceptance.
e. To employ the methods of operation specified by Franchisor in order to insure the highest quality food products and services to the consuming public.
f. To comply with all requests of Franchisor with respect to the appearance and use of the marks and names licensed hereunder, including any requests to change the form or style or discontinue using any said marks and names.
g. Etc., etc., etc. . . . .

EXHIBIT 23-8   (Continued)

Termination.   Upon the occurrence of any of the following events, FRANCHISOR, at its option, shall have the right to terminate this Agreement and all of the Franchisee's rights hereunder, provided Franchisee shall fail to remedy any of the following to FRANCHISOR's satisfaction:

If Franchisee shall: (a) become in default under any lease covering the premises or equipment of his FRANCHISOR SYSTEM, and such default remains unremedied for ten (10) days after notice thereof; or (b) close the business operation for a period of fifteen (15) days without FRAN-CHISOR's prior written consent; or (c) default in the performance of any of the covenants, terms or conditions of this Agreement, and such default remains unremedied for more than five (5) days after written notice thereof to the FRANCHISEE of such default; or (d) become insolvent; be adjudicated a bankruptcy, have a voluntary or involuntary petition in bankruptcy or any other arrangement under the bankruptcy laws filed by or against it, make an assignment for the benefit of creditors, or if a receiver or trustee in bankruptcy appointed to take charge of FRAN-CHISEE's affairs or property; or (e) permit any judgment against the FRANCHISEE to remain unsatisfied or unbonded of record for fifteen (15) days.

MISCELLANEOUS PROVISIONS

The right to have successors and assigns; what happens in the event of death; the right to sub-franchise or sublicense; the right to borrow money against your interest in the business; the designation of the place; where notices are to be sent; the method by which costs are borne in the event of disputes; the use of arbitration boards; which state law will apply; disclaimer by franchisor of liability; and the many other detailed provisions that are usually addressed in a franchise agreement. These additional provision are usually individualized as to the different business fields, and their meaning is usually clear. If all of the other provision are satisfactory, the miscellaneous provision are not usually troublesome or form a basis for rejecting the entire contract.

Source: Handbook of Successful Franchising.

Rubin states that there are several standard clauses in franchise contracts.[16] The franchisor generally agrees to provide some form of managerial assistance to the franchisee. The support typically consists of start-up assistance and training for the franchisee and ongoing support during the term of the franchise contract. The initial fee provides the franchisor with capital to finance the franchisee's initial training and start-up; the ongoing royalty payments provide for the cost of continuing support.

In the franchise contract, the franchisee agrees to run the business in a manner stipulated by the franchisor. The standard of quality specified by the franchsior in the contract becomes more detailed as the risk of agency problems increases. The remedies for default of quality standards can range from fines to termination of the franchise agreement.

The franchise contract also contains a clause specifying the amount of royalties the franchisee will pay. According to Sen, the initial fees and ongoing royalty payments have several functions.[17] The fee structure is in place to achieve channel control, cover the cost of services, provide a risk-sharing mechanism, and reduce capital market imperfections. Channel control is the ability of channel members to achieve the desired outcome in their relationship with other channel members. The monthly fee usually con-

[16] Rubin, p. 224.

[17] Sen, p. 176.

sists of the royalty and a contribution to the franchisor for advertising on a national level. The franchisee's first cash outflow is initial fee, which is never returned. Therefore, only applicants who are confident they will recoup their investment will apply for a franchise. The number of applications received by the franchisor will be less, which means less work for him or her in choosing a franchisee. The fees also act as a disincentive for franchisee free-riding.

Free-riding can occur vertically, in which case a franchisee may "shirk" his or her obligations in order to reduce revenues and hence the royalty paid to the franchisor. The franchisor, too, can free-ride vertically by not maintaining brand-name strength. The franchisee may also engage in horizontal free-riding on other franchisees. In this case the franchisee will rely on the high quality maintained by the other franchisees to attract customers for the first time to his or her store under the same name. However, any diminished quality of service or product on the franchisee's part will reflect on the rest of the franchise chain. The solutions to the free-rider problem include monitoring of franchisees, and the initial fee may be considered as a bond or guarantee to the franchisor that the franchisee will not shirk. An additional solution to free-riding is to reduce royalty rates. The imposition of royalty rates prohibits the franchisor's attempts to free-ride by actively involving the franchisor in maintaining the chain's overall quality and because royalties are based on sales, not on profits.

The royalty payments also cover the cost of services. The franchisor provides initial and continuous services to the franchisee, as specified in the contract. The fees enable the franchisor and franchisee to share in the risk of the franchised outlet. One reason a franchisor franchises a location instead of a company-owned outlet is uncertainty. If the location is successful, then the royalty payment enables the franchisor to share in the success. If the franchised outlet fails, then the franchisor will forego the royalty payments. Despite Rubin's assertion that capital market imperfections are not an explanation of franchising, Sen believes that lack of capital for new franchisors influences initial fees.[18] He points to evidence showing that new entrants to franchising charge higher initial fees than more experienced ones.

The typical franchise agreement will also contain a termination clause. This details the specific circumstances in which either the franchisor or franchisee can terminate the franchise agreement. If the contact specifies longer terms, according to Brickley and Dark, this reduces the problem of quasi-rent appropriation.[19] A contract with renegotiation provisions (i.e., short contracts with detailed renegotiation provisions) reduces the potential for quasi-rent appropriation. As can be seen in Exhibit 23-9, the duration of franchise relationships varies. A 1988 survey showed that 73% of operating business format franchising companies issued franchise agreements of varying lengths. Many of these franchise agreements, especially in the retail field, were associated with a lease. In all companies, these agreements provided an opportunity for the franchisee to enter into a new agreement at the end of the original term. Although the terms of the agreement vary from one year to a perpetual agreement, 34% of them are for 20 years or longer.[20] According to Sen, legislation reduces franchise terminations.[21] Legislation

---

[18] Ibid., p. 179.

[19] Brickley and Dark, p. 409.

[20] Mark P. Friedlander and Gene Gurney, *Handbook of Successful Franchising*, 3rd ed. (Blue Ridge Summit, PA: Liberty Hall, 1990), p. 10.

[21] Sen, p. 177.

EXHIBIT 23-9

DURATION OF FRANCHISE AGREEMENTS

Number of Years	Percentage
1	1.10%
3	1.50
5	14.8
10	33.1
15	14.6
20	19.6
25	0.90
Perpetual	12.5
Others	1.90

Source: Handbook of Successful Franchising.

---

regulates the manner in which franchise terminations occur. It is no longer the case that a franchisor can terminate an agreement without just cause as laid out in the franchise contract.

Franchise contracts include a number of miscellaneous clauses. These control anything from the supplies the franchisee buys to the amount of local advertising the franchisee is obliged to undertake. Brickley and Dark conclude that franchisors can control certain agency problems associated with franchised units such as shirking and perquisite taking, inefficient risk-bearing, free-rider problems, and quasi-rent appropriation.[22] Multiple ownership, whereby a franchisee is offered a discount to run two or more outlets, can be used to control free-riding. The leasing of assets by franchisor to franchisee reduces problems of rent appropriation. If the contract specifies a standard of quality that the franchisee must uphold, then the free-rider problem is not as much of an issue. By specifying a minimum level of input use, the franchisor can also reduce the free-rider problem.

THE FUTURE OF FRANCHISING

The level of franchising in the economy increases annually. Franchising has a predicted 50% growth rate into the twenty-first century.[23] Social and demographic trends, economic cycles, and international expansion have aided in the growth of franchising. Understanding the factors affecting franchising are important for sound business decisions.

---

[22] Brickley and Dark, pp. 408–409.

[23] Richard C. Hoffman and John F. Preble, "Franchising into the Twenty-First Century," *Business Horizons* (November 1993): 35.

REFERENCES

BOND, ROBERT E. *The Source Book of Franchise Opportunities*. 1993 ed. Homewood, IL: Dow Jones-Irwin, 1993.

DICKE, THOMAS S. *Franchising in America: The Development of a Business Method, 1840–1980*. Chapel Hill: University of North Carolina Press, 1992.

FRIEDLANDER, MARK P. AND GENE GURNEY. *Handbook of Successful Franchising*. 3rd ed. Blue Ridge Summit, PA : Liberty Hall, 1990.

GRANT, CLIVE. *Business Format Franchising: A System for Growth*. London: Economist Intelligence Unit, 1985.

International Franchise Association and Howarth International. *Franchising in the Economy, 1988–1990*.

International Franchise Association and Howarth International. *Franchising in the Economy, 1991*.

International Franchise Association and University of Louisville. *Franchising in the Economy, 1991–1993*. August 1994.

MARTIN, ROBERT E. "Franchising and Risk Management." *American Economic Review* (December 1988): 954–968.

MENDELSOHN, MARTIN. *The Guide to Franchising*. 3rd ed. Oxford; New York: Pergamon Press, 1982.

SELTZ, DAVID D. *The Complete Handbook of Franchising*. Reading, MA: Addison-Wesley, 1982.

U.S. Department of Commerce. *Franchising in the Economy*. (Various editions.)

## 24

Tutor Time (B)

Richard Weissman sat in his office at Tutor Time Learning Systems, Inc., a daycare provider based in Boca Raton, Florida. Through the window, the palm trees gently waving in the breeze belied the rush of adrenaline the owner of Tutor Time still felt from reading the day's business news. The headlines of October 14, 1996, announced the acquisition of KinderCare Learning Centers, Inc. (KinderCare) by Kohlberg Kravis Roberts & Co. (KKR), buyout specialists. KinderCare, a giant in the fragmented daycare industry, had been acquired for approximately $600 million. Weissman turned back to John Floegel, Senior Vice President of Corporate Development at Tutor Time. Both men knew that the KinderCare acquisition would focus a lot of attention on the daycare industry. Weissman called the meeting with Floegel and other Tutor Time executives to discuss the company's response to the news of the purchase. A born entrepreneur, Weissman was eager to face the challenges that changing trends would bring to the industry and to Tutor Time.

Set up in 1980 with the first center in Boca Raton, Tutor Time had grown to approximately one-third the size of KinderCare by 1996. Despite several setbacks in the early 1990s, Tutor Time was in a process of rapid expansion. Tutor Time was regarded as one of the industry's most innovative and efficient companies. The main vehicle of growth for Tutor Time had been the franchise market. Franchisees' deposits helped Tutor Time with up-front cash. However, Tutor Time management realized that one-off fees and extended royalty payments from franchisees were not sufficient to finance the development of new centers and product lines. As well as setting up a corporate school (i.e., a Tutor Time wholly-owned center) in each area into which Tutor Time wished to expand, partners for developing sites were sought. The partnership style of ownership provided Tutor Time with initial capital from outside sources and would also produce cash flow once the center was operating.

Weissman knew that with the KinderCare acquisition there would be changes in the daycare industry. Predicting the transformations KKR would make to KinderCare was difficult. No one could tell which way KKR would go with its new acquisition.

Research Associate Catherine Conneely prepared this case under the supervision of Professor Paul Gompers as the basis for class discussion rather than to illustrate either effective or ineffective handling of an administrative situation.

Notwithstanding the upsurge of interest in the child care industry arising from KKR's newly acquired company, management at Tutor Time was certain that the industry itself had been stagnant for far too long. The future held many changes. Floegel, in charge of Corporate Development at Tutor Time, wondered what was in store for the daycare industry in general and for Tutor Time in particular and the transitions that would have to be made to deal with a revitalized KinderCare. It was his job to set a course for expansion. He also wondered about timing. One thing was certain, however: now was either the best or the worst time in the history of the child care industry to expand.

IMPLICATIONS OF KKR'S ACQUISITION FOR TUTOR TIME AND THE DAYCARE INDUSTRY

The October 1996 KKR acquisition of KinderCare held a promise of much change in the daycare industry. KKR's involvement brought a stamp of approval to the industry. On the day of the announced acquisition the stock price of KinderCare and other publicly traded daycare companies increased dramatically. The stock of Childtime, the fifth largest daycare provider, increased by 13% over two days following the KKR announcement, while KinderCare stock rose by 23%. The leader in the child care industry, KinderCare had an enrollment of 120,000 children across 38 states and had expanded internationally to the United Kingdom with a total of 1,148 centers.

Ownership of approximately 85% of KinderCare was to be acquired by an entity organized at the direction of KKR. The terms of the deal included the following: Kinder Care would pay $393 million to reacquire stock, warrants, and options; $118 million in debt would be retired; and the acquisition was to be financed by issuing $404 million in new debt and by $148.75 million in equity invested by KKR. The total value of the transaction was $553 million. KinderCare stockholders were to receive $20.25 per share in cash as part of the agreement. In a separate deal in November 1996, KinderCare also increased its revolving credit facility to $200 million from $150 million.

The acquisition of KinderCare had implications for the industry and for Tutor Time as well. It was possible that Tutor Time would be viewed as an acquisition target by buyout companies eager to include profitable firms in their portfolios. The larger national child care chains would also be on the lookout for possible acquisitions to increase their market share and enable them to compete with KinderCare. KKR's management of KinderCare would also have implications for Tutor Time. If KKR decided to squeeze the company for profit, then Tutor Time and other child care providers would benefit. But if KKR decided to expand KinderCare nationally, any expansion plans by Tutor Time would be made all the more difficult. How would Tutor Time grow in the light of the acquisition? Should the company try to grow using the same method? Company management had seen Children's Discovery Centers of California try to expand by taking over smaller, independent daycare providers. The strategy was not appealing to Tutor Time. The success the company had so far was in developing and building centers from the ground up. The company knew that expansion by building more centers was expensive to finance. Management wondered if there were other feasible alternatives.

THE CHILD CARE INDUSTRY IN 1996

In 1996, the child care industry in the United States was large and highly fragmented. The estimates of the size of the industry varied from $14 billion to $40 billion. The 10 largest providers combined represented less than 7% of the market. (See Exhibits 24-1 and 24-2 for Tutor Time competitors.) Small local providers tended to dominate

EXHIBIT 24-1

TOP 10 U.S. CHILD CARE PROVIDERS

Company	Total Licensed Capacity[a] (# of children)	Total Number of Centers[a]
KinderCare Learning Centers	140,956	1,147
La Petite Academy	95,000	750
Children's World Learning Centers	62,500	500
Children's Discovery Centers	23,600	239
Childtime Learning Centers	18,285	163
Nobel Education Dynamics Inc	15,000	101
Tutor Time Child Care Learning Centers	13,800	92
Bright Horizons Children's Centers	11,400	118
Corporate Family Solutions	10,132	75
Kids 'R Kids International	9,250	37
Top 10 Providers	399,923	3,222
Top 10 as % of Total Market	6.9	4.0
Total "Paid" Market	5,811,000[b]	80,000[c]

[a] Figures as of January 1, 1996. *Source:* Child Care Information Exchange Magazine, March/April 1996. Based solely on information supplied by organizations.

[b] Total number of children in paid arrangements. Figure as of 1993. *Source:* Current Population Reports, U.S. Census Bureau, 1995.

[c] Total number of centers. Excludes family day care and in-home paid arrangements. Figure as of 1990.

Source: Kisker et al., Mathematica Policy Research, Inc., 1991.

Source: William Blair & Co., Childtime Learning Centers Inc., Company Report, June 20, 1996.

the business. However, as the larger national chains began to consolidate, smaller providers found it difficult to compete against the economies of scale and greater financial and managerial resources of the nationwide chains.

Despite the intense competition between the possible substitute forms of child care, such as bringing the children to relatives, having a private sitter come to the house, or bringing the children to a daycare center, the demographic trends were favorable in the short term for the industry as a whole. (See Exhibit 24-3.) The number of children in the under-five age group had grown to 19.7 million in 1994, from 15.6 million in 1977, a 1.4% average annual increase. But growth in the under-five age group was expected to slow down over the next 15 years. Other favorable demographic trends included the higher percentage of mothers in the workforce. The U.S. Bureau of Labor Statistics estimated that the percentage of married women with children under the age of six participating in the labor force totaled 45% in 1980 and had increased to 60% in 1993. The U.S. economy continued to improve in 1996. Single parents and the nonworking spouse in two-parent families joined the workforce in increasing numbers. The outlook for the child care industry looked good in the short term.

Financially, the child care industry had been underrated. There were many negative perceptions about the industry which were unwarranted for the majority of daycare providers. The involvement of KKR brought an aura of respectability to the

EXHIBIT 24-2

FINANCIAL DATA OF PUBLICLY TRADED CHILD CARE COMPANIES, YEARS ENDING 1993–1995

	KinderCare Learning Centers, Inc.[a]			Children's Discovery Centers			Childtime Learning Centers, Inc.[b]			Nobel Education Dynamics, Inc.		
	1993	1994	1995	1993	1994	1995	1993	1994	1995	1993	1994	1995
Sales-Net ($millions)	437.20	488.73	506.51	38.56	55.32	77.63	N/A	55.34	65.62	32.59	34.37	44.15
EBIT ($millions)	27.76	50.34	53.42	1.98	4.70	5.42	N/A	5.13	5.48	3.54	3.21	4.48
Net Income (Loss) ($millions)	(10.72)	17.43	22.07	1.11	2.76	2.64	N/A	1.85	2.41	1.71	2.34	3.84
Debt—Total ($millions)	43.64	178.69	160.39	8.21	15.43	19.96	N/A	19.42	1.24	13.94	10.04	22.02
Price/Earnings	(3.571)	12.887	12.383	25.714	19.956	13.487	N/A	N/A	15.208	8.750	8.654	24.638
Beta	0.641	0.800	0.686	0.617	0.490	0.736	N/A	N/A	N/A	N/A	N/A	0.858

[a] KinderCare changed fiscal year end in 1993 from December to May.
[b] Childtime went public in 1994.

Source: Standard & Poor's Compustat PC Plus CD-ROM, 1996.

EXHIBIT 24-3

PERCENTAGE CHANGE IN POPULATION OF CHILDREN UNDER SIX

Time Period	Percentage Change in Population	
	3–5 years old	Under 6 years old
1983–1988	6.2	4.7
1988–1993	7.7	7.6
1993–1998	4.8	0.1
1998–2003	−2.9	−2.1

Source: U.S. Department of Labor, *Monthly Labor Review*, August 1995.

---

industry. Other financial companies would be eager to follow KKR's lead in buying out or acquiring daycare providers. In an industry overripe for consolidation, the opportunities were many.

TUTOR TIME IN 1996

Tutor Time was eager to grow. With over 90 sites open in 1996, not only did management wish to expand geographically, but it sought to develop new products and new structures in which to expand. (See Exhibit 24-4 for locations.) Tutor Time's analysis indicated that it should consider developing a new identity as an educator rather than a mere daycare provider.

Tutor Time cherished its reputation for innovation. Licensing the Brigham Young University education format and inclusion of a full-time director of education programs led to new ideas and a constantly evolving learning environment. A testament to their success was the numerous awards that Tutor Time had received. Tutor Time attributed part of its success to tighter management of student-to-teacher ratios than other daycare providers and bigger schools—the typical school size was 10,000 square feet—which allowed the Tutor Time centers to serve more students. But given increasing competition in the industry, Tutor Time knew that it would have to carefully manage other factors in order to remain successful in the future. Geographically, Tutor Time began to choose site locations with greater care. The company examined the demographics of the area for a potential site, the average income of the area, and the number of children under five in the area. Competition studies and the typical rent payments in the area were other factors influencing the decision to acquire a site. Tutor Time would then systematically model whether the proposed expansion made sense.

Tutor Time management knew that the company would need to expand in order to survive among the large publicly traded national chains. Several expansion structure options were available to Tutor Time. Management strategy was to set up a corporate school in an area and then sell franchise units in the surrounding area. It would also be possible for Tutor Time to grow by acquiring existing daycare centers. Independent operators were finding it hard to compete with the larger companies and to adhere to the strict regulations set by state accreditation agencies. Tutor Time management was not sure if it would take that route, however.

EXHIBIT 24-4

TUTOR TIME CHILD CARE CENTER LOCATIONS AS OF NOVEMBER 25, 1996

ALABAMA
Vestavia Hills, AL

ARIZONA
Tempe, AZ
*Chandler, AZ (2)
*Glendale, AZ
*Mesa, AZ (2)
*Phoenix, AZ (4)
*Tempe, AZ

CALIFORNIA
Agoura Hills, CA
Escondido, CA
Fair Oaks, CA
Fontana, CA
Highland, CA
Irvine, CA
Laguna Niguel, CA
Montebello, CA
Newport Beach, CA
Oceanside, CA
San Juan Capistrano, CA
Santa Clarita, CA
Thousand Oaks, CA
West Lancaster, CA
*Ceres, CA
*Glendora, CA
*Lakewood, CA
*Missiona Viejo, CA

*Morena Valley, CA
*Rancho Cucamongo, CA
*San Ramon, CA
*Santee, CA
*Ventura, CA
*Yorba Linda, CA

COLORADO
Aurora, CO
Colorado Springs, CO
Denver, CO
Littletown, CO
*Aurora, CO
*Highland Ranch, CO
*Lakewood, CO
*Littleton, CO (2)
*Smokey Hill, CO
*Tower, CO
*Westminster, CO

CONNECTICUT
Brookfield, CT
Monroe, CT
Greenwich, CT
*Branford, CT
*New London, CT
*Milford, CT
*Newington, CT
*Norwalk, CT
*Woodbridge, CT

Bear, CT

DELAWARE
*Newark, DE

FLORIDA
Atlamonte Springs, FL
Boca Raton, FL (2)
Bradenton, FL
Casselberry, FL
Deerfield Beach, FL
Ft. Lauderdale, FL
Jacksonville, FL
Kennedy Space Center, FL
Marketplace, FL
Melbourne, FL
Miami Lakes, FL
Miami, FL
Ocala, FL
Oldsmar, FL
Parkland, FL
Pembroke Pines, FL
Sunrise, FL
Tampa, FL
Temple Terrace, FL
Titusville, FL
Wingate, FL
*Davie, FL
*Jupiter, FL
*Melbourne, FL
*Naples, FL

*Ocoee, FL
Plantation, FL
*Port St. Lucie, FL
*Sarasota, FL
*Tampa, FL

GEORGIA
Lithia Springs, GA
Marietta, GA
Norcross, GA
Asworth, GA
*Marietta, GA
*Norcross, GA
*Smyrna, GA

ILLINOIS
Lombard, IL
Westmont, IL
*Hanover Park, IL
*Lisle, IL
*St. Charles, IL

INDIANA
Evansville, IN
Ft. Wayne, IN
South Bend, IN
*Schererbille, IN

KANSAS
Shawnee, KS (2)

MASSACHUSETTS
Pittsfield, MA

MICHIGAN
*Auburn Hills, MI
*Ann Arbor, MI
*Canton, MI
*West Bloomfield, MI

MINNESOTA
Apple Valley, MN
*Andover, MN
*White Bear Lake, MN

MISSOURI
Independence, MO
*St. Johns, MO

MONTANA
*Bozeman, MT

NEVADA
*Las Vegas, NV

NEW JERSEY
Lindenwold, NJ
Succasunna, NJ
Voorhees, NJ
Edison, NJ
Runnemede, NJ

*Egg Harbor, NJ
*Hamilton, NJ
*Holmdel, NJ
*Hopewell, NJ
*Kingston, NJ
*McKee City, NJ
*Nutley, NJ
*Old Bridge, NJ
*Parsippany, NJ
*Princeton, NJ

NEW YORK
Armonk, NY
Clay, NY
Clifton Park, NY
Deer Park, NY
East Northport, NY
Holbrook, NY
Islandia, NY
Middletown, NY
Mineola, NY
Pleasantville, NY
Syosset, NY
*Bay Ridge, NY
*Carle Place, NY
*Fairport, NY
*Glen Cove, NY
*Hauppauge, NY
*Lebittown, NY
*Medford, NY

*N. Amityville, NY
*Nanuet, NY
*Oakdale, NY
*Peekskill, NY
*Rochester, NY
*Smithtown, NY (2)
*Staten Island, NY
*Vestal, NY

NORTH CAROLINA
Cary, NC
Durham, NC
*Mathews, NC
*Charlotte, NC (2)

OHIO
Loveland, OH
*Hubor Heights, OH
*Cincinnati, OH
*Sylvania, OH

OREGON
*Beaverton, OR

PENNSYLVANIA
Allentown, PA
Erie, PA
Langhorne, PA
*Exton, PA
*Middletown, PA

*Reading, PA
*Warrington, PA

TEXAS
Arlington, TX
Carrolton, TX
Cole Fitzhugh, TX
Dallas, TX (2)
Desoto, TX
Houston, TX
Garland, TX
Lake Worth, TX
North Richland Hills, TX
Richardson, TX (3)
San Antonio, TX (2)
*Fort Worth, TX (2)
*San Antonio, TX (1)

VIRGINIA
*Richmond, VA

WASHINGTON
Olympic, WA
Kirkland, WA
Lacey, WA
*Richland, WA
*Mt. Vernon, WA

INTERNATIONAL
Jakarta, Indonesia

*Opening Soon—Opening Soon Locations may be modified due to zoning or other contingencies.

Management wondered how Tutor Time would expand. The typical franchisee paid an up-front fee of $42,000 and a $125,000 site development fee. The associated expense with site development, in an ideal construction scenario, was minimal. Once established, a 5 to 6% royalty fee was paid to Tutor Time out of the franchisee's revenues before profits. A company-owned corporate school provided no up-front fees, and the initial capital financing for construction and start-up of the center had to be found within the company. But Tutor Time was assured of all profits of such wholly owned sites. (See Exhibits 24-5–24-7 for financial statements.)

Beginning in 1996, Tutor Time developed a partnership arrangement, whereby the equity split was 49% to an outside partner and Tutor Time retained a majority holding in the center. The partnership fee was up to $110,000. In forthcoming partnership agreements, Tutor Time attempted to retain a 70% holding in each center in exchange for an up-front partnership fee of about $75,000. Management wanted to develop the optimal mix between the franchisee-owned, partnership sites, and corporate schools to ensure maximum revenues and profits to internally finance company expansion. While the correct mix between the different center structures would be difficult to achieve in

EXHIBIT 24-5

INCOME STATEMENT FOR TUTOR TIME FOR 1995–1996

	September 30, 1996	September 30, 1995
Revenues:		
Franchise fees	$ 441,500	$ 486,100
Site development fees	1,144,388	1,355,640
Other franchise fees	1,264,514	574,748
Real estate commissions	1,240,883	908,404
Royalties	1,033,681	675,905
Architectural fees	471,340	277,681
Other	863,592	521,370
Total Revenue	$6,459,898	$4,799,848
Operating Expenses:		
General and administrative expenses	$2,923,776	$2,193,707
Salaries and benefits	2,458,147	1,618,239
Construction costs	218,607	279,018
Total operating expenses	$5,600,530	$4,090,964
Income from operations	859,368	708,884
Interest expense	266,011	152,197
Income before taxes	$ 593,357	$ 556,687
Provision for income taxes	222,509	
Net income	$ 370,848	$ 556,687

Source: Company documents.

EXHIBIT 24-6

BALANCE SHEET OF TUTOR TIME FOR 1995–1996

	September 30, 1996	December 31, 1995
Assets		
Current Assets:		
Cash	$ 1,151,270	$ 173,627
Accounts receivable, net	7,688,284	4,277,736
Current portion of notes receivable	161,357	280,376
Due from affiliate		95,515
Subscriptions receivable	1,980,769	
Prepaid expenses and other current assets	40,832	211,729
Deferred tax asset	46,000	46,000
Total current assets	$11,068,512	$ 5,084,983
Property and equipment, net	$ 107,533	$ 68,004
Notes and other receivables, net	2,044,699	1,709,535
Due from officers	136,832	139,783
Other assets	1,814,723	835,764
Total assets	$15,172,299	$ 7,838,069
Liabilities and Stockholders' deficit		
Current Liabilities:		
Accounts payable	$ 2,681,889	$ 3,262,351
Accrued expenses	881,422	982,259
Income taxes payable	451,509	229,000
Current portion of long-term debt	1,052,167	1,279,973
Deferred fees	4,993,520	4,267,900
Other current liabilities	2,176	49,088
Total current liabilities	$10,062,683	$10,070,571
Deferred fees	$ 3,662,374	$ 2,970,450
Long-term debt	1,354,435	835,396
Stockholders' deficit:		
Preferred stock	5,760,307	
Common stock	39,469	39,469
Additional paid-in capital	1,310,931	1,310,931
Accumulated deficit	(7,017,900)	(7,388,748)
Total stockholders' equity	$ 92,807	($ 6,038,348)
Total liabilities and stockholders' equity	$15,172,299	$ 7,838,069

Source: Company documents.

EXHIBIT 24-7

STATEMENT OF CASH FLOWS FOR TUTOR TIME FOR NINE MONTHS ENDED SEPTEMBER 30, 1996

Cash flows from operating activities:

Net income	$ 370,848
Adjustments to reconcile net income to net cash used in operating activities:	
Depreciation and amortization	103,186
Bad debt expense	200,840
Changes in assets and liabilities:	
Accounts, notes and other receivables	(3,827,533)
Due from officers and affiliate	98,466
Other assets	(350,204)
Prepaid expenses and other current assets	170,897
Accounts payable and accrued expenses	(681,299)
Deferred fees	1,417,544
Income taxes payable	222,509
Other current liabilities	(46,912)
Net cash used in operating activities	($2,321,658)
Cash flows from investing activities:	
Purchase of property and equipment	($63,426)
Purchase of territorial rights	(675,595)
Net cash used in investing activities	($739,021)
Cash flows from financing activities:	
Borrowings under long-term debt	$1,005,624
Repayments of long-term debt	(746,840)
Issuance of preferred stock	3,779,538
Net cash provided by financing activities	$4,038,322
Net increase in cash	$ 977,643
Cash, beginning of year	173,627
Cash, end of period	$1,151,270
Supplemental disclosure of cash flow information:	
Cash paid for interest	$ 266,011
Cash paid for taxes	$ 0

Source: Company documents.

the short term, the long-term mix of franchisee-owned sites, partnership-owned centers, and corporate schools would allow the company sufficient cash flow for internal financing of the expansion without having to raise additional outside equity for Tutor Time.

The 1996–1997 estimates for Tutor Time were that about 20,000 children would be served in 97 open sites. Eighty-nine sites would be under construction in 28 states. By the end of 1996, there were approximately 25 corporate schools, 20 partnership schools, and 30 franchise sites in various stages of the design process. Seventy-five sites were planned for construction in 1997 and 110 sites in 1998. (See Exhibit 24-8 for 1997–1998 projections.) The primary areas of expansion in the United States were Ari-

---

EXHIBIT 24-8

PROJECTIONS FOR TUTOR TIME FOR 1997–1998

	1997	1998
Royalty Income	$ 2,332,500	$ 3,104,375
Franchise fees	1,328,000	1,660,000
Site development	2,120,000	2,650,000
Real estate commissions	1,296,000	1,728,000
Architectural fees	600,000	800,000
Risk fees	0	425,000
Other	0	
Construction receipts		
School tuition:		
Partnership schools opened—96	1,060,000	1,685,000
Partnership schools opened—97	1,520,000	5,910,000
Partnership schools opened—98		3,420,000
Corporate schools—96	1,130,000	1,770,000
Corporate schools—97	2,280,000	3,940,000
Corporate schools—98		2,280,000
Total revenue	$13,666,500	$29,372,375
Operating expenses	12,084,800	24,720,900
Earnings before interest and taxes	$ 1,581,700	
Interest expense:	(100,000)	
Interest income ($2,000,000*5%)	100,000	
Earnings before taxes	$ 1,581,700	$ 4,651,475
Provision for taxes (37%)	585,229	1,721,046
Net income	$ 996,471	$ 2,930,429
Number of shares used to calculate EPS		6,867,911

Source: Company documents.

zona, southern California, Colorado, New Jersey, and Florida. These areas had the best demographic characteristics for Tutor Time's expansion. Tutor Time had not intended to expand internationally, but in 1995, the company was approached by a franchisee interested in setting up a center in Jakarta, which proved to be very profitable.

NEW PRODUCTS AT TUTOR TIME

In an effort to more fully utilize the large investment in fixed assets (primarily the centers themselves), Tutor Time continually developed new products. There were several different programs which franchisees could run in the afternoon and on weekends. Tumbling Tots™ was a program designed to offer activities in a fitness-through-play curriculum. The Honors™ was an add-on to after-school activities offering reading and math enhancement in a regimented, proven tutoring system. Insta-Sitta™ was a drop-off babysitting service for children ages two to twelve—parents were issued beepers in case of emergencies. Tutor Time also offered a Summer Program with a more camp-like atmosphere than the typical school year curriculum. Franchisees paid additional fees to avail themselves of after-hours programs. Management felt, however, that although the extra programs were successful, the burden on the center's director did not balance the extra revenues. Franchisee-owners needed to take a break from running the centers.

Management was experimenting with add-ons at different locations. Some sites were exploring video vending machines from which parents could rent children's movies and programs on video; others considered having roasted chicken available so parents could pick up their children and have a hot dinner at the same time. The company was eager to further develop curriculum and technology at the centers. Tutor Time considered new programs or revisions to their curriculum as R&D. Tutor Time had been progressive in offering computer labs in the centers in the late 1980s and early 1990s, but more and more daycare centers were beginning to offer computers. Many other child care providers had variations on Tutor Towne™—a specially constructed village that allowed children to use role-play and develop skills in a microcosm of the real world. The company was looking to expand the services it could offer children and parents and was examining tele- and video-conferencing facilities installed in the centers for parents and children.

The company was very aware of security at each center and had developed policies early on which were becoming standard in the industry. All employees had to be carefully screened before they could work at any Tutor Time center, and the physical plant of each center was designed for security with motion detectors, video monitoring cameras in classrooms, and a special lock at the entrance. Tutor Time also used Safe N Sound™, an electronic automated security and business management system created for the child care industry. A magnetic card was issued to all parents, which enabled a computer to monitor the coming and going of students. With other daycare providers catching up to Tutor Time's technological level, the firm was considering outsourcing its technical needs in order to develop a more sophisticated security and technology package. Management began to experiment with hand-print security features at some centers.

In expanding its role as an educator, Tutor Time became involved in a plan to open a private school in September 1997 in Boca Raton, to be known as the Boca Raton Preparatory. Management felt that the timing might not be wholly appropriate for Tutor Time, but it had to take the opportunity presented to it. The U.S. Olympic diving team's practice complex in an upscale neighborhood of Boca Raton was for sale. Tutor

EXHIBIT 24-9

ECONOMIC INDICATORS

	Real GDP Bn 1992 $	Inflation	Unemployment (%)	T-Bill 1 month	Treasury Bond 5-Year Note	Treasury Bond 10-Year Note	S&P 500 Index	Hambrecht & Quist Growth Index
Q1Y93	6327.9	2.867	7.0	2.760	5.240	6.030	451.67	1057.61
Q2Y93	6359.9	2.703	7.0	2.820	5.050	5.800	450.53	1184.03
Q3Y93	6393.5	2.327	6.7	2.750	4.790	5.400	458.93	1256.01
Q4Y93	6476.9	2.521	6.5	2.800	5.210	5.830	466.45	1285.02
Q1Y94	6524.5	2.224	6.5	3.350	6.230	6.770	445.77	1216.75
Q2Y94	6600.3	2.351	6.1	3.500	6.970	7.340	444.27	1033.96
Q3Y94	6629.5	2.539	5.9	4.430	7.280	7.620	462.69	1241.49
Q4Y94	6688.6	2.664	5.4	3.660	7.830	7.840	459.27	1337.31
Q1Y95	6703.7	2.716	5.4	5.700	7.080	7.200	500.71	1498.24
Q2Y95	6708.8	2.694	5.6	5.240	5.980	6.210	544.75	1686.6
Q3Y95	6759.2	2.406	5.7	5.280	6.010	6.170	584.41	2112.13
Q4Y95	6796.5	2.324	5.6	3.480	5.380	5.580	615.93	2134.9
Q1Y96	6826.4	2.503	5.5	5.130	6.100	6.340	645.5	2253.43
Q2Y96	6926	2.687	5.3	4.750	6.470	6.730	670.63	2406.72
Q3Y96	6943.8	2.733	5.2	4.930	6.460	6.720	687.31	2538.96

Source: Adapted from Citibase.

Time knew that other child care providers (e.g., Childtime) were also looking to develop their involvement in higher levels of education. The site was in almost perfect condition for a school, consisting of swimming pools, dormitories, and three levels of suitably sized rooms for classes, and would need minimum construction to adapt it to a school format. In order to finance the purchase of the property, Tutor Time negotiated the sale. The financing was off-balance sheet, and Tutor Time had a controlling interest in the school. Situated across the road from a prominent year-round tennis camp, Tutor Time hoped to serve between 80 and 100 students from the tennis center and local area within the first two years of operation in grades K-12. Management thought that if the school was successful, Tutor Time could tap a new growth opportunity. As more states and communities debated charter schools and school vouchers, Tutor Time might be able to expand rapidly.

FINANCING TUTOR TIME'S EXPANSION

An important aspect of Tutor Time's expansion was the company's ability to finance growth. Management believed that the company would continue its planned expansion to 1998–1999 with current funding. Tutor Time had been moving from the traditional in-line sites (i.e., sites located in outdoor malls or office buildings) to free-standing sites. While it took the former 7.9 months from the opening of a school to reach 70% capacity, the latter only took 5.9 months to reach the same point in revenues. The hard costs of starting up each center included $40,000 working capital and training costs of up to $75,000 for the director. This $75,000 included training expenses and salary during the training phase. During site build-out, Tutor Time arranged for landlords to pay for the construction of the center. Approximately $10,000 in fees were spent by Tutor Time in the selections and negotiation of a lease for a site. Lease payments only began when the center opened. These expenses were incurred over six to nine months and were offset by any up-front fees. Tutor Time distinguished itself in the level of support and education that it provided to its franchisees. Similar to the different revenue flows from franchisee, partnership, or wholly owned centers, the financing needs of each ownership style also differed. Tutor Time was careful to ensure that even the franchisee sites had enough funds to reach a profit-making point.

Many exit opportunities had been presented to the company since 1994 when Floegel became Senior Vice President. Two potential buyers had approached Tutor Time. Neither company would set a value for the firm hoping that the owners would reveal a price. There were, however, no results from the negotiations. In 1995 Tutor Time had considered merging with a publicly traded clothing manufacturer. Again the negotiations were not completed. The company had plans to go public itself at the beginning of 1996, but a major investor and board member suggested that Tutor Time should finish constructing planned sites and build its position before issuing stock. Management was understandably reluctant to give up control of the company it had built from scratch. A true entrepreneur, the founder had pulled the company through some tough times, without having to resort to venture capital firms or other forms of outside financing.

TUTOR TIME—PAST PROBLEMS

Tutor Time offered potential franchisees a number of competitive advantages over other methods of setting up a business in the daycare industry. The Tutor Time methodology

EXHIBIT 24-10

PROJECTIONS FOR MODEL TUTOR TIME CENTER

Year 1

	1	2	3	4	5	6	7	8	9	10	11	12	Year 1
Revenue													
Total Tuition	$51,708	$56,850	$57,123	$61,452	$63,075	$64,702	$71,203	$73,737	$75,990	$75,990	$76,550	$76,550	$804,930
Capacity Utilization	49.8%	54.7%	55.0%	59.1%	60.6%	62.2%	65.9%	68.2%	70.3%	70.3%	70.8%	70.8%	47.9%
Operating Costs													
Total Fixed Costs	$27,900	$28,375	$26,651	$29,436	$27,563	$27,470	$27,420	$27,420	$27,420	$27,420	$27,420	$27,420	$331,915
Total Variable Costs	$26,028	$27,234	$28,513	$27,943	$26,094	$25,279	$31,482	$28,968	$31,360	$33,450	$30,917	$30,917	$348,635
Total Costs	$53,929	$55,610	$55,164	$57,380	$53,657	$52,749	$58,902	$56,389	$58,781	$60,870	$58,337	$58,337	$679,740
Profits													
EBIT	–$2,220	$1,240	$1,959	$4,072	$9,418	$11,952	$12,301	$17,348	$17,209	$15,120	$18,213	$18,213	$125,190
Operating Margin	*–4.3%*	*2.2%*	*3.4%*	*6.6%*	*14.9%*	*18.5%*	*17.3%*	*23.5%*	*22.6%*	*19.9%*	*23.8%*	*23.8%*	*15.6%*

Year 2

	1	2	3	4	5	6	7	8	9	10	11	12	Year 2
Revenue													
Total Tuition	$80,773	$80,773	$80,773	$88,940	$88,940	$88,940	$88,940	$88,940	$88,940	$88,940	$88,940	$88,940	$1,042,780
Capacity Utilization	74.7%	74.7%	74.7%	82.3%	82.3%	82.3%	82.3%	82.3%	82.3%	82.3%	82.3%	82.3%	80.4%
Operating Costs													
Total Fixed Costs	$27,420	$27,420	$27,420	$27,420	$27,420	$27,420	$27,420	$27,420	$27,420	$27,420	$27,420	$28,321	$329,945
Total Variable Costs	$33,450	$30,917	$33,979	$33,232	$30,917	$33,979	$33,232	$33,232	$33,232	$33,232	$33,232	$33,232	$395,868
Total Costs	$60,870	$58,337	$61,400	$60,653	$58,337	$61,400	$60,653	$60,653	$60,653	$60,653	$60,653	$61,553	$725,812
EBIT	$19,903	$22,436	$19,374	$28,287	$30,603	$27,540	$28,287	$28,287	$28,287	$28,287	$28,287	$27,387	$316,968
Operating Margin	*24.6%*	*27.8%*	*24.0%*	*31.8%*	*34.4%*	*31.0%*	*31.8%*	*31.8%*	*31.8%*	*31.8%*	*31.8%*	*30.8%*	*30.4%*

Source: Company documents.

was tried and tested, and new center directors were trained in the Tutor Time methods of running a child care center. The company helped with site selection and negotiating lease and construction of the center once a site had been chosen. A unique curriculum and state of the art security features made Tutor Time stand out among other daycare centers.

The company's reliance on franchise fees to develop sites, however, meant that a backlog of franchisees who had paid their fees and were waiting for sites had increased considerably by 1992. Construction overruns caused delays in setting up sites. The landlord financed the build-out of the sites. Due to stringent regulations applied to daycare centers and Tutor Time's own unique layout plans, many of the sites ran over the negotiated budgets. Between 1993 and 1994, Tutor Time had a substantial fraction of its capital tied up in site build-outs because it chose to bear any cost overruns. All new site build-outs eliminated this overrun exposure for Tutor Time.

Although his primary focus was on transactions and acquisitions, Floegel played an important role in resolving the problems that plagued Tutor Time in the early 1990s. By 1996, many of the issues had been dealt with satisfactorily. Some of the lasting effects of an unreliable partnership were beginning to die out. Tutor Time had lost opportunities to expand in different directions because of the association with an unstable partner. Notably, the establishment of a production company to make children's programs based on the Tutor Time "Pookie the Panda" character had been shelved. Trying to clean up the problems was one of the biggest cash drains the company faced. Pending litigation had implications for finding outside funds, as companies were understandably wary of financing a company with legal problems. By October 1996, however, Tutor Time was again sailing. Management and Floegel had cleared up legal matters and were focusing on expansion. The issue now was "How quickly could Tutor Time grow?"

"CLOUDS ON THE HORIZON"

The involvement of a buyout firm in the child care industry was not the only foreseeable difficulty in Tutor Time's future. Externally, the Americans with Disabilities Act (ADA) had been used in 1996 against KinderCare to allow a child with diabetes to attend a daycare center in Ohio. Susan Rosario, the head of Tutor Time's development department, changed prototypes and specifications to comply with the ADA.

Proposed welfare reform would also pose potential problems for some daycare providers with a sudden influx of children from low-income families. Some form of federal funding or voucher program would be needed to subsidize the cost of daycare. Some providers might have to raise fees. Because the Tutor Time market was a parent with a typical income of $40,000 to $60,000, however, this was not seen as a big problem for existing Tutor Time centers. Under new legislation, signed by President Clinton in August 1996, additional funding for child care would be available for low-income families as part of welfare reform. It was impossible to tell how much of the funding would be available to the nationwide daycare chains. The company's management felt that Tutor Time should learn how to fill the gap in providing daycare facilities for different income groups.

Internally, Tutor Time needed to examine the management structure at corporate headquarters. Recruiting for management positions had not yet been a problem, but with the proposed rate of expansion, the growing company would soon need to add to the management team. Tutor Time also needed to implement a centralized information technology at the management level. Tutor Time also found it difficult to protect in-house innovations from being adapted and used by other child care companies. Many of the features that had initially brought competitive advantages to the Tutor Time sites gradually became standard for all daycare centers. Tutor Time was continually innovating and creating new features to offer clients.

Another challenge was finding suitable directors for each daycare center. The mandatory training Tutor Time provided for each field director a cost of $75,000 before a center would even open. The stressful nature of the occupation, dealing with the industrywide high employee turnover, children ranging in ages from six months to six years, and parents with changing schedules, made it difficult to attract suitable candidates for the positions. The center director was critical to the success of a unit, combining the skill sets of a caregiver and a businessperson. Labor costs were typically a large percentage of any daycare center's costs. At Tutor Time, however, labor costs constituted a much lower percentage of revenues than industry comparables. During 1996, the U.S. Congress enacted an increase in the minimum hourly wage from $4.25 to $4.75 effective October 1, 1996, with an additional increase to $5.15 to be effective on September 1, 1997. Tutor Time had foreseen the increases in minimum wage and already paid employees above-industry averages to reduce turnover at the centers.

In 1996, all child care providers had to be accredited by the state in order to operate. Strict regulations laid down by each state ensured that parents would be sending their children to safe, clean premises. Most daycare providers considered that state accreditation was adequate testimonial for their centers. But a trend developed among some child care chains and individual centers to gain accreditation from different private organizations such as NACE, the National Association for the Education of Young Children, and the National Corporate Childcare Association. While none of the Tutor Time centers was accredited by any private associations, Tutor Time had begun negotiations with NACE in 1996. The sticking point of the negotiations was the unique curriculum and school layout that Tutor Time had developed and that were integral parts of the Tutor Time system. Tutor Time management considered that the company's centers were superior to many of the other daycare providers despite that lack of accreditation from the private organizations. Having their approval, however, could only work in positive ways for the company.

CONCLUSION

All in all, Tutor Time looked to be in a solid position. Potentially, the sky was the limit for the company's expansion. "You have to think that the industry will consolidate," said a company executive. It was difficult, however, to predict the time frame in which industry consolidation would take place. But over the next 10 years or so, Tutor Time would be able to take advantage of the changes in the fragmented child care industry. With the right mix of corporate schools, franchisee-owned sites, and partnership run centers, Tutor Time would be financially self-sufficient. There would be no urgency to bring the company public. The big decision for Weissman, Floegel, and Tutor Time at the end of 1996 was, how should the company grow and expand?

## 25

Xedia and Silicon Valley Bank (A)

Marty Meyer, CFO of Xedia Corporation, was on a conference call in late October 1997 with Jim Maynard, Senior Vice President of Silicon Valley Bank East (SVB), talking about the deal terms of a bridge loan. Xedia was a networking equipment manufacturer that helped to provide high-speed Internet service and had already taken out a small equipment line of credit with SVB in early 1997. Now, however, Xedia needed additional financing to fund the company until it raised its next round of venture capital financing. Xedia was currently having discussions with a few venture capitalists about investing in the next round, but Meyer was uncertain when the deal would close given the general uncertainty of raising venture capital, including finding investors to commit, negotiating terms, and reviewing all legal documents. Meyer needed to make sure that the company did not run out of cash because, without the bridge loan, his negotiating power with the venture capital firms would weaken.

Meyer wondered whether he and Maynard could come to agreeable terms. After all, Xedia was burning approximately $500,000 per month, and without another venture capital infusion, the company would be unable to pay the loan back. While Meyer believed that Xedia could raise the money, the firm's fast declining cash balances made life more complicated.

BANKS AND ENTREPRENEURIAL FIRMS

Young companies had historically suffered from a lack of debt financing because traditional banking rules about creditworthiness often ruled out firms with little operating history. Bankers traditionally secured loans either with a company's cash flows or only extended credit if the firm had substantial tangible assets. Emerging companies had tremendous difficulty convincing bankers to provide financing under these traditional guidelines because they often had no assets and no track record of positive cash flows. Small loans (also called micro-lending) dropped precipitously in the United States during the banking troubles of the late 1980s and by the late 1990s still had not returned to levels of lending seen in the early 1980s.

Much of the drop in loans to small businesses was a direct result of government regulation, which often required a larger capital base to support such loans. Young, entrepreneurial firms were difficult to evaluate by conventional financial metrics, and government regulators often saw them as very risky.

Three primary problems affected credit availability for young entrepreneurial firms. First, the entrepreneur typically knew substantially more than the banker about the firm's business. The banker was likely only casually aware of new developments and new technologies, much less how to evaluate them.

Second, the level of uncertainty surrounding potential outcomes was quite large. The range of possible returns and cash flows was much wider than would have been the case with the bank's more mature customers. Without some way to ascertain the likelihood of payback, a bank would be unwilling to provide a loan. Because the payment to the bank was fixed interest and principal repayment, any write-off of loans could destroy a bank's profitability.

Finally, many entrepreneurial firms were businesses whose value depended solely on intangible assets (e.g., patents, copyrights, etc.) or the skills of its employees. Intellectual property often made poor collateral. In situations where the bank would have to seize the asset, it would be more likely that the intellectual property was worthless. Similarly, individuals cannot pledge themselves as collateral. Without assets to pledge, companies had difficulty convincing banks to lend money.

HISTORY OF SVB

In early 1981, three senior Silicon Valley businessmen decided over a poker game that the inability of young companies to secure adequate credit represented a business opportunity. From their many years of experience, the three businessmen, Bill Biggerstaff, Bob Medearis, and David Elliot, knew many young companies that had been refused credit because they did not satisfy traditional banking criteria for asset-backed or cash flow-based loans. This group decided to start a bank specializing in lending to young companies in the Silicon Valley area. Ken Wilcox, Executive Vice President of SVB, explained the premise behind the founding of SVB:

> The founding of Silicon Valley Bank was based on the ability to overcome one's prejudice. Because venture capitalists were reluctant to bring an end to a company prematurely, they almost always believed that with some tweaking and additional financing the company could still succeed. Thus, it was very likely that the companies would receive funding for that next round. (See Exhibit 25-1 for info on the likelihood of second round financing.)

SVB's strategy was to serve as the banker of choice for emerging growth and middle-market companies in specific target niches focusing on the technology and life sciences industries. The founders of SVB incorporated the bank in 1982 but did not receive all banking licenses to operate until the end of 1983.

EXHIBIT 25-1

DATA ON SUBSEQUENT ROUNDS OF FINANCING, 1987–1995

Round	Number of Companies	Median Amount Raised	Mean Amount Raised	Median Post-Money Valuation	Mean Post-Money Valuation	Percentage of Previous Round
1	1150	$2.83	$3.85	$ 7.00	$10.00	100.0%
2	986	$3.50	$4.66	$13.50	$17.10	85.0%
3	614	$3.90	$5.10	$19.00	$25.90	62.3%

Source: VentureOne.

SVB PRODUCTS AND ORGANIZATION

Over the years, SVB established teams of lending and support staff along distinct industry lines: software, communications, semiconductors, computers and peripherals, as well as medical devices, biotechnology and health care services. These groups provided most SVB services to companies in that particular industry group that had raised venture capital money. The product lines sold to these industries included equipment financing, working capital lines of credit, asset acquisition loans, and bridge financing. Equipment financing agreements provided loans secured by the borrower's equipment. A working capital loan was secured by the current assets of the client's company: accounts receivable and inventory. Rules of thumb encouraged SVB bankers to lend upwards of 80% of accounts receivable, 20% of inventory, and 80% to 100% of plant and equipment. An asset acquisition loan allowed the borrower to purchase another company and was secured by the assets of the target company. Finally, a bridge loan financed the daily operations of the borrower's company until the company raised its next round of equity financing. Depending on market conditions and competitive factors, SVB made bridge loans with varying degrees of security from fully collateralized to completely unsecured.

SVB also organized itself by financial products and services for clients only requiring specific banking services. These clients were served by employees specially trained to provide a particular service. Examples of SVB's service divisions included business banking, cash management, factoring, asset-based lending, equipment loans, and international banking services. (See Exhibit 25-2 for SVB's group organization.) The business banking division focused on non-venture-backed, emerging growth companies with annual sales under $5 million. Client companies in this division required less than $1 million in loans and represented SVB's strategy of helping young companies grow. Usually, SVB switched these clients into the niche practices as they raised venture capital money. In the cash management group, SVB assisted clients in managing cash collections, disbursements, and investments in an efficient, cost-effective manner by using wholesale lockbox services and PC (computer-linked) banking. SVB's factoring group helped clients raise capital by quickly selling accounts receivable to SVB at a discount. The discount included an implicit interest rate once the full amount of the account receivable was collected by SVB. Of course, risk resided with SVB if the full amount of the account receivable was not collected. The Asset-Based Lending group made loans

EXHIBIT 25-2

SVB GROUP ORGANIZATION

Technology and Life Sciences	Special Industries	Strategic Financial Products and Services
• Communications and Information	• Diversified Industries	• Cash Management Services
• Computers and Peripherals	• Entertainment	• Asset-Based Lending
• Semiconductors	• Premium Wine Industry	• Emerging Technologies
• Software	• Real Estate	• International
• Venture Capital Banking Division	• Religious Financial Resources	• Factoring
• Life Sciences and Health Care		

Source: Company documents.

against the company's accounts receivable and inventory to offer greater financing capacity and flexibility through active monitoring of assets. Finally, the International Services group offered a full range of products and services to clients who conducted business overseas. These services included foreign exchange, import and export letters of credit, documentary collections, and export financing.

GROWTH OF SVB

SVB expanded throughout California and Massachusetts during the 1980s followed by expansion to other markets during the 1990s. (See Exhibit 25-3 for the list of SVB offices and Exhibit 25-4 for historical growth in loans and assets.) The profitability of SVB and its rapid expansion throughout the United States attracted other commercial lenders to make loans to emerging companies. This competition took many different forms: small lenders like Comerica and Imperial with renewed focus on emerging companies;

EXHIBIT 25-3

SILICON VALLEY BANK LOCATIONS

LOCATIONS	
• Santa Clara, CA	• Palo Alto, CA
• Menlo Park, CA	• San Diego, CA
• Beverly Hills, CA	• Irvine, CA
• St. Helena, CA	• Boulder, CO
• Wellesley, MA	• Rockville, MD
• Beaverton, OR	• Austin, TX
• Chicago, IL	• Atlanta, GA
• Bellevue, WA	• Phoenix, AZ

Source: Company documents.

EXHIBIT 25-4

SVB HISTORICAL GROWTH ($MILLIONS)

Year	Loans	Assets	Net Income	Deposits
1983	$7.6	$17.9	$0.24	$13.5
1984	30.1	50.3	0.25	45.3
1985	45.5	73.4	0.46	67.6
1986	102.7	169.4	0.98	158.3
1987	142.3	202.7	1.50	188.1
1988	188.7	275.4	3.50	255.5
1989	286.0	439.4	7.02	412.0
1990	484.6	670.6	10.00	630.7
1991	601.1	860.1	11.99	799.8
1992	606.1	956.2	−2.33	888.9
1993	553.6	992.3	1.61	915.0
1994	702.4	1,161.6	9.07	1,075.4
1995	793.8	1,407.6	18.15	1,298.0
1996	1,001.6	1,924.5	21.47	1,774.3
1997	1,312.8	2,625.1	27.68	2,432.4
14-Year CAGR	44.5%	42.8%	40.3%	44.9%
5-Year CAGR	16.7%	22.4%	NM	22.3%

Source: Company documents.

larger banks like Fleet and Bank of America with increased emphasis on emerging companies; and lastly, equipment leasing and financing companies like Comdisco that were aggressively lending against the special equipment and plant of emerging companies. As a result of this increased competition, SVB's fees and margins had decreased over the last few years. (See Exhibit 25-5 for SVB's most recent financials.) SVB management viewed the increased competition, both in terms of additional competitors as well as additional products offered, as demonstrating the need for differentiation through marketing. (See Exhibit 25-6 for a sample of SVB's marketing material.)

The success of SVB and its competitors over the past 15 years greatly improved the amount of credit provided to young companies, although credit availability did not return to the levels of the early 1980s. (See Exhibit 25-7 for the amounts of loans provided by banks to small companies in the United States.) At the same time, favorable macroeconomic conditions and an improved net interest margin throughout the commercial banking industry improved industry profitability. (See Exhibits 25-8 and 25-9 for commercial banking industry profitability, and Exhibit 25-10 for general macroeconomic conditions).

CREDIT SELECTION AND ANALYSIS

SVB was founded on the premise that traditional sources of principal repayment (i.e., cash flow or asset sales) were not the primary emphasis. Thus, a legitimate source of

EXHIBIT 25-5

SVB FINANCIAL HIGHLIGHTS (DOLLARS AND NUMBERS IN THOUSANDS, EXCEPT PER-SHARE AMOUNTS)

Years Ended December 31,	1997 (Unaudited)	1996	1995	1994	1993
Income Statement Summary:					
Net interest income	$110,824	$87,275	$73,952	$60,260	$50,410
Provision for loan losses	10,067	10,426	8,737	3,087	9,702
Noninterest income	13,265	11,609	12,565	4,922	9,316
Noninterest expense	52,682	52,682	47,925	45,599	47,357
Income before taxes	47,721	35,776	29,855	16,496	2,667
Income tax expense	20,043	14,310	11,702	7,430	1,066
Net income	27,678	21,466	18,153	9,066	1,601
Common Share Summary:					
Net income per share	$ 2.72	$ 2.21	$ 1.98	$1.06	$0.20
Book value per share	17.50	14.51	11.71	9.08	8.48
Weighted average common shares outstanding	9,970	9,702	9,164	8,575	8,201
Year-End Balance Sheet Summary:					
Loans, net of unearned income	$1,174,645	$ 863,492	$ 738,405	$ 703,809	$564,555
Assets	2,625,123	1,924,544	1,407,587	1,161,539	992,289
Deposits	2,432,407	1,774,304	1,290,060	1,075,373	914,959
Shareholders' equity	174,481	135,400	104,974	77,257	70,336
Average Balance Sheet Summary:					
Loans, net of unearned income	NA	$ 779,655	$ 681,255	$592,759	$574,372
Assets	NA	1,573,903	1,165,004	956,336	917,569
Deposits	NA	1,441,360	1,060,333	877,787	846,298
Shareholders' equity	NA	119,788	91,710	73,461	68,198
Capital Ratios:					
Average shareholders' equity to average assets	6.9%	7.6%	7.9%	7.7%	7.4%
Total risk-based capital ratio	11.5%	11.5%	11.9%	10.1%	11.3%
Tier 1 risk-based capital ratio	10.2%	10.2%	10.6%	8.9%	10.1%
Tier 1 leverage ratio	7.1%	7.7%	8.0%	8.3%	6.9%
Select Financial Ratios:					
Net interest margin	NA	6.1%	7.1%	7.2%	6.4%
Efficiency ratio	55.9%	55.9%	60.6%	68.3%	68.9%
Return on average assets	1.3%	1.4%	1.6%	0.9%	0.2%
Return on average shareholders' equity	18.2%	17.9%	19.8%	12.3%	2.3%

Source: Company Annual Report.

TABLE A   Composition of SVB Loans

Type of Loan	1992	1997
Working capital	72%	40%
Equipment	25%	40%
Acquisition financing	1%	1%
Bridge	2%	19%

Source: Company documents.

loan repayment was the next round of financing raised by the company from venture capitalists. Because most young companies lacked profits and assets, most banks were unwilling to lend to these young companies. Most commercial banks would only lend to a company if it had a long track record of profits to repay the debt or if it had assets that could be sold for a price great enough to recover their principal. SVB needed to analyze whether a company would receive the next round of financing to ensure that their loan would be repaid. Dave Fischer, Senior Vice President of SVB, explained the credit analysis process:

> The first screen is whether the company is financeable by equity investors which boils down to whether the company is positioned well to do great things. From our experience, we have found it unusual for a company to grow rapidly without outside money. For example, some companies are what we call "lifestyle" companies with very little desire to either grow rapidly or do an IPO. We look at these companies differently from those that have the potential to skyrocket. Second, we spend time with the venture capitalists to assess their willingness to fund the next round. One of the time-honored principals of this business is that one needs to know who the key decision makers are. The fate of a young company is often in the hands of the investors, not the company's management. In essence, we rely on the investors to perform part of the due diligence for us. For example, if a top venture capitalist brings us a deal, then we almost always do the deal because we trust his instincts and that if it isn't working, he'll do something about it. On the flip side, we will not lend money to portfolio companies of certain other venture firms because of previous bad experiences. Next, we perform internal due diligence on the company's industry and trends within that industry. Basically, we want to understand whether the company is positioned well and how much competition exists for that space. Finally, we analyze how the company intends to spend the money and why the company wants bank debt. We want to do business with people who are confident that their company will do well and think of a loan from SVB as a means to decrease dilution of their equity.

HISTORY OF XEDIA

Xedia was founded in 1993 by Jens Montanana and Ashley Stephenson. During this period, Xedia successfully designed, manufactured, marketed, and sold an Ethernet switch. By 1995, senior management realized, however, that Xedia was late in that product's life-cycle trail, behind well-capitalized competitors like Cisco Systems, Ascend, and 3Com. Furthermore, the Internet's open standards influenced convergence with traditional data networking, broadcast video, and telephony, which also attracted new competitors like Lucent Technologies and Northern Telecom to enter this market. Xedia management believed that this intense competition would depress Ethernet switch prices, creating an industry where scale was the most important success variable. Throughout the mid-1990s, Cisco was buying as many competitors as possible in order

EXHIBIT 25-6

SILICON VALLEY BANK ADVERTISEMENT FROM COMPANY PRESS KIT

Source: Company documents.

EXHIBIT 25-7

BANKING INDUSTRY STATISTICS: AMOUNT OF CREDIT TO YOUNG COMPANIES (BILLIONS OF 1994 DOLLARS)

	1981	1982	1983	1984	1985	1986	1987	1988	1989	1990	1991	1992	1993	1994
Industry Totals														
Total Dollar Volume	523.8	570.9	583.7	588.8	595.5	630.3	603.7	605.4	596.7	565.3	491.7	458.2	449.3	480.6
Dollar Volume by Credit Size:														
Less than $100,000:	54.6	50.2	44.4	46.8	40.5	39.5	37.6	41.0	43.4	33.7	23.7	22.9	23.6	22.5
$100,000 to $250,000:	45.3	38.1	36.6	38.8	36.5	37.3	38.0	40.8	38.9	30.1	25.7	22.2	23.0	25.3
$250,000 to $1 million:	91.9	76.2	66.4	73.5	72.3	77.3	74.2	64.9	61.4	54.0	40.7	43.3	41.1	45.9
$1 million to $10 million:	169.9	194.3	172.2	172.3	176.5	182.0	178.5	154.8	173.0	163.9	142.5	142.9	135.5	152.7
$10 million to $25 million:	53.7	83.5	104.4	114.1	97.1	114.4	101.9	127.3	110.3	134.5	107.4	100.9	116.2	124.4
$25 million to $100 million:	93.5	101.2	118.3	113.5	135.6	134.5	141.6	123.0	137.5	110.3	100.5	95.7	90.9	86.5
Greater than $100 million:	14.8	27.2	41.5	29.8	36.9	45.2	31.8	53.7	32.2	38.8	51.2	30.3	19.0	23.2
Organizations with Greater than *$100 Billion in Total Assets*														
Total Dollar Volume	55.7	59.9	62.7	49.3	42.3	45.2	54.8	37.1	40.1	37.5	81.4	74.0	82.4	92.2
Dollar Volume by Credit Size:														
Less than $100,000:	3.0	2.6	0.8	0.9	0.6	0.3	0.3	0.1	0.0	0.1	0.2	0.3	0.2	0.3
$100,000 to $250,000:	2.0	1.9	0.9	1.0	0.6	0.4	0.3	0.1	0.1	0.2	0.3	0.6	0.5	0.4
$250,000 to $1 million:	3.1	2.7	3.1	3.3	2.8	2.4	1.8	0.4	0.5	0.8	1.3	1.7	2.0	1.6
$1 million to $10 million:	16.3	16.9	13.6	14.8	14.8	14.4	18.8	5.8	8.6	7.2	14.0	14.9	15.3	21.0
$10 million to $25 million:	11.1	12.2	11.9	11.0	8.1	6.4	9.8	7.4	11.5	11.3	17.4	18.0	25.1	28.1
$25 million to $100 million:	16.9	18.9	17.7	15.5	11.9	17.8	17.8	11.8	16.5	10.7	33.5	28.7	32.0	32.3
Greater than $100 million:	3.3	4.9	14.8	2.7	3.4	3.4	6.1	11.6	2.7	7.2	14.7	9.9	7.2	8.5

Source: Brookings Papers on Economic Activity, "The Transformation of the U.S. Banking Industry: What a Long Strange Trip It's Been;" Berger, Allen; Kashyap, Anil; and, Scalise, Joseph; volume 2, 1995, pp. 55–218.

EXHIBIT 25-8

INCOME AND EXPENSES AS A PERCENTAGE OF AVERAGE NET CONSOLIDATED ASSETS, ALL INSURED COMMERCIAL BANKS, 1985–1996[a]

Item	1985	1986	1987	1988	1989	1990	1991	1992	1993	1994	1995	1996
Gross Interest Income	9.58%	8.50%	8.39%	9.00%	9.95%	9.59%	8.58%	7.47%	6.87%	6.66%	7.30%	7.21%
Gross Interest Expense	6.08	5.11	4.97	5.46	6.44	6.14	4.97	3.57	2.96	2.87	3.57	3.45
Net Interest Margin	3.50	3.39	3.42	3.54	3.51	3.46	3.61	3.90	3.90	3.79	3.73	3.76
Noninterest Income	1.20	1.28	1.43	1.50	1.62	1.67	1.79	1.95	2.13	2.00	2.02	2.19
Loss Provisions	0.68	0.78	1.30	0.65	0.98	0.97	1.03	0.78	0.47	0.28	0.30	0.38
Other Noninterest Expense	3.17	3.22	3.35	3.38	3.42	3.49	3.73	3.87	3.94	3.76	3.65	3.73
Securities Gain	0.06	0.14	0.05	0.01	0.03	0.01	0.09	0.11	0.09	−0.01	0.01	0.03
Income Before Tax	0.90	0.80	0.26	1.02	0.76	0.68	0.73	1.32	1.70	1.74	1.81	1.86
Taxes[b]	0.21	0.19	0.19	0.33	0.30	0.23	0.25	0.42	0.56	0.58	0.63	0.65
Extraordinary Items	0.01	0.01	0.01	0.03	0.01	0.02	0.03	0.01	0.06	NM	NM	NM
Net Income	0.70	0.62	0.08	0.71	0.47	0.47	0.51	0.91	1.20	1.15	1.18	1.21
Cash Dividends Declared	0.33	0.33	0.36	0.44	0.44	0.42	0.45	0.41	0.62	0.73	0.75	0.91
Net Retained Earnings	0.37	0.29	0.29	0.28	0.02	0.05	0.07	0.50	0.59	0.42	0.43	0.29
MEMO:												
Net Interest Margin, Taxable Equivalent[c]	3.88%	3.79%	3.63%	3.72%	3.65%	3.57%	3.71%	3.99%	3.99%	3.86%	3.79%	3.81%
Return on Equity	11.18%	9.97%	1.29%	11.61%	7.33%	7.29%	7.71%	12.66%	15.34%	14.64%	14.71%	14.60%

[a] Assets are fully consolidated and net of loss reserves.

[b] Includes all taxes estimated to be due on income, extraordinary gains, and security gains.

[c] For each bank with profits before tax greater than zero, income from tax-exempt state and local obligations was increased by [t/(1 − t)] times the lesser of profits before tax or interest earned on tax-exempt obligations (t is the marginal federal income-tax rate). This adjustment approximates the equivalent pretax return on tax-exempt obligations.

Source: Federal Reserve Bulletin, June 1996.

EXHIBIT 25-9

PROFITABILITY METRICS FOR COMMERCIAL BANKS, BY SIZE

Profitability Metric	1986	1987	1988	1989	1990	1991	1992	1993	1994	1995	1996
Return on Equity											
All Banks	9.83%	1.29%	11.61%	7.33%	7.29%	7.71%	12.66%	15.34%	14.64%	14.71%	14.60%
Ten Largest Banks	9.58	−18.11	23.30	−3.92	10.13	4.23	10.91	16.75	13.86	13.78	13.34
Banks Ranked 11 through 100	12.75	−1.70	9.72	8.41	4.07	7.71	15.21	16.91	16.27	16.45	16.93
Banks Ranked 101 through 1000	10.93	9.25	10.01	10.54	7.41	8.45	12.16	14.94	15.45	14.86	14.42
Banks Not Ranked in Top 1000	6.74	6.99	8.09	9.66	8.60	8.95	11.64	12.66	12.03	12.12	12.38
Return on Assets											
All Banks	0.62%	0.08%	0.71%	0.47%	0.47%	0.51%	0.91%	1.20%	1.15%	1.18%	1.21%
Ten Largest Banks	0.47	−0.80	1.07	−0.19	0.48	0.21	0.61	1.13	0.91	0.88	0.93
Banks Ranked 11 through 100	0.72	−0.09	0.51	0.47	0.23	0.47	1.05	1.26	1.22	1.31	1.35
Banks Ranked 101 through 1000	0.73	0.62	0.67	0.71	0.51	0.60	0.92	1.22	1.29	1.28	1.29
Banks Not Ranked in Top 1000	0.55	0.58	0.68	0.83	0.74	0.77	1.04	1.19	1.15	1.21	1.26

Source: Federal Reserve Bulletin, June 1997.

EXHIBIT 25-10

GENERAL MACROECONOMIC CONDITIONS, 1990–1997[a]

Year	Real GDP (1992 $ Billions)	Inflation	Unemployment Rate	12-Month Treasury Bill Rate	5-Year Government Bond	10-Year Government Bond	Prime Rate	S&P 500 Index
1990	$6,079.0	5.3%	6.3%	6.4%	7.7%	8.1%	10.0%	330.2
1991	$6,105.3	2.6%	7.3%	3.9%	5.9%	6.7%	7.2%	417.1
1992	$6,327.1	2.9%	7.4%	3.5%	6.0%	6.7%	6.0%	435.7
1993	$6,476.9	2.5%	6.5%	3.5%	5.2%	5.8%	6.0%	466.5
1994	$6,688.6	2.7%	5.4%	6.8%	7.8%	7.8%	8.5%	459.3
1995	$6,796.5	2.3%	5.6%	4.9%	5.4%	5.6%	8.7%	615.9
1996	$7,017.4	2.9%	5.3%	5.3%	6.2%	6.4%	8.3%	740.7
Q1 1997	$7,101.6	2.4%	5.2%	5.7%	6.8%	6.9%	8.3%	757.1
Q2 1997	$7,159.6	2.0%	5.0%	5.4%	6.4%	6.5%	8.5%	885.1
Q3 1997	$7,217.6	1.9%	4.9%	4.9%	6.0%	6.1%	8.5%	947.3
Q4 1997	$7,283.3	1.6%	4.7%	5.2%	5.7%	5.8%	8.5%	970.4

[a] Quarterly numbers for GDP represent the trailing four quarters.

to grow. Xedia was forced to sell its product through Bay Networks under an original equipment manufacturer (OEM) agreement. Under this agreement, Bay placed its name on Xedia's product and sold it. Meanwhile, Xedia had no brand name with all its revenues coming from royalties. Xedia senior management did not feel comfortable about the long-term sustainability of their company if they did not reinvent the firm.

Ashley Stephenson, President and CEO, had recruited Marty Meyer as the CFO during 1995. Along with Montanana, this group began to analyze the repositioning of the company. (See Exhibit 25-11 for resumes of Xedia's senior management.) Senior management analyzed the company's core competencies and how they could fund their new strategy. Marty Meyer described this time:

> In February 1996, a plan was put in place to use the $5 million in forecasted royalty revenues which we would receive from Bay Networks over the next nine months to restart the company. The decision was made to swim upstream into communication equipment with an increased level of software content. Ultimately, we decided to focus on developing an access router which would help corporate clients and Internet Service Providers (ISPs) to manage bandwidth for the provision of high speed Internet service, that is, Xedia's proposed product would be able to guarantee a customer access to the Internet at a certain speed.

THE "NEW" XEDIA

The "new" Xedia was repositioned to take advantage of the growth in Internet traffic. The opportunity stemmed from the belief that the Internet would become more integral to the business applications of an enterprise. As a result, companies required increased speed, more consistent performance, and better management control over their Internet access resources. At the same time, Internet Service Providers (ISPs), the firms that provided connections to the Internet, needed a way to manage who had access at what speed.

To attack this market opportunity, Xedia created a single-box solution that integrated high-performance, industry-standard hardware, and highly optimized software technology providing network operators with a scalable Internet access solution that effectively managed Internet traffic. In essence, the Xedia product managed the bandwidth of a network to maximize access. Using fully open, nonproprietary traffic management technology called Class-Based Queuing (CBQ), a customer was able to classify, specifically allocate, and efficiently share, or borrow, bandwidth across the departments of a company, managed server environments, or multi-tenant facilities. This product allowed consistent quality of access to the Internet at well-specified speeds.

Xedia envisioned that the market demand for their product would skyrocket as usage of the Internet increased. In this situation, a firm's network manager would need to establish policies to control (1) who had access, (2) how much bandwidth, and (3) at what service level. With Xedia's product, the network manager could establish and enforce Internet access policies that ensured that service needs were met across the firm's employees users and applications. The company believed there were two major applications to its technology.

First, a company could use Xedia's product to allocate bandwidth space between the different corporate departments. The network manager could allocate bandwidth by department (e.g., sales, marketing, engineering, etc.), by traffic type (e.g., Web, electronic mail, voice over IP, etc.) or by any combination of these criteria. Each class of traffic would then be allocated an explicit bandwidth rate. A second application involved

EXHIBIT 25-11

MANAGEMENT BIOGRAPHIES

Jens Montanana, Chairman

One of the founders of Xedia Corporation, Jens Montanana brought extensive experience in launching and repositioning companies for success.

In 1986, he founded DataTec Ltd., a networking and communications distributor with a market cap of over $200M. In 1989 he led the acquisition of UK-based data communications front-runner Miracom Ltd. as part of a joint venture with U.S. Robotics, Inc., the leading U.S. modem maker. Subsequently, he served as Vice President and Managing Director of U.S. Robotics for five years.

During his tenure with U.S. Robotics, Mr. Montanana increased revenues fivefold for the Miracom division while overseeing a tenfold increase in profits and a rise from an eleventh-place market position to number two in the industry. Previously, he held a range of executive, marketing, and sales positions within the computer industry, including experience with Sperry Corporation, Commodore Computers, Westinghouse, and Computer Science Corporation.

Ashley Stephenson, President & CEO

As a member of the executive team that established Xedia, Ashley Stephenson became President & CEO of the company in August 1995. He was most recently responsible for leading Xedia's expansion beyond its initial successes in workgroup Ethernet switching into the emerging market of Managed Broadband Access to the Internet.

In his previous position as Vice President of Marketing with Xedia, he led the introduction of its first products through indirect channels and established the company's initial OEM relationship with existing firms in the networking field.

His prior experience included senior strategic responsibilities with Groupe Bull, including the founding of the Power PC/PowerOpen consortium with IBM, Motorola, and Apple Computer. He began his career in engineering, holding positions such as Director of CPU Development with Stellar Computer, Architect of SNA and LU6.2 gateway products for Wang Laboratories, and various research and development roles with IBM UK.

Mr. Stephenson conducted postgraduate research in high-energy physics at C.E.R.N., Switzerland (Conseil European pour la Recherché Nucleaire/European Particle Physics Laboratory) after graduating with First Class Honors from the Royal College of Science in London. He served on the Board of Directors for the PowerOpen Association and the Object Management Group.

Karen Barton, Vice President of Marketing

Karen Barton joined Xedia in 1997 as the Vice President of Marketing. Barton had more than 20 years of experience in strategic marketing, product planning, business development, product management, and marketing programs. She joined Xedia from Bay Networks where, as Vice President of Strategic Business Development, she played an executive role in developing corporate strategy, building technology partnerships, mergers and acquisitions, and in corporate and product planning. Previously, she held senior-level management positions in product marketing, market development, and strategic planning at Wellfleet Communications, BBN Comm., and Motorola Codex. Barton received a B.S. from the University of New Hampshire and an MBA from Boston College.

(Continued)

EXHIBIT 25-11 *(Continued)*

Jeremy Greene, Chief Technical Officer

Jeremy Greene joined Xedia in 1996 as the principal architect of the company's new product line designed to address the needs of the Broadband Internet Access marketplace. Greene led the engineering effort to develop the new generation of Xedia products encompassing technologies such as IP Routing, Frame Relay, and ATM.

Before coming to Xedia, Mr. Greene held senior technical and consulting positions with Proteon, Chipcom, Coral Systems and InterLan. Over the course of his career, Mr. Greene has managed and developed a wide variety of networking-related projects ranging from routers, network management systems, and remote access devices.

Born and educated in the United States, Mr. Greene held BSEE and MSEE degrees from the University of Massachusetts.

Rick Lemieux, National Sales Manager

Rick Lemieux was responsible for developing key components of the sales and marketing plan for Xedia's flagship Access Point family of products. Lemieux joined Xedia from UB Networks where he was responsible for launching UB's channel program in the Northeast. Between 1987 and 1995, Mr. Lemieux held senior sales positions at ascom Timeplex, Primary Access Corporation and Network Equipment Technologies. At ascom Timeplex, he was an Executive Account Manager responsible for developing Timeplex's major accounts in the Northeast. At Primary Access, Mr. Lemieux was an Executive Account Manager responsible for launching Primary Access's dial access systems in the Northeast, including key accounts as IBM/Advantis, Digital Equipment Corporation, Prodigy Services, and Travelers Insurance. At Network Equipment Technologies, he was responsible for sales of T1 networking systems in the New England area to key accounts such as Bank of Boston. Commercial Union, and John Hancock Mutual Life Insurance. Prior to entering sales, Mr. Lemieux held a series of technical management positions at Motorola Codex.

Mr. Lemieux had won numerous awards throughout his career, including Rookie of the Year, # 1 New Account closer, and President's Club. He has also served as executive sales advisor.

Martin Meyer, Chief Financial Officer

As Chief Financial Officer, Mr. Meyer was responsible for the financial strategy and management of the company. He was also responsible for operational departments, including Human Resources. Mr. Meyer has over a dozen years of high-tech experience in engineering and finance, and joined the company in 1995. He had extensive experience in tax management, mergers and acquisitions, financial management, and the structuring of corporate benefit programs. Previously, he held several controllerships for Stratus Computer, including controller of Stratus' Isis software subsidiary. Mr. Meyer began his career as a hardware engineer for Raytheon Corporation. He received a technical degree from Boston University and an MBA from Babson College.

Source: Company Web site.

EXHIBIT 25-12

DIAGRAM OF PRODUCT

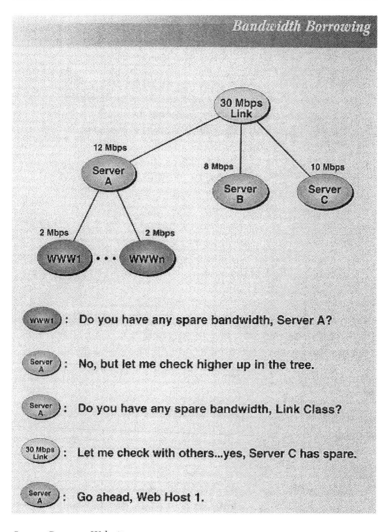

Source: Company Web site.

---

the network service providers who, as a means of differentiating their service, wanted to guarantee the quality and quantity of service to achieve sales. Using the Xedia product, Internet Service Providers could manage their bandwidth capacity more effectively to provide better service to more customers. (See Exhibit 25-12 for an example.)

HISTORICAL FINANCING

Through the end of 1996, Xedia was financed by Montanana, a group of individual investors and two corporate investors, Bay Networks and Japan Tobacco Software Services, a Japanese conglomerate. This group had invested under the old strategy of Ethernet switch product. With its new strategy, Xedia needed more money to finance the research and development of the new product. After depleting a substantial cash position generated from their previous Ethernet switch business and which Xedia senior management used to bring their new product to Alpha stage, Xedia management wanted to raise venture capital money. Marty Meyer explained:

> Xedia was an odd duck because it was a restart. We had good people looking at a large market but with a checkered past. Our story required more explaining than most. We decided that Xedia needed the outside validation that venture capital money brings; this type of validation was worth the dilution of a VC investment. Ultimately, we raised $6.3 million in February 1997 led by Roger Evans of Greylock at a post-money valuation of $20 million. We were definitely right about the validation because as soon as we received the investment from Greylock, we received phone calls from investment banks, commercial banks, many real estate and insurance people, and equipment financing companies. Before, we had to work hard to meet bankers and get bank financing, even for warrants, whereas now they seek us out to offer bank financing. (See Exhibit 25-13 for a list of similar Greylock investments).

Soon after Xedia decided to open a credit line in order to buy equipment and furniture for the company. Taking on debt would allow the company to retain as much of its equity as possible. Xedia maintained a banking relationship with US Trust for checking and deposits but worried about US Trust's inexperience in lending to young companies. Another possible source of lending was venture leasing firms like Comdisco, Lighthouse, and Phoenix. Xedia management believed that most venture leasing firm lenders did not have the time or resources to learn about many different industries like Xedia's access routing business, so any agreement would require a significant number of warrants to make a loan. Xedia was also interested in SVB because of its reputation as the commercial lender of choice for young companies and also because of its reputation for competitive pricing. Ultimately, Xedia arranged a small loan of $700,000 with SVB primarily for the purchase of office furniture and equipment. Meyer discussed their decision:

> We liked the fact that SVB has specific groups that focus on specific industries. Because of this, they knew more about the different technologies than most bankers, allowing them to take more risk. Another place where SVB added value involved their covenant agreements. We felt that SVB understood our business more than the other bankers we talked to. We felt that they would not panic if we ever breached a banking covenant.

CORPORATE STRATEGY

Xedia planned to raise a large amount of money for its next round in order to finance the production rollout of its product. Early indications from beta site users were that the product would be well received by the market. The company was burning $500,000 per month and expected this rate to increase steadily in the future. Without either the bridge loan or the next round of financing, Xedia would reach its fume date by the end of March 1998. Senior management believed that their company was poised for a major breakthrough, resulting in strong growth and profitability. (See Exhibit 25-14 for historical financials, Exhibit 25-15 for Xedia income statement projections created by SVB, Exhibit 25-16 for information on comparable companies to Xedia, and Exhibit 25-17 for volatility calculations.)

EXHIBIT 25-13

LIST OF SIMILAR GREYLOCK INVESTMENTS

Year	Company	Product/Market Focus	Status
Networking Equipment (Hardware)			
1979	Intertel/Infinet	Data modems	Acquired by Memotech Data in 1986
1979	Tellabs	Telecommunications equipment	IPO 1980
1979	Micom	Data multiplexor and data PABX products	IPO 1981; acquired by Odyssey Partners in 1988
1985	Bytex	Matrix switches/equipment	IPO 1989
1989	Ascend Communications	Remote LAN access	IPO 1994
1989	CrossComm Corporation	Internetworking equipment	IPO 1993
1990	Xircom, Inc.	Network adapters and modems	IPO 1992
1991	Shiva Corporation	Remote LAN access	IPO 1994
1992	Sonix Communications Limited	Modems, ISDN products	Acquired by 3Com in 1995
1993	Whitetree Network Technologies, Inc.	ATM networking equipment	Acquired by Ascend in 1997
1995	Endgate Corporation	High frequency radio transmission and receiving	Private company
1995	Sahara Networks	Telephone network products	Acquired by Cascade in 1997
1995	ZeitNet, Inc.	ATM network interface cards	Acquired by Cabletron in 1996
1996	Copper Mountain Communications	xDSL internet access devices	Private company
1996	Ipsilon Networks, Inc.	IP switch	Acquired by Nokia in 1997
1997	Xedia	High-speed internet access devices	Private company
1997	Argon Networks	Terabit switch router	Private company
Networking Software			
1990	Xcellenet, Inc.	Remote distribution of PC applications	IPO 1994
1993	Wildfire Communications	Telephone-based applications	Private company
1994	Cambio Networks, Inc.	Network management application	Private company
1994	Optimal Networks Corporation	Network management application	Private company
1994	Airsoft, Inc.	Wireless communications software	Acquired by Shiva in 1996
1994	Puma Technology, Inc.	Wireless communications software	Private company
1994	Raptor Systems	Internet firewall	IPO 1996; acquired by Axent in 1998
1995	IntelliLink Corporation	Wireless communications software	Acquired by Puma in 1996
1995	Unwired Planet, Inc.	Platform for wireless internet appliances	Private company
1995	Starburst Communications Corporation	IP multicast software solutions	Private company
1996	Frontier Software Development, Inc.	Network monitoring and diagnostics	Private company

Source: Greylock management.

TABLE B   Historical Financing of Xedia ($000s)

Round	Lead Investor	Date	Amount Raised	Post-Money Valuation
1	Xedia Management	1/93	$ 360	$ 6,000
2	Japan Tobacco Software Services	12/93	$1,650	N/A
3	Bay Networks	11/95	$2,400	$17,000
4	Greylock	2/97	$6,300	$20,000

Source: VentureOne

EXHIBIT 25-14

XEDIA HISTORICAL INCOME STATEMENT [a]

Income Statement (000s)	1994	1995	1996	1997 (Estimated)
Revenue	**$491**	**$3,564**	**$4,424**	**$1,000**
Cost of Goods Sold	365	2,645	3,565	750
Gross Profit	**$126**	**$919**	**$859**	**$250**
Operating Expenses:				
Research & Development	906	926	1,052	2,500
Sales & Marketing	448	877	555	2,100
General & Administrative	458	596	771	950
Income from Operations	**($1,686)**	**($1,480)**	**($1,519)**	**($5,300)**
% of Sales	(345%)	(42%)	(35%)	(530%)
Interest (Expense)/Income	10	14	15	25
Taxes	0	0	0	0
Net Income	**($1,696)**	**($1,494)**	**($1,534)**	**($5,275)**
% of Sales	(345%)	(42%)	(35%)	(528%)

[a] Estimates of 1997 income statement and balance sheet were made by SVB after discussions with Xedia management.

Source: Company documents.

(*Continued*)

EXHIBIT 25-14 *(Continued)*

XEDIA HISTORICAL BALANCE SHEET

Balance Sheet (000s)	1994	1995	1996	1997 (Estimated)
Cash	$110	$831	$445	$250
Accounts Receivable	46	305	1	850
Inventory	245	1,569	58	500
Other Current Assets	33	51	62	250
Current Assets	**$434**	**$2,756**	**$566**	**$1,850**
Net Fixed Assets	192	230	384	700
Other Long-Term Assets	0	0	21	50
Intangibles	0	0	0	0
Total Assets	**$626**	**$2,986**	**$971**	**$2,600**
Short-Term Notes	0	0	94	100
Accounts Payable	298	1,580	118	400
Accruals	142	289	366	600
Deferred Revenues	0	0	0	25
Other	84	0	70	100
Current Liabilities	**$524**	**$1,869**	**$648**	**$1,225**
Long-Term Debt	0	0	68	0
Other LT Liabilities	428	436	300	500
Total Liabilities	**$952**	**$2,305**	**$1,016**	**$1,725**
Equity	(326)	681	(45)	875
Total Liabilities & Equity	**$626**	**$2,986**	**$971**	**$2,600**

Source: Company documents.

EXHIBIT 25-15

SVB'S PROJECTIONS OF XEDIA'S INCOME STATEMENT[a]

Income Statement (000s)	1998P	1999P
Revenue	**$13,500**	**$38,500**
Cost of Goods Sold	6,000	15,500
Gross Profit	**$7,500**	**$23,000**
Operating Expenses:		
Research & Development	3,750	5,500
Sales & Marketing	7,000	9,750
General & Administrative	1,500	3,000
Income from Operations	**($4,750)**	**$4,750**
% of Sales	(35%)	12%
Interest (Expense)/Income	150	225
Taxes	0	1,600
Net Income	**($4,600)**	**$3,375**
% of Sales	(34%)	9%

[a] SVB projections are based on conversations with Xedia.

Source: SVB projections.

EXHIBIT 25-16

COMPARABLE COMPUTER COMMUNICATIONS EQUIPMENT COMPANIES

Company	1996 Sales (millions)	1996 Debt to Total Capital (Market Value)	1996 Beta	1996 Shares Outstanding (millions)	1996 Stock Price	1996 Market Value (millions)
SBE, Inc.	$ 13.4	9.6%	1.50	2.2	$ 4.125	$ 9.2
Proteon, Inc.	$ 45.3	0.0%	3.56	15.4	$ 2.50	$ 38.6
Lanoptics	$ 20.6	NA	2.41	NA	$ 7.375	NA
ODS Networks	$ 117.9	0.0%	0.71	16.3	$12.00	$ 195.9
Network Equipment Technology	$ 324.5	8.3%	2.52	21.0	$13.50	$ 284.2
Netframe System	$ 74.4	0.0%	0.32	13.8	$ 2.562	$ 35.5
Madge Networks	$ 482.1	1.2%	0.73	44.5	$ 9.875	$ 439.1
Fore Systems	$ 395.4	0.1%	1.47	97.7	$15.00	$ 1,465.1
Cisco Systems	$4,096.0	0.0%	1.62	973.9	$34.50	$33,600.5
Bay Networks	$2,056.6	2.2%	1.97	188.5	$25.75	$ 4,854.8
Access Beyond	$ 39.4	3.5%	1.49	10.9	$12.625	$ 137.0
Shiva Corporation	$ 201.8	0.1%	2.59	28.9	$34.875	$ 1,007.6
Retix	$ 31.1	0.0%	1.94	22.6	$ 6.75	$ 152.5
Olicom	$ 168.2	0.0%	1.46	14.7	$18.875	$ 277.1
Emulex Corporation	$ 51.3	0.5%	1.75	6.0	$14.625	$ 87.6
Digital Link Corporation	$ 52.1	0.0%	1.96	9.2	$24.25	$ 223.5
Cabletron Systems	$1,406.6	0.0%	1.70	156.3	$30.125	$ 4,708.7
3Com Corporation	$3,147.1	1.3%	1.68	178.4	$48.50	$ 8,651.1
Asante Technologies	$ 67.0	0.0%	0.83	8.9	$ 6.625	$ 58.7
Ascend Communications	$ 549.3	0.0%	3.95	119.4	$62.125	$ 7,418.8
Amati Communications	$ 12.1	0.2%	4.60	17.7	$11.25	$ 199.0
Gandalf Technologies	$ 66.2	15.2%	3.34	43.4	$ 1.687	$ 73.2

[a] These companies were used to calculate the volatility of the different stock returns. The data set used monthly returns from 1993 to 1996; hence, the comparable data table above shows the 1996 information of the comparable companies.

EXHIBIT 25-17

VOLATILITY HISTOGRAM OF COMPARABLE COMPUTER COMMUNICATIONS EQUIPMENT COMPANIES

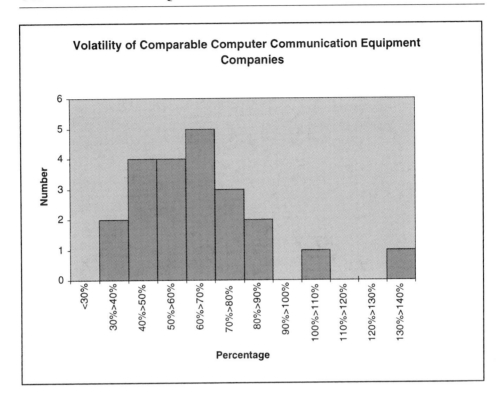

Median Volatility ----- 61.2%   Mean Volatility----- 64.6%

Source: The graph plots the average annualized volatility of 22 Computer Communication Equipment companies over the period 1993 to 1996. Data were sourced from Center of Research for Securities Prices.

CONCLUSION

Notwithstanding senior management's confidence about their company's future, general uncertainty behind fundraising caused Xedia management not to know exactly when they would close on their next round of financing. For this reason, Xedia decided to ask SVB for a bridge loan of $1.5 million in order to give the company more breathing room in its negotiation with its VC investors. Meyer informed SVB in August 1997 about the possibility of needing the bridge loan, given that the company would officially run out of cash in March 1998.

Meyer was confident that the company was now headed in the proper direction since the restart of the company and believed that the creditworthiness of Xedia would influence most lenders to make the bridge loan. He fully realized, however, that time was beginning to become a factor. The company was traveling at a fast speed, and this financing represented a brick wall that Xedia had to get over or else it would be in trouble.

Xedia and Silicon Valley Bank (B-1): The Bank's Perspective

We were at the point where we needed to finalize our initial offer to Xedia. In these situations, I normally round up Ken Wilcox and Dave Fischer to discuss the situation. We needed to analyze a few components of the bridge loan's pricing: the interest rate, negative covenants covering the behavior of Xedia, and the number of warrants we wanted and our registration rights associated with those warrants. We were in agreement that the risk associated with an uncovered bridge loan forced us to negotiate for warrants. After these internal discussions, we sent our initial proposal for the bridge loan to Xedia in mid-October, 1997. (See Exhibit 1 for SVB's initial term sheet.)

—Jim Maynard, Senior Vice President of SVB

DUE DILIGENCE PROCESS

After analyzing the trends in the Internet market space and, more specifically, the access router industry, Maynard decided that Xedia's growth prospects were favorable for the ensuing years. SVB's due diligence showed the importance of improved bandwidth access and management because of the Internet explosion. There were other issues, however, that still needed to be explored. Was Xedia positioned appropriately to compete well within this space? To some extent, SVB relied on the technical knowledge and the due diligence of Greylock, the venture capital firm that funded Xedia's first round, to decide whether Xedia was positioned to succeed in this market space. Further due diligence was completed through public equity analyst reports and SVB's internal research office.

First, Maynard spent time with Ashley Stephenson and Marty Meyer, the President and CFO of Xedia respectively, to assess their operating strategy and subsequent burn rate of cash. In essence, Maynard needed to feel comfortable with Xedia's strategy and the competence of Xedia's senior management. Based on these conversations, Maynard believed that the $1.5 million would last for three to four months if no outside equity financing were raised. Xedia management planned to use the bridge loan to fund daily operations until the next round of financing was raised.

Research Associate Jon M. Biotti prepared this case under the supervision of Professor Paul Gompers as the basis for class discussion rather than to illustrate either effective or ineffective handling of an administrative situation.

Next, Maynard met with Greylock management to assess its intention to fund Xedia's next round as well as its thoughts on how well positioned Xedia was to compete in its market segment. SVB often tapped the technical knowledge and due diligence of the venture capitalists backing the company. Maynard explained SVB's thought process regarding the next round of funding:

> As a part of our due diligence, we must talk with the venture investors to assess their intention to participate in the next round. Usually, the VC firm has a lot more at stake in the company than SVB, and therefore has more to lose by not funding the next round. They could lose their entire first round of invested money. If Xedia didn't raise the next round of financing, however, then we would have very little recourse other than to liquidate what little collateral there was or to continue to assess what Greylock would do with its investment. So we met with Roger Evans to assess his desire to fund the next round and received a favorable impression that they would do so and be supportive beyond the round in question.

NEGOTIATIONS

After the internal discussions with SVB senior management, Maynard decided to initially offer Xedia an interest rate of prime plus .75% for the bridge loan, matching the interest rate on SVB's equipment line already extended to Xedia. The current marketplace was particularly competitive at this time, with most risky loans priced at prime rate plus 1% and normal risk loans priced at flat prime. Furthermore, bridge loans for good customers were priced at prime plus one-half percentage point even after considering the increased risk of a bridge loan. Maynard believed that SVB needed to price aggressively in order to keep Xedia's business.

Given the general riskiness of a bridge loan, Maynard decided to ask Xedia management for some warrants in order to participate in the potential upside of the firm. He tried to place a figure on the number of warrants that he might ask for, ultimately deciding on a fixed amount of $45,000, a 3% coverage ratio on the $1.5 million bridge loan, as priced by the last series of preferred equity sold on or prior to January 31, 1998. If Xedia were unable to raise the next round, then SVB would receive the warrants at the price per share of the previous round. In the previous round, Xedia raised $6.3 million at a post-money valuation of $20 million, which translated into a share price of $1.50. The warrants expired in December 2002 and had a strike price equal to the per share value in the previous venture capital round. The premise was that the warrants would compensate SVB for its additional risk. Maynard was unsure how Xedia would react to this request, especially given the very competitive state of the commercial lending industry. Furthermore, SVB planned to ask for registration rights allowing SVB to sell its Xedia shares in any IPO.

Maynard also planned to ask for specific negative covenants that guided Xedia's ability to borrow money once the next round of financing was raised. Maynard wanted this covenant to state that Xedia could not borrow more than 80% of eligible domestic account receivables.

CONCLUSION

SVB senior management sent the bridge loan proposal to Xedia and waited for Xedia's reply. SVB's main concern was the request for warrants from Xedia. Maynard was completely unsure how Meyer would react to SVB's bridge loan proposal.

EXHIBIT 1

SVB'S INITIAL TERM SHEET FOR THE BRIDGE LOAN

Silicon Valley Bank (the "Bank") has approved and hereby proposes to make a loan ("Loan") to Xedia Corporation ("Borrower") under the terms and conditions in this letter. This letter is not meant to be, nor shall it be construed as, an attempt to define all the terms and conditions of the Loan. Rather, it is intended only to outline certain of the basic points of our understanding around which the final terms and documentation are to be structured. The following is a summary of the basic business points of the Loan which have been approved by the Bank and are proposed to Xedia:

CREDIT FACILITY: $1,500,000 Bridge Loan, converting to a revolving accounts receivable line of credit upon raising new equity.

PURPOSE: To support general working capital needs.

INTEREST RATE: Prime + .75%

COLLATERAL: First Priority Lien on corporate accounts receivable, Inventory and specific equipment (cross-collateralized with existing $500,000 equipment line of credit). Negative Pledge on Intellectual Property.

ADVANCE RATE: Prior to New Equity: None; After New Equity: 80% of eligible domestic A/R under 90 days.

LOAN FEE: $7,500 payable by Borrower upon closing of the subject loan. A formal documentation package will supersede this letter.

WARRANTS: Warrant to purchase $45,000 of preferred stock at the most recent round's pricing (forthcoming round if completed; last round if not).

WARRANTIES AND COVENANTS: Borrower shall make customary representations, warranties, and covenants, together with such other representations, warranties, and covenants as the bank or its counsel may deem reasonably necessary or desirable, including the following:

Financial Covenants: Minimum $5,000,000 of New Equity by January 31, 1998
Minimum Quick Ratio of 1.5
Minimum Tangible Net worth of $500,000

All Covenants are tested monthly.

Financial Reporting:
1. Company-prepared monthly financial reports within 35 days of month-end;
2. After New Equity: Monthly Borrowing Base certificate and A/R Aging Report within 35 days;
3. Audited FYE Report within 90 days;
4. Fiscal Year 1998 operating and balance sheet plan by December 21, 1997.

Other Covenants:
1. Borrower shall maintain an operating account at the Bank.
2. Borrower will allow Bank to complete an annual examination of the Borrower's accounts receivable at the expense of the Borrower.

(Continued)

EXHIBIT 1 (Continued)

EXPENSES: Borrower shall pay all of the Bank's fees and charges in connection with the Loan, including fees of Bank's outside counsel. Such costs payable by Borrower are in addition to the Loan Fee described above. In the event the Loan does not close, the Loan Fee refundable to Borrower shall be reduced by the aggregate of all such expenses and charges.

CONDITIONS OF CLOSING: The following shall be satisfied by borrower prior to closing and shall be conditions precedent to Bank's obligation to fund the Loan:

1. After due diligence inquiry conducted by the Bank (including without limitation, environmental audits and accounts receivable audits, in the sole discretion of the Bank and at the expense of Borrower), there shall be no discovery of any facts or circumstances which would negatively affect or tend to negatively affect, in the Bank's sole discretion, collectability of the Loan against Borrower.
2. No representation, warranty, or disclosure made to the Bank by Borrower shall prove to be false or misleading as of the date made.

This letter is intended to set forth the Bank-approved and Bank-proposed terms of the Loan. Except for your obligation to pay the Bank's expenses and charges described above, this letter and our other communications and negotiations regarding the proposed Loan do not constitute an agreement and do not create any legal rights benefiting, or obligations binding on, either of us. It is intended that all legal rights and obligations of the Bank and Borrower will be set forth in signed definitive loan documents acceptable to the Borrower, the Bank and their respective counsels.

Source: Bank documents.

Xedia and Silicon Valley Bank (B-2): The Company's Perspective

Marty Meyer looked over the initial proposal from Silicon Valley Bank (SVB) and wondered how flexible SVB would be concerning the terms of the bridge loan. Meyer was concerned about the company's burn rate of $500,000 per month and fume date of March 1998. Xedia wanted the bridge loan to put them in a better position to negotiate with the venture capitalists for the next round of financing. In this way, senior management of Xedia would receive a better valuation and suffer from less dilution. Market conditions favored Xedia given the increased banking competition, especially from large banks like Fleet which were placing increased emphasis on small company lending, and the large amounts of venture money raised in the previous 12 months. Given these considerations, Meyer decided to negotiate on the following terms and conditions.

NEGOTIATIONS

First, Meyer decided to ask for a reduction in the interest rate to prime. While aggressive, Meyer believed that other companies were getting regular loans at prime, although not necessarily bridge loans. Second, Meyer wanted to reduce the loan fee but was unsure what was a fair amount. He finally decided to request a reduction to $5,000.

Meyer also wanted to deny SVB's request to receive Xedia warrants. Finally, Meyer wanted to change the advance rate terms of the bridge loan. In its original form, SVB would lend up to $1.5 million in the bridge loan until Xedia raised the next round of money, with Xedia agreeing to raise at least $5 million. As soon as Xedia raised the next round, Xedia was obligated to pay down the bridge loan to a loan amount not exceed-

Research Associate Jon M. Biotti prepared this case under the supervision of Professor Paul Gompers as the basis for class discussion rather than to illustrate either effective or ineffective handling of an administrative situation.

ing 80% of eligible domestic accounts receivable under 90 days old. Meyer wanted to include 50% of inventory in this loan amount covenant once the next round was raised. (See Exhibit 1 for Xedia's proposed deal terms.)

XEDIA PERSPECTIVE

Marty Meyer also needed to consider other factors while achieving these negotiating goals. Other factors included Xedia's good working relationship with SVB, which senior Xedia management wanted to develop for the long term. Given this, Xedia was willing to pay a slight premium to stay with SVB.

EXHIBIT 1

PROPOSED DEAL TERMS BY XEDIA

Silicon Valley Bank (the "Bank") has approved and hereby proposes to make a loan ("Loan") to Xedia Corporation ("Borrower") under the terms and conditions in this letter. This letter is not meant to be, nor shall it be construed as, an attempt to define all the terms and conditions of the Loan. Rather, it is intended only to outline certain of the basic points of our understanding around which the final terms and documentation are to be structured. The following is a summary of the basic business points of the Loan which have been approved by the Bank and are proposed to Xedia:

CREDIT FACILITY:	$1,500,000 Bridge Loan, converting to a revolving accounts receivable line of credit upon raising new equity.
PURPOSE:	To support general working capital needs.
INTEREST RATE:	Prime
COLLATERAL:	First Priority Lien on corporate accounts receivable, Inventory and specific equipment (cross-collateralized with existing $500,000 equipment line of credit). Negative Pledge on Intellectual Property.
ADVANCE RATE:	Prior to New Equity: None; After New Equity: 80% of eligible domestic A/R under 90 days and 50% of inventory.
LOAN FEE:	$5,000 payable by Borrower upon closing of the subject loan. A formal documentation package will supersede this letter.
WARRANTS:	None
WARRANTIES AND COVENANTS:	Borrower shall make customary representations, warranties, and covenants, together with such other representations, warranties, and covenants as the bank or its counsel may deem reasonably necessary or desirable, including the following:
Financial Covenants:	Minimum $5,000,000 of New Equity by January 31, 1998 Minimum Quick Ratio of 1.5 Minimum Tangible Net worth of $500,000 All Covenants are tested monthly.
Financial Reporting:	1. Company-prepared monthly financial reports within 35 days of month-end; 2. After New Equity: Monthly Borrowing Base certificate and A/R Aging Report within 35 days; 3. Audited FYE Report within 90 days; 4. Fiscal Year 1998 operating and balance sheet plan by December 21, 1997.
Other Covenants:	1. Borrower shall maintain an operating account at the Bank. 2. Borrower will allow Bank to complete an annual examination of the Borrower's accounts receivable at the expense of the Borrower.

(Continued)

EXHIBIT 1 *(Continued)*

EXPENSES:

Borrower shall pay all of the Bank's fees and charges in connection with the Loan, including fees of Bank's outside counsel. Such costs payable by Borrower are in addition to the Loan Fee described above. In the event the Loan does not close, the Loan Fee refundable to Borrower shall be reduced by the aggregate of all such expenses and charges.

CONDITIONS OF CLOSING:

The following shall be satisfied by borrower prior to closing and shall be conditions precedent to Bank's obligation to fund the Loan:

1. After due diligence inquiry conducted by the Bank (including without limitation, environmental audits and accounts receivable audits, in the sole discretion of the Bank and at the expense of Borrower), there shall be no discovery of any facts or circumstances which would negatively affect or tend to negatively affect, in the Bank's sole discretion, collectability of the Loan against Borrower.
2. No representation, warranty, or disclosure made to the Bank by Borrower shall prove to be false or misleading as of the date made.

This letter is intended to set forth the Bank-approved and Bank-proposed terms of the Loan. Except for your obligation to pay the Bank's expenses and charges described above, this letter and our other communications and negotiations regarding the proposed Loan do not constitute an agreement and do not create any legal rights benefiting, or obligations binding on, either of us. It is intended that all legal rights and obligations of the Bank and Borrower will be set forth in signed definitive loan documents acceptable to the Borrower, the Bank and their respective counsels.

Source: Company documents.

26

A Note on Strategic Alliances

INTRODUCTION

A study of the financing of emerging companies and innovation must include a discussion on how firms interact, particularly the formation of strategic alliances ("cooperative agreements," "cooperative linkages," "collaborative agreements," "corporate partnering") between firms. A survey of 750 CEOs in *Business Week*'s annual listing of American companies showed that there were 20,000 strategic alliances formed among U.S. firms between 1988 and 1992. This was roughly four times the number formed from 1980 to 1987.

This note will discuss the economic theory underlying strategic alliances, including those between industry and the university-academia complex. Examples will be provided from a cross-section of industries with a particular emphasis on the biotechnology industry. The reference section contains a detailed list of cited texts and articles that offer much greater detail.

TRANSACTION COSTS THEORY

A cooperative agreement can be defined as any long-term, explicit agreement between two or more firms. The exchange can involve financial remuneration, goods and services, information, or any combination of the three. To clarify: (1) a long-term agreement is defined in contrast to a one-time spot exchange, as in the example of General Motors' 10-year exclusive contract in 1919 to purchase substantially all of its closed bodies from Fisher Body (cited in Klein, Crawford, and Alchian, 1978); (2) an explicit agreement must be understood by both parties before to the exchange and can take a variety of legal forms (even verbal agreement).

At the most fundamental level, a firm is an entity that purchases inputs and combines them to produce a product. Firms engage in a series of activities including buying inputs, transforming them into semifinished products, undertaking research activi-

Alex Tsai (Harvard College '98) prepared this note under the supervision of Professor Paul Gompers as the basis for class discussion rather than to illustrate either effective or ineffective handling of an administrative situation.

ties for product innovation, obtaining financing, designing final products, distributing and marketing, and searching for new markets. Many of these activities can be separated and done independently. Transaction cost theory (Williamson 1975, 1979, 1985) explains why firms enter into strategic alliances.

A transaction occurs when a good or service is transferred from one firm to another. For each activity, a firm can choose to execute the transaction either through "hierarchies" (i.e., within the firm) or through "markets" (i.e., externally). Organization costs involve the costs associated with running the vertically integrated firm, and contracting costs involve the costs associated with setting up, running, and monitoring an arm's-length market transaction.

The costs of market transactions increase as the frequency of transactions increases because there is a cost to each transaction (for example, the time-cost of meetings). If transactions recur often and if the terms of the transaction vary little, then perhaps both parties are better off negotiating a long-term contract. One could envision a firm hiring new workers each day on a contract basis, but the contracting would become extremely costly. The costs of market transactions also increase when the terms of exchange are surrounded by uncertainty. Uncertainty arises when contingencies affecting the execution of the contract are complex and therefore difficult to understand or predict. Contracts made under such conditions will therefore be incomplete and require renegotiation when unexpected contingencies arise. This is usually the case with research and development. It is often difficult to contract with another firm to do R&D because it is difficult to know what will come out of those efforts.

It is also the case that if an activity involves investing in assets that have only one potential customer, then it might be hard to ensure that the proper investment is made (Klein, Crawford, and Alchian, 1978). For example, a railroad may build a line to a coal mine to carry its ore to market. If the railroad and the coal mine do not sign a long-term contract, both sides may try to use their bargaining power to gain more favorable terms. The railroad, knowing that the coal mining firm will try to exploit its position later, may choose to not build the line. A long-term contract can often solve this problem.

The potential for opportunistic behavior may make contracting impossible in many situations. Williamson argued that, as external market transactions become more costly, a firm is more apt to internalize its activities to economize on transaction costs. Internalization eliminates the possibility of opportunistic behavior and reestablishes the incentive to commit to transaction-specific assets. For example, a firm might merge with another firm in order to gain access to its marketing and distribution channels. One example is the $800 million acquisition of Chipcom by 3Com, in which 3Com gained access to Chipcom's distribution network, a sales force specializing in large accounts. Walt Disney acquired Capital Cities/ABC Media for $19 billion. Rather than manage the difficulties of an alliance of two independent entities, Disney acquired the other firm in order to deliver its programming through the established Capital Cities/ABC Media network. In the event that a new product is so different that current distribution channels do not suffice, a firm would be forced to develop its own channels internally. Mergers and internal development may involve governance costs so large that the whole may not be greater than the sum of its parts. The firm faced with this decision should carefully weigh the administrative costs and loss in efficiency (if its abilities are inferior to those of an external firm) against the hazards of opportunistic recontracting.

STRATEGIC ALLIANCES BETWEEN ACADEMIA AND INDUSTRY

Universities played an important role in building the scientific foundations of industrial innovation. Recent academic research accounted for about 10% of the new products in U.S. high-technology industries from 1975 to 1985. Statistics released by the U.S. Patent and Trademark Office show that the rate of increase in patents to universities has increased as well. Correspondingly, the rate of industry-financed R&D at universities more than tripled to $1.5 billion from 1984 to 1993. The effects of academic linkages varied by industry: according to Mansfield (1991), the percentage of new products and processes based on academic research was highest in the drug industry and lowest in the oil industry.

In addition, expenditures on academic research collaborations sometimes had a disproportionate impact on a company's output. Stated Howard A. Schneiderman, Monsanto's Senior Vice President for R&D, "We spend 3% of our total research budget on university collaboration. This generates about 15% of our genuine discovery activities." Bell Laboratories, for example, had more than 800 science Ph.D.s. Yet president Ian Ross regarded his company's joint efforts with academic researchers, about 5% of Bell Labs' 900 research projects, as the main source of its R&D knowledge.

Universities provided fundamental contributions to industrial research. This knowledge was protected via the university technology licensing office, which in turn conveyed the information to firms through a variety of contracts. Academic research sometimes resulted in new cost-saving techniques that corporate researchers were able to take advantage of. For example, high-resolution nuclear magnetic resolution (NMR) spectroscopy had become a necessary component of any chemical laboratory ever since its discovery in Stanford and Harvard research laboratories.

Firms investing in university relationships did not always have commercial motives. The United States General Accounting Office's 1988 survey of firms participating in the National Science Foundation Engineering Research Centers (ERCs) found that only a small minority of participating companies regarded the opportunity to develop patentable products as an extremely important motivation for investing. This finding suggested that most firms invested in university-based research consortia simply to support generic research, as opposed to applied research, and relied on in-house staff to advance that knowledge into commercializable products.

TYPES OF AGREEMENTS

University group research programs operated out of the more than 50 university–industry research and engineering centers in the United States. Group programs served to provide corporate sponsors with a window on emerging technologies—members were allowed to attend seminars, place their in-house scientific staff at the research centers, and receive nonexclusive licenses to scientific developments. Some group programs offered individual firm sponsorship as well. For example, the Semiconductor Research Corporation sponsored research on behalf of a consortium, but most participants had direct contracts as well.

The more aggressive independent group sponsorship approach offered more flexibility to sponsor individual projects. Multiple sponsors formed an independent group to sponsor work at selected universities. For example, the Edison Polymer Innovation Corporation, a not-for-profit consortium consisting of 76 member firms, sponsored a variety of materials research programs at Ohio universities. Each member made commitments varying from $2,000 to $50,000 per year.

Finally, if both parties wanted to develop technology in partnership using shared resources, a firm could sponsor a formal research collaboration. Sometimes a firm simply wished to monitor developments by funding universities and small companies of potential strategic interest. These nonspecific objectives were reflected in the more hands-off approach of the sponsoring firm. Tailored research projects were conducted at research centers with a particular scientist. Depending on the type of agreement signed, the firm could receive exclusive patent rights or the right to excise proprietary data from research articles before publication. If a scientific researcher made a discovery and the university's technology licensing office patented it, a firm that wanted the rights to develop and market the product signed a licensing agreement. The Monsanto-Washington University agreement was one such example of a single-firm research collaboration. Some universities even set up independent organizational units. For example, Warwick University created a Rolls-Royce Ceramic Development Unit on campus.

Other types of agreements did not involve official sponsorship. Firms that preferred to keep sensitive R&D in-house had visiting technical staff arrangements with universities, while the university scientists served in a consulting capacity. If neither party wished to pool intellectual resources, they simply signed shared facilities agreements, making it possible to conduct experiments that would otherwise be out of reach of their individual efforts. The University of Michigan, for example, sold time on its nuclear reactor outlet ports for neutron beam experiments in health care. In Switzerland, Ciba-Geigy and Sandoz Pharma contributed 25% each toward the tomograph machine at the University of Basel, and both the university and the companies used the equipment for research.

BENEFITS TO BOTH PARTIES

The company benefited from a relationship with the research institution in a number of different ways. To begin with, if a company could obtain exclusive rights to new technology, it could achieve a competitive advantage in the marketplace and could likely dominate the field of products that resulted from its development. Perhaps more importantly, a working relationship would also keep the company abreast of new developments in scientific research. Because the academic community was highly networked, key researchers could afford to keep up with the weekly discoveries and thousands of publications where even the most highly capitalized firms could not.

Corporate sponsorship provided royalty income, equipment, and employment opportunities for the university. In addition, both faculty and students gained a richer understanding of the process of research commercialization and the world of business, something that they might never be exposed to in the "ivory tower" of academic life. In the case of Norelco's coffee-maker design project with Rensselaer Polytechnic Center for Manufacturing and Productivity, Director Leo Hanifin claimed that it "provided great educational experiences for many of our students who thought manufacturing was the last place they wanted to work." This process also had the potential to increase the visibility of a faculty member so as to attract useful and remunerative consulting work outside the university.

Occasionally conflicts arose, given the different priorities of the business and academic worlds. Sponsorship changed the priorities of academic research. Faculty members supported by industry found that their choice of research area was increasingly affected by the possibility of discovering a commercial application. This change blurred the distinction between pure unfiltered academic research and market-oriented, product-driven corporate research. One underlying tension was between a firm's desire for secrecy and commercially viable "results" on the one hand and the university's openness and pursuit of knowledge on the other. Typical sponsorship contracts reached a compromise; corporate sponsors might be protected by confidentiality clauses, while scientists were assured of the right of publication after their articles were reviewed for proprietary data. If a compromise could not be reached, the collaboration fell through. In one case, Carnegie-Mellon University withdrew from a research project due to unrealistic deadlines that it could not meet with a standard graduate student staff.

INCENTIVES TO ENTER INTO STRATEGIC ALLIANCES

There are a number of reasons why a firm would enter into a strategic alliance with another firm. In general, strategic alliances are established when the internal resources of either firm are insufficient or it is deemed too risky to invest them, to the extent necessary to establish a competitive position in new markets, or to maintain a competitive position in existing markets. Utilizing resources in tandem, the strategic alliance may improve both firms' positions beyond what either firm could accomplish individually. Some of the motivational factors in forming strategic alliances include:

- Information exchange
- Complementary resources
- Economies of scale
- International expansion

INFORMATION EXCHANGE

The motivation of technology transfer is closely related to the desire to reduce risk and search costs. A study of European firms (Mariti and Smiley 1983) found that one of the most common types of strategic alliances involved the exchange of information. This type of agreement might be based on technology transfer (outright purchase or licensing by one firm of the technology of another firm) or technological complementarity (each firm contributes expertise to a joint project). One might also expect to find a higher incidence of technological complementarity alliances in industries with rapidly changing technologies, such as semiconductors, biotechnology, and electronics. Such industries are R&D-intensive, and the rate of new product introduction would therefore be greater in those industries (Pisano and Mang, 1993). Furthermore, the inherent uncertainty in R&D competition presented additional reasons for entering into collaborative competition.

Small firms often attempted to mitigate risk by spreading their involvement among projects sponsored by several large firms. In the face of frequent research setbacks and the prospect of going through the arduous FDA approval process, the typical New Biotechnology Firm (NBF) entered into strategic alliances in order to spread some risk to an established pharmaceutical company. Competition among the more than 1,300 NBFs in the United States occurred largely in research and early product development, thus requiring enormous infusions of capital. Government economists estimated the pretax capitalized cost of commercializing a new drug at $359 million. The "burn rate" referred to the NBF's rate of cash consumption to fund ongoing R&D without corresponding income from a product. Cash burn limited the longevity of 50% of all biotechnology companies to two years or less. One recent survey (Peridis, 1992) indicated that the feeling of security of being allied with a larger firm was reflected in the daily activities and decisions of small firm managers. NBFs also entered into multiple alliances with research laboratories and university scientists. As uncertainty increased, having a multiple alliance network raised the possibility of producing a stream of scientific discoveries. The multiple alliances served as a hedge against the tremendous uncertainty in any one particular project.

NBFs, usually firms with fewer than 1,000 employees, dominated the biotechnology industry and contributed most to product innovation (Kenney, 1986). A study prepared for the Small Business Administration by Gellman Research Associates, Inc. discovered that NBFs produced 2.5 times as many innovations as large firms relative to the number of employees. Another study undertaken by Human Services Research for the National Science Foundation found that NBFs produced 24 times as many major innovations per R&D dollar as did large firms and 4 times as many as did medium-sized firms.

Correspondingly, large firms attempted to mitigate risk by supporting multiple innovative efforts among a set of small firms. The large pharmaceutical companies were the rare exception in the biotechnology industry, with the three Swiss giants (Ciba, Hoffmann-LaRoche, and Sandoz) providing $7 billion in biotechnology equity investments between 1986 and 1996. With the steady stream of revenues provided by their blockbuster drugs, large pharmaceutical companies could comfortably fund ongoing research and development. Overall, research-based pharmaceutical companies had R&D budgets of more than $18 billion in 1997, an 11.5% increase over 1996.

Corporate interest in biotech alliances increased substantially after the stock market crash of 1987, when small companies turned to pharmaceuticals after other sources of financing closed off. This pattern illustrates the role that many large corporations played in dampening cycles in access to capital for small, young companies. This is true across a broad range of industries including telecommunications, computer hardware and software, semiconductors, and life sciences. At the same time, with R&D costs skyrocketing, the conservatism of the larger firms led them to look to biotechnology for innovation. Because of the range of specialized knowledge demanded in biotechnology R&D, even large pharmaceuticals no longer had the capacity to maintain in-house research outfits that were completely self-sufficient.

COMPLEMENTARY RESOURCES

Strategic alliances motivated by resource complementarity are often established by two firms that are not in direct competition with each other but, rather, operate along the same innovation chain. To more precisely examine these types of motivations for forming cooperative linkages, the framework outlined in Abernathy and Clark (1985) is useful. Their "transilience framework" separated innovation into upstream competencies (e.g., R&D, production, operations) and downstream competencies (e.g. distribution, knowledge of customers, etc.). Revolutionary innovations rendered upstream competencies obsolete. Niche creating innovations did not affect upstream competencies but instead opened up new links to the market. The less frequent architectural innovations destroyed both upstream and downstream competencies. An episode of innovation affected both competencies differently. Accordingly, a firm might respond to the innovation by focusing on its preserved competency and entering into a strategic alliance with a firm that had a distinguishing competency in another activity. By cooperating with an existing competitor, the new entrant gained access to efficient production facilities, established channels of marketing and distribution, and customer loyalty. The existing competitor, in turn, might share the new technology on which a rapid expansion of market share would be based.

Shan (1990) argued that an understanding of both transaction cost efficiency and strategic behavior was necessary to obtain a complete understanding of strategic alliance formation. His findings suggested that smaller and late-entering firms with underdeveloped internal capabilities were more likely to enter into cooperative agreements because external market transactions with other firms would be more efficient than expending the resources to acquire the necessary assets internally. He expected this to be a particularly distinctive pattern in the biotechnology industry because the technology life cycle quickly made the technology obsolete.

The pharmaceutical industry is a good example of an industry where revolutionary innovation has taken place. Pisano and Mang (1993) asserted that downstream competencies in the industry were not affected by revolutionary innovations to the same degree as were upstream competencies. As indicated above, the NBFs' major asset consisted of knowledge capital in biotechnology (Pisano, 1990). While synthesis of a new product was the primary innovation in biotechnology, NBFs often lacked the resources necessary to complete the rest of the innovation cycle: engineering know-how for scale-up from laboratory to industrial-scale manufacturing processes; screening/testing facilities and familiarity with the grueling FDA approval process; and finally, networks for marketing and distribution. These assets were typically found among the large pharmaceuticals, in addition to a comparative abundance of financial resources. Because drugs developed from biotechnology utilized the same downstream capabilities as conventional drugs derived from pharmaceutical R&D—they went through clinical trials, were subject to FDA regulation, and could be similarly marketed—the established pharmaceutical companies were not forced to compete with the NBFs as if they were traditional "Schumpeterian" entrants (Pisano and Mang, 1993). Instead, the past two decades saw a division of labor in the biotechnology industry, with NBFs acting as upstream suppliers entering into strategic alliances with established pharmaceuticals acting as downstream buyers.

Consider Cetus Corporation, one of the leading NBFs. It formed a joint venture with Eastman Kodak to market diagnostic kits, allied with Squibb to produce anti-infective drugs, and joined with Ben Venue Therapeutics to market anti-cancer drugs. A common thread of each strategic alliance is that Cetus provided the technological expertise and its partner provided production and marketing expertise. Product speed to market was a crucial determinant of overall profitability. Short product lives and the speedy erosion of technical leadership were characteristic of the semiconductor industry. Appropriability, that is, the ability to maintain one's relative technological advantage, was stronger in the pharmaceutical and biotechnology industries, but innovators still had to be wary of generic competitors once the Orphan Drug Law patent protection expired. Hence, partnership with established marketers and distributors was of strategic importance.

While strategic alliances were the standard arrangement in biotechnology, Pisano (1990) examined the evolution of the industry over time and found that there was a noticeable trend towards vertical integration. He suggested a number of reasons why NBFs were positioning themselves to develop downstream competencies. Vertical integration allowed for know-how accumulation, as the scale-up of innovations from the laboratory to industrial manufacturing was extremely firm-specific. The savings derived from this continuity partially offset the governance costs associated with in-house manufacturing efforts. Because technological know-how was the key asset for most NBFs, outsourcing manufacturing activities was especially difficult if highly proprietary knowledge were at stake. Precautions taken to avoid knowledge leakage introduced extra transactions costs. In addition, because a manufacturing contract often required the other firm to invest in transaction-specific assets, contracting was difficult. Due to one of the idiosyncrasies of drug regulations, switching costs also contributed to the costs of contracting. Vertical integration into distribution was required if preexisting channels did not support a new disease-specific drugs. The contracting firm would have to modify its own distribution network to accommodate the new innovation if it did not have the capability. In the event that it chose to make this transaction-specific investment, it would find itself in the classic small numbers bargaining position; that is, either party might try to hold up the process because they felt they had significant bargaining power.

ECONOMIES OF SCALE

A new entrant to an industry faced a potential barrier to entry if there were large economies of scale. To develop its own production capabilities and continue expansion would require a significant expenditure of resources. Until it achieved its own economies of scale in production, the new entrant was at a significant cost disadvantage. This type of problem was usually not faced by new entrants in a technology-intensive industry because competition in those industries was usually in the upstream competencies (particularly R&D) as detailed above. Entering a strategic alliance would help the new entrant overcome the significant economies of scale currently realized by its competitors. Likewise, by reducing average cost per unit of output, an alliance between established firms could create a preemptive barrier to entry for would-be entrants.

Strategic alliances formed for economies of scale were pervasive in the automobile industry because it was a huge and mature industry. Not only were R&D costs rising, but incremental gains from these investments were shrinking: it could require production of up to two million units to recoup R&D costs. Hence, there was a potential for powerful economies of scale to be realized in the production process. Mariti and Smiley (1983) cited the agreement between Alfa Romeo and Nissan in which Alfa Romeo produced the engine and Nissan produced the body for a new automobile to be marketed in Europe. Both firms benefited from the introduction of a new automobile at reduced investment cost. In addition, both firms saved on learning costs and achieved a larger production output than either firm could have achieved separately.

INTERNATIONAL EXPANSION

Strategic alliances also provided a mechanism by which firms could quickly expand their geographic scope. A partnership provided a way for the domestic company to expand internationally through the alliance partner. In many industries, the traditional boundaries of domestic competition were penetrated by foreign competitors, who were prodded by saturation in their own domestic markets and drawn by the potential that new markets promised. The strategic alliance provided a mechanism for expansion at reduced risk for the firm instead of undertaking the venture independently. Shan (1990) found that strategic alliances were preferred by biotechnology firms as a strategy for commercializing a new product in a foreign market. Moreover, the potential costs of entering a foreign market were more pronounced for a smaller firm than for a transnational corporation. Even if the firm had the resources to eventually achieve capabilities of efficient scope in foreign markets, it might be outdistanced by competitors during the extended length of time required to build up those assets. Once again, where speed of deployment was critical, alliances also proved to be important.

Regulations and government intervention often forced strategic alliances in foreign markets. Governments are frequently pressured by their constituencies to protect local industries from foreign competitors. Absolute barriers to entry rendered the market impenetrable if they could not be overcome. Relative barriers to entry only gave a competitive advantage to existing domestic competitors. Government policies such as tariffs, market share quotas, and foreign ownership restrictions served either as absolute or relative barriers to entry, depending on their nature. A foreign firm might overcome tariffs by constructing a local production facility. High start-up and operating costs, such as the cost of constructing a brand-new facility, might induce collaboration on the part of those anxious to gain an early foothold into the market. Other regulations, such as market share quotas and foreign ownership restrictions, forced a foreign firm to enter into a collaborative agreement with a domestic firm. Other complications were not so explicitly stated in policy. For example, a foreign firm might not have appropriate knowledge of the local customer; even if government policies could be circumvented with innovative organizational structures, its marketing activities would be rendered ineffectual. Finally, firms aiming for a foothold in foreign countries faced a wide range of risks idiosyncratic to each country, such as political risk, regulatory risk, currency risk, and liquidity risk. Careful selection of a strategic partner to help manage those risks was deemed essential.

The alliance between Inland Steel and Nippon Steel accomplished a diverse set of these goals. By enlisting the aid of Nippon Steel's engineers to build its cold steel mill in New Carlisle, Indiana, Inland Steel gained technological know-how. In addition, Nippon Steel supplied low-cost capital. Nippon Steel, as a part owner in the domestic facility, was able to avoid American import quotas and was thus able to supply Japanese automobile plants in the U.S. A recent newspaper article (*New York Times* 1988) indicated that many recent United States-Japan automobile manufacturing alliances involved American production facilities that benefited from Japanese know-how. The Mazda-owned Flat Rock, Michigan assembly plant produced both Ford and Mazda automobiles that relied heavily on designs developed in Japan. As a foreign firm, Mazda gained greater access to the U.S. market, while Ford engineers learned from Japanese auto makers.

TYPES OF STRATEGIC ALLIANCE AGREEMENTS BETWEEN FIRMS

Alliance formation is influenced by the specific nature of the technology and/or the capabilities of the firms involved. The following models should not be considered an exhaustive list of the choices available to firms considering such a strategy, but they are representative of the types of structures employed.

One of the most common types of strategic alliances was the R&D licensing agreement. The sponsor, typically the larger and more established partner (Pisano, 1990), provided the developer with the necessary capital for development of a product. The most limited form of arrangement was the simple product development funding agreement. The developer was free to market its product to third parties; the sponsor only received the right to purchase the finished product on favorable terms and receive royalties on sales by the developer to third parties. If the sponsor wished to control the technology, however, it arranged for a product development agreement with option to acquire the resulting technology. The larger firm acquired exclusive license to develop, manufacture, or market the finished product. Finally, nonspecific development funding allowed the sponsor to invest in more basic research that might not be immediately applicable to its business. Instead, the sponsor wanted to obtain access to a particular area of technology that might be of strategic import in the future, as opposed to specific products. The advantages to the smaller firm were many. The research of Shan, Walker, and Kogut (1994) indicated that a firm with more alliance connections was more likely to have a greater innovative output. Such an alliance was particularly useful to new companies looking to enhance their image in the public markets, because the backing of an established firm provided a partial signal as to the start-up's worth. This made it easier for privately held firms to attract capital, particularly from conservative institutional investors, when going public.

The disadvantage to licensing arrangements, of course, was that the firm often ceded control of proprietary technology to the sponsoring firm. It was often the case that a firm might license several of its peripheral undertakings while keeping certain technologies proprietary. Rather than license out proprietary technology and rely on the corresponding royalty payments, a firm that wished to develop its own capabilities—and had the resources to do so—might undertake the research and development functions internally. Thus, all the risks and rewards of technology development were borne by the firm itself. The small research-intensive firm might still lack the so-called complementary assets needed to bring its product to market, such as sales forces, scale-up know-how, and experience with regulatory agencies. Unable to completely forward integrate, the firm might sign a marketing agreement with a more experienced partner. Marketing agreements gave the sponsoring partner the right to market the product in one or more specified countries or territories. Often the smaller firm would cede worldwide marketing rights while retaining domestic marketing rights, thus simultaneously deferring to the more expansive resources of its partner while gaining valuable marketing experience for itself. Sometimes the marketing arrangement would include clauses for royalty sharing between their respective territories. Other arrangements gave the sponsoring firm exclusive marketing rights while the smaller firm retained an option for co-promotion within a defined territory. In the event that it decided not to co-promote, the smaller firm might receive only a royalty on sales. Many manufacturing agreements were designed as "cost plus"; that is, the smaller firm would receive reimbursement of its costs plus a set profit. The work of Pisano and Mang (1993) shows that, as the biotechnology industry matured, biotechnology firms increasingly retained exclusive manufacturing rights. For the biotech firm aiming to forward integrate, valuable know-how and scale-up experience could be accumulated during the manufacturing process.

The joint venture was formed when two allying firms created a new legal entity. It could be either an operating or nonoperating joint venture. Operating joint ventures created a new entity with its own facilities to perform certain functions. Nonoperating joint ventures were purely legal and administrative entities that contracted with their parents for certain activities. From the perspective of transaction cost theory, joint venturing created a "mutual hostage position" by combining real and financial assets of both firms. Both firms stood to gain or lose from the successes or failures of the joint venture, as the bond was cemented by equity exchange. It thus aligned the performance incentives of both firms, along with their incentives to share technology and information, invest in relationship-specific assets, and monitor each other. Pisano (1989) shows that the use of equity linkages increased as transactional hazards increased in the biotechnology industry. Joint ventures were also created in order to build market power by binding upstream suppliers or downstream distributors, deterring potential entrants into the market, cementing oligopolistic competition, or opening up international markets. Amgen, Inc. (U.S.) performed the research and development functions for Kirin-Amgen, a nonoperating joint venture between an American biotechnology firm and a Japanese brewing company. Each parent was responsible for manufacturing and marketing in its respective domestic market. Joint venturing might also facilitate the exchange of information. For example, joint ventures were prevalent in the automobile industry. Swelling protectionist sentiment in the United States necessitated an alliance for Toyota, leading to the 1981 joint venture between Toyota and General Motors. Toyota was a part legal owner of the New United Motor Manufacturing, Inc. (NUMMI) joint venture. In return, GM was provided with a superior subcompact automobile and was also able to learn Japanese production methods. While a simple supply agreement might operate at lower production or transaction costs, GM was able to build its own internal capabilities for the future. The work by Kogut (1988) provides a survey of the theoretical and empirical literature on joint ventures.

REFERENCES

ABERNATHY, W. AND K. CLARK. 1985. "Innovation: Mapping the winds of creative destruction." *Research Policy* 14: 3–22.

KENNEY, M. 1986. *Biotechnology: The university-industry complex*. New Haven, CT: Yale University Press.

KLEIN, B., R.G. CRAWFORD, AND A.A. ALCHIAN. 1978. "Vertical integration, appropriable rents, and the competitive contracting process." *Journal of Law and Economics* 21: 297–326.

KOGUT, BRUCE. 1988. "Joint Ventures: Theoretical and Empirical Perspectives." *Strategic Management Journal* 9:319–332.

MANSFIELD, E. 1991. "Academic research and industrial innovation." *Research Policy* 20:1–12.

MARITI, P. AND R.H. SMILEY. 1983. "Co-operative agreements and the organization of industry." *Journal of Industrial Economics* 31(4): 437–451.

New York Times. June 5, 1988. "Mixing cultures on the assembly line."

OHMAE, K. 1989. "The global logic of strategic alliances." *Harvard Business Review*, March/April: 143–154.

PERIDIS, T. 1992. "Strategic alliances for smaller firms." *Research in Global Strategic Management* 3: 129–142.

PISANO, G. 1989. "Using equity participation to support exchange: Evidence from the biotechnology industry." *Journal of Law, Economics, and Organization* 5(1): 109–126.

PISANO, G. 1990. "The R&D boundaries of the firm: An empirical analysis." *Administrative Science Quarterly* 35: 153–176.

PISANO, G.P. AND P.Y. MANG. 1993. "Collaborative product development and the market for know-how: Strategies and structures in the biotechnology industry." *Research on Technological Innovation, Management, and Policy* 5: 109–136.

SHAN, W. 1990. "An empirical analysis of organizational strategies by entrepreneurial high-technology firms." *Strategic Management Journal* 11: 129–139.

SHAN, WEI-JIAN, GORDON WALKER, AND BRUCE KOGUT. 1994. "Interfirm Cooperation and start-up innovation in the Biotechnology Industry," *Strategic Management Journal* 15: 387–394.

WILLIAMSON, O.E. 1975. *Markets and hierarchies*. New York: Free Press.

WILLIAMSON, O.E. 1979. "Transaction cost economics: The governance of contractual relations." *Journal of Law and Economics* 22: 233–261.

WILLIAMSON, O.E. 1985. *The economic institutions of capitalism*. New York: Free Press.

## 27

Parenting Magazine

Robin Wolaner was distracted as the waiter at the Rue Lepic Restaurant in downtown San Francisco, California, asked what she wanted to order. Wolaner, her husband, and a legal advisor had just terminated negotiations with a team representing Time Inc. about a much needed $5 million investment in her plan to launch a new magazine called *Parenting*. Negotiations had reached an impasse, with both sides digging in their heels. The Time team had left the all-day negotiating session remarking that they thought a deal would be impossible, given the bargaining intransigence of the Wolaner group. They were headed to the airport to take the "red-eye" back to New York. It was March 27, 1986.

The particular negotiating impasse between the Time representatives and Wolaner concerned the terms under which Time might buy Wolaner's ownership in the magazine venture. Basically, Time wanted to have the option to purchase Wolaner's stake at a point three years from the signing of the contract for a price that would be capped, no matter how well the magazine was doing at that time or what the fair market value would be. Wolaner's advisors were adamant: there should be no cap. Time could buy Wolaner out, but the purchase price should be related to the then-current market value of the magazine.

Wolaner had acceded to her advisors during the meeting but was now having second thoughts. If the project worked, the buyout price would still yield a substantial sum, particularly for someone who had spent the previous five years working as publisher of *Mother Jones*, a nonprofit magazine based in San Francisco. Did it really matter if the price wasn't "fair market value?" Moreover, raising money from venture capitalists would surely entail giving up a substantial piece of the pie, even if there were no cap on the ultimate value.

The probable consequences of losing the Time deal were disconcerting: Wolaner and her partners had exhausted their funds and were confronted with limited options for raising the requisite amount of money in the near future. Some venture capital firms and at least one other publishing company had expressed interest in investing, but no one was as close to a deal as Time. Nor were other investors as knowledgeable about

---

publishing as Time. To make matters worse, Wolaner had a bad case of the flu, but at least that would pass: whether or not she could find a way to launch *Parenting* was another matter.

It wasn't easy for Wolaner to collect her thoughts, but she would have to decide quickly: if not, her dream of starting *Parenting* might go for nought.

BACKGROUND INFORMATION

Robin Wolaner's search for a new venture began in late November of 1984. From 1980 to 1985, she had been publisher of *Mother Jones*, a monthly magazine with a left-leaning editorial bent. Wolaner had joined *Mother Jones* as general manager and circulation director. Two years later, she was promoted to publisher and oversaw all the business aspects of the magazine, including circulation, financial planning, operations, and advertising. (Additional biographical information on Wolaner is included in Exhibit 27-1.)

EXHIBIT 27-1

PARENTING MAGAZINE

Background Information on Robin Wolaner[2]

Robin Wolaner, the Publisher and Founder, was the Publisher of *Mother Jones* (an award-winning, national consumer magazine with a paid circulation of 170,000) from 1982 to February 1985.

Every summer since 1982, Robin has taught at the Radcliffe Publishing Procedures Course at Harvard University where she directs 100 students working on 10 magazine launches, each requiring a three-year business plan, a dummy issue, and so on. She was the winner of a 1984 Gold Award from *Folio*, the Magazine of Magazine Management, for excellence in circulation direct marketing. Her writing has appeared in *Working Woman* and *Glamour* Magazines, and she is a frequent publishing industry speaker.

Her previous positions were:

General Manager/Circulation Director, *Mother Jones*, 1980–1981.

Publishing Consultant, Ladd Associates, 1979–1980, working with clients such as *Quest*, *Food & Wine*, and *Newsweek* International.

Circulation Manager (top circulation executive), *Runner's World* Magazine, 1977–1979, during which time the magazine was launched nationally and grew from 90,000 to 360,000.

Editor, *Impact*, a newsstand trade magazine, 1976–1977.

Features Editor, *Viva* Magazine, 1975–1976.

Promotion Copywriter, *Penthouse* Magazine, 1975.

In the winter and spring of 1985, she served as a direct marketing consultant to Banana Republic, the clothing catalog company owned by the Gap. She graduated from Cornell University with a B.S. in Industrial and Labor Relations. Profiles of Robin have appeared in *Newsday*, *The Boston Globe*, and *USA Today*, and her biography is included in *Who's Who in America*.

[2] This information was included in the business plan prepared by Robin Wolaner in late 1985.

While Wolaner had enjoyed her years at *Mother Jones*, there were frustrations, including her lack of input on the editorial side. Moreover, the business challenges of *Mother Jones* were circumscribed: almost all the magazine's revenues came from circulation, with advertising and other revenues modest in comparison. Though Wolaner had helped improve the operations of the magazine, the company was consistently unprofitable, with losses being subsidized by one wealthy patron. Wolaner was ready to move, and she gave three months notice in November of 1984.

The idea that Wolaner might launch a magazine on parenting was somewhat improbable: Wolaner did not have children. However, many of her friends did, and she had often wondered what magazine they read. After discussions with a number of new parents in her peer group and several visits to the local newsstand, Wolaner came to the conclusion that the existing magazines were not appropriate. The leading magazine, *Parents*, was too lowbrow: the writing was pedestrian and the apparent target audience was not one that would include Wolaner or her friends.

Wolaner's early investigations evolved into a full-blown project to create a new kind of magazine for new parents, one that would be targeted at an upscale audience and would be characterized by great writing. Wolaner believed the time was ripe to introduce such a magazine, given the attractive demographic outlook and the perceived mismatch between the existing magazine offerings and the new wave of affluent, well-educated parents. If such a magazine were successfully introduced, total circulation could exceed 500,000, which would yield substantial profits.

Having selected what she thought was an attractive opportunity. Wolaner set out to find financing for the initial stages of the project. She had modest resources herself—her *Mother Jones* salary was under $40,000—and planned to raise approximately $100,000 for the research phase. Ultimately, she thought, the total capital required would be over $5 million. With the rudiments of a business plan in hand, Wolaner began making calls to friends and then to friends of friends.

Wolaner was beginning to pile up charges on her credit cards, so it was imperative that she get outside financing as soon as possible. One of her early meetings was with Arthur Dubow, a financier from New York, who was visiting San Francisco to look at a possible publishing acquisition. Dubow, was impressed with Wolaner and the business concept. He wrote her a check for $5,000, which he described as "walking around money." That was February 5, 1985. Dubow also committed to help assemble the financing group Wolaner hoped to put together.

Dubow recommended that Wolaner contact Gil Kaplan, publisher of *Institutional Investor* magazine. Kaplan in turn recommended that Wolaner conduct a direct mail test of the idea. Though Wolaner was not enthusiastic about direct mail market research—her experience had shown the results to be somewhat unreliable—she eventually accepted Kaplan's advice. As a result she raised her initial budget to $175,000 and began to design the direct mail test.

Raising capital was not the only task occupying Wolaner's attention. She was also talking to her various contacts in the publishing world, getting advice on how to create *Parenting*. There were a myriad of challenges, including designing the direct mail campaign, assembling a team, including an editor, and building an editorial advisory board. Of course, without money, these efforts would be pointless.

RAISING CAPITAL

After meeting over 70 potential investors, Wolaner managed to line up commitments for $125,000. Included in the investor group were Arthur Dubow, who had increased his commitment to $25,000, and Playboy Enterprises, which agreed to invest $12,500.

However, the $125,000 was $50,000 less than Wolaner's target. At the reduced level of funding, Wolaner would not be able to draw a salary, and there was no contingency funding: any slippage or overruns in the budget would jeopardize the project.

More problematic was the fact that Wolaner could not gain access to the $125,000 without the approval of the limited partners because she fell short of the target. After extensive negotiations with the investor group, which took place during June of 1985, Wolaner reached an agreement to modify the terms of the investment. Originally, the investors were to receive a 3.5% stake in a limited partnership in return for each $25,000 invested. Under the revised terms, the investors would receive at least 5% for each $25,000, with the actual percentage dependent on how much capital was eventually raised. If $150,000 were raised on or before October 31, 1985, the equity share would be 5.5%: if no additional capital were raised, then the share would be 6% for each $25,000. As a result of the agreement, Wolaner was able to spend the $125,000 she had already raised and had strong incentives to raise the additional $50,000 before October. If she were able to raise the full amount, then she would be entitled to a salary of $27,000 during the first six months of the partnership.

Having secured sufficient financing for the market test, Wolaner proceeded on all fronts. By late August of 1985, the test was almost ready for mailing. A copy of the original package is included as Exhibit 27-2. Wolaner had also succeeded in raising an additional $37,500, bringing the total to $162,500. At that level, at least she would be able to draw some salary.

THE AUGUST 30, 1985 MAILING

The actual mailing took place on August 30, exactly on plan. Some 130,000 pieces were mailed to names culled from 27 lists, mostly parents who bought books, educational toys, magazine subscriptions, or apparel for their children. Of the total sample, 90,000 were sent an identical package; 10,000 received an offering with a $15 subscription price (higher than the $12 price in most of the mailings); 10,000 received a package with a "hard" offering (implying a firmer commitment on the part of the respondent to subscribe); and the remaining packages represented variations on other aspects of the mailing (e.g., the envelope used or the text of the letter). Wolaner hoped to receive a 5% positive response rate to her mailing, though any rate higher than 3.5% would be considered a success.

As it turned out, Wolaner's diminutive mail box was inundated with responses: the final tally showed a 5.7% response rate. The figure was even more impressive when the weaker mailing lists were eliminated from the base. The remaining lists, which contained the names of over 4.5 million potential subscribers, had a response rate of 7.2%. Wolaner had clearly identified a market segment not being adequately served. Further analysis of the market test revealed that there was modest price sensitivity—the response rate at the $15 price was 95% of the rate at the $12 price—and that the respondents were strongly committed to buying a magazine like *Parenting*. The project was off and running.

REFINING THE PLAN AND RAISING CAPITAL

The market test results were encouraging, but many formidable and potentially insuperable hurdles remained. Chief among these was Wolaner's estimate that she would need at least $5 million to launch *Parenting*, which she hoped to do in February 1986, a scant six months after the market test. No one in the current investor group was ca-

EXHIBIT 27-2

PARENTING MAGAZINE

Original Mailer

(Continued)

pable of investing that amount of money, but most were willing to help in the process. Among the possible new investors were venture capital firms, wealthy private investors, a private placement by an investment banking firm, and publishing companies. Wolaner's first choice was to raise money from noncorporate sources because of concerns about control.

As a first step in the process of raising capital, Wolaner worked hard on preparing a business plan that reflected what she had learned from the market tests. A Table of Contents from the business plan is included as Exhibit 27-3.

Briefly told, the plan was to create a magazine with two important constituencies: parents and advertisers. By establishing high editorial standards and attracting a well-educated, high-income readership, the magazine would become the vehicle of choice for advertisers.

Wolaner's research had revealed that the demographics of the target readership were very attractive. A followup questionnaire mailed in November of 1985 to the test market respondents indicated a median household income in excess of $40,000, almost

EXHIBIT 27-2 *(Continued)*

Original Mailer

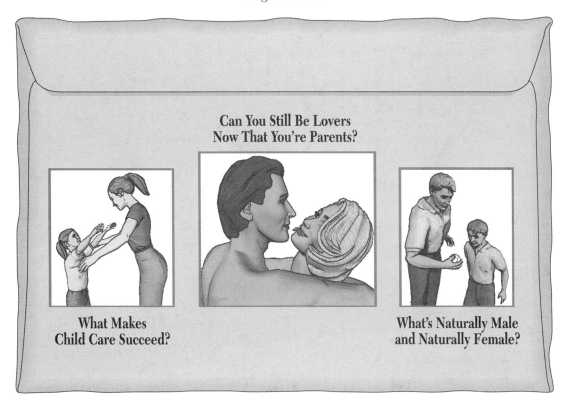

a third larger than the comparable figure for her primary competitors (*Parents, Working Mother*, and *American Baby*). More than half of the respondents were college educated. These characteristics were highly valued by potential advertisers.

The total potential market for a magazine like *Parenting* was very large. There were an estimated 20 million women in the 20–30 year age group. Fully 16 million couples were expected to become parents during the 1980s. There were approximately 1.5 million first-child births each year. By 1990, there were expected to be almost 20 million children under five years old. Finally, many of the women having children in the 1980s and beyond were bearing children later in their lives and were likely to return to the workplace during the child-raising period.

Wolaner had decided to focus on the latter segment of the parenting population. Specifically, the magazine would be targeted at women who were active in the workforce and who were engaged in many activities of which parenting was one. Moreover, the marketing strategy would concentrate on the nine-year period of planning and conception, birth, toddlerhood, and early schooling. Magazines like *Parents* were targeted at broader constituencies (e.g., parents of children of all ages), and, in Wolaner's view, lost much of their editorial impact because of this lack of focus. An overview of the

EXHIBIT 27-3

T.O.C. FROM BUSINESS PLAN FOR *PARENTING* MAGAZINE

Business Plan Table of Contents

Appendixes

Tables

content of *Parenting* and a proposed outline for the inaugural issue are contained in Exhibit 27-4 and Exhibit 27-5.

Wolaner planned to use a number of methods to attract subscribers to *Parenting*. Chief among these was direct mail. Wolaner planned to send out over 3 million pieces of mail in the first year of operation, which would result in approximately 126,000 subscriptions if her assumptions were correct. Gradually, the amount of mail sent out each year would decline as subscription renewals became a more important source of circulation.

In addition to direct mail, *Parenting* would be marketed through a number of other channels. For example, each issue would contain the ubiquitous insert cards. These cards were often an important source of subscriptions. Also, *Parenting* would be made available on newsstands as well as through agents like Publisher's Clearing House. Finally, particularly in the early years, a certain number of free copies of the magazine would be sent to obstetricians' offices, birthing centers, and other similar outlets. Once again, the goal was to get women to read the magazine and subscribe.

The ultimate purpose of these efforts to gain readership was to create an attractive medium for advertisers. Most mature consumer magazines received at least half of their revenues from advertising rather than from circulation. However, attracting advertisers to a new magazine was very difficult and represented a classic "chicken and egg" problem. Wolaner believed that she would be able to overcome the reluctance of advertisers to commit to a new magazine by offering a cost-effective means of reaching an upscale audience. She intended to charge approximately $5,000 per four-color page of advertising, which translated to a $25 CPM[1] rate. For early advertisers in the magazine, Wolaner planned to offer incentives, including the opportunity to receive three ads for the price of two, or ten ads for the price of eight less 5%. Thus, one of the early adopters could place a page of advertising in each of *Parenting*'s first-year issues for a total cost of under $40,000. By contrast, the cost of a page in *Parents* was $38,000 (which represented a CPM of slightly less than $23). Over time, as the circulation of the magazine increased, Wolaner believed she could increase dramatically the revenue generated from each page of advertising.

In the long run, there were other ways to generate revenues from a magazine like *Parenting*. For example, one possibility was introducing a monthly newsletter that would be targeted at specific subgroups in the *Parenting* population. Such a newsletter venture would require modest additional investment in editorial resources but would generate substantial subscription revenues. Also, as with most mass-market publications, Wolaner believed that mailing list rentals would be a very profitable source of income in the future.

According to Wolaner's projections, the payoff from a successful launch of *Parenting* would be high: by 1991, total revenues were expected to exceed $23 million, with pretax income of over $6 million. The magazine would break even in the third full year of operations. Wolaner's assumptions and related financial forecasts are summarized in Exhibit 27-6.

In order to accomplish her plans, Wolaner projected a cash need of over $4 million. She intended to raise $5 million in order to have some safety margin in the event her projections proved optimistic. Wolaner contacted a number of venture capital firms that had previously made investments in consumer marketing companies. She also

[1] CPM refers to the cost to the advertiser for a page of advertising divided by every 1,000 in circulation rate base. For example, if the rate base is 200,000 and the CPM is $25, then the cost of a page of advertising is $5,000.

EXHIBIT 27-4

PARENTING MAGAZINE

Editorial Overview

Parenting will help its readers make their own choices about what's best for their children by providing the most up-to-date information on children's psychological and physical development. It will also address *parents'* emotional and physical needs in major articles about such touchy issues as restoring intimacy to a relationship after the arrival of children. PARENTING will treat tough topics in an accessible yet authoritative way.

The brochure used in the direct mail test shows the general design of the magazine and many typical articles. The following section is a description of the regular columns, departments and features in PARENTING. Then outlines of two sample issues present the departments and features in the order they'd appear in the magazine.

Columns

A column appears in every issue and is usually one page. The headline is the same each issue, anchoring the magazine for readers by providing a familiar landmark. PARENTING's every-issue columns will be:

The Editor's View. Rather than retelling the stories behind the stories, as with most magazine editor's columns, this will be intensely personal. The column will set the tone, the ethic, and the theme of the magazine. It will demonstrate, through its perspective and human touch, that there is no dry approach to life, no sure-fire answers on these pages; that in the sensitive business of being a mother or a father, only caring, hanging in there and paying attention count.

Expert Opinions. Rather than simply printing our readers' letters, our column will offer a real give-and-take. Readers will voice their opinions on subjects covered in PARENTING, and our writers and editors will respond.

NewsBriefs. Up-to-the-minute news in medicine, psychology, law, education, the economy, etc. that affects our readers' lives.

First Choice. What's new and worth recommending for parents and children to read, watch and listen to. Our video, film, book, software, television and music reviews will help parents make educated entertainment choices.

What's In. This monthly underground report will give you an insider's understanding of what your child is saying, why she is straightening only one side of her hair, why he won't put shoelaces in his sneakers and, in general, where he or she is at.

Kidstuff. Our illustrated best-buys page. Our staff will comb American and European specialty catalogues and stores for unique products for parents and children.

PARENTING's Puzzle. On the last page of the magazine will be a challenge for the whole family—an illustrated puzzle for children to solve with or without coaching from their parents.

Cartoons

The subject of parenting lends itself to witty, provocative treatment by the nation's best cartoonists. Their cartoons will appear throughout PARENTING, breaking up solid pages of text and enlivening even the most serious writing.

Departments

Departments appear regularly in a magazine, though not every one appears in every issue and the length can vary: usually one or two pages, sometimes a department is important enough to expand to three or four pages, with photos and/or illustrations. Some run in the back, with the "editorial well" (major features) dividing the front and back. The following are regular headings; each department will also have a headline about the specific coverage in that issue.

Great Expectations. Every pregnancy is like a first pregnancy since no two gestations are predictably alike, and scientific advances made between one birth and the next can make the recommended prenatal care, delivery procedure and postpartum care different for each child. Expecting parents—whether for the first or the fourth time—will find the information they need to make pregnancy as safe and satisfying an experience as possible.

Childhood Profile and American Family Journal. People like to read about people, and these regular departments will showcase fine journalism. *Childhood Profile* will consist of excerpts from new biographies covering the early years of achievers like Georgia O'Keefe, Saul Bellow and Henry Kissinger. *American Family Journal* will be vivid reporting by gifted writers on little-known, but richly interesting, American families.

(Continued)

EXHIBIT 27-4 (Continued)

Single Parenting. Whether single by choice or circumstance, the sole parent of one or more children is faced with a job that can seem overwhelming. No other magazine addresses the special needs and problems of single parents such as the financial strain of patenting alone, the need for setting personal time aside and how to help children adjust to a single parent's social life.

Child Care. To whom do you give the ultimate responsibility of caring for your children while you're unavailable? How can parents choose and evaluate private nannies, small home play groups, and preschool programs for their children?

The Ethical Parent. This department deals thoughtfully with questions of the intelligent and ambitious parent. For example, the ultimate success in many fields means moving to a large city. But are parents sacrificing their young families on the altars of ambition? Is The Big City right for toddlers or adolescents?

Interaction. Is your praise loaded with future expectations? Is your discipline an effective deterrent or an unproductive punishment? When is giving your child what he or she wants giving in? When is it an affirmation of your child's autonomy? How do you shape the parent–child dynamic so that all family members feel respected and loved?

The PARENTING Interview. PARENTING will feature (in both question-and-answer interviews and profiles) those celebrities who make interesting observations about raising children or those who have made real efforts to raise healthy families. One or two magazine covers per year will feature famous faces (with their children when possible). The kinds of people PARENTING would cover include Meryl Streep, John Irving, Steve Wozniak, Sam Shepherd and Jessica Lange, Jane Pauley and Garry Trudeau, etc.

Kids Fashion. Shot on location, photographs of children in wonderful clothes can be visually stunning. PARENTING will examine style and material as well as practicality.

Learning. Too often parents are given a (or impose their own) schedule of normal development against which to judge their children's acquisition of skills. PARENTING will approach learning from a different perspective: Parents will gain insight into what a milestone in intellectual development means to *their* newborn, toddler and preschooler at whatever age that milestone is achieved.

Family Fitness. What feels like a good workout for one member of the family is a strain for another and barely an exertion for a third. How does one plan active outings that are healthy for the whole family? What physical fitness objectives should parents keep in mind for themselves? Their partner? Their children?

The Law. Family law is one of the fastest changing legal fields, and this department will bring human interest as well as guidance for readers. For example, one of the first things expectant or new parents do is *start* to write their wills—but then the process grinds to a halt: choosing a guardian is much more difficult than dividing the property. Some other topics that will be covered include the legal and tax aspects of child care, employment rights of pregnant executives, post-divorce custody and support, etc.

Family Finances. Today's household income has to be allocated and invested wisely to meet the high expenses of raising children now and building up funds for future education expenses and retirement needs. Investment and tax planning strategies will help readers make their income work hard to reach their financial goals.

Interior Design. Becoming a parent doesn't necessitate living in disarray and eating off "Sesame Street" plasticware. Children's furniture can be a welcome addition to the home and break-resistant dishes can grace the table. Parents can display their good taste even when their children are bent on destruction.

En Route. When is it safe to take an infant abroad? When is it *sane* to take an infant abroad? How to evaluate babysitting services offered by hotels, cruise ships or tourist bureaus. The best travel guides for parents. The least traumatic ways to leave the children behind while going on a business trip or away for a romantic weekend.

Family Business. Parenting is a growth industry, and this department will offer likely business reporting about the companies and people making the products PARENTING's reader's buy.

Food. Parents don't have to live on fish sticks, bologna and frozen french toast until their children reach the age of majority. Cultivating young tastes, building menus around flexible foods that can be dressed down or up, and sharing kitchen duties with young children.

Features

Usually four or five pages in length, features include illustrations or photographs and cover varied topics. They form the center, or "editorial well," of the magazine, in recognition of readers' limited time and desire for quick, accessible information.

If PARENTING were now being published, it would run many of the departments and features in the following sample issue.

EXHIBIT 27-5

FEBRUARY *PARENTING*: FIRST ISSUE CONTENT

The Editor's View

Expert Opinions

NewsBriefs. New child care options being considered by companies all over the world . . . The Missouri study that indicates that parents can be taught how to rear their babies—and those babies will be smarter and better-adjusted as a result. . . . The crisis of skyrocketing insurance costs for child care providers.

Great Expectations

When Drugs Are Necessary During Pregnancy. For some women, the ideal of totally restricting intake of drugs during pregnancy is unrealistic. How women with such chronic health problems as diabetes, head, neck or back pain, or hypertension can have a healthy pregnancy despite their need for medication.

Single Parenting

The Courting Dilemma. What happens when two single parents find each other in a romantic way, and things get personal and, well, intimate? How do you get intimate, or should you, when there are small children in the house?

Child Card

English As a Second Language. Babysitters often harken from the far corners of the earth and feel most comfortable speaking their native tongue. Does exposure to two languages delay or retard speech development? Does it have beneficial effects?

The Ethical Parent

Do As We Say, Not As We Did. The almost universal desire of parents to keep their children from experimenting with drugs conflicts with the experience of many people who grew up during the 60s: how do you set a drug-free example for your children when, in fact, your college years were filled with marijuana smoke? What do you say to your child when his or her favorite sports hero is hauled into court on a cocaine charge?

Interaction

Friends for Life. Theorists of the last generation held that children didn't really socialize until they were three or four years old. Many parents of toddlers disagree. They say friendships can begin as far back as 18 months of age. According to the latest research, the parents are right. Does that mean that social calendars for two-year-olds are in order?

Law

Scientific Advances That Pressure Doctors to Pressure Mothers. Chorionic villus sampling, the new alternative to amniocentesis, is an extremely accurate pregnancy test for birth defects—so accurate that its effect is to impose a strict liability standard on physicians, that is, it's the doctor's fault if an unhealthy baby is born. Some doctors react by unnecessary testing.

Learning

"Not in Front of the Children." Most parents act as if their toddlers are deaf—talking about sensitive issues in front of them just as they did when the toddlers were newborns with no language skills. Then one day, the habit catches up with them and the mention of school provokes an anxious crying fit, or a reference to ice cream results in a temper tantrum because none is available. How much more language can toddlers understand than they can speak? When should parents start to edit their conversation?

Features

(COVER) First Love—Fathers and Daughters: Mothers and Sons

It's conventional wisdom that our style of loving a person of the opposite sex is shaped by our first relationship with that sex—our mothers and fathers. If a man has a good relationship with his mother, he'll probably make a stable husband, and likewise for fathers and daughters. But *what* is a good relationship? What makes a bad one? The cover story profiles people willing to speak candidly and insightfully about their parents—and their partners.

The Pregnant Pause: When Is Infertility Counseling Necessary?

Infertility counseling is available for a reasonable cost to just about every couple. But that doesn't mean that every couple will benefit from this sometimes traumatic medical intervention. Who should seek infertility counseling? Who should not?

Forum: Child Care

Periodically, PARENTING will sponsor discussions to address child-rearing issues. Members of the editorial advisory board, other specialists, and noted parents will meet to discuss questions such as "Is quality time a myth?" The focus of this forum will be a survey conducted among PARENTING's readers on how they are

(Continued)

EXHIBIT 27-5   *(Continued)*

solving child care problems. This original research will be newsworthy, and the forum should have room for ground-breaking clashes of opinion as well as valuable information.

The Art of Announcing
PARENTING scours the country for a portfolio of the most beautiful, most original, and most outrageous birth announcements.

Five Years at Sea
Vicky and Sy Carkhuff were tired of fighting the rat race, tired of the stockbroker trade and the parties and suburbia. So they fulfilled many readers' fantasy: they pulled five-year-old David out of kindergarten and began an amazing odyssey, a five-year sail around the world by themselves. David's education became correspondence courses taught by his mother in the belly of the boat. Now that they've re-entered the "real world," Vicki writes candidly of the experience.

Left Handedness: More Than a One-Sided Preference
New findings about left-handedness suggest that being a southpaw may have far-reaching effects much more significant than having trouble finding scissors that fit. From the structure of his brain to the effectiveness of his immune system, the lefty may have a make-up different from his right-handed counterpart.

Growing Up Funny
A noted television-comedy writer's journal of his attempts to instill a sense of humor in his daughter.

Discipline for Different Ages
Yelling at a one-year-old, reasoning with an eighteen-month-old and threatening a two-year-old don't work. What does? Psychologists and educators give their opinions about fashioning discipline for effectiveness at different ages.

Short in the Tooth
Your family dentist may say that brushing habits and dental checkups can wait three or four years until your baby is more mature. However, today's specialists in pedodontics (childhood dental care) disagree. They believe that good oral hygiene—like good personal hygiene—is a habit that should start right after birth to protect emerging teeth. What kind of dental hygiene is important for infants and toddlers?

Back-of-the-Magazine Columns and Departments
First Choice.   A round-up of the best new books—memoirs of well-known parents and children: Yael Dayan on her father Moshe; Wilfred Sheed's *Frank and Maisie: A Memoir with Parents*; John Cheever in his daughter Susan's words.

Family Finance
Options for Tuition Savings.   Tax revisions that are being considered by Congress this year threaten two of the most common tuition savings plans: Clifford Trusts and UGMA (uniform gifts to minors accounts). Both of these investment funds offer parents tax advantages because the money contributed to them is taxed at the lower rate of the child. If both of these savings plans are disallowed, what investment strategies could parents use to replace them?

Interior Design
Two Kids in One Room: Variations on a Theme. How to split up the space in one room to accommodate two children depends on the temperaments, ages, and interests of the children. Design prototypes that can be mixed and matched according to a family's individual needs are pictured here.

En Route
Ski Resorts That Welcome Young Children.   "Children under 12 not allowed" is frequently the last phrase in a brochure about an elegant vacation resort. A review of resorts that do cater to small children while maintaining an atmosphere appreciated by the parents.

Family Fitness
Avoiding Mountain Sickness.   If our readers are moved by the En Route column to take a ski vacation, this column will help them protect their families against high altitude sickness.

Food
Noodles for Them; Pasta for You.   Recipes for turning their plain spaghetti and tomato sauce into your sophisticated pasta dinner for two.

What's In

Kidstuff

PARENTINGS's Puzzle

EXHIBIT 27-6

PARENTING MAGAZINE: FINANCIAL PROJECTIONS

PROFIT & LOSS SUMMARY	1986	1987	1988	1989	1990	1991
REVENUE						
Advertising	$ 0	$1,154,105	$3,036,966	$ 6,086,650	$ 9,460,943	$13,128,416
Subscription	0	1,841,821	2,875,630	4,927,862	5,992,461	7,293,739
Single-copy	0	578,125	681,875	905,438	994,125	1,084,500
List	0	233,625	297,084	383,173	491,761	590,168
Newsletter	0	0	0	921,827	1,115,036	1,265,426
TOTAL REVENUE	0	3,807,676	6,873,555	13,224,950	18,054,326	23,362,249
EXPENSES						
Circulation	898,383	1,569,809	1,705,831	3,118,509	3,126,235	3,084,839
Advertising	373,009	1,023,741	1,293,293	1,667,168	2,021,419	2,231,950
Production	0	1,762,417	2,504,081	4,340,396	5,817,752	7,790,608
Editorial	385,193	1,444,274	1,400,016	1,785,791	2,031,584	2,051,961
Art	78,777	306,888	328,896	397,462	450,516	476,760
Administration	437,300	570,040	588,928	620,711	655,073	691,487
Newsletter	0	0	0	598,515	755,378	752,953
TOTAL EXPENSES	2,172,662	6,677,169	7,821,045	12,528,552	14,857,957	17,080,558
INCOME (LOSS)	(2,172,662)	(2,869,493)	(947,490)	696,398	3,196,369	6,281,691
CUMULATIVE NET INCOME (LOSS)	(2,172,662)	(5,042,155)	(5,989,645)	(5,293,247)	(2,096,878)	4,184,813
CASH FLOW SUMMARY						
RECEIPTS						
Advertising	0	1,142,020	2,999,677	5,921,798	9,360,232	13,047,308
Subscription	0	2,864,803	3,926,836	5,793,966	6,770,542	8,058,000
Single-copy	0	550,891	675,805	859,912	987,104	1,076,695
List	0	202,540	285,388	371,727	484,096	585,621
Newsletter	0	0	0	921,827	1,115,036	1,265,426
TOTAL RECEIPTS	0	4,760,254	7,887,706	13,869,230	18,717,010	24,033,050

(Continued)

EXHIBIT 27-6 *(Continued)*

DISBURSEMENTS

Circulation	$ 898,383	$1,569,809	$1,705,831	$ 3,118,509	$ 3,126,235	$ 3,084,839
Advertising	373,009	1,023,741	1,293,293	1,667,168	2,021,419	2,231,950
Production	0	1,762,417	2,504,081	4,340,396	5,817,752	7,790,608
Editorial	385,193	1,444,274	1,400,016	1,785,791	2,031,584	2,051,961
Art	78,777	306,888	328,896	397,462	450,516	476,760
Administration	437,300	570,040	588,928	620,711	655,073	691,487
Newsletter	0	0	0	598,515	755,378	752,953
TOTAL DISBURSEMENTS	2,172,662	6,677,169	7,821,045	12,528,552	14,857,957	17,080,558
OPERATING CASH FLOW (DEFICIT)	(2,172,662)	(1,916,915)	66,661	1,340,678	3,859,053	6,952,492
CUMULATIVE NET CASH FLOW	(2,172,662)	(4,089,577)	(4,022,916)	(2,682,238)	1,176,815	8,129,307

(Continued)

487

EXHIBIT 27-6 *(Continued)*

PARENTING MAGAZINE: ASSUMPTIONS FOR THE FINANCIAL PROJECTIONS

Major Publishing Assumptions	1987	1988	1989	1990	1991
Number of issues/year	10	10	12	12	12
Average circulation	262,000	326,000	408,000	494,000	551,000
Circulation pricing					
1 year introductory rate	$12	$12/15*	$15	$15	$17
Newsstand cover price	$2.5	$2.5	$2.75	$2.75	$3
Direct Mail**					
Volume (millions)	3.2	1.4	2.1	1.9	1.8
Average response***	5.4%	6.2%	5.6%	5.6%	5.7%
Pay-up	75.0%	67.5%	67.5%	67.5%	67.5%
First-time renewal rate		40.0%	40.0%	40.0%	40.0%
2nd & subsequent renewal			65.0%	65.0%	65.0%
Production costs/per copy					
Printing	$0.38	$0.44	$0.52	$0.59	$0.74
Postage	$0.16	$0.21	$0.26	$0.27	$0.29
Total per copy	$0.54	$0.65	$0.78	$0.86	$1.03
Average total pages/issue	102	115	135	167	182
Average ad pages/issue	30	50	65	80	89
Four-color ad rate 1,000 circulation	$25.09	$26.60	$28.19	$29.88	$31.68
Ad rate base					
	Sept. 86–	Feb 87–	Jan 88–	Jan 89–	Jan 90–	Sept 90–
	Jan 87	Dec 87	Dec 88	Dec 89	Aug 90	Aug 91
	200,000	300,000	350,000	430,000	500,000	550,000
Number of Employees					
Editorial	9	9	10	11	11
Art and Production	4	4	4	4	4
Advertising	7	7	9	10	10
Circulation	4	4	4	4	4
Administration	6	6	6	6	6
Newsletter			2	2	2
TOTAL	30	30	35	37	37
Annual Inflation Rate					
Postage	0%	15%	10%	0%	10%
Phone	10%	10%	10%	10%	10%
All other	5%	5%	5%	5%	5%

* The first price increase is scheduled for the middle of the second year.

** See pages 12–13 and 14 for a complete description of the direct mail assumptions used in the business plan.

*** As a magazine matures, the overall direct mail responsiveness declines so the business plan projections are based on a decreased percentage after the first year. However, because a lower amount of direct mail is planned after the launch, only the best performing lists will be utilized. This more selective mailing strategy results in a higher weighted average.

**** If paper, printing, postage rates or other expenses increase beyond the expectations of this plan, all magazines would be faced with the necessity of raising subscription and advertising prices. So PARENTING could compensate for any unexpected inflation without losing competitive ground.

(Continued)

EXHIBIT 27-6 *(Continued)*

PARENTING MAGAZINE: COMPARISONS WITH OTHER MAGAZINES

Comparison of Vital Statistics	Parents	Working Mother	Parenting Year 1	Parenting Year 5
Subscriptions	1,604,000	504,000	209,000	482,000
Single-copy sales (newsstand)	90,000	16,000	53,000	69,000
Advertising pages				
per year	1,131	945	302	1,062
per issue	94	79	30	89
Cover price	$1.95	$1.95	$2.50	$3.00
Subscription price	$11.95	$11.95	$12.00	$17.00
Advertising Price (CPM)	$22.81	$29.07	$25.09	$31.68

Note: Circulation figures for PARENTS and WORKING MOTHER are from the December 1984 Audit Bureau of Circulation Publisher's Statement. The figures for PARENTING are averages from the business plan. The 1985 advertising figures for PARENTS and WORKING MOTHER are according to ADVERTISING AGE. Subscription and cover prices for PARENTS and WORKING MOTHER are as of January 1986. PARENTING's 1986 CPM was set to equal that of PARENTS' 1986 CPM, plus 10%.

began the process of contacting various publishing companies that might have an interest in financing a magazine like *Parenting*.

The response from the venture capital community was positive but excruciatingly slow. Few venture capitalists had experience with magazines, which resulted in a protracted period of due diligence. Moreover, it was difficult to get the senior partners of the funds to make definitive commitments: most of the background work on the *Parenting* project was handled by associates within the venture capital firm.

The possibility of raising money from existing publishing companies was complicated because few companies were willing to hold minority stakes in ventures. Indeed, these companies were more likely to want to own 100% of the project. On the other hand, there were exceptions to the general rule and Wolaner began to explore options with companies like Times Mirror and Field Publications.

Wolaner had also considered contacting Time Inc., which was known to be considering a new magazine in the same general area. In late December of 1985, one of the venture capitalists who had looked at the *Parenting* deal suggested that Wolaner contact a man named Don Spurdle, a senior executive in the magazine development group at Time.

In January of 1986, Spurdle called Wolaner and suggested she come to New York for a meeting. When Wolaner arrived at Spurdle's office, she was immediately confronted with a dilemma: Spurdle's secretary handed her a release form that she would have to sign before her meeting. The document released Time from any obligations to Wolaner and her magazine and allowed Time to use any and all information Time might receive during discussions. Wolaner immediately headed for the elevators. She called her attorneys back in San Francisco (who had also invested in the partnership) and asked their advice. The attorneys suggested she sign the release, noting that it would probably be cheaper in the long run for Time to buy the magazine than to steal from it.

Wolaner returned to Spurdle's office and proceeded to lay out her plans. She and Spurdle had a very cordial meeting at the end of which Spurdle said it was very unlikely that Time would ever invest in a venture like *Parenting* under terms that would be acceptable to Wolaner. He wished Wolaner luck, joking that Time would probably end up buying her out in five years at some exorbitant price. Wolaner left the office impressed with Spurdle's publishing acumen but convinced that Time would not back her project. She made sure to take all of her direct mail materials with her as she left.

She returned to San Francisco to explore other financing options. The pressure to make progress was enormous. Wolaner had almost exhausted the seed capital, which had lasted well beyond the original October 1985 forecast. In early February 1986 she had sent out an appeal for an additional $50,000 (with each $25,000 receiving a 1.25% stake in the partnership equity). She had already succeeded in raising the full $175,000 targeted seed capital.

In spite of the pressures, progress was modest. Three different venture capital groups were continuing their due diligence. Discussions were also under way with Field Publications about possible participation. However, no one seemed close to a final decision.

Then, in late-February, Wolaner received a phone call from someone at Time Inc., who was a member of the team trying to put together the new magazine project. She said that her boss was interested in talking to Wolaner about a possible joint venture. Out of courtesy, Wolaner then called Don Spurdle who suggested she come back to New York for further discussions. Unbeknownst to Wolaner, Time had come to the conclusion that Wolaner was much further along with her magazine project than Time was internally.

In mid-March, Wolaner flew back to New York for a meeting with a number of Time executives, including Spurdle and Chris Meigher, Executive Vice President of the Magazine Group. The subsequent discussion lasted through lunch and well into the afternoon. Wolaner was peppered with questions by Meigher, Spurdle, Marshall Loeb (Managing Editor of *Fortune*), and a number of members of the Time group investigating the parenting field. The meeting was tough, but Wolaner felt she had more than held her own. Wolaner had made her points forcefully, including insisting that she owns 51% of the venture initially, and she had fielded the publishing questions well. She was also convinced that Time would be a good partner, one that could truly add value and increase the likelihood of success.

In late-March, Wolaner was asked to come back to New York for a meeting that would include Henry Grunwald, the legendary Editor-in-Chief of the Time Inc. Magazine Group. Once again, Wolaner was able to respond effectively to the questions posed by Grunwald and his fellow Time executives. As a result, Don Spurdle and a lawyer for Time agreed to come to California to work on the terms of a potential deal. That meeting was scheduled for March 27.

THE STANFORD COURT MEETING

Early on the morning of March 27, 1986, Wolaner, her husband and a lawyer met with Don Spurdle and Tom McEnerney, a Time Inc. lawyer. The negotiations were difficult, but substantive progress was made at each point. Some key negotiating issues that were resolved included a provision for each party to be able to buy the other party out. Some progress was also made on Time's insistence that Time buy out the interests of all the limited partners who had invested in the venture. Essentially, Time agreed to offer this group an amount equal to three times their original investment, but this proposal was subject to approval by the limited partners.

EXHIBIT 27-7

PARENTING MAGAZINE: *PARENTING* DEAL STRUCTURE OUTLINE OF TERMS

A. *Investment.*
   1. *Original Limited Partners.* The Original Limited Partners have contributed $175,000 and own an aggregate of approximately 34.5% of the equity. Time is to invest $5 million in the business in exchange for 45% of the equity. In addition, Time will offer to buy out the Limited Partners at three times their investment or a total of $525,000. Thus, Wolaner and Time will approach all 10 Limited partners with an offer from Time to buy them out at three times their investment. Rationale is that Time thinks it is preferable to have only the publisher as a partner. Upon the buyout, Time will own an additional 4% or a total of 49%.

   Limited Partners to agree in writing to be bought out at the time the agreement in principle is reached between Wolaner and Time *and prior to*:

   (i)   Time putting any money in the venture; and
   (ii) any publicity or announcement regarding the venture.

   2. *Capital Advance.*
   Upon resolution of the Limited Partners and execution of agreement in principle among Wolaner and Time, Time will make a $500,000 advance available to Wolaner for start-up expenses. These will be documented to Time as spent.

   Wolaner and Associates will sign a non-recourse, interest-free, promissory note which will provide that if the Wolaner-Time deal falls through, the note is re-paid with first money invested by any third party in the "Parenting" venture. The note would be a lien on that venture.

   Wolaner draws money monthly based upon budgeted cash needs for the succeeding month.

   Parties proceed diligently to sign definitive partnership agreement a quickly as practicable, estimated to be mid-May.

   3. *Time Capital Contributions.*
   Upon signing definitive partnership agreement, Time is committed to finance venture up to $3.2 million through July 31, 1987 when the benchmarks are to be met. If the benchmarks are met, Time is committed to fund the venture up to an additional $1.8 million or a total of $5 million. The $500,000 advance described in paragraph 2 is included in the $5 million. However, whatever Time spends to buy-out the Limited Partners will be in addition to the $5 million that goes into the venture.

   Wolaner draws money monthly based upon budgeted cash needs for the following month.

   4. If the venture fails to meet one or more benchmarks, then Time has the choice of whether or not to invest the additional $1.8 million.

   If Time decides not to invest any additional money, then Wolaner has 30 days to find a new investor and if she does, then Time gets bought out for a nominal payment. If Wolaner can't find an additional investor, then Time can sell its interest to a third party or cause the venture to liquidate. Wolaner retains ownership of the Parenting trademark and the idea for the magazine and the other assets are sold and the proceeds are distributed to partners pro rata based on invested capital.

   If Time decides to invest the $1.8 million even if the venture fails to meet the benchmarks, then Time assumes control of the day-to-day operations of the business and control of the management committee or other governing body. Time's equity is increased by 20 percentage points (to 65% or more) and Wolaner's equity is reduced proportionately.

B. *Benchmarks.*
Benchmarks are designed to measure the performance of the venture through July 31, 1987 as follows:

   1. For the period from January 1, 1987 through July 31, 1987, average monthly overhead cost shall not exceed $ _____ (number is 10% higher than budget).

   2. For the period from commencement of the venture through July 31, 1987, aggregate advertising sales revenue of the venture shall be not less than $ _____ (number is 20% less than budget). (Should be bookings plus actual for six or seven issues)

   3. For the period from commencement of the venture through July 31, 1987, certain circulation benchmarks, including subscription response rates, newsstand sales and payment rates must be met (numbers are within 15%).

(Continued)

EXHIBIT 27-7 *(Continued)*

C. *Management*.

Partnership Agreement to provide that day-to-day operation of the business is to be handled by Wolaner and Associates. There will be a five member Management Committee to oversee the business with three members being appointed by Wolaner and two by Time. The Committee will act by majority vote except for certain significant items which will require unanimous approval. Examples of these are as follows:

1. Borrowing money by the venture.

2. Admission of new partners.

3. Sale of Assets.

4. Approval of annual Business Plan and Budget but only so long as the venture has a negative cash flow for the prior 12 consecutive months.

5. Approval of contracts that have a term in excess of 12 months, unless cancelable without penalty on no more than 60 days notice.

6. Contracts in excess of $25,000 unless the expenditure is provided for in the annual Business Plan or Budget.

7. Distributions of cash from the venture to the partners.

8. Removal or appointment of auditors or legal counsel.

9. Commencement or settlement of legal proceedings.

10. Partnership elections under the Internal Revenue Code.

D. *Financials*.

The venture will operate on a calendar year and will have annual audited financial statements. The venture will provide the partners with unaudited quarterly and monthly financial information, including comparisons to budget.

Profits and losses will be divided according to the equity interest of the partners in the venture except that:

1. For tax purposes, Time may, if it desires, receive a special allocation of losses (e.g. 99% of all venture losses). Similarly, Time would then later re-

ceive a special allocation of profits, for tax purposes, that matches the special loss allocation.

2. Time will receive a larger share of profits and distributions (e.g. 80%) until such time as the capital investment of Time has been returned to it.

E. *Divorce*.

Except as otherwise specifically provided, neither Time nor Wolaner can sell, transfer or otherwise dispose of their partnership interests prior to December 31, 1987. In addition, Wolaner cannot resign as Publisher prior to this date. This is the critical initial period when Time's financial commitment and Wolaner's entrepreneurial expertise will be most needed.

After December 31, 1987 (September 1, 1987 if benchmarks are not met), Time may dispose of its interest to a third party, provided Wolaner shall have a right of first refusal.

After December 31, 1987, Wolaner may resign as Publisher in the following circumstances:

1. Time has acquired 51% or more ownership of the venture and has begun exercising day-to-day control of the business.

2. In the good faith judgement of Wolaner, Time's treatment of Wolaner shall be intolerable to her or irreconcilable business differences shall exist on material business matters affecting the venture, provided, however, that at least 45 days prior to any such resignation, Wolaner shall deliver to Time a written notice of her pending resignation, describing the nature of the problems or differences and the parties shall use all reasonable efforts to resolve the problem or differences prior to the end of the 45 days.

In the event Wolaner resigns, Time shall assume control of the Management Committee and the day-to-day operation of the business and Wolaner shall receive a lump-sum severance payment equal to 18 months salary. Time shall also have the right for a period of 90 days after the date of such resignation to purchase from Wolaner a portion of her equity interest in the venture so that Time would have 51% equity ownership. The purchase price would be $150,000 per percentage point of equity in the venture sold by Wolaner to Time.

(Continued)

EXHIBIT 27-7   *(Continued)*

F. *BuyOut.*

1. Time shall have the option to purchase Wolaner's interest in the venture during the period July 1, 1989 through December 31, 1989 at a price equal to her equity interest in the venture multiplied by the fair market value of the venture. For these purposes, fair market values shall equal (a) $XXX (amount to be determined) million minus (b) .75 multiplied by (i) the amount of money invested Time in the venture less (ii) the amount of such investment which has been returned to it prior to the date the option is exercised.

2. During the period March 1, 1990 through April 30, 1990 Time shall have the right to initiate the "shotgun" procedure.

3. During the period May 1, 1990 through June 30, 1990 either Time or Wolaner shall have the right to initiate the "shotgun" procedure.

4. During the period March 1, 1991 and April 30, 1991 (and each such two-month period in each succeeding year), either party shall have the right to initiate the "shotgun" procedure.

5. The "shotgun" procedure.

    • The party initiating the procedure does so by delivering written notice to the other party setting forth a value for the venture.

    • The receiving party has 30 days to decide whether to sell her or its interest or whether to buy the initiating party's interest.

    • The purchasing party must purchase the selling party's interest for cash within 120 days of the date the initiating party delivered the first notice.

    • Failure to pay such purchase price within said 120-day period shall be a default and shall (a) entitle the other party to reimbursement of legal, accounting and other expenses incurred in connection with the proposed buyout and (b) give such party an option to purchase the defaulting party's interest in the venture at 80% of the price set in the initiating party's notice.

G. *Miscellaneous.*

1. Upon a buyout by Time on or before December 31, 1989, Wolaner will remain as publisher for 18 months. For a buyout by Time in 1990 and beyond, Wolaner will remain as publisher for 12 months.

2. Upon Wolaner's resignation as publisher or a purchase by Time of Wolaner's equity interest in the venture, Wolaner will be subject to a 5-year non-compete agreement in the area of magazines relating to parents and/or children and related fields [to be refined further].

Wolaner also accepted the principle that Time would be entitled to a higher percentage of the equity in the event the venture failed to meet its financial projections. Time would also have the option to truncate its commitment at $3.2 million should certain hurdles not be surpassed.

One point that could not be resolved, however, related to granting Time the option to purchase Wolaner's stake in the venture at some point in the future. Time wanted to cap the price that it would pay. Wolaner and her advisors knew that successful publishing ventures were very valuable in the market, with typical valuations of 10 times normalized pretax income. If Time were to cap the amount that Wolaner would receive for her interest, then the actual price might be far less than fair market value.

After working for several hours on the buyout issue, the meeting broke up. Spurdle stated that he believed Time would insist on a cap and that further negotiations were fruitless unless Wolaner and her advisors relented on this issue. Spurdle and McEnerney left for the airport to take the "red-eye" back to New York. Meanwhile, Wolaner, her husband, and her lawyer left for the restaurant to discuss their options.

Wolaner was exhausted. The all-day negotiations had been tense, in addition to which she had a temperature of 103 degrees. While she understood the issue related to Time's right to buy her share in the venture, she was not sure that the position she and her advisors had taken was appropriate. After all, their terms would still result in a handsome payoff if the magazine were successful. And, considering the traditionally conservative posture taken by Time, much progress had been made. (Exhibit 27-7 contains a brief outline of the Time proposal.)

As Wolaner considered the menu at Rue Lepic, she wondered what to do next. She was totally committed to the creation of *Parenting*. Yet, her financing options were limited, and she was desperately short of cash. Moreover, she thought the people at Time could make a substantive contribution to the effort in addition to their capital. On the other hand, did it make sense to accept a contract that was potentially less lucrative?

28

A Note on Government Sources of Financing for Small Businesses

There are many sources of financing available to small businesses from federal, state, and local governments. The main source of funding from the federal government is the Small Business Administration (SBA). Many state governments provided funding for businesses through their state departments of Commerce, Economic Development, Trade, or Industry Development. Local resources include city governments and regional authorities anxious to further economic growth in their area.

According to the SBA, there are approximately 22 million small businesses in the United States. American small businesses employ more than 50% of the private workforce and generate more than half of the U.S. gross domestic product. Small businesses are also considered to be the principal source of new jobs in the United States.

In the United States, small businesses did not always have access to federal lending programs or other sources of government funds. A Department of Commerce study in 1935 on small business financing ascertained that of about 6,000 small manufacturing firms, 47% could not obtain long-term funds from any source.[1] The Reconstruction Finance Corporation (RFC) was established during the Great Depression to help both large and small businesses. During World War II, the Smaller War Plants Corporation (SWPC) was the first governmental agency established to assist small business. One of the functions of the SWPC was a loan program for small firms to assist in production for war and for civilian essentials. The SWPC made about 6,000 loans to small businesses. In 1946, the loan function of the SWPC was transferred to the RFC. During the Korean War, the Small Defense Plans Administration (SDPA) was created to make

---

Research Associate Catherine Conneely prepared this note under the supervision of Professor Paul Gompers as the basis for class discussion rather than to illustrate either effective or ineffective handling of an administrative situation.

[1] Deane Carson, ed., *The Vital Majority: Small Business in the American Economy* (Washington D.C.: Small Business Administration, 1973), p. 61.

recommendations for loan approval to the RFC. Over 400 loans had been approved, totaling $51 million, when the SDPA was abolished in July 1953. The Small Business Administration Act, passed in July 1953, established a new agency that took over the disaster loan program administered by the RFC and a business loan program.[2] According to Deane Carson, "the creation of the Small Business Administration was in response to a widespread belief that our private money and capital markets did not give small business a 'fair deal'."[3] These and other programs form the basis of assistance to new, emerging companies.

This note presents an overview of many federal and state programs designed to aid small business. The motivation and focus of these programs are analyzed, and the magnitude of the programs is profiled. Further information about government sources of financing for small business can be obtained at http://www.people.hbs.edu/pgompers.

MOTIVATIONS FOR GOVERNMENT FINANCING OF ENTREPRENEURIAL FIRMS

Governments around the world often develop programs aimed at financing young, entrepreneurial firms. The stated motivation for such programs usually involves the belief that the market for financing young firms is not efficient. Several arguments are frequently made as to the source of this inefficiency. The important element, however, is that a market failure needs to exist in order to justify a role for government intervention. If there were no market failure, then individuals who had profit motivations would come in and finance these firms in place of the government and would do it more efficiently.

Government officials often argue that young, entrepreneurial firms create a disproportionate number of new jobs and should therefore be subsidized. From an efficiency point of view, however, the government programs can only be justified if the market would not have financed these firms in the first place and if their benefits outweigh the program's costs. If the government money just substitutes for private capital, the program is not justified. Similarly, if the benefits of financing the firm are outweighed by the costs (which include overhead related to running the program and any incentive effects due to taxes), then the firm should not receive the capital. Most programs are not evaluated on this basis.

First, many governments argue that entrepreneurial firms create benefits for other companies and that the start-up cannot capture these benefits. These benefits are known as externalities. If, for example, a firm develops a new way of doing business that is easily imitated, then the start-up may not be able to reap the full profit potential from the innovation because others can copy it. In this case, no one would finance the start-up because the economic returns to the investment would be limited by imitation, even if the innovation improves output and efficiency in the economy. A government could provide the initial capital for the firm, and all citizens would benefit from the government's investment. Similarly, a start-up firm may provide additional value for other companies in the supply chain and may not be able to capture all of those benefits. Government funding would be justified because the public benefits are much larger than the firm's private benefits.

---

[2] Ibid., p. 99.

[3] Ibid., p. 40.

A second inefficiency that is often discussed is the capital constraints that young, start-up firms face. Proponents argue that informational asymmetries and the uncertainty/high risk of very young, start-up firms lead to an inability to finance these companies. The government, it is argued, can fill this funding gap by providing very early-stage, development capital. Little research, however, has been able to show whether this capital is efficiently deployed or substitutes for other forms of capital that would be available in any case.

Finally, government financing of small firms is often a political tool. Many small business groups are powerful political constituencies that politicians try to placate. By providing grants and assistance to young firms, the government can direct resources to its political supporters. This motivation is, however, less than efficiency enhancing.

FEDERAL SOURCES OF FUNDING

The major source of government financing available to small businesses is the Small Business Administration (SBA). The SBA was established in 1953 to "aid, counsel, and protect the interests of the Nation's small business community." The agency worked with intermediaries, banks, and other lending institutions to provide loans and venture capital financing to small businesses that were unable to secure financing through normal lending channels. Small Business Investment Companies (SBICs), licensed and regulated by the SBA, were privately owned and managed investment firms that provide venture capital and start-up financing to small businesses.

Many other federal programs were operated through government departments and agencies. The Small Business Innovation Research (SBIR) program and the Advanced Technology Program (ATP) were among other federal programs that provided funds to small businesses.

PROGRAMS OF THE SMALL BUSINESS ADMINISTRATION[4]

The Small Business Administration (SBA) was established by an act of Congress. Four years after its setup, in 1957, the SBA was granted permanent status. The SBA guarantees approximately $24 billion of total small business debt held by banks and finance companies in 1995. In fiscal year 1995, the SBA approved 55,596 loans totaling $8.259 billion, almost three times and double the dollar value of loans approved in 1991.[5] The SBA had a portfolio of approximately 180,000 companies across the United States in 1996.[6]

The SBA is involved in several aspects of small business financing. There are financial programs whereby the SBA guarantees loans for small businesses. The SBA runs an investment program—the Small Business Investment Company (SBIC). The SBA also assists small businesses in obtaining government procurement contracts. Counseling and development services are offered to small businesses, including SCORE (Service Corps of Retired Executives) and there were many programs designed to assist minority-owned businesses. The 57 Small Business Development Centers (SBDCs)

---

[4] Information in this section was taken from the SBA's Web site.

[5] Nancy Passapera, "SBA Loans: A Reliable Source of New Financing Opportunities," *Journal of Lending and Credit Risk Management* (January 1997): p. 68.

[6] Mitchell Stern, "The Insider's Guide to the SBA," *Working Woman* (October 1996): p. 44.

across the country, with a network of over 1,000 service locations, provide advice and training to new and existing business owners.[7]

The SBA generally provides the guarantee that enables businesses to obtain loans from lenders. Direct loans are available from the SBA under specific circumstances, such as loans for businesses in disaster areas. The 7(a) Loan Guarantee Program and the 504 Program are the SBA's main lending programs. The 7(a) Loan Guarantee Program had over $17 billion worth of loans approved since 1994.[8] Loans are made by lenders approved by the SBA and range from $50,000 to over $1 million.

The specialized programs under the 7(a) program include: LowDoc, which was designed to increase the availability of funds under $100,000 and expedite the loan review process; FA$TRAK, a pilot program that increases the capital available to businesses seeking loans up to $100,000; CAPLines, a program to help small businesses meet their short-term and cyclical working-capital needs with five separate programs; the International Trade Loan Program to help businesses engaged in international trade, or when a business is adversely affected by competition from imports; and the Export Working Capital (EWC) program, which is designed to provide short-term working capital to exporters in a combined effort of the SBA and the Export-Import Bank. Other programs include the Pollution Control program designed to provide loan guarantees to eligible small business for the financing of the planning, design, or installation of a pollution control facility, and the Defense Loan and Technical Assistance (DELTA), a joint SBA and Department of Defense effort to provide financial and technical assistance to defense-dependent small firms adversely affected by cutbacks in defense. The SBA also supports lending to minority and women small business owners. The Minority and Women's Prequalification Loan Program is a pilot program that used intermediaries to assist prospective minority and women borrowers in developing loan application packages and securing loans.

The SBA's 504 Certified Development Company (CDC) Program makes long-term loans available for purchasing land, buildings, and machinery and equipment, and for building, modernizing, or renovating existing facilities and sites. A CDC is a nonprofit corporation set up to contribute to the economic development of its community or region. Such companies work with the SBA and private-sector lenders to provide financing to small businesses. There are about 290 CDCs nationwide, each covering a specific area. A 504 project generally includes a loan secured with a lien from a private-sector lender which covers up to 50% of the project cost, a loan from the CDC covering up to 40% of the cost, and a contribution of at least 10% equity from the small business being helped. The program is designed to enable small businesses to create and retain jobs. The CDCs are obliged, therefore, to create or retain one job for every $35,000 provided by the SBA.

The SBA also has a Microloan Program that works through intermediaries to provide small loans from as little as $100 up to $25,000. Under this program, the SBA makes funds available to nonprofit intermediaries, which in turn make loans to eligible borrowers. The average loan size was $10,000. The turnaround on completed applications was speedy, for they could be processed by the intermediary in less than a week.

---

[7] Ibid.

[8] Ibid.

GENERAL DESCRIPTION OF SBA LOANS

The 7(a) Loan Guarantee Program provided loans to small businesses that had been refused loans from private lenders. Private lenders provided loans for the program which were guaranteed by the SBA. In fiscal year 1996, small minority-owned businesses received 9,099 Section 7(a) Guaranteed Loans worth approximately $1.7 billion. During fiscal year 1996, a total of 1,036 loans under the 504 program were made to small minority-owned businesses equating approximately $455 million. This represented an increase of 57% more loans and an increase of 58% in the loan amount over fiscal year 1995.

For most SBA loans there is no legislated limit to the total loan amount for which a business could apply. In the mid-1990s, the maximum amount the SBA could guarantee, however, was approximately $750,000. The SBA could guarantee up to 80% of loans of $100,000 and less, and up to 75% of loans above $100,000. Businesses could, therefore, receive over $1 million from a lender once approved by the SBA. The main considerations in the loan application for the SBA were a business's ability to repay the loans from cash flow, the owner(s)' exhibit of good character and management ability, and the amount of collateral available and owner's equity contribution. All owners of 20% or more are required to personally guarantee SBA loans. Although most small businesses are eligible for SBA loans, some, such as businesses engaged in illegal activities, loan packaging, speculation, multisales distribution, gambling, investment or lending, or where the owner is on parole, are ineligible. Real estate investment, other speculative activities, lending activities, pyramid sales plans, and charities, religious or other nonprofit organizations are also considered ineligible.

The SBA determines eligibility by four factors: type of business; size of business; use of loan funds; and special circumstances. Businesses are obliged to operate for profit and to do business in the United States. They also must have reasonable owner equity to invest and are obliged to use alternative financial resources first including personal assets. The definition of a small business according to the Small Business Act is one "that is independently owned and operated and not dominant in its field of operation." This definition varies from industry to industry. The SBA size standards defines the maximum size of an eligible small business. (See Table A.)

The proceeds of SBA loans can be used for most business purposes, including the purchase of real estate used for business operations; construction, renovation, or leasehold improvements; acquisition of furniture, fixtures, machinery, and equipment; purchase of inventory; and working capital. Among the special circumstances that the SBA considers for businesses which are otherwise ineligible include if the business is a fran-

TABLE A   SBA Small Business Size Standards (1996)

Industry	Size (revenues/employees)
Retail and Service	$3.5 to $13.5 million
Construction	$7.0 to $17.0 million
Agriculture	$0.5 to $3.5 million
Wholesale	No more than 100 employees
Manufacturing	500 to 1,500 employees

chise, a recreational facility or club, a farm or agricultural business, businesses involving fishing vessels, medical facilities, a change of ownership, or ownership by aliens.

The advantages of SBA loans include the relatively long maturities. Loan maturities are based on the ability to repay, the purpose of the loan proceeds, and the useful life of the assets financed. The maximum loan maturities are generally 25 years for real estate and equipment loans and 7 years for working-capital loans. Another advantage of SBA financing is that the interest rates are generally lower than those available to small businesses from other investors. The interest rate is negotiated between the borrower and the lender but are subject to SBA maximums, pegged to the Prime Rate.[9] Lenders have to pay certain fees to the SBA that could be passed on to the borrower once they have been paid by the lender. The amount of the guaranty fees is determined by the amount of the loan guarantee. In addition, all loans approved are subject to a 0.5% servicing fee. However, other fees such as processing fees, origination fees, application fees, points, brokerage fees, bonus points, and any other fees that can be charged to an SBA loan applicant are prohibited.

SBA SPECIALIZED PROGRAMS

Both the Minority Prequalification Pilot Loan Program and the Women's Prequalification Pilot Loan Program use fee-charging intermediaries to help minority and women borrowers develop loan applications and obtain loans. The loan package is submitted to the SBA for a decision that is usually made within three days. If the application is approved, the SBA issues a letter of prequalification which states that the SBA will guarantee the loan. The maximum amount for loans is approximately $250,000, of which the SBA can guarantee up to 90%. The intermediary then helps the borrower locate a lender offering the most competitive rates.

The Minority Prequalification Loan Program was established in 1995 as a pilot program at 16 sites. Between October 1, 1995, and September 30, 1996, the SBA guaranteed 110 loans totaling $11.6 million. Of the 110 loans, 74.5% were made to businesses owned and managed by men, and 25.5% were made to businesses owned and managed by women. Also, 44.5% of the loans were made to businesses owned and managed by Black Americans, 27.3% to Asian-American-owned and -managed businesses, 23.6% to Hispanic-American-owned and managed businesses, and 4.6% to Native American-owned businesses.

The LowDoc Program was designed to increase the availability of loans under $100,000 and to accelerate the SBA loan review process. The application form is one page long, and completed applications are processed quickly, usually within two or three days. The terms, interest rates, and uses were the same as for any 7(a) loan.

The FA$TRAK Program was another program designed to increase the capital available to businesses seeking loans of up to $100,000 It was a pilot program in the mid-1990s. Under this program, certain lenders were authorized to use their existing documentation and procedures to make and service an SBA guaranteed loan. There are no additional forms to fill and no waiting for SBA loan approval.

[9] Fixed rate loans could not exceed Prime +2.25% for maturities of less than seven years, and Prime +2.75% for maturities of seven years or more. For loans of less than $25,000, the maximum interest rate could not exceed Prime +4.25%, and for a maturity of seven years or more, +4.75%; for loans between $25,000 and $50,000, maximum rates could not exceed +3.25% and +3.75%. Variable rates could be pegged to either the lowest prime rate or the SBA optional peg rate. (Information as of 1996.)

Short Term Loans and Revolving Lines Of Credit (CAPlines) is a program through which the SBA can help small businesses meet their short-term and cyclical working-capital needs. There are five short-term working-capital loan programs for small businesses under the CAPLines umbrella: the Seasonal line, which gives advances against inventory and accounts receivable during peak seasons for businesses that experienced seasonal sales fluctuations; the Contract line, which helps finance labor and material costs under assignable contracts; the Builders Line, which helps small general contractors or builders finance direct labor and material costs; the Standard Asset-based line, which is an asset-based revolving line of credit for businesses which generally provides credit to other businesses; the Small Asset-based line is similar to the Standard line program, but has a lower line of credit available.

The International Trade Loan Program was aimed at businesses that engaged in international trade or that had been affected by import competition. For this program the SBA could guarantee as much as $1,250,000 in combined loans.

The Export Working Capital (EWCP) Program is designed to provide short-term working capital to exporters and is a combined effort of the SBA and the Export-Import Bank (Eximbank). The EWCP uses a one-page application form and has a turnaround of about 10 days. EWCP loan requests of $833,333 or less are processed by the SBA, while loan requests over $833,333 are processed through the Eximbank. In addition to the eligibility standards for all 7(a) program loans, an applicant must have been in business for a full year at the time of application for a EWCP loan.

SMALL BUSINESS INVESTMENT COMPANY PROGRAM

The Small Business Investment Company (SBIC) Program, which Congress established in 1958, had approximately 270 active licensed companies in 1996.[10] The SBIC program, administered by the SBA, was created to fill the gap in equity financing left by the SBA's credit provision programs. The goal of the program was to encourage the provision of long-term capital to small firms. The first two SBICs were licensed by the SBA on March 19, 1959.[11] There were two types of SBICs—the original SBICs and Specialized Small Business Investment Companies (SSBICs). In 1976, SSBICs were developed to target "the needs of entrepreneurs who have been denied the opportunity to own and operate a business because of social or economic disadvantage." The official name for such SBICs was Section 301(d) SBICs, so-called because they were organized under Section 301(d) of the Small Business Investment Act. From the beginning of the program through March 1996, regular SBICs financed approximately 60,636 different small business concerns, and specialized SBICs financed approximately 18,595 different small business concerns for a total of $14,036 million.[12] Many well-known companies were financed by SBICs during their initial growth, including the following: America OnLine; Apple Computer; Federal Express; Gymboree Corporation; Intel Corporation; Outback Steakhouse; Staples; and Sun Microsystems.[13]

SBICs are licensed by the SBA as privately organized and managed investment firms. SBICs used their own capital as well as funds borrowed from the government to provide financing to small businesses starting up or that are already established. Many

---

[10] Stern, "The Insider's Guide," p. 44.

[11] Carson, *The Vital Majority*, p. 70.

[12] SBIC Program Statistical Package, Table 3.

[13] Ibid., Table 16.

SBICs are owned by small groups of individuals, some are publicly held, and some are subsidiaries of large financial institutions. SBICs operate in much the same manner as venture capitalists. The majority of SBICs are motivated by profit. They hope to earn returns from the success of the small business.

The SBIC program benefits small businesses that qualify for assistance, venture capitalists investing in the program, and the public in general from additional tax revenue and job creation. The small businesses are able to receive equity capital, long-term loans, and expert management assistance. The SBA requires a minimum private capital investment of $5 million for a group to be granted an SBIC license. SBICs can obtain financing by acquiring private equity capital, publicly selling stock, taking advantage of government leverage, issuing debt securities, and obtaining loans. In return, the SBIC has the responsibility of financing small businesses. The SBIC can finance a small business in a variety of ways. Long-term loans with maturities of up to 20 years can be made to small businesses. The SBIC can also loan money in the form of debt securities whereby the SBIC holds a convertible security or the right to purchase equity in the business. The SBIC can also purchase equity securities in providing equity capital to the small business.

The SBA has certain regulatory requirements that protect the small business interests during the SBIC financing process. SBICs can invest only in qualifying small business concerns. The SBIC must avoid conflicts of interest by not engaging in "self-dealing" to the advantage of its associates. An SBIC is not permitted to control any small business on a permanent basis. The SBIC could not invest more than 20% of its private capital in a single business. Certain real estate investment and relending or reinvesting procedures are prohibited. Investment funds used to purchase securities have to go directly to the small business concern issuing the securities. The minimum period of financing is a five-year term.

The SBIC program did not prove to be very successful. The SBA reported that 1,361 SBICs were licensed over the 1959–1994 period. Of these, 455, or 33%, were transferred into liquidation between 1967 and 1994.[14] The failure of many of the SBICs can be linked to risky investments that were made in the early 1970s. Many of these investments were highly levered and had little operating history. Because many of the SBICs had little experience investing in young, start-up firms, the recession of the early 1970s resulted in the failure of many SBIC-backed companies and, hence, along with them the liquidation of many SBICs.

SMALL BUSINESS INNOVATION RESEARCH PROGRAM

The Small Business Innovation Research (SBIR) Program was initiated in 1982 with the enactment of the Small Business Innovation Development Act. Following submission of proposals, agencies make SBIR awards based on small business qualification, degree of innovation, technical merit, and future market potential. The SBIR Program consists of three phases. Phase I is the start-up phase. The project is evaluated, and

---

[14] Elijah Brewer, Hesna Genay, William Jackson, Paula Worthington, "Performance and Access to Government Guarantees: The Case of Small Business Investment Companies," *Economic Perspectives* (September/October 1996): 16. This study showed that of the 280 active SBICs in 1986, over 56% had failed by 1993. "As of September 1995, 189 SBICs were in liquidation with SBA-guaranteed debentures outstanding of over $500 million. The U.S. General Accounting Office estimated that only $200 million would ultimately be repaid."

grants of up to $100,000 are made. Only those businesses that are awarded Phase I grants are eligible for a Phase II grant. Phase II awards are up to $750,000, over a two-year period, to expand results obtained in Phase I. Private or non-SBIR funds are used to support Phase III. In this phase the product, service, or technology is brought to market.

In the first year of the program, 686 Phase I awards were made for $44.5 million to small high-technology firms. In fiscal year 1995, awards increased to 3,085 in Phase I and 1,263 in Phase II for a total of over $864 million. SBIR funding was expected to grow in fiscal year 1996 as legislation was passed requiring the participating agencies to increase their funding requirement from 2.0% to 2.5%.

All federal agencies with R&D budgets greater than $100 million are required to set up SBIR programs. Departments with SBIR programs include Agriculture, Commerce, Defense, Education, Energy, Health and Human Services, Transportation, the Environmental Protection Agency, NASA, the National Science Foundation, and the Nuclear Regulatory Commission. These agencies designate R&D topics and accept proposals.

Any funding received under the SBIR program is a grant, not a loan, and consequently the application procedure is a competitive process. Small businesses submit proposals for technological research and development. The SBIR applicants have to be American-owned and independently operated. The principal researchers have to be employed by the business, the companies have to be for-profit, and firm size is limited to 500 employees.

The SBA is the coordinating agency for the SBIR program. It collects the information from all participating agencies and publishes it in a Pre-Solicitation Announcement (PSA), which is the single source for the topics and closing dates for submission of solicitations to each agencies.

SMALL BUSINESS TECHNOLOGY TRANSFER PROGRAM

The Small Business Technology Transfer (STTR) program is similar to the SBIR program in that it fosters R&D by small businesses. The major difference between the programs was that funding was provided to joint ventures or partnerships between nonprofit research institutions and small businesses. Like the SBIR, the STTR program has three phases. An award of $100,000 is made during the year-long Phase I. Phase II awards are of up to $500,000 in a two-year expansion of Phase I results. Funds for Phase III of STTR must be found outside the STTR program. By this time, however, the research project should be ready for commercialization. The STTR Pilot program began making awards in fiscal year 1994. In that year it made 198 awards for almost $19 million to small high-technology businesses that collaborated with nonprofit research institutions to undertake R & D projects. In fiscal year 1995, 238 Phase I and 22 Phase II awards were made for a total of over $34 million.

The Departments of Defense, Energy, and Health and Human Services, and the federal agencies of NASA and the National Science Foundation are required to set aside a percentage of their R&D funds for small business/nonprofit research institution partnerships annually. As with the SBIR program, STTR is a highly competitive application procedure. Small businesses have similar eligibility limits in STTR and SBIR. The nonprofit institution must also meet certain criteria; namely, it has to be located in the United States and must meet one of the following definitions: that it be a nonprofit college or university, a domestic nonprofit research organization, or a federally funded R&D center.

ADVANCED TECHNOLOGY PROGRAM[15]

The Advanced Technology Program (ATP) was established by Congress in 1988 and operated at the National Institute of Standards and Technology (NIST) from fiscal year 1990 to fiscal year 1993 as an experimental effort. The program continued in 1994 on a more permanent basis. The ATP's mission is to provide support for the development of technologies to the economic advantage of the United States. ATP works in partnership with industries to accelerate the development of key technologies, which without the help of ATP, would be obsolete by the time they came to market. ATP did not fund companies that implemented product development. Projects are selected from proposals submitted by U.S. firms on a competitive basis. The recipients of the awards share the overhead cost of project R&D with ATP funds.

Between 1990 and 1996, the ATP made a total of 288 cost-sharing awards to individual companies or industry-led joint ventures. The ATP's cost-shared funding—with more than $1 billion in private-sector investment since 1991—enabled industry to pursue promising technologies that otherwise would be ignored or developed too slowly to compete in rapidly changing world markets. Nearly half (46%) of a total of 288 awards went to individual small businesses or to joint ventures led by a small business. There were 184 single applicants and 104 joint venture applications, and a total of 134 of the projects involved small businesses.

The ATP has a "unique mission—to support civilian technologies in the nation's economic interest." Some features of the program are that the ATP has "a broad mission to promote large economic benefits for the nation, works as a partner with industry, emphasizes cost sharing (ATP recipients on average pay more than half the total costs of the R&D), and has a comprehensive plan for monitoring and evaluating its performance." The program also takes an active role in ensuring the success of projects that are awarded funds. Projects are selected in a competition on the basis of technical and business merit. Each proposal is reviewed by experts in the subject area. An evaluation was made of the potential economic impact of the project. The proposer must be committed to the project in order to pass the review. Semifinalists receive in-depth oral reviews. Proposals are then ranked according to published selection criteria, and funding is awarded on the basis of the ranking.

The ATP implemented several new strategies in 1994. The program began taking a more active role in building cooperative programs among businesses, universities, and government agencies. It also pledged to assist interested companies in planning for future commercialization and in developing linkages with investors as well as intensifying the program's outreach efforts.

OTHER LOANS AND GRANTS FROM FEDERAL SOURCES

Agriculture

Financing for agriculture includes not only farmers' loan programs, but also aid to businesses involved in agriculture or the production of commodities. The Farmers Home Administration (FmHA), a division of the Department of Agriculture, and the Farm Credit Administration, a federal government agency, are the two main sources of funds for agricultural purposes. The Department of Agriculture's Farmers Home Adminis-

---

[15] Information in this section is from the ATP Web page.

tration Business and Industry Loan Program was established in the early 1970s.[16] FmHA provides loans to small agricultural enterprises and businesses in rural areas. The Farm Credit Administration runs the Farm Credit Program, which helps small businesses in commodity and agricultural operations. The Federal Land Bank Cooperative Associations provides long-term loans, and the Production Credit Associations provides short-term loans under the auspices of the Farm Credit Program. The Commodity Credit Corporation is another federal agency that helps entrepreneurs produce and market agricultural products abroad.

Community Development

Assistance is available from the federal government for community development through loans to businesses for local development, construction, or modernization of buildings; for projects servicing low-income areas with high unemployment or that had experienced natural disasters; or for projects serving disadvantaged individuals. The Rural, Economic, and Community Development Service guarantees loans up to $10 million to support projects that impacted the rural economic community.

The Department of Housing and Urban Development provides mortgage loans for builders of housing and renewal projects. The Economic Development Administration of the Department of Commerce, through its Business Development Assistance Program, helps businesses in redevelopment areas finance the cost of land, buildings, equipment, and working capital. It also runs a special economic and development and adjustment assistance program, which provides grants to businesses in regions threatened with economic deterioration due to the loss of a major employer or several smaller employers.

Export Programs

Many agencies make financing available for export-related purposes. The Export-Import Bank is a government agency whose primary purpose is to facilitate the export of American products and services through financing. The Exporter Credit Insurance Program provides insurance to exporters against loss due to nonpayment by overseas credit customers. The Commercial Bank Exporter Guarantee Program guarantees repayment of medium-term export debt obligations.

The Overseas Private Investment Corporation provides medium- to long-term financing for U.S. business ventures in developing countries through direct loans and loan guarantees. The Department of Commerce supports U.S. companies overseas in the Overseas Company Promotion program.

Financing for Minorities and Women

As well as the programs run by the SBA, assistance is widely available for minority-owned businesses or for businesses serving minorities or the disadvantaged from the federal government. The definition of a minority-owned business is one that is 51% or more owned by one or more, either minority or woman owners. Federal assistance is available to native American-owned businesses and programs that promote the business and economic development of reservations.

---

[16] The Insider's Guide to Small Business Financing. p. 84–85.

The SBA division of the Office of Minority Enterprise Development (MED) assists economically and socially disadvantaged business owners. The MED is authorized by Section 7(j) of the Small Business Act to provide assistance, through the Division of Management and Technical Assistance, to "socially and economically disadvantaged individuals and firms owned by such individuals, businesses located in areas of low income or high unemployment, and firms owned by low-income individuals." Fiscal year 1996 marked the twenty-eighth year of the SBA's 8(a) Minority Enterprise Development program, a government procurement program for minorities. During that fiscal year, a total of 6,115 businesses participated in the 8(a) Program and were awarded approximately $5.3 billion in contracts by the federal government. These firms contributed an estimated 158,648 jobs to the workforce.

Other federal offices and agencies that give assistance to minority firms and individuals for business expansion and development are the Bureau of Indian Affairs, the Office of Small and Disadvantaged Business Utilization, and the Minority Business Development Agency.

OTHER FEDERAL PROGRAMS

Among other programs established by government departments or federal agencies is the guaranteeing of loans for contractors engaged in national defense works by the Federal Reserve Board. The Maritime Administration guarantees loans for shipbuilding. The Department of the Interior makes and guarantees loans for businesses engaged in mineral and fishing activities.

The Department of Energy makes loans for many different R&D programs, including Electric and Hybrid Vehicle Loan Guarantees, to assist the manufacture or distribution of electric or hybrid vehicles. Other programs include: Research and Development in Energy; Research and Development in Fission, Fossil, Solar, and Geothermal; Electrical Storage Systems and Magnetic Fusion; Basic Energy Sciences; High Energy and Nuclear Physics; Advanced Technology and Assessment Projects; Biomass Loan Guarantees; Coal Loan Guarantees; and Geothermal Loan Guarantees.

The Catalog of Federal Domestic Assistance, which is available from the Government Printing Office and is published annually, lists many federal programs, including those that provide financing for small businesses.

STATE AND LOCAL SMALL BUSINESS FINANCING INITIATIVES

While too numerous to detail, most states have programs that provide financial assistance or incentives to small businesses. Such programs are administrated by departments and agencies within state or local government. There are many different programs available in each state, but most states have a department of trade or commerce that runs loan assistance, investment, procurement, and other programs. Small businesses assistance at the state level can be in the form of direct financial assistance, tax benefits, technical assistance, or through small business incubators.

The state can have a program for lending directly to small businesses. Loan guarantee programs, similar to those run by the SBA, are also available in some states. Other programs include security deposit programs, whereby funds are deposited into financial institutions that agree to provide low-interest loans to businesses specified by the state, and industrial development bonds (IDBs). The interest earned on the bonds is federally tax exempt, so IDBs are attractive to investors. The money from the sale of the bonds is loaned to businesses at low interest rates to subsidize the financing of land, site development, or other large fixed assets. The bonds can be pooled to meet the financing needs of several small projects. There is an annual limit on the amount of IDBs that can be issued in each state. Grants, equity venture capital programs, and target programs for small, minority or disadvantaged businesses are also popular state programs. Some states have chartered Business Development Corporations that make loans to small businesses.

At the local level, small business owners can contact city and county or township governments for assistance. In many areas, local development authorities can also be a useful resource in finding financing for new or existing businesses.

REFERENCES

BLECHMAN, BRUCE JAN AND JAY CONRAD LEVINSON. *Guerrilla financing: alternative techniques to finance any small business*. Boston: Houghton Mifflin, 1991.

BLUM, LAURIE. *Free money from the federal government for small businesses and entrepreneurs*. New York: Wiley, 1993.

BREWER, ELIJAH; GENAY, HESNA; JACKSON, WILLIAM; WORTHINGTON, PAULA; "Performance and Access to Government Guarantees: The Case of Small Business Investment Companies." *Economic Perspectives* (September/October 1996): 16.

CARSON, DEANE, ed. *The Vital Majority: Small Business in the American Economy*. Washington, DC: Small Business Administration, 1973.

GUMPERT, DAVID E., AND JEFFRY A TIMMONS. *The insider's guide to small business resources* Garden City, NY: Doubleday, 1982.

HAYES, RICK STEPHAN AND JOHN COTTON HOWELL. *How to finance your small business with government money: SBA loans*. New York: Wiley, 1980.

PASSAPERA, NANCY. "SBA Loans: A Reliable Source of New Financing Opportunities." *Journal of Lending and Credit Risk Management* (January 1997): 68.

SBIC directory and handbook of small business finance. Merrick, NY: International Wealth Success, 1989.

STERN, MITCHELL. "The Insider's Guide to the SBA." *Working Woman*, October 1996: 44.

United States. Office of Management and Budget. *Catalog of federal domestic assistance*. Washington, DC: Office of Management and Budget, annual.

United States. Small Business Administration. Office of the Chief Counsel for Advocacy. *The states and small business, programs and activities*. Washington, DC: Office of the Chief Council for Advocacy, U.S. Small Business Administration, 1983–

United States. Small Business Administration. Service Corps of Retired Executives. *Small business start-up information package*. Denver, CO: U.S. Small Business Administration, 1993.

Web Sites

Advanced Technology Program   http://www.atp.nist.gov/

Small Business Administration   http://www.sbaonline.sba.gov/

## 29

Torrent Systems

Rob Utzschneider slammed down the phone in disgust. He had just spent two gruel-ing hours trying to convince officials at the Department of Commerce's Advanced Tech-nology Program (ATP) that Torrent had, in fact, done nothing wrong. But it had been no use. Like a shark circling its prey, the ATP was sending a team of five bloodthirsty auditors to the offices of the Cambridge, Massachusetts-based company. They were scheduled to spend an entire week tearing apart Torrent's files and individually ques-tioning the company's personnel. The "inquisition" was about to begin.

Further complicating matters was the stack of unpaid bills that were piled high on Utzschneider's desk—bills that would have to wait until the whole mess was resolved. Although Torrent had been close to completing its ATP-sponsored R&D project—research that had progressed with flying colors—the ATP had suspended the company's funding pending further investigation. Unfortunately, Utzschneider had counted on those funds. And now he didn't even have enough cash to cover the payroll.

Utzschneider knew he had to face the harsh reality: There was a chance that the company he had co-founded three years earlier might soon go under. But why should the ATP penalize Torrent's success? Why should a company that was about to reach its goals be placed in an adversarial relationship with its strongest financial backer? To Utzschneider, it just didn't make any sense. Did the ATP realize that it was on the verge of destroying everything it had helped build?

TORRENT'S CORE TECHNOLOGY

During the late 1980s and early 1990s, information processing had become an increas-ingly pressing issue for corporate America. Growing numbers of companies—from com-mercial airlines to credit card vendors—had been capturing more detailed information about their customers and core business operations. Government agencies, too, had been developing new computer systems for tracking large volumes of data. And while this information accumulation had yielded some impressive gains in the form of higher

Research Associate Benjamin Kaplan prepared this case under the supervision of Professor Paul Gompers as the basis for class discussion rather than to illustrate either effective or ineffective handling of an administrative situation. Some information in this case has been disguised.

sales, lower operating costs, and improved customer retention, it had also heightened the need for more powerful data processing tools.

Torrent Systems was founded on the idea that converting these enormous transaction databases into meaningful information often required data processing power that was in excess of the capabilities of conventional mainframes, minicomputers, and workstations. Torrent further believed that parallel computers—machines with multiple processors that could break a problem into pieces and address those pieces simultaneously—represented the best and most cost-effective way to address these performance issues. By harnessing the power of parallel processing, Torrent emphasized, more sophisticated "database mining" techniques could be developed—methods that would better enable organizations to extract value from large volumes of data.

But Torrent's founders also stressed that widespread use of parallel processing had been constrained by the limited supply of programmers with the knowledge base necessary to take advantage of the hardware's capabilities. Because parallel programming was inherently difficult and required specialized expertise and training, many businesses ended up shying away from the technology due to the added risk and expense. Torrent aimed to dramatically reduce these development bottlenecks.

To achieve this goal, Torrent intended to use object-oriented design—a programming approach that encapsulated data within reusable objects—to insulate software developers from the complexities of parallel architectures. This would enable software developers to build applications for the emerging class of parallel computers without having to learn new languages, algorithms, or programming paradigms. Furthermore, "scalability" features would allow developers to build applications that easily adapt to large and growing volumes of data. The result, Torrent hoped, would be a substantial savings in time and cost, as well as improvements in portability and adaptability for businesses utilizing Torrent's software.

FAILURES BY "MASSIVELY PARALLEL" HARDWARE VENDORS

In 1994, a series of high-profile failures by "massively parallel processing" (MPP) hardware vendors illustrated the collapse of an industry built on a market that was precarious at best. The most notable of these failures was Thinking Machines Corp. (of Cambridge, Massachusetts) which filed for Chapter 11 bankruptcy protection in August 1994, following a nine-month attempt to attract a major new investor. Started by a group of MIT students a decade earlier, Thinking Machines had pioneered massively parallel processing—linking hundreds, even thousands, of inexpensive microprocessors into what it hoped would be a cheaper version of the traditional supercomputer. But the company had been unable to turn its technical wizardry into financial success. According to Richard Fishman, who assumed the helm of Thinking Machines in 1993, "There was a view that our technology was so superior that no one could challenge us. We were wrong."[1] Likewise, Kendall Square Research Corp. (also based in Cambridge) was unable to popularize a massively parallel processing machine and so followed Thinking Machines into Chapter 11 bankruptcy. Kendall Square Research, a publicly traded company, had been in such dire straits that its managers had improperly booked millions of dollars in sales. Other massively parallel computer manufacturers that fell by the wayside in the early 1990s included Alliant Computer Systems; Bolt, Beranek & Newman; and Wavetracer, Inc. In a mere five years, massively parallel processing had been trans-

---

[1] *The New York Times*, August 7, 1994.

formed from a promising technology with vast market potential, to an overpriced remnant of a disappearing industry.

The demise of these parallel hardware vendors had been the result of several interrelated factors. First, as the Cold War era ended and government funding for expensive computers began to shrink, the market for supercomputers began to collapse. Many universities, government agencies, and national research laboratories—organizations that depended on government funding—could no longer justify purchasing parallel supercomputers that had price tags ranging between $1 million and $20 million. Unfortunately for companies like Thinking Machines and Kendall Square Research, such organizations had accounted for most of their revenues. Furthermore, with the end of the Cold War, government subsidies for the design of supercomputers had seemingly evaporated overnight.

Second, parallel computers had gained little acceptance by commercial users. The hefty price of the hardware, combined with the substantial costs of software development, had created a scenario in which adopting a parallel processing system required large financial investments. Because of these substantial up-front costs, commercial customers tended to favor less expensive systems that were compatible with what they had used in the past. And with the future beginning to look bleak for such companies, potential commercial customers backed away from investing in their expensive hardware.

Third, small parallel computing vendors had faced increased competition in the race to design powerful computers for banks, retailers, and other commercial enterprises—the expected source of the industry's future profits. The promise of big sales in the commercial sector had drawn such established companies as IBM, Intel, Silicon Graphics, and Digital Equipment to the industry, luring customers away from smaller and less stable companies. The large companies that entered the market squeezed out the massively parallel manufacturers by selling increasingly more powerful machines that started in price at between $300,000 and $500,000. Furthermore, linked clusters of smaller computers and workstations were increasingly being used to do chores that once could only be handled by the biggest supercomputers. Research labs and companies alike were thus able to obtain some of the advantages of parallel processing, without the huge price tags and software headaches that accompanied massively parallel computers.

Venture capitalists had invested heavily in both Thinking Machines and Kendall Square Research, and had suffered heavy losses. Thinking Machines, for instance, had raised more than $120 million in private equity capital before its bankruptcy, including funds from the late William Paley, founder of the CBS television network. The high-profile downfall of both companies caused many venture investors to shy away from practically any investment that was related to parallel processing.

ESTABLISHING THE COMPANY: SEARCHING FOR FUNDING SOURCES

Torrent Systems (formerly Applied Parallel Technologies, Inc.) was founded in February 1993 and existed for 18 months before receiving ATP funding. During its infancy, the Cambridge-based company consisted solely of its two founders, Rob Utzschneider and Frank Carter. While Carter brought to the table the necessary technical know-how, Utzschneider provided the business acumen (see Exhibits 29-1 and 29-2 for individual biographies). During these early years, the founders spent most of their energy conducting background research on software architecture and market opportunities. They

EXHIBIT 29-1

PROJECT STAFFING

Torrent will staff the proposed project with a team of research scientists and engineers who will join the company upon an ATP funding commitment. A research team from NPAC [Northeast Parallel Architectures Center] at Syracuse University will contribute to the project as a subcontractor. In addition, three leading systems integrators and one major end-user involved in building large-scale parallel database mining systems will collaborate with Torrent to provide software developer and user requirements and to test the technology prototype developed in this project.

Torrent has a qualified candidate and at least one qualified backup candidate for every position in the project. The team has more than 100 man-years of experience in both research and technology development in several relevant technology areas. The team has published many technical papers and has completed federal R&D contracts and commercial technology development successfully in related technical areas. Torrent's affiliation with Geoffrey Fox and NPAC will provide direct access to one of the world's leading research scientists and university research centers in parallel processing. (See below.) Torrent's collaboration with leading systems integrators will provide important input from the commercial sector as well as technical direction and support reflecting hundreds of man-years in parallel programming, database mining, and systems integration. Abbreviated resumes of key team members are presented below.

Frank S. A. Carter is a co-founder of Torrent and the company's Chief Technology Officer. He has more than eight years of experience in parallel computing architectures, applications development, technical marketing, and systems support with a range of companies. Prior to founding Torrent, he was Director of Technical Marketing at Wavetracer, Inc. Prior to joining Wavetracer, Mr. Carter provided consulting on parallel architectures to Motorola and Nixdorf. Mr. Carter spent more than three years at Thinking Machines Corporation, where he worked in a range of positions in systems engineering, applications development, and project management. Mr. Carter has worked in development of neural networks and parallel computing architectures at Martin Marietta. Mr. Carter has spoken and written on many aspects of parallel computing. He has written technical reports on text-retrieval algorithms and programming in C/Paris. He holds a B.S. in Biophysics and Electrical Engineering from Johns Hopkins.

Dr. Geoffrey Fox is an advisor to Torrent and will direct NPAC's research efforts on the project. He is an internationally recognized expert in the use of parallel architectures and the development of concurrent algorithms. He is a leading proponent for the development of computational science as an academic discipline and a scientific method. His research on parallel computing has focused on development and use of this technology to solve large-scale computational problems. Dr. Fox is currently professor of Computer Science and Physics, and Director of the Northeast Parallel Architectures Center and InfoMall, all at Syracuse University. He established and directs the New York State founded program ACTION which is focused on accelerating the introduction of parallel computing into New York State industry. ACTION has excellent access to industry in computational science and established Master's and Ph.D. programs in this area at both Caltech and Syracuse. He earned his Ph.D. in theoretical physics from Cambridge University in 1967. He co-authored *Solving Problems on Concurrent Processors* and edits *Concurrency: Practice and Experience* and the *International Journal of Modern Physics*. His research experience includes work at the Institute for Advanced Study at Princeton; Lawrence Berkeley Laboratory; Cavendish Laboratory; Brookhaven National Laboratory; and Argonne National Laboratory. He has served as Dean for Educational Computing and Associate Provost for Computing at Caltech.

(Continued)

EXHIBIT 29-1 (Continued)

Stephen J. Smith is a scientist and Product Development Manager of Database Analysis Tools at Thinking Machines Corporation. His interests include the application of evolutionary coding techniques to classification and prediction problems involving large databases. He has led several projects recently, including TMC's development of the Darwin suite of pattern-finding and forecasting tools for commercial database mining, the SUPERSORT project comparing parallel implementations of the bitonic, radix, and sample sort algorithms, the XSORT project building an in-place, fault-tolerant external sort on the Connection Machine CM-5, and the building of a hand printed character recognition system. He has recently published works in journals, including the *Communications of the ACM, IEEE Transactions, Pattern Analysis and Machine Intelligence*, and *Complex Systems*. Mr. Smith holds an M.S. in Engineering from Harvard and a B.S. in Electrical Engineering from MIT.

Michael J. Beckerle is a Technical Staff Member of the Motorola Cambridge Research Center. His research interests include parallel processing, computer architecture, software engineering, performance measurement, compilation, and operating systems. Mr. Beckerle is Chief Architect for the software system of the START (*T) parallel processing system being implemented by the MIT Laboratory for Computer Science and Motorola. *T is a scalable computer architecture designed to support a broad variety of parallel programming styles, including those that use multithreading to tolerate the increases in memory latency which occurs as the machine size is scaled up. Motorola has recognized Mr. Beckerle's technical leadership on the *T project by promoting him to manage all software development efforts on this project. Mr. Beckerle developed a performance measurement system for the Monsoon hardware prototype created jointly by Motorola and the MIT Laboratory for Computer Science. Mr. Beckerle holds an M.Sc. in Electrical Engineering and Computer Science from MIT.

Dr. Brahm A. Rhodes has consulted with Torrent since the company's formation in early 1993. Dr. Rhodes has extensive experience conducting basic and applied research in a number of fields, including visualization and computer graphics; object-oriented, parallel, and distributed computing; and human–computer interaction technologies. Dr. Rhodes is recognized for his expertise in object-oriented software design. In recent work, he has headed several projects to develop advanced decision support, visualization, parallel computing, and user interface technologies. These include development of: an environmental visualization system; visualization, graphics, computational and simulation techniques using parallel processors; an object-oriented system using physically based modeling and rendering methods; and advanced user interface technologies for visualization, interactive multimedia, and decision support. Dr. Rhodes holds a B.S. in Electrical Engineering and an M.S. in Aerospace Engineering from Boston University's Graduate School of Arts and Sciences.

Dr. Andrea Carnevali is a Principal Investigator at Motorola Cambridge Research Center, where his research work has involved multithreading systems and fine grain computer architectures. Dr. Carnevali has participated in the development of an HPF FPRTRAN compiler. As a member of the MIT and Motorola *T research team, he has worked on system and application-level software design, including low-level split-phase transaction software. Dr. Carnevali designed and implemented message passing packages based on Active Messaging. He implemented a behavioral model of the *T multiprocessor which simulates program execution on *T and derives performance measures, including network statistics and parallel scalability. He has also developed a neural tree networks package and a parallel translator to the C language. Dr. Carnevali holds a doctoral degree in Electronic and Computer Science from Rome University. He graduated with a grade of 110 out of 110. His doctoral thesis was titled: "A Language Processor Generator: General Instruments and Application to Four Pascal Dialects."

Source: Company's ATP Proposal.

EXHIBIT 29-2

MANAGEMENT BIOGRAPHY

Robert Utzschneider.   Robert Utzschneider is a co-founder of Torrent and the company's Chief Executive Officer. He is responsible for Torrent's business direction, business development, and product commercialization. Mr. Utzschneider will participate in commercial aspects of collaborative efforts with systems integrators and end-users on this project. He has nearly 15 years of consulting and operating experience in corporate and start-up environments. Prior to founding Torrent, Mr. Utzschneider was vice president of product marketing at Wavetracer, Inc., a start-up developer of low-cost massively parallel computers. Prior to joining Wavetracer, Mr. Utzschneider provided strategy consulting, operating management, and investment banking to venture-backed start-up firms and public firms. He has been involved in market development and technology commercialization for technology start-ups in markets such as two-way interactive videoconferencing, paging, data communications, software and related services, voice messaging, and parallel processing. He has formulated business strategies for corporate clients while employed at Booz, Allen & Hamilton, Inc. Mr. Utzschneider graduated from Dartmouth College with honors in economics. He holds an MBA in finance and marketing from the University of Chicago Graduate School of Business Administration.

Source: Company's ATP Proposal.

---

also spent time cultivating relationships with leading systems integrators, hardware vendors, and end-users.

As their business plan began to crystallize, Utzschneider and Carter started to search for venture capital funding sources. But raising capital proved to be an extremely difficult task because most investors deemed parallel programming to be an extremely risky technology with a precarious commercial market. "A lot of venture investors saw hardware failures in parallel computers, and were consequently reluctant," said Utzschneider. "It was difficult to get a venture capitalist interested when companies back then didn't yet have the computers needed to use the software."

As a result, Utzschneider and Carter broadened their search to include government funding sources. They first examined the Small Business Innovation Research (SBIR) program—the largest U.S. public venture capital initiative—but concluded that the structure of the program was not a good fit for the demands of their technology. Because the SBIR program used a two-phase grant process, Phase I grant awardees needed to show substantial progress to be among the companies selected for the more substantial Phase II awards. But in the case of Torrent, a Phase I SBIR award (at the time no more than $50,000) was not a large enough sum to significantly advance their research. And even if the company did win a Phase II award, it still would need substantially more capital than the $500,000 Phase II funding ceiling would permit.

When Utzschneider and Carter examined the Advanced Technology Program, however, it was immediately attractive because Torrent could apply for up to $2 million in funds. Moreover, the government would not take a chunk of their equity stake in the company. The ATP funding would provide Torrent with the opportunity to develop its technology, construct a prototype, and thus demonstrate the value of its ideas to the private sector—investors who could fund the ultimate commercialization of the product. To Utzschneider, the ATP seemed to be a capital source tailor-made for a company like Torrent.

THE ADVANCED TECHNOLOGY PROGRAM

Program Overview

The Technology Competitiveness Act of 1988 created the Advanced Technology Program in the hopes of improving the competitive position of the U.S. economy. According to the statute that established the ATP, the program was initiated for the purpose of "assisting United States businesses in creating and applying the generic technology and research results necessary to (1) commercialize significant new scientific discoveries and technologies rapidly, and (2) refine manufacturing technologies."[2] The ATP began operation in 1990 with an appropriation of only $10 million. But the program, a component of the Department of Commerce's National Institute of Standards and Technology, rapidly grew to a 1995 budget of $341 million under the Clinton Administration. As of September 1996, the Advanced Technology Program had received more than 2,200 proposals in 22 merit-based competitions and had awarded 280 grants totaling $970 million in ATP funds.

ATP grants were awarded to companies that push the scientific or technical state-of-the-art. Some ATP-funded projects advanced technologies that would enable lower cost, higher quality, or faster-to-market products. Other projects would develop the know-how to provide new-to-the-world or radically improved products and services. But the common denominator of such research projects was that they involved "high-risk technologies"—defined by the ATP as "technical challenges which display significant recognized uncertainty of success, where success will dramatically change the direction of technology and its market impact."[3] A further condition of ATP funding was that projects needed to have the potential to generate substantial "spillover" benefits—positive externalities that accrued to others besides the direct recipients of the funding. In essence, the ATP selected projects for which it thought the potential return to the nation far exceeded the private rate of return on the investment.

The ATP allowed both individual firms and joint ventures to be eligible for its grants. The ATP did specify, however, that awards to individual companies were limited to $2 million over a maximum three-year duration; grants awarded to joint ventures were not subject to this size limitation and could last for up to five years. Over the course of the ATP's history, roughly two-thirds of ATP-sponsored projects had been conducted by individual companies, although a majority of the ATP's financial support had been allocated to joint venture projects. Universities, federal laboratories, and independent research organizations could also participate in ATP projects, but as subcontractors or members of joint ventures.

Within this framework, a wide variety of U.S. businesses, ranging from start-up companies to major industrial firms, had been selected for ATP grants. In some instances, the ATP aimed to "incubate" young companies whose technology was too early-stage to attract private capital. For more established companies, the ATP tried to fund projects that were of great benefit to the national interest but that might be too expensive, long-term, and high-risk for a company to pursue on its own. Since the program's inception, 36% of ATP funding had gone to small businesses, with an additional 10% going to joint ventures led by small businesses.

A unique aspect of ATP criteria, compared to other government R&D programs, was the emphasis on a project's commercial potential. Not only was each proposal re-

---

[2] Omnibus Trade and Competitiveness Act of 1988 (P.L. 100–418, 15 U.S.C. 278n), as amended by the American Technology Preeminence Act of 1991 (P.L. 102–245).

[3] 1996 ATP Bidders' Converence Materials.

viewed by scientific experts in the field, but ATP proposals that scored well in this technical review went on to a further evaluation of the business-related factors that affected the likelihood that a project would ultimately be commercialized. In addition, reducing the time it took for a technology to reach the commercialization phase was a prominent program goal:

> The ATP accelerates technologies that, because they are risky, are unlikely to be developed in time to compete in rapidly changing world markets without such a partnership of industry and government.[4]

But despite this emphasis on commercialization, the ATP made it clear that the program did not fund product development. Although the program took into account the business merits of a proposal in its selection process, ATP funds could only be used for *pre-product* R&D. According to program materials, the ATP "operates in the middle ground between basic research and product development."[5]

An equally important ATP objective was that the program foster, rather than replace, private-sector involvement. To avoid "crowding out" private investment, the ATP selected projects that were unlikely to receive adequate or timely financing by the private sector. The ATP also required cost sharing; individual companies were required to pay for all of their "indirect" costs, while joint ventures needed to provide more than 50% of a proposed project's resources. Such requirements were designed to ensure that companies had a vested interest in the completion and timely commercialization of their ATP-sponsored projects. On average, ATP grant recipients paid for more than half of the total research costs of their ATP-sponsored projects.

To select the projects best-suited for ATP funding, the program conducted merit-based competitions. Hoping to avoid conflict-of-interest and proprietary information problems, the ATP's scientific and technical reviewers were typically federal and academic experts. Business reviews were conducted primarily by business experts from the private sector who agreed to abide by non-disclosure requirements. And after these experts reviewed a company's written proposal, a select group of "semifinalists" had in-depth oral interviews.

Since 1994, the ATP had tried to maximize its leverage by devoting the bulk of its funding to focused program areas—multiyear efforts of approximately $20 million to $50 million per year targeted at specific industries. In selecting these industries, the ATP solicited suggestions from the private sector and evaluated potential focused program areas on such criteria as the impact on the U.S. economy, the quality of the scientific and technical concepts, the strength of the private-sector commitment, and the opportunity for the ATP to make a major difference. By 1996, the ATP had established 11 focused programs, including "Tools for DNA Diagnostics," "Digital Data Storage," "Vapor Compression Refrigeration Technology," and "Component-Based Software." The ATP also sponsored at least one general competition each year, which was open to U.S. businesses in all technology areas. Overall, ATP-funded projects spanned a broad range of industries, with particular concentrations in information technology, electronics, biotechnology, and advanced materials.

Despite the ATP's unique attributes, the program had been a frequent target of attack by congressional Republicans. Some tax-cutters and deficit hawks had claimed the program offered special favors and was wasteful corporate welfare. These outspoken

[4] 1996 ATP Program Overview.
[5] 1996 ATP Guidelines for Economic Evaluation.

critics of the ATP threatened, but were not able to achieve, total elimination of the program in 1995. In response to the continued controversy, however, the ATP's pace of awarding grants did slow in 1996. That year the agency funded only 8 projects, compared to 17 in 1995 and 32 in 1994.

Initial Submissions

Torrent first submitted a 10-page "white paper" to the ATP's 1994 general competition—a contest open to all U.S. technology-based companies. The ATP had encouraged companies to submit this abbreviated proposal before sinking extensive time and energy into writing a full proposal. In response to Torrent's white paper, the ATP informed the company that it was unlikely to receive an ATP grant, and it recommended that Torrent refrain from submitting a full proposal. According to Utzschneider, the rejection was likely a consequence of a competition "that was so general, it was hard to get anyone's attention."

Despite the setback in the general competition, in May 1994, Torrent submitted a new white paper to a specialized ATP competition designed to target component-based software development. Because this new competition specified judging criteria that was custom-tailored to a particular industry (which happened to match Torrent's core technology), Utzschneider and Carter felt they had a much higher probability of success in this focused contest than in the general competition. Furthermore, the founders believed that writing a full proposal would be a much simpler endeavor now that the ATP had outlined a detailed proposal framework that took into account the specific demands of the technology. The proposal could therefore be tailored to the specific criteria listed in the proposal.

By mid-June, the ATP had responded to Torrent's initial white paper and had encouraged the company to submit a full proposal. Torrent had been one of 10 companies that had received a positive response. And although the ATP had been vague about the number of grants that would ultimately be awarded, Utzschneider and Carter felt good about their chances. The founders spent the remainder of June and all of July drafting a full proposal, and focused special attention on adapting the company's R&D plans to better meet the ATP's detailed component-based software requirements.

The ATP's Component-Based Software Program

The ATP's focused program in component-based software was launched in April 1994, with an emphasis on improving software development technology for complex, large-scale commercial and industrial applications. A primary motivation for the program came from private industry itself; the ATP had received dozens of white papers discussing the need for improved software development techniques. These white papers repeatedly stressed the need for more systematic reuse, interoperation, and automation in the software design process.

To address this need, the ATP created a five-year program designed to fundamentally change the way software was produced. The program explicitly targeted component-based software—programming tools that streamlined and automated the software development process. The objective of component-based software was to create a programming environment in which software developers had minimal direct involvement with issues of syntax, form, representation, and implementation. Instead, the component tools would be sophisticated enough to compose software based on the intent of the developer rather than on following a huge number of error-prone instructions. Software developers would thus be able to concentrate on the needs of the specific end application; only a specialized group of component developers would focus on traditional design and implementation processes.

A key rationale for the ATP's component-based software program was the large potential impact on the U.S. economy. Because software provided infrastructure in a wide range of industries, enhancements in software development could result in large benefits to the economy as a whole. In the same way that interchangeable parts fueled the industrial revolution a century ago, it was hoped that component-based software could create massive gains in the productivity and reliability of software production. An additional impetus for the program came from the increased competition that the U.S. software industry faced from countries that could offer programming services at a fraction of the U.S. cost. The ATP hoped that a new component-based software paradigm would help the United States maintain its leadership position in software technology by enabling U.S. developers to concentrate on higher value, more specialized roles in software design.

The ATP held its first component-based software competition in 1994 and its second in 1995. There were 110 white papers and 96 full proposals submitted in the two competitions combined. The ATP's evaluation boards selected 18 of those proposals for ATP awards.

TORRENT'S COMPONENT-BASED SOFTWARE PROPOSAL

Project Overview and Timeline

In its submission to the component-based software competition, Torrent proposed to develop a technology prototype of an automated parallel software development environment. Torrent's proposed project was organized into four research and development activities:

1. *Applications R&D:* "Research, investigate, and validate that the proposed software system meets the software development requirements, application requirements, and performance requirements of commercial software development partners and users in the chosen commercial application."

2. *Parallel Primitives:* "Determine and create the appropriate subset of communication and system primitives as well as the mathematical subroutines to be used in the construction of the higher level components."

3. *Performance Optimization:* "Determine, measure and minimize any system performance degradation caused by the multi-layered hierarchical structure of the proposed component-based software environment."

4. *Design of the Object-Oriented Parallel Environment:* "Investigate, create and validate a general framework for the higher level component-based system that supports application portability, scalability, and extensibility."

As for the project's key personnel, Frank Carter, Torrent's Chief Technology Officer, assumed the role of Project Director for all aspects of the research. Dr. Geoffrey Fox, director of the Northeast Parallel Architectures Center (NPAC), was to serve as a project advisor to Carter. In addition, a separate principal investigator was assigned to manage each of the project's four main research activities. The proposal further specified that Torrent "had one candidate and at least one backup candidate for each of these four positions."

Selling the Proposal

In appealing to the ATP's selection criteria, the most prevalent theme throughout Torrent's proposal was the emphasis placed on the vast national returns that would result from the successful commercialization of the technology. Torrent stressed that its software would make parallel database mining techniques substantially more efficient and effective by "transforming a hand-crafted cottage industry into an automated process." And the proposal underscored the fact that parallel database mining could impact any sector of the U.S. economy:

> Solutions to many of these [information] problems could yield economic value totaling billions and even tens of billions of dollars throughout the U.S. economy. For example, application of parallel database mining could recover much of the $20 to $100 billion lost annually to health care fraud. . . . Parallel processing will enable U.S. airlines to save more than $1 billion annually from more efficient scheduling of crews.

In accordance with the ATP's objective of funding promising but high-risk technologies, the proposal further highlighted the project's significant technical challenges. Most notable was the challenge of creating components that were general enough to support many different applications, yet powerful enough to provide significant value for specific applications—an especially difficult task when dealing with infant technologies that had yet to achieve industry standardization. But at the same time that Torrent's proposal emphasized the substantial *technical* risks of the research, it also stressed that the *commercialization* risks of the project had been minimized. Because Torrent's potential product would address the largest commercial application in a market that was predicted to increase by at least $5 billion in the next five years, the company felt there would be a substantial window of opportunity.

Furthermore, Torrent had already lined up initial customers and distribution channels for its future product (see Exhibit 29-3). As a result, the founders felt strongly that Torrent would not require large marketing expenditures to generate the company's first $1 million in sales. And with commercial database mining systems costing from $1 million to $10 million each, the company expected that the technology would support rapid growth in revenues. The key, the proposal stressed, was conquering the initial technological challenges. Once that was accomplished, the founders believed that everything else would fall into place. The proposal boldly projected that the company "could generate $5–$10 million in annual revenues within two years of product completion, and accelerate growth in subsequent years." (Exhibit 29-4 outlines Torrent's commercialization plans.)

Last, the proposal emphasized that ATP funding of the project was essential to the timely development of industry-standard parallel software development technology. Each ATP dollar, the proposal suggested, would be highly leveraged through the stimulation of private-sector investment:

> Torrent's management has raised venture start-up funding several times during the past ten years, and has maintained contacts with venture investors since company formation. These investors have few concerns about the market for parallel software development technology, but have significant concerns about the technical risks associated with the proposed technology. These investors have no interest in funding Torrent's research and technology development. Such investors would fund product development and commercial-

EXHIBIT 29-3

PARTNERSHIPS WITH POTENTIAL CUSTOMERS

Management has positioned Torrent at the leading edge of paradigm shifts in computing and in software design. A core element of Torrent's technology development and commercialization plan is to work closely with the most innovative systems integrators and end-users to research, develop, and provide the proposed software technology. By linking Torrent's technologists with the brightest thinkers in leading-edge systems integration and end-user firms, Torrent will apply these new paradigms to real-world problems successfully. Such collaborations also supports the validity of Torrent's proposed research, technology development, product development, and business development efforts. This combining of technologists with innovative customers is the most proven method of researching, developing, and introducing paradigm-shifting technologies quickly and successfully, particularly for start-ups. Pursuit of this project in a commercial vacuum would lead to business failure.

Torrent has formed research and technology development partnerships with the three leading U.S. systems integrators involved in developing large-scale parallel database mining systems and with one major end-user. The systems integration firms share several characteristics: significant experience in building parallel software systems, organizational commitment to building businesses in parallel database mining; ambitious growth prospects; and understanding of parallel programming complexities. The four organizations include Epsilon, a subsidiary of American Express; Booz, Allen & Hamilton, Inc.; Fidelity Investments; and MRJ, Inc. . . .

Each organization has no viable alternative to the proposed technology and believes that software development bottlenecks will restrict their exploitation of emerging market opportunities. The three systems integration firms are working with more than 20 large commercial and government organizations in database mining and expect this client group to grow rapidly during the next two to three years. . . . The systems integration firms will eventually provide high-volume distribution of Torrent's proposed parallel software development technology.

Source: Company's ATP Proposal.

---

ization of an ATP-funded prototype of this technology. Some investors may also fund Torrent's indirect costs during the project if ATP funds the risks of research and technology development. . . . The provision of such funding by outsiders is contingent upon ATP funding of the proposed project. Torrent's founders have serious concerns about financing the company's research and technology development plans in the absence of ATP funding.

In actuality, the solicitation of venture capital support for the project had been far more difficult than the proposal indicated. Torrent had initiated casual meetings with potential venture capital investors beginning in the summer of 1994. North Bridge Venture Partners (of Waltham, Massachusetts) had shown interest in the project, but in light of the recent demise of hardware vendors such as Thinking Machines and Kendall Square Research, the venture capital firm clearly thought that Torrent would be a highly risky venture. And North Bridge had been optimistic compared to the other venture capitalists that had reviewed Torrent's business plan. Even assuming that the ATP was willing to cover the company's direct R&D costs, several other venture investors had deemed Torrent far too risky a prospect.

EXHIBIT 29-4

COMMERCIALIZATION PLANS

[The] ATP needs to assemble research and technology development funding, product development funding, and industry support to provide sufficient parallel software technology to attract enough applications developers to build a critical mass of parallel software systems to bring parallel processing into the commercial mainstream. Because of this, Torrent's research and technology development plan, product development plan, and commercialization plan are linked inextricably.

Since company formation, Torrent has oriented its research and technology development to reflect market requirements and minimize commercialization risks. This approach ensures that: (1) the company develops the right parallel software technology (technology focus); (2) the technology solves one critical real-world application and can be extended to other applications (application focus); and (3) the company develops relationships with partners who can disseminate Torrent technology broadly and rapidly once available (distribution focus). . . .

Following the proposed research and technology development, Torrent will commercialize parallel software in stages. Initially, Torrent will develop and market parallel software development technology for database mining. This will establish customers and cash flow required to support ongoing product development. Torrent's partnerships will ensure that its product technology addresses market requirements and will establish distribution prior to completing research, technology development, and product development. After building a base business in database mining, Torrent will extend its software technology and market it to leading developers in other applications. Torrent's next target applications may include seismic processing in the oil industry, financial analytics in the securities industry, and capacity optimization in transportation and process industries (refining, petrochemicals). Torrent management has initiated preliminary discussions with systems integrators and end-users involved with these applications. Success with developers in these applications will enable Torrent to extend its software technology and bundle it with leading low-cost parallel hardware, increasing Torrent's installed base and market momentum, and driving the software as an industry standard.

Source: Company's ATP Proposal.

Winning an Award

Torrent's proposal was due on August 1, and by the end of August, the ATP had notified the company that it had been selected as a semifinalist. The next hurdle for Torrent was an in-depth oral interview conducted by a panel of experts in the field. According to Utzschneider, the interview lasted more than four hours, with 90% of the time devoted to technological elements of the project and the remaining 10% focused on the business opportunity. Weeks after the interview, Torrent was notified that it had been awarded an ATP grant of nearly $2 million for its proposed three-year project. At the time, Torrent had been financed entirely out of the pockets of the founders, with no appreciable revenues yet generated. Torrent's full-time staffing consisted solely of the two founders, with four scientists and engineers contributing to the company as part-time consultants.

The Aftermath

Soon after Torrent received the ATP grant, North Bridge Venture Partners added $500,000 in seed funding to cover the project's indirect costs. According to Utzschneider, North Bridge may not have invested in Torrent if the company had failed to win an ATP grant. "We felt that the ATP grant sent a very strong signal to the venture capital firm that this is a good technology," said Utzschneider. "We wouldn't have gotten sufficient venture capital funding for the technology development without the ATP."

From November 1994 to February 1996, Torrent's research and development activities proceeded with flying colors. In September 1995, Carter was removed from his duties as day-to-day manager of software development because it was felt that Rick Burns could better manage the project. Carter, however, remained as Torrent's Chief Technology Officer and Principal Investigator for the ATP project. When the ATP visited Torrent in February 1996 as part of its annual review, the agency praised the company for the progress that had been made on its project. The company had already overcome most of its major technological challenges, had met all of its major milestones on schedule, and had developed a prototype. (See Exhibit 29-5 for Torrent's assessment of its progress.) In fact, Torrent's research had progressed so well that the company had begun discussions with North Bridge to invest in a second round of venture financing to help Torrent commercialize its technology. The February presentation emphasized the need to move forward on the commercialization front and outlined steps that Torrent would take in 1996 to get the technology into the market. Torrent had, however, planned to make a clear separation of expenses to ensure commercialization efforts were not paid from ATP funds.

Following the February meeting, however, Carter left Torrent. Even before Carter's departure, however, the day-to-day management of the ATP project had already been handed over to Rick Burns. This development had been discussed at the ATP presentation in February, and ATP had raised no objection. Following Carter's exit, Mike Beckerle, a full-time Torrent employee and the Principal Investigator for the performance optimization stage of the project, assumed the position of Chief Technical Officer and ATP Project Director. Even after his departure, Carter maintained a major equity stake in the company.

Carter's departure, however, created substantial tension with Torrent's ATP administrators. The ATP told Torrent that it was disturbed by such a development because a project director had never left an ATP-funded research project. ATP also did not feel that Beckerle was qualified to manage the project, even though his credentials were as good as or better than those of Carter.

From Utzschneider's perspective, however, the ATP was taking an inappropriate academic-based approach—one that assumed that a grant was given to a particular person. (See Exhibit 29-6 for ATP regulations regarding changes in project leadership.) Utzschneider further emphasized that such an approach was not appropriate for a business. He stressed that the grant had been awarded to the company, not Carter, and that the matter was an intellectual property issue—making the company free to hire the personnel it wanted. In addition, Torrent pointed out that Beckerle brought more than 10 years of research experience in data-flow architectures, parallel processing, and software engineering to the job, and was actually far more qualified for the position than his predecessor. Utzschneider sent ATP a package of nearly a dozen letters of recommendation for Beckerle from leading computer scientists. Similarly, the departure of a founding partner was not unheard of in young, venture capital-backed start-ups. If the skills of the founder no longer matched the needs of the company, a new manager was hired.

But the most significant aspect of the Carter issue was that it triggered a more heated debate over the extent of Torrent's commercialization activities. And it would be the issue of commercialization and the ATP's strict stipulation that its funds only be

---

EXHIBIT 29-5

TECHNICAL PROGRESS RELATIVE TO PROJECT RESEARCH GOALS (SPRING 1996)

As discussed earlier in this report, this project had four original research goals that were to be achieved by means of a research plan containing four activities, each of which contained a number of tasks. Torrent's realized progress relative to each task is discussed below.

1. Research Goal One: Applications R&D

   • Task 1: Applications Requirements Definition

   Status: Completed
   The application requirements for a basic parallel component framework have been reasonably well understood. Note, however, that applications requirements specifically related to data mining technology are discussed under task 3.

   • Task 2: User Environment Design

   Status: Open
   This task involved design of a visual programming environment for component-based application development. Only a cursory initial investigation into this area has been done, and Torrent plans to continue this work beyond the completion of the NIST project.

   • Task 3: Development of Application Expertise

   Status: Ongoing
   The application requirements for the predictive modeling subarea within the chosen application area of data mining are well understood. Other subareas of data mining remain to be investigated, and Torrent will continue its work in this area beyond the NIST project. In addition we need to understand the relationship between component algorithms and business problems soluble by data mining.

   • Task 4: Prototype Testing and Validation

   Status: Ongoing, though completed with respect to Basic Framework.
   With respect to the basic parallel software component framework, only internal testing and application partner testing have occurred. Requirements for significantly increased ease-of-use have been found, and we propose to carry out research beyond the NIST project. The purpose of this research will be to achieve improved usability by creating a new framework with much higher-level interfaces supporting semantic applications specification.

   With respect to data mining, we have substantial work to do to complete and evaluate technology, addressing even just the basic predictive modeling subarea of data mining. We plan to continue this area of investigation following the completion of the NIST project.

2. Parallel Primitives

   • Task 1: Data Transfer Operations

   Status: Completed

   • Task 2: Computational Intrinsics

   Status: Ongoing
   We expect to continue work in data-mining-related advanced analytical algorithms beyond the completion of the NIST project.

   • Task 3: Memory Management Functions

   Status: Completed
   Our framework design obviated the need for the work described under this task item.

3. Performance Optimization

   Status: All three tasks completed.

4. Design of the Object-Oriented Parallel Environment

   We propose to revisit some issues in this activity area as part of our ongoing work in semantic and usability enhancements. Torrent will continue this work beyond the completion of the NIST research project.

---

used for pre-product research and development, that would rapidly deteriorate the relationship between Torrent and the ATP. (Exhibit 29-7 examines the specifics of the ATP's rules concerning use of funds.) At about the same time as the Carter departure, Torrent had participated in what it called "an innocuous little announcement" with IBM. The press release stated that Torrent would introduce its flagship product, Orchestrate,

EXHIBIT 29-6

ATP REGULATIONS REGARDING CHANGES IN PROJECT LEADERSHIP

If a company in an ATP project (joint venture participant or single company) undergoes or foresees major structural changes (e.g., a company is being acquired by another company or is acquiring another company) that affects the management or organizational structure responsible for the ATP project, then the new management responsible for committing resources to the ATP project will need to provide ATP with written confirmation of continued commitment consistent with the approved project goals as part of the overall project change requirements.

Source: Advanced Technology Program: Proposal Preparation Kit.

later in the year. (See Exhibit 29-8.) But according to Utzschneider, the ATP accused the company of misrepresenting to the agency the extent of its product development. "The ATP thought the announcement meant that we were already far enough along to ship products," said Utzschneider. "They didn't realize that even before a product is ready, you have to build market awareness." Utzschneider added that he had no idea that such an announcement would be an issue with the ATP. "Where in the guidelines did it say that I have to clear such a statement with the ATP?" stressed Utzschneider. "We were careful not to allocate any ATP money to anything remotely commercial. I didn't think there would be a problem."

From Utzschneider's perspective, Torrent had made it clear to the ATP that during the project's second year the company would begin commercialization of the technology it had already developed—using non-ATP funds to cover product development costs. Furthermore, the company had clearly delineated two separate groups—a product group and an R&D group—funded by entirely different sources. The ATP grant would continue to fund research and development that would push the programming interface to much higher levels and would advance the technology's core algorithms. But while pursuing this research, Torrent wanted to establish a presence in the market.

EXHIBIT 29-7

ATP USE OF FUNDS REGULATIONS

There are certain types of projects that ATP will not fund because they are inconsistent with the ATP mission. These include:

1. Straightforward improvements of existing products or product development.
2. Projects that are predominantly basic research.
3. Precommercial scale demonstration projects where the emphasis is on demonstration that some technology works on a large scale rather than on R&D.
4. Projects involving military weapons R&D or R&D that is of interest only to some mission agency rather than to the commercial marketplace.
5. Projects that ATP believes would likely be completed with or without ATP funds in the same time frame or nearly the same time frame.

Source: Advanced Technology Program: Proposal Preparation Kit.

EXHIBIT 29-8

TORRENT'S PRODUCT ANNOUNCEMENT WITH IBM

TORRENT INTRODUCES PARALLEL DATA WAREHOUSING AND DATA MINING APPLICATION DEVELOPMENT ENVIRONMENT FOR IBM RS/6000 SP SYSTEM

BOSTON, Massachusetts, March 26, 1996—Torrent Systems (formerly Applied Parallel Technologies, Inc.) today announced ORCHESTRATE*, an advanced data mining application development environment for the IBM RS/6000** Scalable POWERparallel** Systems (SP**) server using the IBM DB2** Parallel Edition** (PE**) relational database management system.

Torrent has designed the ORCHESTRATE Development Environment to support construction of large-scale data warehousing and data mining software systems which fully exploit the capabilities of parallel computing and parallel RDBMS systems. By hiding the complexities of both parallel programming and the handling of large data, ORCHESTRATE enables commercial systems integrators and application developers to build these systems faster and at a far lower cost.

"ORCHESTRATE represents an important addition to the RS/6000 SP system software environment" stated Ben C. Barnes, general manager of IBM's newly formed worldwide Decision Support Solutions organization. "By making it simpler for application developers and systems integrators, including IBM, to build data mining software products and systems for the RS/6000 SP, Torrent and IBM can accelerate customer exploitation of large databases."

Data mining is the process of discovering hidden patterns and relations in large databases using a variety of advanced analytical techniques. Torrent intends to take advantage of the rich set of these techniques offered by IBM. In many applications, data mining offers distinct advantages over more traditional decision support techniques such as querying (e.g., SQL querying) and statistical analysis. Examples of problems which can be addressed using data mining software include finding fraud in credit card transactions, predicting which subscribers are likely to drop a magazine subscription, and identifying customer buying patterns in retailing chains.

Customer demand for large-scale data mining is growing quickly. Businesses are generating increasing volumes of data about their customers. Rapid declines in disk storage costs now make it possible to store massive amounts of data. Parallel computing and RDBMS systems provide the enabling technology required for building large-scale data warehouses and applying complex data mining techniques against the data. However, the complexities of both parallel programming and operating on large data has limited the development of data warehousing and data mining software systems which fully exploit the information contained in very large databases.

ORCHESTRATE facilitates migrating data from source repositories to the RS/6000 SP server and performing complex data conversions and transformations prior to loading the data warehouse. ORCHESTRATE also supports parallel data connections between advanced data mining applications and large-scale warehouses based on DB2 Parallel Edition. ORCHESTRATE includes an expanding analytical toolkit, incorporating neural networks and proprietary techniques, for parallel data mining. ORCHESTRATE also supports more traditional decision support techniques.

ORCHESTRATE provides the capability to run sequential third-party software packages in parallel transparently across the processors of the SP server. This allows software vendors and systems integrators to leverage the functionality of leading data warehousing and data mining software tools against large data without the complexities of running multiple instances across processing nodes of a parallel computing system. To provide the performance advantages of sorting large data sets in parallel, Torrent has integrated SyncSort***, the high-performance sort product from Syncsort, Inc., Woodcliff Lake, NJ, into ORCHESTRATE.

Coinciding with the product announcement, Torrent and IBM also announced a joint initiative to support third-party software developers and systems integrators in building data mining software tools and systems for SP systems and ORCHESTRATE. The program intends to support a variety of software groups: vendors of sequential data warehousing and data mining software tools; software developers interested in building advanced data mining software tools using ORCHESTRATE; and systems integrators building large-scale data warehousing and data mining software systems. Details about this initiative are available from Torrent. Torrent plans to release the initial commercial version of ORCHESTRATE by the end of the second quarter of 1996.

The RS/6000 platform, IBM's high-performance line of technical and commercial workstations and servers offer customers one of the most extensive families of UNIX-based solutions available in the marketplace.

From PowerPC-based workstations and servers for small and large businesses to symmetric multiprocessor and parallel computing systems for the most demanding of client/server or commercial on-line transaction processing applications, the RS/6000 offers powerful performance and price/performance to customers.

IBM's Software Solutions Division provides data management, application development and workgroup solutions for mission-critical applications on personal computers, workstations, LANs and host systems.

Source: Company documents.

An early commercial presence, Utzschneider believed, would help establish Torrent's software as an industry standard and would allow the company to benefit from the accelerated learning curves that often accompany early interactions with customers. In fact, the ATP had previously indicated that the company's well-designed commercialization plans had been a strength of Torrent's initial proposal.

The commercialization issue was especially frustrating to Utzschneider because he believed that in Torrent's case, the strict application of the regulation ran counter to the agency's fundamental objectives. It was creating a divergence between Torrent's agenda and ATP rules as the company moved closer to product development. ATP regulations stipulated that Torrent could only use the ATP funding in pre-product R&D, although it did not specify that the company could not undertake commercial activity. Many companies that had received ATP grants were selling products in the commercial market. In fact, Torrent had already begun commercialization efforts several months earlier using venture capital money, being sure to keep all ATP funding devoted entirely to R&D. It seemed ironic to Utzschneider that the ATP's mission was to rapidly commercialize enabling technologies and now they were about to stand in the way of that goal. In effect, Utzschneider believed the company was being penalized for its success. "A company shouldn't be terrified of writing a press release or of talking with a company," said Utzschneider. "In an effort to watch dimes, you lose sight of the big picture. The increased tax revenues alone would likely make up for the costs."

Utzschneider further highlighted the blurry distinction between pre-product R&D and the beginnings of commercialization. He stressed that the ATP had never clearly delineated between the two, and had in fact, told the company that it was supposed to use its best judgment in determining what was R&D and what was product development. "The company came to feel that there was a substantial risk involved in making the distinction between research and commercialization," Utzschneider said. It was also the case that Torrent had not changed anything since the February review. In February Torrent was a model company. By April, they were accused of misusing government funds. Utzschneider found it difficult to reconcile those two pictures of the same company.

As the relationship between Torrent and the ATP continued to unravel, other points of contention surfaced between the two organizations. Foremost among the controversy was the issue of personnel. Torrent's ATP proposal had included resumes of personnel that ended up not participating in the project. Because the labor market was competitive, the company had been unable to sign all of the prospective candidates that had been included in its initial proposal. The company had instead brought replacements on-board—personnel whom Utzschneider stressed were at least as qualified as those candidates included in the proposal. In addition, he had notified ATP about who was hired and who was working on the project in each quarterly report to the ATP.

As a result of all of these issues, the ATP told Torrent that they needed to thoroughly examine all of the company's records during a week-long, on-site audit. Utzschneider was shocked. "At the annual review in February, the ATP couldn't have been happier," Utzschneider said. "They called us a model project, and said that we had advanced faster than everyone else. But only a few weeks later, the ATP acted as if funding us had been a disaster." And because ATP grants are doled out in monthly installments, the ATP suspended Torrent's funding first for a week and then indefinitely, pending a thorough investigation. According to Utzschneider, one ATP auditor even threatened to shut down the company. Adding insult to injury was the fact that Continuum Software, a direct competitor of Torrent, continued to receive ATP funding even though its efforts lagged far behind those of Torrent. Moreover, the ATP's drawn-out investigation had created costly

EXHIBIT 29-9

PROJECT BUDGET

Torrent is submitting this proposal for ATP-funded R&D as a single applicant. Torrent plans to subcontract with NPAC at Syracuse University for portions of the proposed work and has budgeted $314,995 for this subcontracting work. Torrent proposes to cover all indirect costs (facilities, utilities, project administration, etc.) associated with the project. Torrent will also cover any direct costs associated with Robert Utzschneider's participation in the project. Torrent is requesting that ATP fund all of the direct costs of this project. These direct costs include one-half of the costs of employing Frank Carter, who will spend the majority of his time working directly on the project. Because the proposed R&D project involves software design and development, the majority of project costs are for direct labor, direct labor benefits, and equipment (workstation leases). These three categories account for 82% of the total budget requested from ATP.

Equipment costs include the costs of leasing Unix workstations under a three-year operating lease. Torrent has received a lease quotation of $607 per month from Electro Rent Corporation (Quotation #34880) for a three-year operating lease of a Sun SPARCstation 10. Torrent has added 20% to this quotation to cover software costs and system administration. Travel costs have been budgeted for trips to and from the subcontractor and systems integration partners. Torrent has assumed 4% annual increases in employee salaries.

Torrent requests a total of $1,983,493 in ATP funding for completing the proposed R&D project over a period of 28 months. Of this total, Torrent will require $872,731 during year 1, $835,271 during year 2, and $275,491 during year 3 of the project.

Detailed Project Cost Schedule

	Year One	Year Two	Year Three	Total Project
Total Project Direct Costs By Activity				
Activity One: Application R&D				
Principal Investigator direct labor (Stephen J. Smith)	$ 65,000	$ 67,000	$23,209	$155,209
Other Investigator direct labor	97,500	75,725	23,209	196,434
Direct labor benefits	43,875	38,698	12,533	95,106
Equipment	21,840	18,564	5,824	46,228
Travel	8,652	5,052	1,684	15,388
Subcontracts (NPAC)	50,052	50,052	16,684	116,788
Materials and supplies	1,368	1,368	456	3,192
Total Research Activity	$288,287	$257,059	$83,599	$628,345
Activity Two: Parallel Primitives				
Principal Investigator direct labor (Dr. Andrea Carnevali)	$ 65,000	$ 67,600	$23,435	$156,035
Other Investigator direct labor	60,000	62,400	21,632	144,032
Benefits	33,750	35,100	12,168	81,018
Equipment	17,472	17,472	5,824	40,768
Travel	4,452	4,452	1,484	10,388
Subcontracts (NPAC)	80,751	88,092	29,364	198,207
Materials and Supplies	1,368	1,368	456	3,192
Total Research Activity	$262,793	$276,484	$94,363	$633,640

(Continued)

EXHIBIT 29-9 (Continued)

Detailed Project Cost Schedule

	Year One	Year Two	Year Three	Total Project
Activity Three: Performance Optimization				
Principal Investigator direct labor (Michael J. Beckerle)	$ 65,000	$ 67,600	$23,435	$156,035
Other Investigator direct labor	30,000	31,200	10,816	72,016
Direct labor benefits	25,650	26,676	9,248	61,574
Equipment	13,104	13,104	4,368	30,576
Travel	1,170	1,404	468	3,042
Materials and supplies	855	1,026	342	2,223
Total Research Activity	135,779	144,010	48,677	325,466
Activity Four: Object-Oriented Design				
Principal Investigator direct labor (Dr. Brahm A. Rhodes)	$ 65,000	67,600	22,533	155,133
Other Investigator direct labor	65,000	45,067	11,717	121,784
Direct Labor Benefits	35,100	30,420	9,248	74,768
Equipment	17,472	14,560	4,368	36,400
Travel	1,932	1,932	644	4,508
Materials and Supplies	1,368	1,140	342	2,850
Total Research Activity	$185,872	160,719	48,852	395,443
Total Project Direct Costs (Four Activities)	872,731	835,272	275,491	1,983,493
Total Project Direct Costs By Cost Category				
Direct labor before benefits	$512,500	484,792	159,987	1,157,278
Direct labor benefits @27%	138,375	130,894	43,196	312,465
Equipment	69,888	63,700	20,384	153,972
Travel	16,206	12,840	4,280	33,326
Subcontracts (NPAC)	130,803	138,144	46,048	314,995
Materials and supplies	4,959	4,902	1,596	11,457
Total Project Direct Costs (All Cost Categories)	$872,731	$835,272	$275,491	$1,983,493
Total Project Direct Costs (ATP funded)	872,731	835,271	275,491	1,983,493
Total Project Indirect Costs (Torrent)	135,550	141,800	47,267	324,617
Total Project Direct and Indirect Costs	1,008,281	977,071	322,758	2,308,110
Total ATP Funding By Participant				
APT	741,928	697,127	229,443	1,668,498
NPAC	130,803	138,144	46,048	314,995
Total Budget Requested From ATP	872,731	835,271	275,491	1,983,493

Source: Company's ATP Proposal

EXHIBIT 29-10

TORRENT FINANCIAL STATEMENTS: 1995

TORRENT SYSTEMS, INC. (Balance Sheets)	1995
ASSETS	
CURRENT ASSETS:	
Cash and cash equivalents	$190,244
Grant receivable	$ 85,529
Prepaid expenses	$ 17,198
Total current assets	$292,971
PROPERTY AND EQUIPMENT, AT COST:	
Equipment under equipment line of credit	$233,508
Computer equipment	$ 14,044
Furniture and fixtures	$ 7,540
Office equipment	$ 1,649
Leasehold improvements	$ 1,456
	$258,196
Less − Accumulated depreciation and amortization	$ 82,901
	$175,295
OTHER ASSETS	$ 38,578
TOTAL ASSETS	$506,844
LIABILITIES AND STOCKHOLDERS' EQUITY	
CURRENT LIABILITIES:	
Current portion of equipment line of credit	$ 77,836
Accounts payable	$ 7,942
Accrued expenses	$ 26,940
Unearned grant revenue	$125,599
Total current liabilities	$238,317
EQUIPMENT LINE OF CREDIT, NET OF CURRENT PORTION	$105,382
STOCKHOLDERS EQUITY:	
Series A convertible preferred stock, $.01 par value—Authorized—616,000 shares	$ 6,160
Common stock, $.01 par value—	
Authorized—4,004,902 shares, Issued and outstanding—1,447,000 shares	$ 14,476
Additional paid-in capital	$647,064
Accumulated deficit	−$504,556
Total stockholders' equity	$163,145
TOTAL LIABILITIES AND STOCKHOLDERS' EQUITY	$506,844

(*Continued*)

EXHIBIT 29-10   (Continued)

TORRENT SYSTEMS, INC.	1995
REVENUES:	
License revenue	$ 0
Other income	$ 0
Total revenues	$ 0
EXPENSES:	
Research and development, net	$ 84,470
Selling and marketing	$0
General and administrative	$305,546
Total expenses	$390,016
Loss from operations	−$390,016
INTEREST INCOME, NET	$ 5,750
Net loss	−$384,266

(Continued)

---

time delays for the company. Utzschneider likened the whole ordeal to "Chinese water torture."

The sudden withdrawal of funds created great risks for Torrent. The company did not even have the cash to cover its payroll, and there existed a substantial chance that Torrent—which had practically nothing in the bank—would have to file for bankruptcy. (See Exhibit 29-9 and 29-10 for Torrent budgets.) Utzschneider was also concerned that the ATP would take back equipment that had already been counted upon for future projects. Furthermore, with Utzschneider trying to negotiate the $3.2 million infusion of capital from venture capital investors during this time frame, he was concerned that the company's ATP-induced financial crisis would get in the way of a deal. At the very least, Utzschneider now had almost no bargaining power with his venture capitalists. This venture capital investment was necessary to continue the commercialization efforts that had begun several months earlier. To Utzschneider, the ATP seemed to not recognize that it had paralyzed Torrent and was on the verge of destroying the company and all of the successful research Torrent's computer scientists had already completed. In addition, the ATP seemed inexperienced in dealing with fragile start-ups. "During a moment of crisis, a venture capitalist would be asking, 'How can we help you?'" Utzschneider emphasized. "The ATP did exactly the opposite."

What Now?

Despite the impending onslaught of ATP auditors, Rob Utzschneider still had positive feelings toward the program. Although Torrent's latest battle with the ATP was placing the company under tremendous financial strain, Utzschneider recognized that without the ATP, Torrent would either not exist at all or else would have been substantially

EXHIBIT 29-10   (Continued)

TORRENT SYSTEMS, INC.	1995
Statements of Cash Flows for the Year Ended December 31, 1995	
CASH FLOWS FROM OPERATING ACTIVITIES:	
Net loss	−$384,266
Adjustments to reconcile net loss to net cash used in operating activities–	
Depreciation and amortization	$ 77,082
Loss from retirement of property and equipment	
Changes in assets and liabilities–	
Grand receivable	−$ 85,529
Prepaid expenses	−$ 11,838
Accounts payable	−$ 437
Accrued expenses	$ 12,380
Unearned grant revenue	$ 56,623
Net cash used in operating activities	−$335,985
CASH FLOWS FROM INVESTING ACTIVITIES:	
Purchase of property and equipment	−$ 17,670
Increase in other assets	−$ 26,740
Net cash used in investing activities	−$ 44,410
CASH FLOWS FROM FINANCING ACTIVITIES:	
Issuance of restricted common stock	$ 10,780
Proceeds received under sale/leaseback of property and equipment	$111,369
Payments on equipment line of credit	−$ 50,290
Net cash provided by financing activities	$ 71,859
NET INCREASE (DECREASE) IN CASH AND CASH EQUIVALENTS	$308,536
CASH AND CASH EQUIVALENTS, BEGINNING OF PERIOD	$498,781
CASH AND CASH EQUIVALENTS, END OF PERIOD	$190,244
SUPPLEMENTAL DISCLOSURE OF CASH FLOW INFORMATION:	
Cash paid during the year for–	
Interest	$ 14,521
Income taxes	$ 4,674
SUPPLEMENTAL SCHEDULE OF NONFAT INVESTING AND FINANCING ACTIVITIES:	
Equipment acquired under line of credit	$122,138

Source: Company documents. (Data disguised.)

further behind in its research and development cycle. At a core level, much of what his company had been able to achieve could be attributed to its ATP award.

He just wished that he could have recognized in advance the substantial strings that would be attached to the grant money. But that was all in the past. Now he had to devise a workable resolution to the conflict. Legal action was an option, but he felt that such an action would likely only make a bad situation worse. Another option was the creation of a "rolling research agenda," in which other research activities could be substituted for projects that were deemed too close to the commercialization phase. But although the ATP had seemed willing to discuss alternative project models when the company was still on good terms, now the ATP seemed to be unwilling to consider alternatives. How would Torrent ever survive such an onslaught?

30

A Note on the Initial Public Offering Process

As has been often noted in "Entrepreneurial finance," the process of taking portfolio firms public is very important for entrepreneurial firms. While the claim of Black and Gilson that "a well developed stock market . . . is critical to the existence of a vibrant venture capital market"[1] may be overstated, there is clearly a strong relationship. To be a successful entrepreneur, an understanding of the initial public offering (IPO) process is important.

This note summarizes the mechanisms by which firms go public. It highlights some of the key institutional features associated with these offerings and suggests some explanations for why the process works as it does. While we note differences across countries, our focus will be on the major industrialized country with the greatest volume of offerings, the United States. Although the note must of necessity summarize the complexity and details of these offerings, the references suggests some sources for further reading for those who wish to learn more about this often-mysterious process.[2]

WHY DO FIRMS GO PUBLIC?

Firms and their investors typically have several motivations for going public. At the same time, some real costs may also be associated with such a transaction. The relative importance of these competing factors may vary across time and circumstances.

Professor Josh Lerner prepared this note as the basis for class discussion.

[1] Bernard S. Black and Ronald J. Gilson, "Venture Capital and the Structure of Capital Markets: Banks versus Stock Markets," *Journal of Financial Economics* 47 (1998): 243–277.

[2] This discussion is based in part on a variety of sources, especially Jay R. Ritter, "Initial Public Offerings," in Dennis Logue and James Seward (eds.), *Warren, Gorham, and Lamont Handbook of Modern Finance* (New York: WGL/RIA, 1998); Josh Lerner, "ImmuLogic Pharmaceutical Corporation" (case series), Harvard Business School case Nos. 292-066 through 292-071, 1992; and Katrina Ellis, Roni Michaely, and Maureen O'Hara, "When the Underwriter Is the Market Maker: An Examination of Trading in the IPO Aftermarket," unpublished working paper, Cornell University, 1999.

Potential Advantages   One important motivation for going public is the need to raise capital. Many technology companies, such as new semiconductor manufacturers and biotechnology firms, require hundreds of millions of dollars to successfully introduce a new product. This kind of capital may be difficult to raise from other sources. Banks and other debt financiers, for instance, may consider the firm too risky to lend funds to. Meanwhile, even if a venture capital group was willing to finance such a company's initial activities, it might not be able to continue funding the firm until it achieved positive cash flow. For instance, most private equity groups are restricted to investing no more than 10% or 15% of their capital in a single firm. Thus, the need to raise capital to finance projects may be an important motivation to go public.[3]

A second motivation is the desire to achieve liquidity. Entrepreneurs are likely to worry about placing "all their eggs in one basket" and will seek to achieve diversification by selling some of their shares. Private equity investors are also likely to desire to liquidate their investments in a timely manner, whether through outright sales of the shares or through the distribution of the shares to their investors, in order to achieve a high rate of return.[4]

Achieving liquidity, however, is typically not done at the time of the IPO. This is because of the fears of investment bankers, who worry that if insiders such as entrepreneurs and board members are seen as "bailing out" at the time of the offering, new investors will be unwilling to purchase shares. (Insider sales at the time of the IPO are more common among private equity-backed firms in Europe.) Thus, they seek to prohibit or severely limit the sale of shares at the time of offering and to restrict any additional sales during a "lock-up" period. (In addition, the speed and timing of sales by insiders may be restricted by government regulations, as is the case in the United States.) After the lock-up period expires, however, insider sales are likely.

A third motivation is that going public may help the firm in its interactions with customers or suppliers. Being a public firm can help a firm project an image of stability and dependability. This is particularly important in industries where products do not represent a one-time purchase but require ongoing service or upgrades. For instance, a corporation may be unwilling to purchase software to run a critical function from a small private firm that might soon disappear and not be available to offer upgrades or address problems. Enhanced visibility is a particularly important rationale for foreign technology companies seeking to break into the U.S. market, who have increasingly chosen to go public on the NASDAQ exchange in New York rather than on their local exchange.

Potential Disadvantages   At the same time, going public involves some real costs, which lead many firms to resist going public:

- The legal, accounting, and investment banking fees from an offering are substantial, frequently totaling 10% of the total amount raised in the offering or more.
- The degree of disclosure and scrutiny associated with being a publicly traded concern may be troubling, especially for a family business that has been run as a private firm for several decades.

---

[3] It should be noted that many firms raise far more in follow-on offerings than they do in their IPOs. But the IPO may provide important advantages: even if the firm does not raise all the financing that it needs in the initial offering, it is likely to find a follow-on offering to raise more equity substantially quicker to arrange and less expensive after it is publicly traded.

[4] For more about private equity distributions, see "Rogers Casey Alternative Investments," Harvard Business School case No. 296-024.

- If a firm files to go public and the offering must be subsequently withdrawn, even due to factors beyond the company's control, some managers fear that the company may be "tainted." In particular, other investors may be reluctant to even consider investing in the concern, presuming that the reason that it was forced to withdraw its IPO was due to some ethical lapse or fundamental business problem.

Another complication is introduced by the fact that the market's appetite for new issues appears to vary dramatically over time. In particular, the volume of IPOs changes dramatically from year to year. These periods of high IPO activity appear to follow periods when stock prices have risen sharply. The bunching of offerings is even more dramatic when patterns are examined on an industry basis. During these periods, firms may find it significantly easier to sell shares in IPOs to investors.

WHAT IS THE IPO PROCESS?

The process by which firms go public is a complex one. This summary highlights the crucial steps along this journey.

First Steps The first step in the going public process is the selection of the underwriter. Firms considering going public will frequently be courted by several investment banks. Among the criteria used by firms and their private equity investors to evaluate banks are the reputation of the research analyst covering the firm's industry, the commitments made to provide analyst coverage in the months or years after the offering, and the performance of past IPOs underwritten by the investment bank. One arena where investment banks very infrequently compete is in the pricing of the transactions. A fee of 7% of the capital raised, plus the legal and other costs borne by the bank, is standard across investment banks of both high and low caliber.[5]

In many cases, firms select multiple underwriters to manage the offering. These might include, for instance, a smaller investment bank that specializes in a particular industry and a larger bank with the ability to market equities very effectively. (For instance, many high-quality venture backed deals are underwritten by a technology specialist such as Hambrecht & Quist and one of the largest, most prestigious underwriters such as Goldman, Sachs or Salomon Smith Barney, termed a "bulge bracket" bracket firms in Wall Street parlance.) Only one of the banks, however, will be designated as the lead, or book, underwriter. This firm will be responsible for the most critical function, the management of the records of who desires shares in the new offering and the allocation of the shares among investors. The managing or co-managing banks will in turn recruit other banks and brokerage houses to join the "syndicate," the consortium that will actually sell the offering to its clients. Thus, while only one to three banks will actually underwrite the offering, the number of financial institutions involved is actually much larger.

Even before the offering is marketed, the underwriter plays several important roles. These include undertaking due diligence on the company ensure that there are no "skeletons in the closet," determining the offering size, and preparing the marketing material. In collaboration with the law firm representing the firm, the investment bank will also assist in the preparation of regulatory filings.

---

[5] In some small offerings, less prestigious underwriters may demand warrants from the firm in addition to a fee in cash. In some of the very largest offerings, the fee may fall as low as 5%. For a detailed discussion, see Hsuan-Chi Chen and Jay R. Ritter, "The Seven Percent Solution," *Journal of Finance*, forthcoming.

In most major industrialized nations, permission from one or more regulatory bodies is required before a firm can go public. In the United States, these are the Securities and Exchange Commission (SEC) and state regulatory bodies. The review of the SEC focuses on whether the company has disclosed all material information, not on whether the offering is priced appropriately. In past years, state regulators occasionally sought to assess whether an offering was fairly priced. (To cite one example, Massachusetts regulators had in December 1980 initially barred the sales of shares of Apple Computer in the state, even though it was an operating profitable company, on the grounds that its IPO price was too high.) Since 1996, however, all offerings being listed on one of the three major exchanges have been exempt from state-level scrutiny.

The extent of the disclosure required varies with the size of the offering and the firm. Many nations have provisions for simplified filings for smaller firms or for those that will be listed on one of the smaller exchanges. In the United States, for instance, firms going public with less than $25 million in revenues can use file Form SB-2 rather than the much more exhaustive S-1 statement; those raising less than $5 million can file under Regulation A, which requires even less disclosure.

There may be other regulatory requirements as well. For instance, in the United States, the SEC designates the weeks before and after the offering as the "quiet period." The firm's ability to communicate with potential investors during this period (aside from the distribution of the offering document, also known as the prospectus, and formal investor presentations) is severely limited.

Marketing the Offering   As the firm undergoes regulatory scrutiny, the investment bank begins the process of marketing the offering. It typically circulates a preliminary prospectus, or "red herring" (so named for the disclaimers typically printed in red on the document's cover), to prospective institutional and individual investors in the firm. In many cases, the firm will also undertake a "road show," in which the management team describes the company's lines of business and prospects to potential investors.

The actual mechanism used to determine the price varies across countries. In the United States, "book-building" is the most frequently employed approach. In particular, the underwriter learns from potential investors how many shares will be demanded at each proposed price, which enables him to set the best price for the company. All indications of interest are recorded in a central "book" compiled by the lead underwriter. In many other countries, however, the share price is set before the information about demand is gathered (though a number of these countries, such as Great Britain and Japan, have recently adopted the U.S. system in hopes of stimulating IPO activity). Elsewhere, other systems are employed, such as formal auctions to determine the offering price.

Reputable investment banks in the United States typically undertake only "firm commitment offerings." In these transactions, unlike "best efforts" offerings, the investment bank commits to sell the shares to investors at a set price. This price, however, is not set until the night before the offering, so the actual risk that the investment bank runs of not being able to sell the shares is very small. This information gathered about demand proves invaluable during the "pricing meeting" on the night before the IPO. In this session, the investment bank and firm bring together all the information about demand in order to determine the price at which the shares will be sold to the public. In determining a price, the bankers are also likely to factor in information about valuation of comparable firms, as well as discounted cash-flow analyses of the firm's projected cash flows.

The Day of the Offering and Beyond   Whatever valuation is set at the time of the offering, the share price is likely to increase on the next trading day. (On average, even the first trade of the stock is at a substantial premium to the IPO price.) While the median firm undergoes only a very modest increase in its price, a small but significant number of firms have experienced a significant jump in their share price after going public. This has been particularly true in recent years in the United States, where Internet companies such as Yahoo!, TheGlobe.com, and the Internet Capital Group, have all experienced jumps of several hundred percent on their first day of trading. But more generally, these types of high returns have been observed on the first day of trading across many nations and time periods.

Several explanations have been offered for this frequently observed pattern of high first-day returns:

- One possibility is that the increase in price (or the discount offered to investors who purchase IPO shares) is necessary to attract investors. Otherwise, uninformed investors might fear that they would be taken advantage of in offerings: for instance, informed investors would purchase most of the shares of promising firms, while leaving them holding the bulk of the unpromising offerings.

- A second possibility is that there is a "bandwagon" effect at work. Once sophisticated institutional investors indicate interest in a stock by buying shares, other less sophisticated investors "rush in" to purchase shares.

- A third explanation is that the investment bank frequently has "market power." This view suggests that bankers deliberately set offering prices too low in order to transfer wealth to the select investors whom they let participate in the IPO. These investors, having reaped big returns on the first trading day, will presumably reward the bank by steering other transactions, such routine custodial services, to the bank.

Each of these explanations is likely to capture some, but not all, of the complex phenomenon of IPO pricing.

Another commitment made by underwriters in the United States is to stabilize the price in the days and weeks after the offering. Typically, the underwriter will try to prevent the share price from falling below the offering price. In undertaking this stabilizing activity, the investment bank will almost always employ the "Green Shoe" option, a complex feature named after the 1963 offering where it was first employed. Essentially, investment bankers reserve the option to sell 15% more shares than the stated offering size. The investment banker will often sell 115% of the projected offering size: for instance, if the firm announced its intention to sell 2 million shares, the investment bank would actually sell 2.3 million. If the share price rises in the days after the offering, the bank simply declares the offering to have been 15% larger than the size projected initially. If the share price drops below the initial offering price, however, the bank will buy back the additional 15% of shares sold. This will allow the bank to help fulfill its commitment to support the stock price (the purchase of the shares may drive up the share price) while profiting by disparity between the price at which it sold the shares and the lower price at which it repurchased them.[6]

The relationship between the underwriter and the portfolio company does not end in the weeks after the offering. Rather, at least in the United States, a complex relationship continues, with many points of interaction. These include the analyst coverage

[6] When the bank is particularly worried that the share price will drop, it may sell even more than 15% of shares that the "Green Shoe" option allows. Essentially, the bank has then constructed a "naked short" position: it must buy back the excess shares, whether the share prices rise or drops. If the share price falls, it will once again have supported the price more effectively while profiting from its trading strategy. If the share price rises, however, it will need to purchase the additional shares at a loss.

noted above,[7] but also a variety of other roles. In virtually all cases, a U.S. investment bank will serve as a market maker: a trader responsible for insuring orderly day-to-day transactions in a security (including holding excess shares if necessary). In fact, the lead underwriter is virtually always the most important source of market-making activities in the months after the IPO. Finally, the underwriter of the IPO continues to serve as a financial advisor in most cases: about two-thirds of the firms completing a follow-on offering in the United States in the three years after the IPO employ the same underwriter.

ADDITIONAL INFORMATION SOURCES

BARRY, CHRISTOPHER B., CHRIS J. MUSCARELLA, JOHN W. PEAVY III, and MICHAEL R. VETSUYPENS. "The Role of Venture Capital in the Creation of Public Companies: Evidence from the Going Public Process." *Journal of Financial Economics* 27 (October 1990): 447–471.

BLACK, BERNARD S. and RONALD J. GILSON. "Venture Capital and the Structure of Capital markets: Banks versus Stock Markets." *Journal of Financial Economics* 47 (1998): 243–277.

CHEN, HSUAN-CHI, and JAY R. RITTER. "The Seven Percent Solution." *Journal of Finance*, forthcoming.

GOMPERS, PAUL A. and JOSH LERNER, *The Venture Capital Cycle*. MIT Press, Cambridge, MA, 1999, Section III.

HALLORAN, MICHAEL J., LEE F. BENTON, ROBERT V. GUNDERSON, JR., KEITH L. KEARNEY, and JORGE DEL CALVO. *Venture Capital and Public Offering Negotiation*. Volume 2. Aspen Law and Business, Englewood Cliffs, NJ, 1995.

MEGGINSON, WILLIAM C. and KATHLEEN A. WEISS. "Venture Capital Certification in Initial Public Offerings." *Journal of Finance* 46 (July 1991): 879–893.

RITTER, JAY R. "Initial Public Offerings." In Dennis Logue and James Seward (eds.), *Warren, Gorham, and Lamont Handbook of Modern Finance*. WGL/RIA, New York, 1998.

---

[7] Perhaps not surprisingly, it has been shown that investment banks issue more buy recommendations on companies that they underwrite than on other firms and that these recommendations seem to be excessively favorable (relative to the firms' subsequent performance).

31

Amazon.com—Going Public

Joy Covey, chief financial officer of online bookseller Amazon.com, settled into her airline seat and opened the day's *Financial Times* as her plane pulled back from its gate at London's Heathrow airport. It was April 30, 1997, and Covey and Jeff Bezos, Amazon.com's founder and CEO, had just completed the European leg of Amazon.com's "road show." Over the past three days, they had presented the company's investment story to dozens of European institutional investors interested in Amazon.com's pending initial public offering. They were returning to San Francisco to attend Hambrecht & Quist's Technology Investor Conference the next day, where they would meet scores of technology investors and analysts. Following the conference, they would launch the domestic leg of Amazon.com's road show, during which they would make 48 presentations in 20 U.S. cities in 16 days.

Covey was tired from their European tour but encouraged by the reception she and Bezos had received. Though she had not seen the "book"—the list of investors who tentatively had subscribed to purchase shares in the offering—she believed that the Amazon.com story had been well received. Frank Quattrone, Amazon.com's investment banker at lead underwriter Deutsche Morgan Grenfell, had told her that he had never seen a road show presentation as heavily attended. Covey and Bezos had fielded many difficult questions about the company's aggressive spending plans and sustained losses, but investors had seemed to understand the company's long-term investment strategy. They also had been willing to accept Covey's reluctance to disclose key operating metrics that she and Bezos felt were strategically sensitive.

As Covey flipped through the *Financial Times*, she noticed a headline that was becoming all too familiar: "Investors Skeptical on Internet Flotations." Despite a surge in the technology sector and a recent spike in IPOs of venture-backed technology start-ups, several prominent Internet commerce companies had recently encountered difficulties. Most notably, Auto-By-Tel, a leading online car retailer, had pulled its much-anticipated IPO the previous week. Covey was cautiously observing this market, uncertain of the impact that these events would have on Amazon.com's offering.

Senior Researcher Laurence E. Katz prepared this case at the HBS California Research Center under the supervision of Professor William A. Sahlman as the basis for class discussion rather than to illustrate either effective or ineffective handling of an administrative situation.

As the plane took off, she was hopeful that attendees at H&Q's conference would respond as favorably to Amazon.com's story as she felt their European counterparts had. She knew a successful IPO would be critical to the company's long-term success—both in raising capital to fund future operating requirements and in extending its brand—and knew that the next several weeks would determine the offering's success. She expected that she would continue to face difficult questions about the company's still unproven business model, its bold spending plans, recent competitive entries, and the weak technology market. She also thought ahead to the upcoming pricing meeting that would occur the day before the offering. Given recent events, she wondered whether Amazon.com's registered offering price of $12 to $14 was still appropriate. Would negative market conditions overcome Amazon.com's strong long-term story, or would the offering be so heavily subscribed that they would be able to increase the offering price? If the offering gained significant interest and visibility, would they see a major stock price spike on the first day of trading, as Netscape had experienced, which might put additional pressure on the company to live up to the expectations embedded in the stock price? She leaned back in her seat and closed her eyes, knowing that she would need to be well rested for her whirlwind U.S. tour.

BACKGROUND

Company History

Since its founding[1] in July 1994, Amazon.com had become the poster child of Internet commerce. Jeff Bezos, a 32-year-old computer science and electrical engineering major from Princeton University, had started the online bookseller after becoming intrigued by the rapid penetration of the Internet. He believed that retail could become the Internet's "killer application," offering a unique customer value proposition at a relatively low cost to customers around the world. While still working as a vice president at D.E. Shaw, a New York City brokerage firm, Bezos drew up a list of 20 retail categories in which he thought consumers might want to purchase online. He "force-ranked" them according to a list of self-selected criteria and researched the top five, ultimately pinning his hopes on bookselling. In 1995, Bezos packed up his car (and dog) and headed out to Seattle, which offered proximity to the Roseburg, Oregon, warehouse of leading book distributor Ingram and a large concentration of technical talent. His wife drove as Bezos tapped out the draft of the business plan on his laptop and contacted potential seed investors on his cellular phone.

Amazon.com opened its "doors" in July 1995 in Bezos's 400-square-foot garage, calling itself "Earth's Biggest Bookstore." From its beginnings, Amazon.com's mission was to become a leader in online bookselling. Amazon.com initially offered customers a selection of 1 million titles (later increased to 2.5 million), which included most of the estimated 1.5 million English-language books in print. In addition to the largest book selection, Amazon.com promoted its discounted prices (40% off on best-sellers and 10% off on hundreds of thousands of other books), the convenience of its service, its efficient search and retrieval interface, and the ability to interact with other readers. Amazon.com complemented its catalog of books with content that users could access to evaluate a book, including jacket images, synopses, reviews, customer testimonials, and

---

[1] *Amazon.com* (Jeffrey Rayport and Dickson Louie, HBS Case No. 897-128: 1997) presents a more detailed account of the founding of Amazon.com.

recommendations. Customers ordered books online and received them through delivery services of their choice, usually within two to five days.

Amazon.com sourced 350,000 titles, which accounted for nearly 60% of its orders, from Ingram—and the remainder from other distributors and publishers. Rather than warehousing its entire inventory, Amazon.com stocked only the top best-sellers and ordered other titles on demand. This sourcing model reduced Amazon.com's capital requirements while also limiting its need for warehouse space and distribution centers. As a result, Amazon.com had approximately 50 inventory turns per year in its single distribution facility in Seattle.

The company was founded with $10,000 from Bezos and personal loans of $74,000 that he made to the business. In January 1995, Bezos raised $1.2 million from private investors, issuing 4.2 million shares of common equity at a $4 million pre-money valuation. In March 1996, Bezos raised $8 million at a $60 million pre-money valuation from legendary Silicon Valley venture capital firm Kleiner Perkins Caufield & Byers. (See Exhibit 31-1 for share purchase history.)

By the end of the first quarter of 1996, Amazon.com had grown rapidly to $875,000 in sales. It doubled its sales during each of the next four quarters, reaching $16 million in sales in the first quarter of 1997. By March 1997, Amazon.com had a customer database of approximately 340,000 names from over 100 countries. Average daily visits had increased from approximately 2,200 in December 1995 to approximately 80,000 in March 1997, and repeat customers accounted for over 40% of orders. During the first 30 months of operations, Amazon.com had accumulated a deficit of $9.0 million. (See Exhibits 31-2 and 31-3 for historical financial performance.)

EXHIBIT 31-1

AMAZON.COM SHARE PURCHASE HISTORY

Name	Date	Number of Common Shares	Capital Contributed	Price/Share
Jeffrey P. Bezos	July 1994	10,200,000	$10,000	$0.001
Private Investors	Feb. 1995 through May 1996	1,410,244	275,000	0.1845
Thomas A. Alberg[a]	December 1995	150,000	50,000	0.3333
Other Angel Investors	Dec. 1995 through March 1996	2,793,000	931,000	0.3333
Kleiner, Perkins, Caufield, & Byers	June 1996	3,401,376[b]	8,000,000	2.35
Scott Cook[c]	January 1997	15,000	100,000	6.66
Patricia Stonesifer[c]	February 1997	15,000	100,000	6.66

[a] Thomas Alberg is a director of the company.

[b] Represents 3,315,966 shares and 85,410 shares of common stock issuable upon conversion of Series A Preferred Stock held by Kleiner Perkins Caufield & Byers VIII and KPCB Information Sciences Zaibatsu Fund II, respectively.

[c] Scott Cook and Patricia Stonesifer are directors of the company. Represents common shares issuable upon conversion of Series A Preferred Stock.

Source: Amazon.com.

EXHIBIT 31-2

AMAZON.COM INCOME STATEMENT ($000)

	1994[a]	1995	1996	Quarter Ended				
				March 31, 1996	June 30, 1996	September 30, 1996	December 31, 1996	March 31, 1997
Net sales	$ —	$ 511	$15,746	$ 875	$ 2,230	$ 4,173	$ 8,468	$16,005
Cost of sales	—	409	12,287	695	1,753	3,262	6,577	12,484
Gross profit	$ —	$ 102	$ 3,459	$180	$477	$911	$ 1,891	$ 3,521
Operating expenses								
Marketing and sales	—	200	6,090	205	696	2,251	2,938	3,906
Product development	38	171	2,313	263	394	755	901	1,575
General and administrative	14	35	1,035	48	163	377	447	1,142
Total operating expenses	$ 52	$ 406	$ 9,438	$ 516	$ 1,253	$ 3,383	$ 4,286	$ 6,623
Operating profit	$ (52)	$ (304)	$ (5,979)	$ (336)	$ (776)	$ (2,472)	$ (2,395)	$ (3,102)
Interest income	—	1	202	5	9	92	96	64
Net loss	$ (52)	$ (303)	$ (5,777)	$ (331)	$ (767)	$ (2,380)	$ (2,299)	$ (3,038)
Net loss per share	$ (0.00)	$ (0.02)	$ (0.25)	$ (0.02)	$ (0.03)	$ (0.10)	$ (0.10)	$ (0.13)
Fully diluted shares	17,730	18,933	22,655	22,251	22,431	22,967	22,969	23,018

[a] For the period July 5, 1994 to December 31, 1994.

Source: Amazon.com Prospectus.

EXHIBIT 31-3

AMAZON.COM BALANCE SHEET, DECEMBER 31, 1995, TO MARCH 31, 1997 (IN THOUSANDS, EXCEPT SHARE AND PER SHARE DATA)

	December 31, 1995	December 31, 1996	March 31 1997
ASSETS			
Current assets:			
Cash and cash equivalents	$ 996	$6,248	$ 7,162
Inventories	17	571	939
Prepaid expenses and other	14	321	937
Total current assets	1,027	7,140	9,038
Equipment, net	57	985	2,491
Deposits	—	146	193
Total assets	$1,084	$8,271	$11,722
LIABILITIES AND STOCKHOLDERS' EQUITY			
Current liabilities:			
Accounts payable	$ 99	$2,852	$ 5,650
Accrued advertising	—	598	1,254
Accrued product development	—	500	—
Other liabilities and accrued expenses	8	920	2,055
Total current liabilities	107	4,870	8,959
Stockholders' equity:			
Preferred stock, $0.01 par value:			
Authorized shares—10,000,000			
Issued and outstanding shares—569,396 at December 31, 1996 and 574,396 at March 31, 1997 (none pro forma), aggregate liquidation preference—$8,200	—	6	6
Common stock, $0.01 par value:			
Authorized shares—100,000,000			
Issued and outstanding shares—14,555,244, 15,900,229 and 17,352,406 at December 31, 1995 and 1996 and March 31, 1997, respectively (20, 798, 782 pro forma)	1,075	159	173
Advances received for common stock	150	—	—
Additional paid-in capital	—	9,873	14,737
Deferred compensation	—	(612)	(3,090)
Accumulated deficit	(248)	(6,025)	(9,063)
Total stockholders' equity	977	3,401	2,763
Total liabilities and stockholders' equity	$1,084	$8,271	$11,722

Source: Amazon.com Prospectus.

Covey commented on the rapid success of the service:

> Amazon.com's service is better for everyone in the value chain. Book buyers have access to a broader selection of titles, lower prices, value-added content, customer interaction, and personalized services, all from the convenience of their home. Publishers get a respite from the pain they have been experiencing over the past several years with the explosion of returns. Amazon.com's publisher return rates are far below average because most orders are not placed until the customer places his/her order. Additionally, we help them promote mid-list books, which are much harder for publishers to promote. Not to be forgotten, authors benefit by getting their books, which otherwise might not get widely distributed, into readers' hands.

Joy Covey's Background

Covey, 33 years old, had joined Amazon.com in the fall of 1996. A high school dropout, she had graduated from California State University, Fresno, in 1982 with a CPA at 19 years old. After graduation, she worked at Arthur Young and Co. (now Ernst and Young LLP) as a certified public accountant for four years. In 1986, she entered the joint law and business program at Harvard University, graduating with honors from both Harvard Business School and Harvard Law School in 1990. Upon graduation, she joined Wasserstein Perella & Co., the New York mergers and acquisitions advisory boutique, as an associate. In April 1991, Covey left Wall Street and returned to the West Coast as chief financial officer of Digidesign, a digital audio software company. After going public in 1993, Digidesign merged with Avid Technology, a Boston-based digital video company, in January 1995. (See Exhibit 31-4 for Covey's resume.)

After serving in a transitional role at Avid as vice president of Business Development, Covey left the company in February 1996 to return to an entrepreneurial environment. She described her job search and introduction to Amazon.com:

> I had interviewed with nearly 40 high-tech companies in Silicon Valley. I was very particular, though I was not focused on a specific role. I wanted to help build something significant, I wanted to work with very high quality teammates, I wanted to build a business with a strong, virtuous-cycle business model, and I wanted it to be on the Peninsula. In August, I met an executive recruiter who wanted me to meet Jeff but I told him that there was no way I was moving to Seattle. He convinced me to meet Jeff as a favor to him. After our meeting, I couldn't sleep. I could not stop thinking about Amazon. It was clearly a "category formation" time and I wanted to be part of the team. The next day, I called Jeff to ask whether he would consider a commuting role.

Covey and Bezos worked out a commuting arrangement in which she spent weekdays in Seattle and weekends in San Francisco. After eight months, Covey moved to Seattle.

The Book Industry

The worldwide book industry in 1996 was large, growing, albeit slowly, and highly fragmented. Domestic wholesale book sales were estimated to be approximately $26 billion in 1996 and were expected to grow to $33 billion in 2001. (See Exhibit 31-5.) Worldwide wholesale book sales were estimated to be approximately $82 billion in 1996 and were expected to grow to $90 billion by 2000. The consumer book market represented approximately $15 billion of domestic wholesale sales.

EXHIBIT 31-4

JOY COVEY'S RÉSUMÉ, FEBRUARY 1996

Joy Covey

Work experience

1995–1996   **AVID TECHNOLOGY, INC.**   **TEWKSBURY, MA**

Vice President of Operations, Broadcast Division.   Integrative role across functional and organizational lines in $100 million division of $400 million digital media technology company. Developed planning and product line P&L models. Implemented forecasting, scheduling and reporting tools for manufacturing, sales and margin. Improved complex system sales processes.

Vice President, Business Development.   Acquired two imaging technology companies in separate but simultaneous transactions; structured deals for quick close prior to major tradeshow and coincident with purchase agreement and public announcement. Coordinated Digidesign-Avid post-merger integration.

1991–1995   **DIGIDESIGN, INC.**   **MENLO PARK, CA**

Chief Financial Officer.   CFO role in management team that built company valuation from $20 million to $225 million; achieved 50%+ annual growth with consistent high margins and positive cash flow; and solidified market leadership position through open system, standard platform strategy. Managed successful IPO and five public quarters that consistently exceeded analyst expectations and established sterling reputation for financials "among the tightest, cleanest ever seen" by our analysts. Negotiated and executed Avid merger, including SEC filings and HSR process. Created and implemented all public company processes, including investor relations, SEC reporting, annual report, investment conferences. Built infrastructure and processes to manage growth through excellent information flow, planning and execution. Led smooth system conversion prior to IPO. Managed, drafted, and negotiated many contracts. Managed all finance, planning, accounting, investor relations, human resource and legal activities.

1990–1991   **WASSERSTEIN PERELLA & CO.**   **NEW YORK, NY**

Mergers and Acquisitions Associate.   Executed a broad range of merger and acquisition assignments, including analysis of acquisitions, divestitures, strategic alternatives, financing mechanisms and defense scenarios.

1985–1986   **INDEPENDENT CONSULTANT**   **ORANGE COUNTY, CA**

Various projects for Denny's, Inc. arising from its LBO and for another company in connection with a system implementation.

1982–1985   **ARTHUR YOUNG & COMPANY**   **ORANGE COUNTY, CA**

Supervising Senior Accountant. Planned and directed financial statement audits for a wide range of businesses, including Denny's, Inc. $800 million LBO purchase valuation and related financial statements.

Education

1986–1990   **HARVARD GRADUATE SCHOOL OF BUSINESS ADMINISTRATION**   **BOSTON, MA**

Earned Master of Business Administration degree with high distinction. Designated Baker Scholar (top 5%).

          HARVARD LAW SCHOOL   **CAMBRIDGE, MA**

Earned Juris Doctor degree, *magna cum laude*. One of four third-year students invited to join the *Harvard Law Review* for 1989–1990 academic year.

1980–1982   **CALIFORNIA STATE UNIVERSITY, FRESNO**   **FRESNO, CA**

Earned Bachelor of Science degree, *summa cum laude,* in Business Administration. Graduated with 4.0 GPA in 2-1/2 years. Honors included President's List, Beta Gamma Sigma Award, and election to Beta Gamma Sigma. Elected Secretary of Gamma Omicron Chapter of Beta Alpha Psi, National Accounting Honor Society.

Designations, honors, publications

Member California Bar
Certified Public Accountant, California
Awarded Elijah Watt Sells Silver Medal Award for placing second in the United States out of 73,000 candidates on the November 1982 CPA examination.
Note, *Review of Board Actions: Greater Scrutiny for Greater Conflicts of Interest*, 103 Harv. L. Rev. 1697 (1990).
Case Comment, *Restrictions on Prisoners' Rights to Receive Publications*, Thornburgh v. Abbott, 103 Harv. L. Rev. 239 (1989).

Personal   Enjoy windsurfing, kayaking, bicycling, scuba, climbing, symphony, and reading.

EXHIBIT 31-5

DOMESTIC BOOK EXPENDITURES (IN MILLIONS)

	1991		1996		1997E		1998E		1999E		2000E		2001E	
	$	%	$	%	$	%	$	%	$	%	$	%	$	%
Adult Trade	5,147.0	26%	6,924.6	27%	7,104.9	26%	7,371.5	26%	7,659.7	25%	7,908.7	25%	8,141.8	25%
Juvenile Trade	1,965.0	10%	2,549.1	10%	2,704.1	10%	2,858.4	10%	2,994.6	10%	3,101.8	10%	3,147.6	10%
Mass Market Paperbacks	1,923.1	10%	2,374.5	9%	2,488.5	9%	2,589.6	9%	2,715.4	9%	2,872.4	9%	3,012.3	9%
Book Clubs	728.8	4%	1,061.4	4%	1,151.5	4%	1,240.8	4%	1,337.0	4%	1,426.8	4%	1,528.6	5%
Mail Order Publications	755.2	4%	598.6	2%	594.9	2%	590.8	2%	590.8	2%	592.7	%	603.9	2%
Religious	1,476.4	7%	1,909.1	7%	2,039.1	7%	2,170.0	8%	2,317.6	8%	2,477.9	8%	2,636.7	8%
Professional	3,060.5	15%	4,287.6	16%	4,540.9	17%	4,801.6	17%	5,066.2	17%	5,338.9	17%	5,619.6	17%
University Press	307.7	2%	405.6	2%	431.1	2%	460.1	2%	491.8	2%	525.6	2%	559.6	2%
Elementary/High School	1,973.7	10%	2,521.7	10%	2,687.2	10%	2,831.3	10%	2,974.1	10%	3,127.7	10%	3,277.6	10%
College	2,329.1	12%	2,920.0	11%	3,098.6	11%	3,271.9	11%	3,476.3	11%	3,698.7	12%	3,813.3	12%
Subscription Reference	436.7	2%	556.9	2%	572.5	2%	594.2	2%	621.7	2%	647.8	2%	678.3	2%
Total	20,103.2	100%	26,109.1	100%	27,413.3	100%	28,780.2	100%	30,245.2	100%	31,719.0	100%	33,019.3	100%

Source: Book Industry Study Group, 1997.

The book publishing industry in 1996 was highly fragmented. The leading consumer publisher, Random House, controlled less than 10% of the market. *Books in Print*, the leading industry catalog, listed approximately 50,000 publishers, many of them with only a single title imprint. In recent years, book publishers had been suffering from sustained losses due to the explosion of book returns, declining adult hard cover and soft cover book sales, and escalating author advances. Liberal book return policies had been introduced during the Depression to entice booksellers to order books from publishers. Recently, book returns had increased to 35% to 50% from standard levels of 15% to 25%. In addition, unit sales of adult trade books, the most profitable consumer titles, had fallen nearly 11% over the previous two years, further depressing publishers' earnings.

The book seller industry was also highly fragmented. Despite the consolidation of the retail book channel over the previous 10 years, the largest retailers, Barnes and Noble and Borders, represented only 11% and 10% of total domestic book sales, respectively. No bookseller had successfully built a leading global brand. Land-based superstores stocked, on average, 130,000 titles, with the largest stores carrying up to 175,000 titles on site. Independent booksellers carried approximately 25,000 to 30,000 titles. Other channels, including mail order and warehouse clubs, collectively represented over 50% of all consumer purchases. (See Exhibit 31-6 for detail on reseller market shares.)

Book distributors served as the primary vendors for many retailers, carrying up to 350,000 of the best-selling titles. Domestic distribution was led by the two largest domestic wholesalers—Baker and Taylor, and Ingram. These distributors bought inventory from publishers in large volumes at attractive prices and sold the books in smaller volumes to retailers and other resellers.

ELECTRONIC RETAILING

By 1997, online retail was growing with the rapid acceptance of the Internet. The ability of online retailers to interact directly with customers by customizing their featured

---

EXHIBIT 31-6

FRAGMENTATION OF DOMESTIC BOOK INDUSTRY

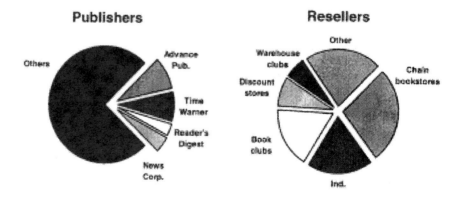

Source: William J. Gurley, "Amazon.com: The Quintessential Wave Rider," Deutsche Morgan Grenfell, June 9, 1997.

selections, "store designs," pricing, and presentation made the Web an attractive commercial medium. Among the early products sold on the Web were computers, travel services, brokerage services, automobiles, and music. The total value of goods sold over the Web in the United States was estimated to have grown from $318 million in 1995 to $5.4 billion in 1996 and was expected to reach $95 billion by 2000.[2]

The demographics of Web users made them an attractive customer base. Web users had grown to approximately 35 million in 1996 and were expected to grow to approximately 163 million, or 60% of Americans, by 2000.[3] The majority of Web users were highly educated, with over 50% holding a college degree or higher, and over 62% of the worldwide Internet users earning at least $40,000 in annual salary.

Covey compared electronic retailing to traditional retailing:

> There are several limitations to traditional resellers' ability to provide deep selection and personalized services. Physical land-based retailers need to invest significant capital resources in inventory, real estate and personnel for each retail location. This capital and real estate intensive business model limits the amount of inventory that can be economically carried in any one location. It's also impossible to build a customized store for every customer or to provide customized recommendations without significantly increasing selling costs.
>
> Internet retailers have the advantages of centralized inventory management, low occupancy costs, and high sales per employee. The minimal cost to publish on the Web and the ability to reach a large and global group of customers from a central location makes the model very scalable and provides additional economic benefits for online retailers. Moreover, the Internet provides an easy way for retailers to track consumer purchasing patterns to better anticipate demand. From a service perspective, the Internet can store vast amounts of data and allow the consumer to drill down to whatever level he/she desires without significantly increasing the cost to serve. This data in combination with power of technology provides unprecedented opportunity for personalized services, such as a customized storefront.

Several services had launched or announced plans to introduce competing online bookstores. Notable competitors included retail bookstore chains such as Barnes & Noble, which operated more than 1,000 physical stores and planned to launch its Web site (barnesandnoble.com) in May 1997, and Borders, which had announced plans to be online by the end of 1997. (Exhibits 31-7 and 31-8 present financial statements for these two companies; Exhibits 31-9 and 31-10 present their respective stock price charts.) CUC International, a $2.3 billion consumer services company, was developing a subscription-based marketplace called NetMarket which would sell a wide range of goods to members, including books.

Covey continued to describe why she strongly believed in Amazon.com's business model:

> Though our gross margins are lower than those for land-based book retailers, we have the potential to realize meaningful structural economic advantages over traditional book retailers at scale. Every time a retailer rolls out a new physical store, it increases its labor, inventory, and occupancy costs. Although we have variable costs such as fulfillment and customer service costs, many other costs of online retail are relatively fixed.

[2] International Data Corporation.
[3] Ibid.

EXHIBIT 31-7

BARNES & NOBLE, FINANCIAL STATEMENTS ($000, EXCEPT PER SHARE DATA)

	1996	1995	1994
Revenues	$2,448,124	$1,976,900	$1,622,731
Cost of sales (includes occupancy)	1,569,448	1,269,001	1,050,011
Gross profit	878,676	707,899	572,720
Selling and administrative expenses	456,181	376,733	311,344
Rental expense	225,450	182,473	147,225
Depreciation and amortization	59,806	47,881	36,617
Pre-opening expenses	17,571	12,160	9,021
Restructuring charge	—	123,768	—
Operating profit (loss)	119,668	(35,156)	68,513
Interest (net of interest income of $2,288, $2,138 and $3,008, respectively) and amortization of deferred financing fees	38,286	28,142	22,955
Earnings (loss) before provision (benefit) for income taxes	81,382	(63,298)	45,558
Provision (benefit) for income taxes	30,157	(10,322)	20,085
Net earnings (loss)	$ 51,225	$ (52,976)	$ 25,473
Net earnings (loss) per common share	$1.48	(1.70)	0.81
Weighted average common shares outstanding	34,576,000	31,217,000	31,344,000

Source: Barnes & Noble 10-K, February 1, 1997.

(*Continued*)

We also have an unusually capital efficient model. Our inventory turns are high and we have a rapid cash conversion cycle—1 day of receivables, 7 days of inventory, and 41 days of payables. As we grow, we generate cash, which helps offset our cash used for operating expenses. As a result, we have more cash to invest in systems and services, such as branding, product features, and customer service, to create a closer relationship with our customer. This, in turn, can drive sales growth, which is necessary if we are to develop sourcing economies, promotion and co-marketing leverage, and operational and logistical efficiencies. This also means that the potential return on invested capital is high if critical volume levels are achieved and we manage to realize the potential of our business model. (See Exhibits 31-11, 31-12, and 31-13.)

We think the underlying dynamics of our business model are, in many ways, analogous to that of Dell. By going direct to its customers, Dell was able to remove layers of the distribution chain and their associated costs. This allowed Dell to provide added value to customers and vendors and to extract value out of the chain for their shareholders. They were able to drive a very efficient operating cycle and minimize inventory levels, which freed up capital to invest in building better systems and a closer relationship with the customer. Their negative working capital cycle has enabled triple-digit return on invested capital (ROIC) even with relatively low margins.

EXHIBIT 31-7   *(Continued)*

BARNES & NOBLE, CONSOLIDATED BALANCE SHEETS
($000, EXCEPT PER SHARE DATA)

	1996	1995
Assets		
Current assets:		
Cash and cash equivalents	$ 12,447	$ 9,276
Receivables, net	45,558	49,019
Merchandise inventories	732,203	740,351
Prepaid expenses and other current assets	76,747	49,542
Total current assets	$ 866,955	$ 848,188
Property and equipment:		
Land and land improvements	681	681
Buildings and leasehold improvements	326,392	249,603
Fixtures and equipment	289,684	204,528
Total property and equipment	$ 616,757	$ 454,812
Less accumulated depreciation and amortization	181,983	134,932
Net property and equipment	$ 434,774	$ 319,880
Intangible assets, net	$ 93,494	$ 96,799
Other noncurrent assets	51,424	50,475
Total assets	$1,446,647	$1,315,342
Liabilities and shareholders' equity		
Current liabilities:		
Revolving credit facility	$ 40,000	$ —
Accounts payable	373,340	415,698
Accrued liabilities	240,923	205,990
Total current liabilities	$ 654,263	$ 621,688
Long-term debt	$ 290,000	$ 262,400
Other long-term liabilities	46,395	31,019
Shareholders' equity:		
Common stock: $.001 per value: 100,000,000		
shares authorized; 33,188,125 and 32,958,614		
shares issued and outstanding, respectively	33	33
Additional paid-in capital	446,298	441,769
Retained earnings (deficit)	9,658	(41,567)
Total shareholders' equity	$ 455,989	$ 400,235
Commitments and contingencies	—	—
Total liabilities and shareholders' equity	$1,446,647	$1,315,342

Source: Barnes & Noble 10-K, February 1, 1997.

(Continued)

EXHIBIT 31-7 *(Continued)*

BARNES & NOBLE, CONSOLIDATED STATEMENTS OF CASH FLOWS ($000)

Fiscal Year	1996	1995	1994
Cash flows from operating activities:			
Net earnings (loss)	$ 51,225	$ (52,976)	$ 25,473
Adjustments to reconcile net earnings (loss) to net cash flows from operating activities:			
Depreciation and amortization	61,652	50,185	38,921
(Gain) loss on disposal of property and equipment	(130)	4,657	2,959
Deferred taxes	6,604	(32,110)	(5,394)
Restructuring charge	—	123,768	—
Increase in other long-term liabilities for scheduled rent increases in long-term leases	15,663	10,670	7,266
Changes in operating assets and liabilities, net:			
Receivables, net	3,461	(19,191)	(9,474)
Merchandise inventories	8,148	(241,432)	(137,576)
Prepaid expenses and other current assets	(19,502)	(17,340)	1,751
Accounts payable and accrued liabilities	(7,584)	116,925	93,957
Net cash flows from operating activities	$ 119,537	$ (56,844)	$ 17,883
Cash flows from investing activities:			
Purchases of property and equipment	$(171,885)	$(154,913)	$ (88,763)
Proceeds from sales of property and equipment	177	551	3
Net increase in other noncurrent assets	(16,787)	(2,378)	(15,876)
Net cash flows form investing activities	$(188,495)	$(156,740)	$(104,636)
Cash flows from financing activities:			
Net (decrease) increase in revolving credit facility	$ (32,400)	$ 72,400	$ —
Proceeds from issuance of long-term debt	100,000	—	—
Proceeds from issuance of common stock, net	—	88,725	—
Proceeds from exercise of common stock options	4,529	6,313	3,859
Net cash flows from financing activities	$ 72,129	$ 167,438	$ 3,859
Net increase (decrease) in cash and cash equivalents	$ 3,171	$ (46,146)	$ (82,894)
Cash and cash equivalents at beginning of year	9,276	55,422	138,316
Cash and cash equivalents at end of year	$ 12,447	$ 9,276	$ 55,422

EXHIBIT 31-8

BORDERS GROUP, INC., FINANCIAL STATEMENT ($ MILLIONS, EXCEPT PER COMMON SHARE DATA)

	1996	1995	1994
Sales	$1,958.8	$1,749.0	$1,511.0
Cost of merchandise sold (includes occupancy)[a]	1,437.8	1,302.3	1,127.1
Gross margin	$ 521.0	$ 446.7	$ 383.9
Operating Expenses			
Selling, general and administrative expenses	409.6	374.5	333.3
Pre-opening expense	7.2	7.3	5.7
Goodwill amortization and writedown	1.1	205.5	7.4
Other	—	59.8	(6.3)
Operating income (loss)[b]	$ 103.1	$ 200.4	$ 43.8
Interest expense	7.0	4.6	1.0
Income (loss) before income tax	$ 96.1	$ (205.0)	$ 42.8
Income tax provision	38.2	6.1	21.9
Net income (loss)	$ 57.9	$ (211.1)	$ 20.9
Earnings (loss) per common share data—Unaudited and pro forma for 1995 and 1994 (Note 3):			
Earnings (loss per common share)	$ 0.70	$ (2.53)	$ 0.24
Weighted average common shares outstanding (in thousands)	82,554	83,358	87,140

[a] Rental expenses totaled $167.1 million in 1996 and $143.8 million in 1995.

[b] Includes FAS 121 Impairment, operating losses of stores identified for closure, and restructuring provisions.

Source: Borders Group, 10-K, January 26, 1997.

(*Continued*)

PREPARING TO GO PUBLIC

The process of preparing the company to go public had been a time-consuming one for Bezos and Covey. Since the company's beginnings, Bezos had hoped to take the company public in order to extend the brand and build consumer awareness. In the summer of 1996, he had begun the process of informally meeting with investment banks to become familiar with their different styles and cultures. Though he wanted to build a solid foundation for the business before considering an offering, he also wanted to prepare himself for the time when the company was ready to present itself to the public markets.

Covey joined the company expecting to take it public "as soon as it was ready." For three months after Covey's hiring, she made a concerted effort to keep the investment banks out of Amazon.com's offices. She knew that the IPO would be the first day of its public life, and she believed that it was very important to be prepared to meet the

EXHIBIT 31-8 *(Continued)*

BORDERS GROUP, INC., CONSOLIDATED BALANCE SHEET
($ MILLIONS, EXCEPT SHARE AMOUNTS)

	1996	1995
Assets		
Current assets:		
Cash and cash equivalents	$ 42.6	$ 36.5
Merchandise inventories	737.5	637.5
Accounts receivable and other current assets	44.1	34.0
Property held for resale	8.1	28.7
Deferred income taxes	14.1	3.5
Total current assets	$ 846.4	$ 740.2
Property and equipment, net	289.2	243.5
Other assets	18.4	6.3
Deferred income taxes	18.5	22.7
Goodwill, net of accumulated amortization of $41.5 and $40.4, respectively	38.5	39.6
Total Assets	$1,211.0	$1,052.3
Liabilities and Stockholders' Equity		
Current liabilities:		
Short-term borrowing and current portion of long-term debt	$ 30.5	$ 60.5
Trade accounts payable	350.1	304.8
Accrued payroll and other liabilities	197.8	164.0
Taxes, including income taxes	56.1	13.6
Total current liabilities	$ 634.5	$ 542.9
Long-term debt and capital lease obligations	6.2	8.1
Other long-term liabilities	24.8	29.3
Commitments and contingencies	—	—
Total liabilities	665.5	580.3
Shares subject to repurchase	$ 34.1	$ —
Stockholders' equity		
Common stock	0.1	—
Additional paid-in capital	648.0	669.2
Deferred compensation and officer receivable	(0.8)	(3.4)
Accumulated deficit	(135.9)	(193.8)
Total stockholders' equity	$ 511.4	$ 472.0
Total Liabilities and Stockholders' Equity	$1,211.0	$1,052.3

Source: Borders Group 10-K, January 26, 1997.

(Continued)

EXHIBIT 31-8 *(Continued)*

BORDERS GROUP, INC., CONSOLIDATED STATEMENTS OF CASH FLOWS ($ MILLIONS)

	1996	1995	1994
Cash flows from operations			
Net income (loss)	$ 57.9	$(211.1)	$ 20.9
Adjustments to reconcile net income (loss) to operating cash flows:			
Restructuring provision	—	—	6.4
Depreciation and amortization	42.9	42.0	45.6
Goodwill writedown	—	—	201.8
FAS 121 impairment	—	63.1	—
Loss on disposal of property and equipment	—	1.8	5.3
Deferred income taxes	(6.4)	(0.4)	22.3
Increase (decrease) in other long-term assets and liabilities	(16.0)	(14.6)	8.3
Other—net	—	1.5	—
Changes in current assets and current liabilities:			
Increase in inventories	(100.0)	(109.7)	(88.8)
Decrease in property held for resale	—	(7.0)	—
Decrease in restructuring reserve	(2.1)	(38.0)	(38.2)
Increase in accounts payable	45.3	33.6	10.5
Increase (decrease) in taxes payable	44.2	7.6	(1.3)
Other—net	35.2	41.1	(17.5)
Net cash flows from operations	$101.0	$ 11.7	$ (26.5)
Cash flows from investing activities			
Investing			
Capital expenditures	(97.2)	(116.0)	(123.0)
Purchase of Planet Music	—	—	(12.3)
Proceeds from sale of property and equipment	4.7	34.2	3.4
Other	(0.4)	—	—
Net cash flow from investing activities:	$(92.9)	$ (81.8)	$(131.9)
Cash flows from financing activities			
Repayment of long-term debt and capital lease obligations	(2.0)	(7.2)	(2.2)
Proceeds from sale of put options	4.5	—	—
Proceeds (advances) for construction funding	19.8	(9.6)	8.0
Proceeds from initial public offering	—	248.0	—
Proceeds from (repayments to) Kmart	—	(360.0)	112.0
Net funding from credit facility	(30.0)	60.0	—
Issuance of common stock	5.7	11.1	—
Purchase of shares held by Kmart	—	(72.7)	—
Net equity transactions with Kmart	—	—	247.4
Net cash flow from financing activities	$ (2.0)	$(130.4)	$ 365.2
Net increase (decrease) in cash and equivalents	6.1	(200.5)	206.8
Cash and equivalents at beginning of year	36.5	37.0	30.2
Cash and equivalents at end of year	$ 42.6	$ 36.5	$ 237.0

EXHIBIT 31-9

BARNES & NOBLE STOCK PRICE GRAPH, OCTOBER 1, 1993–APRIL 25, 1997 (66 MILLION SHARES OUTSTANDING)

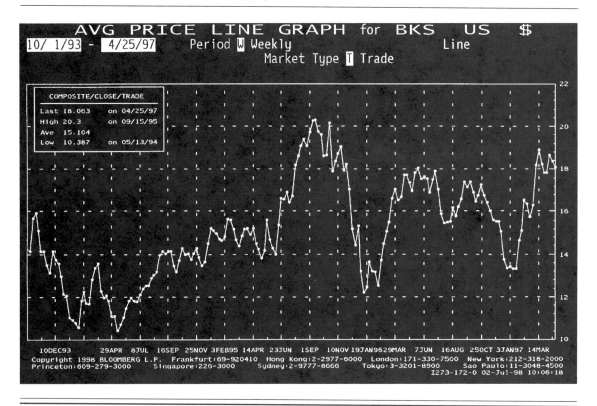

company's responsibilities to its new shareholders and for life in the public spotlight. Covey spent the first three months preparing the company to take it public, developing the financial reporting infrastructure and systems that would enable it to meet the demands placed on public companies. By February 1997, with the business performing at a $60 million run rate, Covey believed Amazon.com was ready for discussions with the banks.

Covey reflected on the decision to go public:

> While Jeff and I fully understood the benefits of going public, the decision to do so wasn't a no-brainer. The company did not need to go public at the time to raise capital—though we had only $7 million of cash available, our operating cycle reduced our capital requirements and we had received many inquiries from parties interested in privately financing the company. We decided that the brand exposure would be invaluable to the company, but we were committed to not giving in to the short-term pressures which public companies often feel. We were committed to focusing on the long-term value of the business and on value to our customers, which we believed to be the best approach if we wanted to build an enduring global franchise.

Market Conditions

Over the previous two months, the market for technology IPOs had softened. During the previous two years, several Internet-related companies had completed successful

EXHIBIT 31-10

BORDERS GROUP STOCK PRICE GRAPH, MAY 26, 1995–APRIL 25, 1997 (82.6 MILLION SHARES OUTSTANDING)

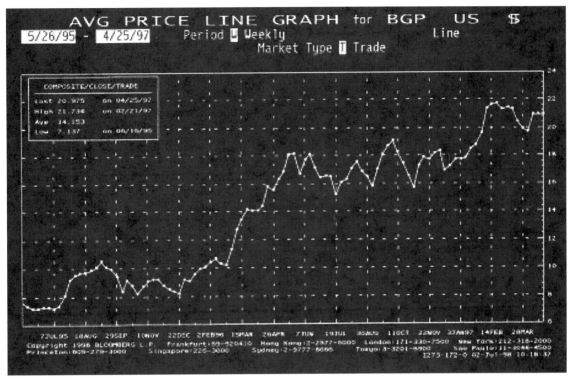

Source: Bloomberg.

EXHIBIT 31-11

BUSINESS MODEL COMPARISON

	Land-based	Amazon.com
Superstores	439	1
Titles per superstore	175,000	2,500,000
Occupancy costs (% of sales)[a]	12%	<4%
Sales per operating employee	$100,000	$300,000
Inventory turnover	2–3×	50–60×
Sales per square foot	$250	$2,000
Rent per square foot	$20	$8.00

[a] Includes Rental, Depreciation, Amortization, and Pre-opening expenses.

Source: William J. Gurley, "Amazon.com: The Quintessential Wave Rider," Deutsche Morgan Grenfell, June 9, 1997.

EXHIBIT 31-12

OPERATING CYCLE OF AMAZON.COM AND TYPICAL BOOK RETAILER

Amazon.com Operating Cycle

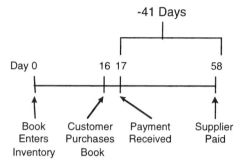

Typical Book Retail Operating Cycle

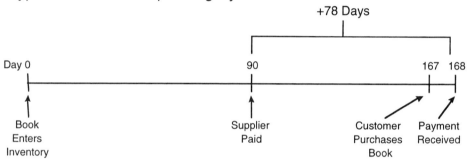

Source: Amazon.com.

---

public offerings, including Netscape's offering in 1995 and Yahoo's successful IPO in 1996. But while 1996 had set record levels for IPO activity with 104 technology companies going public in the first half of 1996, raising about $8.6 billion, the first four months of 1997 had seen only 40 technology companies go to the public markets to raise $1.2 billion. Only three Internet companies had gone public by April 1997, raising a meager $52 million.[4]

The overall market had become skittish in December 1996 following Federal Reserve Chairman Alan Greenspan's "irrational exuberance" comment, which had cast doubt on the underlying strength of the longest-running bull market in history. Following this comment, the Dow Jones Industrial Average had fallen 2.6% within 10 days and investors had fled small-cap stocks for more secure investments. (See Exhibit 31-14 for selected capital markets data.) The technology IPO market had chilled in March 1997 because of the underperformance of many Internet companies. Of those that had gone public since August 1995, nearly 75% were trading below their offering prices. (See Exhibits 31-15 and 31-16 for IPO pricing trends and Exhibit 31-17 for de-

---

[4] Securities Data Company.

EXHIBIT 31-13

AGGREGATE VALUE/REVENUE MATRIX ($ MILLIONS)

	Aggregate Value	Aggregate Value/ 1997 Revenue
Internet Content/Commerce/Search:		
CUC International	6,475	2.6×
Yahoo!	796	17.4×
E*Trade	508	5.3×
CNET	269	7.3×
Lycos	166	6.2×
Excite	159	4.4×
Infoseek	101	3.7×
Retail Booksellers:		
Barnes & Noble	1,652	0.6×
Borders Group	1,624	0.7×
Retail Booksellers (Adjusted):[a]		
Barnes & Noble	4,471	1.5×
Borders Group	3,713	1.7×

[a] Adjusted value recognizes the aggregate value of the operating leases as debt.

Source: William J. Gurley, "Amazon.com: The Quintessential Wave Rider," Deutsche Morgan Grenfell, June 9, 1997.

tail on Internet companies' post-IPO performance.) One industry analyst commented: "Investors are beginning to sour on Internet plays without earnings. The hype surrounding Internet content and search engines is beginning to wear off as earnings forecasts are revised downward."

Among the companies that had been unsuccessful accessing the public markets, Wired Ventures, a multimedia publisher, and N2K, a leading online music retailer, had pulled their offerings at the last minute during the previous summer. More recently, Auto-By-Tel, the online car and truck shopping service considered a visible Internet commerce company had pulled its offering at the end of March. With the market softening immediately before the pricing meeting, its bankers had told the company that they would have to lower its offering price $2 to $3 because of market conditions. Auto-By-Tel decided to withdraw the offering rather than accept a lower valuation. Most recently, rumors had spread that OnSale, a leading online auction site, would pull its filing prior to its April 17 offering. Though the company successfully had sold through at its registration price, the stock price had not moved since its offering.

A Decision to Go Ahead

Mistrustful of the strength of the IPO market in early 1997, Covey solicited proposals in February 1997 from eight leading investment banks with strong technology practices: Alex Brown, Deutsche Morgan Grenfell, Goldman Sachs, Hambrecht & Quist,

EXHIBIT 31-14

SELECTED DATA ON THE CAPITAL MARKETS, 1990 TO APRIL 1997

Financial Markets Data	1990	1991	1992	1993	1994	1995	I Qtr. 1996	II Qtr. 1996	III Qtr. 1996	IV Qtr. 1996	Jan 1997	Feb 1997	March 1997
3-Month U.S. Treasury Bill Yield[a]	6.4	3.9	3.1	3.0	5.5	5.0	5.0	5.0	4.9	5.1	5.0	5.1	5.2
30-Year U.S. Treasury Bond Yield[a]	8.3	7.4	7.4	6.3	7.9	6.0	6.7	6.9	6.9	6.6	6.8	6.8	7.1
Corporate Aaa Bond Yield	9.1	8.2	7.9	7.0	8.5	6.7	7.4	7.5	7.5	7.3	7.4	7.4	7.7
Prime Interest Rate[a]	9.8	6.5	6.0	6.0	8.5	8.5	8.3	8.3	8.3	8.3	8.3	8.3	8.5
Standard & Poor's 500 Index[a]	330.2	417.1	435.7	468.6	459.3	615.9	645.5	670.6	687.3	740.7	786.2	790.8	757.1
Standard & Poor's 500 Dividend Yield—Annualized	3.8	2.9	2.8	2.6	2.9	2.3	2.1	2.3	2.3	2.0	1.3	2.3	2.0
Standard & Poor's 500 Price/Earnings Ratio[a]	15.5	26.2	22.8	21.3	15.0	18.1	19.0	19.2	19.1	19.1	20.3	20.4	18.8
Nasdaq Composite Index	373.8	586.3	677.0	776.8	752.0	1,052.1	1,101.4	1,185.0	1,226.9	1,291.0	1,379.9	1,309.0	1,221.7
Hambrecht & Quist: Growth Index	635.0	1266.0	1227.0	1346.0	1390.0	2318.0	2392.0	2619.0	2617.0	2426.0	2552.0	2276.0	2016.0
Hambrecht & Quist: Technology Index	225.0	326.0	385.0	450.0	539.0	803.0	818.0	876.0	929.0	996.0	1102.0	1012.0	1070.0

[a] Rates are quoted at end of year, end of quarter, or end of month.

Source: Compustat, DRI, Datastream, Moody's, Standard & Poor's, and Hambrecht and Quist.

EXHIBIT 31-15

IPO PRICING TRENDS, JANUARY 1996 TO APRIL 1997

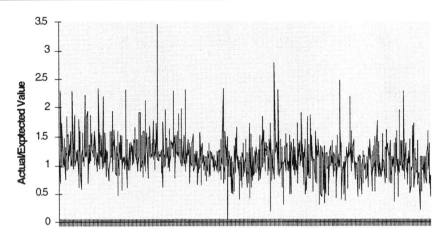

Explanation: This graph depicts the ratio of the total amount of capital actually raised (total shares sold times offering price per share) to the amount of capital listed in the preliminary prospectus filed with the Securities and Exchange Commission.

Source: Securities Data Company.

EXHIBIT 31-16

INTERNET IPO PRICING TRENDS, JANUARY 1996 TO APRIL 1997

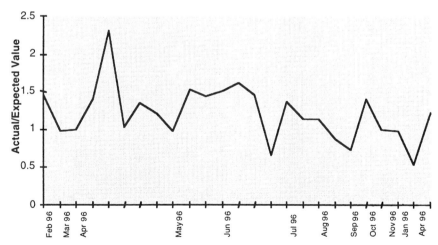

Explanation: This graph depicts the ratio of the total amount of capital actually raised (total shares sold times offering price per share) to the amount of capital listed in the preliminary prospectus filed with the Securities and Exchange Commission.

Source: Securities Data Company.

EXHIBIT 31-17

INTERNET IPO MARKET ENVIRONMENT, APRIL 30, 1997

		Offering		Offer to Current (4/30/97)			
Issuer	IPO Date	Market Cap. at Offer	Price at Offer	4/30/1997 Price	Price % Change	Market Cap.	Market Cap. Gain/(Loss)
		($MM)	($)	($)	(%)	($MM)	($MM)
Netscape Communications	08/08/95	$1,068	$14.00	$27.06	93%	$2,349	$1,281
VictorMaxx Technologies	08/10/95	26	6.00	0.24	(96%)	1	(25)
Desktop Data	08/11/95	123	15.00	7.25	(52%)	63	(60)
Premenos	09/19/95	178	18.00	6.50	(64%)	73	(105)
Secure Computing	11/17/95	223	16.00	7.25	(55%)	109	(114)
Kinetiks.Com	12/06/95	32	6.00	.375	(94%)	2	(30)
Meta Tools	12/12/95	202	18.00	9.13	(49%)	121	(81)
CKS Group	12/14/95	210	17.00	21.13	24%	271	61
DeltaPoint	12/20/95	12	6.00	2.00	(67%)	5	(7)
ForeFront	12/20/95	38	8.00	3.00	(63%)	19	(19)
Open Text	01/23/96	228	15.00	7.50	(50%)	124	(104)
Raptor	02/06/96	178	15.00	11.50	(23%)	150	(28)
VocalTec	02/06/96	162	19.00	6.25	(67%)	53	(109)
CyberCash	02/15/96	175	17.00	14.00	(18%)	150	(25)
CyLink	02/15/96	361	15.00	9.25	(38%)	238	(123)
MindSpring Enterprises	03/14/96	60	8.00	8.63	8%	65	5
IDT	03/15/96	187	10.00	5.50	(45%)	115	(72)
Individual	03/15/96	163	14.00	5.88	(58%)	84	(79)
Eagle River Interactive	03/21/96	145	13.00	10.875	(16%)	121	(24)
Lycos	04/10/96	219	16.00	12.88	(20%)	178	(41)
Excite Inc.	04/03/96	183	17.00	9.13	(46%)	109	(74)
Worldtalk Communications	04/12/96	77	8.00	4.38	(45%)	42	(35)
Yahoo!	04/12/96	334	13.00	34.13	163%	907	573
CompuServe	04/18/96	2,706	30.00	9.13	(70%)	845	(1,861)
Infonautics	04/29/96	131	14.00	1.88	(87%)	18	(113)
Edify	05/02/96	233	15.00	10.88	(27%)	177	(56)
Open Market	05/22/96	485	18.00	7.50	(58%)	214	(271)
OnLine Systems	05/22/96	20	6.75	2.50	(63%)	8	(12)
Security First Network Bank	05/22/96	187	20.00	8.13	(59%)	66	(121)
OzEmail	05/28/96	143	14.00	6.50	(54%)	0	(143)
Infoseek	06/11/96	305	12.00	6.13	(49%)	159	(146)
BroadVision	06/21/96	137	7.00	5.31	(24%)	106	(31)
Check Point Software	06/28/96	458	14.00	23.63	69%	773	315
CNET	07/01/96	211	16.00	20.25	27%	269	58
OneWave	07/02/96	236	16.00	2.00	(88%)	30	(206)
Connect	08/15/96	111	6.00	1.36	(77%)	25	(86)
E*Trade Group	08/16/96	308	10.50	15.00	43%	444	136
Rocky Mountain Internet	09/05/96	14	3.50	4.75	36%	65	51
The Leap Group	09/27/96	136	10.00	2.25	(78%)	10	(126)
Trusted Info Sys.	10/10/96	142	13.00	9.00	(31%)	103	(39)
DIGEX	10/16/96	107	10.13	8.13	(20%)	92	(15)
V-One	10/23/96	63	5.00	5.00	0%	63	0
VoxWare	10/30/96	87	7.50	4.56	(39%)	57	(30)
Dr. Solomon's	11/26/96	313	17.00	24.88	46%	459	146
TMP Worldwide	12/12/96	327	14.00	20.00	43%	471	144
First Virtual	12/13/96	79	9.00	4.00	(56%)	22	57
EarthLink Network	01/12/97	123	13.00	9.00	(31%)	87	(36)
OnSale	04/17/97	98	6.00	4.75	(21%)	79	(19)
Auto-By-Tel	withdrawn	—	—	—	—	—	—
PrimeNet	withdrawn	—	—	—	—	—	—
N2K (Need to Know)	withdrawn	—	—	—	—	—	—
Wired Ventures	withdrawn	—	—	—	—	—	—

Source: Based on analysis in: Mary Meeker and Sharon Pearson, *Internet Retail Report*, Morgan Stanley, May 28, 1997.

Montgomery Securities, Morgan Stanley, Robertson Stephens, and Smith Barney. Covey reflected on the conversations:

> We called the investment bankers and said "This is not yet an official bake-off but we want to meet you on February 26 and 27. Bring your team because we may move quickly when we actually decide to begin our IPO and may not conduct another full round of meetings." We didn't share with them any internal numbers—we were less concerned about valuation and more about banker quality, judgment, commitment, distribution and analyst quality.

Covey flew to San Francisco to meet each of the investment banking teams, including analysts and brokerage teams, in Kleiner Perkins's offices. Covey quarterbacked the process without Bezos's involvement, remembering John Doerr's advice that "the CFO should be the CEO of the going public process." Covey returned to Seattle the next day and proposed to Amazon.com's board of directors that they select Deutsche Morgan Grenfell (DMG), the highly publicized group that had recruited a team of technology investment bankers led by Frank Quattrone from Morgan Stanley, to lead the offering, with Hambrecht & Quist and Alex Brown as co-managers. Covey described the selection:

> We decided that we liked DMG's approach. We were entrepreneurial and focused on long-term value and we wanted a bank that shared our approach. We also wanted a bank that had as much to win or lose, if our IPO was a success, as we did—DMG was a relatively new team and we were their first highly visible lead-managed IPO. We knew we would have their full attention.

Preparing the Prospectus

With their bankers selected, Covey turned to drafting the "red herring," or S-1 filing, that the company would submit to the Securities Exchange Commission (SEC) in advance of their filing. Back in December and January, she had drafted much of the company background late at night and on the weekends. Covey now focused on how to position the company for its investors:

> From the beginning, Jeff and I very much saw the IPO as just another step in our business development process. We saw an opportunity to access the public markets while helping to build our brand. We made a strategic choice to focus on the long-term opportunity, which would involve significant investment in marketing and promotion, site development, and technology and operating infrastructure development, rather than short-term profitability. We hoped these investments would help us provide more value to customers and enable us to build scale faster. We believed that the right thing for our customers and for the long-term development of the business, and therefore, for our shareholders, was to extend our brand position and achieve sufficient sales volume to realize economies of scale.
>
> In writing our prospectus and preparing for the road show, we had some very real decisions to make. We needed to balance our long-term strategy, which required indicating that we would not be profitable for some time, with traditional earnings expectations of investors. We decided to remain true to our long-term approach and hope that enough investors would agree with our strategic philosophy. We realized that in this evolving space, flexibility would also be very important, and expectations drawn too narrowly would be a significant problem. Our guiding principle was to share with people the decision-making approach and strategic perspective that we actually used, rather than what might sound "better." This way, investors could make informed decisions. In the prospectus, we presented risks very candidly. [See Exhibit 31-18.] For example, we said, "The Company

EXHIBIT 31-18

EXCERPTS FROM AMAZON.COM'S PROSPECTUS

PROSPECTUS SUMMARY

The following summary should be read in conjunction with, and is qualified in its entirety by, the more detailed information and financial statements and notes thereto appearing elsewhere in this Prospectus.

The Company

Amazon.com is the leading online retailer of books. Since opening for business as "Earth's Biggest Bookstore" in July 1995, the Amazon.com bookstore has quickly become one of the most widely known, used and cited commerce sites on the World Wide Web (the "Web"). Amazon.com strives to offer its customers compelling value through innovative use of technology, broad selection, high-quality content, a high level of customer service, competitive pricing and personalized services. As an online bookseller, Amazon.com has virtually unlimited online shelf space and can offer customers a vast selection through an efficient search and retrieval interface. The Company offers more than 2.5 million titles, including most of the estimated 1.5 million English-language books believed to be in print, more than one million out-of-print titles believed likely to be in circulation and a smaller number of CDs, videotapes and audiotapes. Beyond the benefits of selection, purchasing books from Amazon.com is more convenient than shopping in a physical bookstore because online shopping can be done 24 hours a day and does not require a trip to a store. Furthermore, Amazon.com's high inventory turnover, lack of investment in expensive retail real estate and reduced personnel requirements give it meaningful structural economic advantages relative to traditional booksellers.

Through March 31, 1997, Amazon.com had sales of more than $32 million to approximately 340,000 customer accounts in over 100 countries. Average daily *visits* (not "hits") have grown from approximately 2,200 in December 1995 to approximately 80,000 in March 1997, and repeat customers currently account for over 40% of orders. *Time* magazine rated Amazon.com one of the 10 "Best Websites of 1996."

The Offering

Common Stock offered	2,500,000 shares
Common Stock to be outstanding after this offering	23,298,781 shares(1)
Use of proceeds	For working capital and other general corporate purposes.
Proposed Nasdaq National Market symbol	AMZN

(1)   Excludes 2,940,774 shares, 339,075 shares and 264,000 shares of Common Stock issuable upon exercise of options outstanding at March 31, 1997 under the Company's Amended and Restated 1994 Stock Option Plan (the "1994 Stock Option Plan"), the Company's 1997 Stock Option Plan (the "1997 Stock Option Plan," and together with the 1994 Stock Option Plan, the "Plans") and outside the Plans, respectively, at a weighted average exercise price of $1.76 per share. See "Management—Employee Benefit Plans" and Note 3 of Notes to Financial Statements.

Summary Financial Data
(in thousands except per share data)

	For the Period from July 5, 1994 (Inception) to December 31, 1994	Year Ended December 31, 1995	Year Ended December 31, 1996	Quarter Ended March 31, 1996	Quarter Ended June 30, 1996	Quarter Ended Sept. 30, 1996	Quarter Ended Dec. 31, 1996	Quarter Ended March 31, 1996
Statement of Operations Data:								
Net sales	$—	$511	$15,746	$875	$2,230	$4,173	$8,468	$16,005
Loss from operations	(52)	(304)	(5,979)	(336)	(776)	(2,472)	(2,395)	(3,032)
Net loss	(52)	(303)	(5,777)	(331)	(767)	(2,380)	(2,299)	(2,968)
Net loss per share (1)	(0.00)	(0.02)	(0.26)	(0.02)	(0.04)	(0.10)	(0.10)	(0.13)
Shares used in computation of net loss per share (1)	17,577	18,780	22,543	22,098	22,279	22,897	22,899	22,955

	At March 31, 1997 Actual	At March 31, 1997 As Adjusted (2)
Balance Sheet Data:		
Cash and cash equivalents	$7,162	$36,537
Working capital	79	29,454
Total assets	11,722	41,097
Stockholders' equity	2,763	32,138

(1)   See Note 1 of Notes to Financial Statements for information concerning the determination of net loss per share.

(2)   Adjusted to give effect to the sale by the Company of the shares of Common Stock offered hereby at an assumed initial public offering price of $13.00 per share and after deducting the estimated underwriting discount and offering expenses, and the receipt of the net proceeds therefrom. See "Use of Proceeds" and "Capitalization."

(Continued)

EXHIBIT 31-18 *(Continued)*

RISK FACTORS

In addition to the other information contained in this Prospectus, investors should carefully consider the following risk factors before making an investment decision concerning the Common Stock. All statements, trend analysis and other information contained in this Prospectus relative to markets for the Company's products and trends in net sales, gross margin and anticipated expense levels, as well as other statements including words such as "anticipate," "believe," "plan," "estimate," "expect" and "intend" and other similar expressions, constitute forward-looking statements. These forward-looking statements are subject to business and economic risks, and the Company's actual results of operations may differ materially from those contained in the forward-looking statements.

Limited Operating History; Accumulated Deficit; Anticipated Losses. The Company was founded in July 1994 and began selling books on its Web site in July 1995. Accordingly, the Company has a limited operating history on which to base an evaluation of its business and prospects. The Company's prospects must be considered in light of the risks, expenses and difficulties frequently encountered by companies in their early stage of development, particularly companies in new and rapidly evolving markets such as online commerce. Such risks for the Company include, but are not limited to, an evolving and unpredictable business model and the management of growth. To address these risks, the Company must, among other things, maintain and increase its customer base, implement and successfully execute its business and marketing strategy, continue to develop and upgrade its technology and transaction-processing systems, improve its Web site, provide superior customer service and order fulfillment, respond to competitive developments, and attract, retain and motivate qualified personnel. There can be no assurance that the Company will be successful in addressing such risks, and the failure to do so could have a material adverse effect on the Company's business, prospects, financial condition and results of operations.

Since inception, the Company has incurred significant losses, and as of March 31, 1997 had an accumulated deficit of $9.0 million. The Company believes that its success will depend in large part on its ability to (i) extend its brand position, (ii) provide its customers with outstanding value and a superior shopping experience, and (iii) achieve sufficient sales volume to realize economies of scale. Accordingly, the Company intends to invest heav-

ily in marketing and promotion, site development and technology and operating infrastructure development. The Company also intends to offer attractive pricing programs, which will reduce its gross margins. Because the Company has relatively low product gross margins, achieving profitability given planned investment levels depends upon the Company's ability to generate and sustain substantially increased revenue levels. As a result, the Company believes that it will incur substantial operating losses for the foreseeable future, and that the rate at which such losses will be incurred will increase significantly from current levels. Although the Company has experienced significant revenue growth in recent periods, such growth rates are not sustainable and will decrease in the future. In view of the rapidly evolving nature of the Company's business and its limited operating history, the Company believes that period-to-period comparisons of its operating results are not necessarily meaningful and should not be relied upon as an indication of future performance. See "Management's Discussion and Analysis of Financial Condition and Results of Operations."

The Company expects to use a portion of the net proceeds of this offering to fund its operating losses. If such net proceeds, together with cash generated by operations, are insufficient to fund future operating losses, the Company may be required to raise additional funds. There can be no assurance that such financing will be available in amounts or on terms acceptable to the Company, if at all.

Unpredictability of Future Revenues; Potential Fluctuations in Quarterly Operating Results; Seasonality. As a result of the Company's limited operating history and the emerging nature of the markets in which it competes, the Company is unable to accurately forecast its revenues. The Company's current and future expense levels are based largely on its investment plans and estimates of future revenues and are to a large extent fixed. Sales and operating results generally depend on the volume of, timing of and ability to fulfill orders received, which are difficult to forecast. The Company may be unable to adjust spending in a timely manner to compensate for any unexpected revenue shortfall. Accordingly, any significant shortfall in revenues in relation to the Company's planned expenditures would have an immediate adverse effect on the Company's business, prospects, financial condition and results of operations. Further, as a strategic response to changes in the competitive environment, the Company may from time to

(Continued)

EXHIBIT 31-18 *(Continued)*

time make certain pricing, service or marketing decisions that could have a material adverse effect on its business, prospects, financial condition, and results of operations. See "Business—Competition."

The Company expects to experience significant fluctuations in its future quarterly operating results due to a variety of factors, many of which are outside the Company's control. Factors that may adversely affect the Company's quarterly operating results include (i) the Company's ability to retain existing customers, attract new customers at a steady rate and maintain customer satisfaction, (ii) the Company's ability to manage inventory and fulfillment operations and maintain gross margins, (iii) the announcement or introduction of new sites, services and products by the Company and its competitors, (iv) price competition or higher wholesale prices in the industry, (v) the level of use of the Internet and online services and increasing consumer acceptance of the Internet and other online services for the purchase of consumer products such as those offered by the Company, (vi) the Company's ability to upgrade and develop its systems and infrastructure and attract new personnel in a timely and effective manner, (vii) the level of traffic on the Company's Web site, (viii) technical difficulties, system downtime or Internet brownouts, (ix) the amount and timing of operating costs and capital expenditures relating to expansion of the company's business, operations and infrastructure, (x) the number of popular books introduced during the period, (xi) the level of merchandise returns experienced by the Company, (xii) governmental regulation, and (xiii) general economic conditions and economic conditions specific to the Internet, online commerce and the book industry.

The Company expects that it will experience seasonality in its business, reflecting a combination of seasonal fluctuations in Internet usage and traditional retail seasonality patterns. Internet usage and the rate of Internet growth may be expected to decline during the summer. Further, sales in the traditional retail book industry are significantly higher in the fourth calendar quarter of each year than in the preceding three quarters.

Due to the foregoing factors, in one or more future quarters the Company's operating results may fall below the expectations of securities analysts and investors. In such event, the trading price of the Common Stock would likely be materially adversely affected.

Risk of Capacity Constraints; Reliance on Internally Developed Systems; System Development Risks. . . .

Risk of System Failure; Single Site and Order Interface. . . .

Management of Potential Growth; New Management Team; Limited Senior Management Resources. . . .

Dependence on Continued Growth of Online Commerce. The Company's future revenues and any future profits are substantially dependent upon the widespread acceptance and use of the Internet and other online services as an effective medium of commerce by consumers. Rapid growth in the use of and interest in the Web, the Internet and other online services is a recent phenomenon, and there can be no assurance that acceptance and use will continue to develop or that a sufficiently broad base of consumers will adopt, and continue to use, the Internet and other online services as a medium of commerce. Demand and market acceptance for recently introduced services and products over the Internet are subject to a high level of uncertainty and there exist few proven services and products. The Company relies on consumers who have historically used traditional means of commerce to purchase merchandise. For the Company to be successful, these consumers must accept and utilize novel ways of conducting business and exchanging information.

In addition, the Internet and other online services may not be accepted as a viable commercial marketplace for a number of reasons, including potentially inadequate development of the necessary network infrastructure or delayed development of enabling technologies and performance improvements. To the extent that the Internet and other online services continue to experience significant growth in the number of users, their frequency of use or an increase in their bandwidth requirements, there can be no assurance that the infrastructure for the Internet and other online services will be able to support the demands placed upon them. In addition, the Internet or other online services could lose their viability due to delays in the development or adoption of new standards and protocols required to handle increased levels of Internet or other online service activity, or due to increased governmental regulation. Changes in or insufficient availability of telecommunications services to support the Internet or other online services also could result in slower response times and adversely affect usage of the Internet and other online services generally and Amazon.com in particular. If use of the Internet and other online services does not continue to grow or grows

(Continued)

EXHIBIT 31-18 (Continued)

more slowly than expected, if the infrastructure for the Internet and other online services does not effectively support growth that may occur, or if the Internet and other online services do not become a viable commercial marketplace, the Company's business, prospects, financial condition and results of operations would be materially adversely affected.

Rapid Technological Change. To remain competitive, the Company must continue to enhance and improve the responsiveness, functionality and features of the Amazon.com online store. The Internet and the online commerce industry are characterized by rapid technological change, changes in user and customer requirements and preferences, frequent new product and service introductions embodying new technologies and the emergence of new industry standards and practices that could render the Company's existing Web site and proprietary technology and systems obsolete. The Company's success will depend, in part, on its ability to license leading technologies useful in its business, enhance its existing services, develop new services and technology that address the increasingly sophisticated and varied needs of its prospective customers, and respond to technological advances and emerging industry standards and practices on a cost-effective and timely basis. The development of the Web site and other proprietary technology entails significant technical and business risks. There can be no assurance that the Company will successfully use new technologies effectively or adapt its Web site, proprietary technology and transaction-processing systems to customer requirements or emerging industry standards. If the Company is unable, for technical, legal, financial or other reasons, to adapt in a timely manner in response to changing market conditions or customer requirements, its business, prospects, financial condition and results of operations would be materially adversely affected. See "Business—Technology."

Dependence on Key Personnel; Need for Additional Personnel. . . .

Online Commerce Security Risks. . . .

Competition. The online commerce market, particularly over the Internet, is new, rapidly evolving and intensely competitive, which competition the Company expects to intensify in the future. Barriers to entry are minimal, and current and new competitors can launch new sites at a relatively low cost. In addition, the retail book industry is intensely competitive. The Company currently or potentially competes with a variety of other companies. These competitors include (i) various online booksellers and vendors of other information-based products such as CDs and videotapes, including Book Stacks Unlimited, Inc., a subsidiary of CUC International, Inc. ("CUC"), (ii) a number of indirect competitors that specialize in online commerce or derive a substantial portion of their revenues from online commerce, including America Online, Inc. ("AOL") and Microsoft Corporation, through which other bookstores may offer products, and (iii) publishers and retail vendors of books, music and videotapes, including large specialty booksellers, with significant brand awareness, sales volume and customer bases, such as Barnes & Noble, Inc. ("B&N") and Borders Group, Inc. ("Borders"). Both B&N and Borders have announced their intention to devote substantial resources to online commerce in the near future and B&N, specifically, has a relationship with AOL through which B&N offers a broad selection of titles at discount prices.

The Company believes that the principal competitive factors in its market are brand recognition, selection, personalized services, convenience, price, accessibility, customer service, quality of search tools, quality of editorial and other site content and reliability and speed of fulfillment. Many of the Company's current and potential competitors have longer operating histories, larger customer bases, greater brand recognition and significantly greater financial, marketing and other resources than the Company. In addition, online retailers may be acquired by, receive investments from or enter into other commercial relationships with larger, well-established and well-financed companies as use of the Internet and other online services increases. Certain of the company's competitors may be able to secure merchandise from vendors on more favorable terms, devote greater resources to marketing and promotional campaigns, adopt more aggressive pricing or inventory availability policies and devote substantially more resources to Web site and systems development than the Company. Increased competition may result in reduced operating margins, loss of market share and a diminished brand franchise. There can be no assurance that the Company will be able to compete successfully against current and future competitors, and competitive pressures faced by the Company may have a material adverse effect on the Company's business, prospects, financial condition and results of operations. Further, as a strategic response to changes in the competitive environment, the Company may from time

(Continued)

EXHIBIT 31-18   (Continued)

---

to time make certain pricing, service or marketing decisions or acquisitions that could have a material adverse effect on its business, prospects, financial condition and results of operations. New technologies and the expansion of existing technologies may increase the competitive pressures on the Company. For example, client-agent applications that select specific titles from a variety of Web sites may channel customers to online booksellers that compete with the Company. In addition, companies that control access to transactions through network access or Web browsers could promote the Company's competitors or charge the Company a substantial fee for inclusion. See "Business—Competition."

Reliance on Certain Suppliers.   The Company purchases a substantial majority of its products from two major vendors, Ingram Book Group ("Ingram") and Baker & Taylor, Inc. ("B&T). Ingram is the single largest supplier and accounted for 59% of the company's inventory purchases in 1996. The Company carries minimal inventory and relies to a large extent on rapid fulfillment from these and other vendors. The Company has no long-term contracts or arrangements with any of its vendors that guarantee the availability of merchandise, the continuation of particular payment terms or the extension of credit limits. There can be no assurance that the Company's current vendors will continue to sell merchandise to the Company on current terms or that the Company will be able to establish new or extend current vendor relationships to ensure acquisition of merchandise in a timely and efficient manner and on acceptable commercial terms. If the Company were unable to develop and maintain relationships with vendors that would allow it to obtain sufficient quantities of merchandise on acceptable commercial terms, its business, prospects, financial condition and results of operations would be materially adversely affected. See "Business—Warehousing and Fulfillment."

Risks Associated with Entry into New Business Areas. . . .

Trademarks and Proprietary Rights. . . .

Governmental Regulation and Legal Uncertainties. The Company is not currently subject to direct regulation, by any domestic or foreign governmental agency, other than regulations applicable to businesses generally, and laws or regulations directly applicable to access to online commerce. However, due to the increasing popularity and use of the Internet and other online services, it is possible that a number of laws and regulations may be adopted with respect to the Internet or other online services covering issues such as user privacy, pricing, content, copyrights, distribution and characteristics and quality of products and services. Furthermore, the growth and development of the market for online commerce may prompt calls for more stringent consumer protection laws that may impose additional burdens on those companies conducting business online. The adoption of any additional laws or regulations may decrease the growth of the Internet or other online services, which could, in turn, decrease the demand for the Company's products and services and increase the Company's cost of doing business, or otherwise have an adverse effect on the Company's business, prospects, financial condition and results of operations. Moreover, the applicability to the Internet and other online services of existing laws in various jurisdictions governing issues such as property ownership, sales and other taxes, libel and personal privacy is uncertain and may take years to resolve. Any such new legislation or regulation, the application of laws and regulations from jurisdictions whose laws do not currently apply to the Company's business, or the application of existing laws and regulations to the Internet and other online services could have a material adverse effect on the Company's business, prospects, financial condition and results of operations.

Sales and Other Taxes. . . .

Control of the Company.   Immediately upon completion of this offering, the outstanding Common Stock will be beneficially owned approximately 42% by Jeffrey P. Bezos, the Company's President, Chief Executive Officer and Chairman of the Board, and 10% by members of Mr. Bezos' family and trusts controlled by members of Mr. Bezos' family (42% and 10%, respectively, if the over-allotment option is exercised in full). The above persons and entities will hold an aggregate of approximately 52% of the outstanding voting power of the Company immediately upon completion of this offering. As a result, upon completion of this offering, the Bezos family will be able to (i) elect, or defeat the election of, the Company's directors, (ii) amend or prevent amendment of the Company's Restated Certificate of Incorporation or By-laws, or (iii) effect or prevent a merger, sale of assets or other corporate transaction. The Company's public stockholders, for so long as they hold less than 50% of the outstanding voting power of the Company, will not be able

(Continued)

EXHIBIT 31-18 *(Continued)*

to control the outcome of such transactions. The extent of ownership by the Bezos family may have the effect of preventing a change in control of the Company or discouraging a potential acquirer from making a tender offer or otherwise attempting to obtain control of the Company, which in turn could have an adverse effect on the market price of the Common Stock. See "Management," "Certain Transactions" and "Principal Stockholders."

Recent and Continuing Publicity. . . .

No Prior Public Market; Possible Volatility of Stock Price. . . .

Shares Eligible for Future Sale. Sales of substantial amounts of the Company's Common Stock in the public market after this offering could adversely affect prevailing market prices for the Common Stock. The 2,500,000 shares of Common Stock offered hereby will be freely tradable without restriction in the public market. Taking into account restrictions imposed by the Securities Act of 1933, as amended (the "Securities Act"), rules promulgated by the Securities and Exchange Commission (the "Commission") thereunder, the Company's contractual right to repurchase shares and lock-up agreements between certain stockholders and the Company or Deutsche Morgan Grenfell Inc., the number of additional shares that will be available for sale in the public market, subject in some cases to the volume and other restrictions of Rule 144 under the Securities Act, will be as follows: approximately 44,213 additional shares will be eligible for sale beginning 91 days after the date of this Prospectus and approximately 19,258,913 additional shares will be eligible for sale beginning 181 days after the date of this Prospectus. Approximately 681,300 remaining shares will be eligible for sale pursuant to Rule 144 upon the expiration of one-year holding periods or the expiration of the Company's contractual right to repurchase the shares between November 1997 and May 1998. Deutsche Morgan Grenfell Inc. may, in its sole discretion and at any time without notice, release all or any portion of the shares subject to such lock-up agreements. Upon the closing of this offering, holders of 13,286,376 shares of Common Stock are entitled to certain rights

with respect to the registration of such shares under the Securities Act. In addition, the Company intends to file a registration statement on Form S-8 under the Securities Act approximately 180 days after the date of this Prospectus to register approximately 9,534,648 shares of Common Stock reserved for issuance under the 1994 Stock Option Plan and the Company's 1997 Stock Option Plan. See "Description of Capital Stock—Registration Rights" and "Shares Eligible for Future Sale."

Antitakeover Effect of Certain Charter Provisions. . . .

No Specific Use of Proceeds. The Company has not designated any specific use for the net proceeds from the sale by the Company of the Common Stock offered hereby. The Company expects to use the net proceeds for general corporate purposes, including working capital to fund anticipated operating losses and capital expenditures. A portion of net proceeds may also be used to acquire or invest in complementary businesses, products and technologies. From time to time, in the ordinary course of business, the Company expects to evaluate potential acquisitions of such businesses, products or technologies. However, the Company has no present understandings, commitments or agreements with respect to any material acquisition or investment. Accordingly, management will have significant flexibility in applying the net proceeds of this offering. The failure of management to apply such funds effectively could have a material adverse effect on the Company's business, prospects, financial condition and results of operations. See "Use of Proceeds."

Immediate and Substantial Dilution. The initial public offering price is substantially higher than the book value per outstanding share of Common Stock. Accordingly, purchasers in this offering will suffer an immediate and substantial dilution of $11.66 per share in the net tangible book value of the Common Stock from the initial public offering price. Additional dilution will occur upon exercise of outstanding options granted by the company. See "Dilution."

* * * *

believes that it will incur substantial operating losses for the foreseeable future, and that the rate at which such losses will be incurred will increase significantly from current levels." This was a somewhat unusual statement at the time, but we thought the right one in order to enable investors to make an informed investment decision.

My experience at Digidesign helped inform my perspective on Amazon.com's IPO. At Digidesign, we also had a very open and financially conservative culture. I had learned a key bit of advice from Roger McNamee, a well-known growth company investor formerly with T. Rowe Price who is a general partner at Integral Capital Partners. Roger told me, "You don't have to convince everyone of your story on day one—only enough to complete the IPO. Make the right choices for your long-term strategy."

THE ROAD SHOW

As Covey settled into her airplane seat, she reflected on the past three days of the European leg of the road show. She had visited four cities—Zurich, Geneva, Paris, and London—making nearly five presentations each day:

So far, Jeff and I have received very positive feedback. Our story is good. We have doubled our sales every quarter for six consecutive quarters, and our customer focus and business model are compelling.

It's really a relief to me. We have adopted a philosophy of openness and candor about our long-term philosophy. We held to our investment plans despite the weak market. Moreover, we maintained the confidentiality of many metrics of our business despite inquiries by investors. They wanted to know details on customer mix, repeat buyer patterns, and successful marketing programs. We understand why investors are interested in these metrics—they are important underpinnings to our business model. But we truly believe that we will be a much better investment for them if we keep that learning proprietary vis-a-vis our competitors. We think that our new investors will reap the benefits of these choices in the future.

Covey thought ahead to the upcoming pricing meeting. Amazon.com had indicated a filing range of $12 to $14 per share for 2.5 million shares, but their underwriters had not yet given Covey an indication of investor interest. Would the "book" be hopelessly oversubscribed? In this case, the company could either raise the offering price or be assured of a big run up in the market price in the first days of trading. Did the company want a big first day pop or a slow steady rise? What would Covey do if the book were weaker than hoped? Would she have to consider lowering the price or even pulling the offering? To date, the company had invested considerable management and capital resources in the public filing and did not want a disappointing offering.

Covey turned to review industry reading in preparation for the H&Q conference. She paused as she came across one U.S. analyst's comment about their much anticipated offering: "Wired fell out of bed, Auto-By-Tel didn't pop, and even with Amazon.com's top-tier investment bankers, I think they'll have trouble selling the book." Covey knew that she and Bezos had their work cut out for them.

32

ArthroCare

Dr. Hira Thapliyal rubbed his eyes and looked at the digital clock beside his bed. Was it 2 A.M. or 3 A.M.? Dr. Thapliyal was having a difficult time falling asleep; he couldn't help thinking about the board meeting that would take place later that week, where several important decisions affecting the future direction of his company—ArthroCare— would be made. ArthroCare was a young company in the medical devices arena; the company made small, disposable, electrosurgical tools that could be used for cutting and shaping tissue through minute incisions in the body. ArthroCare had gone public in February 1996, at $14/share, raising $32 million for the company, and placing a market capitalization of roughly $120 million on the enterprise. One month later, the stock was as high as $26. Now, Monday, August 12, 1996—six months later—the stock was trading at $13.75, slightly below the offering price. The most immediate cause for the drop in the price of ArthroCare's stock related to issues with the medical device sector overall. As Paul Brown, an equity analyst with Volpe, Welty put it:

> ArthroCare went public at the height of the feeding frenzy. Companies were going public based upon a view of their earnings three or four years out. Now as several other medical device companies have reported sales and earnings figures below expectations, the sector overall has been slammed.[1]

As the first half of 1996 unfolded, ArthroCare had made its first quarter earnings target. Several weeks earlier, on July 25, the company had announced its second quarter earnings, which were also in line with analysts' estimates. During the prior week, however, ArthroCare's stock had dropped. On Tuesday, August 6, Phil Nalbone, an analyst at one of ArthroCare's investment banks—Volpe, Welty—had issued a downward revision to their near-term earnings estimates. ArthroCare stock had closed for the week at $13.75.

Lecturer Michael J. Roberts prepared this case at the Harvard Business School California Research Center with the assistance of Professor William Sahlman and Professor Jack McDonald of Stanford University Graduate School of Business, as the basis for class discussion rather than to illustrate either effective or ineffective handling of an administrative situation.

[1] Casewriter Interview.

At the upcoming board meeting, the company would confront several issues that could have a serious impact on its ability to make the future earnings numbers that analysts had forecast during the IPO. Specifically, the company needed to deal with several issues:

- Marketing executives at ArthroCare wanted to drop the price of one of the company's products—the "controller" (see more below)—in order to increase market penetration. This would have a serious impact on the company's near-term margins, making it highly unlikely that the company would be able to meet its near-term earnings estimates.

- ArthroCare was also spending heavily to "extend its technology platform." Thapliyal was an ardent believer in the fundamental electrode technology that underlay ArthroCare's device. He believed that this technology could be extended from its current orthopedic use to other applications, including dermatology, gynecology, cardiology and ear, nose, and throat surgical procedures. But, the cost of doing this fundamental R&D and getting the devices through the Food and Drug Administration (FDA) approval process had raised ArthroCare's break-even to more than $25 million in sales, roughly double what it would have been had the company pursued a more narrowly focused strategy of simply trying to "get profitable quickly" with its first device, which was targeted towards orthopedic procedures.

Thapliyal explained the difficulty these choices presented:

As we have begun to apply our proprietary technology, we see more and more applications for it. Thus, we face a complicated set of choices about whether to move as quickly as possible to reach profitability, or whether to try to maximize the value of the enterprise by staking out the broadest spectrum of opportunities, getting both the market and technical advantages that we will need to be successful. Similarly, with respect to the pricing of the controller, it is a question of short term profits vs. the long-term benefits of increasing our market penetration. People said that being a public company would present us with a host of additional issues to manage. It looks like they were right.

BACKGROUND

Hira Thapliyal, Ph.D., was 47. He was born in the small village of Thapli in India's Northern Himalayan Mountains and had come to the United States in 1969 to attend college at Washington State University. He received a Master's from the University of Idaho and a doctorate in Materials Science & Engineering from Cornell in 1977. Dr. Thapliyal then joined Corning Corporation, in upstate New York, to work on advanced medical device projects. After four years at Corning, he received an offer to join Amdahl Corp. in Silicon Valley as a process engineer. Gene Amdahl, the founder of Amdahl Corp., had virtually invented disk storage at IBM, and he had then left to form his own business. Soon after Dr. Thapliyal joined Amdahl, however, Gene Amdahl left to start Trilogy, another business aimed at making high-speed computers. Dr. Thapliyal joined Trilogy in its start-up phase and stayed for about a year: "My interest in medical devices had been piqued at Corning, and I wanted to get back to that industry."

In 1982, Dr. Thapliyal joined Oximetrix, a company that made cardiac medical devices. And one and one-half years later, he was offered "the chance of a lifetime":

Through a mutual friend, I was introduced to Dr. John Simpson, one of the pioneers in the cardiac device field. Simpson had been one of the inventors of balloon angioplasty.

With this technique, a cardiac catheter—a slim tube—is fed through an artery in the leg up to the chambers and blood vessels of the heart. Typically, catheters were used to take readings and measurements for diagnostic purposes. But Simpson had the idea of putting a small balloon at the tip of the catheter, feeding it up to the blood vessels that feed the heart, and then inflating the balloon, to "crack" and compress the plaque—the fatty deposits—that can block the vessel and cause a heart attack.

Anyway, Dr. Simpson was starting a new company—Devices for Vascular Intervention— DVI. Simpson's approach at DVI was actually to remove the plaque with a very small cutting tool on a catheter, rather than compress it with a balloon.

Dr. Thapliyal joined DVI in 1984 as vice president of engineering. He worked not only on perfecting the device design, but also managed the research and clinical trials, quality control, administrative and regulatory functions, including dealing with the FDA. Dr. Thapliyal recalled his work at that time:

In 1985, we got interested in imaging the interior of blood vessels via ultrasound. It was a seductively defocusing project. Up until then, all of the cardiac catheter imaging devices could only see the inner wall—the lining—of the blood vessel. But Dr. Yock at Stanford came to us with the idea of imaging the blood vessel in three dimensions by using ultrasonic techniques.

We started work on this project on 1985, and decided to spin out the company—CVIS— in 1986 for the purpose of focusing on this opportunity. I was president of CVIS until 1988. I'd gotten married in 1986 and had my first child in 1988. I decided to take a break and recharge my batteries, and we hired another president to run CVIS. DVI was sold to Eli Lilly in 1989 for about $200 million. CVIS went public in 1992 and was bought in 1995 by Boston Scientific for approximately $100 million.

After a year I was offered the opportunity to run another company—MicroBionics. Between 1989 and 1993, I served as president and CEO of this privately held company that was in the business of continuous monitoring of blood gas levels. Again, it used a catheter technology, this time to measure a vital sign for patients who were critically ill. This was technically a very difficult task, and I was not able to raise sufficient capital to take the idea to a clinical solution.

I left the company in 1993 to pursue another idea that had come to me during my work in the cardiovascular arena. One of the most serious problems in cardiology is a total occlusion—or blockage—of the blood vessel. Balloon angioplasty is often successful in opening clogged arteries, but—with a total occlusion—there is no space in which the catheter can be worked through. In this case, the patient must have a coronary artery bypass graft (CABG). The CABG is a very common procedure that solves this problem. Yet it is a very debilitating procedure. The entire chest is cracked open at the breastbone, and veins cut from the leg are grafted onto the heart to replace those that are blocked. There are 400,000 CABGs performed every year in the United States.

During my years at Corning, I had worked with a very bright medical device expert who was a consultant in the medical device business—Phil Eggers. I went to Phil with the germ of an idea, and together we developed the concept of taking an electrode and supplying it with an electric current, and basically melting the fatty deposits—like you would melt butter in a frying pan—so that you could then pass a catheter through the occlusion and break it up using traditional angioplasty. We filed an early patent, and in 1992 we founded a company—AngioCare—to pursue this technology.

Together, Thapliyal and Eggers worked on perfecting the electrode devices that could be used for this purpose. While the technique showed promise in cadaver studies, it proved problematic in early tests: "The electricity took the path of least resistance—

which was through the blood—and wouldn't travel through the fatty deposits sufficiently to warm and melt them."

Thapliyal and Eggers worked to devise a strategy to overcome this problem:

> One day we were at a gas station in Columbus, Ohio and looked around and saw all these cars at all these gas pumps, all these nozzles simultaneously pumping gas to all these cars. And we thought—why not use *multiple* electrodes to deliver current to the tissue? In this way, we could activate only those electrodes that were actually touching the fatty deposits, and not give the electricity a chance to avoid the deposits. Phil and I talked, we tried it, and it worked. We quickly sought patent protection for this technology, and moved towards trying to make a business out of it.

In late 1992, as the men were working to perfect the technology, they were also trying to raise money to finance the new company:

> I knew several venture capitalists from my prior experiences in the medical device business. But everyone I talked to felt the total occlusion market was too small—only 50,000 cases per year. Finally one of our eventual co-founders—Robert Garvie—said, "Would this technology work in orthopedics?" Garvie's thinking was that there are over two million cases a year of arthroscopic surgery of the knee, shoulder, elbow, wrist and ankle. In an arthroscopic surgical procedure, a small incision is made near the joint, and a tiny tool and video camera are used to cut and remove tissue.

> We didn't know if it would work, but we said we would try. We tested the tool in some animal tissue studies and it worked. It was better than using conventional metal blades that cut tissue because one tool through one incision could be made to do the work of multiple mechanical tools inserted through multiple incisions via the more traditional procedure. And, the electrode approach had the added benefit of cauterizing the blood vessels as it cut, sealing them up and stopping the bleeding of these blood vessels immediately.

> Just as the results were starting to come in, I ran into Annette Campbell-White, a VC from Paragon Venture Partners. Annette had been an investor at DVI and CVIS, and when she heard what we were up to, she said to come see her. Phil and I went in to see her in April 1993. One week later, she and her partner, John Lewis, had written us a check for $1 million.

AngioCare was put on "hold," and a new company called ArthroCare was started to pursue the orthopedics opportunity. (For a more complete description of Arthro-Care, see Exhibit 32-1, which presents detailed background material from the company's IPO prospectus.) A fourth co-founder, Tony Manlove (a Harvard MBA and past president of Oximetrix), joined Thapliyal, Eggers, and Garvie to co-found ArthroCare and to serve as its CFO. Upon the advice of their lawyers, Thapliyal and Eggers put their patents into a limited partnership and then licensed the orthopedics applications to ArthroCare. The company raised another $800,000 from wealthy individuals on the same terms as the Paragon investment—a $4 million post-money valuation.

This first $1.8 million of financing was intended to take the company to the point of submitting necessary animal data to the FDA for market approval of the device. (See below for information on the FDA approval process.) By mid-1994, animal tests showed that the device worked well in removing cartilage and other tissues in the joint. The next step in the process required human testing, which the company initiated in France; because of the significant time lag imposed by the FDA regulatory pathway, very few medical device companies performed human testing in the United States.

Meanwhile, in January of 1994, the company raised another round of $4 million, at an $11 million post-money valuation. This was followed by two more rounds prior to the IPO, raising $5.8 million at a $19 million valuation, and $4.1 million at a $37 million

EXHIBIT 32-1

EXCERPTS FROM ARTHROCARE'S IPO PROSPECTUS

Overview

Since commencing operations in April 1993, ArthroCare Corporation has primarily engaged in the design, development, clinical testing and manufacturing of its Arthroscopic System. ArthroCare Corporation designs, develops, manufactures and markets arthroscopic surgical equipment for use in orthopedics. The Arthroscopic System is designed to replace the multiple surgical tools used in arthroscopic procedures with one multi-purpose, electrosurgery system that ablates (removes) soft tissue while simultaneously achieving homeostasis (sealing small bleeding vessels). This allows the surgeon to remove damaged tissue while reducing the need for the frequent exchange of instruments that is common in arthroscopic procedures. The company received clearance of its 510(k) premarket notification from the FDA in March 1995 to market its Arthroscopic System for use in arthroscopic surgery of the knee, shoulder, elbow and ankle.

The company has experienced significant operating losses since inception and, as of December 31, 1995, had an accumulated deficit of $9.9 million. The company expects to generate substantial additional losses due to increased operating expenditures primarily attributable to the expansion of marketing and sales activities, scale-up of manufacturing capabilities, increased research and development and activities to support regulatory and reimbursement applications.

The company has only sold a small number of units and does not have any experience in manufacturing or selling its Arthroscopic System in commercial quantities. Whether the company can successfully manage the transition to a larger-scale commercial enterprise will depend upon the successful development of its manufacturing capability, the further development of its distribution network, obtaining foreign regulatory approvals for the Arthroscopic System, obtaining domestic and foreign regulatory approvals for potential products and strengthening its financial and management systems, procedures and controls.

Liquidity and Capital Resources

Since inception, the company has financed operations primarily from the sale of Preferred Stock. As of December 31, 1995, the company had raised $15.7 million. As of that date, cash and cash equivalents equaled $4.8 million. The company's cash used in operations increased to $6.6 million for the year ended December 31, 1995 from $2.1 million for the year ended December 31, 1994,

reflecting expenditures made primarily to increase research and development, to form a marketing and sales organization, to support administrative infrastructure, to expand to a 22,000 square foot facility, to purchase equipment and to begin building product inventory.

The company believes that the net proceeds from this offering together with interest thereon and the company's existing capital resources, will be sufficient to fund its operations at least through fiscal 1997.

Use of Proceeds

The net proceeds to the company from the sale of the 2,200,000 shares of Common Stock offered by the company hereby are estimated to be approximately $32,140,000 (assuming the Underwriters' over-allotment option is exercised in full), after deducting the underwriting discounts and commissions and estimated offering expenses payable by the company.

The company anticipates using the net proceeds from this offering as follows: approximately $6.0 million to increase manufacturing capacity; approximately $6.0 million to expand its marketing and sales efforts; approximately $5.0 million to fund its research and development efforts; approximately $3.0 million for working capital; and approximately $7.8 million for general corporate purposes.

The ArthroCare Arthroscopic System

The Arthroscopic System is an instrument used to perform surgery upon a site which is visualized with an arthroscope. The company does not manufacture arthroscopes.

The company's Arthroscopic System is comprised of the disposal ArthroWand, a connecting cable and a radio frequency power controller. The controller, approximately 14 inches by 11 inches by 5 inches, is used to deliver high-frequency power to the ArthroWand. The list price of the controller, including the cable, is $12,500. The voltage level can be changed by the user to ablate different tissues using the keys on the front panel of the controller. The cable, which is approximately 10 feet in length, connects the controller to the ArthroWand. Power is transmitted through the cable to the ArthroWand by depressing the foot pedal, thereby enabling surgeons to utilize the ArthroWand as a conventional probe as well as an instrument that ablates and coagulates. Accordingly, the surgeon using the Arthroscopic System need not remove and insert a variety of instruments to

(Continued)

EXHIBIT 32-1   (Continued)

perform different tasks as is required when using conventional arthroscopic instruments. The ArthroWand is approved for sale in tip sizes from 1.5mm to 4.5mm with angles ranging from 0 to 90 degrees. It is currently available in two tip sizes, 2.5mm and 3mm, and each size is available in tip angles of 0, 15 and 90 degrees. These different tip sizes and tip angles enable the surgeon to ablate different volumes of tissue and to access treatment sites not readily accessible by existing mechanical instruments and motorized cutting tools. The list price of the ArthroWand is $120.

The company's patented multi-electrode, bipolar, electrosurgical technology offers a number of benefits that the company believes may provide advantages over competing surgical methods and devices. The principal benefits include:

- Ease of Use. The Arthroscopic System performs many of the functions of mechanical tools, power tools and electrosurgery instruments allowing the surgeon to use a single instrument. The lightweight probe is simple to use and complements the surgeon's existing tactile skills without the need for extensive training.

- Precision. In contrast to conventional tools, the Arthroscopic System permits surgeons to perform precise tissue ablation and sculpting. The company believes this may result in more rapid patient rehabilitation.

- Simultaneous Ablation and Hemostasis. The Arthroscopic System efficiently seals small bleeding vessels during the tissue ablation process. In procedures involving the shoulder, the capability to ablate tissue hemostatically removes the need to introduce coagulating instruments and improves the surgeon's visibility of the operative site.

- Cost Reduction. The Arthroscopic System eliminates the need to introduce multiple instruments to remove and sculpt tissue and seal small bleeding vessels. The company believes this may reduce operating time and thereby produce cost savings for health care providers.

In order to secure these benefits, however, a hospital or surgical center must purchase a specially designed power control unit (controller) which has a list price of $12,500. At hospital sites or surgical centers where several arthroscopic surgery procedures may be performed simultaneously, the purchase of multiple controllers may be required. In addition, motorized and mechanical instruments and electrosurgery systems currently used by hospitals and surgical centers for arthroscopic procedures have a history of success and have become widely accepted by orthopedic surgeons.

ArthroCare Strategy

The company's objective is to utilize its proprietary technology to design, develop, manufacture and sell innovative, clinically superior electrosurgical devices for the arthroscopic surgical treatment of joint injuries and for the surgical treatment of other soft tissue conditions. The key elements of the company's strategy to achieve this objective include:

- Penetrate Existing Arthroscopic Surgical Instrument Market. The company's initial sales efforts are focused on marketing the company's products to orthopedic surgeons performing high volume arthroscopy and to opinion-leaders in orthopedic surgery.

- Expand into New Arthroscopic Surgical Markets. The company intends to encourage surgeons to use its Arthroscopic System to treat joints that have been primarily treated by open surgery, such as the shoulder, elbow and ankle. Because of the small size, varying shapes and tactile feel of the company's ArthroWand, surgeons will be able to arthroscopically access areas difficult to reach by conventional arthroscopic surgical tools.

- Target Key International Markets. The company intends to market its Arthroscopic System in certain international markets if required regulatory approvals are received. The company is developing a network of independent distributors in Europe and intends to collaborate with one or more marketing partners to assist with regulatory requirements and to market and distribute the Arthroscopic System in Japan.

- Leverage Broadly Applicable Proprietary Technology. The company expects to leverage its proprietary technology by developing additional wands for use in a variety of surgical procedures, including urology (e.g., trans-urethral resection of the prostate), dermatology (e.g., abnormal skin growth and wrinkle removal), gynecology (e.g., endometrial ablation), and periodontics (e.g., gingivectomy).

(Continued)

EXHIBIT 32-1 (Continued)

- Pursue Regulatory Approvals Through 510(k) Applications. The company intends to pursue additional applications of its technology in indications that will require FDA clearance through the shorter, less costly 510(k) regulatory process.

Products Under Development

The company believes that its core technology is applicable to other surgical applications that will utilize the current Arthroscopic System, including the controller. The company is currently developing a urology product designed for use with a conventional resectoscope, a device used to visualize the urethra and bladder during surgical procedures. The company is currently developing a gynecology product designed for use with a conventional hysteroscope, a device used to visualize the uterus during surgical procedures.

Research and Development

The company has undertaken preliminary animal studies and wand development for the use of its ablation technology with its current controller in the following areas: i) dermatology and plastic surgery for skin resurfacing and for the treatment of epidermal (the outermost layer of skin) and dermal (the deep bed of vascular connective tissue beneath the epidermal layer) disorders; ii) gynecology for the laparoscopic treatment (a surgical treatment utilizing a miniature video camera and miniature surgical instruments manipulated through small portals in the abdominal wall) of endometriosis (a condition in which tissue growth occurs in the pelvic cavity, accompanied by abdominal pain); iii) oral surgery for the treatment of gingivitis (inflammation of the gums) and other disorders of mucosal tissue; and iv) general surgery for use in the dissection, resection and ablation of soft tissue in open surgical procedures and in endoscopically assisted surgery.

Stock Plans

Incentive Stock Plan A total of 1,536,025 shares of Common Stock has been reserved for issuance under the company's Incentive Stock Plan. Under the Incentive Stock Plan, as of December 31, 1995, options to purchase an aggregate of 493,350 shares were outstanding, 123,750 shares of Common Stock had been purchased pursuant to the exercise of stock purchase rights and 918,925 shares were available for future grant.

Principal Stockholders

Beneficial Owner	Shares Beneficially Owned	Percentage of Shares Beneficially owned	
		Prior To Offering	After Offering
Entities affiliated with InterWest Partners	1,227,695	20.0%	14.7%
Entities affiliated with Institutional Venture Partners	1,212,694	19.8%	14.6%$
Entities affiliated with Paragon Venture Partners	1,088,088	17.7%	13.1%
Hira V. Thapliyal, Ph.D.	628,750	10.3%	7.5%
Philip E. Eggers	593,750	9.7%	7.1%
Annette J. Campbell-White	230,467	3.8%	2.8%
Robert T. Hagen	123,334	2.0%	1.5%
Al Weinstein	100,000	1.6%	1.2%
A. Larry Tannenbaum	18,334	*	*
All Directors and executive officers as a group (8 persons)	4,010,418	65.4%	48.1%

(Continued)

EXHIBIT 32-1   (Continued)

Financial Statements

See Tables 1A and 1B below for ArthroCare's balance sheets and income statements. [NOTE: Columns listing 1996 YTD results were *not* included in the original prospectus, but *are* included here for ease of comparison.]

TABLE 1A   ArthroCare Corporation Balance Sheets ($000)

			December 31,	
			1996 YTD[a]	
	1994	1995	Q1	Q2
Assets				
Current assets:				
Cash and cash equivalents	$2,599	$4,774	$33,041	$30,223
Accounts receivable, net	—	212	863	1,176
Inventories	—	315	1,143	1,301
Prepaid expenses and other current assets	31	891	355	334
Total current assets	2,630	6,393	35,402	33,034
Property and equipment, net	275	1,135	1,090	1,477
Related party receivables[b]	—	228	—	1,609
Other	12	49	1,896	329
Total assets	$2,917	$7,800	$38,388	$36,449
Liabilities				
Current liabilities				
Accounts payable:				
Trade	$ 104	$ 732	$ 1,051	$ 439
Related parties	17	35	36	45
Accrued liabilities	35	472	577	922
Capital lease obligation, current portion	8	34	35	36
Total current liabilities	163	1,274	1,699	1,442
Capital lease obligations, less current portion	15	43	44	35
Deferred rent	12	148	163	163
Total liabilities	$ 190	$1,475	$ 1,906	$ 1,640
Stockholders' Equity				
Convertible preferred stock	$ 4	$ 9	$ —	$ —
Common stock	1	2	9	9
Additional paid-in capital	5,685	16,869	48,767	48,787
Notes receivable from stockholder	—	(92)	(92)	(92)
Deferred compensation	—	(550)	(509)	(469)
Unrealized loss on investment	—	—	(37)	(35)
Accumulated deficit	(2,963)	(9,913)	(11,656)	(13,391)
Total Stockholders' Equity	2,727	6,325	36,482	34,809
Total Liabilities and Stockholders' Equity	$2,917	$ 7,800	$38,388	$36,449

[a] Unaudited.

[b] Related party receivables consists primarily of several loans made to officers of the company.

(Continued)

EXHIBIT 32-1 (Continued)

TABLE 1B ArthroCare Statements of Operations

[NOTE: Columns listing 1996 YTD results were *not* included in the original prospectus, but *are* included here for ease of comparison.]

	Period from April 29, 1993 (date of inception) to December 31, 1993	Year Ended December 31,		YTD 1996[a]	
		1994	1995	Q1	Q2
Net sales	—	—	$218	$1,159	$1,406
Cost of sales	—	—	447	1,065	1,236
Gross margin	—	—	(229)	94	170
Costs and expenses:					
Research and development	750	2,119	4,009	864	950
Sales and marketing	—	—	1,351	658	872
General and administrative	108	128	1,321	576	527
Nonrecurring charge for acquired technology	—	—	260	—	—
Total operating expenses	857	2,247	6,940	2,098	2,349
Loss from operations	(857)	(2,247)	(7,169)	(2,004)	(2,179)
Interest and other income	15	126	219	263	444
Net loss	$(842)	$(2,121)	$(6,950)	$(1,743)	$(1,735)
Pro forma net loss per share	$(0.18)	$(0.33)	$(1.00)	$(0.25)	$(0.20)
Shares used in computing pro forma net loss per share	4,768,466	6,414,664	6,929,202	6,856,086	8,675,055

[a] Unaudited.

valuation (all valuations post-money). All these financings were done in the form of a convertible preferred stock, and the original VC firms of Paragon Ventures Partners, InterWest Partners, Institutional Venture Partners, and MedVenture Associates participated. Each firm (except IVP) had a board representative. (See table below for details of financing rounds.)

ArthroCare Financings

Preferred Stock Round	Date Financed	Total Capital Raised	Purchase Price per Share	Preferred Stock Sold— Number of Shares	Conversion Ratio Preferred: Common	Effective Price/ Common Share	Common Shares Outstanding[a]
A	5-12/93	$1,730,816	$0.95	1,856,127	2:1	$1.90	1,176,475
B	1/94	$3,956,159	$1.60	2,500,000	2:1	$3.20	1,186,475
C	5/95	$5,827,777	$2.00	2,922,500	2:1	$4.00	1,792,725
D	10/95	$4,190,251	$3.00	1,399,109	2:1	$6.00	1,792,725

[a] After financing, but excluding the employee stock option pool (see Exhibit 32-1 for details).

Dr. Thapliyal described the company's strategy:

> We figured our best strategy was to develop the core technology, sort out the range of possible applications, stake out a broad set of patent claims, get the FDA approvals, and sell the company to one of the established players. That is basically the model that most of these venture-backed medical device companies are based upon, simply because the cost of setting up a proprietary distribution channel is so high. But then we realized, in order to do this "plan A"—and get the highest price, we had to actually do "plan B"—to ramp up and market the product ourselves. Otherwise, we would appear to a prospective buyer as though a sale was our only option, and we'd have a lot less negotiating strength. And, it was also clear that we could command a higher price if we actually started taking sales and margin away from some of the established players. Our device would compete with mechanical shavers made by Bristol-Myers, for instance, so we knew we'd attract their attention if we started affecting their revenue numbers.

As the company's R&D effort proceeded, relationships with the VC's did become contentious over one issue—intellectual property. Another early investor—Bob Momsen, a partner at InterWest Partners—described the tension:

> When Hira first came to us, ArthroCare owned a license on the Eggers/Thapliyal electrode patents for application in orthopedic uses only. The two men had retained the rights to use the technology in other applications in other areas for themselves. I felt strongly that the company in which the VCs were investing should own all the intellectual capital—the rights to apply this technology in all markets. It was clear to us that this technology had broad application. And, I've learned that the business model often changes as you move down the learning curve. Why should we finance this learning, only so it can be applied more profitably in another segment that we wouldn't get to participate in? Dr. Thapliyal and I could not agree on this issue during the first round, so I agreed to invest on his terms, with the understanding that this would be a continuing item of discussion. By the time the third round came up in 1995, I think everyone understood that we were going to have a lot of complicated choices about which markets to pursue on what kind of schedule, and the last thing we wanted was a conflict of interest injected into these discussions as a result of different ownership stakes in different parties' hands.[2]

At the time of the third round of financing, the Eggers and Thapliyal patents were folded into ArthroCare, and the owners received additional cash compensation and stock in exchange for their contribution.

THE FDA AND REGULATIONS AFFECTING MEDICAL DEVICES

Medical devices are subject to stringent FDA regulations and approval processes. The FDA regulates the testing, manufacture, labeling, packaging, marketing, distribution, and recordkeeping for all classes of medical devices.

Most devices require a "premarket" approval from the FDA to ensure their safety and effectiveness. Life-sustaining and life-supporting devices, as well as implantable devices, are subject to Class III restrictions. And any new device that has not been found to be "substantially equivalent" to an existing device is subject to Class III regulation. Approval for this type of device can take from three to five years.

Class II devices are subject to a lower level of regulation. ArthroCare sought Class II approval to market its device (the ArthroWand) on the basis of its "substantial equiv-

[2] Casewriter Interview.

alency," through a process known as a 510(k) premarket notification. ArthroCare had been successful in its applications to the FDA, winning 510(k) clearance for the ArthroWand for the knee, shoulder, elbow, and ankle joint applications prior to its IPO. And in December of 1995, the company submitted 510(k) notifications for urological and gynecological applications; FDA clearance was received for the urological applications in March 1996. In general, it took from 4 to 12 months to obtain the 510(k) clearance from the FDA.

RAMPING UP THE BUSINESS

In March of 1995, the company received a 510(k) clearance from the FDA on its first product—aimed at surgery of the knee. The company had contracted with manufacturers and third-party distributors, and in the summer of 1995, the product was announced.

As this was happening, the company was wrestling with the issue of how to finance the next stage of development. The most conservative estimates of the capital that ArthroCare would require were in the $10 to $20 million range. This was for a very minimal strategy of simply proceeding with the knee product and distributing it using a third party. As financing estimates grew to include developing the other applications which Thapliyal and the board believed had merit, as well as building a distribution network for the product, financing requirements grew to the $20 to $40 million range.

As ArthroCare was coming to grips with these figures, the IPO market for medical device companies heated up (see Exhibit 32-2 for overall state of equity market and device company IPOs).

The board asked Dr. Thapliyal to initiate discussions with investment banks and to get some sense of the valuation the company might fetch in an IPO. By Fall, the board had selected Robertson Stephens and Volpe, Welty as lead underwriters for an IPO, tentatively scheduled for year-end. The thinking behind the decision was expressed by Dr. Thapliyal:

> We knew we could raise $10 to $15 million in private capital, but that simply was not going to take us where we wanted to go. Public equity is less expensive money, and we knew we could get sufficient capital to fund our aggressive growth strategy.

> As far as the selection of Robertson Stephens and Volpe, Welty, we talked to eight different investment banks. Of nine medical device IPOs, Robertson had done four—they knew the pulse of the market. I had known Paul Brown, the head of Volpe, Welty's research group for 10 years. They had a well-respected analyst following medical device companies. Some of the other investment banks didn't even have analysts covering this industry.

> Once we picked these underwriters, we never haggled over valuation or pricing. Since the company had negative earnings, they had to look out to 1999 to get a "normalized" year, and discount it back to get a 1996 value. The board was comfortable with the result.

The rationale for a year-end offering was clear—ArthroCare would have its first quarter of sales history behind it, and the bankers felt that this would allow the company to make more credible projections of future revenues and earnings, and thus, command a higher valuation. In October of 1995, however, the company discovered that it had a problem with the sterile packaging in which the ArthroWands were shipped, and had to undertake a product recall. Dr. Thapliyal recalled the experience:

> This was my first experience with an IPO, and I thought that a product recall would present a big problem. We worked like mad, and within a week we had the units recalled, the problem fixed, and the company "closed-out" the issue with the FDA. When I talked with

---

EXHIBIT 32-2

**PUBLIC EQUITY MARKET—MEDICAL DEVICE COMPANIES
INDEX AT TIME OF IPO**

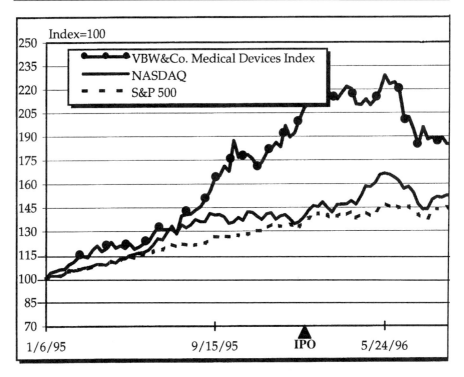

Source: Volpe, Welty.

---

the bankers, I expected bad news about the impact this would have on the IPO. But when they heard how we'd handled it, they said not to worry.

The company submitted a draft of an S-1 registration statement in December, and the SEC approved of the company's offering in January.

THE IPO

Dr. Thapliyal went to speak with potential investors on the company's "road show" from January 15 through February 2, 1996. The company went public at $14 on February 5, 1996. The offering raised $32 million for the company, and the $14 share price valued the company at $120 million. As is typical in such cases, "insiders" including officers, directors, and significant shareholders were prohibited from selling their shares during the first six months of public trading. By the end of the first day of trading ArthroCare stock was up and closed near $17. Dr. Thapliyal described the experience:

The IPO was very exciting. It was grueling—15 cities in two weeks. I gave the same presentation more than 50 times. But, here I was, a fellow from the Himalayas, living the

EXHIBIT 32-3

MEDICAL DEVICE: VENTURE CAPITAL AND IPO STATISTICS

	1991	1992	1993	1994	1995	1996
VENTURE CAPITAL INVESTMENTS						
# Deals	99	113	114	99	111	123
# Initial Venture Rounds	35	36	42	29	22	37
Total Amount Raised ($millions)	$475	$470	$452	$507	$603	$594
Mean Raised ($millions)	—	$4.2	$4.0	$5.1	$5.4	$4.8
INITIAL PUBLIC OFFERINGS*						
Total IPOs	—	24	11	9	16	36
Amount Raised in IPO ($million)	—	$691	$159	$210	$410	$1,268
Avg IPO Amount ($million)	—	$ 29	$ 14	$ 23	$ 26	$ 35
Avg Pre-$ Valuation ($million)	—	$ 80	$ 42	$ 74	$ 63	$ 94
Avg Post-$ Valuation ($million)	—	$109	$ 57	$ 98	$ 89	$ 130

* Categorized as venture-backed start-ups, venture-backed buyouts, and venture-backed consolidations deals.

Source: 1996 Venture Capital Annual Report © 1997 by VentureOne Corporation.

American Dream. It was thrilling to see the stock come across the ticker. We still had a lot of work ahead of us, but it was a very satisfying milestone.

Paul Brown of Volpe, Welty, described the market context in which ArthroCare had gone public (see Exhibit 32-3 for an overview of Medical Device investment trends):

Like all industry segments, the market for medical device companies goes through cycles. ArthroCare went public near the peak of the cycle that started in the summer of 1995. The cycle prior to that had been stopped dead in its tracks in 1993—the industry was devastated by the Clinton Health Care proposals. By the time analysts determined that the Clinton Plan was not going to pass, they had figured out that managed care was going to force tremendous change. Analysts began to revise their income statement models for these companies, reducing the price of devices, and flowing through the effect to revenues and earnings. And, they were right. By mid-1995, people began to see that some companies had sorted through the managed care model, and that you could make money. The cloud began to lift. This had a follow-on effect in the deal market, as companies that had tried to go public earlier in the year—and failed—now came back up to the plate and were successful. By the end of 1995, it was a feeding frenzy. People were willing to buy stock in companies that hadn't established their sales or earnings model. Institutional investors were willing to play venture capitalists, at least until the waters got choppy again.[3]

Brown, who was involved in ArthroCare's offering, explained how the company had been valued in the IPO:

The only way you could rationalize a valuation for any of the early-stage companies that went public during this cycle was off of projected 1999 or year 2000 earnings. So, when we began discussions with ArthroCare about going public, we had to construct a revenue

[3] Casewriter Interview.

model going out through 2000. We had discussions with Hira about how he saw Arthro-Care's strategy playing out. We were impressed with the technology, and did believe that it had broad application. But the company was already going public relatively early, and we encouraged him to focus on the orthopedic market. We wanted to focus the story around orthopedics and prove out the business model in this application.

Phil Nalbone—our analyst—came out with a full-blown research report on ArthroCare dated March 4, 1996. This was 30 days after the IPO—pretty much the minimum to live within the SEC's quiet period requirements. This report pretty well captured the argument that Hira had made during the road show. And—while the company is not allowed to share its projections with prospective purchasers of the stock—we as analysts are allowed to present *our* view.[4] (See Exhibit 32-4 for excerpts from this report.)

The earnings model on which these forecasts were based had several assumptions. The first product ArthroCare had introduced (Q4:95) was for the orthopedic application; it included a "controller," which supplied the electric current, and the "wand," which was the disposable tool. First, Volpe, Welty's analyst forecast the average selling price of the wand at $100 and assumed the product had a 68% gross margin at this price. The analyst estimated that the controller would have an average realized selling price of $8,500 and assumed that the unit had a cost to ArthroCare of $2,750. (See Table 4E of Exhibit 32-4 for the analyst's volume forecasts.) The Volpe, Welty analyst also estimated that, in the base scenario for 1996, at least 75% of ArthroCare's R&D spending was associated with the application of technology to the orthopedic application and less than 25% was associated with extending the technology to other markets.

THE FIRST SIX MONTHS

ArthroCare's stock traded within the $17 to $26 range for first four to five months. (See Exhibit 32-5 for price history and valuation relative to Volpe, Welty medical device index; Exhibit 32-6 for excerpts from follow-on research reports; and Exhibit 32-7 for ArthroCare Institutional shareholdings.) In April, ArthroCare announced its first quarter results: "Better than expected Q1 sales of nearly $1.2 million beat our $750,000 projection," was the report from Volpe, Welty (see Tables 1A and 1B of Exhibit 32-1 for quarterly financial results). By mid-May, the stock was trading around $25. Then, the price began to drop. According to Paul Brown, this was due to a slide in the market for device companies overall: "A large number of the companies that went public early in the year were having problems meeting the expectations that were set during the IPO. These problems taint the entire sector."

By mid-July, ArthroCare's stock price had briefly dipped below the offering price for the first time. Dr. Thapliyal explained his views: "We looked at 44 medical device IPOs that had been done for the 18 months through mid-1996. Of the 44, 40 were below the offering price." On July 16, an analyst at the investment banking firm DLJ began covering ArthroCare and rated the stock "outperform." He noted:

Over the past several weeks, the shares have been particularly weak on little volume. We believe that there could be some investor fall-out from the recent slide in Orthologic (another niche player in the orthopedic segment) shares and general weakness in small capitalization OTC stocks.[5]

---

[4] Casewriter Interview.

[5] DLJ research report on ArthroCare dated July 16, 1996.

EXHIBIT 32-4

EXCERPTS FROM FIRST VOLPE, WELTY RESEARCH REPORT DATED MARCH 4, 1996

Investment Thesis

ArthroCare Corporation has created a superior product for performing arthroscopic surgery, one of the last great growth markets in the orthopedics industry. We expect significant appreciation in ArthroCare's stock over the next year. We expect this technology to be adapted to several other surgical fields, such as urology, gynecology, dermatology, and periodontics—all of which will add value to the company over time. We are initiating coverage of Arthro-Care with a STRONG BUY (1) recommendation and 12-month price target of $30.

Introduction

ArthroCare has developed a core technology platform that simplifies the removal of soft tissue from the body. This technology, which has broad patent protection, has applications in several fields of medicine, including orthopedics, urology, gynecology, dermatology, and periodontics.

ArthroCare's technology entails a razor/razor blades approach. The capital components include a radio-frequency energy power controller and connecting cable, which together sell for approximately $12,500. The disposable component is a bipolar, multielectrode catheter, or wand, which carries a list price of $120.

TABLE 4A ArthroCare Target Markets

Target Markets	Applications	510(k) Filing	U.S. Launch	U.S. Procedures/ Year (Est.)
Orthopedics	Arthroscopy	7/94 (App 3/95)	12/95	2,300,000
Urology	Prostatic soft tissue, bladder tumors	12/95	Expected 2H:97	250,000
Gynecology	Intrauterine soft-tissue resection	12/95	Expected 2H:97	625,000
Dermatology	Wrinkles, discoloration	Expected mid-96	Expected 2H:98	500,000
Periodontics	Gingivectomy	Expected mid-96	Expected 2H:98	1,000,000

Source: ArthroCare Corp. and Volpe, Welty & Co. estimates.

TABLE 4B ArthroCare Sales by Product Category (US$ in thousands)

	1996E	1997E	1998E	1999E	2000E
Arthroscopy	$7,200	$24,700	$40,200	$49,730	$ 60,000
Urology		300	4,800	10,800	14,000
Gynecology		600	6,300	12,800	15,500
Dermatology			600	3,220	5,000
Periodontics	—	—	600	3,450	5,500
TOTAL	$7,200	$25,600	$52,500	$80,000	$100,000

Source: Volpe, Welty & Co. estimates.

In 1995, we estimate that approximately 2.3 million arthroscopies were performed in the United States. Procedures have grown at a compounded rate of 12% over the past couple of years and we are projecting a slight acceleration in this rate of procedure growth to 14% over the next several years.

We have surveyed several surgeons who have tested the ArthroCare system. The majority of these surgeons tell us that they believe the ArthroCare system is the most advanced method of performing arthroscopic surgery today. Most say they consider the system a superior tool for arthroscopy: the project simplifies the procedures, makes maneuvering in tight spaces faster and easier and reduces time required to perform the procedure.

(Continued)

EXHIBIT 32-4   (Continued)

Several surgeons have mentioned another advantage of the ArthroCare system: The product fits into the current Medicare reimbursement codes and guidelines for arthroscopic surgery. It is not like a device that requires a completely different surgical technique to be instituted, which often necessitates a new reimbursement code.

ArthroCare has developed a true platform technology that will give it a multitude of opportunities to add to the company's revenue stream over time. We think arthroscopy will be the main driver of the company's growth. In December 1995, the company filed separate 510(k) applications for use of the system in urology and gynecology. In our models, we assume that the product will be cleared for these indications and launched in the U.S. market in late 1997.

Management

ArthroCare has a strong and experienced management team. Directors and executive officers of the company own approximately 48% of the company's shares outstanding.

Financial Results and Projections

ArthroCare received net proceeds from its February 5, 1996, initial public offering of $31.8 million which, added to the company's previous balance of cash and equivalents of $4.8 million, gave the company cash and equivalents of approximately $36.6 million. We project that this sum will be more than sufficient to carry ArthroCare through to a cash-flow-positive position in the middle of 1997. We are forecasting cumulative losses of approximately $5.4 million between the first quarter of 1996 and the second quarter of 1997.

For 1996, the company's first full year of sales, we are forecasting that sales will reach $7.2 million—entirely from sales of the Arthroscopic System. Our model assumes that 35% of the year's sales, or $2.5 million, will be from sales of the capital component of the product, the controller and connecting cables, and that 65% of the total, or $4.7 million, will be derived from sales of the disposable ArthroWand component of the system. We assume that the product will be available in overseas markets in late 1996.

For 1997, we are projecting a jump in sales to $25.6 million, comprised mostly (96.5%) of sales of the Arthroscopic System. We project that the company will launch versions of its tissue ablation and coagulation technology for the urology and gynecology market in the second half of the year, and that sales of those products will comprise 1.2% and 2.3% of total sales for the year, respectively.

For 1998, we forecast that sales will more than double to $52.5 million. Our model assumes that ArthoCare will launch versions of its product for the dermatology and periodontics markets in the second half of that year and that sales into these new markets will add an incremental $1.2 million to sales for the full year (2.3% of total sales for the year). Our earnings estimate of the year is $9.4 million, or $1.01 per share ($5.6 million, or $0.63 per share, fully taxed).

In 1999, with all five currently contemplated versions of the company's technology on the market, we forecast sales growth of nearly 52% to $80 million. Of this total, 62.2% is expected from the core Arthroscopy System, 13.5% from urology applications, 16.0% from gynecology, 4.0% from dermatology, and 4.3% from periodontics. For 1999, we assume a tax rate for the entire year of 38%. On this fully taxed basis, we are projecting earnings of $10.2 million, or $1.08 per share.

Valuation

At the current price of $21 3/4, ArthroCare has a market capitalization of approximately $195 million. We think that the stock could carry a valuation of approximately $268 million, or $30 per share, within 12 months. This would represent a gain of 38%.

In our valuation models, we are using 1999 as our reference year, since this represents the first full year of "normalized" operations—the first year in which ArthroCare's products for each target-use should be on the market. We are projecting approximately $10.2 million in fully taxed net income for ArthroCare in 1999. We think the stock could trade in late 1998 at a forward multiple of 35 times our projected net income figure, for a market capitalization of approximately $357 million, or nearly $40 per share. That forward multiple would represent a discount to our projected three-year compounded fully taxed earnings growth rate of 85%. If we discount this anticipated late 1998 market capitalization back by 25% a year to the end of Q1:97, this gives us a one-year target market cap of $268 million, or a $30 per share price target.

(Continued)

EXHIBIT 32-4 (Continued)

TABLE 4C Comparable Company Valuation Analysis of Selected Medical Device Companies

Company	LTM[a] Ended	LTM Financial Performance Measures					MarketCap 3/1/96 ($mil)	Ratio MarketCap to LTM Revenue	Ratio Price To				Projected 5YR EPS Growth Rate (%)	Ratio '96 PE To 5 YR EPS Growth Rate
		Margins	Gross Margins	Net Margins	LTM ROA[b]	LTM ROE[c]			Operating Income	LTM EPS	'96 EPS	'97 EPS		
Arrow International Inc.	Nov-95	53.5%	25.3%	16.2%	14.6%	21.0%	$923	4.2×	16.6×	260×	215×	18.0×	19.5	110.4×
ArthroCare Corp.	Dec-95	nm	nm	nm	nm	nm	187	858.0	nm	nm	nm	94.6	50.0	nm
Avecor Cardiovascular	Dec-95	45.5	10.5	9.9	13.5	15.6	99	3.0	28.2	29.9	26.8	19.2	40.0	67.1
Cardiometrics, Inc.	Dec-95	57.4	nm	nm	nm	nm	55	4.9	nm	nm	nm	nm	nm	nm
Circon Corp.[c]	Dec-95	55.1	7.4	2.7	2.4	5.1	161	1.0	13.5	36.6	11.9	9.9	20.0	59.4
EndoSonics Corp.[d]	Dec-95	30.0	nm	nm	nm	nm	196	11.5	nm	nm	nm	56.3	30.0	nm
ESC Medical Systems Ltd.	Dec-95	75.5	31.7	32.9	14.5	15.7	339	40.3	127.1	122.5	90.7	67.2	35.0	259.2
Gynecare Inc.	Dec-95	5.9	nm	nm	nm	nm	78	92.4	nm	nm	nm	nm	35.0	nm
MediSense Inc.	Dec-95	66.6	18.8	17.8	3.7	54.2	540	3.2	17.1	18.1	17.3	14.7	18.0	96.2
VidaMed Inc.	Dec-95	nm	nm	nm	nm	nm	87	33.3	nm	nm	nm	25.7	nm	nm
HIGH		75%	31.7%	32.9%	33.7%	54.2%		92.4×	127.1×	122.5×	90.7	67.2×	50	259.2%
LOW		5.9	7.4	2.7	2.4	5.1		1.0	13.5	18.1	11.9	9.9	18	59.4
MARKET WEIGHTED AVERAGE		55.9%	22.5%	17.9%	18.4%	27.0%		72.4×	35.2×	40.8×	31.3×	32.3×	25.1	125.1%
MEDIAN		55.1	14.6	13.8	14.0	15.6		8.2	22.7	33.3	22.1	22.4	27.1	81.6
AVERAGE		48.0	17.1	15.8	16.0	22.6		23.7	46.5	51.8	36.7	32.1	30.5	120.5

[a] LTM = Latest 12 months.

[b] Return on average assets and equity for LTM.

[c] Circon Corp. data exclude nonrecurring charges related to the company's 1995 acquisition of Cabot Medical.

[d] EndoSonics Crop Q4:95 and FY:95 financial data are preliminary, and were released by the company on January 23, 1996.

Source: Volpe, Welty & Company estimates, First Call, Zack's Investment Research and 1/B/E/S.

(Continued)

EXHIBIT 32-4 (*Continued*)

TABLE 4D ArthroCare: Quarterly Results and Volpe, Welty Forecasts ($ in 000)

	Revenue	COGS	Gross Margin	S,G & A	R&D	Operating Income	Operating Margin	Pretax Income	Pretax Margin	Tax Rate	Net Income	Net Margin	EPS
Q1:95a	$ 0	$ 0	NM	$ 395	$ 658	$(1,053)	NM	$(1,033)	NM	0.0%	$(1,033)	NM	(0.15)
Q2:95a	0	0	NM	540	890	(1,430)	NM	(1,365)	NM	0.0	(1,365)	NM	(0.20)
Q3:95a	0	0	NM	730	1,600	(2,330)	NM	(2,265)	NM	0.0	(2,265)	NM	(0.33)
Q4:95a	218	447	NM	1,007	1,121	(2,357)	NM	(2,288)	NM	0.0	(2,288)	NM	(0.33)
FY 95 Total Actual	218	447	NM	2,672	4,269	(7,170)	NM	(6,951)	NM	0.0%	(6,951)	NM	(1.00)
Q1:96e	750	880	NM	1,015	1,140	(2,285)	NM	(2,121)	NM	0.0	(2,121)	NM	(0.27)
Q2:96e	1,200	980	18.3%	1,020	1,150	(1,950)	NM	(1,694)	NM	0.0	(1,694)	NM	(0.20)
Q3:96e	1,840	1,200	34.8	1,030	1,200	(1,590)	NM	(1,260)	NM	0.0	(1,260)	NM	(0.14)
Q4:96e	3,410	1,500	56.0	1,050	1,400	(540)	NM	(290)	6.3	0.0	(290)	6.3	(0.03)
FY 96 Total Est.	7,200	4,560	36.7%	4,115	4,959	(6,365)	NM	(5,365)	NM	0.0%	(5,365)	NM	(0.65)
Q1:97e	5,000	2,000	60.0	1,600	1,750	(350)	NM	(120)	NM	0.0	(120)	NM	(0.01)
Q2:97e	5,800	2,300	60.3	1,850	1,780	(130)	NM	70	1.2	0.0	70	1.2	0.01
Q3:97e	6,800	2,500	63.2	1,950	1,790	560	8.2	750	11.0	0.0	750	11.0	0.08
Q4:97e	8,000	2,700	66.3	2,300	1,800	1,200	15.0	1,380	17.3	0.0	1,380	17.3	0.15
FY 97 Total Est.	25,600	9,500	62.9%	7,700	7,120	1,280	5.0%	2,080	8.1%	0.0%	2,080	8.1%	0.23
Q1:98e	10,000	3,300	67.0	3,200	2,000	1,500	15.0	1,700	17.0	0.0	1,700	17.0	0.19
Q2:98e	12,250	4,000	67.3	4,200	2,050	2,000	16.3	2,210	18.0	0.0	2,210	18.0	0.24
Q3:98e	14,000	4,550	67.5	5,000	2,100	2,350	16.8	2,530	18.1	0.0	2,530	18.1	0.27
Q4:98e	16,250	5,280	67.5	5,900	2,270	2,800	17.2	2,930	18.0	0.0	2,930	18.0	0.31
FY 98 Total Est.	52,500	17,130	67.4%	18,300	8,420	8,650	16.5%	9,370	17.8%	0.0%	9,370	17.8%	1.01
FY 99 Total Est.	80,000	25,500	68.1	28,400	10,285	15,815	19.8	16,465	20.6	38.0	10,208	12.8	1.08
FY 00 Total Est.	100,000	30,000	70.0%	35,000	12,500	22,500	22.5%	23,000	23.0%	38.0%	14,260	14.3%	1.50

Note: Amounts may not total due to rounding.

(*Continued*)

EXHIBIT 32-4 (Continued)

TABLE 4E ArthroCare Sales Forecast—Units and Revenue ($000)

	1996					1997					1998					1999				
	Q1	Q2	Q3	Q4	YEAR	Q1	Q2	Q3	Q4	YEAR	Q1	Q2	Q3	Q4	YEAR	Q1	Q2	Q3	Q4	YEAR
SALES—UNITS																				
CONTROLLERS																				
Arthroscopy	48	76	117	217	458	118	130	131	93	472	109	111	108	150	478	191	158	184	146	678
Urology	0	0	0	0	0	0	0	4	8	12	15	22	33	42	113	31	37	41	44	152
Dermatology	0	0	0	0	0	0	0	0	0	0	0	0	5	9	14	8	11	13	14	45
Gynecology	0	0	0	0	0	0	0	8	16	25	19	33	42	54	148	38	42	47	54	181
Peridontics	0	0	0	0	0	0	0	0	0	0	0	0	5	9	14	8	11	13	16	49
Total	48	76	117	217	458	118	130	143	117	509	143	166	188	264	753	268	259	298	274	1105
WANDS																				
Arthroscopy	4,875	7,800	11,960	22,165	46,800	44,444	52,200	56,489	64,533	217,667	79,718	90,047	97,412	109,741	376,918	114,750	123,200	130,500	139,500	507,950
Urology	0	0	0	0	0	0	0	733	1,444	2,167	6,118	8,941	13,176	16,941	45,176	24,200	28,600	31,900	34,100	118,800
Peridontics	0	0	0	0	0	0	0	0	0	0	0	0	1,882	3,765	5,647	6,600	8,800	10,450	12,100	37,950
Total	4,875	7,800	11,960	22,165	46,800	44,444	52,200	57,222	65,977	219,834	85,836	98,988	112,460	130,447	427,741	181,300	193,050	219,270	238,500	840,920
SALES—(000$)																				
CONTROLLERS																				
Arthroscopy	263	420	644	1,194	2,520	1,000	1,102	1,116	792	4,010	924	946	920	1,272	4,062	1,620	1,344	1,560	1,240	5,764
Urology	0	0	0	0	0	0	0	35	70	105	130	190	280	360	960	264	312	348	372	1,296
Dermatology	0	0	0	0	0	0	0	0	0	0	0	0	40	80	120	66	90	110	120	386
Gynecology	0	0	0	0	0	0	0	70	140	210	160	280	360	460	1,260	324	360	396	456	1,536
Peridontics	0	0	0	0	0	0	0	0	0	0	0	0	40	80	120	72	96	114	132	414
Total	263	420	644	1,194	2,520	1,000	1,102	1,221	1,002	4,325	1,214	1,416	1,640	2,252	6,522	2,346	2,202	2,528	2,320	9,396
WANDS																				
Arthroscopy	487	780	1,196	2,217	4,700	4,000	4,698	5,084	5,808	19,590	6,776	7,654	8,280	9,328	32,038	9,180	9,856	10,440	11,160	40,636
Urology	0	0	0	0	0	0	0	65	130	195	520	760	1,120	1,440	3,840	1,936	2,288	2,552	2,728	9,504
Dermatology	0	0	0	0	0	0	0	0	0	0	0	0	160	320	480	484	660	810	880	2,834
Gynecology	0	0	0	0	0	0	0	130	260	390	640	1,120	1,440	1,840	5,040	2,376	2,640	2,904	3,344	11,264
Peridontics	0	0	0	0	0	0	0	0	0	0	0	0	160	320	480	528	704	836	968	3,036
Total	487	780	1,196	2,217	4,700	4,000	4,698	5,279	6,198	20,175	7,936	9,534	11,160	13,248	41,878	14,504	16,148	17,542	19,080	67,274
TOTAL SALES (000$)																				
Total Arthroscopy	750	1,200	1,840	3,410	7,200	5,000	5,800	6,200	6,600	23,600	7,700	8,600	9,200	10,600	36,100	10,800	11,200	12,000	12,400	46,400
Total Urology	0	0	0	0	0	0	0	100	200	300	650	950	1,400	1,800	4,800	2,200	2,600	2,900	3,100	10,800
Total Dermatology	0	0	0	0	0	0	0	0	0	0	0	0	200	400	600	550	750	920	1,000	3,220
Total Gynecology	0	0	0	0	0	0	0	2,000	400	2,400	800	1,400	1,800	2,300	6,300	2,700	3,000	3,300	3,800	12,800
Total Periodontics	0	0	0	0	0	0	0	0	0	0	0	0	200	400	600	600	800	950	1,100	3,450
TOTAL $	750	1,200	1,840	3,410	7,200	5,000	5,800	8,300	7,200	26,300	9,150	10,950	12,800	15,500	48,400	16,850	18,350	20,070	21,400	76,670

EXHIBIT 32-5

ARTHROCARE STOCK PERFORMANCE POST-IPO

ArthroCare Share Price (Index) vs. Medical Device, S&P 500 and NASDAQ Indices

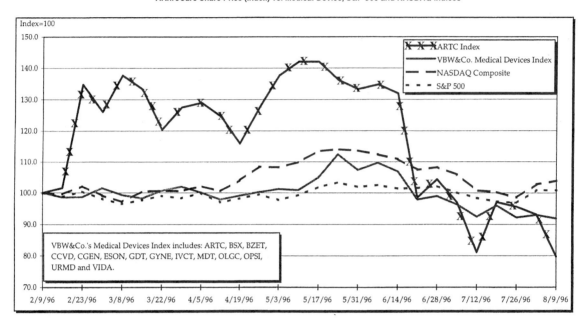

Source: Volpe, Welty.

In the same report, the analyst for DLJ estimated that ArthroCare was realizing an average price of $3,500 to $4,000 for controller and $100 for the wand. On July 25, the company announced its second quarter results: "Revenues of $1.4 million exceed our estimates of $1.2 million . . . a loss of $0.20 per share in line with forecasts," said Volpe, Welty. The stock was trading at about $16. The Volpe, Welty analyst estimated that ArthroCare had sold the following unit volumes of controllers and wands during the first half of 1996:

Unit Volume	Q1:96	Q2:96
Controllers	140	125
Wands	8,200	10,300

The Company's 10-Q filing for the first quarter indicated that approximately 75% of that quarter's sales were attributable to "initial stocking orders" from the 30 dealers/distributors through whom ArthroCare had chosen to sell its product. The Company further indicated that these sales were at or near cost.

In its 10-Q for the second quarter, ending June 29, 1996, the Company indicated that it had established an installed base of 300 controllers and that it had engaged in several promotional programs in which controller prices were discounted in exchange

EXHIBIT 32-5 *(Continued)*

ArthroCare Stock: Price and Volume History

Note: Volume for days 1 and 2 of trading is excluded.

Source: Bloomberg.

for wand purchase commitments. The company reported that the revenue mix was approximately 33% controllers and 67% wands for the first six months of the year.

Finally, in just the week leading up to August 6, Volpe, Welty had issued its latest research report, in which the analyst revised ArthroCare's sales and earnings forecasts for the first time since the offering (see Exhibit 32-6): the forecast loss for the remainder of the year increased from $0.17 per share to $0.35, largely as a result of an increase in the analyst's estimates of R&D costs associated with moving the technology to additional applications. For FY 1997, 1998, 1999, and 2000, sales and earnings estimates remained unchanged, as the benefits of ArthroCare's investments in the technology platform were seen to pay off.

THE ISSUE

In preparation for the company's August 15 board meeting later that week, ArthroCare's CFO had begun preliminary work on its budget and business plan for the coming year. Dr. Thapliyal described the issues that had arisen:

> First, an immediate issue was the price of the controller. The ArthroCare system depends upon a reliable, steady source of electrical current to deliver the energy to the electrode tip. The source of this electrical current was the "controller." This unit, which had a list

EXHIBIT 32-6

EXCERPTS FROM FOLLOW-ON VOLPE, WELTY RESEARCH REPORTS

March 12, 1996
Price $25
Opinion: Strong Buy (1)

ArthroCare Gets 510(k) Clearance for Urology Device—the clearance, which covers ARTC's bipolar urological loop device, came within 90 days, much sooner than we had expected.

April 26, 1996
Price $22
Opinion: Strong Buy (1)

ArthroCare Reports Better-Than-Expected Q1:96 Sales—Sales for Q1:96 of nearly $1.2 million beat our $750,000 projection, reflecting not only higher-than-expected sales of demonstration units to distributors, but also higher sell-through of wands to physicians. The loss of $1.74 million ($0.25 per share) was slightly better than the estimated $2.1 million ($0.26 per share).

June 6, 1996
Price $23
Opinion: Strong Buy (1)

ArthroCare Gets Second 510(k) Clearance for a Urology Device—The 510(k) clearance, which was approved in less than 90 days, covers a multielectrode, bipolar device. This complements the company's previously approved urological loop device. The clearance supports ArthroCare's efforts to develop its platform technology beyond its initial use in arthroscopy.

July 26, 1996
Price $16 1/2
Opinion: Strong Buy (1)

ArthroCare's Q2:96 revenues of $1.4 million exceeded our estimate of $1.2 million. A reported loss per share of $0.20 was in line. Product sales were up 21% over the previous quarter, reflecting growing demand for the company's bipolar Arthroscopic system. Ninety controllers were placed in the second quarter, bringing the total base of installed controllers to roughly 30–40% of those in hospitals where wand usage per controller should be higher. Q2:96 wands sales were approximately 10,000 units.

Q2:96 gross margins of 12% exceeded the 8% we had anticipated, and we expect this margin to continue to improve.

The FDA recently cleared ArthroCare's 510(k) application to market the Arthroscopic system for use in the wrist and the hip. The wrist indication was approved in 35 days, the hip in 65 days. The system is now approved for use in all six of the major joints in the body.

We think that upcoming events, including evidence of continued market penetration in arthroscopy, FDA-clearance of the periodontal and dermatology indications, the signing of a U.S. marketing partner for the company's urological devices, agreements with international distributors and the commencement of international sales in early 1997, will help investors recognize the tremendous potential behind the stock. Our 12-month price target: $30.

(Continued)

EXHIBIT 32-6   (Continued)

August 6, 1996
Price $14 1/2
Strong Buy (1)

We have revised our sales and earnings estimates for ArthroCare Corp. to reflect the following: We expect higher 2H:96 and FY:97 SG&A expenses associated with aggressive growth plans for U.S. marketing of the company's Arthroscopic System, as well as for the FY:97 launch of devices for the urology and periodontal markets. We have raised our estimate of Q3:96 R&D costs by $50,000 and our estimates of Q4:96 R&D costs by $100,000 to account for development of ArthroCare's technology for the urology and periodontal markets following sooner-than-anticipated 510(k) clearance for these indications. We have also lowered our Q4:96 sales estimates slightly because we now expect ArthroCare to move the launch of its System overseas from late 1996 to the first half of 1997. Accordingly, we have revised our 1997 sales ramp while our FY:97 revenue estimate remains the same. We also expect slightly higher FY:96 and FY:97 interest income.

We think ArthroCare will continue to reap benefits from its 510(k) strategy to gain U.S. marketing clearance for its core technology in several different indications. In orthopedics, the company's Arthroscopic System can now be marketed for use in all major joints in the body, and we expect the company to remain focused on this market in the United States for the rest of 1996. We continue to rate the stock a STRONG BUY (1). Our 12-month price target is $30.

Volpe, Welty Earnings Estimate Change

Period	Estimate	Former	Current	% Change
Q3:96E	Revenues (000)	$1,840	$1,840	0.00%
	Earnings Per Share	($0.14)	($0.20)	NM
Q4:96E	Revenues(000)	$3,410	$3,150	(7.62%)
	Earnings Per Share	($0,03)	($0.15)	NM
FY:96E	Revenues(000)	$7,815	$7,555	(3.33%)
	Earnings Per Share	($0.63)	($0.80)	NM
Q1:97E	Revenues (000)	$5,000	$4,600	(8.00%)
	Earnings Per Share	($0.01)	($0.03)	NM
Q2:97E	Revenues (000)	$5,800	$5,400	(6.90%)
	Earnings Per Share	$0.01	$5,400	NM
Q3:97E	Revenues (000)	$6,800	$7,200	5.88%
	Earnings Per Share	$0.08	$0.10	25.00%
Q4:97E	Revenues (000)	$8,000	$8,400	5.00%
	Earnings Per Share	$0.15	$0.16	6.67%
FY:97E	Revenues (000)	$25,600	$25,600	0.00%
	Earnings Per Share	$0.23	$0.23	0.00%
FY:98E	Revenues (000)	$52,500	$52,500	0.00%
	Earnings Per Share	$1.01	$1.01	0.00%
FY:99E	Revenues (000)	$80,000	$80,000	0.00%
	Earnings Per Share	$1.08	$1.08	0.00%
FY:00E	Revenues (000)	$100,000	$100,000	0.00%
	Earnings Per Share	$1.50	$1.50	0.00%

EXHIBIT 32-7

ARTHROCARE CORPORATION: INSTITUTIONAL SHAREHOLDINGS

(Ranked based on 6/30/96 Ownership)

OWNER	HOLDINGS 3/30/96	HOLDINGS 6/30/96
Putnam Inv. Mgt.	352,600	505,200
Geocapital Corp	38,000	363,000
Crown Advisors	35,800	168,800
AIM Mgt Group	228,400	100,000
BZW Barclays	0	71,500
Columbia Mgt Co	11,500	59,000
USAA Inv Mgt	40,000	54,000
Sunamer Asset Mgt.	0	31,500
General Motors	21,500	21,500
Strong/Cornelius	11,300	17,900
Calif. Teachers	0	16,100
Bankers Trust	6,400	8,200
Dean Witter Intercapital	0	7,000
Wells Fargo	0	3,350
Merrill Lynch & Co	0	2,200
Westfield Capital	1,100	1,100
Fred Alger Mgt.	24,000	0
Berkeley Capital Mgt	120,800	0
Furman Selz	28,000	0
Husic Capital	12,000	0
Jack's National	120,500	0
Nich-Apple Capital	139,400	0
Oppenheimer Mgt	75,500	0
Piper Capital Mgt	1,000	0
Frank Russell Co.	81,700	0
Sirach Capital Mgt	285,500	0
Yale University	0	0
Mellon Bank	0	0
RCM Capital	0	0
Mellon Capital Mgt	0	0
Travelers, Inc	0	0
American General	0	0
Bear Sterns	0	0

Source: Carson Group.

price of $12,500, was required in order to power the disposable wand. We had some luck selling these controllers to the very "early adopters," but as we attempted to broaden the penetration of the market, we discovered that it was very difficult to sell these units for anything like the list price. In the old days, the surgeons ruled the roost. If a doctor wanted a new piece of equipment, the hospital would buy it. Today, the managed care environment has shifted a great deal of power to the purchasing manager. It's bad enough for the doctor to say he needs a wand that costs two or three times as much as the old mechanical shaver. But, layer on top of that the need for a $12,500 box, and the purchasing manager is going to give the physician a very hard time. Some doctors may choose to really fight for this, and some of those will win the fight. But many will simply throw up their hands. Conversely if you will *give* the doctor a $12,500 piece of equipment, that is a very compelling argument for the physician to use with the purchasing manager about why the hospital should be willing to stock the wands.

ArthroCare had already discounted the price of the controller unit to help achieve its marketing objectives.

Allan Weinstein, ArthroCare's vice president marketing, wanted to take further discounts on the price of the controller and simply place the controller units doctors and hospitals in exchange for an agreement to purchase a minimum number of wands over the coming year. Larry Tannenbaum, ArthroCare's CFO, was worried that this action would cause a further erosion of the company's margins. He was anxious to live up to the expectation that ArthroCare would turn profitable during the second quarter of 1997. He felt that any further reduction in the controller's price would adversely effect the company's ability to achieve this objective.

Dr. Thapliyal found the decision a difficult one:

We have worked hard to make our numbers. The board has been very supportive in terms of telling me to pay attention to the business and not worry about the stock price. But it is hard. It does affect the way people inside the company think about the business. We have 65 employees, and all have stock options. Lots of our employees are young people who have signed on for the classic start-up: work hard but reap the big rewards. Many people's options are set at the IPO price. When the stock is at $26, they love it. When it's back at $14, or below, it takes its toll on morale. As the stock has been dropping, it has taken more and more of my time to pay attention to this and attempt to manage it.

A second issue that the board would have to take up revolved around ArthroCare's investment in R&D to expand to other product market applications. Dr. Thapliyal explained:

As we get further down the technology learning curve, we keep finding new and profitable market opportunities: cardiology, dermatology, urology, and gynecology. There are procedures in all of these fields that could be revolutionized by our technology. We spend almost $1 million per quarter on R&D, so it is a large expense for us.

Moreover, some of these other segments offer more margin than the orthopedic segment, even if they are not as large. In the arthroscopy field, we are competing with mechanical shavers that sell for $70 to $90. So, we can price our product somewhat higher than this number because we are delivering a superior result. But we can't price it at two or three times the price—in the managed care environment, it just won't fly. However, there are certain applications where there is currently no device out there establishing a price point. Take surgery to the head and neck, for example. This is performed today in the "old-fashioned" way—you have to cut to get where you want to be. If our tool enables a surgeon to perform what used to be a $20,000, three-day, in-the-hospital procedure on an outpatient basis, now we are competing against the $20,000 price. There is a lot more room for pricing the wand in this application and getting an outstanding margin. The same kind of argument applies in certain other areas, say cardiovascular applications, where you are competing against a $1,000 device. Again, a lot more pricing flexibility.

We have continued to build our intellectual property base, and have received additional patents since we went public. Still, time is our scarcest resource. When we went public, we indicated to the market that we would be profitable by the second quarter of 1997. We could probably drive the company to profitability by this point if we focus narrowly on this goal. But we are trying to build long-term value, not simply become profitable.

## 33

Nantucket Nectars

Well, we knew we were in an interesting position. We had five companies express interest in acquiring a portion of the company. Sometimes you have to laugh about how things occur. Tropicana (Seagram) and Ocean Spray became interested in us after reading an article in Brandweek *magazine that erroneously reported that Triarc was in negotiations to buy us. (See Exhibit 33-1 for a copy of this article.) At the time, we hadn't even met with Triarc, although we knew their senior people from industry conferences. We have no idea how this rumor began. Within weeks Triarc and Pepsi contacted us. We told no one about these on-going negotiations and held all the meetings away from our offices so that no Nectars employee would become concerned. It was quite a frenetic time.*

The most memorable day was just a few days ago actually. Firsty and I were in an extended meeting with Ocean Spray, making us late for our second round meeting with Pepsi. Ultimately, Tom and I split up: Firsty stayed with Ocean Spray and I met with Pepsi. Ocean Spray never knew about the Pepsi meeting. Tom and I have learned under fire throughout our Nectars experience, but this experience was a new one for us.

—Tom Scott, co-founder of Nantucket Nectars

It was certainly exciting to have some companies interested in acquiring Nantucket Nectars. But should the founders sell at this time? They had originally planned to take the company public. The company was doing great, better than they had ever imagined. See Exhibit 33-2 for historical financials and Exhibit 33-3 for recent valuations of initial public offerings. But many people, particularly company founders who were running their newly public companies, were telling them that going public wasn't a completely positive experience. They wondered whether the company was even ready to go public. Regardless of their decision about going public, should they continue negotiating with potential buyers to find out the market value of their company? Ultimately, they needed to decide whether to sell the company or begin the initial public offering process. Of course, operating Nantucket Nectars as a stand-alone company was always an option.

Research Associate Jon M. Biotti prepared this case under the supervision of Professors Joseph B. Lassiter III and William A. Sahlman as the basis for class discussion rather than to illustrate either effective or ineffective handling of an administrative situation.

EXHIBIT 33-1

BRANDWEEK ARTICLE ON POTENTIAL TRANSACTION

Deals

Triarc May Be on Trail Of Nantucket Nectars

By Karen Benezra

Triarc Cos., eager to add to its premium beverage portfolio following its purchase of Snapple, is said to be holding discussions with Nantucket Nectars about a possible acquisition.

Nantucket, founded in 1989 by college pals Tom First and Tom Scott and now a $30 million brand, is one of the few attractive independent juice makers, along with Arizona, at the center of buyout speculation as the once booming new age drinks market has ebbed. Triarc already owns Mistic and Royal Crown.

The talks, said to be initiated months ago by Triarc principals Nelson Peltz and Peter May, grew stronger last month following Triarc's $30 million offer for Cable Car Beverages, the Denver maker of Stewart's Root Beer. Early word had Nantucket's price at a hefty $100 million, but sources last week said more "sane" discussions had since taken place.

Triarc rep Martin Shea would not comment on any talks, but said: "Our strategy is to add brands that are of premium quality and Nantucket Nectars would be under that banner."

A Nantucket rep said there was "no truth" to any talks, saying it is often presented deals. A sale would spell a nice finale for the self-styled "juice guys," who began selling flavored drinks off the side of a boat and then hit the college campus circuit touting the 100% juice brand's bohemian image and natural ingredients.
—*with Gerry Khermouch* ∎

BACKGROUND

Tom Scott and Tom First met while students at Brown University. (See Exhibit 33-4 for their résumés.) During their summers, the two created Allserve, a floating convenience store serving boats in the Nantucket Harbor. The founders decided to return to Nantucket after graduation to continue this service business. At the time, they sold ice, beer, soda, cigarettes and newspapers and performed services such as pumping waste and delivering groceries and laundry for boats in the Harbor. The founders did not even sell juice at that time. As First recalled, "we started what was basically a floating 7-Eleven."[1]

During the winter of 1990, First recreated a peach fruit juice drink that he had discovered during a trip to Spain. The drink inspired the two founders to start a side-

---

[1] *Beverage Aisle*, February 1996.

EXHIBIT 33-2

HISTORICAL FINANCIALS OF NANTUCKET NECTARS ($000s)

December 31 of each year	1991	1992	1993	1994	1995	1996
Total Revenue	$233	$379	$978	$8,345	$15,335	$29,493
Cost of Sales	172	317	765	6,831	11,024	20,511
Gross Profit	61	62	213	1,514	4,311	8,982
Marketing and Advertising	0	0	0	320	875	2,581
General and Administrative	82	62	90	3,290	3,344	5,432
Total Expenses	82	62	90	3,610	4,219	8,013
EBITDA	−21	0	123	−2,096	91	969
Amortization and Depreciation	0	4	0	104	137	247
EBIT	−21	−4	123	−2,199	−45	722
Interest Expense	0	5	7	53	139	301
Earnings before Taxes	−21	−9	116	−2,252	−184	421
Income Tax Expense	0	0	0	0	16	52
Net Income (Loss)	−21	−9	116	−2,252	−200	369

business of making fresh juices. In the spring of 1990, the founders decided to hand bottle their new creation and sell them off their Allserve boat. "We started by making it in blenders and selling it in cups off the boat. But we also put it in milk cartons and wine bottles—there was a wine guy on the island—basically anything that we could find."[2] Everyone loved the product, prompting the founders to open the Allserve General Store on Nantucket's Straight Wharf. Soon thereafter, other Nantucket stores started carrying the product. In its first year, Nantucket Allserve sold 8,000 cases of its renamed juice, Nantucket Nectars, and 20,000 the following year.

FINANCING

In the first two years, the two founders invested their collective life savings, about $17,000, in the company to contract an outside bottler and finance inventory. For the next two years, Nantucket Nectars operated in an undercapitalized state on a small bank loan. Tom Scott recalled the situation:

> We were scraping along. Everything was going back into the company. By early 1993, our few employees hadn't been paid in a year, never mind that Tom and I hadn't paid ourselves in three and a half years. But we worked all sorts of odd jobs on the side, especially during the winter. It was especially tough because we could see the juice really taking off.

Ultimately, the two founders and Ned Desmond, who would later become the Regional Director of Sales and Marketing, persuaded Mike Egan to invest $600,000 in

[2] Ibid.

EXHIBIT 33-3

IPO DATA FROM SDC

Company	Description	IPO Date	Proceeds (millions)	Offer Price	Shares Offered (millions)	Market Value at IPO (millions)	FYE[a] Sales in IPO Year (millions)	FYE EBIT in IPO Year (Millions)	LTM[b] Sales at IPO (millions)	LTM EBIT at IPO (millions)	Current Market Value (millions)
Saratoga Beverage	Bottled Spring Water	6/23/93	6.00	$ 5.00	1.20	$ 10.4	$ 6.2	$ −2.5	$ NA	$ NA	$ 6.3
Panamerican Beverages	Bottles Spring Water	9/21/93	293.3	$25.50	11.5	854.6	1110.8	122.0	1060.5	NA	3249.2
Odwalla	Juice	12/15/93	6.3	$ 9.00	0.700	13.5	12.6	−0.16	17.1	NA	38.3
Redhook Ale Brewery	Specialty Beer	8/16/95	38.3	$17.00	2.25	114.3	25.9	5.4	19.9	NA	49.0
Pete's Brewing	Specialty Beer	11/06/95	62.1	$18.00	3.45	248.9	59.2	2.8	51.5	1.9	52.5
Boston Beer	Specialty Beer	11/20/95	71.3	$20.00	3.56	491.5	151.3	10.6	142.1	NA	153.2
Lion Brewery	Specialty Beer	5/02/96	11.3	$ 6.00	1.88	21.9	26.4	3.1	25.2	NA	14.6
American Craft Brewing	Specialty Beer	9/11/96	10.0	$ 5.50	1.82	18.9	0.43	−0.36	0.42	−0.10	4.6
Independence Brewing	Specialty Beer	2/11/97	4.5	$ 5.00	0.900	12.1	0.51	−0.85	0.51	−0.9	1.5

[a] FYE stands for Fiscal Year Ending.
[b] LTM stands for Last Twelve Months.

EXHIBIT 33-4

RÉSUMÉS OF TOM SCOTT AND TOM FIRST

Tom Scott. Born in Alexandria, Virginia, in 1966, Tom Scott spent his childhood in Chevy Chase, Maryland. He attended Landon School in Bethesda, Maryland where he lettered in football, basketball, and lacrosse. He continued his education at Brown University in Providence, Rhode Island. Brown offered Tom the opportunity to pursue his various interests including varsity football, theater, and outdoor leadership programs. While garnering accomplishments in these areas, Tom also managed to earn a degree in American Civilization and start a business during his summers on Nantucket Island.

In the summer of 1988, Tom founded Nantucket Allserve, a boat business that serviced boats in Nantucket Harbor; he was soon joined by his current partner, and college friend, Tom First. From this first business grew their second venture and most notable accomplishment to date, Nantucket Nectars.

Tom currently lives in Boston and Nantucket and is accompanied at all times by his dog, Becky.

Tom First. Tom First was born in Boston in 1966 and raised in Weston, Massachusetts. He attended Concord Academy and played soccer, basketball, and baseball. He continued his education at Brown University in Providence, Rhode Island, where he met his current partner and close friend, Tom Scott. While earning a degree in American History at Brown, Tom spent some of his time at the neighboring art institute, Rhode Island School of Design, aspiring to continue on to architecture school. In addition to these academic endeavors, Tom enjoyed playing lacrosse and sailing for Brown. During the summer between his junior and senior year, Tom First joined Tom Scott in Nantucket and helped get their then fledgling business, Allserve, up and running. After graduating from Brown in 1989, the two Toms moved to Nantucket and concentrated on strengthening their boat business. Tom First is credited with the initial Nantucket Nectars inspiration. Driven by a passion for cooking, he was determined to recreate the taste of a peach nectar that he had sampled during his travels in Spain. After mixing fruits in a blender, both Toms were thrilled with the results. With no business experience to speak of, the two embarked on a true adventure that has now developed into a company that boasts ever increasing sales and national as well as international distribution. Tom resides in Cambridge and Nantucket with his wife Kristan and dog, Pete.

Nantucket Nectars in exchange for 50% of the company. The founders originally met Mike Egan while serving his boat in Nantucket Harbor during the early days of Allserve. Mike Egan was the founder and former CEO of Alamo Car Rentals and still maintained 93% of that company's stock. While the founders were concerned about ceding a controlling share to an outsider, they needed the money and had no other options.

Egan performed the function of trusted advisor while not meddling in the day-to-day operations of the business. As Egan explained, "I really made the investment because it makes me wake up in the morning and feel like I'm twenty-five again, trying to grow another company."

The founders used the capital to improve distribution and increase inventory. First, they secured better, independent bottlers. Given their lack of credit history and Snapple's fantastic growth, which utilized the majority of good bottler capacity, Nantucket Nectars previously had difficulty finding quality bottlers at an affordable price. Second, they built their own distribution arm with the equity capital. The founders needed to decide how to distribute their beverages in the early days, deciding between three options:

- implement a large advertising campaign to build brand awareness while moving their product through an independent distributor channel that would carry multiple brands at the same time;
- contact retailers directly to create trade promotions; or
- distribute the product yourself.

Given that Nantucket Nectars could not afford the first two strategies, the founders created a unique private distribution strategy whereby they themselves sold, delivered, and stocked the product. Ned Desmond explained:

> We were doing it all. We leased some warehouse space, bought an old van, and went up and down the street selling Nantucket Nectars and our passion to make the brand succeed. The retailers immediately loved our story and enjoyed seeing us stock the shelves ourselves. Becoming our own distributor allowed us to control the positioning of the product. We often rearranged the shelves to ensure that Nantucket Nectars was better positioned than Snapple.

In order to speed up their growth, the founders obtained the exclusive rights to distribute Arizona Iced Tea in Massachusetts. Boston was one of the top 5 New Age beverage markets in the United States, and Arizona Ice Tea needed a strong Boston position in its own race with Snapple. While hoping to harness the "on-the-street, upstart energy" of the Nantucket Nectars team, Arizona Iced Tea was more than prepared to cancel the contract if Nantucket Nectars did not perform.

The founders wanted to piggyback off the strong brand and higher volumes of Arizona Iced Tea to build their own distribution arm and to get more outlets for their own products in the market. Within three months the distribution division grew from 7 to 100 employees and from 2,000 to 30,000 cases sold per month. At the same time, the founders repackaged and reformulated their own product while convincing small stores to carry Nantucket Nectars alongside the red-hot Arizona Iced Tea. By the end of 1994, revenues surpassed $8 million.

MARKETING AND THE CREATION OF A BRAND

Most New Age[3] beverage companies must have clear differentiation because undercapitalization did not allow traditional, expensive advertising strategies and slotting charges for garnering shelf space. Nantucket Nectars relied on creative packaging, rapid and original product introductions, word-of-mouth, and a memorable story line. Achieving this combination of low-priced but effective marketing was extremely difficult. Knowing this difficulty, the founders decided to focus on a simple vision without the help of any outside agencies: create a high-quality product and sell a persona. The result was the creation of a unique brand personality based on the start of the company on Nantucket. In the early days, Nantucket Nectars focused on creative but mundane ways of creating name recognition at a minimal cost. The company set up samplings, giveaways, sponsorship for road races and summer sports leagues which usually required only donation of product. In addition, the company set up publicity stunts including salespeople dressed up as fruits.

---

[3] Term given to trendy, healthier beverages such as ready-to-drink teas, sports drinks, and juices.

With the increased capital raised from Egan, the founders segued into radio ads as a means to push the Nantucket "story." The founders described early mishaps in radio ads and placed messages underneath their bottle caps in order to attract consumer interest. See Exhibits 33-5, 33-6, and 33-7. For example, an early radio ad described how Ned Desmond, on the first sales trip to Boston, crashed the Nantucket Nectars van on Storrow Drive destroying all the juice. Another radio ad explained how early employee Larry Perez accidentally dropped the proceeds from the first sale into the harbor.[4]

GROWTH

The early days were extremely frustrating for the two founders. While customers clearly liked the product, Nantucket Nectars only had three flavors—Cranberry Grapefruit, Lemonade, and Peach Orange—and the founders were completely unsure of how to grow the business. Tom Scott explained: "The frustrations that we dealt with were immense. We didn't know what point-of-sale was, we didn't know what promotion was, we didn't know what margin we should be making."[4]

Product Development   As a means to differentiate, Nantucket Nectars committed to creating high-quality, all natural juice beverages without regard for the margins; the quality of the product came first. This strategy translated into replacing high-fructose corn syrup with only pure cane sugar. The founders believed that using pure cane sugar would improve the taste without leaving the consumer thirsty like other sweetened beverages. Furthermore, the founders used four times the juice of other major brands to improve on their mantra of quality and taste. The founders also differentiated their product by introducing a proprietary 17.5-ounce bottle to complement their existing 12 ounce line as compared to their competitors' standard 16-ounce bottle. From the original three juice flavors, Nantucket Nectars developed 27 flavors across three product lines during the first three years: 100% fruit juices, juice cocktails, and ice teas/lemonades.

Sales and Distribution   Having started out as a "floating 7-Eleven," the founders had been distributors long before they had been suppliers and marketers of juice. At first, the founders structured their in-house distribution arm to target delis, sandwich shops, small markets, gourmet food shops, convenience stores and food service cafeterias. The Arizona Iced Tea contract and their own self-confidence lead them to launch a broader distribution business with the hopes of carrying multiple brands and higher volumes at lower costs into the New England market. This new business allowed them to penetrate even more of the small outlets and to begin building up a presence in the larger stores and chains. They learned the "ins and outs" of the distribution business and forged relationships with many independent distributors around the country. Unfortunately, they also learned that the economics of the distribution business really required one of the "big brands" or you just could not carry the overhead. Having "made every mistake in the book," the founders gained a new respect for the talent and time it took to scale up a business. In 1995, the founders sold their distribution arm after losing $2 million in the previous year. They believed that their brand was firmly entrenched on the shelves and were confident that any adverse effects on revenue growth caused by selling the distribution business would be small. The founders concentrated on marketing their own product and developing the Nantucket Nectars brand name. The priority at Nantucket Nectars was "moving the juice."

---

[4] *Beverage Aisle*, February 1996.

EXHIBIT 33-5

NANTUCKET NECTAR SALES CREDO

"We simply make good tasting juices, from the best ingredients." *—Tom First*

Hi I'm Tom, and I'm Tom. We're juice guys.™

We started Nantucket Nectars because we believe in providing a top quality product. Our goal at Nantucket Nectars mirrors our philosophy behind our first business *Allserve*. We are determined to provide a reliable service and to offer the consumers the quality that they want without complication.

Nantucket Nectars is a team effort, and we are proud of the commitment to quality and hard work that has been undertaken by each one of our company members. For Nantucket Nectars employees, being a juice guy means more than simply enjoying a great tasting product. Being a juice guy means providing honest and reliable service and taking pride in each one of our bottles that stand on the shelf. Juice guys share a strong commitment to quality and a desire to create a product that remains on the shelf long after the thrill of newness has passed.

The term *juice guy* is not gender specific. Webster's Dictionary defines *guys* as "persons of either sex; people". Continuing in Webster's tradition, our juice guys are really anyone who enjoys Nantucket Nectars. If you buy Nantucket Nectars, you're a juice guy. If you sell Nantucket Nectars, you're a juice guy. And if you make Nantucket Nectars, you're a juice guy.

Nantucket Nectars is not a flash in the pan product, for it is grounded by a work ethic that focuses on forging strong relationships with both our distributors and individual consumers. We started Nantucket Nectars simply because we wanted to make the highest quality and best tasting juice in a bottle. From the beginning this is how it has always been, and this is how it continues to be for the two of us and all the rest of the juice guys at Nantucket Nectars.

Everyone is always asking us what our next step is. All we can promise is that whatever we do, we won't let you down.

TOM&TOM

EXHIBIT 33-6

NANTUCKET NECTARS COLLATERAL

We're juice guys.™

The company switched the distribution of Nantucket Nectars to a combination of in-house salesforce and outside distributors. The company granted exclusive rights to sell Nantucket Nectars products within a defined territory while allowing those distributors to carry other beverage products as well. The company wrote multiyear agreements with most of its distributors. When an order was placed at company headquarters from the outside distributor, the company selected an outside trucking source to pick up the products from the bottler of the beverage to deliver to the appropriate distributors. The distributors then sold and delivered the product to retail outlets from their warehouses using their own salespeople and delivery drivers. The company initiated incentive programs aimed at distributors and their salespeople to promote Nantucket Nectars through stocking, merchandising, and retail sales deals. These programs, which were budgeted individually by territory, were meant to gain shelf space and visibility.

With the direct salesforce, Nantucket Nectars called the store accounts to sell the product. The salesforce also employed the strategy of visiting all small retailers to make sure that the product was displayed well, "eye to thigh" and also to check the distribu-

---

EXHIBIT 33-7

NANTUCKET NECTARS TYPICAL BOTTLE CAP

---

tor's work. The strategy was to build steadily a sustainable organization through strong relations with either the best distributors or individual vendors. As Tom Scott explained, "we were not trying to build a house of cards, we wanted solid long-term growth."

CONSUMER TASTES AND PREFERENCES

Nantucket Nectars was fortunate to have caught a new wave emerging in the beverage industry, the New Age segment, including ready-to-drink teas, water, juices and sports drinks. Tremendous growth occurred in this segment from 1992 through 1995:

TABLE A   Three-Year Compound Annual Growth Rate for New Age Beverage Segments

Category	Three-Year CAGR (1992–1995)
Ready-to-Drink Teas	24%
Water	34%
Juices	32%
Sports Drinks	12%

Driving this strong growth were trendy young consumers pursuing healthier lifestyles, yet faced with fast-paced lifestyles and shortened lunches. For these reasons, they appreciated large, single-serve packaging of New Age beverages and the "gulpability" of lighter, noncarbonated, natural fruit juices.

COMPETITION

Competition surfaced in three major ways in the New Age beverage world. First, a competitor might simply undercut in pricing to flood the market while also offering a high-quality or innovative product. The second way of competing involved image and brand strength: brand advertising, packaging, trade, and consumer promotions. Lastly, brands competed, especially the large players in the beverage industry, by blocking the smaller, less powerful players from the retailer shelf space. At Christy's in Harvard Square, the New Age beverages held over 75% of the chilled beverage space, with the remainder controlled by traditional carbonated beverages. The proliferation of brands and flavors confused and distracted even the most loyal juice drinker. Promotions, new flavors, and even new brands tempted the consumer to try new products. See Exhibit 33-8 for a list of New Age beverages at the Harvard Square Christy's. So far, more than 100 companies from traditional beverage companies like Coca-Cola to regional start-ups like Arizona had launched New Age beverages hoping to capture shifting consumer tastes. Product innovation was a critical element of competitiveness and created an incredibly fierce battle for shelf space, especially among regional companies focused on differentiating themselves through flavors, packaging, and image. Commenting on this competition, Tom First stated:

EXHIBIT 33-8

NEW AGE BEVERAGE PRODUCT SELECTION, CHRISTY'S OF HARVARD SQUARE

Product Selection at Christy's, New Age Beverages

Apple Quenchers (Very Fine line extension)

Arizona Iced Tea

Boku

Crystal Light

Chillers (Very Fine line extension)

Evian

Fruitopia

Gatorade

Jones Soda

Lipton

Minute Maid

Mistic

Nestea

Ocean Spray

Orangina

Poland Springs

Powerade

Snapple

Tropicana Season's Best

Very Fine

If we had known how unattractive the industry dynamics were before we started our business, we probably would not have started Nantucket Nectars. However, now that we're in the business, we think that the odds of someone replicating what we did are very slim. The industry dynamics and the fast-paced changes within the industry really decrease the probabilities of an early entrant's success.

Many industry analysts believed that competition would increase as New Age beverages became the latest battleground in the Cola Wars. Coke, Pepsi, and Seagrams were all fighting to become the best "total beverage company" to serve the masses while also responding to new beverage trends. New Age beverages were an opportunity to bolster flattening cola and alcohol businesses with short-term profits, and to improve their competencies at serving niche markets. These firms supported a portfolio of beverage brands with expensive marketing and sophisticated distribution skills. Their access to supermarkets through controlling shelf space, vending machines, convenience stores and fountain distribution channels combined with mass marketing and brand awareness provided them with distinct advantages in developing brands, even though their procedures and image inhibit their ability to exploit nontraditional, rapidly changing market opportunities. Furthermore, scale lowered a beverage company's cost structure by decreasing the cost of per unit ingredients and distribution.

Meanwhile, the customer clearly had many substitutes from which to choose (water, carbonated sodas, alcoholic beverages, sports drinks, and other fruit juices and ready-to-drink teas) and had no switching costs. Furthermore, some people questioned the sustainability of any New Age beverage brand given the "fad" status of this segment.

PROFITABILITY AND COST MANAGEMENT

Fiscal year 1995 represented the first year of profitability for the company. The company's margins were among the lowest in the New Age beverage category given the founders' emphasis on quality. Unfortunately, high sales growth forced the founders to focus on increasing production to meet high demand, rather than delivering quality at a favorable cost. Their lower margins were a result of higher quality ingredients in the juices and limited futures contracts in commodity procurement. All-natural juice beverages depended on commodities for their raw inputs, placing their margins at risk to the markets. Furthermore, Nantucket Nectars juice cocktails were made with real cane sugar, which was more expensive than the high-fructose corn syrup used in most competitive products. The company also used four times more fruit juice in its products instead of relying on water and artificial flavorings. Lastly, unlike many competitors, the company offered a full line of 100% unsweetened juices.

The company's rapid growth and emphasis on quality ingredients accentuated its competitive disadvantages in raw material procurement and plant scheduling. Because of difficulty in predicting growth, the founders were unable to institutionalize future contracts on ingredients. As a consequence, the company was heavily dependent on the harvests as competitors were more likely to secure products if there were a shortage. For example, due to the poor 1995 cranberry harvest, Nantucket Nectars got no cranberries because Ocean Spray controlled all the supplies. This competitive disadvantage in procurement had an even greater impact on Nantucket Nectar's margins because of the higher fruit content in their products.

NANTUCKET NECTARS' STRATEGY

In August 1997, responding to the launch of competitors' new product lines, Nantucket Nectars launched a new line of beverages, called Super Nectars, which were herbally enhanced and pasteurized fruit juices and teas. Four of the six new flavors were made from no less than 80% real fruit juice, while the remaining two were naturally steeped from green tea and flavored with real fruit juice and honey. Each Super Nectar was created with a concern for both great taste and good health.

TABLE B List of Super Nectars

Product Name	Description
Chi'I Green Tea	Green tea and ginseng mix flavored with white clover honey, lemon, gardenia; offered the health benefits of traditional green tea and the revitalizing powers of ginseng.
Protein Smoothie	Combined the power of natural soy protein with the great tasting juices of strawberries, bananas, oranges, and coconuts. Super Nectars Protein Smoothie offered the nine essential amino acids that the body cannot manufacture on its own.
Vital-C	100% real fruit juice made primarily from the acerola berry, a fruit native to the West Indies and known as a vitamin C powerhouse. Acerola was blended with the juices of other fruits including strawberries, kiwifruits, and oranges to offer 140% of the recommended daily allowance of vitamin C.
Ginkgo Mango	Blended with 100% orange and mango juices, offered the health benefits of ginkgo, an ancient Chinese medicinal herb derived from the ginkgo biloba tree. The medicinal uses of ginkgo can be traced back to ancient healing practices where it was valued for its ability to benefit the brain.
Green Angel	Combined the valued herbs of spirulina, echinacea, wheat grass, and angelica with the juices of white grapes, bananas, and pineapple. Echinacea was an herb known to enhance the immune system, and spirulina was one of nature's richest protein foods. Wheat grass was a natural vitamin supplement that offered minerals, amino acids, and enzymes, and angelica was valued for its ability to promote healing and balance.
Red Guarana Tea	An herbal tea mixed with white clover honey, cranberry juice, and guarana nut berry, a plant native to the Amazon region. Guarana was naturally high in caffeine and a valuable source of energy.

Furthermore, there was evidence to suggest that Nantucket Nectars should maintain their growth for at least the next five years:

TABLE C Projected U.S. Retail Sales of New Age Beverages, by Product Category from 1991 to 2000 (in millions)[a]

Category	1991	1995	2000	CAGR (1991–2000)
Alternative Fruit Drinks	$236.8	$857.0	$1,328.8	21.1%
Gourmet/Natural Sodas	371.9	627.7	697.5	7.2
Flavor-essenced Waters	304.1	329.7	259.2	(1.8)
Juice Sparklers	232.9	238.4	231.2	(0.1)
Total	$1,145.7	$2,052.8	$2,516.7	9.1%

[a] *Beverage Industry*, March 1997, p. 51.

TABLE D   Location of All New Age Beverages Sold, 1996[a]

Location	Percentage Sold
Supermarkets	55%
Convenience Stores and Smaller Mass-Volume Stores	35%
Health/Natural Food and Gourmet Stores	10%
Total	100%

[a] *Beverage Industry*, March 1997, p. 50.

As one compares the channel location of all New Age beverages sold with Nantucket Nectar's current sales, one sees the tremendous upside with supermarket distribution:

TABLE E   Sales Location (Channels) for Nantucket Nectars, 1996

Location	Percentage Sales
Supermarket Channel	1%
Convenience Chains	6%
All Others (delis, educational institutions, etc.)	93%
Total	100%

This apparent growth potential was also demonstrated by the potential geographic expansion capabilities of the Nantucket Nectars brand. Table F represents the current geographic sales of the brand:

TABLE F   Current Geographic Sales Percentages

Location	Sales Percentage
Northeast U.S.	38%
Mid-Atlantic/Southeast U.S.	29%
Midwest	9%
West	9%
International	15%
Total	100%

Based on these growth opportunities, the founders wondered whether a buyer would possibly pay an appropriate price given the negative publicity associated with the Snapple transaction, a previous high-growth beverage company.

The founders were also aware that their success to date was accomplished through the more fragmented channels like convenience stores, delis, educational institutions and health and gourmet stores which demanded single-serve product. They also wanted to market their product through the supermarket channel which demanded multi-serve product.

The Snapple Deal   Outside of macro-economic conditions and the stock market jitters of October 1997, the Snapple deal profoundly affected the New Age beverage market. In November, 1994, Quaker Oats purchased Snapple from Thomas Lee for $1.7 billion. By 1997, Quaker Oats conceded its defeat, selling Snapple to Triarc for $300 million, while firing their chief executive officer, William Smithburg. Industry experts blamed Snapple's decline on Quaker's problems with Snapple's distributors as well as a new marketing strategy. Quaker Oats replaced Howard Stern and "Wendy the Snapple Lady" with the corporate "Threedom is Freedom" advertising campaign. Quaker Oats also attempted to take away the most profitable distribution business from the distributors in order to utilize its own Gatorade distribution arm. Due to expensive legal agreements called "Take or Pay" contracts, Quaker Oats was forced to keep their old distributors or pay exorbitant fees to break away from them. Ultimately, they decided to stay with the old distribution system. However, the old distributors by that time had relegated Snapple to secondary status causing Snapple sales to decline precipitously. Quaker's strategy to drop their old distribution network became known as Snappleization within the distribution industry: a distributor lost its distribution contract after a beverage company was acquired by a bigger player. The acquirer moved distribution either in-house or simply to larger distributors after the first distribution network helped build the market for the beverage.

CORPORATE STRATEGY

The founders wondered what to do with the company. They wanted to grow the company but were worried about the associated risks. Given their growth needs, they needed to decide whether to sell a part or all of the company, operate under status quo, or undergo an IPO. Mark Hellendrung, Nantucket Nectars CFO, described the consensus of senior management: "The decision was difficult because we felt comfortable operating our company independently with our current capital structure, under an IPO scenario, or with a strategic partner making an investment in our company."

If they decided to proceed with a sale, they wondered how to handle the negotiations in order to maximize the price. How could they hold all the meetings so that their employees would not find out prematurely about the transaction? The founders also worried about whether the ownership structure of the company helped or hindered the negotiation process. By the time of the case, Mike Egan, the individual investor, had aggregated 55% of the company due to follow-on investments which permitted early operating losses.

With all these issues, Tom and Tom wondered if they needed advisors to help them with the process? If so, should they hire a local investment banker from Boston or a large investment bank from New York? Should they organize a full blown auction of Nantucket Nectars? Would there be any adverse effects if, after a high profile auction, the founders decided not to sell? Should they pick two strategic players and ask them for a preemptive offer for the company? Or should they identify six or so potential bidders and contact them to assess their interest in entering a bidding process. See Exhibit 33-9 for descriptions of major potential bidders. Also, how should the founders handle the beginning of a negotiation: should they specify a minimum bid or force the buyers to submit their first bids?

Lastly, Tom Scott and Tom First wondered how to structure the potential transaction. They both believed strongly in the upside potential of their company but were also concerned about holding the stock of a different company. Should they negotiate the best cash deal possible without a long-term management responsibility or should they

EXHIBIT 33-9

LIST OF POTENTIAL BUYERS AND STRATEGIC MATCH

Potential Bidder	Strategic Match
Seagram (Tropicana)	Tropicana maintains the strongest distribution in the grocery segment for juices which should provide Nantucket Nectars with a strong platform to expand. Furthermore, Tropicana's strength in the Northeast US (70% market share) matches Nantucket Nectar's business perfectly. Given Tropicana's strategic push into the single-serve business, the company should have interest in exploring an acquisition of Nantucket Nectars. From Tropicana's 1996 annual report: "Strategic direction is to continue growing its North American market share in chilled juices, broaden its product mix, expand its presence in attractive global markets and diversify into new distribution channels."

Tropicana has also made a strong international push with the acquisition of Dole as almost 20% of revenues come from abroad with increased cheaper production capabilities overseas (China). Furthermore, Tropicana has restructured its operations since its purchase of Dole in 1995. This cost improvement makes Tropicana perhaps the best platform to wring big savings out of Nantucket Nectars. Tropicana also could help the cost structure of Nantucket Nectars by having the strongest buyer power in the juice business (e.g. 25% of FLA. orange crop each year). |
| Ocean Spray | The founders knew the Ocean Spray senior management from industry conferences and believed that there was a good match of culture. Ocean Spray was private which would allow Nantucket Nectars to operate in a similar fashion: less disclosure, less hassle, and less short-term pressure to hit earnings. The founders also knew that Ocean Spray generated a good internal cash flow which could be used to fund Nantucket Nectar growth. They also knew that Nantucket Nectars might be able to exploit Ocean Spray's loss of Pepsi distribution which might cause them to bid aggressively. Ocean Spray is the world's largest purchaser of non-orange fruit juice, especially berries, tropicals and other exotics. Lastly, Ocean Spray maintained a network of five captive bottling plants plus several long-term arrangements with bottlers giving secure, national manufacturing coverage at advantageous cost and quality control.

The founders were worried by the loss of Pepsi distribution. Industry experts believed that the distribution agreement would terminate in May 1998, with 50% of current single-serve distribution handled by Pepsi-owned bottlers (approx. $100MM) with another $100MM handled by Pepsi franchisees.[1] Thus, Ocean Spray could lose as much as $200 million in sales (from a base of $1.05 billion) if they could not find a good distributor or could not distribute effectively themselves. Ocean Spray, however, maintained strong power on the grocery shelves, especially in the Northeast. |
| Pepsi | Pepsi seems more prepared to take risks with new products in the New Age segment. Pepsi recently terminated its distribution arrangement with Ocean Spray which will take effect sometime in early 1998. Many industry insiders believe that Pepsi entered into this distribution arrangement to learn as much as possible about single-serve New Age beverages before entering the market themselves. Skip Carpenter, a Donaldson, Lufkin & Jenrette equity analyst, described the action as a "move that clearly signals a bold new way in which PepsiCo will compete in the juice segment going forward."[2]

In late 1996, Pepsi launched a cold, ready-to-drink sparkling coffee drink with Starbucks coffee called Mazagran. In 1995, Pepsi also launched Aquafina, a bottled water drink. One major concern for the founders was that Pepsi has a history of downscaling the quality of products, such as Lipton Brisk Tea, in order to achieve higher volume. |

[1] DLJ Research report, July 14, 1997.

[2] Donaldson, Lufkin & Jenrette Beverage Industry Report; Skip Carpenter; July 14, 1997.

(Continued)

EXHIBIT 33-9   *(Continued)*

Potential Bidder	Strategic Match
Triarc (Snapple and Mistic)	The founders believed that Triarc provided the best platform to grow the Nantucket Nectars business the most over the next two years. Through ownership of Snapple, RC Cola and Mistic, Triarc has immediate access to a national single-serve () network to push the Nantucket Nectar product.
	One concern was that Triarc would want to replace many of Nantucket Nectar's distributors because of redundancy. While the written contracts with the distributors were favorable concerning termination without too much cost, Nantucket Nectars worried about reprise from distributors (similar to what happened to Quaker Oats after they bought Snapple, which created the term "Snappleization").
Cadbury (Schweppes Ginger Ale)	Cadbury owns Schweppes Ginger Ale, 7 Up and Dr. Pepper. The firm has come under pressure in the past two years to improve its management team, set up a succession plan, and reduce its dependence on the Cadbury family. Stagnant sales in the carbonated soda segments, a vulnerable production structure, and perceived lack of direction have created takeover rumors. The sheer size of Cadbury makes a takeover unlikely. The production strategy is to use an assorted group of independent bottlers as well as long-term agreements with Coke and Pepsi.
	While there have been no public indications to date, Cadbury might have plans to diversify its beverage portfolio away from slow-growing carbonated sodas toward the faster growing New Age beverage segments. While Cadbury has deep pockets to operate a New Age beverage company appropriately and for strategic reasons might decide to bid aggressively for Nantucket, their current company strategy does not create much operating improvements or increased distribution strength.
Starbucks	Nantucket Nectars had recently consummated an agreement with Starbucks calling for all Starbucks coffee shops to carry the Nantucket Nectar product. While Starbucks was clearly not in the New Age beverage business, Howard Schultz was considered to understand the tastes and trends of the new generation. Throughout the negotiations with Starbucks, Schultz expressed that he very much liked the Nantucket Nectars brand and that maybe there was something more which could be done between these two companies.
Welch's	Welch's was very similar to Ocean Spray, private with a cooperative of grape farmers as the parent. Founded in 1868, the company maintained sales in the $600 million range, with grape frozen concentrate as the company's main product. Welch's rolled out new product lines in 1997: a shelf-stable concentrate that did not require freezing and a full complement of single-serve, 16-ounce product. Flavors included white grape peach, apple cranberry, guava peach, apple, watermelon strawberry, strawberry kiwi, fruit punch, pink grapefruit, tropical punch, apple orange pineapple, and white grape raspberry.
	Concerning product innovation, Welch's has maintained a strong philosophy of reacting to the marketplace. CEO Dan Dillon described corporate strategy: "The whole industry seemed to be going in one direction, with faddish kinds of products. We have gone in a different direction, by giving the consumer products that have got substance to them. With our grape-based items, that means providing a very distinct, robust-tasting product."
Coca-Cola	The Nantucket Nectars founders were uncertain about Coca-Cola's interest in the New Age beverage market given their lack of success with the Fruitopia product. Coca-Cola spent $180 million developing Fruitopia, of which $60 million was spent on the 1994 product launch. Coca-Cola has demonstrated strong concern in the past about acquiring businesses with smaller margins than their core carbonated soda business.

negotiate for acquirer stock in order to participate in the company's continued upside? How would the chosen strategy affect the valued employees who had helped build the company? With all these issues swirling around in their minds, Tom Scott and Tom First turned their attention to the potential valuation of their company.

VALUATION ANALYSIS

Beyond the numbers and the marketplace, the founders wondered what significant assets and skills within Nantucket Nectars drove their corporate value. The founders decided to hold internal brainstorming sessions to analyze why Nantucket Nectars succeeded and therefore deserved a premium for the brand. The founders came up with the following list of value drivers:

- Great product: great tasting, all-natural product
- Current management team
- Value of the brand: quirky, eccentric, and *memorable*
- Geographic expansion capabilities: current sales base and future sales base
- Management's knowledge of and experience with the single-serve business: ability to add value to large player rolling out new single-serve products
- Guerrilla marketing skills
- Ability to exploit small, rapidly changing market opportunities
- A more appealing story than any other juice beverage company (great material for a company with a large marketing budget and more distribution power);
- A stabilizing cost structure
- Access to 18–34 market
- Last good access to single-serve distribution in the New Age beverage market
- Best vehicle for juice companies to expand into juice cocktail category without risking their own brand equity

The founders wondered how all these assets were reflected in the pro formas and the actual valuation of the company. They decided to analyze the valuation in three different ways: discounted cash flow, comparable acquisitions and comparable trading. They wondered if these analyses prepared them for the potential negotiations with the buyers. As Tom First described the situation, "this kind of analysis tells us nothing about what certain buyers can do for Nantucket Nectars concerning improved cost structure or increased sales through wider distribution. The difficult question is how do we figure out what the value of Nantucket Nectars is to someone else, not just us." The founders believed that most acquirers would provide scale economies on costs of goods sold decreasing costs approximately 10% to 20% depending on the acquirer. See Exhibit 33-10 for comparable trading, Exhibit 33-11 for comparable operating statistics, and Exhibit 33-12 for comparable acquisitions. Exhibit 33-13 shows a basic discounted cash flow based on company pro formas. Furthermore, Nantucket Nectars had rolled out a larger-sized bottle (36-ounce bottle) for the supermarkets, but the company was having difficulty securing shelf space in the larger supermarket chains.

EXHIBIT 33-10

LATEST 12 MONTHS TRADING STATISTICS FOR SELECTED COMPARABLE COMPANIES ($MM)

Company	As of 7/31/97: Price per Share	Shares Outstanding	Market Cap	Earnings per Share CY1997E	CY1998E	P/E Multiples CY1997E	CY1998E	(1997–98) Growth Rate	1998 P/E to Growth	Market Cap/LTM Net Revenue	ROE	Market Cap/ Book Value
Food and Beverage Growth Brands												
Ben & Jerry's	$12.88	6.4	$ 82	$0.50	$0.65	26 ×	20 ×	30%	0.70 ×	0.5 ×	2%	1.1 ×
Boston Beer	9.38	16.2	152	0.35	0.40	27	23	14	1.60	0.8	10	2.9
Celestial Seasonings	12.00	8.1	97	1.44	1.65	17	15	15	1.00	1.2	13	2.3
Cott Corp.	10.00	63.9	639	0.54	0.73	19	14	35	0.40	0.6	13	1.8
Dreyers Ice Cream	21.13	26.8	566	0.60	1.42	NM	30	NM	NM	0.6	1	5.8
Robert Mondavi	46.75	7.5	349	2.02	2.36	23	20	17	1.20	1.2	13	3.5
Starbucks	20.47	156.7	3,208	0.80	1.10	51	37	38	1.00	3.9	8	7.5
Weider Nutrition	18.50	8.2	152	0.74	0.95	25	19	28	0.70	0.7	21	5.7
Mean						26.9 ×	22.5 ×	25%	0.9 ×	1.2 ×	10.1%	3.8 ×

EXHIBIT 33-11

LATEST 12 MONTHS OPERATING STATISTICS FOR SELECTED COMPARABLE COMPANIES ($MM)

Company	Latest 12 Months	Latest 12 Months Revenue	EBITDA	EBIT	Net	Margins Gross	EBITDA	EBIT	Net	Enterprise Value	Enterprise Value/LTM Revs.	EBITDA	EBIT	A/R DSO	Inv. Turns	Debt/ Mkt. Cap.
Food and Beverage Growth Brands																
Ben & Jerry's	3/97	$ 165	$ 11	$ 3	$ 2	30%	7%	2%	1%	$ 94	0.57 ×	8.7 ×	27.6 ×	34	6.9 ×	34%
Boston Beer	6/97	186	13	10	6	50	7	5	3	168	0.90	12.7	17.1	41	7.0	6
Celestial Seasonings	6/97	78	12	10	6	62	16	12	7	101	1.29	8.2	10.5	46	4.2	7
Cott Corp.	4/97	1,015	95	59	47	16	9	6	5	851	0.84	8.9	14.4	45	NA	39
Dreyers Ice Cream	6/97	886	51	22	1	22	6	2	0	857	0.97	16.9	39.8	36	15.4	44
Robert Mondavi	6/97	301	67	55	28	45	22	18	9	912	3.03	13.6	16.6	60	1	24
Starbucks	3/97	827	117	60	41	53	14	8	5	3,593	4.34	30.7	52.3	9	5.1	5
Weider Nutrition	5/97	219	37	30	17	37	17	14	8	508	2.32	13.7	17.0	58	3.6	11
Wholesome and Hearty Foods	3/97	40	2	1	1	49	4	2	2	57	1.43	37.3	71.4	36	NA	0
Mean:						40.4%	11.3%	7.7	4.4%		1.7 ×	16.7	29.6 ×	40.6	6.2 ×	18.9%

Source: Hambrecht & Quist.

EXHIBIT 33-12

SELECTED FOOD AND BEVERAGE M&A TRANSACTIONS

Date Announced	Acquirer Name	Name	Business Description	Value of Transaction ($ mil.)	Net Sales LTM ($ mil.)	Value/ LTM Sales	LTM EBIT ($ mil.)	Value/ LTM EBIT
08/11/92	Investor Group	Lincoln Snack (Sandoz Nutrition)	Produce, whole pre-popped popcorn	$ 12	$ 30	0.4 ×	—	NM ×
08/31/92	Nabisco Foods Group	Stella D'Oro Biscuit Co.	Produce breakfast treats	100	65	1.5	—	NM
09/17/92	President Banking Co.	Famous Amos Chocolate Chip	Produce cookies	61	75	0.8	—	NM
11/16/92	Kraft General Foods	RJR Nabisco Holdings-Ready-to-Eat	Ready-to-eat cereal business	450	230	2.0	—	NM
11/23/92	Thomas J. Lipton Inc.	Isaly Klondike Co.	Produce ice cream	155	101	1.5	—	NM
03/08/93	Russell Stover Candies Inc.	Per Inc.-Whitman's Chocolates	Produce and whole chocolate	35	85	0.4	—	NM
03/25/93	American Home Products Corp.	M. Polaner Inc.	Produce fruit spreads, spices	70	65	1.1	—	NM
07/26/93	Specialty Foods (Specialty)	Mother's Cake & Cookies, 7 Other	Produce cookies, cake, bread	1,100	2,100	0.5	—	NM
07/23/93	Nestle SA	Italgel SpA	Produce ice cream	715	489	1.5	—	NM
09/08/93	Unilever U.S. Inc.	Kraft General Foods-Ice Cream	Produce ice cream	300	500	0.6	—	NM
09/28/93	Jacobs Suchard (KGF)	Freia Marabou	Produce candy and chocolate	1,374	905	1.5	—	NM
10/08/93	Gourmet Coffee of America Inc.	Hillside Coffee of California	Produce coffee	42	28	1.56	7.0	
11/01/93	Dean Foods Co.	Kraft General Foods-Birds Eye	Produce frozen vegetables	140	250	0.6	—	NM
04/18/94	ConAgra Inc.	Universal Foods-Frozen Foods	Produce frozen foods	202	239	0.8	—	NM
05/23/94	Sandoz AG	Gerber Products Co.	Manufacture baby foods and products	3,823	1,203	3.2	184	20.8
07/19/94	Pillsbury Co. (Grand Met PLC)	Martha White foods (Windmill)	Produce flour and cake mixes	170	137	1.2	—	NM
08/29/94	Brach Acquisition Co.	Brock Candy Co.	Produce candy	140	145	1.08	17.5	
09/12/94	Kohlberg Kravis Roberts & Co.	Borden Inc.	Produce dairy prods. snacks	3,606	4,000	0.9	115	31.4
10/18/94	Trefoil Investors II LP	Fantastic Foods Inc.	Manufacture instant soups, grain prod.	—	30	NM	—	NM
11/02/94	Quaker Oats Co.	Snapple Beverage Corp.	Produce, wholesale soft drinks	1,703	700	2.4	127	13.4
11/28/94	Campbell Soup Co.	Pace Foods	Produce pickled vegetables	1,115	220	5.1	42	26.5
01/01/95	Pillsbury Co. (Grand Met PLC)	Pet Inc.	Dairy products, canned foods	3,225	1,573	2.1	217	14.9
01/04/95	Seagram Co. Ltd.	Dole Food Co-Juice Business	Produce, wholesale juice beverages	285	325	0.9	—	NM
01/06/95	Interstate Bakeries	Continental Baking (Wonder, etc.)	Produce bakery products	1,021	2,000	0.5	—	NM
06/27/95	Triarc Cos. Inc.	Mistic Beverage Co.	Produce soft drinks	94	150	0.6	—	NM

(Continued)

EXHIBIT 33-12 *(Continued)*

Date Announced	Name	Acquirer Name	Business Description	Value of Transaction ($ mil.)	Net Sales LTM ($ mil.)	Value/ LTM Sales	LTM EBIT ($ mil.)	Value/ LTM EBIT
11/22/95	Wine World Estates (Nestle S.A.)	Investor Group	Produce wine	350	210	1.7	40	8.8
12/01/95	Millstone Coffee Inc.	Procter & Gamble Co.	Wholesale coffee products	—	90	NM	—	NM
02/15/96	Earth's Best Inc.	H.J. Heinz Co.	Produce baby food	40	28	1.4	—	NM
04/08/96	Koala Springs International	Nestle Beverage (Nestle USA)	Produce beverages, spring water	—	—	NM	—	NM
05/06/96	Eagle Snacks Inc.	Procter & Gamble Co.	Produce nuts, potato chips	—	—	NM	—	NM
06/05/96	Sunshine Biscuits	Keebler (United Biscuits PLC)	Produce biscuits and snacks	—	—	NM	—	NM
07/29/96	Cascadian Farms	Trefoil natural Foods	Produce grapes	—	—	NM	—	NM
08/14/96	Ralcorp Holdings-Branded Cereal	General Mills Inc.	Produce cereals and snack food	570	300	1.9	—	NM
09/19/96	Hansen Juices Inc.	Fresh Juice Co. Inc.	Produce, wholesale juices	8	11	0.7	—	NM
11/18/96	Lenders Bagel Bakery Inc.	Kellogg Co.	Produce, wholesale bagels	455	275	1.7	—	NM
12/04/96	Mother's Cake & Cookie Co.	President International Inc.	Cookies and crackers	130	—	NM	—	NM
03/27/97	Snapple Beverage Corp.	Triarc Cos. Inc.	Produce, wholesale soft drinks	300	550	0.5	—	NM
05/02/97	Bumble Bee Seafoods Inc.	International Home Foods Inc.	Manufacture canned seafood products	203	—	NM	—	NM
05/07/97	Campbell Soup-Marie's Salad	Dean Foods Co.	Produce salad dressings	—	35	NM	—	NM
05/12/97	Kraft Foods-Log Cabin	Aurora Foods Inc.	Manufacture maple-flavored syrup	220	100	2.2	—	NM

Average	1.4 ×	17.5 ×
Median:	1.2 ×	16.2 ×
Range:	0.4–5.1 ×	7.0–31.4 ×

EXHIBIT 33-13

DISCOUNTED CASH FLOW ANALYSIS UNDER STAND-ALONE SCENARIO ($000s)

	1997	1998	1999	2000	2001	2002
Revenues	$50,026	$69,717	$93,700	$122,981	$148,499	$174,635
Growth	94.1%	30.0%	28.0%	25.0%	15.0%	12.0%
Gross Profit	17,246	26,634	35,796	46,982	56,730	66,715
Gross Margin	34.5%	38.2%	38.2%	38.2%	38.2%	38.2%
EBITDA	2,234	4,610	7,459	11,344	15,461	20,139
EBITDA Margin	4.5%	6.6%	8.0%	9.2%	10.4%	11.5%

Valuation

	EBIT Exit Multiple		
	9.0 ×	10.0 ×	11.0 ×
Discount Rate	Equity Value		
12.0%	$106,877	$117,767	$128,658
14.0%	$ 97,646	$107,614	$117,581
16.0%	$ 89,323	$ 98,461	$107,598
18.0%	$ 81,806	$ 90,195	$ 98,584

Valuation

	Terminal Growth Rate		
	4.0%	6.0%	8.0%
Discount Rate	Equity Value		
12.0%	$74,634	$98,243	$145,460
14.0%	$56,094	$69,291	$ 91,286
16.0%	$43,874	$52,081	$ 64,391
18.0%	$35,255	$40,730	$ 48,394

	Sales Exit Multiple		
	1.0 ×	1.4 ×	1.8
Discount Rate	Equity Value		
12.0%	$107,960	$153,666	$193,303
14.0%	$104,706	$140,986	$177,266
16.0%	$96,301	$129,559	$162,818
18.0%	$88,709	$119,243	$149,777

(Continued)

EXHIBIT 33-13 (Continued)

INCOME STATEMENT (000s)

		Historical Fiscal Years Ended December 31,			Projected Years Ending December 31,					
		1994	1995	1996	1997	1998	1999	2000	2001	2002
Total Revenue		$8,345	$15,335	$29,493	$50,026	$69,717	$93,700	$122,981	$148,499	$174,635
Cost of Sales		6,831	11,024	20,511	32,780	43,083	57,904	75,999	91,769	107,920
Other Expenses/Adjustments		—	—	—	—	—	0	0	0	0
Total Cost of Sales		6,831	11,024	20,511	32,780	43,083	57,904	75,999	91,769	107,920
Gross Profit		1,514	4,311	8,982	17,246	26,634	35,796	46,982	56,730	66,715
Marketing & Advertising		320	875	2,581	5,601	9,238	11,529	14,069	15,819	17,345
General & Administrative		3,290	3,344	5,432	9,410	12,785	16,808	21,569	25,450	29,231
EBITDA		(2,096)	91	969	2,234	4,610	7,459	11,344	15,461	20,139
Amortization and Depreciation		104	137	247	209	331	495	710	763	947
EBIT		(2,199)	(45)	722	2,025	4,279	6,964	10,633	14,698	19,192
Interest Expense										
Notes Payable	8.5%	0	0	0	337	323	323	323	323	323
Current Maturities	8.5%	0	0	0	0	0	0	0	0	0
Interest Income (Excess Cash)	5.0%	0	0	0	(34)	(95)	(187)	(345)	(601)	(996)
Subordinated Debt	9.0%	0	0	0	102	204	204	204	204	204
Total Interest Expense/(Income)		53	139	301	405	432	340	182	(74)	(469)
Earnings Before Taxes		(2,252)	(184)	421	1,620	3,847	6,624	10,451	14,772	19,661
Income Tax Expense	39.6%	—	16	52	641	1,523	2,623	4,139	5,850	7,786
Net Income (Loss)		$(2,252)	$ (200)	$ 369	$ 978	$ 2,324	$ 4,001	$ 6,312	$ 8,922	$ 11,875

(Continued)

EXHIBIT 33-13 (Continued)

BALANCE SHEET (000s)

	Historical Fiscal Years Ended December 31,					Projected Fiscal Years Ended December 31,			
	1994	1995	1996	1997	1998	1999	2000	2001	2002
ASSETS									
Current Assets									
Cash	$ 109	$ 38	$ 2	$ 100	$ 139	$ 187	$ 246	$ 297	$ 349
Excess Cash (Plug)	0	0	0	1,346	2,455	5,025	8,769	15,260	24,590
Inventories	1,139	1,328	4,754	5,409	6,032	6,948	9,120	11,012	12,950
Accounts Receivable	772	1,356	2,063	4,382	6,106	8,207	10,772	13,007	15,296
Prepaid Expenses	145	105	145	200	209	281	307	297	349
Other Current Assets	71	115	335	500	697	937	1,230	1,485	1,746
Total Current Assets	2,235	2,942	7,300	11,937	15,639	21,586	30,444	41,358	55,281
Property, Plant & Equipment, gross	322	332	680	1,030	1,518	2,174	3,305	4,075	5,297
Accumulated Depreciation	(99)	(137)	(204)	(410)	(739)	(1,232)	(1,940)	(2,701)	(3,645)
Property, Plant & Equipment, net	223	195	477	620	779	943	1,096	1,374	1,652
Other Assets	99	49	85	100	139	187	123	148	175
Goodwill & Intangibles	0	77	92	89	87	85	82	80	78
	$2,557	$3,263	$7,953	$12,747	$16,644	$22,801	$31,745	$42,961	$57,186
LIABILITIES & EQUITY									
Current Liabilities									
Notes Payable	$1,303	$1,438	$4,130	$ 3,800	$ 3,800	$ 3,800	$ 3,800	$ 3,800	$ 3,800
Accounts Payable	667	1,078	2,157	3,442	4,524	6,080	7,980	9,636	11,332
Accrued Expenses	270	382	428	950	1,325	1,780	2,337	2,821	3,318
Current Maturities	0	0	0	0	0	0	0	0	0
Capital Lease Obligations	0	16	47	0	0	0	0	0	0
Total Current Liabilities	2,240	2,914	6,762	8,192	9,648	11,660	14,116	16,257	18,449
Capital Lease Obligation	51	0	0	0	0	0	0	0	0
Other Debt	0	0	0	176	176	176	176	176	176
Subordinated Debt	0	0	0	2,094	2,094	2,094	2,094	2,094	2,094
Total Long-Term Debt	51	0	0	2,270	2,270	2,270	2,270	2,270	2,270
Other Long-Term Liabilities	0	22	184	300	418	562	738	891	1,048
Excess Debt (Plug)	0	0	0	0	0	0	0	0	0
Total Liabilities	2,292	2,935	6,946	10,762	12,336	14,492	17,124	19,417	21,767
Shareholders' Equity									
Common Stock	1	1	1	1	1	1	1	1	1
Additional Paid-In Capital	2,282	2,282	2,282	2,282	2,282	2,282	2,282	2,282	2,282
Retained Earnings	(2,019)	(1,956)	(1,277)	(299)	2,025	6,025	12,338	21,260	33,135
Total Shareholders' Equity	265	328	1,006	1,985	4,308	8,309	14,622	23,544	35,419
Total Liabilities & Equity	$2,557	$3,263	$7,953	$12,747	$16,644	$22,801	$31,745	$42,961	$57,186

(*Continued*)

EXHIBIT 33-13 (Continued)

STATEMENT OF CASH FLOWS (000s)

Fiscal Year Ended	1994	1995	1996	1997	1998	1999	2000	2001	2002
					Projected Years Ending December 31,				
Cash Flow from operating activities									
Net income (loss)	$(2,252)	$(200)	$369	$978	$2,324	$4,001	$6,312	$8,922	$11,875
Adjustments made to reconcile net income (loss) to net cash used by operating activities									
Depreciation and amortization	104	137	247	209	331	495	710	763	947
Deferred Taxes	0	0	0	0	0	0	0	0	0
Changes in operating assets and liabilities:									
Net assets available for sale	0	0	0	0	0	0	0	0	0
Accounts Receivable		(584)	(707)	(2319)	(1725)	(2101)	(2565)	(2235)	(2289)
Inventory		(189)	(3426)	(655)	(623)	(917)	(2171)	(1892)	(1938)
Prepaid expenses		40	(41)	(55)	(9)	(72)	(26)	10	(52)
Other current assets		(45)	(220)	(165)	(197)	(240)	(293)	(255)	(261)
Accounts Payable		411	1079	1285	1082	1556	1900	1656	1696
Accrued Expenses		112	46	522	374	456	556	485	497
Other Non-Current Liabilities		22	162	116	118	144	176	153	157
Net cash used by operations		(298)	(2490)	(83)	1675	3322	4599	7607	10631
Cash flows from investing activities									
Net additions to property and equipment		(10)	(348)	(350)	(488)	(656)	(861)	(1039)	(1222)
Proceeds from extraordinary items		0	0	0	0	0	0	0	0
Net additions (payments) on capital lease obligations		(36)	31	(47)	0	0	0	0	0
Net additions on LT Assets		51	(36)	(15)	(39)	(48)	64	(26)	(26)
		5	(353)	(412)	(527)	(704)	(796)	(1065)	(1249)
Cash flows from financing activities									
Increase in notes payable		135	2692	(330)	0	0	0	0	0
Increase in working capital facility		0	0	(0)	0	0	0	0	0
Increase in other debt		0	0	176	0	0	0	0	0
Increase in subordinated debt		0	0	2094	0	0	0	0	0
Dividend Payments		0	0	0	0	0	0	0	0
Stock Repurchases		0	0	0	0	0	0	0	0
Proceeds from issuance of common stock		87	115	0	0	0	0	0	0
Net cash (used) supplied by financing activities		$222	$2807	$1939	$ 0	$ 0	$ 0	$ 0	$ 0
Total change in cash		(71)	(36)	1444	1148	2618	3803	6542	9382
Cash at the beginning of period		109	38	2	1446	2594	5213	9015	15557
Cash at end of period		38	2	1446	2594	5213	9015	15557	24939

EXHIBIT 33-13 (Continued)

DISCOUNTED CASH FLOWS (000S)

CASH FLOW FORECASTS	Historical				Projected Years Ending				
	1995	1996	1997	1998	1999	2000	2001	2002	
Total Revenues	$15,335	$29,493	$50,026	$69,717	$93,700	$122,981	$148,499	$174,635	
EBITA	(45)	722	2,025	4,279	6,964	10,633	14,698	19,192	
Income Taxes (Benefit) on Unlevered Income	(18)	286	802	1,695	2,758	4,211	5,820	7,600	
Unlevered Net Income (EBIAT)	(27)	436	1,223	2,585	4,206	6,423	8,878	11,592	
Depreciation	137	247	209	331	495	710	763	947	
Working Capital Requirements	(185)	(3,232)	(1,484)	(1,137)	(1,365)	(2,658)	(2,283)	(2,401)	
Capital Expenditures	(295)	(315)	(350)	(488)	(656)	(861)	(1,039)	(1,222)	
Free Operating Cash Flow	$ (371)	$ (2,864)	$ (402)	$ 1,291	$ 2,680	$ 3,614	$ 6,319	$ 8,916	
Tax Rate	39.6%	39.6%	39.6%	39.6%	39.6%	39.6%	39.6%	39.6%	

621

EXHIBIT 33-14

BOSTON GLOBE ARTICLE ON NANTUCKET NECTAR CULTURE

Emerging *Business*

Fostering corporate culture

By Joann Muller
GLOBE STAFF

It could have much to do with a firm's success – or it's failure

When Brown University buddies Tom First and Tom Scott launched their juice company, Nantucket Nectars, six years ago, they deliberately made things as informal as possible.

No hierarchy. No dress code. No stodgy corporate culture.

The free-spirited attitude of the blonde beach boys is flaunted throughout their Brighton-based company – from the dogs roaming the purple-toned offices to the naked man pictured jumping into the harbor on their juice labels.

But now, as juice sales approach $20 million, Nantucket Nectars is outgrowing its fraternity house culture, and "Tom and Tom" (as they're known) are grappling with how to manage that growth without destroying the entrepreneurial spirit that has made the company special.

"It's one of my biggest fears," admits First, 29, whose baby face belies his intensity. "Once you start departmentalizing, you lose that."

Whether identified by purple walls or conservative blue suits, a company's culture has everything to do with its success – or failure.

That's especially true within start-up companies, where hard-driving employees typically put in long hours for relatively low pay.

"If you look at the failures of many companies, it wasn't the failure of the technology or the products or the market. It was the failure of the management to create a positive culture," says Gary Eichhorn, who became chief executive of Open Market, a fast-growing Internet company, two months ago after 21 years with large corporations.

Sometimes, the lack of a clearly defined culture can keep a company from ever getting off the ground. And that is why it is important and why, say specialists, it should rank high on the priority list for fledgling companies.

Eileen Richardson, vice president of Atlas Venture in Boston, says her venture capital firm won't invest in a technology company that has promising ideas but no shared sense of mission.

"What makes a good corporate culture is that everyone in the company, from the secretaries to the CEO, understands what business they're in and who their customer is," she says.

A strong, but flawed company cul-
CORPORATE CULTURE, Page 76

NANTUCKET NECTARS: Company founders Tom First (left) and Tom Scott hoop it up in the storage area of their company in Brighton.

cul·ture *n* **1**: cultivation, tillage **2**: the set of shared attitudes, values, goals and practices that characterize a company or corporation

---

Reprinted courtesy of *The Boston Globe*, © 1996.

EXHIBIT 33-14   **(Continued)**

Using culture to advance mission

To a company, it may mean success or failure

EMERGING BUSINESS
Continued from page 72

...have can bring down even the mightiest of corporations. One reason Kmart Corp., the nation's No. 2 retailer, has faltered against rival Wal-Mart Stores Inc. is that Kmart's inbred corporate culture stifled creativity and change.

At the same time, the right culture can push a company forward, and, sometimes, become its identity.

* * *

What makes culture?

If it's paternalistic culture – often, identified by its propensity toward blue suits and red ties – fostered deep employee loyalty with promises of good benefits, good pay and, until recently, a lifetime job.

Too often, company cultures – especially at start-up firms – are measured by what people wear to work or how much time they spend playing games in the corridors. But while blue jeans and Nerf basketball games might inspire creativity or relieve tension, they are not what make the culture.

A company's culture has more to do with its employees' behavior, values and expectations. When employees understand and share a company's mission and values, specialists say, they are more productive, and the company is more prosperous.

So where does a company's culture come from?

Whether intentional or not, it's typically spawned by the founder early in the company's life.

First and Scott, 30, set the work ethic for Nantucket Nectars long before selling a single bottle of juice. During summers in Nantucket, they spent long hours selling supplies from a boat, shucking scallops, even walking dogs – anything to earn money and a reputation for service.

"Nantucket's a close-knit community. We needed to be respected as business people, and not just seen as college kids passing through," First says.

Doing by example

Today, Nantucket Nectars' employees put in equally long hours. The office is lit up well past 8 p.m., and many staffers drop in on weekends to take care of business.

The founders didn't initially realize the example they were setting. About two months ago, First called the staff together and encouraged them to leave at 6 p.m. each night.

The problem, says staffer Wink Mierko, is that employees thought they were guilty of being inefficient.

"I'm like a tornado," First confesses. "I have tunnel vision. People look at their leaders and I have to be real careful about the tone I set."

Whether or not the founder of a company thinks much about cultural issues

during its start-up phase, these issues become critical as a company matures, specialists and entrepreneurs agree.

"How you maintain a culture during explosive growth is probably the No. 1 thing that I worry about," says Frank Ingari, chief executive of Shiva Corp., a $118 million company that makes equipment and software for telecommuters.

In his view, a company's culture has to fit not only the employee, but the employee's family, too. Not surprisingly, then, Shiva encourages employees to work from home on flexible schedules, if it fits their lifestyle.

"I don't care whether people are working here or there, as long as they are self-starters, self-motivators and hard workers," Ingari says.

Pamela Reeve, president and chief executive of Lightbridge Inc., a Waltham-based provider of software for the cellular communications industry, shares Ingari's obsession with managing culture.

"You have to pay as much attention to cultural issues as you do to your financing or marketing. To me, it's one of the assets that has to be managed and fertilized and watered."

Without a clearly defined culture, employees may try to clone themselves in the image of the company's leader – by wearing similar clothes or adopting various personality traits – rather than embrace the leader's ideas and principles, says William Bygrave, director of the Center for Entrepreneurial Studies at Babson College.

* * *

Teamwork, not titles

Another problem as companies grow, adds Babson colleague Julian Lange, is that "people try to divine what's happening in the company by reading titles."

At Lightbridge, Reeve tried to head off that situation by giving her company a very flat organization. "We have very little structure," she says. "Sure, someone has to have spending responsibility and someone has to have responsibility for hiring and training. But that's all in the background. We're very team-oriented. I don't run the team. I'm just on it."

She compares the situation to her first whitewater rafting trip. The guide led the group through tumultuous waters, but he steered from the back of the boat.

To promote teamwork among the company's 380 employees, Lightbridge holds frequent brown bag lunches where goals are discussed, and ties performance incentives to companywide accomplishments, not individual ones.

* * *

Place called 'home'

When the company moved into larger office space at the end of a particularly stressful period of growth, Reeve invited art therapists in for a day to help employees design artwork

that reflected the company's culture.

"We needed to put our soul in the building," she says.

In one exercise, each employee was assigned to paint a small area on a large canvas, which was their "home." The space between each area was their "neighborhood." Together, employees decided how to paint those common areas. The result is an eclectic mix of colorful abstract paintings displayed throughout Lightbridge's offices.

The art helps the employees bond together, something that becomes more difficult as companies grow beyond the start-up phase.

At Nantucket Nectars, weekly staff meetings include a guest speaker – an employee "who has to stand up and talk about their whole life, and what inspires them," First says. "We're so busy, sometimes we don't respect what other people do. I wanted everyone to understand who the people are and how they're helping this company."

"You have to respect the fact that your employees are smart," says David Blohm, president of software company Virtual Entertainment, who has used similar team-building tactics.

At his last company, Mathsoft Inc., which he founded in 1984 and took public in 1992, Blohm made sure every employee was plugged in by requiring them to demonstrate the company's software products to colleagues.

"My wanted them to talk about the product benefits, like they were demonstrating them to their in-laws. We wanted them to talk about it at that level. That raises the level of understanding and empathy for the customer," Blohm says.

* * *

Coming together

To keep the cultural flavor of a small company, many entrepreneurs search for ways to bring employees together, whether for Halloween parties, pizza and beer blasts, or summer barbecues.

At Molten Metal Technology Inc. in Waltham, it's breakfast.

Each Friday, two of the company's most recent hires are responsible for preparing breakfast for the rest of their colleagues.

In the beginning, when there were only a dozen or so employees, it was easy. "You just stopped and got a bag of bagels," says Ian Yates, vice president of sales and market development for the environmental technology company.

Now, however, Molten Metal has 300 employees, including 180 at its Waltham headquarters.

But the tradition continues, with some newcomers going all out, preparing everything from pancakes to exotic ethnic favorites as breakfast burritos. The company picks up the tab.

"It's a small price to pay for the benefit, which is bringing people together," says Yates. "We don't want the first chance for people to meet to be in a meeting or on a project. If you know someone first, you'd

be surprised how much better you listen to them."

Another meeting place at Molten Metal is the fifth-floor atrium, where employees and executives talk over business issues while shooting pool or playing table tennis or air hockey.

Having fun is actually part of the 7-year-old company's mission statement. But in the end, what makes any company's culture work is a shared sense of passion for the company's objectives.

"We're part of a team that is dedicated to changing the way the world deals with waste," Yates says. "We're pulling on the same end of the rope together. That's pretty powerful. It makes the time playing table tennis more fun."

SALES AFTERMATH

The founders were also very concerned with the outcome after a sale. Nantucket Nectars currently has 100 employees, of which there are 15 accountants, 20 marketers, 57 salespeople, 5 sales administrators, and 3 quality control people. Depending on the structure of the potential transaction, what would happen to these people?

Another major concern was that the culture of the firm would change drastically depending on whether a transaction was consummated and with whom. Nantucket Nectars still maintained a nonformal dress code; it was very uncommon to see anyone dressed in business attire. The organization of the firm was still nonhierarchical with all employees able to approach the two Toms. See Exhibit 33-14. Tom First described this concern: "Destroying the entrepreneurial spirit that has made the company special is one of my biggest fears. Once you start departmentalizing, you lose that. It is essential that we maintain our culture so that work is still fun."

The founders were also concerned about the management involvement of any potential strategic partner. Both founders wanted to continue to run the company if possible. Lastly, the founders did not want to have their effective sales and marketing story negatively affected because of ownership issues. Would consumers continue to enjoy the Nantucket Nectars story if the company were actually owned by a large public company?

34

HIMSCORP, Inc.

Kent Dauten, CEO of Health Information Management Services Corporation (HIMSCORP), anxiously waited for his fax machine to begin printing. Just minutes earlier, Richard Reese, CEO of Iron Mountain, had called to announce that he was faxing a letter detailing the terms of Iron Mountain's offer to purchase HIMSCORP. It was August 1, 1997, and it had been more than three months since Dauten and Reese had first initiated discussions about a sale of HIMSCORP to Iron Mountain. Since then, Iron Mountain had continued its aggressive acquisition pace and expansion plans into new industry segments. With this fax, Dauten hoped to be able to assess whether Iron Mountain recognized the value that he believed his team had created at HIMSCORP and that Iron Mountain could capture by continuing to grow the business.

HIMSCORP was a leading provider of record and information management services to the health-care industry. The company provided active medical record storage and retrieval services to health-care institutions, primarily hospitals. Iron Mountain, a publicly traded Boston-based company, was the nation's largest records management company, providing records management services to numerous industries, including law, banking, health-care, and government organizations.

Dauten, 41 years old, had not expected this day to come so soon when he initiated his "roll-up" of the health-care records management industry in 1995. A former general partner at Chicago-based private equity investment firm Madison Dearborn Partners, Inc. (MDP), he had decided at that time to pursue his life-long entrepreneurial interest by buying and running a company. In February 1995, Dauten had led the buyout of four franchisees of Record Masters for $12.5 million, incorporating them under the name HIMSCORP. Over the past 30 months, he had completed eight add-on acquisitions. In 1997, the company forecasted $29 million in sales and $9 million of earnings before interest, taxes, depreciation, and amortization (EBITDA).

Despite his initial intentions to run HIMSCORP for at least five years, Dauten had been thinking about selling the company or taking it public over the past year. While HIMSCORP's performance to date had exceeded projections, he was concerned about

Senior Researcher Laurence E. Katz prepared this case under the supervision of Professor William A. Sahlman and Lecturer Michael J. Roberts as the basis for class discussion rather than to illustrate either effective or ineffective handling of an administrative situation.

its ability to sustain these results because industry dynamics were beginning to change. Many of his customers—the larger hospital chains—were trying to cut costs by consolidating and re-bidding service contracts to national service providers. With 13 businesses in only 12 cities, Dauten was concerned that HIMSCORP might not be able to compete against the two larger national enterprises. At the same time, Iron Mountain and Pierce Leahy were engaged in a race to become the largest records storage company in the country. Each had closed several dozen acquisitions of local or regional storage companies over the previous three years.

Dauten thought that the current competitive dynamics, together with the favorable stock market, tax, and interest rate environment, might make this an opportune time to sell the company. Recently, he had initiated discussions with both Iron Mountain and Pierce Leahy about a possible sale of HIMSCORP. Both had indicated strong interest, but no valuations had been formally discussed. Simultaneously, he had approached other publicly traded companies with related lines of business about a possible sale. He believed that several other players might be interested in purchasing HIMSCORP as a means of entering the growing document services industry. He also had begun discussions with several investment banks about an initial public offering. All the investment bankers had indicated that HIMSCORP would be an attractive initial public offering.

Dauten, however, was not committed to exiting the company at this time. While he felt that tremendous value already had been created, he was confident that additional opportunities still existed to grow HIMSCORP. He believed that the company had an opportunity to expand into several of the top 50 metropolitan markets where off-site record storage for health-care providers had been virtually untapped. In addition, he believed that the company could diversify its service offerings into other services that were increasingly being outsourced by its customer base. As the fax machine rang and began printing, Dauten considered his position:

> Though the market and competitive climate might make this the perfect time to sell, we have a lot of unfinished business and a lot of emotion and commitment tied up here. I truly believe that we could double the size of our business over the next few years by starting-up or acquiring archival storage companies in new markets and diversifying our service offerings. We also have a high-quality group of people at HIMSCORP whom I enjoy working with and being a part of their development. But it's always nice to prove the value that you think has been created and there's always a price at which I'll sell. Even though I've been involved in buying and selling companies for the past 18 years, this decision is probably the most significant one to me personally. Is this the right time to exit? If so, what is HIMSCORP worth and what is the best harvest option, for the business and me?

RECORD MASTERS BUYOUT[1]

Upon graduating from Harvard Business School in 1979, Dauten joined First Chicago Venture Capital, the private equity investment arm of First Chicago Corporation and a pioneer in the venture capital industry. Dauten and his partners spun out of First Chicago in 1992 to form Madison Dearborn Partners, Inc. (MDP), where they continued to execute middle-market buyouts with a $550 million pool of equity capital.

While Dauten's 15 years of investment experience ranged across industries and stages of investment, he had extensive experience leading transactions in the health-

---

[1] Dauten's initial investment decision in the Record Masters franchisees is the subject of *Record Masters* (William A. Sahlman, HBS Case 899-020: 1999).

care industry. Among other investments, he had led growth equity investments in HMA, a hospital management company which increased in value by 400×, and in Genesis Health Ventures which had become one of the leading publicly traded long-term care management companies. In 1994, he decided to leave MDP to personally sponsor a middle-market buyout in which he might play a more active management role than he could at MDP. He reflected on the decision:

> I wanted to pursue my entrepreneurial instinct and try to build a business. After a successful venture capital career, I felt that I had the experience and financial security to make a successful run at buying and building a business without risking my family's future. It was only a question of which one to buy—I knew I wanted to buy because it is so much easier to build a business which already has a proven market and an existing customer base than it is to green-field a company. At MDP, we consistently had greater success with buyouts than with early-stage venture deals.
>
> After I left the firm, I sat down in my office with a blank page of paper and asked myself what critical lessons I had learned at MDP about successful deals. I came up with this list of business characteristics of successful buyouts:

- Recurring revenue stream
- Service a definable and protected niche
- High entry barriers
- Customer diversity
- High customer retention
- Industry size too small to attract big players
- High-quality people
- Limited existing competition
- Strong cash flow characteristics
- Strong internal customer growth rate
- Stable industry with growth potential

> I hired one of my former MDP analysts, Scott Gwilliam, who was attending Northwestern's Kellogg Graduate School of Management and was tapped into the private equity community in Chicago, to look for and pass along any business opportunities that he thought looked attractive. In particular, I mentioned that something in the records management business, perhaps for the health-care industry, would be interesting. At the time, I didn't even know if such a business existed. After looking at 30 to 40 different businesses, Scott referred to me a selling memorandum from Coopers and Lybrand for Record Masters. From the moment I looked at the memo, I was *extremely* interested.

Record Masters Background

In 1994, the Record Masters Network was an eight-year-old records storage company providing management and retrieval services of active medical records to health-care institutions. Record Masters provided open-shelved storage and retrieval services, including ancillary services such as purging, relocation, and copying.

The Record Masters Network was the franchisor to 12 franchisees, each incorporated as a subchapter S corporation and locally operated under the name Record Masters. The Network operated as a cooperative, owned by the shareholders of the franchisees, with equal board representation from each franchisee. The Network provided administrative help for the franchisees but did not control their strategic decisions or day-to-day operations. The Network primarily provided a common name ("Record Masters") and a common software file tracking system ("HealthRx") to the franchisees.

The records management industry was estimated to be $1.0 billion in sales in 1994, growing 10% per year. The potential market was estimated to be much larger, as three-quarters of all services were still "unvended," or internally managed. Active records, which referred to current or frequently accessed records, were estimated to account for 20% of all records management services. The market was highly fragmented, with approximately 2,800 companies offering services in the United States. Over the previous five years, the industry had been rapidly consolidating, as Iron Mountain and Pierce Leahy had been developing a national presence and increased market share by purchasing smaller, regional firms. In 1996, Iron Mountain and Pierce Leahy each controlled about 18% of the vended market.

Medical records were among the fastest growing segments of the records management industry, having grown in excess of 20% annually for the previous five years. In recent years, record storage had become an increasing cost for professionals in the health-care service industry. Despite talk of moving toward a paperless organization, the growth of low-cost computers, fax machines, and printers had led to the proliferation of paper documents. Increases in litigation and regulatory requirements for medical providers also had led to larger volumes and longer retention periods for documents. At the same time, growing pressures on medical providers to reduce costs had led them to increasingly outsource management of nonclinical activities. Outsourcing records management allowed medical providers to reduce space dedicated to file storage, which cost approximately $400 per square foot annually in hospitals, and convert that space for use by revenue-generating activities. Outsourcing also reduced their need for qualified personnel trained in records management, who were often hard to find and expensive to employ.

Record Masters had initiated a revolution in records storage for the health-care industry. Prior to Record Masters, hospitals outsourced their active heath-care records management to traditional archival facilities, which stored records in closed boxes. These facilities charged monthly storage fees and "a la carte" fees for retrieval and delivery. While such a system worked well for industries without frequent retrieval needs, traditional archival facilities did not adequately serve hospitals because of the high frequency and volume of retrieval requests for active medical records. To guarantee rapid turnaround services, Record Masters reproduced the open-shelf filing system[2] of the hospitals, storing all files in the health-care industry standard "terminal digital order." Warehouses were lined with row upon row of floor-to-ceiling storage systems, each with 14 rows of shelving filled with color-coded files. The company made at least two daily deliveries to each hospital, which were usually located within one hour's drive of the warehouse. Clients were charged fixed fees that covered storage, retrieval, refiling, and delivery services. Record Masters offered ancillary services, such as coding or temporary staffing, on a fee-for-service basis. In 1994, approximately 78% of revenues were generated by traditional management services, while 22% were derived from ancillary services.

In 1994, the largest four of the twelve Record Masters franchisees, located in Philadelphia, Pittsburgh, New Orleans, and Detroit, decided to collectively sell their businesses. These owners, who together controlled 33% of the shares of the Network, wanted to sell because they felt threatened by the risk of computerized record storage and lim-

---

[2] Open-shelf filing referred to the storing of files of charts or X-rays side-by-side on shelves, rather than in boxes that were than placed on shelves.

ited by the franchise structure in their ability to change the strategic direction of the business. The owners hoped to find a buyer who would invest in new processes, services, and technology to meet the growing needs of their clients. After the sale, all four owners wanted to continue to manage their businesses.

Doing the Deal

When Dauten first reviewed the Coopers and Lybrand selling memorandum, he was excited. Ten years earlier, he had competed with and lost to Iron Mountain in the auction for Bell + Howell's commercial records business. He had been enthusiastic about the document storage business model since then:

> From an investment perspective, the records management industry had a terrific business model. It was a growing industry with strong profitability. It required little working capital investment, as accounts were billed a month in advance, and small maintenance capital expenditures, as most facilities were leased. The only capital commitments were for shelving, which grew proportionately with revenue, and for delivery vehicles and computers. The industry had stable, annuity-like revenue streams because it was insensitive to business cycles and customer switching costs were high. Customers were reluctant to remove files not only because of the inherent risks of misplacing them but also because contracts specified one- to three-year commitments and significant "exit fees" upon removal of files. The "exit fees" could amount to six months of storage fees. As a result, customer retention approached 99% and internal customer growth neared 15% per year because existing customers added new files to storage each year.

He continued to explain his interest in the Record Masters franchisees:

> I thought Record Masters, in particular, was exciting because it had a strong brand name in its markets, which I thought was critical in a business in which customer confidence was important. In each of the four markets, Record Masters had a strong competitive position, with 50% to 80% market share, which discouraged new entrants. Additionally, it had focused on a specific niche in the records management business, which was the fastest growing segment. Finally, it had reinforced customer switching costs by developing a database of individual medical records, which was used for online retrieval and to track file history. Customers did not have copies of this database and would have to recreate it if they removed their files.

Despite the strategic appeal of the business, Dauten recognized that the deal had several issues that might scare away other investors. He enumerated his concerns:

> As we say in the buyout business, this was a very "hairy" deal. First, the proposed deal was to buy four disparate companies, each of which had individual operating histories, but none of which had operated together. There was no reason to believe that they would perform well together and there was no team in place to manage the consolidated company. In fact, the sellers, who were the only ones who knew anything about the business, were cashing out and it was not clear that they planned to stick around after the deal. Clearly, only a strategic buyer—one which had a related business or existing management team in place—would do this deal. Second, the financials were messy and unaudited, which often scares away traditional institutional investors. Third, the companies had no meaningful assets other than receivables. This would make bank financing difficult to line up. Fourth, the selling memorandum screamed of technology risk. Everyone expected that electronic storage would replace paper-based storage. Finally, the legal details of the franchise agreement were tricky. Specifically, the Network had the right of first refusal to match any offer for

the purchase of any franchisee's business. This meant that a suitor could spend lots of time trying to put the deal together, only to be trumped by the Network. Furthermore, the franchise governance structure was cumbersome and could infringe on the buyer's ability to control the businesses.

After submitting an initial indication of interest of $6 million, Dauten focused on several of the key risks in order to assess their significance. To understand the threat of electronic storage, Dauten and Gwilliam talked to industry experts at the American Health Information Management Association about trends in the industry. These experts predicted that the costs associated with computerized records and the risks to patient security would discourage conversion for at least the next 10 years. To gain comfort with the financial condition of the company, Dauten hired Ernst and Young's Mergers and Acquisitions team to perform accounting due diligence to validate the financial condition of the business. Their study gave him a strong degree of confidence that the cash-generating power of the businesses was significantly higher than the selling memorandum had reported.

Dauten ultimately won the auction with a bid of $12.5 million, outbidding a field of larger industry buyers, including Iron Mountain. He financed the deal with a 9% senior term loan of $8.0 million which carried two primary covenants: (1) the total senior debt to EBITDA ratio could not exceed 3.5× and (2) the total senior debt to net worth ratio could not exceed 3:1. The sellers accepted $1.975 million in seller notes paying 7.75% annually. Dauten personally invested $3.0 million in preferred stock yielding a 9% preferred return and $342,000 for 8,050 shares of common stock. Each of the four Record Masters sellers invested $20,750 in common equity on the same terms at which Dauten invested. Table A presents HIMSCORP's initial sources and uses of capital:

TABLE A   HIMSCORP Sources and Uses of Capital, February 1995

July 13, 1998 Sources	$	Uses of Funds	$
Senior Revolver	$ 500,000	Purchase Record Masters Common stock	$12,500,000
Term Debt	$ 7,500,000	Fees and Expenses	$ 400,000
Seller Notes	$ 1,975,000	Excess Funding	$ 500,000
Dauten Preferred Stock	$ 3,000,000		
Dauten Common Stock	$ 342,000		
Management Common Stock	$ 83,000		
Total	$13,400,000	Total	$13,400,000

Dauten reflected on the buyout process:

My private equity experience really paid off in closing this deal. When we showed up in the first round of bidding, no one took us seriously. But doing the deal required the same skills of valuing, negotiating letters of intent, and establishing relationships with an unsophisticated seller. During the process, we gained a lot of credibility because we knew what we were doing. We also never could have lined up the financing for the deal if I hadn't had a successful track record with the lender. Even though I knew a lot of lenders well, many of them didn't want to touch this deal—we needed to aggressively capitalize the deal and we had no assets to secure it with other than receivables. Several lenders offered to do the deal if I personally guaranteed their loans, but I wasn't willing to do that. I ultimately secured financing without guarantees from a lender who had confidence in me because of a very successful prior transaction.

Dauten anticipated making several add-on acquisitions, but the ultimate pace exceeded his expectations. Shortly after closing the first four acquisitions, HIMSCORP began discussions with the San Diego and Los Angeles Record Masters franchisees to acquire their businesses. HIMSCORP closed these acquisitions in June 1995 and followed over the next 24 months with acquisitions of the Record Masters franchisees in Houston, Cleveland, St. Louis, and Portland, Oregon. Although the Los Angeles and San Diego add-ons required an additional $450,000 equity investment, the remaining deals were financed strictly with bank borrowings and seller notes. In October 1996, HIMSCORP completed its first non-Record Masters acquisition of Copyright, a Philadelphia medical records copying company that provided a complimentary service line to HIMSCORP's existing storage business in that city. In January 1997, HIMSCORP bought a medical records storage franchisee from its competitor, Deliverex, which had a strong hold on the Baltimore market. (See Exhibit 34-1 for a history of acquisitions.) In February 1997, HIMSCORP started its first "green-field" location in Milwaukee, hiring a local general manager with a strong health-care sales background and committing $250,000 to the start-up effort. By June 1997, Dauten had built HIMSCORP into a business with a run-rate approaching $29 million in sales, serving approximately 350 hospitals in 12 cities. Exhibit 34-2 presents HIMSCORP's financial history.

EXHIBIT 34-1

HIMSCORP INC. ACQUISITION HISTORY, 1995–1997

Location	Acquisition Date	Run-Rate Revenues (Millions)	Run-Rate EBITDA (Millions)	Purchase Price (Millions)	EBITDA Multiple
Detroit	2/1/95	$1.9	$0.7	$ 3.5	5.1×
New Orleans	2/1/95	2.1	0.8	4.4	5.1×
Philadelphia	2/1/95	2.1	0.5	2.7	5.1×
Pittsburgh	2/1/95	1.5	0.4	1.9	5.1×
Total		$7.6	$2.5	$12.5	5.1×
Los Angeles	6/30/95	$1.2	$0.4	$1.6	4.0×
San Diego	6/30/95	$1.0	$0.3	$1.2	4.0×
Houston	3/31/96	$1.0	$0.1	$1.2[a]	N/A
Cleveland	3/31/96	$1.0	$0.35	$1.9	5.8×
Copyright (Philadelphia)	9/30/96	$2.8	$0.75	$3.0	4.0×
Baltimore	12/31/96	$1.2	$0.6	$3.9	6.0×
St. Louis	12/31/96	$1.8	$0.7	$4.3	6.4×
Portland	5/30/97	$2.0	$0.5	$3.2	6.4×

[a] Structured as an earn-out based on forward 1996 and 1997 EBITDA.

Source: HIMSCORP Internal.

EXHIBIT 34-2

HIMSCORP, INC., CONSOLIDATED FINANCIAL HISTORY, 1995–1997

	1995		1996		1997 (Actual 6 mos)[a]		1997 (Full Year Forecast)[a]	
	$	%	$	%	$	%	$	%
Revenue								
Record management services	$6,831	71.8%	$10,780	68.9%	$ 7,841	60.0%	$18,045	61.8%
New material processing	1,643	17.3	2,414	15.4	1,718	13.1	4,493	15.4
Release of information	470	4.9	1,585	10.1	2,325	17.8	5,240	18.0
Other services	570	6.0	873	5.6	1,188	9.1	1,432	4.9
Total revenue	$9,513	100.0%	$15,652	100.0%	$13,072	100.0%	$29,210	100.0%
Expenses								
Payroll	$3,096	32.5%	$ 5,125	32.7%	$ 4,539	34.7%	$10,225	35.0%
Vehicles	253	2.7	408	2.6	291	2.2	641	2.2
Uniforms & supplies	76	0.8	119	0.8	111	0.8	178	0.6
Royalties	94	1.0	164	1.0	157	1.2	324	1.1
Start-up costs	0	0.0	0	0.0	0	0.0	200	0.7
General/administrative	1,293	13.6	2,261	14.4	1,883	14.4	4,182	14.3
Depreciation	394	4.1	636	4.1	443	3.4	1,100	3.8
Indirect (rent)	1,477	15.5	2,327	14.9	1,714	13.1	3,963	13.6
Corporate	202	2.1	376	2.4	415	3.2	471	1.6
Total expenses	$6,885	72.4%	$11,416	72.9%	$ 9,553	73.1%	$21,284	72.9%
Operating profit	$2,628	27.6%	$ 4,236	27.1%	$ 3,518	26.9%	$ 7,926	27.1%
EBITDA	$3,022	31.8%	$ 4,872	31.1%	$ 3,961	30.3%	$ 9,026	30.9%
Other income & expenses								
Other expense	$ 60	0.6%	$ 321	2.1%	$162	1.2%	$0	0.0%
Interest expense	996	10.5	1,278	8.2	1,118	8.5	2,526	8.6
Amort. of goodwill & def. fin.cost	548	5.7	809	5.2	661	5.1	1,425	4.9
Total other expense	$1,604	16.9%	$ 2,315	14.8%	$ 1,750	13.4%	$ 3,900	13.4%
Profit before taxes	$1,024	10.8%	$ 1,827	11.7%	$ 1,577	12.1%	$ 3,935	13.5%
Provision for income taxes	359	3.8	789	5.0	570	4.4	1,377	4.7
Net Income	$ 665	7.0%	$ 1,038	6.6%	$ 1,007	7.7%	$ 2,558	8.8%

[a] Reported as of June 30, 1997 (does not include the first five months of financial results for the Portland acquisition which occurred on June 1, 1997).

Source: HIMSCORP Internal.

(Continued)

EXHIBIT 34-2   (Continued)

	1995	1996	1997 Actual 6 Months[a]	1997 Full-Year Forecast
Assets				
Current assets				
Cash & equivalents	($ 170)	$ 15	$ 135	$ 0
Accounts receivable	2,100	2,710	4,196	4,802
Prepaid expenses	133	183	319	240
Total current assets	$ 2,064	$ 2,907	$ 4,651	$ 5,042
Fixed assets				
Property, plant, and equipment	$ 3,481	$ 4,786	$ 6,787	$ 7,326
Accumulated depreciation	(2,033)	(2,551)	(2,946)	(3,536)
Total fixed assets	$ 1,447	$ 2,236	$ 3,840	$ 3,790
Other assets				
Investment in network	$ 1	$ 1	$ 1	$ 1
Goodwill, gross	13,643	19,162	29,149	34,295
Accum. amortization	(455)	(1,111)	(1,656)	(2,219)
Goodwill, net	$13,188	$18,051	$27,493	$32,076
Deferred financing and organizational cost, gross	617	1,039	1,385	1,039
Accum. amortization	(93)	(246)	(361)	(401)
Deferred financing and organizational cost, net	$ 524	$ 792	$ 1,024	$ 638
Total other assets	$13,712	$18,845	$28,519	$32,714
TOTAL ASSETS	$17,223	$23,987	$37,010	$41,547
Liabilities				
Current liabilities				
Accounts payable	$ 700	$ 1,258	$ 1,613	$ 1,601
Accrued liabilities	594	803	1,081	1,681
Total current liabilities	$ 1,294	$ 2,061	$ 2,694	$ 3,281
Long-term liabilities				
Other long-term liabilities	$ 0	$ 925	$ 525	$ 0
Working capital loan	0	0	0	0
Term/revolver loan	9,138	13,044	24,236	27,606
Subordinated notes	2,259	2,259	2,759	2,259
Total long term liabilities	$11,397	$16,228	$27,520	$29,864
TOTAL LIABILITIES	$12,691	$18,289	$30,215	$33,146
Stockholders' equity				
Stockholders' equity	$ 3,867	$ 4,059	$ 5,787	$ 7,156
Retained earnings	665	1,640	1,007	1,245
TOTAL EQUITY	$ 4,532	$ 5,698	$ 6,795	$ 8,401
Total Liabilities & S/E	$17,223	$23,987	$37,010	$41,547

[a] Reported as of June 30, 1997 (does not include the first five months of financial results for the Portland acquisition which occurred on June 1, 1997).

(Continued)

EXHIBIT 34-2   *(Continued)*

	1995	1996	1997 Actual 6 Months[a]	1997 Full Year Forecast
Cash flow from operations				
Net income	$ 665	$1,038	$1,007	$2,558
Adjustments to reconcile net income:				
Depreciation and amortization	942	1,362	1,102	2,525
Payment of corporate expenses	0	(259)	0	0
Decrease (Increase) net receivables	(584)	(99)	(914)	(1,506)
Decrease (Increase) prepaid expenses	(40)	(41)	(27)	(58)
Increase (Decrease) acc. payables	84	252	(100)	390
Increase (Decrease) def. Increase tax	(347)	0	0	0
Increase (Decrease) acc. expenses	360	191	(93)	400
Total cash from operations	$1,080	$2,444	$ 975	$4,309
Cash flow from investing				
Increase (Decrease) capital expenditures	($ 502)	($986)	($988)	($1,365)
Increase (Decrease) fixed assets	0	0	0	(1,000)
Total cash from investing	($ 502)	($986)	($988)	($2,365)
Cash flow from financing				
Increase (Decrease) in equity	$ 0	$ 641	$116	$ 0
Increase (Decrease) in goodwill	0	(4)	9	(8,400)
Increase (Decrease) in long-term liab.	0	0	(400)	0
Increase (Decrease) in term loan	(740)	(1,909)	410	0
Total cash from financing	($748)	($1,272)	($135)	($8,400)
Net increase in cash	($171)	$ 185	$123	($6,458)
Beginning cash balance	1	(170)	15	138
Ending cash balance	($170)	$ 15	$138	($6,320)

[a] Reported as of June 30, 1997 (does not include the first five months of financial results for the Portland acquisition which occurred on June 1, 1997).

Dauten described the process of identifying and buying additional franchisees:

The industry wasn't very big and we had met most of the Record Masters owners during the buyout of the first four franchisees. These owners all knew each other and talked. After a few months, they heard from the first four sellers that we were capable, honest, hardworking guys who were helping them improve their businesses. While these owners were reluctant to give up their annuity for a lump sum payment, I tried to convince them to view the world a bit differently. I helped them realize that their entire net worth was wrapped up in this business and that every month, they were gambling their entire nestegg in an undiversified asset. I offered them a choice: they could sell today and eliminate their personal financial risk, or they could continue to build their business with the hope that the favorable competitive climate and strong merger and acquisition market would continue. This was a highly emotional process for the sellers, but it got easier with later sellers as they saw that our strategy was working.

With each acquisition, we learned a bit more about the earnings power of the businesses and how to value each franchisee. Over time, we could look at a business and have confidence about what we could do with it—either that we could increase revenues with a new salesperson, or more fully utilize warehouse space and spread fixed costs, or reduce payroll expense by consolidating three buildings into one. These insights into target acquisitions proved important as acquisition prices trended upward.

As the roll-up progressed, Iron Mountain and other strategic buyers clearly became more of a competitive threat. How did we beat them? We rolled up our sleeves a bit more and developed a deeper understanding of the projected cash flows, but we also sold our strengths. Unlike a corporate buyer, we were willing to customize our deal to each seller's needs, we promised a quick and reliable closing, we guaranteed a minimum disruption to the business, and we conveyed our entrepreneurial spirit, which they clearly related to. We also tried to convince sellers not to shop their companies, knowing that this would only slow down the process and drive prices up.

CREATING VALUE AT HIMSCORP

Dauten explained in detail his strategies for creating value at HIMSCORP:

From my days at MDP, I had come to believe that value is created by good managers who are steered in the right direction, encouraged to focus on drivers of economic value, and given the tools and incentives to succeed. At HIMSCORP, we bought businesses that were strong before we ever arrived on the scene. Our job was to offer leadership and discipline to the business and create a unified business out of disparate entities.

From the beginning, our key goals were sales growth, EBITDA margin, and cash flow management. These three measures were our mantra because they were the drivers of economic value of the business. To the extent that we could improve these key variables, we knew that we could increase our leverage and our equity returns.

Prior to our acquisitions, the sellers ran these businesses with varying degrees of attention, professionalism, and efficiency. Most of them stayed on as our day-to-day managers, but we needed to help them focus on the right indicators of economic value. Immediately after signing the final purchase and sale agreements, we drafted their new employment contracts with them, tying their bonuses to EBITDA targets and working capital metrics. (See Exhibit 34-3.) We also did little corny things to reinforce our goals, like sending out bumper stickers that said, "Have you checked your EBITDA today?" At our annual managers' conference, we passed out awards to reward sales growth and EBITDA achievements.

To get the GMs to focus on the right targets initially required helping them to understand the new format of our financial statements. Although they were very capable individuals, most GMs didn't understand how EBITDA, growth, and cash flow determined value. Scott prepared a simple training package and periodically walked our managers through a basic presentation that explained how these variables could drive our share price up.

While setting the goals was important, developing financial systems to generate timely and accurate reports to track these indicators was equally important. These organizations had no standard reporting system—in fact some franchisees reported on a cash basis, some on an accrual basis, and some didn't report any numbers until tax time. We started by installing the same financial software in each location and centralizing cash management with one bank in Chicago. Within six weeks of the first closing, Scott developed a standard financial reporting format that reported the performance of each business. This package was sent out monthly to each GM with a letter from me describing recent developments at

---

EXHIBIT 34-3

HIMSCORP SAMPLE OPERATING AND INCENTIVE PLAN

Philadelphia, 2/1/95

1. Complete transition to new ownership by carefully managing customer and employee relationships

2. Achieve 1995 budget of:

Revenues	$2,375,000
EBITDA	$ 580,000
Capital Expenditures	$ 45,000
Days A/R	60 days

3. Develop a game plan for improving profit margins by 5 percentage points within the next two years.

   a. Evaluate ways to either streamline the current organizational structure or better absorb its overhead expense.

   b. Take a creative and hard look at other expense items.

4. Continue to develop a strong Management Team by broadening the experience base of Nannette Low, Bill Walker, and Bob Keyser.

5. Support HIMSCORP Corporate in the establishment of a corporate controller function performed by Bob Keyser (approximately one to two days per month).

6. Develop a Marketing Plan for the potential implementation of an Imaging Service during the last half of 1995.

7. Incentive Plan: Maximum available bonus is 35% of base salary. 70% of available bonus is tied to achieving annual EBITDA target, 15% to meeting Accounts Receivable target, and 15% to achieving individual objectives.

Source: HIMSCORP Internal.

---

each location. These financial systems were important in keeping our managers focused and critical to keeping our lender informed.

Somewhat incidentally, we found that an ancillary benefit to our financial reporting was to reinforce a healthy competition among our managers. Included in each package was a one-page detailed summary of financial performance, measured by key indicators, of all locations. (See Exhibit 34-4.) It was very easy for any GM to look at this page and compare their results to the other locations with similar operating characteristics. We found that GMs would call each other and ask questions like "What's going on with your employee productivity? or "How did you win that new account?"

Because we were highly leveraged, we needed to build discipline into the system to make sure that we were meeting our loan covenants. To encourage financial discipline, we initiated a budgeting process that involved each of our GMs. Each November, we required GMs to forecast growth of their top customer accounts, predict new customer sales, and estimate expenses for the coming year. Initially, we found that the GMs were overly optimistic in their forecasts, but it was our job to make the forecasts more realistic. We also tracked cash very closely. In an LBO, cash is a measure of the financial health of the business. Everyday, I would come to work and ask Scott if we were net borrowers or had paid down debt the previous day.

EXHIBIT 34-4

MONTHLY LOCATION REPORT, KEY OPERATING STATISTICS

Month Ending June 30, 1997

	RMDT	RMNO	RMPT	RMPH	RMLA	RMSD	RMHO	RMCL	CRI	RMSL	RMBW	RMPD (a)	Cons.
Operating Statistics													
Revenues	$210,047	$264,891	$229,273	$380,784	$132,412	$117,789	$134,190	$105,616	$244,842	$232,506	$144,857	$194,523	$2,425,541
EBITDA	$ 82,376	$104,644	$ 59,710	$158,836	$ 40,017	$ 50,498	$ 18,988	$ 20,056	$ 58,624	$ 79,738	$ 66,913	$ 41,436	$ 754,262
EBITDA %	39.2%	39.5%	26.0%	41.7%	30.2%	42.9%	14.2%	19.0%	23.9%	34.3%	46.2%	21.3%	31.1%
Growth Statistics													
Revenue growth vs. prior year	10.3%	24.8%	25.7%	21.4%	3.9%	20.1%	36.6%	12.7%	12.8%	31.2%	28.4%	19.3%	22.1%
EBITDA growth vs. prior year	18.8	−2.1	−1.4	20.1	−28.5	27.9	38.7	−28.6	6.1	32.9	48.7	20.3	10.2
EBITDA % of plan	99.8	126.8	111.3	154.3	80.2	107.3	76.7	88.4	63.2	128.9	115.9	128.9	112.1
Expense Statistics													
Payroll as % of revenues	28.7%	36.5%	38.2%	30.2%	32.9%	25.2%	47.0%	28.1%	44.0%	31.7%	19.4%	40.3%	34.2%
Indirect expense as a % of rev.	14.9	8.8	11.7	16.0	19.2	17.1	17.7	21.8	1.7	14.4	11.2	19.1	13.7
G&A expense as a % of rev.	12.9	8.3	14.5	7.6	14.8	12.1	13.9	23.1	17.4	12.4	18.4	13.5	14.3
Annualized Productivity Statistics													
Ann. Revenues/Employee	$63,014	$59,975	$61,140	$50,213	$52,965	$94,231	$50,321	$74,552	$53,420	$69,752	$86,914	$66,694	$61,536
Ann. FF revenues/square foot	$28.71	$38.64	$23.79	$23.41	$25.86	$28.39	$17.05	$15.30	NA	$24.86	$35.10	$21.00	$28.13
# of employees (FTE's)	40	53	45	91	30	15	32	17	55	40	20	35	473
# of salaried/# of hourly	7/33	2/51	8/37	8/84	4/26	3/12	2/27	2/15	6/49	4/36	4/16	4/31	57/416
# of square feet	64,600	52,500	61,825	115,000	54,000	38,772	70,000	57,000	NS	65,000	40,000	84,500	618,697
Cash Flow Statistics													
Days accounts receivable	59	59	60	93	49	32	52	63	26	26	35	38	53
Capital Expenditures	$20,130	$20,581	$11,087	$8,994	$2,109	$2,727	$91,514	$19,614	$ 0	$38,760	$18,376	$9,955	$243,848
Increase(Decrease) in term/ revolver balance	($44,775)	($88,135)	$40,007	$151,059	($10,317)	($10,254)	($18,984)	$25,961	$15,735	($33,831)	($46,293)	($31,959)	$154,182

(*Continued*)

EXHIBIT 34-4 (Continued)

Year-to-Date June 30, 1997

	RMDT	RMNO	RMPT	RMPH	RMLA	RMSD	RMHO	RMCL	CRI	RMSL	RMBW	RMPD (a)	Cons.
Operating Statistics													
Revenues	$1,413,130	$1,586,900	$1,309,556	$1,950,243	$803,249	$659,138	$777,200	$610,650	$1,532,348	$1,298,921	$811,987	$194,523	$13,071,594
EBITDA	$ 584,209	$ 646,946	$ 367,510	$ 580,596	$251,746	$248,322	$ 96,644	$124,096	$ 412,645	$ 427,521	$363,587	$ 41,436	$ 3,961,056
EBITDA %	41.3%	40.8%	28.1%	29.8%	31.3%	37.7%	12.4%	20.3%	26.9%	32.9%	44.8%	21.3%	30.3%
Growth Statistics													
Revenue growth vs. prior year	15.4%	21.5%	23.1%	22.3%	11.0%	11.2%	39.1%	17.1%	13.0%	22.1%	20.5%	19.3%	20.6%
EBITDA growth vs. prior year	27.0	20.5	28.5	25.7	−12.1	6.0	15.5	16.6	−2.1	34.4	45.7	20.3	16.8
EBITDA % of plan	123.6	136.9	119.7	102.4	88.1	92.1	68.2	95.5	77.6	120.6	109.9	128.9	107.9
Expense Statistics													
Payroll as % of revenues	27.2%	34.4%	38.3%	36.1%	34.3%	26.6%	54.5%	31.7%	38.5%	33.8%	19.5%	40.3%	34.7%
Indirect expense as a % of rev.	14.7	8.6	11.1	17.9	15.3	18.2	15.7	24.0	1.8	13.0	13.7	19.1	13.1
G&A expense as a % of rev.	11.9	9.0	12.6	10.8	14.2	13.4	13.2	15.5	17.6	14.1	17.0	13.5	14.4
Annualized Productivity Statistics													
Ann. Revenues/Employee	$70,656	$59,883	$58,202	$42,862	$53,550	$87,885	$48,575	$71,841	$55,722	$64,946	$81,199	$11,116	$55,271
Ann. FF revenues/square foot	$28.39	$39.83	$22.96	$22.28	$25.00	$28.66	$17.20	$15.03	NA	$23.69	$35.44	$3.50	$25.35
# of employees (FTE's)	40	53	45	91	30	15	32	17	55	40	20	35	473
# of salaried/# of hourly	7/33	2/51	8/37	8/84	4/26	3/12	2/27	2/15	6/49	4/36	4/16	4/31	57/416
# of square feet	64,600	52,500	61,825	115,000	54,000	38,772	70,000	57,000	NA	65,000	40,000	84,500	618,697
Cash Flow Statistics													
Days accounts receivable	59	59	63	109	48	34	58	65	25	28	38	38	59
Capital Expenditures	$110,562	$85,993	$125,972	$91,789	$75,577	$2,727	$206,151	$60,921	$0	$145,738	$67,376	$9,955	$987,583
Increase(Decrease) in term/ revolver balance	($320,168)	($133,345)	$52,949	$350,369	($29,051)	($161,638)	$568,764	$35,429	($240,523)	($5,944)	$146,467	($31,959)	$410,433

a Does not include the first five months of financial results for the Portland (RMPD) acquisition which occurred on June 1, 1997.

Source: HIMSCORP Internal.

While we generally stayed out of the tactical, day-to-day operations of the business, we did support our locations whenever they needed us. We would often assist them in preparing proposals and developing a bidding strategy for major competitive RFPs (requests for proposal). Each year in June, we held an operations meeting with our top 50 people attending roundtables on best practices and encouraged them to share their trade secrets. It's unbelievable how people benefited and enjoyed sharing their knowledge on things like employee productivity, space configuration, and project management. For $1,000 per head in travel and hotel cost, we got a ton of value out of those meetings.

To encourage sales growth, we encouraged our managers to think more broadly about what additional services we could provide to our customers. We pushed a more expansive definition of our business strategy and encouraged them to focus on selling new services, such as purging, copying, and coding, to our existing customer base. In Philadelphia, we acquired a medical records copying business which complemented our existing product line and allowed us to cross sell our services to their customer base and vice versa. On a day-to-day level, Scott and I would reinforce sales growth as an objective by asking the GMs how the monthly sales figures looked, what new customers were in the pipeline, and how the next few months were shaping up.

Whenever possible, we tried to pull out cost savings by consolidating purchases to receive better prices from our vendors. For example, Scott was able to reduce the costs of storage boxes from $1 to $0.70 by offering all of our business to one vendor. He negotiated a 25% reduction in business insurance costs while significantly upgrading the level of coverage. At the unit level, we tried to tailor our help to meet their needs. In Houston, for example, we identified labor productivity as a problem and sent a "SWAT" team of managers with strong operational skills down there. In Cleveland, we promoted a #2 manager from another location to become the GM in order to put greater emphasis on sales growth.

All of these practices clearly allowed us to improve our operating leverage. Within 24 months in Philadelphia, for example, we were able to double our sales and improve our EBITDA margin 8%—from 25% to 33%. (See Exhibit 34-5.) But just as important, our operating leverage allowed us to maximize our financial leverage. Our rapid growth allowed us to increase our credit facility to $26.5 million while maintaining our debt to EBITDA ratios that the bank required. (See Exhibit 34-6.) After the first two rounds of acquisitions, we were able to finance them entirely with debt.

Although Dauten believed that his change programs had been effective, he acknowledged the limitations of the process:

> Getting our managers to focus on the economic drivers had its costs as well. I've learned that you can't avoid all problems—you can only pick which ones you want to deal with. In particular, encouraging our GMs to focus on EBITDA had its risks—it sometimes encouraged GMs to be short sighted by focusing on short-term gains at the expense of long-term investments. For example, our Pittsburgh GM wanted to replace a college-educated accountant who was earning $35,000 with a less expensive, high school educated accountant who probably couldn't get the job done. Scott and I had to remind our GMs that, while EBITDA was important, they couldn't ignore decisions that would increase the long-term value of the business.

GROWTH OR HARVEST?

In early June 1997, HIMSCORP completed its buyout of the final independent Record Masters franchisee in Portland, Oregon. It had been a busy two and one-half years for Dauten and Gwilliam, but HIMSCORP's performance had exceeded projections. (See Exhibit 34-7 for unit economics.) Over the past two years, however, Dauten had

EXHIBIT 34-5

RECORD MASTERS OF PHILADELPHIA ($000s)

	1994[a]		1995[b]		1996		1997		Estimated 1998	
	$	%	$	%	$	%	$	%	$	%
Revenue										
Record management services	$1,612.3	76.0%	$1,928.2	77.3%	$2,326.5	73.3%	$2,806.1	65.9%	$3,260.4	65.0%
New material processing	509.7	24.0	539.3	21.6	649.9	20.5	849.1	20.0	1,003.2	20.0
New services	—	0.0	27.9	1.1	199.4	6.3	600.3	14.1	752.4	15.0
Release of information	—	0.0	—	0.0	—	0.0	—	0.0	—	0.0
Total revenue	$2,122.0	100.0%	$2,495.6	100.0%	$3,175.8	100.0%	$4,255.5	100.0%	$5,016.0	100.0%
Year-over-year revenue growth	17.6%		17.6%		27.3%		33.9%		17.8%	
Expenses										
Payroll	$ 727.0	34.3%	$ 735.6	29.5%	$1,039.2	32.7%	$1,528.4	35.9%	$1,791.6	35.7%
Vehicle	76.1	3.6	72.4	2.9	89.9	2.8	106.6	2.5	120.2	2.4
Uniforms & supplies	43.3	2.0	24.7	1.0	31.8	1.0	48.1	1.1	45.5	0.9
Royalties	25.1	1.2	24.5	1.0	32.1	1.2	33.7	0.8	—	0.0
General & administrative	298.6	14.0	344.7	13.8	400.9	12.6	430.1	10.1	501.8	10.0
Depreciation	112.2	5.3	122.0	4.9	113.1	3.6	147.9	3.5	156.4	3.1
Indirect (rent)	363.7	17.1	463.6	18.5	596.7	18.8	731.0	17.2	860.1	17.1
Other	57.9	2.7	44.2	1.8	32.3	1.0	47.0	1.1	46.9	0.9
Total expenses	$1,703.9	80.3%	$1,831.7	73.4%	$2,335.3	73.5%	$3,072.8	72.2%	$3,522.4	70.2%
Operating profit	$ 418.1	19.7%	$ 663.9	26.6%	$ 840.5	26.5%	$1,182.7	27.8%	$1,493.6	29.8%
EBITDA	$ 530.3	25.0%	$ 785.9	31.4%	$ 953.6	30.0%	$1,330.6	31.3%	$1,650.0	32.9%
Year-over-year EBITDA growth	12.1%		48%		21.3%		39.5%		24.0%	

[a] Based on Ernst & Young Due Diligence Report.

[b] Expense figures are annualized from 11 months of operations (February–December). Revenues are 12-month actuals.

Source: HIMSCORP Internal.

EXHIBIT 34-6

HIMSCORP SELECTED MONTH-END BALANCE SHEET STATISTICS ($000)

	2/1/95	6/30/95	3/31/96	9/30/96	12/31/96	6/30/97
Acquisition(s)	Detroit, New Orleans, Philadelphia, Pittsburgh	Los Angeles, San Diego	Houston, Cleveland	Copyright, Inc.	Baltimore, St. Louis	Portland
Debt Commitments						
Senior Debt Commitment	$8,000	$11,000	$14,000	$16,000	$23,000	$25,000
Total Seller Subordinated Debt[a]	1,959	2,259	2,959	2,959	2,959	3,459
Total Debt Commitments	$9,959	$13,259	$16,959	$18,959	$26,159	$28,859
Invested Equity						
Preferred Stock	$3,000	$ 3,000	$ 3,000	$ 3,000	$ 3,000	$ 3,000
Common Stock[b]	425	900	900	900	900	900
Total invested equity	$3,425	$ 3,900	$ 3,900	$ 3,900	$ 3,900	$ 3,900
Senior Debt/Total Invested Capital	70%	75%	79%	81%	86%	88%
Total Debt Commitments/ Total Invested Equity	2.91	3.40	4.35	4.86	6.71	7.40

[a] Houston acquisition had a minimum earn-out provision worth $700k over two years. For purposes of this analysis, assume that the $700K earn-out payments are Seller Subordinated Debt.

[b] Excludes key employee stock investment program proceeds.

Source: HIMSCORP Internal.

become aware that industry dynamics were changing. Many of its customers, including such health-care giants as Columbia/HCA and Tenet, were consolidating at a rapid pace. To realize cost synergies, many of these hospitals were rationalizing their outsourcing agreements by rebidding them to national providers. With 13 businesses in only 12 cities, Dauten was concerned that HIMSCORP would not be able to compete against larger national records management enterprises. At the same time, Iron Mountain and Pierce Leahy had been driving consolidation of the records management industry by acquiring numerous independent operations. Dauten was unsure that HIMSCORP could continue its aggressive growth under such competitive pressures. In other markets, he had seen Iron Mountain use its size and significant financial resources to aggressively price services.

Dauten was proud of what he and his team had accomplished, but knew that he was clearly at a strategic crossroads:

At this point, I think that we have several strategic growth options. Most of the acquisition targets in the active health-care records industry have been pretty well picked over, but that doesn't mean we are done growing—clearly there are opportunities to continue to

EXHIBIT 34-7

HIMSCORP UNIT ECONOMICS AT ACQUISITION VS. 1997 FORECAST ($000)

Location	Acquisition Year	Pre-Acquisition			1997 Forecast		
		Sales	EBITDA	EBITDA %	Sales	EBITDA	EBITDA %
Detroit	1995	$1,927	$755	39.2%	$3,000	$1,275	41.5%
New Orleans	1995	2,048	780	38.1	3,100	1,250	40.3
Philadelphia	1995	2,122	530	25.0	4,000	1,175	29.4
Pittsburgh	1995	1,459	366	25.1	2,600	790	30.4
Los Angeles	1995	1,067	458	41.9	1,650	575	34.8
San Diego	1995	962	304	31.6	1,325	530	40.0
Houston	1996	1,018	146	14.3	1,700	215	12.6
Cleveland	1996	1,142	325	28.5	1,200	275	22.9
Copyright	1996	3,004	860	28.6	3,400	980	28.8
Baltimore	1997	1,412	562	39.8	1,600	680	42.5
St. Louis	1997	2,253	688	30.5	2,700	900	33.3
Portland	1997	2,000	402	20.1	2,300	450	19.6

Source: HIMSCORP Internal.

build the business. Our market research indicates that five to ten markets in the top 50 cities are underserved. We certainly could green-field new sites, as we have done in Milwaukee, which we expect would cost about $250,000 each. Additionally, we could expand the scope of services we offer to our customer base. We could develop new services that our customers want, such as release of information, facilities management, and temporary fileroom staffing. In particular, our coding and imaging businesses seem to be on track and could create a lot of value. We also could expand into other industry segments and try to create a third national storage company to compete with Iron Mountain and Pierce Leahy. HIMSCORP has already identified a number of leading independent archival storage companies that are looking to sell to a buyer interested in building another national archival player.

During the previous six months, Dauten also had begun to think more actively about selling the business. The bidding war for SafeSite, the fifth largest records storage company, had spurred his interest. In March 1997, Iron Mountain had outbid Pierce Leahy after several rounds of escalating bidding, finally closing the deal for $60 million or approximately 3 times reported 1996 revenues and 30 times reported 1996 EBITDA.[3] The SafeSite acquisition capped the previous three years of activity in which Iron Mountain and Pierce Leahy had acquired several dozen archival storage companies. In several other transactions, private companies that were eager to sell also had benefited by successfully engaging both companies in a bidding war. (See Exhibit 34-8 for compa-

---

[3] Meaningful consolidation synergies due to overlap in 10 of Safesite's 14 markets were expected to raise the "steady-state post-acquisition" EBITDA, and therefore, sharply lower the effective multiple paid to 10× EBITDA.

EXHIBIT 34-8

SAMPLE IRON MOUNTAIN ACQUISITION DATA ($000)

Company	Date of Acquisition	Acquisition Structure	Purchase Price	LTM Revenue[a]	LTM EBITDA[a]	Mult. of LTM EBITDA[a]	Adjusted LTM EBITDA[a,b]	Adjusted Mult. of LTM EBITDA[a,b]
Company A	Dec-95	Asset	$14,500	$5,151	$1,328	10.92	$1,528[c]	9.49×
Company B	Mar-95	Asset	$15,700	$6,698	$1,728	9.09	$1,928[d]	8.14×
Company C	Jan-96	Asset	$ 3,450	$1,375	$ 548	6.30	$ 548	6.30×
Company D	Sep-96	Asset	$24,200	$9,173	$1,647	14.69	$2,647[e]	9.14×
Company E	Sep-96	Asset	$ 3,800	$1,724	$ 393	9.67	$ 593[d]	6.41×

[a] LTM refers to last 12 months.

[b] EBITDA has been adjusted to reflect expected acquisition synergies. Financials and multiples may not reflect all acquisition synergies. Industry acquisition multiples had generally ranged between 6× and 8× EBITDA.

[c] EBITDA has been adjusted to eliminate $738k of nonrecurring gain on sale of assets and to reflect $200 potential saving from potential synergies.

[d] EBITDA has been adjusted to reflect $200k potential savings from potential synergies.

[e] Purchase price was $20,200k and a $4,000k earn-out based on 1997 and 1998 revenue targets. Financials have been adjusted to increase EBITDA by $1,000k of potential synergies.

Source: Iron Mountain Senior Debt Prospectus, HIMSCORP Internal.

643

EXHIBIT 34-9

IRON MOUNTAIN STOCK PERFORMANCE, MARCH 15, 1996–JULY 31, 1997

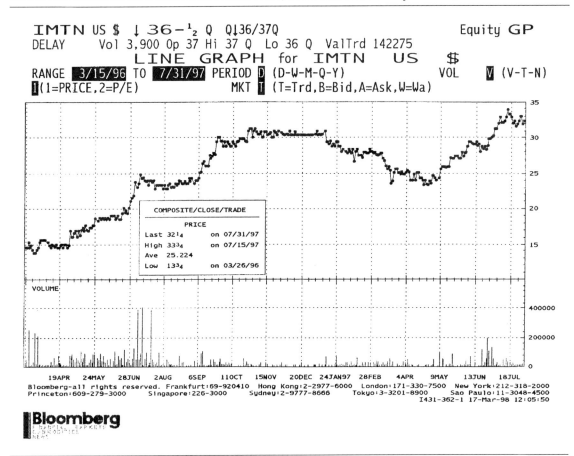

rable Iron Mountain transactions.) Dauten commented on how this event had impacted his thinking:

> The bidding frenzy for SafeSite opened my eyes to the opportunity to sell HIMSCORP. It was clear to me that there was a race to be the biggest records storage company. In our case, I thought Iron Mountain or Pierce Leahy might be interested in acquiring us because we provided access to a high-growth market—health-care services—in which both were underpenetrated and we had a leadership position. Clearly, both could take the intellectual capital that we built at HIMSCORP and leverage it throughout their organization to create value in their own health-care storage business. Pierce Leahy, which is more centralized than Iron Mountain and makes more of an effort to integrate acquisitions into its central operating system, also could capture some overhead savings but at the risk of hurting our high service standards. The chemistry and "fit" was clearly better with Iron Mountain. The key question to me was whether they would recognize the value that HIMSCORP's business model could bring to them in a merger. (See Exhibit 34-9 and 34-10 for historical stock quotes for Iron Mountain and Pierce Leahy and Exhibit 34-11 for a sample analyst report on Iron Mountain.)

EXHIBIT 34-10

PIERCE LEAHY STOCK PERFORMANCE, JULY 1, 1997–AUGUST 1, 1997

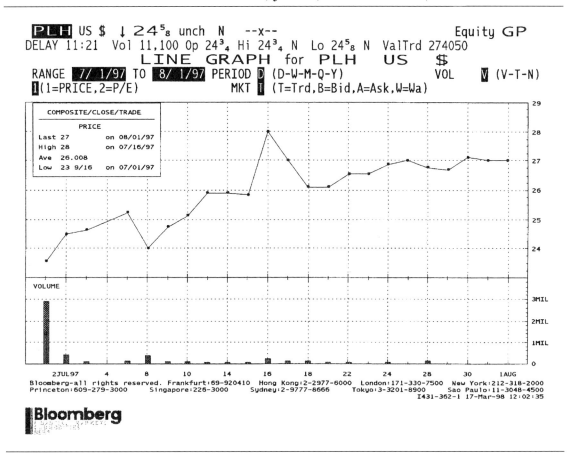

Over the past couple of months, Dauten had invited several investment banks, including DLJ, William Blair, and Allen and Co., to evaluate HIMSCORP as a potential public offering. Dauten thought that going public would allow HIMSCORP to accumulate funds to support their expansion into new industry segments and the archival storage business. Several signs indicated that this might be an attractive time to access the public markets. In particular, Iron Mountain was trading at 12 times 1997 forecast EBITDA, and Pierce Leahy had gone public on July 1, 1997 at over a $500 million valuation, or approximately 10 times trailing EBITDA. (See Exhibit 34-12 for sample public company comparables.) Moreover, the markets had been receptive to other recent public offerings of service industry "roll-ups." (Exhibit 34-13). Capital gains tax rates had recently been cut and interest rates were low. HIMSCORP had pulled together five-year financial forecasts which it had shared with these investment banks (Exhibit 34-14).

The investment bankers had also pulled together a list of potential strategic buyers should HIMSCORP be interested in moving in that direction (Exhibit 34-15). Dauten already had initiated conversations with several potential strategic buyers,

EXHIBIT 34-11

SAMPLE IRON MOUNTAIN ANALYST REPORT

Donaldson, Lufkin & Jenrette

Donaldson, Lufkin & Jenrette Securities Corporation • 277 Park Avenue, New York, NY 10172-0002

Corporate Services

Ty Govatos
Vice President
(212) 892-4254

Robert Callagy
(212) 892-8949

August 8, 1997
1896-97
RESEARCH BULLETIN

IRON MOUNTAIN, INC. (IMTN) +

A Solid Second Quarter

Rating: Market Performanc   **Relative Return Projection:** 0% to 15%

Price		EBITDA Per Share			EBITDA Multiple		Dividend	
08/07/97	52-Week Range	12/96	12/97E	12/98E	12/97E	12/98E	Rate	Yield
30⅞	34½–21½	$3.30	$4.30	$6.00	12.2	8.5	—	—

DIJA: 8165.70   Shares Outstanding (mil.):   10.1
S&P 500: 945.06   Market Capitalization (mil.): $325

VIEWPOINT

On August 1, Iron Mountain reported second quarter earnings per share at a negative nine cents per share. Iron Mountain continues to accelerate the consolidation of the records storage and management industry. Margins, although slightly down, continue to be fairly stable. We should, however, begin to see improvements in 1998. With EPS momentum, cash flow should also improve dramatically in 1998. Investors with a long-term perspective should consider purchase of IMTN shares. Although we are maintaining our *market performance* rating on IMTN common shares, we believe the company is well positioned to be *the* market leader in this industry and has an extremely favorable long-term outlook.

(Continued)

EXHIBIT 34-11 *(Continued)*

IMPORTANT POINTS

Revenues: Revenues increased 41.5% for the quarter to $46.6 million. Of this 41.5% increase, 34.7 percentage points are attributed to acquisition activity in 1996 and 1997. Only 6.8 percentage points were attributed to internal growth. Excluding the New Jersey plant fire, internal growth would have been 9.6%. This is at the high-end of management's target of 5–10%. Storage revenues increased 38.5%, from $20.2 million. Storage revenues are a predominately recurring revenue base in the records management business. Such growth is a healthy indication that business is good. Storage revenues were 60.1% of total revenues versus 61.4% last year. Service revenues increased 46.3%, to $18.6 million. Services revenues were 39.9% of revenues versus 38.6% last year. The slight transition to service revenues was primarily the result of some acquisitions that were more service oriented.

Five Acquisitions occurred in the quarter. The most significant was Safesite Records Management. Despite the fact that Safesite has annualized second quarter revenues of around $23 million, it had only 18 days' worth of impact in the quarter. The remaining four companies acquired had (pre-acquisition) second quarter run-rate revenues of approximately $27 million. This pace of acquisitions continues as three acquisitions were announced in July.

Margins: Gross margins were 48.3%, compared with 49.2% last year. This was to be expected due to the acquisition activity. EBITDA was $11.2 million or 24.0% of revenues versus $7.9 million or 24.1% last year. Year over year, it grew 40.7%, more or less in line with top-line growth. This slight reduction in EBITDA margin was primarily driven by SG&A. SG&A as a percent of revenues were 51.8% of revenues versus 50.8% of revenues last year. Operating margins were 10.6% versus 12.2% last year. This reduction was driven by D&A. For the quarter, it was $6.2 million or 13.4% of revenues versus $3.9 million or 11.9% of revenues last year.

Valuation: On a valuation basis, the common's multiple range lies between a 50% to a 65% discount, based on a EBITDA per share basis to the market. Currently, the common is at a 61% discount to the market, the lower end of its range. On an Enterprise value to EBITDA multiple basis, the common is at 14.2 times trailing twelve.

Ty Govatos
(212) 892-4254

Robert Callagy
(212) 892-8949

+ WITHIN THE PAST THREE YEARS DONALDSON, LUFKIN & JENRETTE SECURITIES CORPORATION HAS BEEN A MANAGING OR CO-MANAGING UNDERWRITER OF THE COMPANY'S SECURITIES.

EXHIBIT 34-12

MULTIPLES OF PUBLICLY TRADED COMPARABLE COMPANIES

Company	Share Price As of 1/7/97	Shares (000)	Equity Value	Net Debt	Enterprise Value	Revenue	EBITDA	Enterprise Value as Multiple of	
								Revenue	EBITDA
Record Storage-Consolidators									
Iron Mountain	$29.00	10,505	$304,645	$148,165	$452,810	$144,076	$34,464	3.14	13.14
FYI, Inc.	$22.00	6,165	$135,640	$ 13,620	$149,260	$ 85,200	$11,632	1.75	12.83
					Median			**2.45**	**12.99**
Outsource/Systems									
ACS	$51.00	35,484	$1,809,679	$ 42,775	$1,852,454	$ 577,328	$ 89,412	3.21	20.72
ServiceMaster	$25.25	145,496	$3,673,761	$544,517	$4,218,278	$3,235,039	$325,855	1.30	12.95
					Median			**2.26**	**16.83**
Medical Outsource Service									
MedQuist	$24.00	5,528	$132,672	$33,000	$165,672	$56,219	$8,321	2.95	19.91
Cohr, Inc.	$24.38	4,582	$111,686	($6,784)	$104,902	$66,254	$7,030	1.26	11.85
					Median			**2.10**	**15.88**
Computerized Patient Record									
Imnet	$23.63	9,977	$235,718	($33,158)	$202,560	$41,539	$ 4,398	4.88	46.06
Sunquest	$13.25	15,360	$203,519	($39,957)	$163,562	$40,913	$15,377	4.00	10.64
Lan Vision	$ 7.38	8,986	$ 65,608	($31,762)	$ 33,846	$ 8,888	($2,618)	3.81	NM
					Median			**4.00**	**28.35**

Source: HIMSCORP Internal.

EXHIBIT 34-13

RECENT INITIAL PUBLIC OFFERINGS OF CONSOLIDATIONS, MAY 1994 TO AUGUST, 1997

Offer Date	Issuer	Offering Size ($Mil)	Offer Price	Split-Adj. Offer Price	Price 8/26/97	% Change Offer Price to 8/26/97
5/13/94	U.S. Delivery Systems	$ 30.0	$10.0	$10.00	$37.88[a]	278.8%
6/9/94	Consolidated Graphics	26.5	11.50	5.75	52.81	818.5%
7/13/94	Golf Enterprises	31.7	13.50	13.50	12.13	(10.2%)
8/16/94	AccuStaff	21.0	10.50	5.25	26.38	402.4%
9/23/94	Corporate Express	120.0	16.00	7.11	16.75	135.5%
9/38/94	Protection One	17.6	6.50	6.50	17.25	165.4
2/14/95	US Office Products	32.5	10.00	10.00	30.50	205.0%
2/21/95	MedPartners	57.2	13.00	13.00	20.88	60.6%
4/6/95	Boise Cascade Office Products	115.6	25.00	12.50	21.00	68.0%
6/23/95	Physicians Resource Group	40.3	13.00	13.00	8.31	(36.1%)
6/27/95	Global DirectMail Corp.	126.4	17.50	17.50	22.56	28.9%
7/31/95	Pet Practice	64.5	15.00	15.00	NA	NA
10/10/95	Central Parking Corp.	50.4	18.00	12.00	47.75	297.9%
11/7/95	COREStaff	56.1	17.00	17.00	29.88	142.4%
11/16/95	CORT Business Services	36.9	12.00	12.00	37.38	211.5%
12/15/95	United TransNet	56.9	14.50	14.50	13.50[b]	(6.9%)
1/23/96	F.Y.I. Incorporated	24.7	13.00	13.00	24.38	87.5%
2/14/96	Cotelligent Group	21.3	9.00	9.00	16.63	84.7%
4/24/96	Outdoor Systems	44.3	15.00	4.44	25.75	480.0%
5/14/96	Coach USA	50.4	14.00	14.00	26.38	88.4%
5/16/96	The Fortress Group, Inc	27.0	9.00	9.00	4.75	(47.2%)
6/5/96	The Registry	37.4	17.00	17.00	46.00	170.6%
6/20/96	Keystone Automotive	24.3	9.00	9.00	18.88	109.7%
7/17/96	Coinmach Laundry	57.7	14.00	14.00	21.88	56.3%
8/8/96	Telespectrum Worldwide	159.3	15.00	15.00	5.84	(61.0%)
8/15/96	Service Experts, Inc.	33.6	13.00	13.00	26.25	101.9%
8/15/96	Signature Resorts	73.5	14.00	14.00	36.06	157.6%
9/24/96	StaffMark	66.0	12.00	12.00	25.38	136.5%
9/26/96	American Residential Services	54.6	15.00	15.00	21.81	45.4%
10/9/96	Lason, Inc	51.0	17.00	17.00	24.00	41.2%
10/23/96	United Auto Group, Inc	172.2	30.00	30.00	23.19	(22.7%)
11/6/96	NCO Group	32.5	13.00	13.00	36.75	182.7%
1/29/97	Medical Manager Corp.	66.0	11.00	11.00	16.00	45.5%
3/19/97	PalEx, Inc.	22.5	7.50	7.50	12.00	60.0%
5/27/97	Carey International, Inc.	30.5	10.50	10.50	14.75	40.5%
6/26/97	Comfort Systems USA	79.3	13.00	13.00	17.63	35.6%
7/10/97	Metals USA, Inc.	59.0	10.00	10.00	10.94	9.4%
7/22/97	Travel Services International	35.0	14.00	14.00	22.00	57.1%
	Total	$2,105.75		Average (not weighted)		124.9%

[a] Acquired by Corporate Express effective 3/4/96. Price reflects acquisition price per share.

[b] Acquired by Corporate Express effective 11/11/94. Price reflects acquisition price per share

Source: Adjusted from Montgomery Securities, "Main Street Meets Wall Street: Mom & Pop Give Way to the Consolidators," September, 1997

EXHIBIT 34-14

HIMSCORP, INC., FINANCIAL FORECAST 1997–2003 ($000)[a]

	1997	1998	1999	2000	2001	2002	2003
Revenue							
Record management services	$18,045	$26,037	$32,196	$38,218	$44,858	$52,330	$60,511
New material processing	4,493	6,208	7,135	8,401	9,777	11,325	13,005
Release of information	5,240	6,931	9,967	11,502	13,186	14,961	16,908
Other	1,432	1,391	1,754	2,090	2,462	2,907	3,427
Total Revenue	$29,210	$40,566	$51,051	$60,210	$70,284	$81,524	$93,851
Expenses							
Payroll	$10,225	$13,977	$17,505	$20,606	$24,020	$27,815	$31,989
Vehicles	641	889	1,154	1,374	1,617	1,895	2,206
Uniforms & supplies	178	244	319	381	449	526	610
Royalties	324	470	597	718	851	1,002	1,166
Start-up costs	200	200	225	250	250	275	275
General & administrative	4,182	5,789	7,179	8,497	9,831	11,407	13,070
Depreciation	1,100	1,485	1,855	2,257	2,705	3,225	3,812
Indirect	3,963	5,787	7,150	8,511	10,005	11,687	13,521
Other	471	696	902	1,057	1,223	1,408	1,608
Total expenses	$21,284	$29,536	$36,884	$43,650	$50,950	$59,239	$68,257
Operating Profit	$ 7,926	$11,030	$14,167	$16,560	$19,333	$22,285	$25,594
EBITDA	$ 9,026	$12,515	$16,021	$18,816	$22,038	$25,510	$29,406
EBITDA %	30.9%	30.9%	31.4%	31.3%	31.4%	31.3%	31.3%
Other Income and Expenses:							
Interest expense	2,566	3,064	2,818	1,977	911	160	0
Amortization	1,425	1,757	1,877	1,877	1,806	1,704	1,704
Total other expense	$ 3,990	$ 4,821	$ 4,695	$ 3,854	$ 2,717	$ 1,864	$ 1,704
Profit Before Taxes	$ 3,935	$ 6,209	$ 9,472	$12,706	$16,616	$20,421	$23,890
Income taxes	1,377	2,173	3,315	4,447	5,816	7,147	8,361
Net income	$ 2,558	$ 4,036	$ 6,156	$ 8,259	$10,801	$13,274	$15,528

[a] Assumes three new acquisitions per year in 1997 and 1998.

Source: HIMSCORP Internal for investment bank presentations.

(*Continued*)

EXHIBIT 34-14 (Continued)

	1997	1998	1999	2000	2001	2002	2003
Assets							
Current Assets							
Cash	$ 0	$ 0	$ 0	$ 0	$ 0	$12,154	$30,455
Accounts receivable	4,802	6,668	8,392	9,898	11,553	13,401	15,428
Prepaid expenses	240	333	420	495	578	670	771
Total current assets	$ 5,042	$ 7,002	$ 8,812	$10,392	$12,131	$26,225	$46,654
Fixed assets							
Property, plant and equipment	7,326	9,676	11,176	12,926	14,926	16,926	18,926
Accumulated depreciation	(3,536)	(5,021)	(6,875)	(9,132)	(11,837)	(15,061)	(18,874)
Total fixed assets	$ 3,790	$ 4,655	$ 4,301	$ 3,794	$ 3,089	$ 1,865	$ 52
Other assets							
Investment in network	$ 1	$ 1	$ 1	$ 1	$ 1	$ 1	$ 1
Goodwill, gross	34,295	42,595	42,595	42,595	42,595	42,495	42,595
Accumulated amortization	(2,219)	(3,787)	(5,491)	(7,195)	(8,899)	(10,603)	(12,306)
Goodwill, net	$32,076	$38,808	$37,104	$35,400	$33,696	$31,993	$30,289
Deferred financing and organizational costs, gross	$ 1,039	$ 1,039	$ 1,039	$ 1,039	$ 1,039	$ 1,039	$ 1,039
Accum. amortization	(401)	(590)	(763)	(936)	(1,039)	(1,039)	(1,039)
Deferred financing and organizational costs, net	$ 638	$ 449	$ 276	$ 102	$ 0	$ 0	$ 0
TOTAL ASSETS	$41,547	$50,915	$50,493	$49,690	$48,918	$60,083	$76,996
Liabilities							
Current Liabilities							
Accounts payable	$ 1,601	$ 2,223	$ 2,797	$ 3,299	$ 3,851	$ 4,467	$ 5,143
Accrued liabilities	1,681	2,334	2,937	3,464	4,044	4,690	5,400
Total current liabilities	$ 3,281	$ 4,558	$ 5,734	$ 6,763	$ 7,895	$ 9,158	$10,542
Long term liabilities							
Working capital loan	$ 0	$ 0	$ 0	$ 0	$ 0	$ 0	$ 0
Term/revolver loan	27,606	31,662	24,301	14,606	3,371	0	0
Subordinated notes	2,259	2,259	1,864	1,468	0	0	0
Total long term liabilities	$29,865	$33,921	$26,165	$16,075	$ 3,371	$ 0	$ 0
TOTAL LIABILITIES	$33,146	$38,478	$31,899	$22,838	$11,265	$ 9,158	$10,542
Stockholder's Equity							
Stockholder's Equity	$ 7,156	$ 7,156	$ 7,156	$ 7,156	$ 7,156	$ 7,156	$ 7,156
Retained Earnings	1,245	5,281	11,437	19,696	30,497	43,771	59,299
TOTAL EQUITY	$ 8,401	$12,437	$18,593	$26,852	$37,652	$50,926	$66,454
Total Liabilities & S/E	$41,547	$50,915	$50,493	$49,690	$48,918	$60,084	$76,996

(Continued)

651

EXHIBIT 34-14 (Continued)

	1997	1998	1999	2000	2001	2002	2003
Cash Flow from Operations							
Net income	$ 2,558	$ 4,036	$6,156	$ 8,259	$10,801	$13,274	$15,528
Adjustments to reconcile net income							
Depreciation and Amortization	$ 2,525	$ 3,242	$3,732	$ 4,134	$ 4,511	$ 4,929	$ 5,516
Decrease (Increase) in net receivables	(1,506)	(1,867)	(1,724)	(1,506)	(1,656)	(1,848)	(2,026)
Decrease (Increase) in prepaid expenses	(58)	(93)	(86)	(75)	(83)	(92)	(101)
Decrease (Increase) in accounts pebbles	390	622	575	502	552	616	675
Decrease (Increase) in accrued liabilities	400	653	603	527	580	647	709
Total cash flow from operations	$ 4,309	$ 6,593	$9,257	$11,841	$14,705	$17,525	$20,301
Cash flow from investing							
Decrease (Increase) capital expenditures	($ 1,365)	($ 1,350)	($1,500)	($1,750)	($ 2,000)	($ 2,000)	($ 2,000)
Decrease (Increase) acquisition of goodwill	(8,400)	(8,300)	0	0	0	0	0
Decrease (Increase) acquisition of fixed assets	(1,000)	(1,000)	0	0	0	0	0
Decrease (Increase) acquisition of network stock	0	0	0	0	0	0	0
Total cash flow from investing	($10,765)	($10,650)	($1,500)	($1,750)	($ 2,000)	($ 2,000)	($ 2,000)
Cash flow from financing							
Increase (Decrease) revolver	$ 0	$ 0	$ 0	$ 0	$ 0	$ 0	$ 0
Increase (Decrease) term loan	0	0	0	0	0	0	0
Increase (Decrease) sub. debt	0	0	(395)	(395)	(1,468)	0	0
Total cash flow from financings	$ 0	$0	($ 395)	($395)	($ 1,468)	$ 0	$ 0
Free cash flow	($ 6,458)	($ 4,056)	$7,361	$ 9,695	$11,236	$15,525	$30,455
Term debt paydown	6,458	4,056	(7,361)	(9,695)	(11,236)	(3,371)	0
Ending cash	$ 0	$ 0	$ 0	$ 0	$ 0	$12,154	$30,455

EXHIBIT 34-15

LIST OF POTENTIAL STRATEGIC PARTNERS

Company Name	Location	Business Description
Affiliated Computer Services, Inc.	Dallas, TX	Provides information processing services, such as data processing outsourcing, electronic funds transfer transactions processing, and information and image management. The Company's services are provided to customers with time critical and transaction intensive processing needs nationwide.
Arcus, Inc.	Los Angeles, CA	Provides secure off-site data storage of magnetic media (i.e., computer tapes, cartridges, and disks) in order to safeguard against natural and manmade disasters.
F.Y.I. Inc.	Dallas, TX	Provides document management services, including microfilm processing and microfilm distribution; photocopying and electronic imaging of documents; computerized correspondence management systems to hospital medical records departments; record storage and destruction; data processing and information management services; and offsite active and inactive retrieval service of medical records.
Iron Mountain, Inc.	Boston, MA	Operates as a full-service records management company providing storage and related services for all major media, including paper, computer discs and tapes, microfilm and microfiche, master audio and videotapes, film and optical discs, X-rays, and blueprints.
MedQuist, Inc.	Morton, NJ	Provides electronic transcription and document management services to the health-care industry. The Company's customized outsourcing services enable clients to improve the accuracy of transcribed medical reports.
MRC	Chicago, IL	Provides medical transcription and document management services to the health-care industry.
Olsten Corp.	Melville, NY	Provides health-care personnel in home, health-care facilities, and business settings as well as temporary personnel to business, industry, and governments sectors. Also provides on-site paramedical examination services and offers a full range of permanent and temporary placement services to the U.K.
On Assignment, Inc.	Calabasas, CA	Provides temporary and permanent placement of scientific personnel with laboratories and other institutions. Also provides temporary and permanent placement of credit collection and medical billing professionals to the financial services and health-care industries.
Pierce Leahy Corp.	King of Prussia, PA	Provides records storage and management services with operations in Denver, Colorado; Fort Wayne, Indiana; and Albuquerque, New Mexico. The largest archive records management company in North America as measured by the approximately 39 million cubic feet of records currently under its management.
ServiceMaster Corp.	Downers Grove, IL	Provides housekeeping, plant operations, food services, laundry and linen care, lawn care and landscaping, clinical equipment management, and energy services. Also provides pest control, radon testing, carpet, upholstery, and janitorial services, disaster restoration, and window cleaning services.

Source: HIMSCORP Internal

including ServiceMaster, a large, diversified services company with a strong health-care business, and Medquist, the leading medical transcription company. He believed that these companies might be interested in purchasing HIMSCORP as a means of entering the growing document management services industry.

Dauten reflected on his impending decision:

> I think we could have a fun, financially successful run with HIMSCORP as a private, independent company. But if this is the best time to sell—for me and for the business—then that's what I'll do.

35

Dell Ventures

We have great market share, a low-cost model and low working-capital needs. The more we grow the more cash we generate, which is unusual for a company that makes things. So a few years ago we were asking—What should we do with our cash? What can we do to extend our intellectual capital reach into the community and develop long-term strategic products and services? We decided that venture capital-type investments were a good way for us to continue to see what was happening in the market, leverage that, and enjoy some very healthy returns in the process.

—Kevin Nater, Treasurer, Dell Computer Corporation

We need to be careful that we don't dilute the Dell name, and that it remains meaningful. I have heard rumors about other corporate investors that their name does not carry as much weight because they are doing so many investments in non-strategic areas.

—Steve Bailey, Principal, Dell Ventures

Tom Meredith, managing director, Dell Ventures (DV), Dell Treasurer Kevin Nater, and DV portfolio manager Paul Legris were having a sandwich at the Dell cafeteria. While standing in line, Legris mentioned the May 8, 2000 *Business Week* article reporting the impact of the market downturn in April 2000 on some corporate venture capital portfolios. As of early May 2000, Microsoft had lost roughly $14 million on its investment in Careerbuilder Inc, an online job service. The value of Dell's shares of NaviSite, a Web-hosting company, had dropped by $279 million; its shares in Selectica, which sold computer systems for e-commerce, had fallen by 70%, or $140 million, from its high; its shares in Calico Commerce, which sold applications for e-commerce, had declined by $93 million. "It is an interesting perspective that some of these articles are taking," Legris mused. "They try to sensationalize some of these investments. The intent is strategic and we get in substantially below the IPO price. Some of them will be extremely volatile. That is the nature of venture investing." And Dell was doing better than most (see Exhibit 35-1).

Cate Reavis, Senior Researcher, Global Research Group, prepared this case under the supervision of Professor Paul Gompers and Carin-Isabel Knoop, Executive Director, Global Research Group, as the basis for class discussion rather than to illustrate either effective or ineffective handling of an administrative situation. The authors thank Research Associate Suma Raju for her assistance.

EXHIBIT 35-1

VALUE GENERATED BY CORP. FROM IPOS IN 2000

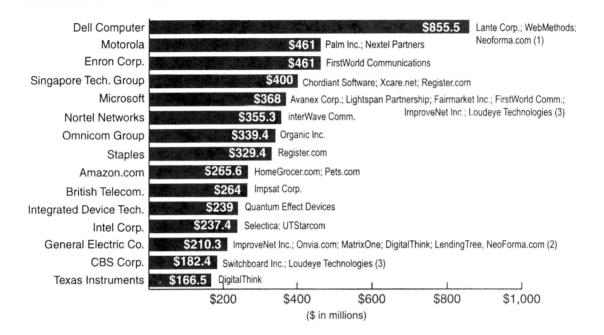

Based on value of shares held by corporations minus original equity investment. Calculated using SEC filings and share price of company as of March 17. Does not include stakes that corporations acquired through spinoffs or transfers of technology or assets.

(1) Amount it invested in WebMethods not disclosed in S-1, so IPO price of $35 is being used to calculate investment. (2) Stake in Neoforma not disclosed. (3) Stake in Loudeye not disclosed in S-1.

Copyright © 2000 *Asset Alternatives Inc.*

Source: The Corporate Venturing Report, April 2000.

"You're exactly right," Nater agreed. "We did not lose from the correction. Our portfolio is well in the money. The market correction is not scaring us at the moment. And this does not change the fundamental reasons we are doing this." They did admit that the market correction delayed potential liquidity in the portfolio because some IPOs were being delayed, and the value of the portfolio was way down from its high. "From a financial perspective," Nater said, "market adjustments are a risk, but we are not using an enormous amount of liquidity so a market adjustment would never endanger Dell's core liquidity requirements. We could get caught up in the opportunistic nature of investment, given some valuations out there. We need to keep a focus on strategic relationships."

This seemed like a good time to take stock of their work since March 1999, when Dell's board of directors agreed to establish a venture capital group responsible for making strategic investments that would benefit Dell's existing businesses and help the company become the premier Internet infrastructure company. Originally called the Strategic Business Development Center of Excellence, the group later became known as Dell Ventures, reflecting the group's focus on venture investing. Under the leadership of Alex Smith, Dell's former treasurer, DV had since invested over $700 million in 90 companies (see Exhibit 35-2) in four areas of strategic importance: data transfer and storage, Internet services, B2B and B2C online commerce, and Internet access and content (see Exhibit 35-3). They had expected to invest $100 million in the first year, in 10 to 12 deals. In the Spring of 2000, Tom Meredith, Dell's former CFO, joined Dell Ventures as a managing director.

Meredith, Nater, and Legris felt DV had the brand, the deal-flow, money, and resources to continue to create value for Dell shareholders. But there were challenges lurking: managing market and people risks, educating Wall Street on the value of corporate venture capital, and finding the appropriate structure and systems for DV to flourish.

HISTORY

Founded in 1984 by 19-year-old college student Michael Dell, Austin, Texas-based Dell Computer Corporation, was the world's leading direct seller of computers as well as a "premier" supplier of technology for Internet infrastructure. With over 36,500 employees worldwide (75% had joined since 1997), Dell was the world's fastest growing computer company. With earnings of $1.9 billion on revenue of $25 billion in 1999,[1] Dell ranked number 78 on the Fortune 5000, number 210 on the Fortune Global 500, and number three on Fortune's "most admired list of companies." Annual sales and earnings had increased more than 40% since 1996. Meanwhile, since the early 1990s, Dell had been the best-performing stock measured against other companies in the S&P 500 Index (see Exhibits 35-4 and 35-5). Dell predicted annual revenue growth of 30% in 2000.[2]

Nearly 70% of Dell's systems were sold to government entities and large businesses. More than 70% of sales came from North and South America, 22% from Europe, and 7% from Asia. With offices in 34 countries, Dell sold its products and services in more than 170 countries. Dell also had regional headquarters in England to serve the European, Middle East, and African markets; Hong Kong to serve Asia-Pacific; and Japan for the Japanese market. Manufacturing plants were located in Austin, Texas; Nashville, Tennessee; Brazil; Ireland; Malaysia; and China.

"Some people take offense when others refer to Dell as a broker of technology, not a technology company," noted Meredith. "It's okay to be a broker if you're changing the whole paradigm of supply chain management. We are also a technology company, but if our competitors want to think we are not, we are a stealth technology company." "We are committed to be leading-edge fast followers," added Manish Mehta, a five-year Dell veteran who joined DV in early May.

---

[1] Lisa Gibbs, "Tech investing . . . ," *Money Magazine* (April 1, 2000).
[2] Ibid.

EXHIBIT 35-2

INVESTMENTS IN EACH AREA OF STRATEGIC IMPORTANCE

A. Communications

2nd Century Communications offers small and medium businesses a range of broadband communication and desktop management solutions.

Go to 2nd Century Communications

2Wire makes products that enhance home use of broadband communications.

Go to 2Wire

Avici Systems Develops high-performance routers and switches.

Go to Avici Systems, Inc.

Cidera delivers content via satellite to the edge of the Internet.

Go to Cidera

Com2001 makes communication servers that handle, fax, data, and messaging.

Go to Com20001

GoAmerica is a wireless service provider for e-mail, Internet, and corporate data.

Go to GoAmerica

Rangestar Wireless develops next-generation components for wireless networking.

Go to Rangestar

(Continued)

EXHIBIT 35-2 (Continued)

B. Internet (Business-to-Business Ecommerce)

DigitalWork.com provides a range of services to assist owners in managing and growing their small businesses.
Go to DigitalWork.com

Divine Interventures incubates early-stage companies specializing in business-to-business e-commerce.
Go to Divine Interventures

Equinix sets up carrier-neutral business exchanges for e-commerce.
Go to Equinix

Hire.com helps businesses to automate their Internet recruiting efforts.
Go to Hire.com

Internet Capital Group invests in business-to-business e-commerce companies.
Go to Internet Capital Group

The National Capital Group invests in business-to-business e-commerce companies.
Go to Internet Capital Group

Neoforma.com facilitates business-to-business interactions between buyers and suppliers in the medical industry.
Go to Neoforma.com

Niku develops software to assist corporations in the management and delivery of professional services.
Go to Niku

TechPacific.com incubates high-technology companies in the Asia-Pacific region.
Go to TechPacific.com

zoho (Z)*

Zoho Corporation operates the premier online marketplace for the hospitality industry
Go to Zoho

(Continued)

EXHIBIT 35-2   (Continued)

C. Server/Storage

Brocade develops advanced technology for fiber channel networks.
Go to Brocade

Crossroads Systems provides storage routers for Storage Area Networks.
Go to Crossroads Systems, Inc.

Finisar Corp. develops fiber optic subsystems and performance test systems for high-speed serial data communications.
Go to Finisar Corp.

The Intel 64 fund invests in technology companies that develop solutions for servers and workstations based on Intel's 64-bit processors.
Go to Intel 64 Fund

Interactive Silicon makes chips for parallel computing compression and de-compression.
Go to Interactive Silicon, Inc.

Linuxcare provides technical support and training for companies using the Linux operating system.
Go to Linuxcare

NSI Software develops products for server management and for maintaining a high level of server availability.
Go to NSI Software

Red Hat Software provides support to Linux users and aggregates Linux-compatible software.
Go to Red Hat Linux

Scenix specializes in embedded processors for Internet-enabled "smart" products.
Go to Scenix

StorageNetworks sells data storage services to enterprises and Web-based companies.
Go to StorageNetworks

Turbolinux, Inc. provides Linux software and support.
Go to TurboLinux, Inc.

VM Ware provides an environment for running multiple virtual computers from a single PC/workstation.
Go to VM Ware, Inc.

(Continued)

EXHIBIT 35-2 *(Continued)*

D. Service

All.com provides technical support information for the online consumer.

Go to All.com

Aveo Corp. delivers PC monitoring/diagnostic solutions for Web-enabled support.

Go to Aveo Corp

Centerbeam provides turnkey solutions for small- and home businesses

Go to Centerbeam

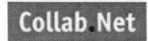

Collab.net provides tools and services for managing open source development projects.

Go to Collab.net

eOnline hosts enterprise application solutions for small and mid-sized companies.

Go to eOnline

Interrelate provides analytics infrastructure for its clients, delivered through an ASP.

Go to Interrelate

Interliant offers Web site and application hosting services to companies of all sizes.

Go to Interliant

Lante Corp. provides expert Internet commerce consulting.

Go to Lante

LivePerson provides a service for delivering chat-based customer support and sales.

Go to LivePerson

Medicalogic, Inc. connects patients and physicians by delivering medical records over the Internet.

Go to Medicalogic, Inc.

Navisite Offers Web site and hosting/management solutions.

Go to Navisite

NetYear assists companies to expand their e-commerce operations to or from Japan.

Go to NetYear

Xuma Inc. makes applications for enterprise-level e-commerce.

Go to Xuma, Inc.

Source: http://www.dell.com/us/en/gen/corporate/ventures_004_dvg_portfolio.htm

EXHIBIT 35-3

INVESTED BALANCE BY SECTOR

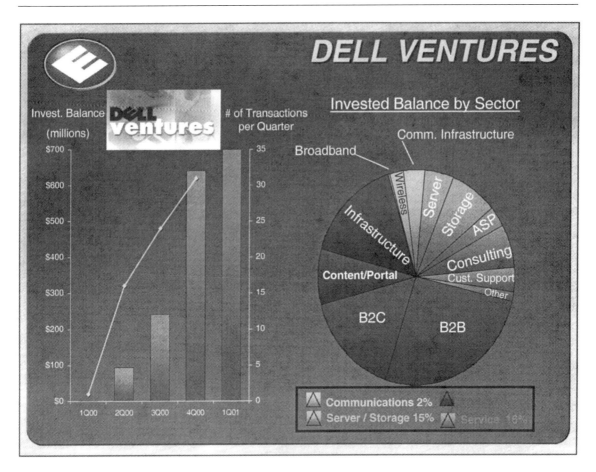

Source: Company documents.

THE DIRECT MODEL

From its inception, Dell bypassed the traditional retail channels by shipping products directly to customers through a 1-800 number. "We entered the business with no channel conflicts," Dell explained. "We were and still are the entire channel, from procurement through service. As a result, we control all the aspects in between."[3]

Dell's products were made-to-order. In 1994, through its Dell.com Web site, Dell led the way to e-commerce. "Michael had the vision for a much more efficient and effective form of distribution of technologies than his predecessors and current competitors," Meredith stated. "In doing so, he not only changed our industry sector, but has been a primary cause for fairly significant change in every industry." "There is a term that has sprung up recently," he continued, " 'to be Delled' which signifies 'to be

[3] "The Dell Advantage," *Michael Dell keynote address* (March 3, 1999).

EXHIBIT 35-4A

DELL COMPUTER CORPORATION—CONSOLIDATED STATEMENT OF FINANCIAL POSITION (IN MILLIONS)

Assets	January 28, 2000	January 29, 1999	February 1, 1998
Current Assets:			
Cash and cash equivalents	$ 3,809	$1,726	$ 320
Short-term investments	323	923	1,524
Accounts receivable, net	2,608	2,094	1,486
Inventories	391	273	233
Other	550	791	349
Total Current Assets	7,681	5,807	3,912
Property, plant and equipment	765	523	342
Long-term investments	1,048	532	—
Equity securities and other investments	1,673	—	—
Goodwill and other	304	15	14
Total Assets	$11,471	$6,877	$4,268
Liabilities and Stockholders' Equity			
Current liabilities:			
Accounts payable	$3,538	$2,397	$1,643
Accrued and other	1,654	1,298	1,054
Total current liabilities	5,192	3,695	2,697
Long-term debt	508	512	17
Other	463	349	261
Commitments and contingent liabilities	—	—	—
Total liabilities	$6,163	$4,556	$2,975
Stockholders' equity:			
Preferred stock and capital in excess of $0.01 par value; shares issued and outstanding: none	—	—	—
Common stock and capital in excess of $0.01 par value; shares issued and outstanding: 2,575 and 2,543, respectively	$ 3,583	$1,781	$ 747
Retained earnings	1,260	606	607
Other comprehensive income	533	(36)	—
Other	(68)	(30)	(61)
Total stockholder equity	5,308	2,321	1,293
Total Liabilities and Stockholders' Equity	$11,471	$6,877	$4,268

Source: Dell Computer Corporation FY 2000 Annual Report.

(*Continued*)

EXHIBIT 35-4A   (Continued)

CONSOLIDATED STATEMENT OF INCOME (IN MILLIONS)

	Fiscal Year Ended		
	January 28, 2000	January 29, 1999	February 1, 1998
Net revenue	$25,265	$18,243	$12,327
Cost of revenue	20,047	14,137	9,605
Gross margin	5,218	4,106	2,722
Operating expenses:	2,387	1,788	1,202
Selling, general, and administrative	374	272	204
Research, development, and engineering	194	—	—
Purchased in-process research and development	2,955	2,060	1,406
Total operating expenses	2,263	2,046	1,316
Operating income	188	38	52
Financing and other	2,451	2,084	1,368
Income before income taxes	785	624	424
Provision for income taxes	$ 1,666	$ 1,460	$ 944
Net income			
Earnings per common share:			
Basic	$ 0.66	$ 0.58	$ 0.36
Diluted	$ 0.61	$ 0.53	$ 0.32
Weighted average shares outstanding			
Basic	2,536	2,531	2,631
Diluted	2,728	2,772	2,952
Cash flows from operating activities:			
Net income	$ 1,666	$ 1,460	$ 944
Adjustments to reconcile net income to net cash provided by operating activities:			
Depreciation and amortization	156	103	67
Tax benefits of employee stock plans	1,040	444	164
Purchased in-process research and development	194	—	—
Other	(24)	11	24
Changes in:			
Operating working capital	812	367	365
Noncurrent assets and liabilities	82	51	28
Net cash provided by operating activities	$3,926	$2,436	$1,592
Cash flows from investing activities:			
Investments:			
Purchases	(3,101)	(1,938)	(1,492)
Maturities and sales	2,319	1,304	1,022
Cash payments for acquisition, net of cash acquired	(4)	—	—
Capital expenditure	(397)	(296)	(187)
Net cash used in investing activities	(1,183)	(930)	(657)
Cash flows from financing activities:			
Purchase of common tock	(1,061)	(1,518)	(1,023)
Issuance of common stock under employee plans	289	212	88
Proceeds from issuance of long-term debt, net of issuance costs	20	494	—
Cash received from sale of equity options and other	63	—	37
Repayments of borrowings	(6)	—	—
Net cash used in financing activities	(695)	(812)	(898)
Effect of exchange rate changes on cash	35	(10)	(14)
Net increase in cash	2,083	684	23
Cash and cash equivalents at beginning of period	1,726	1,042	1,019
Cash and cash equivalents at end of period	$3,809	$1,726	$1,042

Source: Dell Computer Corporation FY 2000 Annual Report.

(Continued)

EXHIBIT 35-4B

PRODUCT REVENUE SPLITS ($ MILLIONS)

	FY1996	FY1997	FY1998	FY1999	FY2000	FY20001E
Revenue by Segment:						
Enterprise	158.9	306.9	1,138.4	2,349.7	4,178.1	6,178.5
Desktops	4,289.8	6,036.7	8,786.2	11,770.8	14,805.9	17,757.0
Portable	847.4	1,415.4	2,402.3	5,121.5	6,280.0	9,564.5
Peripheral and Other	582.6	755.7	1,037.9	1,194.4	1,842.4	3,015.0
Gross Revenue	**$5,296.0**	**$7,759.0**	**$12,327.0**	**$18,242.0**	**$25,264.0**	**$33,500.0**
Revenue Split (%)						
Enterprise	3.0%	4.0%	9.2%	12.9%	16.5%	18.4%
Desktops	81.0%	77.8%	71.3%	64.5%	58.5%	53.0%
Portables	16.0%	18.2%	19.5%	22.6%	24.9%	28.6%
Peripheral and Other	11.0%	9.7%	8.4%	6.5%	7.3%	9.0%
Total	**100.0%**	**100.0%**	**100.0%**	**100.0%**	**100.0%**	**100.0%**
Growth						
Enterprise (year-to-year)	82.9%	93.2%	270.9%	106.4%	77.8%	47.9%
Enterprise (quarter-to-quarter)						
Desktops (year-to-year)	53.3%	40.7%	45.5%	34.0%	25.8%	19.9%
Desktops (quarter-to-quarter)						
Portables (year-to-year)	43.4%	67.0%	69.7%	71.6%	52.4%	52.3%
Portables (quarter-to-quarter)						

Source: Company reports and U.S. Bancorp Piper Jaffray estimates.

Webified', or to make more efficient." By early 2000, while Amazon.com drew roughly five times the traffic, its sales were approximately 7% of Dell's.[4] The company claimed to be the only top tier e-business provider that dealt 100% directly with each customer.

Dell generated 50% of its sales over the Internet, $40 million daily. Gateway and Compaq had Internet sales of 25% and 5%, respectively.[5] Meanwhile, nearly 40% of Dell's technical support and 70% of its order-status transactions occurred online. Dell.com drew more than 25 million visitors each quarter. Each of Dell's online transactions produced an average of 40% fewer order calls for Dell, and 15% fewer technical support calls, a savings of $3 to $8 per call. At Dell, even performance reviews were online.

Dell's built-to-order PCs meant lower inventories, which translated to lower costs and higher margins, and combined with direct customer feedback, allowed the company to offer the latest technologies and improve product quality. "If you look at Dell's asset efficiency," Meredith pointed out, "we have six days of inventory [versus 60 for competitors] and negative working capital. It was not conventional wisdom until recent

[4] Andrew Tausz, "The Internet rewards Dell's directness," *Financial Post* (April 17, 2000).
[5] Ashok Kumar, "Dell Computer Corporation," *US Bancorp Piper Jaffray* (March 2000).

EXHIBIT 35-5

**DELL COMPUTER RELATIVE STOCK PRICE PERFORMANCE,
FIRST QUARTER 1996–FIRST QUARTER 2000**

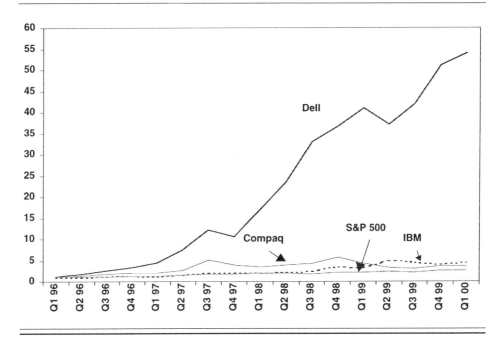

---

years that a company our size could grow at our rate and not consume cash. The faster we grow, the more cash we generate. Ten years ago that was heresy."

Products and Services

Dell's products included desktop and notebook computers, network servers, workstation products, and storage products. Dell also sold more than 30,000 software and peripheral products from industry-leading manufacturers that complemented the company's system offerings. Desktop sales accounted for 55% of systems revenue; notebook sales, 17%; enterprise products, 17%; and sales outside core computer business ("beyond the box"), 16%. Dell's server market share had increased from 16% to 26% since spring of 1999.

In addition to Microsoft's Windows NT operating system (OS), Dell offered Red Hat Software Inc.'s Red Hat Linux OS as a factory-installed option on its Precision workstations and PowerEdge servers, as well as on its OptiPlex desktop PCs. A rival of Microsoft, Linux was a low-cost, openly configured OS. While Linux was quickly gaining market share, 85% of the world's computers ran off of Microsoft's Windows OS.[6] Dell was the industry's first company to sign a major deployment agreement with Linux, which it did in March 1999.

---

[6] Doug Levy, "Linux creator: Next Bill Gates? Operating system could rival Windows," *USA Today* (January 7, 2000).

With PC sales under pressure, Dell was branching out into services including consulting, installation, Internet access, systems integration, and Web hosting. The company provided a number of Internet-based services, including DellEworks.com, a Web site launched in the first quarter of 1999 that provided small businesses with advice on running a business online; Direct from Dell, a site that provided advanced online customer support capabilities; Dell Talk, an online customer-to-customer discussion forum; Ask Dudley, a natural language search engine; Dellnet Internet access; and the Dellnet.com portal site. Dell developed custom Internet sites called Premier Pages for corporate, government and education customers worldwide. The pages enabled approved employees to purchase products specifically configured for their organization. As of early 2000, the company provided more than 40,000 of these customized Web sites.

According to Michael Dell, Dell's future was in Internet infrastructure. The company estimated that by 2003, companies would spend up to $370 billion annually on Internet infrastructure, up from $124 billion in 1999. Dell managers noted that 63% of Fortune 500 CIOs chose e-commerce as their top strategic priority in 2000; 76% planned to spend as much, or more, on Internet infrastructure; while 48% believed Dell would be the biggest beneficiary by a very wide margin.[7] "The scope of what we can do has gone from inside a PC to the whole enterprise," noted David Lunsford, Director of Strategic Investments. "People associate us with the PC and Windows," Michael Dell noted. "That's an easy association to make, but it's not really an accurate description of the company anymore."

Corporate Structure and Culture

Dell executives described the company as a flat and segmented organization (see Exhibit 35-6). Dell was organized in a product/market matrix. Products included Web sites, desktop computers, laptops, workstations, servers, storage, and hosting. Markets included international, consumer, small business, health care, government, education, and enterprise. Each customer-oriented business segment controlled its own product, manufacturing, sales, and support operations.

Employees described Dell as fast, informal, high-energy, fact-based, execution-focused, and tactically focused on quarterly results. Most of the company's senior managers had technology and/or operating experience prior to joining Dell. According to Larry Polizzoto, director of Business Development, "Dell operates on the 80/20 rule. When you get 80% of information, you go ahead and execute. The last 20% is not worth waiting for. You have to be first in the market. Dell is about speed. We call it 'dellocity': evaluate quickly, make a decision, move on it and if you make a mistake, correct it and continue on."[8] "Nobody is stuck in their own little world pushing paper," explained Steve Bailey, a Principal with DV. "People are interested in the success of the company. On any given day, everyone knows our market share versus Compaq and how much revenue is going through Dell.com." "People think it is fun to be part of history," a manager added.

Meredith added there was a sense of fear in the corporation. "There's a healthy skepticism that we are not as good as others may think we are," he explained. "Therefore we operate not just out of desire but also out of fear. Michael Dell calls it 'confident paranoia'."

[7] "The Internet Infrastructure Company," presentation given by Dell Co-Chairman Jim Vanderslice, April 4, 2000.

[8] Velocity—compression of space and time.

EXHIBIT 35-6

DELL MANAGEMENT ORGANIZATION

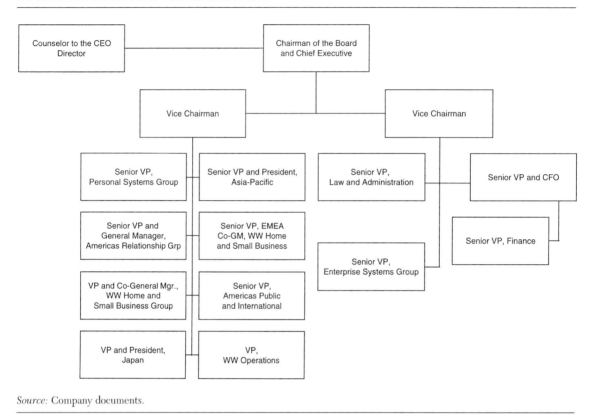

Source: Company documents.

Businesses were very focused on their particular line of business. According to Mike Lazorik, a Principal for DV, "there is not a centralized ability to look at the overall picture for Dell and its venture landscape." Business segments were compensated for meeting quarterly metrics, and minimizing capital requirements. No group had specific incentives to "deploy strategic funds," Lazorik explained. "We focus on investments that look 'over the dashboard,' not ones made for immediate quarterly impact." Lunsford explained that performance based on sector had its costs. "We had an opportunity to invest in a company that was related to digital imaging," he recalled.

> We could put $5 million into it and within a year we believed it would generate a $20 million capital gain. But that company needed the support of a particular segment. The product and the service that they had really wasn't a high revenue maker for that segment. So the segment was unwilling to implement the commercial arrangement because it only meant $200,000 in additional revenue. They weren't going to do it because it would cost their P&L a couple of people to support it and it wasn't going to bring them much. The capital gain was going to show up in DV's P&L. So we start doing things that aren't good for the company at large but are good for a particular sector.

DELL VENTURES

Meredith explained why DV was formed in March 1999:

> It was becoming increasingly apparent to us in the finance group that there were a variety of efforts inside Dell that seemed to be focused on venture investing between dot.coms, the new economy companies, and Dell. What we concluded was that there was no one person in charge of strategic investments. Thought was given to where and why we should be focusing our efforts in terms of new economy companies. Yet we were a new economy company because of our supply chain management capabilities, our asset efficiency, and our Web-enabled revenues. So after a few months our Board of Directors agreed to fund a venture arm.

"The goal was to tap new technologies and business models that were still mostly experimental, but if successful, could radically alter our business," a Dell manager explained.

> DV allowed us to get in earlier in technology curves, and hedge our bets regarding sales models and service capabilities. We were also very challenged as an organization to promote and nurture opportunities within our organization that cut across segments and products. DV allowed us to prioritize on a corporate basis, and presented an alternative to "starving our youngest" which can easily happen in a now very large company that is traveling very fast. We talked a lot about how to foster a unified strategic effort that cuts across segments. This is the origin for Dell Ventures.

"We had been talking about it for a while but we were really focused on executing the core business," Nater added. "But then, Michael recognized what was happening in the financial marketplace and the rate of growth of new companies. We realized that we can add and get value. Our liquidity was strengthened and our management team had matured."

There was also the Network Appliance deal. In early 1998, Dell was presented with the opportunity to make a significant investment in the maker of high-speed data storage servers. Dell, at that time, was starting up its own storage business. According to Polizzoto, Dell was not ready mentally to make such an investment even though the company had plenty of cash. On May 1, 2000, Network Appliance was worth $17.6 billion. "We look at it as the one that got away," Polizzoto reflected.

The success Microsoft and Intel were having with their venture capital arms was another motivating factor. Intel, which began investing in the early 1990s, had turned investments of $2 billion into a portfolio of nearly $10 billion by March 2000.[9] As of December 1999, Microsoft had $6.2 billion in unrealized gains from similar investments.[10] DV was also seen as a way to keep Dell at the forefront of Internet infrastructure and reduce its reliance on PCs, or "boxes." With the slow decline of PC sales, Dell was looking to expand its "beyond the box" revenue stream. Furthermore, a growing number of investment opportunities were being presented to Dell, while the company was generating about $1 billion of cash every quarter. "We have thus far been unable to create businesses which consume cash," Dell noted.

---

[9] Norm Alster, "The tech meltdown's other victims," *Business Week* (May 8, 2000).

[10] Michael Kwatinetz, "Considering investment portfolios in valuing companies," *SoundBytes* (February 4, 2000).

Deals with start-ups such as Red Hat were seen as a way to capture value for the Dell brand. "The endorsement by Dell of a technology or service is like the Good Housekeeping seal, an endorsement that brings with it distribution that is unrivaled," Meredith said.[11] DV was seen as a way to keep the company abreast of strategic targets in a broader way than what the product groups could provide. Finally, DV hoped to attract talent at a time when Internet start-ups were drawing talent away from companies like Dell, Microsoft, and Cisco.

DV, according to Smith, was "a grass roots effort. We had to sell the concept." Smith went to a number of leading venture capital firms in Silicon Valley prior to DV's launch and asked them what types of corporate partners they looked for and what were the biggest issues they had working with corporations.

Mission

DV's mission was to "drive Dell's long-term growth by creating a relentless flow of competitive advantage gained through a constantly evolving array of alliances and investments that execute corporate strategy and build customer advocacy."[12] It was responsible for making equity investments that supported Dell's business initiatives, partnering with companies whose products, services or ideas could enhance and expand Dell's own offerings. "Our strategy," Meredith explained, "is to make money for Dell's shareholders. You do that by insuring that Dell understands where the next technology play is."

In March 2000, DV activity expanded to include equity investments and incubation services for early-stage private companies. "We are particularly interested," Dell explained,

> in early-stage companies with products and services which have the potential to create breakthroughs in the evolving Internet age, with an aim to integrate those products and services in Dell's business and drive our future growth. Our investments in these companies will accelerate their development and allow us to continue to lead the industry in computing and services for the Internet.[13]

DV would not control or limit strategy at the line of business level but would rather help communicate and enable it. It would also not manage alliances on a day-to-day basis. The businesses would remain the owners and managers of individual alliances, and

[11] John Peltz, "Dell Computer's chief financial officer to head venture-capital unit," *Austin-American Statesman* (March 30, 2000).

[12] "Dell: The business center of excellence," Dell company documents (January 7, 1999).

[13] "Dell ventures activity expanded to include incubation," Dell company press release (March 29, 2000).

TABLE A   Accounting Methods for Investments in Equity Securities

Equity Investment	Cost Method	Equity Method	Consolidation	Mark-to-market
Public company	N/A	Ownership between 20% and 50%	Ownership greater than 50%	Less than 20% ownership
Private company	Less than 20% ownership	Ownership between 20% and 50%	Ownership greater than 50%	N/A

Source: Dell Computer Corporation.

an executive sponsor from a line of business would be heavily involved in the alliance. DV used Dell's available cash for its investments and was not given its own pool.[14] Realized gains flowed through Dell's P&L in the "financing and other" line, below the Operating Income line. A change in the value of an investment was reflected in the balance sheet as a change in the asset basis. See Table A for details on Dell accounting procedures for equity securities.

Differentiation

According to Meredith, Dell's strategy differed from that of Cisco, Intel, and Microsoft:

> Cisco is using their venture activity to ultimately place bets on companies and their technologies and then they acquire the companies. They also use it to do R&D off the P&L.
>
> Microsoft is more aligned with Cisco. They place their bets and then acquire the company or technology. They tend to look at a broader swatch of investment activity, some of which is outside their core business such as Web TV. Intel is highly diversified. They are as much opportunistic investors as they are tactical and strategic investors, as an offset to an undiversified distribution channel. We on the other hand use our venture activity not because it is a device where we can sort through which companies to acquire, but to actually understand how to collaborate more virtually with companies that are innovating in and around the edge of our space. Dell's distribution channel is highly diversified and is an asset in itself.

According to Meredith, the Dell brand differentiated DV from traditional venture capital companies:

> We have infinitely greater resources in terms of money and talent, and we have customers. By definition if we invest and endorse commercially, our investment is worth that much more. Traditional venture capitalists can't do that. They can endorse all they want. They still can't hook the seller to the buyer. Our model fosters this and we want to maximize the value of these relationships.

As a result, Dell managers felt that venture capitalists had an interest in cultivating relationships with DV. "We can put $5 million in a company, and that company can generate $30 to $40 million in revenue because of Dell," a DV manager pointed out.

Dell's Web site highlighted the advantages of partnering with DV: acceleration, by helping bring products to market faster using Dell's efficient business model; validation, a vote of confidence in your business by the world's second largest computer systems company; and distribution, an additional outlet through which to deliver your products or services.[15]

Staffing

Smith and Lazorik were the first members of DV. In March 2000, Meredith, who had been Dell's CFO for eight years, was named co-managing director of DV. Meredith's position change was typical of how Dell utilized its talent. One executive explained that the top people were often taken from their positions and put into a start-up situation.

[14] Marla Dial, "Dell turns spotlight on startups," dbusiness.com (March 30, 2000).
[15] www.dell.com, accessed April 27, 2000.

Meredith focused on early-stage investments, incubations, and Asia; Smith, later-stage investments and Europe.

In May 2000, DV's 28 employees included three dealmakers ("principals"), one of whom was an ex-investment banker from Morgan Stanley Dean Witter and was based in Silicon Valley; three portfolio managers whose work started after the initial investment was made; and an operations group that focused on incubator services to early-stage companies and managed DV public relations. Through targeted efforts, DV cultivated relationships with venture capitalists such as Accel Partners, Benchmark, and Austin Ventures, and invested with them frequently. Time management was an issue DV contended with. Bailey and Lazorik assessed deals on weekends. "The opportunity costs of sleeping grew higher and higher through the spring of 2000," Lazorik joked.

DV was also expanding internationally. "There may be different opportunities in Europe and Asia-Pacific," explained Legris.

> For example [foreign markets] are ahead in wireless. Whereas here there are opportunities in telecom, optical networking, photonics companies, etc. We are developing the teams in Europe (London) and Asia-Pacific (Singapore, Japan, and possibly Hong Kong). The general managers in those regions are establishing teams and sourcing deals. In many markets, we might team up with an investment bank or a venture capital firm. Dell lets other people establish the market and then we expand. This will be no exception.

Establishing a compensation plan had been one of the biggest challenges in setting up DV, as it was for many other corporate venture groups. "Compensation for corporate venture capitalists is an extreme challenge because of the way traditional venture capitalists get paid," Tom Welch, Dell's deputy corporate counsel, explained. "Most corporate venture capitalists don't have this type of program. As a result, attracting and retaining talent is also an issue." "There are many examples of corporations, Intel and GE, which have experienced turnover in this space because they have not effectively addressed the issue of compensation," Smith explained.

> We have been successful in addressing this issue. We have not totally emulated the venture capital model because we don't feel it's needed or appropriate. We have the benefit of the Dell brand name. Our model is driven by our performance but it is not exactly the same as traditional venture capital funds. Furthermore, we don't feel that we need to have a salary structure that is the same as a traditional venture capital firm. We aren't going to compete for operational talent that traditional VC firms seek for their top positions. We do have a structure that is different than Dell's traditional compensation to provide incentives to the DV team to attract and retain them as they build the network value of our organization.

DV's culture was very similar to Dell's. "Michael Dell is very involved and he has a lot to do with the culture of DV," Nater underlined. "There is a consistency because of the leadership. That will be infused into the companies we invest in."

Hub-and-Spokes

DV was set up as a hub-and-spokes system. (See Exhibit 35-7 for the hub structure.) As the hub, DV was the central body of financial/market analysts who were responsible for investment activity. All principals, associates, and directors in DV were hub members and responsible for architecting the financial side of each deal, usually executed in coordination with one of the spoke organizations. The spokes included the personal

EXHIBIT 35-7

DELL VENTURES ORGANIZATIONAL MODEL

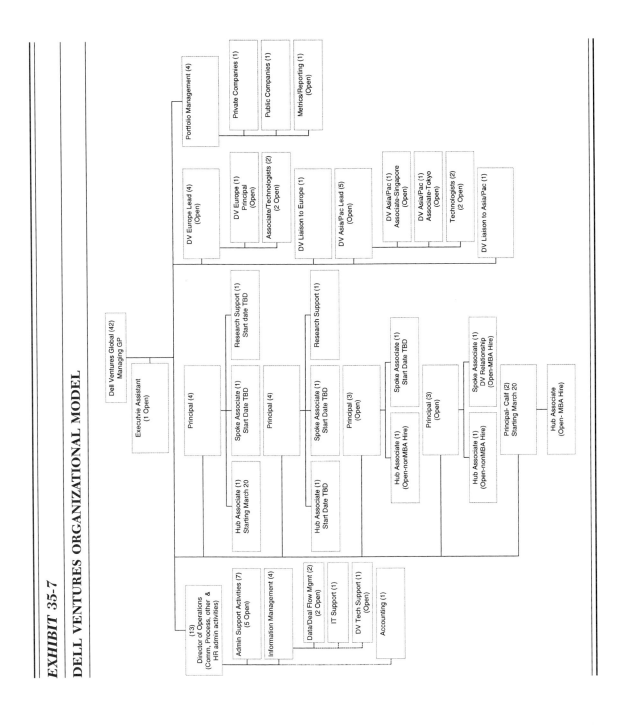

673

systems group, enterprise systems group, Dell home sales, business selling division, public and education, relationship group, preferred accounts division, and Internet partners division. The spokes acted as liaisons between business divisions within Dell and the DV hub, and were involved with technical and business diligence during the assessment process. The spokes usually worked directly with the division leadership but devoted most of their time to driving relationships generated in the course of the department's business activity.

DV met weekly with one representative from each product and marketing group to discuss investment opportunities. All the principals, in addition to Smith and Meredith, were expected to attend. The DV team told business units about what they were seeing and hearing from the market and their venture capital contacts; the business units told the DV people about their plans and needs. Occasionally, a new initiative might make a presentation. Bailey provided an example: "We launched a business called Dell Host a few weeks ago. The hosting business explained what Dell Host was a long time before it was launched to let us know what type of partners made sense for them. We've made a couple of investments since then that support the business."

DV's structure enabled it to keep in close contact with business groups, which in turn helped the company keep investments strategic. "We don't require a business unit to sponsor a deal for us to make an investment," Smith stated. "Although we do prefer to do it this way, it is not a requirement." When deploying capital, Lazorik explained, "it is important that you have a centralized system. You take all of the collective knowledge of the opportunities in front of you and you are able to review them on a relative basis."

According to Smith, the structure allowed DV to move quickly and preserve institutional memory. "One of the unanimous issues that venture capitalists had with corporate venture capital arms is that they can't move quickly enough," he explained. "We knew early on that we wanted a structure that would allow us to move quickly. We have been successful in our structure in how it is tied into the business units. There is only one place where an investment decision can be made and that is within the core DV team."

Part of the hub-and-spokes intent, therefore, was to establish processes that were repeatable. "With all the new people coming into the company and the firm growing so fast," Nater elaborated, "we needed to form a commonality and memory of all the business deals that are being done." "We should not let the business heads make the final investment decisions," Lazorik noted, "because they are compensated to make decisions that are good for their own line of business."

DEALS

DV received, on average, between 50 and 80 business plans a week. One of its most recent investments was in the Web hosting company Interliant, which sold a stake to Dell in January 2000. By February, Dell was reselling Interliant's service. Deals such as the one with Interliant were advantageous for Dell for three reasons: Dell steered customers to Interliant and took a cut; Dell sold its servers to Interliant to support new customers; and Dell's support boosted Interliant's sales. "They buy our infrastructure, we put them in front of our customers," stated Dell.[16] The deal reportedly drove away Verio, the leading Web hosting company, as a Dell customer. With a server budget of

---

[16] Daniel Lyons, "Michael Dell's second act . . . ," *Forbes* (April 17, 2000).

$50 million, Verio had bought Intel-based servers from Dell.[17] A Dell manager refuted the idea that Verio was still an ongoing Dell customer with a buying history but that sales to Interliant were growing handily as a result of the business relationship.

Dell often made investments in companies it competed with. In June 1999, Dell invested in Web hosting company NaviSite, even though Dell was in the midst of creating its own hosting business. According to Polizzoto, NaviSite was positioned in the enterprise space, whereas Dell was focusing on small and medium-sized companies. "When there is an opportunity that Dell Host can't handle, then NaviSite is our preferred partner and they get that business," he explained. "Most companies recognize that there is competition and cooperation that goes on because it is the nature of the business."

According to Smith, the deal process typically took six to eight weeks, although DV had been involved in some deals, which required a decision within days. The process involved five phases. Phase one was the initial assessment of alternatives; phase two entailed due diligence and recommendation to the investment committee, comprised of the Office of the Chairman (OCC), Meredith and Smith; phase three was negotiation; phase four was execution and "hand off" to the businesses; and phase five was monitor, measure, and report results versus objectives.

"At the front end," Lazorik explained, "we look at the management team and cash flows. We look at companies that have the ability to be cash positive at least on an operating level. From a strategic point of view, we look at how well we know the competition and understand the market. Senior management looks only at the best deals."

Initially, all deals had to receive investment committee approval. Starting in the winter of 2000, Smith could invest up to $10 million without other internal approvals. All deals over $10 million had to be approved by the investment committee. According to one of the four initial DV members, the approval process was quite efficient. "Michael Dell is very responsive. I remember sending him a memo at 11:00 P.M. on a Friday night describing a potential investment opportunity. He sent a response back at 4:00 A.M. on Saturday blessing the deal. I think he was in a very different time zone. Michael loves the technology and the information it carries. He's plugged in."

Investment opportunities generally came about in a number of ways: "referrals," that is, executive staff, spokes, hubs, venture capital partners (33% came from venture capital partners), e-mail, mail, or phone calls to Dell, the CEO's office, or the Internet (40%) where a Direct Submit form for an investment offering (IO) was posted. Meredith stated that deal origination was not a problem. "We have Dell's brand, Michael, our commercial success, and we don't have to go out and raise money. The efforts of the team are largely spent on understanding transactions and making decisions on them, not originating deals, fighting to compete in them and raising money. Those are nonissues for our team."

The Data Flow Analyst, an individual familiar with DV's investment criteria, prequalified the IO using a standardized checklist. The following attributes had to be included in any deal before DV considered it: Public/private (reject if public); category (had be one of DV's categories); sector (needed to be similar to one of DV's sectors); number of employees (had to be greater than 20); requested investment amount from Dell (had to be greater than $1 million); and there had to be at least a round B. The Data Flow Analyst then compiled all the basic information into a Deal Concept form. Information included company name and overview, investment overview including spon-

---

[17] Ibid.

sors, investment description and strategic rationale for investment, key concerns/risks, and an exit strategy.

The deal file was then assigned to a hub owner. The hub principal screened the business plan and then either rejected the proposal, or sent it on to the appropriate spokes to pursue the opportunity. Spokes performed technical due diligence and worked directly with the hub to assess the strategic fit.

To get an investment approved after a Deal Concept was accepted, the Principal collected information, managed a diligence process, validated the business model and valuation, oversaw the preparation of an investment proposal that included all the necessary information to support an investment decision by the investment committee, including DV peers and senior management. According to Bailey, "We are collectively smarter about an individual opportunity. Everyone should provide input, in order to maximize the knowledge of the network." Smith continued:

> There is one guiding principal to making smart investments and that is communication. Venture investing is, by its nature, starved for information. There are no S's K's or Q's filed with the SEC. All data points come from the network. That's why I want to embody the collective communication of Dell, of DV, and of the external community into our approval process.

During a Monday investment review meeting, the group would seek the appropriate level of approval for the investment size and scope, and then follow a standard process involving the business, Legal, and Treasury to close investments in an orderly manner.

Once the deal was completed, the spokes provided updates on the performance of commercial agreements. Any communication with the deal companies was done via the relevant spokes but often at the behest of DV managers when companies didn't have immediate relevancy to a spoke's business group. In a few select cases, Dell's associated business executives held board seats; more typically, Dell would ask for observation rights and rely on familiar venture investors with board seats. "We focus on finding great investments," Bailey noted, "and we distribute the back end to our organizations, like most venture capitalists do." Lazorik added:

> Capital is oxygen. Its initial deployment doesn't ensure success. People change. Plans change. DV's role is to stay engaged where it makes sense financially and strategically. Time is the most valuable asset that we manage. Once the capital is spent, we must focus on devoting time from the right groups of people within and outside of Dell to promote the truly innovative companies.

Meredith referred to Dell's investment activity as an "ecosystem model," in which Dell, in the middle, united the expertise of dozens of partners. Meredith believed that alliances made more sense than acquisitions, "freeing Dell to dump one ally's switching technology in favor of a rival with the next big thing."[18]

To Lazorik, success for DV meant investing time and resources in deals that got done.

> If we ran ten deals through our entire process, including seeking approval, and didn't disqualify it early, but only got one funded, then we have not been very effective in our abil-

[18] Daniel Lyons, "Michael Dells second act . . . ," *Forbes* (April 17, 2000).

ity to manage our time. If we choose to only spend five minutes with a deal and it gets shut down but three months later the company goes public and ends up being worth ten times what it was when we had our chance, then we have failed. We didn't spend enough time understanding the company. We have to maximize our time with the winners and vice versa.

In the case of a private company, there might be opportunities for additional investments. Post-IPO, Legris explained,

we look for the right times to monetize our gains. The nature of the investments is strategic but the securities are trading as public entities so at a point in time we will work to monetize our positions. Eventually, if we didn't sell, we'd own a disproportionately large portfolio of mature public companies, and that's not our mandate.

The investment relationship also represented a long-term commitment to a company, and this relationship commitment was judged based on a weighting of several components, including market, commercial relationship, strategic value, company progress, valuation, and capital risk.

CHALLENGES

According to a number of Dell executives, Wall Street's view of corporate venture capital was ambiguous. Nater explained the challenge:

It is unclear how Wall Street values corporate venture capital. Our message is that it is a long-term strategic fit. But an Intel can have decent operating margins and put $300 million through profits and Wall Street is not impressed. When Intel did not make its operating income line the stock got hammered. PEs are still driven from operating income. I think the whole corporate investment community needs to educate Wall Street. As Treasurer, I like deploying cash strategically with Dell's partners because eventually they throw off lots of cash. This is a use of cash that leverages Dell's deployment of other noncash resources, like management's time. But it is unclear how the investment community views this activity.

Some felt that the market would not properly value DV's activities as long as the group was internal to Dell. Lazorik, for one, felt that DV should be more autonomous, but that it should also keep in close contact with the spokes. For Welch, DV was "a brand name for an activity conducted within our corporate subsidiary structure."

Some DV managers worried about overconfidence fueled by the Internet bubble. "Our key motivation is strategic," explained Smith. "[Not all venture] investments will be home runs."[19] "We need to look for singles and doubles," Polizotto added.

Others worried about focus. "The amount of opportunity is enormous and overwhelming," Mehta noted. "To know where to focus is our biggest challenge. If you don't you will not be able to execute. And in Ventures there is so much deal-flow, the problem is even worse." Polizzoto pointed out, however, that "nearly every investment we have made can, in one form or another, be pointed directly to the Internet whether it's pure technology or storage servers."

[19] Norm Alster, "The tech meltdown's other victims," *Business Week* (May 8, 2000).

With the prevalence of CMGI, ICGE and others, another issue had emerged that companies engaging in corporate venture capital had to monitor and address, namely, what differentiated an operating from an investment company and the tax repercussions of increased investment activities.

Identifying, emulating, and targeting DV's competitors also continued to be a challenge. The need for an empowered venture capital organization continued to be tantamount. Meredith noted,

> Dell is inherently the most scalable organization I have ever seen, in terms of raw capital that can be processed through our model. Couple that with Dell's current market share around 11%, this is a powerful weapon, and the right model for a company driven to profitably grow its share over a sustained period. Wall Street has validated this. However, in DV's business, the firm that scales in areas that are strategic, wins. The largest funds don't always have the best returns. Those that provide services and advice are strengthening their ecosystem. The venture firm that scales only in its ability to invest more capital across the entire universe of opportunities, inherently migrates towards the average and that's not our goal. I believe we have access to more opportunities than most firms, but we need to continue to only invest in the percentage of those deals that are both financial and strategic winners for Dell Computer. In brief, long-term DV is successful if we contribute to the growth of Dell's core business.

As they finished lunch it was clear to Meredith, Nater, and Legris that they faced an entirely different set of challenges than they did when launching DV. Their primary goal was to continually evolve the organization to meet new challenges, as the nature of venture capital called for.

Glossary

In this glossary, we have sought to define the technical terms most frequently used in this volume.

Agency problem   A conflict between managers and investors, or more generally an instance where an agent does not intrinsically desire to follow the wishes of the principal that hired him.

Agreement of limited partnership   See partnership agreement.

Angel   A wealthy individual who invests in entrepreneurial firms. While angels perform many of the same functions as venture capitalists, they invest their own capital rather than that of institutional and other individual investors.

Associate   A professional employee of a private equity firm who is not yet a partner.

Asymmetric information problem   When because of his day-to-day involvement with the firm, an entrepreneur knows more about his company's prospects than investors, suppliers, or strategic partners.

Bogey   See hurdle rate.

Book-to-market ratio   The ratio of a firm's accounting (book) value of its equity to the value of the equity assigned by the market (*i.e.,* the product of the number of shares outstanding and the share price).

Capital under management   See committed capital.

Carried interest   The substantial share, often around 20%, of profits that are allocated to the general partners of a venture capital partnership.

Closed-end fund   A publicly traded mutual fund whose shares must be sold to other investors (rather than redeemed from the issuing firm, as is the case with open-end mutual funds). Many early venture funds were structured in this manner.

Closing   The signing of the contract by an investor or group of investors that binds them to supply a set amount of capital to a venture capital fund. Often a fraction of that capital is provided at the time of the closing. A single venture capital fund may have multiple closings.

Co-investment   See syndication.

Committed capital   Pledges of capital to a venture capital fund. This money is typically not received at once, but rather taken down over three to five years starting in the year the fund is formed.

Common stock   The equity typically held by management and founders. Typically, at the time of an initial public offering, all equity is converted into common stock.

Consolidation   A private equity investment strategy that involves merging several small firms together and exploiting economies of scale or scope.

Convertible equity or debt   A securities that can be converted under certain conditions into another security (often into common stock). The convertible shares often have special rights that the common stock does not have.

Conversion ratio   The number of shares for which a convertible debt or equity issue can be exchanged.

Corporate venture capital   An initiative by a corporation to invest either in young firms outside the corporation or units formerly part of the corporation. These are often organized as corporate subsidiaries, not as limited partnerships.

Disbursement   An investment by a venture capitalist into a company in his portfolio.

Distressed debt   A private equity investment strategy that involves purchasing discounted bonds of a financially distressed firm. Distressed debt investors frequent convert their holdings into equity and become actively involved with the management of the distressed firm.

Distribution   The transfer of shares in a (typically publicly traded) portfolio firm or cash from a venture capitalist to each limited partner and (frequently) themselves.

Draw down   See take down.

Due diligence   The review of a business plan and assessment of a management team prior to a venture capital investment.

Employee Retirement Income Security Act (ERISA)   The 1974 legislation that codified the regulation of corporate pension plans. See prudent man rule.

Exercise price   The price at which an option or warrant can be exercised.

First closing   The initial closing of a fund.

First fund   An initial fund raised by a venture capital organization.

Follow-on fund   A fund that is subsequent to a venture capital organization's first fund.

Follow-on offering   See seasoned equity offering.

Form 10-K   An annual filing required by the U.S. Securities and Exchange Commission of each publicly traded firm, as well as certain private firms. The statement provides a wide variety of summary data about the firm.

Float   In a public market context, the percentage of the company's shares that is in the hands of outside investors, as opposed to being held by corporate insiders.

Free cash flow problem   The temptation to undertake wasteful expenditures that cash not needed for operations or investments often poses.

Fund   A pool of capital raised periodically by a venture capital organization. Usually in the form of limited partnerships, venture capital funds typically have a ten-year life, though extensions of several years are often possible.

Fund of funds   A fund designed that invests primarily in other venture capital funds rather than portfolio firms, often organized by an investment advisor or investment bank.

Gatekeeper   See investment advisor.

General partner   A partner in a limited partnership is responsible for the day-to-day operations of the fund. In the case of a venture funds, the venture capitalists are either general partners or own the corporation that serves as the general partner. The general partners assume all liability for the fund's debts.

Grandstanding problem   The strategy, sometimes employed by young private equity organizations, of rushing young firms to the public marketplace in order to demonstrate a successful track record, even if the companies are not ready to go public.

Herding problem   A situation when investors, particularly institutions, make investments that are more similar to one another than desirable.

Hot issue market   A market with high demand for new securities offerings, particularly for initial public offerings.

Hurdle rate   Either (*i*) the set rate of return that the limited partners must receive before the general partners can begin sharing in any distributions, or (*ii*) the level that the fund's net asset value must reach before the general partners can begin sharing in any distributions.

In the money   An option or warrant that would have a positive value if it was immediately exercised.

Initial public offering (IPO)   The sale of shares to public investors of a firm that has not hitherto been traded on a public stock exchange. These are typically underwritten by an investment bank.

Insider   A director, officer, or shareholder with ten percent or more of a company's equity.

Intangible asset   A patent, trade secret, informal know-how, brand capital, or other non-physical asset.

Investment advisor   A financial intermediary who assists investors, particularly institutions, with investments in venture capital and other financial assets. Advisors assess potential new venture funds for their clients and monitor the progress of existing investments. In some cases, they pool their investors' capital in funds of funds.

Investment bank   A financial intermediary that, among other services, may underwrite securities offerings, facilitate mergers and acquisitions, and trade for its own account.

Lemons problem   See asymmetric information problem.

Leveraged buyout (LBO)   The acquisition of a firm or business unit, typically in a mature industry, with a considerable amount of debt.

Leveraged buyout fund   A fund, typically organized in a similar manner to a venture capital fund, specializing in leveraged buyout investments. Some of these funds also make venture capital investments.

Limited partner   An investor in a limited partnership. Limited partners can monitor the partnership's progress, but cannot become involved in its day-to-day management if they are to retain limited liability.

Limited partnership   An organizational form that entails a finitely lived contractual arrangement between limited and general partners, governed by a partnership agreement.

Lock up   A provision in the underwriting agreement between an investment bank and existing shareholders that prohibits corporate insiders and private equity investors from selling at the time of the offering.

Management fee   The fee, typically a percentage of committed capital or net asset value, that is paid to the by a venture capital fund to the general partners to cover salaries and expenses.

Market-to-book ratio   The inverse of the book-to-market ratio.

Mezzanine   Either (*i*) a venture capital financing round shortly before an initial public offering or (*ii*) a investment that employs subordinated debt that has fewer privileges than bank debt but more than equity and often has attached warrants.

Net asset value (NAV)   The value of a fund's holdings, which may be calculated using a variety of valuation rules.

Net present value   The expected value of one or more cash flows in the future, discounted at a rate that reflects the cash flows' riskiness.

Option   The right, but not the obligation, to buy or sell a security at a set price (or range of prices) in a given period.

Out of the money   An option or warrant whose exercise price is above the current value of a share.

Partnership agreement   The contract that explicitly specifies the compensation and conditions that govern the relationship between the investors (limited partners) and the venture capitalists (general partners) during a venture capital fund's life. Occasionally used to refer to the separate agreement between the general partners regarding the internal operations of the fund (e.g., the division of the carried interest).

Private equity   Private equity includes organizations devoted to venture capital, leveraged buyouts, consolidations, mezzanine and distressed debt investments, and a variety of hybrids such as venture leasing and venture factoring.

Post-money valuation   The product of the price paid per share in a financing round and the shares outstanding after to the financing round.

Pre-money valuation   The product of the price paid per share in a financing round and the shares outstanding before the financing round.

Preferred stock   Stock that has preference over common stock with respect to any dividends or payments in association with the liquidation of the firm. Preferred stockholders may also have additional rights, such as the ability to block mergers or displace management.

Prospectus   A condensed, widely disseminated version of the registration statement that is also filed with the U.S. Securities and Exchange Commission. The prospectus provides a wide variety of summary data about the firm.

Proxy statement   A filing with the U.S. Securities and Exchange Commission, that, among other information, provides information on the holdings and names of corporate insiders.

Prudent man rule   Prior to 1979, a provision in the Employee Retirement Income Security Act (ERISA) that essentially prohibited pension funds from investing substantial amounts of money in venture capital or other high-risk asset classes. The Department of Labor's clarification of the rule in that year allowed pension managers to invest in high-risk assets, including venture capital.

Registration statement   A filing with the U.S. Securities and Exchange Commission (e.g., a S-1 or S-18 form) that is must be reviewed by the Commission before a firm can sell shares to the public. The statement provides a wide variety of summary data about the firm, as well as copies of key legal documents.

Road show   The marketing of a venture capital fund or public offering to potential investors.

Roll-up   See consolidation.

Rule 10(b)-5   The U.S. Securities and Exchange Commission regulation that most generally prohibits fraudulent activity in the purchase or sale of any security.

Rule 16(a)   The U.S. Securities and Exchange Commission regulation the requires insiders to disclose any transactions in the firm's stock on a monthly basis.

Rule 144   The U.S. Securities and Exchange Commission regulation that prohibits sales for one year (originally, two years) after the purchase of restricted stock and limits the pace of sales between the first and second (originally, second and third) year after the purchase.

Seasoned equity offering   An offering by a firm which has already competed an initial public offering and whose shares are already publicly traded.

Secondary offering   An offering of shares that are not being issued by the firm, but rather are sold by existing shareholders. The firm consequently does not receive the proceeds from the sales of these shares.

Shares outstanding   The number of shares that the company has issued.

Small business investment company (SBIC)   A federally guaranteed risk capital pool. These funds were first authorized by the U.S. Congress in 1958, proliferated during the 1960s, and then dwindled after many organizations encountered management and incentive problems.

Staging   The provision of capital to entrepreneurs in multiple installments, with each financing conditional on meeting particular business targets. This helps ensure that the money is not squandered on unprofitable projects.

Syndication   The joint purchase of shares by two or more venture capital organizations or the joint underwriting of an offering by two or more investment banks.

Take down   The transfer of some or all of the committed capital from the limited partners to a venture capital fund.

Takedown schedule   The contractual language that describes how and when the venture capital fund can (or must) receive the committed capital from its limited partners.

Tangible asset   A machines, building, land, inventory, or another physical asset.

Uncertainty problem   The array of potential outcomes for a company or project. The wider the dispersion of potential outcomes, the greater the uncertainty.

Tombstone   An advertisement, typically in a major business publication, by an underwriter to publicize an offering that it has underwritten.

Unrelated business taxable income (UBTI)   The gross income from any unrelated business that a tax-exempt institution regularly carries out. If a venture partnership is generating significant income from debt-financed property, tax-exempt limited partners may face tax liabilities due to UBTI provisions.

Underpricing   The discount to the projected trading price at which the investment banker sells shares in an initial public offering. A substantial positive return in the first trading day is often interpreted by financial economists as evidence of underpricing.

Underwriting   The purchase of a securities issue from a company by an investment bank and its (typically almost immediate) resale to investors.

Unseasoned equity offering   See initial public offering.

Valuation rule   The algorithm by which a venture capital fund assigns values to the public and private firms in its portfolio.

Venture capital   Independently managed, dedicated pools of capital that focus on equity or equity-linked investments in privately held, high growth companies. Many venture capital funds, however, occasionally make other types of private equity investments. Outside of the U.S., this phrase is often used as a synonym for private equity.

Venture capitalist   A general partner or associate at a venture capital organization.

Venture factoring   A private equity investment strategy that involves purchasing the receivables of high-risk young firms. As a part of the transaction, the venture factoring fund typically also receives warrants in the young firm.

Venture leasing   A private equity investment strategy that involves leasing equipment or other assets to high-risk young firms. As a part of the transaction, the venture leasing fund typically also receives warrants in the young firm.

Warrants   An option to buy shares of stock issued directly by a company.

Window dressing problem   The behavior of money managers of adjusting their portfolios at the end of the quarter by buying firms whose shares have appreciated and selling "mistakes." This is driven by the fact that institutional investors may examine not only quarterly returns, but also end-of-period holdings.

Withdrawn offering   An equity issue where a registration statement with the U.S. Securities and Exchange Commission but the firm either writes to Commission withdrawing the proposed offering before it is effective or the offering is not completed within nine months of the filing.

Index